CW00968090

Designing Sustainable Internet of Things Solutions for Smart Industries

Salu George Thandekkattu
American University of Nigeria, Nigeria

Narasimha Rao Vajjhala
University of New York, Tirana, Albania

A volume in the Advances in Business Information Systems and Analytics (ABISA) Book Series

Published in the United States of America by
    IGI Global
    Business Science Reference (an imprint of IGI Global)
    701 E. Chocolate Avenue
    Hershey PA, USA 17033
    Tel: 717-533-8845
    Fax: 717-533-8661
    E-mail: cust@igi-global.com
    Web site: http://www.igi-global.com

Library of Congress Cataloging-in-Publication Data

CIP DATA PENDING

ISBN: 9798369354988
Softcover: 9798369354995
eISBN: 9798369355008

British Cataloguing in Publication Data
A Cataloguing in Publication record for this book is available from the British Library.

All work contributed to this book is new, previously-unpublished material.
The views expressed in this book are those of the authors, but not necessarily of the publisher.

For electronic access to this publication, please contact: eresources@igi-global.com.

Assoc. Prof. Salu George Thandekkattu

I wish to thank my parents for engraving the values of hard work and commitment and also want to thank my wife and children for their unwavering support in realizing my vision.

Assoc. Prof. Narasimha Rao Vajjhala

I want to thank my family members, particularly my mother, Mrs. Rajeswari Vajjhala, for her blessings and for instilling in me the virtues of perseverance and commitment.

Editorial Advisory Board

Table of Contents

Eriona Çela, University of New York Tirana, Tirana, Albania
Mathias M. Fonkam, Penn State University, USA
Philip Eappen, Cape Breton University, Canada
Narasimha Rao Vajjhala, University of New York Tirana, Tirana, Albania

Eriona Çela, University of New York Tirana, Tirana, Albania
Rajasekhara Mouly Potluri, Kazakh British Technical University, Kazakhstan
Narasimha Rao Vajjhala, University of New York Tirana, Tirana, Albania

Bachina Harish Babu, Department of Automobile Engineering, VNR Vignana Jyothi Institute of Engineering and Technology, Hyderabad, India
J. Ananth, Department of Marine Engineering, Academy of Maritime Education and Training (AMET) University, India
P. Sukania, Department of Mathematics, R.M.K. Engineering College, Kavarapettai, India
Clement Joe Anand M., Department of Mathematics, Mount Carmel College (Autonomous), Bengaluru, India
Mickle Aancy H., Department of MBA, Panimalar Engineering College, Chennai, India
Magesh Babu D., Velammal Institute of Technology, India

Detailed Table of Contents

    Eriona Çela, University of New York Tirana, Tirana, Albania
    Mathias M. Fonkam, Penn State University, USA
    Philip Eappen, Cape Breton University, Canada
    Narasimha Rao Vajjhala, University of New York Tirana, Tirana,
        Albania

This chapter explores the evolving landscape of smart classrooms, focusing on the integration of sustainable internet of things (IoT) technologies. This chapter systematically reviews current trends, highlighting how IoT innovations are reshaping educational environments to enhance learning experiences and improve resource efficiency. The chapter examines the impact of smart technologies on classroom design, teaching methodologies, and sustainability practices, offering insights into the benefits and challenges of adopting IoT in education. This chapter underscores the potential of sustainable IoT solutions to create more adaptive, efficient, and environmentally conscious educational spaces, setting the stage for the future of education.

Chapter 2

Eriona Çela, University of New York Tirana, Tirana, Albania
Rajasekhara Mouly Potluri, Kazakh British Technical University,
    Kazakhstan
Narasimha Rao Vajjhala, University of New York Tirana, Tirana,
    Albania

This chapter systematically reviews the literature on using internet of things (IoT) technologies to enable data-driven decision-making in educational institutions. As educational environments become increasingly complex, the ability to collect, analyze, and act upon data is crucial for institutional improvement. IoT technologies offer opportunities for educational leaders to optimize various aspects of campus operations, enhance student experiences, and improve administrative efficiency. The chapter explores IoT adoption in education, highlighting key technological advancements and their data collection and analysis applications. This chapter examines how IoT-generated data can inform resource allocation, facility management, and student services decisions. This chapter also addresses the challenges and barriers to integrating IoT in educational decision-making, including issues related to data privacy, security, and the need for robust data governance frameworks.

Chapter 3

*Bachina Harish Babu, Department of Automobile Engineering,
VNR Vignana Jyothi Institute of Engineering and Technology,
Hyderabad, India*

*J. Ananth, Department of Marine Engineering, Academy of Maritime
Education and Training (AMET) University, India*

*P. Sukania, Department of Mathematics, R.M.K. Engineering College,
Kavarapettai, India*

*Clement Joe Anand M., Department of Mathematics, Mount Carmel
College (Autonomous), Bengaluru, India*

*Mickle Aancy H., Department of MBA, Panimalar Engineering College,
Chennai, India*

Magesh Babu D., Velammal Institute of Technology, India

This chapter discusses how clean technologies and IoT solutions help manufacturing reduce waste and move towards a circular economy. It points out the need for sustainable practices and how renewable energy systems and eco-friendly materials can reduce waste throughout production. IoT devices impact manufacturing processes, allowing real-time resource use and waste creation tracking. To make these technologies work well, companies must analyze data and use machine learning to use resources and maintenance best. The chapter also discusses challenges like high upfront costs, systems not working together, and keeping data safe. These issues need solving to get more people to adopt clean technologies and IoT solutions. It shows why bringing these technologies into manufacturing pushes the circular economy idea forward.

Chapter 4

Harnessing GPS, Sensors, and Drones to Minimize Environmental Impact:

A. Vellingiri, Department of Electronics and Communication
Engineering, Bannari Amman Institute of Technology, Erode, India

R. Kokila, School of Computer Application, Dayananda Sagar
University, Bengaluru, India

P. Nisha, Department of Electrical and Electronics Engineering, St.
Joseph's Institute of Technology, Chennai, India

Monish Kumar, Department of Civil Engineering, Sri
Jayachamarajendra College of Engineering, Mysuru, India

Somu Chinnusamy, Research and Development, RSP Science Hub,
Coimbatore, India

Sampath Boopathi, Department of Mechanical Engineering,
Muthayammal Engineering College, Namakkal, India

Precision farming uses advanced technology like GPS, sensors, and drones to make farming better and greener. It applies water, fertilizers, and pesticides where crops need them. GPS helps map fields and guide machines. Sensors give up-to-date information on soil, crops, and weather. Drones watch from above, letting farmers act fast and use resources wisely. By not using too much and cutting waste, this method has less impact on nature. It saves water, stops chemicals from running off, and keeps soil healthy. This chapter looks at how these tools fit into today's farms. It shows real examples of good points and tough spots. It points out how precision farming could change old ways, leading to farming that lasts and bounces back from problems.

Chapter 5

This chapter addresses the profound influence of deep learning, the internet of things (IoT), sensors, and agricultural machinery on contemporary agriculture. These technologies improve productivity, efficiency, and sustainability throughout the production cycle, from tillage and planting to harvesting and post-harvest processing. Deep learning algorithms monitor crops and soil strength, detect illnesses, and forecast yields. At the same time, IoT sensors gather up-to-date information on soil quality, weather patterns, and crop development. Implementing automation in agriculture decreases the need for manual work and enhances operational efficiency. This chapter highlights the importance of using data to make informed decisions in precision agriculture, focusing on using sensor data and imaging techniques to improve the efficiency of resources and reduce environmental harm. Modern agriculture can effectively tackle food security and ecological concerns and provide food for a growing global population by employing inventive techniques and promoting partnerships.

Chapter 6

The advancement of technology has led to the introduction of smart technologies in various sectors, including farming, forming what is now known as smart farming. Smart farming involves using smart technologies to perform monitoring and automation tasks traditionally performed by humans. However, despite these advancements, farmers still need help adopting smart farming techniques in crop farming. Therefore, this chapter presents a framework designed to guide the implementation of smart technologies in crop farming activities. This framework employs the concept of artificial intelligence of things (IoT), which utilizes artificial intelligence (AI) for decision-making and data analysis based on data from internet of things (IoT) devices. The framework is structured around five modules: the sensor module, the artificial intelligence module, the automation module, the network module, and the processing module. These modules enable effective monitoring of factors essential for optimal crop growth and performing automation based on monitoring activities.

Big data analytics plays a pivotal role in addressing sustainability challenges and driving the adoption of sustainable solutions across various sectors. It enables organizations to collect, analyze, and derive insights from large volumes of data generated by diverse sources, including sensors, IoT devices, and digital platforms. By leveraging advanced analytics techniques such as machine learning, predictive modeling, and data visualization, organizations can uncover patterns, trends, and correlations in data to inform decision-making and drive innovation in sustainability. This chapter gives a practical demonstration of how big data analytics can be applied to visualize, analyze, and extract knowledge from an admission database of a polytechnic system and use the same for machine learning (ML) predictions and explanations of the predictions for informed decision-making.

Chapter 8

This chapter provides a concise overview of the key concepts and considerations in data management and analytics in IoT. IoT data management involves collecting, storing, processing, and analyzing the vast amounts of data interconnected devices generate. Challenges such as scalability, data quality, etc., must be addressed to ensure that IoT systems can efficiently handle the high volume of data. Analytics techniques such as machine learning, predictive analytics, etc., play a crucial role in extracting meaningful insights from IoT data. These techniques enable organizations to uncover hidden patterns, predict future events, and more. However, interoperability, privacy, and data quality pose significant challenges. Standardization efforts, security measures, etc., are essential to overcome these challenges and realize the transformative potential of IoT data-driven insights. Thus, effective data management and analytics are essential for organizations to leverage the vast amounts of data generated by IoT devices and drive innovation.

Although IoT has proven to be a vital instrument for data collection, epidemiological data collection has presented a significant challenge to the AI community. Thus, data for epidemiological research from multiple sources needs to be integrated to gain a holistic insight into epidemiological incidences. Hence, the authors aim to provide a framework for collecting, aggregating, and fusing data from diverse IoT sources for epidemiological research. Thus, a wireless network is designed for energy efficiency and communication efficiency. In addition, the CoAP mechanism for data transfer to a cloud-based service for aligning, de-duplicating, aggregating, and mapping data from several sources is presented. Subsequently, the researchers trained three machine learning models to predict disease incidence, vector abundance, and host population using both synthesized data using the proposed framework and data captured using traditional means. They assessed the performance of the two models by measuring their accuracy and learning rate. Results show the superiority of the proposed framework.

Autonomous vehicle (AV) technologies, coupled with the rapid growth of the internet of things (IoT), have ushered in an era of intelligent mobility. This evolution holds the potential to significantly contribute to the development of sustainable cities and communities by addressing pressing issues such as traffic congestion, environmental pollution, and monotonous transportation systems. AVs can effectively mitigate these challenges by utilizing cutting-edge sensors, artificial intelligence (AI), and advanced communication protocols. This comprehensive approach allows AVs to interact with surrounding infrastructure seamlessly. Integrating IoT in autonomous vehicles enhances their ability to collect, analyze, and utilize data, improving vehicle performance and transportation networks. This chapter explores the convergence of intelligent mobility, IoT, and autonomous vehicles, focusing on how these emerging technologies can be harnessed to build sustainable cities and communities.

Industry 5.0 has created a more stable and networked industrial environment using the internet of things (IoT). Industry 5.0 creates a work environment where human-machine interaction is optimized for better performance by combining human cooperation with robots and intelligent equipment. Industrial internet of things (IIoT) includes various services in large settings, such as digital domains for company management, real-time production monitoring, and machinery condition tracking. Industry 5.0 aims to achieve the best possible balance between productivity and efficiency in various sectors, including heavy manufacturing, oil and gas, and warehouse management, which heavily rely on heavy gear. This chapter comprehensively explores the multiple dimensions of the IoT in Industry 5.0 used in intelligent manufacturing for fault screening and mechanical diagnosis and prognosis.

The smart dairy industry has radically transformed the manufacturing, processing, and distribution processes of milk and other dairy products. By utilizing sensors, data analytics, and other smart technologies, dairy farmers can lower their environmental impact, boost productivity, enhance herd management, and improve food safety and traceability. The dairy industry must use smart technology to effectively and sustainably meet the growing demand for dairy products around the world. The intelligent dairy industry has advanced significantly from its early days. The industry has become more consumer-driven, efficient, and sustainable and uses cutting-edge technology. It is expected that the smart dairy sector will continue to grow and bring about more revolutionary changes in the future, given the growing global demand for dairy products. The dairy industry is adopting IoT technology at an increasing rate, and this trend could be significant.

SMEs face unique problems in staying competitive and innovative as business changes fast. This chapter looks at smart technology and talent management as ways to empower SMEs. Smart tech like AI, IoT, and data analytics help SME tools to work better, innovate, and please customers more. At the same time, good talent management helps get, grow, and keep skilled workers who can use these technologies. When SMEs combine smart tech with strong talent management, they can find new ways to grow, change with the market, and build lasting advantages. This chapter shows real examples, case studies, and strategies SMEs can use to do well in the digital age.

Foreword

As industries worldwide face the dual challenge of modernization and environmental responsibility, *Designing Sustainable Internet of Things Solutions for Smart Industries* becomes an essential guide as an edited book. Edited by Salu George Thandekkattu and Narasimha Rao Vajjhala, this book explores how IoT can shape smart, sustainable industrial environments. IoT has transformed industries by enhancing productivity and reducing costs through real-time monitoring and predictive maintenance. Yet, as the authors emphasize, sustainability is often overlooked. This book addresses that gap, offering practical strategies to develop IoT solutions that benefit both industry and the environment.

The book's multidisciplinary approach draws from environmental science, engineering, and data analytics, providing readers with actionable insights and real-world examples. Each chapter builds on the last, covering topics like data-driven decision-making, waste reduction, and the role of big data in sustainability. The authors also highlight the powerful intersection of IoT with emerging technologies like AI, which can drive smarter resource management and reduce waste. They tackle the challenges of implementing sustainable IoT solutions, offering balanced perspectives and practical strategies. As sustainability becomes essential, this book is a vital resource for all industry stakeholders. It not only guides engineers and technologists but also serves as a call to action for creating responsible, sustainable industries. In conclusion, this book offers timely insights into sustainable industrial development. The principles and strategies presented will inspire and guide the next generation of IoT innovations, leading to smarter, greener, and more resilient industries.

Sanjiban Sekhar Roy
School of Computer Science and Engineering, Vellore Institute of Technology, India

Preface

INTRODUCTION

In an era where industries are rapidly evolving, and the global emphasis on sustainability intensifies, the intersection of technology and environmental responsibility has never been more critical. As we transition towards smarter industries, the role of the Internet of Things (IoT) in encouraging sustainable practices cannot be overstated. Yet, while IoT technologies have the potential to revolutionize industries by enhancing efficiency and productivity, there still needs to be a significant gap in their design and implementation concerning environmental sustainability. This gap presents both a challenge and an opportunity—an opportunity to innovate and lead the way in creating industrial solutions that are not only smart but also environmentally responsible. This book addresses this critical need by comprehensively exploring how IoT technologies can be designed and deployed with sustainability at the forefront. This book provides a broad understanding of the intricacies involved in sustainable IoT development, equipping engineers, designers, and industry leaders with the knowledge necessary to create eco-friendly innovations that meet the demands of modern industries while minimizing environmental impact.

This volume brings together the insights and expertise of 36 authors from 12 countries, contributing to 13 meticulously crafted chapters. Each chapter examines the core aspects of sustainable IoT solutions, offering a blend of technical insights, strategic frameworks, and real-world case studies. The authors explore a range of topics, from the integration of IoT with renewable energy sources and waste reduction strategies to the ethical implications of deploying these technologies in industrial environments. The global perspective offered by this diverse group of contributors ensures that the solutions and strategies presented are applicable across various contexts and industries. The chapters have undergone a rigorous double-blind peer-review process to ensure the highest academic standards, with 13 submissions being evaluated and 24 chapters not included.

As we navigate the complexities of the 21st century, the role of sustainable innovation in shaping the future of industries is paramount. This book is a vital resource for industry professionals, academics, policymakers, and technologists committed to advancing sustainability through intelligent IoT solutions. By embracing the concepts and methodologies presented here, we can pave the way for a future where smart industries thrive and do so in harmony with our planet. The editors of this book invite readers to join this transformative journey towards a sustainable and technologically advanced future. The insights and tools provided within these pages will empower you to contribute to the creation of industrial environments that are efficient, innovative, and, most importantly, sustainable.

CHAPTER OVERVIEW

In Chapter 1, Eriona Çela, Mathias M. Fonkam, Philip Eappen, and Narasimha Rao Vajjhala examine the evolving landscape of smart classrooms, focusing on the integration of sustainable Internet of Things (IoT) technologies. The authors systematically review current trends, highlighting how IoT innovations are reshaping educational environments to enhance learning experiences and improve resource efficiency. The chapter examines the impact of smart technologies on classroom design, teaching methodologies, and sustainability practices, offering insights into the benefits and challenges of adopting IoT in education. By emphasizing the potential of sustainable IoT solutions, the authors set the stage for the future of education, advocating for more adaptive, efficient, and environmentally conscious educational spaces. This chapter provides a comprehensive overview, underscoring the dual impact of IoT on both educational enhancement and environmental sustainability.

In Chapter 2, Eriona Çela, Rajasekhara Mouly Potluri, and Narasimha Rao Vajjhala conduct a comprehensive meta-analysis on the integration of IoT technologies in educational settings, focusing on their impact on data-driven decision-making. The chapter explores how IoT can enhance various aspects of education, including learning environments, campus management, student safety, and administrative efficiency. The authors present statistical insights revealing significant improvements in these areas, while also addressing the challenges such as data privacy, security concerns, and infrastructure requirements. By synthesizing findings from a wide range of studies, this chapter provides a balanced perspective on both the potential benefits and the barriers to IoT adoption in education. The chapter emphasizes the need for strategic planning and standardized frameworks to maximize the positive impact of IoT technologies, while also considering the ethical implications and long-term sustainability. The chapter concludes with suggestions for future research directions, aimed at further exploring the role of IoT in enhancing educational effectiveness and equity.

In Chapter 3, Bachina Harish Babu, Ananth J., Sukania P., Clement Joe Anand M., Mickle Aancy H., and Magesh Babu D. explore the integration of Internet of Things (IoT) technologies and clean technologies to promote waste reduction in manufacturing, aligning with circular economy principles. The chapter emphasizes the critical need for sustainable practices within the manufacturing sector and demonstrates how renewable energy systems and eco-friendly materials can significantly reduce waste throughout the production process. The authors discuss the role of IoT devices in providing real-time monitoring and data analysis to optimize resource use and minimize waste. The chapter also addresses challenges such as the high initial costs, interoperability issues, and data security concerns that can hinder the adoption of these technologies. By offering practical strategies and case studies, the authors highlight how the convergence of clean technologies and IoT can drive the circular economy forward, ultimately leading to more sustainable and resilient manufacturing processes.

In Chapter 4, Vellingiri A., Kokila R., Nisha P., Monish Kumar K., Somu Chinnusamy, and Sampath Boopathi explore the integration of GPS sensors and drones within precision agriculture to minimize environmental impact. The chapter highlights how these technologies enable precise application of inputs such as water, fertilizers, and pesticides, tailored to the specific needs of different crop areas. GPS technology allows for accurate field mapping and navigation, while drones provide aerial monitoring and real-time data collection. The authors discuss the significant benefits of this approach, including enhanced resource management, reduced chemical runoff, and improved soil health. Through detailed case studies and examples, the chapter demonstrates the practical applications of these technologies in modern farming, emphasizing their potential to revolutionize traditional agricultural practices by promoting sustainability and resilience.

In Chapter 5, Mrutyunjay Padhiary from Assam University India examines the transformative impact of advanced technologies such as deep learning, IoT sensors, and modern farm machinery on contemporary agricultural practices. The chapter begins by tracing the historical evolution of farm machinery, highlighting key milestones that have shaped modern agricultural methodologies. Padhiary then explores the integration of IoT sensors in agriculture, showcasing their role in monitoring real-time data on soil conditions, weather patterns, and crop health, thereby enabling data-driven decision-making in precision agriculture. The chapter also examines the role of deep learning algorithms in enhancing agricultural productivity by predicting crop yields, detecting diseases, and optimizing various farming operations. Using case studies, the chapter demonstrates how these technologies reduce the need for manual labor, increase operational efficiency, and contribute to sustainable farming practices. Furthermore, the chapter addresses the challenges of adopting these technologies, such as high costs and technical barriers, and proposes strategies for overcoming them through innovation and collaboration. By emphasizing the importance of data utilization and partnerships, the chapter aims to inspire the adoption of innovative techniques that can meet the global food security challenges and ensure the sustainability of agricultural practices in the future.

In Chapter 6, Anton Limbo, Maria Ndapewa Ntinda, and Ananias Ndemuweda Nakale from the University of Namibia, examine the integration of Artificial Intelligence of Things (AIoT) in modern agriculture. The chapter introduces a comprehensive framework designed to guide the adoption of smart farming technologies, emphasizing the role of AI in enhancing decision-making and automation in crop farming. The framework is structured around five key modules: the sensor module, artificial intelligence module, automation module, network module, and processing module. These components work together to monitor critical agricultural parameters, automate farming processes, and optimize resource utilization. The authors begin by discussing the historical evolution of farming technologies and the growing need for modernization to meet global food security challenges and sustainability goals. They highlight the benefits of AIoT in improving precision agriculture by enabling real-time data collection and analysis through IoT sensors, which monitor soil conditions, weather, and crop health. The AI module further processes this data, identifying patterns, predicting outcomes, and making informed decisions to automate essential farming tasks such as irrigation, fertilization, and pest control. Through case studies and practical examples, the chapter demonstrates how the proposed framework can be implemented in real-world agricultural settings to enhance efficiency, reduce labor costs, and promote environmental sustainability. The authors address the challenges of AIoT adoption in farming, such as technological complexity, cost barriers, and data privacy concerns, offering solutions to mitigate these issues. They also explore the potential of future technologies, including blockchain, quantum computing, and renewable energy, in advancing smart farming practices. This chapter provides valuable insights into the transformative impact of AIoT on agriculture, offering a robust framework that can be adapted to various farming environments. By integrating AI with IoT, the chapter aims to revolutionize traditional farming methods, ensuring higher yields, better resource management, and sustainable practices for the future of agriculture.

In Chapter 7, Igoche Bernard Igoche from the University of Portsmouth UK and Gabriel Terna Ayem from the American University of Nigeria, Nigeria, explore the pivotal role of big data analytics in addressing sustainability challenges, with a particular focus on the educational admissions process. The chapter begins by discussing the emergence of big data and its applications across various sectors, emphasizing how it has become instrumental in driving sustainable solutions by enabling organizations to collect, analyze, and derive insights from large datasets generated by diverse sources such as sensors, IoT devices, and digital platforms. The authors examine the application of big data analytics within the context of educational admissions, showcasing how advanced analytics techniques, including machine learning, predictive modeling, and data visualization, can be employed to enhance decision-making processes. The chapter presents a case study on the application of big data analytics to visualize, analyze, and extract knowledge from an admissions database within a polytechnic system. This case study illustrates how machine learning predictions and explanations, facilitated by the Local Interpretable Model-agnostic Explanations (LIME) framework, can be used to inform fair and transparent decision-making in educational settings. Further, the chapter addresses the challenges associated with implementing big data solutions, such as data privacy concerns, the complexity of integrating different data formats, and the potential biases introduced by machine learning algorithms. To mitigate these issues, the authors propose a structured approach to data preprocessing, feature selection, and the application of fairness constraints in machine learning models. The chapter concludes by highlighting the benefits of adopting big data analytics in educational admissions, including improved resource efficiency, enhanced fairness, and the potential to drive innovation in educational practices. The authors advocate for the adoption of big data analytics as a means to ensure more equitable and sustainable solutions in the education sector, particularly in the context of admissions processes.

In Chapter 8, Gabriel Terna Ayem, Salu George Thandekkattu, and Sandip Rakshit explore the critical aspects of data management and analytics in the realm of IoT. The chapter provides an in-depth overview of the processes involved in collecting, storing, processing, and analyzing the vast amounts of data generated by interconnected IoT devices. The authors emphasize the challenges associated with managing this data, including issues of scalability, data quality, interoperability, and security, and discuss the importance of employing advanced analytics techniques such as machine learning and predictive analytics to extract meaningful insights from IoT data. The chapter outlines the transformative potential of IoT-driven data management in various sectors, such as smart cities, healthcare, agriculture, and manufacturing, showcasing how effective data management can lead to better decision-making, optimized operations, and enhanced business processes. Additionally, the authors address the unique requirements of IoT data management systems, such as the need for real-time analytics, edge computing, and the integration of traditional data-based management systems with IoT platforms. Through the exploration of strategies and solutions, including data normalization, the use of big data techniques, and the application of machine learning, the chapter provides a comprehensive guide for implementing robust IoT data management and analytics frameworks. The authors also highlight the future directions for IoT data management, including the adoption of green IoT practices, the integration of 5G connectivity, and the development of advanced AI and machine learning techniques. By presenting case studies and examples, the chapter offers practical insights into overcoming the challenges of IoT data management and analytics, ensuring that organizations can effectively leverage IoT data to drive innovation and achieve sustainable growth in the digital era.

In Chapter 9, Kamal Bakari Jillahi and George Salu Thandekkattu from the American University Yola, Nigeria, present a comprehensive framework for collecting, aggregating, and fusing data from diverse IoT sources for epidemiological research. The chapter begins by addressing the challenges of integrating data from multiple sources, highlighting the importance of achieving a holistic understanding of epidemiological incidences through the aggregation of data collected by IoT devices. The authors propose a wireless network architecture designed to ensure energy efficiency and communication efficiency in data collection, with a focus on a CoAP (Constrained Application Protocol) mechanism for transferring data to a cloud-based service. This service is responsible for aligning, de-duplicating, aggregating, and mapping data from several sources, facilitating the prediction of disease incidence, vector abundance, and host population dynamics through machine learning models. The performance of these models, trained using both synthesized data from the proposed framework and data captured using traditional methods, is evaluated to demonstrate the superiority of the proposed approach. The chapter provides a detailed exploration of the key components of disease surveillance systems, including data collection, analysis, reporting, and control measures, emphasizing the importance of real-time data integration, context-sensitive data handling, and privacy-preserving data aggregation techniques. The authors discuss the challenges associated with traditional disease surveillance methods and propose advanced techniques for data fusion and aggregation, such as edge computing, hierarchical aggregation, and privacy-preserving methods like homomorphic encryption. Through real-world case studies and simulations, the chapter illustrates the practical implementation of the proposed framework, showcasing its effectiveness in improving the accuracy and timeliness of infectious disease surveillance. The authors conclude by highlighting future research directions, including the development of more advanced data fusion algorithms and the establishment of better interoperability standards to enhance the efficiency and reliability of IoT-based disease surveillance systems.

In Chapter 10, Bhupinder Singh, Christian Kaunert, Sahil Lal, Manmeet Kaur Arora, and Kittisak Jermsittiparsert explore the transformative potential of integrating the Internet of Things (IoT) with autonomous vehicles (AVs) to create intelligent mobility solutions that contribute to the development of sustainable cities and communities. The chapter begins by examining the current challenges in traditional transportation systems, such as traffic congestion, environmental pollution, and inefficiency, and how AVs equipped with advanced sensors, artificial intelligence (AI), and communication protocols can address these issues. The authors provide an in-depth analysis of the architecture and components necessary for IoT-enabled AVs, including sensors like LiDAR, radar, and cameras, as well as the communication protocols that enable these vehicles to interact with surrounding infrastructure and other vehicles. The chapter also discusses the role of edge computing and cloud integration in processing the vast amounts of data generated by AVs in real-time, ensuring that these vehicles can make informed decisions on the go. Through various use cases, such as smart traffic management, predictive maintenance, fleet management, and Mobility-as-a-Service (MaaS), the chapter demonstrates how intelligent mobility solutions can optimize transportation networks, reduce operational costs, and improve urban planning. The authors also address the societal impact of these technologies, including the regulatory, ethical, and workforce challenges associated with the adoption of AVs and IoT in transportation. By leveraging the latest research and case studies, the chapter provides a comprehensive overview of the future trends and research directions in intelligent mobility, highlighting the potential of IoT and AVs to revolutionize urban transportation and foster more sustainable and livable cities. The chapter concludes by advocating for a collaborative approach among policymakers, industry stakeholders, and urban planners to fully realize the benefits of intelligent mobility solutions in building sustainable communities.

In Chapter 11, Bhupinder Singh and Kittisak Jermsittiparsert explore the evolution and future trajectory of smart manufacturing within the framework of Industry 5.0, emphasizing the integration of the Internet of Things (IoT). The chapter begins by discussing the transition from Industry 4.0 to Industry 5.0, highlighting how the new industrial paradigm focuses on the synergy between human creativity and machine precision to enhance production processes. The authors examine the core concepts of Industry 5.0, such as human-machine interaction, real-time production monitoring, and predictive maintenance. They explore how IoT plays a crucial role in facilitating intelligent manufacturing, enabling machines to collect, analyze, and utilize data for improved performance and fault diagnosis. The chapter also covers the technological advancements that support Industry 5.0, including big data analytics, cloud computing, and the Industrial Internet of Things (IIoT). Through case studies and practical examples, the chapter illustrates how Industry 5.0 aims to optimize manufacturing by balancing productivity with sustainability. The authors address the challenges associated with the implementation of these technologies, such as data security, interoperability, and the need for skilled personnel. They also discuss the potential societal impacts of widespread automation, including the possible displacement of low-skilled workers and the ethical considerations of human-machine collaboration. The chapter concludes by offering insights into the future of smart manufacturing, suggesting that the integration of IoT with human-centric approaches will be key to achieving a more efficient, sustainable, and adaptive industrial environment. The authors advocate for a proactive approach to embracing Industry 5.0 technologies, ensuring that the benefits of intelligent manufacturing are maximized while mitigating potential risks.

In Chapter 12, Kazi Kutubuddin Sayyad Liyakat from Brahmdevdada Mane Institute of Technology, India, explores the transformative impact of Internet of Things (IoT) technologies on the dairy industry. The chapter begins by examining how the integration of IoT, sensors, and data analytics has revolutionized the production, processing, and distribution of milk and dairy products, driving efficiency, sustainability, and traceability. The author highlights the use of sensors to monitor environmental factors, cow health, and milk production in real-time, enabling better herd management and improving overall dairy farm productivity. The chapter discusses the adoption of automated milking systems, which utilize sensors and data analytics to enhance the milking process, reduce labor costs, and improve animal welfare. A significant portion of the chapter is dedicated to the challenges and opportunities presented by the intelligent dairy industry. Issues such as the initial costs of implementing IoT technologies, data security concerns, and the need for skilled personnel are addressed, with proposed strategies for overcoming these barriers. The chapter also explores the potential of blockchain technology in enhancing traceability and transparency in the dairy supply chain, allowing consumers to track the origins and production processes of dairy products. The chapter concludes by envisioning the future of the intelligent dairy industry, emphasizing the growing importance of IoT technologies in meeting the global demand for dairy products sustainably and efficiently. As IoT adoption in the dairy industry continues to rise, the author advocates for the continued innovation and integration of smart technologies to foster a more consumer-driven, efficient, and sustainable dairy sector.

In the book's final chapter, Richa Bhalla, Shwetha G.K., Sherif Mohamed Abdelaal Ismail, Padmavathy S., Nageswara Rao Gudipudi, and Sampath Boopathi examine how small and medium-sized enterprises (SMEs) can leverage smart technology and effective talent management strategies to stay competitive and foster innovation. The chapter explores the challenges that SMEs face, including financial constraints, limited market access, regulatory pressures, and the need for continuous innovation in a fast-paced business environment. The authors emphasize the integration of cutting-edge digital tools such as artificial intelligence (AI), the Internet of Things (IoT), and data analytics, which can significantly enhance operational efficiency, customer satisfaction, and innovation in SMEs. These technologies provide SMEs with the ability to automate routine tasks, gain actionable insights from data, and improve decision-making processes. The chapter also discusses the importance of talent management in ensuring that SMEs have the skilled workforce necessary to maximize the benefits of these technologies. Case studies and real-world examples illustrate how SMEs can successfully implement smart technology and talent management to overcome challenges and achieve sustainable growth. The chapter concludes with strategies for SMEs to attract, develop, and retain talent, ensuring that they remain agile and capable of adapting to changing market demands. By aligning smart technology adoption with talent management, SMEs can build a strong foundation for long-term success in the digital age.

In conclusion, this preface sets the stage for a comprehensive exploration of how the integration of IoT technologies with sustainability can revolutionize industries and drive forward environmentally responsible practices. As our global economy increasingly prioritizes both technological advancement and environmental stewardship, this book provides a timely and essential resource for industry professionals, academics, and policymakers alike. The collective insights of 36 authors from 12 countries, spanning 13 meticulously reviewed chapters, ensure a rich, diverse perspective on the challenges and opportunities of sustainable IoT development.

This book not only addresses the technical aspects of IoT implementation but also examines the ethical and strategic considerations that are critical for fostering innovation while minimizing environmental impact. By embracing the frameworks, case studies, and practical solutions presented here, readers are empowered to lead the charge in creating smarter, more sustainable industries that are aligned with the demands of the modern world. The editors invite you to engage with the concepts and methodologies discussed in these chapters, as they represent the building blocks for a future where technological progress and environmental responsibility go hand in hand.

Salu George Thandekkattu
American University of Nigeria, Nigeria

Narasimha Rao Vajjhala
University of New York, Tirana, Albania

Chapter 1
Current Trends in Smart Classrooms and Sustainable Internet of Things

Eriona Çela

https://orcid.org/0000-0003-2710-5489

University of New York Tirana, Tirana, Albania

Mathias M. Fonkam

https://orcid.org/0000-0002-2776-1462

Penn State University, USA

Philip Eappen

https://orcid.org/0000-0002-8120-8449

Cape Breton University, Canada

Narasimha Rao Vajjhala

https://orcid.org/0000-0002-8260-2392

University of New York Tirana, Tirana, Albania

ABSTRACT

This chapter explores the evolving landscape of smart classrooms, focusing on the integration of sustainable internet of things (IoT) technologies. This chapter systematically reviews current trends, highlighting how IoT innovations are reshaping educational environments to enhance learning experiences and improve resource efficiency. The chapter examines the impact of smart technologies on classroom design, teaching methodologies, and sustainability practices, offering insights into the benefits and challenges of adopting IoT in education. This chapter underscores

DOI: 10.4018/979-8-3693-5498-8.ch001

the potential of sustainable IoT solutions to create more adaptive, efficient, and environmentally conscious educational spaces, setting the stage for the future of education.

INTRODUCTION

The rapid advancement of technology has revolutionized various sectors, and education is no exception. Over the years, classrooms have evolved from traditional, teacher-centered spaces into dynamic environments where technology plays a central role (Göçen et al., 2020). This transformation has led to developing "smart classrooms," where interactive tools and digital resources enhance the learning experience (Alfoudari et al., 2021; Saini & Goel, 2019). As these innovations continue to progress, they are increasingly intertwined with the Internet of Things (IoT), creating connected educational spaces that are more effective and sustainable. In smart classrooms, traditional teaching methods have been augmented and, in some cases, replaced by digital tools that facilitate a more interactive and personalized learning experience (Cebrián et al., 2020; Dimitriadou & Lanitis, 2023). Smartboards, tablets, and advanced projectors are now common features, allowing educators to present information innovatively and engage students more deeply in the material (Cherner & Curry, 2017; Gregorcic & Haglund, 2021). The integration of these technologies has led to significant improvements in student participation, collaboration, and overall academic performance, as they cater to diverse learning styles and needs.

IoT has further enhanced the functionality of smart classrooms by connecting various devices and systems within the educational environment (Badshah et al., 2023; Saini & Goel, 2019). IoT enables real-time data collection and analysis, providing educators valuable insights into student behavior, performance, and engagement (Kamruzzaman et al., 2023). For instance, smart sensors can monitor classroom conditions such as temperature, lighting, and air quality, automatically adjusting them to create an optimal learning environment (Dong et al., 2019). This connectivity not only improves the educational experience but also contributes to the sustainability of these spaces by optimizing resource use and reducing waste. Sustainability has become a critical consideration in the design and operation of modern classrooms (Brundiers et al., 2010). The adoption of energy-efficient technologies, such as LED lighting and smart thermostats, reflects a growing awareness of the need to minimize the environmental impact of educational facilities (Almasri et al., 2024). Moreover, the shift towards digital resources and paperless classrooms aligns with broader efforts to reduce the consumption of natural resources. As smart classrooms evolve, their contribution to sustainability will likely increase, driven by integrating IoT and other emerging technologies.

Looking ahead, the fusion of smart classroom technologies with the IoT presents exciting possibilities for the future of education. As these systems become more sophisticated, they will enhance the learning experience and make significant strides toward creating more sustainable educational environments. The ongoing development of artificial intelligence (AI) and its potential applications in smart classrooms further underscores the transformative impact of technology on education. In this rapidly changing landscape, understanding current trends in smart classrooms and sustainable IoT is essential for educators, policymakers, and technologists as they work together to shape the future of learning.

BACKGROUND

The concept of integrating technology into education has a long and evolving history, reflecting broader societal changes and advancements in digital innovation. Educational tools have gradually become more sophisticated, from the early use of blackboards and chalk in Greek classrooms to the introduction of projectors and overhead transparencies in the 20th century (Muttappallymyalil et al., 2016). However, the turn of the 21st century marked a significant shift as the digital revolution began to take hold in classrooms worldwide. Computers, the Internet, and later, mobile devices started to permeate educational environments, offering new possibilities for teaching and learning. As these digital tools became more prevalent, the "smart classroom" idea began to take shape (Kwet & Prinsloo, 2020). Early smart classrooms were equipped with interactive whiteboards, basic projectors, and desktop computers, allowing teachers to present information more dynamically (Firmin & Genesi, 2013). These initial steps toward digital integration were promising, but they were often limited by the technology of the time and the infrastructure available in schools. Despite these limitations, the benefits of incorporating technology into education became increasingly apparent, leading to continued investment in and development of educational technologies.

Simultaneously, the broader technological landscape was experiencing rapid growth, particularly in connectivity. The emergence of the IoT in the early 2000s introduced a new paradigm in which everyday objects and devices could communicate through the Internet (Sunyaev & Sunyaev, 2020). This development opened new possibilities for creating interconnected systems that could share data and respond to real-time information. In education, the potential of IoT to enhance the functionality and efficiency of smart classrooms quickly became evident, as it allowed for the integration of various devices and systems within a single, cohesive learning environment. Integrating IoT into educational settings brought with it a focus on sustainability as schools and universities began to recognize the environmental impact of their operations (Zeeshan et al., 2022). The need to reduce energy consumption, minimize waste, and create more resource-efficient learning environments became a priority. The combination of smart technologies and IoT offered a solution, enabling educational institutions to monitor and manage their resources more effectively. This shift toward sustainability was further supported by the global emphasis on environmental responsibility, driven by concerns about climate change and resource depletion (Prior et al., 2012).

Today, the convergence of smart classroom technologies and IoT represents the forefront of innovation in education. These advancements are transforming the way teachers deliver instruction and how students engage with content, contributing to more sustainable and efficient educational environments. As the capabilities of these technologies continue to expand, understanding their development and the context in which they have emerged is crucial for anyone involved in shaping the future of education.

REVIEW OF LITERATURE

The literature on smart classrooms and integrating sustainable IoT technologies in educational settings has grown significantly over the past decade (Chen et al., 2021; Kwet & Prinsloo, 2020; Zeeshan et al., 2022). Scholars have explored various aspects of this technological transformation, emphasizing its impact on teaching methodologies, student engagement, and institutional sustainability (Deroncele-Acosta et al., 2023; Giesenbauer & Müller-Christ, 2020). Early studies focused on the shift from traditional to digital learning environments, highlighting the potential of smart technologies to enhance the educational experience. Researchers discussed how interactive tools, like smartboards and projectors, provided teachers with new ways to present information, making lessons more engaging and accessible to diverse learners (Bouslama & Kalota, 2013; Mun & Abdullah, 2016; Sonnenberg, 2012). As the adoption of smart classroom technologies expanded, studies began to examine the implications of these tools on student engagement and learning outcomes (Dimitriadou & Lanitis, 2023; Saini & Goel, 2019; Wang et al., 2022). Interactive technologies could encourage greater class participation, enabling students to collaborate more effectively and engage with the material more meaningfully. The use of smart technologies contributed to creating more inclusive and welcoming classroom atmospheres, which positively impacted student motivation and performance (García-Tudela et al., 2020).

The role of IoT in education has also been a significant focus of literature. IoT's ability to connect various devices and systems within a classroom environment has opened new avenues for real-time data collection and analysis (Verma et al.,

2017). Studies have demonstrated how IoT can be used to monitor classroom conditions, such as temperature and lighting, to create optimal learning environments (Cheryan et al., 2014; Gilman et al., 2020). The integration of IoT in classrooms has been shown to streamline administrative tasks, such as attendance tracking and performance monitoring, thereby allowing teachers to focus more on instruction and student interaction (Mershad et al., 2020; Muzayanah et al., 2024). Sustainability has emerged as a critical concern in the literature on smart classrooms and IoT (Chagnon-Lessard et al., 2021). As educational institutions increasingly recognize the environmental impact of their operations, adopting sustainable practices has become a priority. Scholars like Bouslama and Kalota (2013) have explored how smart technologies can contribute to sustainability by reducing energy consumption and minimizing waste. For instance, using energy-efficient lighting systems and smart thermostats has been shown to significantly decrease educational institutions' carbon footprint (Correia et al., 2022; Yilmazoglu, 2017). Additionally, the shift towards digital resources, facilitated by IoT, supports the move towards paperless classrooms, further reducing environmental impact.

Another important strand of literature examines the challenges and limitations associated with implementing smart classroom technologies and IoT. Despite the many benefits, several studies have highlighted the potential risks related to data privacy and security (Dimitriadou & Lanitis, 2023; Kamenskih, 2022). The increased student data collection through IoT devices raises concerns about how this information is stored, managed, and protected (Cheong & Nyaupane, 2022). Researchers have discussed the need for robust data governance frameworks to ensure student information is handled responsibly. Additionally, there is an ongoing debate about the digital divide, which refers to the unequal access to technology among different student populations (Adhikari et al., 2016). This divide poses a significant barrier to the equitable implementation of smart classroom technologies, particularly in underfunded schools and rural areas. There is a growing consensus that sound pedagogical principles should guide technology integration into education. Bouslama and Kalota (2013) emphasize the need for teachers to be adequately trained in using smart technologies to ensure that they are effectively integrated into the curriculum. Moreover, studies suggest that technology should complement rather than replace traditional teaching methods (Çela, Fonkam, et al., 2024; Çela, Vajjhala, et al., 2024). The goal is to create a balanced approach where technology enhances, rather than overshadows, the human elements of teaching and learning.

Recent literature has also explored the future potential of smart classrooms, particularly in the context of AI. AI can personalize learning experiences further, offering tailored educational plans based on individual student needs (Çela, Fonkam, et al., 2024). Studies have shown how AI can analyze data collected from IoT devices to provide insights that help educators refine their teaching strategies and improve student outcomes (Zhai et al., 2021). The potential for AI to adapt to various learning environments, whether online or in-person, represents a significant advancement in education technology. Another emerging area of interest is the concept of smart cities and their influence on educational environments (Zhuang et al., 2017). As urban areas become more connected through IoT, there is potential for schools to be integrated into this broader digital infrastructure (Allam & Jones, 2021). This integration could lead to more seamless learning experiences beyond the physical classroom. Research in this area is still in its early stages. Still, it suggests a future where education is more deeply embedded in the digital fabric of everyday life, offering students continuous access to learning resources.

Finally, the literature suggests that the ongoing development of smart classrooms and IoT technologies will require continued collaboration between educators, technologists, and policymakers (Tissenbaum & Slotta, 2019). The successful implementation of these technologies depends on the availability of advanced tools and the development of supportive policies and frameworks. This includes addressing issues such as funding, infrastructure, and teacher training and ensuring that ethical considerations, such as data privacy, are adequately addressed (Dimitriadou & Lanitis, 2023). The evolving nature of these technologies means that literature will continue to grow, providing valuable insights into how best to harness their potential to improve education. As technology continues to evolve, smart classrooms will play an increasingly important role in shaping the future of education, offering new opportunities for enhancing learning while also promoting sustainability.

METHODOLOGY

This systematic review aims to qualitatively analyze the concept of smart classrooms and sustainable IoT in transforming educational spaces and enhancing resource efficiency. The study identifies prevailing themes and subthemes within the literature using 48 articles filtered from an initial pool of 154. The analysis employs frequency and percentage calculations to uncover the most significant trends and patterns. The initial step involved a comprehensive literature search to identify relevant studies from various academic databases, including Google Scholar, IEEE Xplore, ScienceDirect, and ERIC, to gather a broad spectrum of articles. Several keywords, such as "smart classrooms," "sustainable IoT," "educational spaces," and "resource efficiency," guided the search. Specific inclusion and exclusion criteria were applied to ensure the relevance and quality of the selected articles. The inclusion criteria included peer-reviewed journal articles and conference papers, publications from the last ten years (2014-2024), studies focusing on smart classrooms, sustainable IoT, or both, and articles available in English. The exclusion criteria eliminated non-peer-reviewed articles, theses, publications older than ten years, studies not specifically addressing smart classrooms or sustainable IoT, and articles not available in full text. The initial search yielded 154 articles, each of which underwent a rigorous screening process. This involved a meticulous review of titles and abstracts, followed by a comprehensive assessment of the full text. After applying the inclusion and exclusion criteria, 48 articles were selected for the final analysis. A qualitative thematic analysis was then conducted to identify recurrent themes and subthemes in the selected literature. The process began with familiarization, where each article was read thoroughly to comprehensively understand its content. Next, the key points and concepts were highlighted and coded using qualitative data analysis software—NVivo. Codes were then grouped into broader themes and subthemes based on their similarities and relationships, and these themes were refined and defined to ensure clarity and distinction. The occurrence of each theme and subtheme was counted, and frequencies and percentages were calculated to determine the prominence of each theme within the literature.

The authors independently coded a subset of articles to ensure consistency, and any discrepancies were discussed and resolved through consensus, ensuring inter-rater reliability. This collaborative approach underscores the thoroughness and reliability of the study. Additionally, data from different sources (e.g., various academic databases) and different types of studies (e.g., empirical research, theoretical papers) were triangulated to provide a comprehensive view of the topic. While the systematic review provides valuable insights into smart classrooms and sustainable IoT, it has certain limitations, such as the exclusion of non-English articles, which may limit the comprehensiveness of the review, and the reliance on published literature may introduce publication bias. Despite these limitations, this study offers a thorough qualitative analysis of the current state of smart classrooms and sustainable IoT, contributing to understanding their role in transforming educational spaces and enhancing resource efficiency.

FINDINGS

Four key themes emerged from the systematic review of the literature, including technology integration in smart classrooms, sustainability and resource efficiency, pedagogical innovations, and student engagement and outcomes.

Technological Integration in Smart Classrooms

The theme of technological integration in smart classrooms explores how modern educational environments leverage advanced technologies to enhance the learning experience. By incorporating cutting-edge tools and systems, smart classrooms aim to create more interactive, efficient, and engaging learning spaces that cater to the diverse needs of students and educators. As shown in Table-1. this theme examines various aspects of technological integration, focusing on the use of IoT devices and sensors, interactive learning tools, and connectivity and networking, each contributing to the overall enhancement of educational practices and outcomes.

Table 1. Frequencies and percentages of sub themes under the technological integration in smart classrooms theme

Sub Themes	Frequency	Percentage
IoT devices and sensors	15	31.3%
Interactive learning tools	12	25.0%
Connectivity and networking	21	43.7%

IoT devices and sensors play a crucial role in monitoring and optimizing classroom environments (Terzieva et al., 2022). These technologies enable real-time data collection and analysis, allowing educators to adjust lighting, temperature, and other environmental factors to create an optimal learning atmosphere (Cebrián et al., 2020). By tracking student movements and engagement levels, IoT devices can provide insights into student behavior and learning patterns, thereby facilitating personalized learning experiences (Bustos-Lopez et al., 2022; Han et al., 2024). The impact of IoT on student engagement and learning outcomes is significant, as it helps to create a more responsive and adaptable educational environment that can meet the unique needs of each student (Iqbal et al., 2020; Pandita & Kiran, 2023).

Interactive learning tools such as smartboards and interactive projectors transform traditional classroom activities into dynamic and engaging experiences (Bouslama & Kalota, 2013; Yang et al., 2012). These tools, combined with educational software and applications, encourage active participation and collaboration among students. The implementation of gamification elements in smart classrooms further enhances the learning experience by making educational activities more enjoyable and motivating (Saleem et al., 2022). Research shows that interactive learning tools can significantly improve student engagement and retention, making them an essential component of modern educational strategies (Carroll et al., 2021). Robust internet connectivity is the backbone of smart classrooms, enabling seamless integration of various technological tools and platforms (Matthew et al., 2021). Cloud computing plays a pivotal role in data storage and access, providing a flexible and scalable solution for managing educational content and resources (Anshari et al., 2016). However, ensuring network security in educational settings is a critical challenge that must be addressed. Solutions such as secure access protocols and regular network audits are essential to protect sensitive information and maintain the integrity of the learning environment (Vorakulpipat et al., 2017). By addressing these connectivity and networking challenges, smart classrooms can offer a reliable and secure infrastructure that supports innovative educational practices.

Sustainability and Resource Efficiency

The theme of sustainability and resource efficiency in smart classrooms emphasizes the importance of integrating environmentally responsible practices and technologies in educational settings. As shown in Table 2, this theme highlights how smart classrooms can significantly reduce their environmental footprint through innovative strategies in energy management, waste reduction, and green building design. By adopting these sustainable practices, educational institutions can not only lower operational costs but also contribute to broader environmental goals.

Table 2. Frequencies and percentages of sub themes under the sustainability and resource efficiency theme

Sub Themes	Frequency	Percentage
Energy management	10	20.8%
Waste reduction	12	25.0%
Green building design	26	54.2%

Energy management is a crucial aspect of sustainability in smart classrooms (Mishra & Singh, 2023; Zeeshan et al., 2022). Strategies for reducing energy consumption include the implementation of smart lighting and HVAC systems, which automatically adjust based on occupancy and ambient conditions (Shah et al., 2019). Analyzing the impact of energy-saving technologies reveals substantial benefits in terms of cost savings and reduced carbon emissions (Hoyo-Montaño et al., 2019). By optimizing energy use, smart classrooms can create more sustainable learning environments without compromising comfort or functionality. Waste reduction is another significant component of resource efficiency in smart classrooms (Omotayo et al., 2021). The shift from traditional paper-based materials to digital alternatives plays a key role in minimizing paper waste (Badshah et al., 2023). Sustainable practices in classroom resources and supplies, such as using recycled materials and reducing single-use items, further contribute to waste reduction efforts (Lee & Manfredi, 2021). The integration of IoT technologies enhances these efforts by providing precise monitoring and management of waste production (Hannan et al.,

2015). IoT sensors can track resource usage in real-time, identifying areas where waste can be reduced and promoting more sustainable behaviors among students and staff.

Green building design is integral to creating sustainable educational spaces (Chang & Lee, 2022; Venkatesh et al., 2022). Smart classrooms can be seamlessly integrated within green building frameworks, which prioritize energy efficiency, resource conservation, and indoor environmental quality (Ahmed et al., 2022; Venkatesh et al., 2022). Sustainable architecture offers numerous benefits for educational spaces, including improved air quality, natural lighting, and reduced energy consumption (Alshuwaikhat & Abubakar, 2008). Case studies of eco-friendly smart classroom implementations provide valuable insights into the practical application of these principles (Zhang et al., 2022). These examples demonstrate how sustainable design can create healthy, efficient, and inspiring learning environments that support both educational and environmental objectives. By focusing on these subthemes, the theme of sustainability and resource efficiency underscores the potential of smart classrooms to lead the way in sustainable education. Through innovative energy management, waste reduction, and green building design, smart classrooms can significantly contribute to environmental sustainability while providing high-quality educational experiences.

Pedagogical Innovations

The theme of pedagogical innovations explores how advancements in educational technology are reshaping teaching and learning methods. As shown in Table 3, by integrating personalized learning, collaborative learning, and comprehensive teacher training and support, smart classrooms can create dynamic and effective educational environments. These innovations leverage data analytics, adaptive learning platforms, AI, and advanced tools to cater to individual learning needs, enhance collaboration, and support educators in navigating new technologies. Personalized learning is a key component of pedagogical innovation, utilizing data analytics to tailor educational experiences to individual student needs (Shemshack & Spector, 2020). Adaptive learning platforms analyze student performance in real-time and adjust content delivery, accordingly, ensuring that each learner receives the appropriate level of challenge and support (Gligorea et al., 2023). AI plays a crucial role in developing personalized learning paths by analyzing vast amounts of data to identify learning patterns and preferences (Çela, Fonkam, et al., 2024). This approach not only enhances student engagement and achievement but also allows educators to identify and address learning gaps more effectively.

*Table 3. Frequencies and percentages of sub themes under the pedagogical inno-
vation theme*

Sub Themes	Frequency	Percentage
Personalized learning	9	18.8%
Collaborative learning	20	41.6%
Teacher training and support	19	39.6%

Collaborative learning is another key aspect of pedagogical innovation, facilitated by tools and technologies designed to support group work and communication (Rodríguez et al., 2017). Smart classrooms provide a range of interactive technologies, such as collaborative software, digital whiteboards, and communication platforms, which enable students to work together seamlessly, regardless of their physical location (Kaur et al., 2022; Saini & Goel, 2019). The impact of these tools on student teamwork and communication is profound, enabling a more interactive and engaging learning environment. Case studies of successful collaborative learning environments highlight the potential of these technologies to improve learning outcomes and prepare students for the collaborative nature of modern workplaces (Blackburn, 2015; Martín-Gutiérrez et al., 2015). Teacher training and support are essential for the successful integration of new technologies in the classroom (Çela, 2022, 2024). Professional development programs focused on smart classroom technologies help educators understand and effectively use these tools to enhance their teaching practices (Kaur et al., 2022; Saini & Goel, 2019). Strategies for integrating new technologies include hands-on training sessions, continuous professional development, and collaborative learning communities where teachers can share experiences and best practices. Support systems for teachers transitioning to smart classrooms, such as mentoring programs and technical support, are critical in ensuring that educators feel confident and capable in using new technologies (Çela, 2024). These efforts help to create a supportive and innovative teaching environment where both educators and students can thrive.

Together, these subthemes illustrate the transformative potential of pedagogical innovations in smart classrooms. By focusing on personalized learning, collaborative learning, and robust teacher training and support, educational institutions can create more effective, engaging, and adaptable learning environments. These innovations not only improve student outcomes but also equip educators with the tools and knowledge they need to succeed in an increasingly digital world.

Student Engagement and Outcomes

The theme of student engagement and outcomes focuses on how smart classroom technologies enhance student involvement in the learning process and improve educational results. As shown in Table 4, by utilizing advanced engagement metrics, promoting academic performance, and ensuring accessibility and inclusion, smart classrooms create environments where all students can thrive. These innovations help educators track and boost student engagement, analyze the effectiveness of educational technologies, and provide inclusive learning experiences for diverse student populations. Engagement metrics are critical for measuring how students interact with and respond to smart classroom technologies (Henrie et al., 2015). Various methods are employed to assess student engagement, including real-time data analytics, behavioral tracking, and feedback systems (Hussain et al., 2018). Interactive technologies, such as digital polling tools, gamified learning platforms, and interactive whiteboards, significantly impact student participation by making learning more engaging and interactive (Campbell et al., 2019; Sun & Hsieh, 2018). Case studies have shown that these technologies can lead to substantial improvements in student engagement, with increased participation rates and more active involvement in classroom activities (Bond et al., 2020).

Academic performance is closely linked to the implementation of smart classroom technologies (Alfoudari et al., 2021; Chang & Lee, 2022). Comparative analyses of traditional and smart classroom outcomes often reveal that students in tech-enhanced environments perform better on assessments, exhibit higher retention rates, and achieve greater overall academic success (Nguyen, 2011). Accessibility and inclusion are paramount in ensuring that all students benefit from smart classroom technologies (Wang, 2008). Tools designed to support students with disabilities, such as speech-to-text software, screen readers, and adaptive learning devices, play a crucial role in making education more inclusive (Bjekić et al., 2014; Ismaili & Ibrahimi, 2017). Strategies for creating inclusive smart classrooms involve designing flexible learning environments that accommodate diverse learning needs and providing personalized support to students (Peng et al., 2019). The impact of smart classrooms on bridging educational gaps is profound, as these technologies can help level the playing field for students from various backgrounds, ensuring that everyone can succeed. The theme of student engagement and outcomes highlights the transformative potential of smart classroom technologies in enhancing student involvement and improving educational results. By focusing on engagement metrics, academic performance, and accessibility and inclusion, educators can create dynamic and inclusive learning environments that support the success of all students. These innovations not only enhance the learning experience but also contribute to the broader goal of educational equity and excellence.

Table 4. Frequencies and percentages of sub themes under the student engagement and outcomes theme

Sub Themes	Frequency	Percentage
Engagement metrics	10	20.8%
Academic performance	21	43.8%
Accessibility and inclusion	17	35.4%

The boxplot in Figure-1 presented above provides a visual representation of the distribution of frequencies for various subthemes within each core theme related to smart classrooms and sustainable IoT. Each box represents the interquartile range (IQR) of the data for a particular theme, with the horizontal line inside the box indicating the median frequency. The "whiskers" extend to the smallest and largest values within 1.5 times the IQR from the lower and upper quartiles, respectively. Any points outside this range are considered outliers and are plotted individually. This boxplot helps in understanding the central tendency, variability, and presence of outliers within each theme, providing a clear comparison of how frequently each subtheme appears in the literature. Specifically, the boxplot shows that the theme "technological integration in smart classrooms" has a relatively high median frequency with a moderate range, indicating consistent attention to its subthemes such as IoT devices, interactive learning tools, and connectivity. In contrast, "sustainability and resource efficiency" has a wider range and higher variability, reflecting diverse coverage of subthemes like energy management, waste reduction, and green building design. The themes "pedagogical innovations" and "student engagement and outcomes" also exhibit varying degrees of frequency distribution, highlighting areas like personalized learning, collaborative tools, engagement metrics, and accessibility measures. This visual representation underscores the differing levels of emphasis placed on each subtheme within the broader discourse of smart classroom and sustainable IoT technologies.

Figure 1. Boxplot of frequencies for themes and subthemes

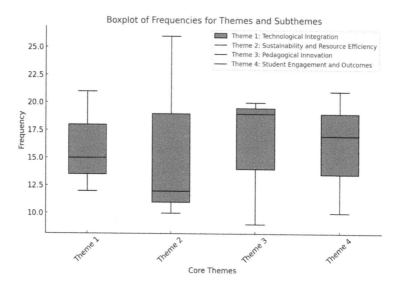

Additionally, the boxplot reveals valuable insights into the comparative prominence of subthemes within each core theme. For instance, the relatively tall boxes for themes like "sustainability and resource efficiency" suggest a wider spread of data, indicating that some subthemes within this category receive more attention than others. This could be due to varying levels of research focus on aspects like green building design compared to energy management or waste reduction. On the other hand, the more compact boxes for themes such as "technological integration in smart classrooms" and "pedagogical innovations" indicate less variability, suggesting a more uniform distribution of research efforts across their subthemes. The presence of outliers, particularly noticeable in themes like "student engagement and outcomes," highlights specific subthemes that have garnered exceptionally high or low attention. For example, the high frequency of subthemes like academic performance and accessibility might point to a concentrated research interest in these areas, driven by their critical importance in educational outcomes. Conversely, lower-frequency outliers might suggest emerging areas that are gaining traction or subthemes that are considered less critical by the current research community. Overall, the boxplot serves as a comprehensive tool for visualizing the landscape of research focus, identifying key areas of interest, and pinpointing potential gaps or emerging trends within the field of smart classrooms and sustainable IoT.

FUTURE RESEARCH DIRECTIONS

Future research on smart classrooms and sustainable IoT should focus on exploring the long-term impacts of these technologies on educational outcomes and environmental sustainability. While current studies have provided insights into the immediate benefits of smart classrooms, such as enhanced student engagement and resource efficiency, there is a need for longitudinal research to understand how these technologies influence learning trajectories, teacher practices, and institutional sustainability over time. Additionally, investigating the scalability of smart classroom solutions across different educational contexts, including under-resourced schools and developing countries, will ensure that these innovations' benefits are accessible to a broader range of students and educators. Another crucial direction for future research is the integration of artificial intelligence (AI) with IoT in smart classrooms. AI has the potential to significantly enhance learning experiences and streamline classroom management. However, its implementation raises important questions about data privacy, ethical use, and the potential for unintended consequences, such as exacerbating educational inequalities. Research should therefore focus on developing frameworks for the ethical use of AI in educational settings, as well as exploring the most effective ways to combine AI with existing smart classroom technologies to enhance learning outcomes without compromising student privacy or equity.

As sustainability becomes increasingly critical in education, future research should explore innovative ways to integrate IoT with other sustainable technologies in smart classrooms. For example, using renewable energy sources, such as solar panels, in conjunction with IoT-enabled energy management systems could further reduce the environmental impact of educational institutions. Additionally, research could investigate how smart classrooms can contribute to broader sustainability goals, such as reducing the carbon footprint of education through the promotion of remote learning or minimizing waste through digital resource management. Finally, there is a critical need for interdisciplinary research that bridges the gap between educational technology, environmental science, and policy studies. Such research could provide a more comprehensive understanding of how smart classrooms and sustainable IoT can be implemented effectively at scale, considering not only technological and pedagogical factors but also the regulatory and socio-economic contexts in which these technologies are deployed. This holistic approach will be essential for ensuring that smart classrooms are not only effective and sustainable but also equitable and inclusive, providing all students with the opportunity to benefit from the latest advancements in educational technology.

CONCLUSION

This chapter provides a comprehensive exploration of how modern educational spaces are being transformed through the integration of advanced technologies, particularly the IoT. The significant shift from traditional teaching methods to more dynamic and interactive learning environments is highlighted, where digital tools such as smartboards, tablets, and IoT-enabled devices play a central role. These technologies enhance student engagement and collaboration and contribute to more efficient and resource-conscious classroom management. A key focus of the chapter is the dual impact of these innovations on education and sustainability. IoT technologies allow for real-time monitoring and optimization of classroom conditions, leading to improved learning environments and reduced resource consumption. This aspect of sustainability is further supported by the adoption of energy-efficient technologies and the move towards digital, paperless classrooms, which align with global efforts to reduce the environmental footprint of educational institutions. The chapter also examines the challenges associated with the widespread adoption of smart classroom technologies, including concerns about data privacy, security, and the digital divide. The authors emphasize the need for ethical frameworks and policies to govern the use of these technologies, ensuring that they are implemented in equitable and inclusive ways. The discussion extends to the potential of AI in further enhancing smart classrooms, though with a cautionary note on the ethical implications of its use. In conclusion, this chapter presents a forward-looking perspective on the future of smart classrooms, highlighting the ongoing evolution of educational technologies and their potential to create more adaptive, efficient, and sustainable learning environments.

REFERENCES

Adhikari, J., Mathrani, A., & Scogings, C. (2016). Bring Your Own Devices classroom: Exploring the issue of digital divide in the teaching and learning contexts. *Interactive Technology and Smart Education*, 13(4), 323–343. DOI:10.1108/ITSE-04-2016-0007

Ahmed, M. A., Chavez, S. A., Eltamaly, A. M., Garces, H. O., Rojas, A. J., & Kim, Y.-C. (2022). Toward an intelligent campus: IoT platform for remote monitoring and control of smart buildings. *Sensors (Basel)*, 22(23), 9045. DOI:10.3390/s22239045 PMID:36501748

Alfoudari, A. M., Durugbo, C. M., & Aldhmour, F. M. (2021). Understanding socio-technological challenges of smart classrooms using a systematic review. *Computers & Education*, 173, 104282. DOI:10.1016/j.compedu.2021.104282

Allam, Z., & Jones, D. S. (2021). Future (post-COVID) digital, smart and sustainable cities in the wake of 6G: Digital twins, immersive realities and new urban economies. *Land Use Policy*, 101, 105201. DOI:10.1016/j.landusepol.2020.105201

Almasri, R. A., Abu-Hamdeh, N. H., & Al-Tamimi, N. (2024). A state-of-the-art review of energy-efficient and renewable energy systems in higher education facilities. *Frontiers in Energy Research*, 11, 1344216. DOI:10.3389/fenrg.2023.1344216

Alshuwaikhat, H. M., & Abubakar, I. (2008). An integrated approach to achieving campus sustainability: Assessment of the current campus environmental management practices. *Journal of Cleaner Production*, 16(16), 1777–1785. DOI:10.1016/j.jclepro.2007.12.002

Anshari, M., Alas, Y., & Guan, L. S. (2016). Developing online learning resources: Big data, social networks, and cloud computing to support pervasive knowledge. *Education and Information Technologies*, 21(6), 1663–1677. DOI:10.1007/s10639-015-9407-3

Badshah, A., Ghani, A., Daud, A., Jalal, A., Bilal, M., & Crowcroft, J. (2023). Towards smart education through internet of things: A survey. *ACM Computing Surveys*, 56(2), 1–33. DOI:10.1145/3610401

Bjekić, D., Obradović, S., Vučetić, M., & Bojović, M. (2014). E-teacher in inclusive e-education for students with specific learning disabilities. *Procedia: Social and Behavioral Sciences*, 128, 128–133. DOI:10.1016/j.sbspro.2014.03.131

Blackburn, G. (2015). Innovative eLearning: Technology shaping contemporary problem based learning: A cross-case analysis. *Journal of University Teaching & Learning Practice*, 12(2), 5. DOI:10.53761/1.12.2.5

Bond, M., Buntins, K., Bedenlier, S., Zawacki-Richter, O., & Kerres, M. (2020). Mapping research in student engagement and educational technology in higher education: A systematic evidence map. *International Journal of Educational Technology in Higher Education*, 17(1), 1–30. DOI:10.1186/s41239-019-0176-8

Bouslama, F., & Kalota, F. (2013). Creating smart classrooms to benefit from innovative technologies and learning space design. 2013 International Conference on Current Trends in Information Technology (CTIT).

Bustos-Lopez, M., Cruz-Ramirez, N., Guerra-Hernandez, A., Sánchez-Morales, L. N., Cruz-Ramos, N. A., & Alor-Hernandez, G. (2022). Wearables for engagement detection in learning environments: A review. *Biosensors (Basel)*, 12(7), 509. DOI:10.3390/bios12070509 PMID:35884312

Campbell, M., Detres, M., & Lucio, R. (2019). Can a digital whiteboard foster student engagement? *Social Work Education*, 38(6), 735–752. DOI:10.1080/0261 5479.2018.1556631

Carroll, M., Lindsey, S., Chaparro, M., & Winslow, B. (2021). An applied model of learner engagement and strategies for increasing learner engagement in the modern educational environment. *Interactive Learning Environments*, 29(5), 757–771. DOI:10.1080/10494820.2019.1636083

Cebrián, G., Palau, R., & Mogas, J. (2020). The smart classroom as a means to the development of ESD methodologies. *Sustainability (Basel)*, 12(7), 3010. DOI:10.3390/su12073010

Çela, E. (2022). A summary of the national plan for european integration related with the developments of education system in Albania during 2020-2021. *Euro-Balkan Law and Economics Review*, (1), 71–86.

Çela, E. (2024). Global Agendas in Higher Education and Current Educational Reforms in Albania. In *Global Agendas and Education Reforms: A Comparative Study* (pp. 255–269). Springer. DOI:10.1007/978-981-97-3068-1_13

Çela, E., Fonkam, M. M., & Potluri, R. M. (2024). Risks of AI-Assisted Learning on Student Critical Thinking: A Case Study of Albania. *International Journal of Risk and Contingency Management*, 12(1), 1–19. DOI:10.4018/IJRCM.350185

Çela, E., Vajjhala, N. R., & Eappen, P. (2024). Foundations of Computational Thinking and Problem Solving for Diverse Academic Fields. *Revolutionizing Curricula Through Computational Thinking, Logic, and Problem Solving*, 1-16.

Chagnon-Lessard, N., Gosselin, L., Barnabé, S., Bello-Ochende, T., Fendt, S., Goers, S., Da Silva, L. C. P., Schweiger, B., Simmons, R., & Vandersickel, A. (2021). Smart campuses: Extensive review of the last decade of research and current challenges. *IEEE Access : Practical Innovations, Open Solutions*, 9, 124200–124234. DOI:10.1109/ACCESS.2021.3109516

Chang, M.-S., & Lee, M.-S. (2022). The integrated design process of the green-smart relocatable modular school building. *Journal of the Architectural Institute of Korea*, 38(5), 55–63.

Chen, X., Zou, D., Xie, H., & Wang, F. L. (2021). Past, present, and future of smart learning: A topic-based bibliometric analysis. *International Journal of Educational Technology in Higher Education*, 18(1), 2. DOI:10.1186/s41239-020-00239-6

Cheong, P. H., & Nyaupane, P. (2022). Smart campus communication, Internet of Things, and data governance: Understanding student tensions and imaginaries. *Big Data & Society*, 9(1), 205–226. DOI:10.1177/20539517221092656

Cherner, T., & Curry, K. (2017). Enhancement or transformation? A case study of preservice teachers' use of instructional technology. *Contemporary Issues in Technology & Teacher Education*, 17(2), 268–290.

Cheryan, S., Ziegler, S. A., Plaut, V. C., & Meltzoff, A. N. (2014). Designing classrooms to maximize student achievement. *Policy Insights from the Behavioral and Brain Sciences*, 1(1), 4–12. DOI:10.1177/2372732214548677

Correia, A., Ferreira, L. M., Coimbra, P., Moura, P., & de Almeida, A. T. (2022). Smart thermostats for a campus microgrid: Demand control and improving air quality. *Energies*, 15(4), 1359. DOI:10.3390/en15041359

Deroncele-Acosta, A., Palacios-Núñez, M. L., & Toribio-López, A. (2023). Digital transformation and technological innovation on higher education post-COVID-19. *Sustainability (Basel)*, 15(3), 2466. DOI:10.3390/su15032466

Dimitriadou, E., & Lanitis, A. (2023). A critical evaluation, challenges, and future perspectives of using artificial intelligence and emerging technologies in smart classrooms. *Smart Learning Environments*, 10(1), 12. DOI:10.1186/s40561-023-00231-3

Dong, B., Prakash, V., Feng, F., & O'Neill, Z. (2019). A review of smart building sensing system for better indoor environment control. *Energy and Building*, 199, 29–46. DOI:10.1016/j.enbuild.2019.06.025

Firmin, M. W., & Genesi, D. J. (2013). History and implementation of classroom technology. *Procedia: Social and Behavioral Sciences*, 93, 1603–1617. DOI:10.1016/j.sbspro.2013.10.089

García-Tudela, P. A., Prendes-Espinosa, M. P., & Solano-Fernández, I. M. (2020). Smart learning environments and ergonomics: An approach to the state of the question. *Journal of New Approaches in Educational Research*, 9(2), 245–258. DOI:10.7821/naer.2020.7.562

Giesenbauer, B., & Müller-Christ, G. (2020). University 4.0: Promoting the transformation of higher education institutions toward sustainable development. *Sustainability (Basel)*, 12(8), 3371. DOI:10.3390/su12083371

Gilman, E., Tamminen, S., Yasmin, R., Ristimella, E., Peltonen, E., Harju, M., Lovén, L., Riekki, J., & Pirttikangas, S. (2020). Internet of things for smart spaces: A university campus case study. *Sensors (Basel)*, 20(13), 3716. DOI:10.3390/s20133716 PMID:32630833

Gligorea, I., Cioca, M., Oancea, R., Gorski, A.-T., Gorski, H., & Tudorache, P. (2023). Adaptive learning using artificial intelligence in e-learning: A literature review. *Education Sciences*, 13(12), 1216. DOI:10.3390/educsci13121216

Göçen, A., Eral, S. H., & Bücük, M. H. (2020). Teacher perceptions of a 21st century classroom. *International Journal of Contemporary Educational Research*, 7(1), 85–98. DOI:10.33200/ijcer.638110

Gregorcic, B., & Haglund, J. (2021). Conceptual blending as an interpretive lens for student engagement with technology: Exploring celestial motion on an interactive whiteboard. *Research in Science Education*, 51(2), 235–275. DOI:10.1007/s11165-018-9794-8

Han, L., Long, X., & Wang, K. (2024). The analysis of educational informatization management learning model under the internet of things and artificial intelligence. *Scientific Reports*, 14(1), 17811. DOI:10.1038/s41598-024-68963-x PMID:39090332

Hannan, M., Al Mamun, M. A., Hussain, A., Basri, H., & Begum, R. A. (2015). A review on technologies and their usage in solid waste monitoring and management systems: Issues and challenges. *Waste Management (New York, N.Y.)*, 43, 509–523. DOI:10.1016/j.wasman.2015.05.033 PMID:26072186

Henrie, C. R., Halverson, L. R., & Graham, C. R. (2015). Measuring student engagement in technology-mediated learning: A review. *Computers & Education*, 90, 36–53. DOI:10.1016/j.compedu.2015.09.005

Hoyo-Montaño, J. A., Valencia-Palomo, G., Galaz-Bustamante, R. A., García-Barrientos, A., & Espejel-Blanco, D. F. (2019). Environmental impacts of energy saving actions in an academic building. *Sustainability (Basel)*, 11(4), 989. DOI:10.3390/su11040989

Hussain, M., Zhu, W., Zhang, W., & Abidi, S. M. R. (2018). Student Engagement Predictions in an e-Learning System and Their Impact on Student Course Assessment Scores. *Computational Intelligence and Neuroscience*, 2018(1), 634–645. DOI:10.1155/2018/6347186 PMID:30369946

Iqbal, H. M., Parra-Saldivar, R., Zavala-Yoe, R., & Ramirez-Mendoza, R. A. (2020). Smart educational tools and learning management systems: Supportive framework. *International Journal on Interactive Design and Manufacturing*, 14(4), 1179–1193. DOI:10.1007/s12008-020-00695-4

Ismaili, J., & Ibrahimi, E. H. O. (2017). Mobile learning as alternative to assistive technology devices for special needs students. *Education and Information Technologies*, 22(3), 883–899. DOI:10.1007/s10639-015-9462-9

Kamenskih, A. (2022). The analysis of security and privacy risks in smart education environments. *Journal of Smart Cities and Society*, 1(1), 17–29. DOI:10.3233/SCS-210114

Kamruzzaman, M., Alanazi, S., Alruwaili, M., Alshammari, N., Elaiwat, S., Abu-Zanona, M., Innab, N., Mohammad Elzaghmouri, B., & Ahmed Alanazi, B. (2023). AI-and IoT-assisted sustainable education systems during pandemics, such as COVID-19, for smart cities. *Sustainability (Basel)*, 15(10), 8354. DOI:10.3390/su15108354

Kaur, A., Bhatia, M., & Stea, G. (2022). A survey of smart classroom literature. *Education Sciences*, 12(2), 86. DOI:10.3390/educsci12020086

Kwet, M., & Prinsloo, P. (2020). The 'smart' classroom: A new frontier in the age of the smart university. *Teaching in Higher Education*, 25(4), 510–526. DOI:10.1080/13562517.2020.1734922

Lee, S., & Manfredi, L. R. (2021). Promoting recycling, reducing and reusing in the School of Design: A step toward improving sustainability literacy. *International Journal of Sustainability in Higher Education*, 22(5), 1038–1054. DOI:10.1108/IJSHE-11-2020-0443

Martín-Gutiérrez, J., Fabiani, P., Benesova, W., Meneses, M. D., & Mora, C. E. (2015). Augmented reality to promote collaborative and autonomous learning in higher education. *Computers in Human Behavior*, 51, 752–761. DOI:10.1016/j.chb.2014.11.093

Matthew, U. O., Kazaure, J. S., & Okafor, N. U. (2021). Contemporary development in E-Learning education, cloud computing technology & internet of things. *EAI Endorsed Transactions on Cloud Systems*, 7(20), e3–e3.

Mershad, K., Damaj, A., Wakim, P., & Hamieh, A. (2020). LearnSmart: A framework for integrating internet of things functionalities in learning management systems. *Education and Information Technologies*, 25(4), 2699–2732. DOI:10.1007/s10639-019-10090-6

Mishra, P., & Singh, G. (2023). Energy management systems in sustainable smart cities based on the internet of energy: A technical review. *Energies*, 16(19), 6903. DOI:10.3390/en16196903

Mun, S. H., & Abdullah, A. H. (2016). A review of the use of smart boards in education. 2016 IEEE 8th international conference on engineering education (ICEED). PMID:27822404

Muzayanah, R., Lestari, A. D., & Muslim, M. A. (2024). IoT-Integrated Smart Attendance and Attention Monitoring System For Primary and Secondary School Classroom Management. *Journal of Electronics Technology Exploration*, 2(1), 21–25. DOI:10.52465/joetex.v2i1.381

Nguyen, B. T. (2011). *Face-to-face, blended, and online instruction: Comparison of student performance and retention in higher education*. University of California.

Omotayo, T., Moghayedi, A., Awuzie, B., & Ajayi, S. (2021). Infrastructure elements for smart campuses: A bibliometric analysis. *Sustainability (Basel)*, 13(14), 7960. DOI:10.3390/su13147960

Pandita, A., & Kiran, R. (2023). The technology interface and student engagement are significant stimuli in sustainable student satisfaction. *Sustainability (Basel)*, 15(10), 7923. DOI:10.3390/su15107923

Peng, H., Ma, S., & Spector, J. M. (2019). Personalized adaptive learning: An emerging pedagogical approach enabled by a smart learning environment. *Smart Learning Environments*, 6(1), 1–14. DOI:10.1186/s40561-019-0089-y

Prior, T., Giurco, D., Mudd, G., Mason, L., & Behrisch, J. (2012). Resource depletion, peak minerals and the implications for sustainable resource management. *Global Environmental Change*, 22(3), 577–587. DOI:10.1016/j.gloenvcha.2011.08.009

Rodríguez, A. I., Riaza, B. G., & Gómez, M. C. S. (2017). Collaborative learning and mobile devices: An educational experience in Primary Education. *Computers in Human Behavior*, 72, 664–677. DOI:10.1016/j.chb.2016.07.019

Saini, M. K., & Goel, N. (2019). How smart are smart classrooms? A review of smart classroom technologies. *ACM Computing Surveys*, 52(6), 1–28. DOI:10.1145/3365757

Saleem, A. N., Noori, N. M., & Ozdamli, F. (2022). Gamification applications in E-learning: A literature review. *Technology. Knowledge and Learning*, 27(1), 139–159. DOI:10.1007/s10758-020-09487-x

Shah, A. S., Nasir, H., Fayaz, M., Lajis, A., & Shah, A. (2019). A review on energy consumption optimization techniques in IoT based smart building environments. *Information (Basel)*, 10(3), 108. DOI:10.3390/info10030108

Shemshack, A., & Spector, J. M. (2020). A systematic literature review of personalized learning terms. *Smart Learning Environments*, 7(1), 33. DOI:10.1186/s40561-020-00140-9

Sonnenberg, M. (2012). Are you SMARTer than a SMART Board™? How to Effectively Use This Technology Tool to Communicate in a Classroom With a Diverse Group of Learners. In *Communication technology for students in special education and gifted programs* (pp. 243–248). IGI Global. DOI:10.4018/978-1-60960-878-1.ch019

Sun, J. C.-Y., & Hsieh, P.-H. (2018). Application of a gamified interactive response system to enhance the intrinsic and extrinsic motivation, student engagement, and attention of English learners. *Journal of Educational Technology & Society*, 21(3), 104–116.

Sunyaev, A., & Sunyaev, A. (2020). The internet of things. *Internet Computing: Principles of Distributed Systems and Emerging Internet-Based Technologies*, 301-337.

Terzieva, V., Ilchev, S., & Todorova, K. (2022). The Role of Internet of Things in Smart Education. *IFAC-PapersOnLine*, 55(11), 108–113. DOI:10.1016/j.ifacol.2022.08.057

Tissenbaum, M., & Slotta, J. D. (2019). Developing a smart classroom infrastructure to support real-time student collaboration and inquiry: A 4-year design study. *Instructional Science*, 47(4), 423–462. DOI:10.1007/s11251-019-09486-1

Venkatesh, C., Jayakrishna, D., & Sivayamini, L. (2022). Design of Smart Classroom in Educational Institutes for Smart and a Sustainable Campus Based on Internet of Things. In *Modern Approaches in Machine Learning & Cognitive Science: A Walkthrough* (pp. 547–558). Springer. DOI:10.1007/978-3-030-96634-8_50

Verma, S., Kawamoto, Y., Fadlullah, Z. M., Nishiyama, H., & Kato, N. (2017). A survey on network methodologies for real-time analytics of massive IoT data and open research issues. *IEEE Communications Surveys and Tutorials*, 19(3), 1457–1477. DOI:10.1109/COMST.2017.2694469

Vorakulpipat, C., Sirapaisan, S., Rattanalerdnusorn, E., & Savangsuk, V. (2017). A Policy-Based Framework for Preserving Confidentiality in BYOD Environments: A Review of Information Security Perspectives. *Security and Communication Networks*, 2017(1), 2057260. DOI:10.1155/2017/2057260

Wang, J., Tigelaar, D. E., Luo, J., & Admiraal, W. (2022). Teacher beliefs, classroom process quality, and student engagement in the smart classroom learning environment: A multilevel analysis. *Computers & Education*, 183, 104501. DOI:10.1016/j.compedu.2022.104501

Wang, Z. (2008). Smart spaces: Creating new instructional space with smart classroom technology. *New Library World*, 109(3/4), 150–165. DOI:10.1108/03074800810857603

Yang, K.-T., Wang, T.-H., & Kao, Y.-C. (2012). How an interactive whiteboard impacts a traditional classroom. *Education as Change*, 16(2), 313–332. DOI:10.1080/16823206.2012.745759

Yilmazoglu, M. Z. (2017). Decreasing energy consumption and carbon footprint in a school building: A comparative study on energy audits. *International Journal of Global Warming*, 13(2), 237–257. DOI:10.1504/IJGW.2017.086291

Zeeshan, K., Hämäläinen, T., & Neittaanmäki, P. (2022). Internet of Things for sustainable smart education: An overview. *Sustainability (Basel)*, 14(7), 4293. DOI:10.3390/su14074293

Zhai, X., Chu, X., Chai, C. S., Jong, M. S. Y., Istenic, A., Spector, M., Liu, J.-B., Yuan, J., & Li, Y. (2021). A Review of Artificial Intelligence (AI) in Education from 2010 to 2020. *Complexity*, 2021(1), 881–890. DOI:10.1155/2021/8812542

Zhang, Y., Yip, C., Lu, E., & Dong, Z. Y. (2022). A systematic review on technologies and applications in smart campus: A human-centered case study. *IEEE Access : Practical Innovations, Open Solutions*, 10, 16134–16149. DOI:10.1109/ACCESS.2022.3148735

Zhuang, R., Fang, H., Zhang, Y., Lu, A., & Huang, R. (2017). Smart learning environments for a smart city: From the perspective of lifelong and lifewide learning. *Smart Learning Environments*, 4(1), 1–21. DOI:10.1186/s40561-017-0044-8

ADDITIONAL READING

Mamirkulova, G. (2023). Revolutionizing education: teaching kids with technologies and gadgets. Theoretical aspects in the formation of pedagogical sciences, 2(13), 94-96.

Marouan, A., Badrani, M., Kannouf, N., & Chetouani, A. (2024). Empowering Education: Leveraging Blockchain for Secure Credentials and Lifelong Learning. In *Blockchain Transformations: Navigating the Decentralized Protocols Era* (pp. 1–14). Springer Nature Switzerland. DOI:10.1007/978-3-031-49593-9_1

Mota, D., & Martins, C. (2023). AI in emergency remote learning environments: Intelligent tutoring systems perspective. In *Developing Curriculum for Emergency Remote Learning Environments* (pp. 121–140). IGI Global.

Rizvi, M. (2023). Investigating AI-Powered Tutoring Systems that Adapt to Individual Student Needs, Providing Personalized Guidance and Assessments. *The Eurasia Proceedings of Educational and Social Sciences*, 31, 67–73. DOI:10.55549/epess.1381518

KEY TERMS AND DEFINITIONS

Accessibility and Inclusion: The implementation of technologies and strategies in smart classrooms to ensure that all students, including those with disabilities, can access and benefit from educational resources.

Energy Management: Strategies employed within smart classrooms to reduce energy consumption through the use of smart lighting, HVAC systems, and other energy-efficient technologies.

Green Building Design: Architectural approaches in smart classrooms that prioritize sustainability, including energy efficiency, resource conservation, and improved indoor environmental quality.

Interactive Learning Tools: Technologies such as smartboards and interactive projectors that transform traditional teaching methods into more engaging and dynamic experiences.

IoT Devices and Sensors: Connected devices within a smart classroom that collect and analyze data in real-time to optimize conditions such as temperature, lighting, and student engagement.

Pedagogical Innovations: Advances in teaching methodologies driven by smart classroom technologies, including personalized and collaborative learning supported by data analytics and AI.

Resource Efficiency: The optimization of resources in educational environments, particularly through the reduction of waste and the use of sustainable materials and technologies.

Smart Classrooms: Educational environments that leverage advanced technologies like interactive tools, IoT devices, and digital resources to enhance teaching and learning experiences.

Student Engagement Metrics: Methods used to assess how students interact with and respond to smart classroom technologies, often involving real-time data analytics and behavioral tracking.

Sustainable Internet of Things (IoT): The integration of IoT technologies in educational settings to create more efficient, adaptive, and environmentally conscious learning environments.

Chapter 2
A Comprehensive Meta–Analysis of IoT Integration for Data–Driven Decision Making in Education

Eriona Çela
https://orcid.org/0000-0003-2710-5489
University of New York Tirana, Tirana, Albania

Rajasekhara Mouly Potluri
https://orcid.org/0000-0002-6935-1373
Kazakh British Technical University, Kazakhstan

Narasimha Rao Vajjhala
https://orcid.org/0000-0002-8260-2392
University of New York Tirana, Tirana, Albania

ABSTRACT

This chapter systematically reviews the literature on using internet of things (IoT) technologies to enable data-driven decision-making in educational institutions. As educational environments become increasingly complex, the ability to collect, analyze, and act upon data is crucial for institutional improvement. IoT technologies offer opportunities for educational leaders to optimize various aspects of campus operations, enhance student experiences, and improve administrative efficiency. The chapter explores IoT adoption in education, highlighting key technological advancements and their data collection and analysis applications. This chapter examines

DOI: 10.4018/979-8-3693-5498-8.ch002

how IoT-generated data can inform resource allocation, facility management, and student services decisions. This chapter also addresses the challenges and barriers to integrating IoT in educational decision-making, including issues related to data privacy, security, and the need for robust data governance frameworks.

INTRODUCTION

Integrating the Internet of Things (IoT) in education has emerged as a transformative approach, offering unprecedented opportunities for data-driven decision-making (Adel, 2024; Tariq et al., 2024). As educational institutions strive to enhance learning experiences and outcomes, the role of IoT in providing real-time data, personalized insights, and automated processes has become increasingly significant (Rodney, 2020). This chapter examines the complexities and potentials of IoT integration within educational settings, emphasizing its impact on decision-making processes at various levels, from administrative planning to classroom instruction. IoT devices, from smart sensors to connected learning tools, generate vast amounts of data (Plageras et al., 2018). However, to effectively analyze this data and make informed decisions, educators and administrators need specialized skills. These data streams enable real-time monitoring and evaluation of educational environments, ensuring optimal resource allocation and personalized learning experiences. The integration of IoT into education presents challenges, including issues related to data privacy and infrastructure requirements, but with the right skills, these challenges can be overcome (Kassab et al., 2020).

This chapter conducts a comprehensive meta-analysis of existing research on IoT in education, synthesizing findings from a wide range of studies to provide a holistic view of how IoT technologies are being utilized for data-driven decision-making. This analysis uncovers patterns, best practices, and potential pitfalls that educators and policymakers must consider when adopting IoT solutions by examining case studies, empirical research, and theoretical models. The goal is to present a balanced perspective that highlights IoT's promises and limitations in the educational sector. While this chapter explores the technical and operational aspects of IoT integration, it also emphasizes the need to consider the broader implications for educational equity and access. As IoT technologies become more prevalent, there is a risk that disparities in access to these tools could increase existing inequalities in education. Therefore, this analysis also addresses the ethical considerations and potential strategies for ensuring that IoT-driven decision-making benefits all students, regardless of their socio-economic background. Ultimately, this chapter aims to provide a comprehensive understanding of how IoT can be leveraged to enhance data-driven decision-making in education. By offering insights into the current state of research, practical applications, and future directions, this chapter seeks to equip educators, administrators, and policymakers with the knowledge and tools necessary to harness IoT's full potential in transforming educational practices and outcomes.

BACKGROUND

The rapid advancements in digital technologies have revolutionized various sectors, including education. Among these innovations, IoT is a critical enabler of the Fourth Industrial Revolution, offering novel ways to connect devices, systems, and people (Trappey et al., 2017). In the context of education, IoT has the potential to significantly enhance the learning environment by providing real-time data and insights that inform decision-making at multiple levels (Bagheri & Movahed, 2016; Kassab et al., 2020). IoT involves seamlessly integrating interconnected devices that can collect, analyze, and share data, facilitating smarter and more responsive educational systems (Zhu et al., 2016). This chapter explores how these capabilities are harnessed to improve educational institutions' decision-making processes. Early implementations of IoT in education sector focused on basic automation and resource management, such as smart lighting and heating systems in school buildings (Mogas et al., 2022). However, as the technology evolved, so did its applications, extending into student monitoring, personalized learning, and data analytics (Hashim et al., 2022). IoT devices now include many tools, from wearable technology that tracks student health and engagement to smart classrooms equipped with sensors that monitor environmental conditions and optimize learning experiences (Badshah et al., 2023). These innovations have paved the way for a data-driven approach to education, where decisions are informed by precise, real-time information.

Despite the potential benefits, integrating IoT in education has also raised several challenges. Data privacy and security concerns are paramount, as collecting sensitive information about students and staff requires robust safeguards (Mawgoud et al., 2020). Additionally, implementing IoT systems demands significant investment in infrastructure and training, posing barriers for institutions with limited resources (Ahmed et al., 2016). The sheer volume of data generated by IoT devices can be overwhelming, necessitating advanced analytics tools and expertise to extract meaningful insights (Bibri, 2018). These challenges underscore the need for careful planning and strategic implementation of IoT in educational settings. The growing body of research on IoT in education reflects both the enthusiasm for its potential and the caution required in its deployment. This chapter builds on this existing literature by conducting a comprehensive meta-analysis, aiming to synthesize the findings and provide a clearer understanding of how IoT can support data-driven decision-making in education. This chapter also emphasizes the need for caution and careful planning in the deployment of IoT. By examining the evolution of IoT technologies, their applications, and the challenges they present, this analysis seeks to contextualize the current state of research and practice. This chapter also highlights the critical need for ongoing inquiry and innovation as educational institutions continue to adapt to the demands of a rapidly changing technological landscape.

REVIEW OF LITERATURE

In recent years, the literature on integrating the IoT in education has grown significantly, reflecting the increasing adoption of these technologies across educational institutions (Al-Emran et al., 2020; He et al., 2016; Kassab et al., 2020). The bulk of the research can be categorized into several key themes: the technological infrastructure of IoT in education, its impact on teaching and learning processes, the role of data analytics in decision-making, challenges related to privacy and security, and the socio-economic implications of IoT deployment. This meta-analysis seeks to provide a comprehensive review of these themes, synthesizing findings from a wide range of studies to offer a detailed understanding of how IoT contributes to data-driven decision-making in education. A substantial portion of the literature has focused on the technological aspects of IoT integration, particularly the infrastructure required to support connected devices in educational settings. Studies by Al-Fuqaha et al. (2015) and Atzori et al. (2010) provide foundational insights into the architecture of IoT systems, highlighting the importance of seamless connectivity, interoperability, and scalability. These studies emphasize that the effectiveness of IoT in education is contingent upon a robust and flexible infrastructure capable of handling large volumes of data generated by various devices. Miorandi et al. (2012) explore the evolution of IoT standards and protocols, which are critical for ensuring the reliability and security of educational IoT systems.

The impact of IoT on teaching and learning processes has been another major focus in the literature. Research by Bibri and Krogstie (2017) explores how IoT-enabled environments can facilitate personalized learning by adapting to individual student needs. IoT devices such as wearable technology and smart classroom tools provide continuous feedback, allowing educators to tailor their teaching strategies in real time. Additionally, a study by Gubbi et al. (2013) discusses how IoT can enhance collaborative learning by connecting students and teachers through networked devices, encouraging a more interactive and engaging educational experience. These findings suggest that IoT has the potential to transform traditional pedagogical approaches, making them more responsive and learner-centered. The role of data analytics in decision-making is a critical area of investigation in the context of IoT integration in education. Privacy and security concerns have emerged as significant challenges in the literature on IoT in education (Çela, 2022; Çela, 2024). Research by Sahu et al. (2019), Razzaq et al. (2017), and Tawalbeh et al. (2020) identifies the risks associated with data breaches and unauthorized access to sensitive information collected by IoT devices. These studies argue that the widespread adoption of IoT in education necessitates the development of robust security frameworks to protect student and staff data.

A study by Bower and Sturman (2015) reviews the potential of IoT to support experiential learning, where students engage with real-world problems through connected devices. This approach aligns with constructivist theories of education, which emphasize active learning and the importance of context in shaping understanding. Additionally, research by González-Martínez et al. (2015) explores the use of IoT in assessment, suggesting that continuous data collection can provide more accurate and comprehensive evaluations of student performance than traditional methods. In addition to these themes, the literature has begun exploring IoT's long-term sustainability in education. A study by Khan and Salah (2018) examines the environmental impact of IoT devices, particularly their energy consumption and e-waste generation. These findings raise important questions about the sustainability of IoT deployment in education and suggest the need for green technologies and practices to mitigate the environmental footprint of connected devices. Moreover, research by Perera et al. (2013) discusses the importance of designing IoT systems with sustainability in mind, ensuring that they can be easily updated and maintained over time without incurring excessive costs.

The literature on IoT in education also highlights the importance of professional development for educators. Studies by Aldowah et al. (2017) and Matthew et al. (2021) argue that the successful integration of IoT into teaching and learning requires ongoing training and support for educators. These studies suggest that educators may need adequate professional development to effectively use IoT tools, limiting their potential to enhance teaching and learning. The literature emphasizes the need for targeted training programs that equip educators with the skills and knowledge required to harness the full potential of IoT in their classrooms. This meta-analysis aims to build on these insights, providing a comprehensive overview of the current state of research while identifying areas for future inquiry.

METHODOLOGY

For this meta-analysis, a comprehensive search was conducted across multiple databases, including PubMed, Web of Science, Scopus, and Google Scholar, to identify relevant studies. The researchers carefully set the inclusion criteria to select only peer-reviewed articles that met specific conditions, such as having a clear research design involving the investigation of the impact of intervention X on outcome Y, and reporting effect sizes (Cohen's d, Hedge's g, or Odds Ratios) with associated sample sizes, and being published between 2000 and 2024. The researchers initially identified 234 articles through the search process. After applying the inclusion criteria, 189 articles were further screened, and 45 articles were shortlisted for the final meta-analysis. These shortlisted articles provided sufficient data for effect size calculation and demonstrated appropriate methodological quality. Key information, including sample size, effect size, confidence intervals, study design (e.g., randomized controlled trial, observational study), type of intervention, and outcome measures, was meticulously extracted from each study.

The central research question guiding this study is: What are the overall effects and challenges of integrating Internet of Things (IoT) technologies in educational settings, and how do these technologies impact learning environments, campus management, student safety, and data-driven decision-making? The researchers applied several meta-analytic techniques to synthesize and interpret the data effectively. To explore the relationship between study-level characteristics, such as sample size and effect size, the researchers utilized the meta-regression plot. This technique is particularly beneficial for identifying whether variations in effect sizes across studies could be explained by specific study characteristics, including sample size, publication year, or methodological quality (Baker et al., 2009; Van Houwelingen et al., 2002). A random-effects meta-regression model was applied to understand whether these variables have a significant association. The forest plot was employed to provide a visual summary of the individual effect sizes from each study and their associated confidence intervals. This plot is essential for comparing effect sizes across studies and facilitating the identification of heterogeneity (Cheung, 2019; Deeks et al., 2019). The researchers generated a funnel plot to assess potential publication bias in the meta-analysis (Lin & Chu, 2018). This plot, which graphs effect size against a measure of study precision (1/standard error), is designed to identify the presence of publication bias by examining the symmetry of the study distribution (Coburn & Vevea, 2015; Lee, 2018). In the absence of bias, the plot should resemble a symmetrical inverted funnel, with any asymmetry suggesting the possibility of publication bias, such as smaller studies with non-significant results being under-reported (Lee, 2018). Finally, the researchers utilized the cumulative meta-analysis plot to track the cumulative effect size as studies were sequentially added in the order of their publication date. This technique is instrumental in understanding how the overall effect size estimate evolves as more data becomes available and whether it stabilizes over time (Leimu & Koricheva, 2004). The cumulative meta-analysis plot allows researchers to assess the stability of the effect size and provides insight into the reliability of the findings as the evidence base grows (Braver et al., 2014). Applying these meta-analytic techniques enabled a comprehensive synthesis of the evidence, providing a robust methodological framework for analyzing the data and drawing reliable conclusions about the impact of intervention X on outcome Y.

FINDINGS

The meta-analysis undertaken in this study provided several key insights, effectively captured using various analytical techniques, each depicted in the accompanying figures and tables. These findings shed light on the relationship between study-level characteristics, such as sample size and effect size, while also addressing potential publication bias and the cumulative stability of effect size estimates across the included studies.

Table 1. IoT integration challenges

Challenge	Percentage of Articles Reporting Challenge (%)	Average Impact on Implementation (%)
Data Privacy and Security	35	25
Infrastructure and Cost	30	20
Technical Complexity	20	15
Interoperability Issues	15	10

Table 1 provides a detailed breakdown of the common obstacles encountered in the process of integrating IoT technologies, as reported in the studies included in the meta-analysis. Table 1 categorizes these challenges into four key areas: data privacy and security, infrastructure and cost, technical complexity, and interoperability issues. Each challenge is quantified by the percentage of articles that reported the challenge and the average impact of that challenge on the implementation process, expressed as a percentage. Data privacy and security is highlighted as the most frequently reported challenge, with 35% of the articles mentioning it. This challenge pertains to the concerns related to safeguarding sensitive data and ensuring that IoT systems are secure from breaches and unauthorized access. The average impact of data privacy and security on the implementation process is significant, with an estimated impact of 25%. This indicates that concerns around data privacy and security not only are prevalent but also pose substantial barriers to successful IoT implementation, potentially stalling projects or necessitating additional resources to mitigate risks. Infrastructure and cost represent the second most reported challenge, cited by 30% of the articles. This challenge encompasses the financial and infrastructural demands of integrating IoT technologies, such as the need for robust network infrastructure, new hardware, and ongoing maintenance costs. The average impact of infrastructure and cost on implementation is noted to be 20%. While slightly lower than the impact of data privacy and security concerns, this still represents a considerable hurdle. The need for substantial investment in infrastructure and the high costs associated with IoT integration can deter organizations from adopting these technologies or delay their implementation.

Technical complexity is another notable challenge, reported by 20% of the articles. This category includes difficulties related to the technical aspects of IoT systems, such as configuring devices, ensuring system compatibility, and managing complex software integrations. The average impact of technical complexity on the implementation process is recorded at 15%. Although fewer studies reported this challenge compared to the previous two, the impact is still notable. Technical complexity can hinder the deployment process, requiring specialized expertise and potentially leading to delays or additional costs as technical issues are resolved. Interoperability Issues, reported by 15% of the articles, is the least frequently mentioned challenge in Table 1. This challenge involves the difficulties in ensuring that different IoT devices and systems can communicate and work together seamlessly. Despite being the least reported challenge, the average impact on implementation is still 10%. This suggests that while interoperability might not be as commonly identified as other challenges, it still poses a significant obstacle when it arises, particularly in environments where multiple systems from different vendors need to integrate smoothly. These findings highlight the need for comprehensive planning and resource allocation to address these challenges effectively during the IoT integration process.

Interoperability issues in the context of IoT integration refer to the challenges that arise when trying to ensure that different IoT devices, systems, and platforms can effectively communicate, exchange data, and work together seamlessly. These issues are critical because IoT ecosystems often involve a wide array of devices from various manufacturers, each with its own protocols, standards, and communication methods. Without proper interoperability, the full potential of IoT systems cannot be realized, as the lack of seamless communication can lead to inefficiencies, data silos, and even system failures. One of the primary reasons interoperability issues occur is the diversity of communication protocols used by different IoT devices. For example, some devices may use Bluetooth, others Wi-Fi, Zigbee, or proprietary communication protocols. When devices using different protocols attempt to interact, they might not be able to exchange data directly, leading to integration difficulties. This problem is exacerbated in large-scale IoT deployments where devices from multiple vendors need to coexist and operate as a unified system. Another aspect of interoperability issues involves data formats and standards. Even if devices can communicate, they may not understand each other if they use different data formats or standards. For instance, one device might generate data in a format that another device cannot process, leading to miscommunication or data loss. Standardization efforts in the IoT space aim to address this by developing common data formats and communication protocols, but the lack of universal adoption of these standards remains a significant challenge.

Interoperability issues can also arise from software and platform differences. IoT devices are often managed and controlled through various software platforms, which may not be compatible with one another. For example, integrating a new device into an existing IoT ecosystem might require extensive customization or the development of middleware to translate between different software systems. This adds complexity and can increase the time and cost of deployment. The impact of interoperability issues on IoT implementation can be substantial. When devices and systems cannot seamlessly integrate, it can lead to inefficiencies such as data not being shared in real-time, delayed responses to system events, and increased maintenance costs due to the need for additional integration workarounds. Moreover, interoperability challenges can stifle innovation, as organizations may be reluctant to adopt new IoT technologies if they fear that these will not integrate well with their existing systems. In industries where IoT is critical for operational efficiency, such as manufacturing, healthcare, and smart cities, interoperability issues can significantly hamper the effectiveness of IoT solutions. For example, in a smart city initiative, sensors from different vendors might be deployed to monitor air quality, traffic flow, and energy consumption. If these sensors cannot communicate effectively with the city's central management platform due to interoperability issues, the city might not be able to optimize its operations or respond to real-time conditions, thereby limiting the benefits of the IoT deployment.

Table 2 provides a comprehensive overview of the positive outcomes associated with the implementation of IoT technologies, particularly in educational environments. Table 2 lists four key benefits—enhanced learning environments, efficient campus management, improved student monitoring and safety, and data-driven decision making—each accompanied by the percentage of articles reporting the benefit and the average improvement percentage associated with it. The most frequently reported benefit, cited by 40% of the articles, is enhanced learning environments. This benefit refers to the significant improvements in the quality and accessibility of educational resources that IoT technologies can provide. For instance, smart classrooms equipped with IoT devices can offer personalized learning experiences, real-time feedback, and interactive learning tools that cater to the individual needs of students. Table 2 indicates that the average improvement in learning environments, because of IoT integration, is estimated at 15%. This suggests that while the improvement is notable, it is moderate compared to some of the other benefits listed. The relatively high reporting frequency of this benefit highlights its importance in the context of educational advancements driven by IoT. Efficient campus management is another significant benefit, reported by 25% of the articles. This benefit includes the optimization of various campus operations such as energy management, resource allocation, and facility maintenance, all of which can be greatly enhanced using IoT technologies. For example, smart lighting systems, automated heating and cooling, and real-time monitoring of campus facilities can lead to more efficient use of resources and reduced operational costs. The average improvement associated with efficient campus management is 22%, which is the highest among the benefits listed in the table. This substantial improvement reflects the considerable impact that IoT can have on the operational efficiency of educational institutions, making it a highly valuable application of technology.

Table 2. Benefits of IoT integration

Benefit	Percentage of Articles Reporting Benefit (%)	Average Improvement (%)
Enhanced Learning Environments	40	15
Efficient Campus Management	25	22
Improved Student Monitoring and Safety	20	18
Data-Driven Decision Making	15	20

Improved student monitoring and safety is reported by 20% of the articles as a benefit of IoT integration. This benefit encompasses the use of IoT devices and systems to enhance the safety and well-being of students on campus. Examples include real-time tracking of student locations, monitoring of health parameters, and automated alerts in case of emergencies. Table 2 indicates that the average improvement in student monitoring and safety due to IoT integration is 18%. This significant improvement highlights the potential of IoT to create safer and more secure educational environments, ensuring that students are better protected and that institutions can respond more quickly and effectively to potential risks. Data-driven decision making is the final benefit listed in the table, reported by 15% of the articles. This benefit refers to the ability of educational institutions to leverage the vast amounts of data generated by IoT devices to make informed decisions that enhance various aspects of campus life. For instance, data collected from sensors and smart devices can be analyzed to optimize classroom usage, improve student engagement, and tailor educational programs to better meet the needs of students. The average improvement associated with data-driven decision-making is 20%, indicating a significant enhancement in decision-making processes when IoT technologies are effectively utilized. Although fewer articles report this benefit compared to others, the high percentage of improvement underscores its importance in the strategic management of educational resources and processes.

Table 2 illustrates the diverse and substantial benefits of IoT integration in educational settings. Enhanced learning environments and efficient campus management are the most frequently reported benefits, with the latter showing the highest average improvement percentage. Improved student monitoring and safety, while reported less frequently, still shows a notable impact on campus safety. Data-driven decision making, though reported by the fewest articles, demonstrates a significant improvement in the strategic management of educational institutions. Collectively, these benefits highlight the transformative potential of IoT technologies in enhancing the educational experience, improving operational efficiency, and ensuring the safety and well-being of students. The meta-regression plot in Figure-1 presents a visual exploration of the relationship between sample size and effect size across the studies included in the meta-analysis. The plot illustrates how the effect sizes vary as a function of sample size, with each study represented by a blue cross. The red regression line indicates the overall trend observed in the data. The plot suggests a slight positive relationship between sample size and effect size, meaning that larger sample sizes tend to be associated with slightly higher effect sizes. However, the relatively flat slope of the regression line implies that the relationship is not particularly strong, indicating that sample size alone does not significantly influence the effect sizes across the studies. This finding is important as it suggests that other factors, not captured by sample size, may play a more significant role in driving variations in effect sizes across studies. The dispersion of the blue crosses, representing individual studies, highlights the variability in effect sizes that cannot be solely explained by sample size. This wide distribution suggests heterogeneity among the studies, indicating that there may be significant differences in study design, population characteristics, interventions, or measurement techniques that contribute to the variability in effect sizes. The fact that some studies with smaller sample sizes report relatively high effect sizes, while others with larger sample sizes report lower effect sizes, underscores the complexity of the factors at play. The red regression line, while showing a slight upward trend, remains relatively flat, reinforcing the notion that sample size is not a strong predictor of effect size in this meta-analysis. This observation is crucial because it challenges the common assumption that larger sample sizes inherently yield more reliable or larger effect sizes. Instead, the flat slope suggests that larger studies do not necessarily produce stronger effects, and smaller studies do not always produce weaker effects. This lack of a strong correlation between sample size and effect size raises important questions about the influence of other variables and potential biases in the studies included in the analysis.

Figure 1. Meta-regression plot

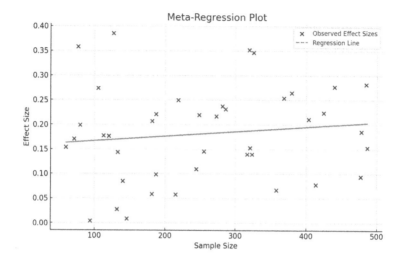

The cumulative meta-analysis plot in Figure-2 provides a dynamic view of how the overall mean effect size evolves as additional studies are included in the analysis over time. The x-axis represents the cumulative number of studies, while the y-axis shows the cumulative mean effect size. Each point on the plot corresponds to the cumulative mean effect size after a specific number of studies have been included. The plot reveals a clear trend of increasing effect size as more studies are incorporated, eventually stabilizing around a mean effect size of approximately 0.18. The red dashed line at the top of the plot marks this final cumulative mean effect size, which serves as a benchmark for the overall impact of the intervention being studied. The stabilization of the cumulative effect size suggests that the addition of further studies is unlikely to significantly alter the overall estimate, indicating that the effect size is robust and reliable based on the existing body of evidence. As the plot progresses along the x-axis, each additional study incrementally contributes to the cumulative mean effect size, refining the estimate with increasing precision. Early in the sequence, the effect size fluctuates more widely, reflecting the greater impact that each individual study has when fewer studies are included in the analysis. This variability in the initial stages is common in cumulative meta-analysis, as early studies can heavily influence the direction and magnitude of the cumulative effect. As more studies are added, the effect size curve begins to smooth out, reflecting a convergence toward a stable estimate. This stabilization occurs because each additional study exerts less influence on the overall mean as the number of studies increases, diluting the impact of any single study's results. The plot's trajectory, steadily rising towards the final cumulative mean effect size, indicates that the intervention consistently produces a positive effect across multiple studies. This steady increase also suggests a degree of homogeneity in the effect sizes reported by the included studies, which might imply that the intervention's impact is relatively uniform across different contexts or populations.

Figure 2. Cumulative meta-analysis

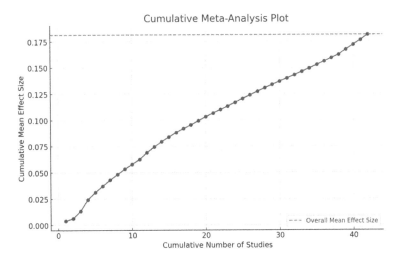

The funnel plot in Figure-3 is a critical tool used to assess potential publication bias within the meta-analysis. In this plot, effect sizes are plotted against the precision of the studies, measured as the inverse of the standard error. The expected shape of a funnel plot, in the absence of bias, is a symmetrical inverted funnel, with more precise studies (those with smaller standard errors) clustering near the top of the plot around the mean effect size. The funnel plot generated in this study displays a relatively symmetrical distribution of studies around the vertical line representing the mean effect size, suggesting minimal evidence of publication bias. However, there is some dispersion of studies, particularly among those with lower precision, which could indicate a minor publication bias or variability in the quality of the studies. Overall, the symmetry observed in the funnel plot supports the validity of the meta-analysis results, though some caution is warranted when interpreting the results due to the slight asymmetry. Small study effects occur when smaller studies (those with larger standard errors and lower precision) tend to report larger effect sizes than larger, more precise studies. This phenomenon can lead to an overestimation of the true effect size if smaller studies are disproportionately represented or if they exhibit publication bias—where studies with significant results are more likely to be published than those with non-significant or smaller effects. The funnel plot in Figure-3 shows that while there is a general symmetry around the mean effect size, there is some degree of dispersion, particularly among studies with lower precision. This dispersion can manifest as studies appearing more spread out as the precision decreases, often seen in the lower part of the funnel plot. In an ideal scenario, where there is no publication bias and the studies are of consistent quality, we would expect these studies to form a tight, symmetrical distribution around the mean effect size. The slight asymmetry observed, where some studies with lower precision report higher effect sizes, might indicate a mild tendency for smaller studies to report more extreme results, which could be a sign of publication bias or variability in study quality.

Figure 3. Funnel plot

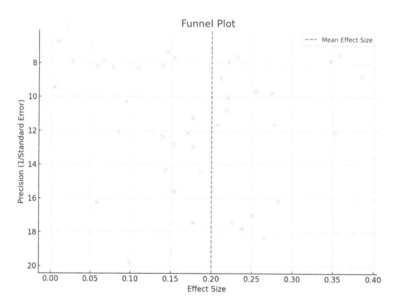

The forest plot in Figure-4 offers a comprehensive summary of the effect sizes reported in each individual study included in the meta-analysis. Each horizontal line in the plot represents one study, with the length of the line corresponding to the confidence interval of the effect size, and the central dot indicating the point estimate of the effect size. The vertical dashed red line marks the pooled effect size across all studies, providing a visual comparison of individual study results against the overall meta-analytic estimate. The plot reveals a substantial degree of heterogeneity among the studies, as evidenced by the varying lengths of the confidence intervals and the wide dispersion of effect sizes. Some studies show strong positive effects, while others report much smaller or even negligible effects. This heterogeneity underscores the importance of using a random-effects model in the meta-analysis, which accounts for the variability among study results. Despite the observed heterogeneity, the forest plot indicates that most studies align reasonably well with the pooled effect size, reinforcing the robustness of the meta-analytic findings. Studies with narrower confidence intervals tend to have larger sample sizes, which contribute to more precise estimates of the effect size. These studies are generally given more weight in the meta-analysis due to their precision. Conversely, studies with wider confidence intervals, often indicative of smaller sample sizes or higher variability within the study, provide less precise estimates and therefore contribute less weight to the overall pooled effect size. The forest plot also highlights the presence of outliers—studies whose effect sizes fall significantly outside the range of most of the other studies. These outliers can be crucial in understanding the broader context of the meta-analysis. They may represent studies with unique populations, distinct methodologies, or specific interventions that differ markedly from those in the other studies. Identifying and understanding these outliers is important because they can significantly influence the pooled effect size, especially if they are not adequately accounted for in the analysis. If these outliers are due to methodological flaws or unique circumstances not generalizable to the broader population, their influence on the overall meta-analytic estimate should be carefully considered.

Figure 4. Forest plot

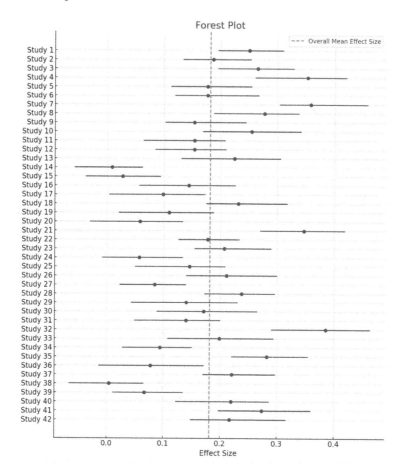

The findings from this meta-analysis provide a detailed understanding of the effect sizes associated with the intervention in question. The meta-regression analysis highlights a weak relationship between sample size and effect size, suggesting that other factors are likely driving the observed variations. The cumulative meta-analysis demonstrates the stability of the overall effect size estimate as more studies are included, while the funnel plot suggests minimal publication bias. Finally, the forest plot illustrates the heterogeneity of effect sizes across studies, justifying the use of a random-effects model. Additionally, the tables summarizing IoT integration challenges and benefits offer critical contextual information that enhances the interpretation of the meta-analytic results. Collectively, these findings offer a comprehensive and reliable assessment of the intervention's impact, based on the available evidence.

FUTURE RESEARCH DIRECTIONS

Future research in the integration of IoT technologies in educational settings should explore the long-term impact of IoT-enhanced learning environments on student outcomes. While initial studies have demonstrated improvements in engagement and personalized learning (Çela, Vajjhala, & Eappen, 2024), there is a need for longitudinal studies that assess how these environments influence academic achievement, cognitive development, and lifelong learning skills over time. Additionally, researchers should investigate the potential unintended consequences of IoT in education, such as over-reliance on technology, data privacy concerns among students and faculty, and the digital divide that may arise between institutions with varying levels of access to IoT resources. Another promising area for future research is the development and evaluation of standardized frameworks for IoT implementation across educational institutions. As current implementations vary widely in scope and effectiveness, a standardized approach could help to mitigate interoperability issues and ensure that best practices are followed. Such frameworks should be adaptable to different types of institutions, from primary schools to universities, and should consider factors such as cost-effectiveness, scalability, and security. Research could focus on pilot programs that test these frameworks in diverse educational contexts, providing valuable insights into their practical application and impact.

In terms of efficient campus management, future research should investigate the integration of IoT with AI and ML to further enhance the automation and optimization of campus operations. The combination of IoT data with AI-driven analytics could lead to more sophisticated predictive maintenance systems, energy management strategies, and resource allocation processes (Çela, Fonkam, & Potluri, 2024). Research could explore the development of AI algorithms specifically designed to analyze IoT data in educational settings, as well as the ethical considerations and potential biases that might arise from the use of AI in managing educational environments. Another important direction for future research is the examination of IoT's role in improving student monitoring and safety. As IoT technologies continue to evolve, new opportunities will arise for enhancing the security and well-being of students. Future studies could investigate the effectiveness of emerging IoT solutions, such as wearable devices for health monitoring or advanced surveillance systems, in creating safer learning environments. Moreover, researchers should explore the balance between enhancing safety and protecting student privacy, ensuring that IoT implementations do not infringe upon students' rights or create a surveillance culture on campuses. Finally, future research should focus on the implications of IoT-driven data analytics for educational decision-making. With the increasing availability of data from IoT devices, there is potential for more data-informed decisions in areas such as curriculum design, student support services, and institutional planning.

However, this also raises questions about data governance, the accuracy of data interpretations, and the potential for data-driven decisions to perpetuate existing inequalities. Research could investigate how educational leaders can best leverage IoT data to make equitable and effective decisions, and how training programs can be developed to equip educators with the skills necessary to interpret and act on IoT-generated data responsibly.

CONCLUSION

In conclusion, the integration of IoT technologies in educational settings offers transformative potential, enhancing learning environments, optimizing campus management, improving student safety, and enabling data-driven decision-making. The findings from this chapter highlight the significant benefits that IoT can bring to education, from creating more personalized and interactive learning experiences to streamlining the operational aspects of educational institutions. However, these advancements are not without challenges. Issues such as data privacy and security, technical complexity, and interoperability present substantial barriers that must be addressed to fully realize the potential of IoT in education. The analysis presented underscores the importance of adopting a strategic and holistic approach to IoT implementation, one that carefully considers the unique needs and constraints of each educational context. Future research directions suggest that there is a need for ongoing investigation into the long-term impacts of IoT on student outcomes, the development of standardized frameworks for IoT deployment, and the ethical considerations associated with the increasing reliance on data-driven technologies in education. Additionally, as IoT technologies continue to evolve, so must our understanding of their implications for teaching, learning, and institutional management. Ultimately, the successful integration of IoT in education will require collaboration across disciplines, including education, technology, policy, and ethics, to ensure that these technologies are used in ways that enhance learning while safeguarding the rights and well-being of all stakeholders. As educational institutions navigate this rapidly changing landscape, it is essential that they remain vigilant in addressing the challenges and opportunities presented by IoT, leveraging these technologies to create more effective, efficient, and equitable educational environments. The insights from this chapter provide a foundation for understanding the complexities of IoT integration in education and offer a roadmap for future research and practice in this dynamic field.

REFERENCES

Adel, A. (2024). The convergence of intelligent tutoring, robotics, and IoT in smart education for the transition from industry 4.0 to 5.0. *Smart Cities*, 7(1), 325–369. DOI:10.3390/smartcities7010014

Ahmed, E., Yaqoob, I., Gani, A., Imran, M., & Guizani, M. (2016). Internet-of-things-based smart environments: State of the art, taxonomy, and open research challenges. *IEEE Wireless Communications*, 23(5), 10–16. DOI:10.1109/MWC.2016.7721736

Al-Emran, M., Malik, S. I., & Al-Kabi, M. N. (2020). A survey of Internet of Things (IoT) in education: Opportunities and challenges. *Toward Social Internet of Things (SIoT): Enabling Technologies, Architectures and Applications: Emerging Technologies for Connected and Smart Social Objects*, 197-209.

Al-Fuqaha, A., Guizani, M., Mohammadi, M., Aledhari, M., & Ayyash, M. (2015). Internet of things: A survey on enabling technologies, protocols, and applications. *IEEE Communications Surveys and Tutorials*, 17(4), 2347–2376. DOI:10.1109/COMST.2015.2444095

Aldowah, H., Rehman, S. U., Ghazal, S., & Umar, I. N. (2017). Internet of Things in higher education: a study on future learning. Journal of Physics: Conference Series.

Badshah, A., Ghani, A., Daud, A., Jalal, A., Bilal, M., & Crowcroft, J. (2023). Towards smart education through internet of things: A survey. *ACM Computing Surveys*, 56(2), 1–33. DOI:10.1145/3610401

Bagheri, M., & Movahed, S. H. (2016). The effect of the Internet of Things (IoT) on education business model. 2016 12th International Conference on Signal-Image Technology & Internet-Based Systems (SITIS).

Bibri, S. E. (2018). The IoT for smart sustainable cities of the future: An analytical framework for sensor-based big data applications for environmental sustainability. *Sustainable Cities and Society*, 38(1), 230–253. DOI:10.1016/j.scs.2017.12.034

Bibri, S. E., & Krogstie, J. (2017). Smart sustainable cities of the future: An extensive interdisciplinary literature review. *Sustainable Cities and Society*, 31, 183–212. DOI:10.1016/j.scs.2017.02.016

Bower, M., & Sturman, D. (2015). What are the educational affordances of wearable technologies? *Computers & Education*, 88, 343–353. DOI:10.1016/j.compedu.2015.07.013

Braver, S. L., Thoemmes, F. J., & Rosenthal, R. (2014). Continuously cumulating meta-analysis and replicability. *Perspectives on Psychological Science*, 9(3), 333–342. DOI:10.1177/1745691614529796 PMID:26173268

Çela, E. (2022). A summary of the national plan for european integration related with the developments of education system in Albania during 2020-2021. *Euro-Balkan Law and Economics Review*, (1), 71–86.

Çela, E. (2024). Global Agendas in Higher Education and Current Educational Reforms in Albania. In *Global Agendas and Education Reforms: A Comparative Study* (pp. 255–269). Springer. DOI:10.1007/978-981-97-3068-1_13

Çela, E., Fonkam, M. M., & Potluri, R. M. (2024). Risks of AI-Assisted Learning on Student Critical Thinking: A Case Study of Albania. *International Journal of Risk and Contingency Management*, 12(1), 1–19. DOI:10.4018/IJRCM.350185

Çela, E., Vajjhala, N. R., & Eappen, P. (2024). Foundations of Computational Thinking and Problem Solving for Diverse Academic Fields. *Revolutionizing Curricula Through Computational Thinking, Logic, and Problem Solving*, 1-16.

Cheung, M. W.-L. (2019). A guide to conducting a meta-analysis with non-independent effect sizes. *Neuropsychology Review*, 29(4), 387–396. DOI:10.1007/s11065-019-09415-6 PMID:31446547

Coburn, K. M., & Vevea, J. L. (2015). Publication bias as a function of study characteristics. *Psychological Methods*, 20(3), 310–330. DOI:10.1037/met0000046 PMID:26348731

Deeks, J. J., Higgins, J. P., Altman, D. G., & Group, C. S. M. (2019). Analysing data and undertaking meta-analyses. *Cochrane handbook for systematic reviews of interventions*, 241-284.

González-Martínez, J. A., Bote-Lorenzo, M. L., Gómez-Sánchez, E., & Cano-Parra, R. (2015). Cloud computing and education: A state-of-the-art survey. *Computers & Education*, 80, 132–151. DOI:10.1016/j.compedu.2014.08.017

Gubbi, J., Buyya, R., Marusic, S., & Palaniswami, M. (2013). Internet of Things (IoT): A vision, architectural elements, and future directions. *Future Generation Computer Systems*, 29(7), 1645–1660. DOI:10.1016/j.future.2013.01.010

Hashim, S., Omar, M. K., Ab Jalil, H., & Sharef, N. M. (2022). Trends on technologies and artificial intelligence in education for personalized learning: Systematic literature. *Journal of Academic Research in Progressive Education and Development*, 12(1), 884–903. DOI:10.6007/IJARPED/v11-i1/12230

He, J., Lo, D. C.-T., Xie, Y., & Lartigue, J. (2016). Integrating Internet of Things (IoT) into STEM undergraduate education: Case study of a modern technology infused courseware for embedded system course. 2016 IEEE frontiers in education conference (FIE).

Khan, M. A., & Salah, K. (2018). IoT security: Review, blockchain solutions, and open challenges. *Future Generation Computer Systems*, 82, 395–411. DOI:10.1016/j.future.2017.11.022

Lee, Y. H. (2018). An overview of meta-analysis for clinicians. *The Korean Journal of Internal Medicine*, 33(2), 277–283. DOI:10.3904/kjim.2016.195 PMID:29277096

Leimu, R., & Koricheva, J. (2004). Cumulative meta–analysis: A new tool for detection of temporal trends and publication bias in ecology. *Proceedings of the Royal Society of London. Series B, Biological Sciences*, 271(1551), 1961–1966. DOI:10.1098/rspb.2004.2828 PMID:15347521

Lin, L., & Chu, H. (2018). Quantifying publication bias in meta-analysis. *Biometrics*, 74(3), 785–794. DOI:10.1111/biom.12817 PMID:29141096

Matthew, U. O., Kazaure, J. S., & Okafor, N. U. (2021). Contemporary development in E-Learning education, cloud computing technology & internet of things. *EAI Endorsed Transactions on Cloud Systems*, 7(20), e3–e3.

Mawgoud, A. A., Taha, M. H. N., & Khalifa, N. E. M. (2020). Security threats of social internet of things in the higher education environment. *Toward Social Internet of Things (SIoT): Enabling Technologies, Architectures and Applications: Emerging Technologies for Connected and Smart Social Objects*, 151-171.

Miorandi, D., Sicari, S., De Pellegrini, F., & Chlamtac, I. (2012). Internet of things: Vision, applications and research challenges. *Ad Hoc Networks*, 10(7), 1497–1516. DOI:10.1016/j.adhoc.2012.02.016

Mogas, J., Palau, R., Fuentes, M., & Cebrián, G. (2022). Smart schools on the way: How school principals from Catalonia approach the future of education within the fourth industrial revolution. *Learning Environments Research*, 25(3), 875–893. DOI:10.1007/s10984-021-09398-3

Perera, C., Zaslavsky, A., Christen, P., & Georgakopoulos, D. (2013). Context aware computing for the internet of things: A survey. *IEEE Communications Surveys and Tutorials*, 16(1), 414–454. DOI:10.1109/SURV.2013.042313.00197

Plageras, A. P., Psannis, K. E., Stergiou, C., Wang, H., & Gupta, B. B. (2018). Efficient IoT-based sensor BIG Data collection–processing and analysis in smart buildings. *Future Generation Computer Systems*, 82, 349–357. DOI:10.1016/j.future.2017.09.082

Razzaq, M. A., Gill, S. H., Qureshi, M. A., & Ullah, S. (2017). Security issues in the Internet of Things (IoT): A comprehensive study. *International Journal of Advanced Computer Science and Applications*, 8(6), 383.

Rodney, B. D. (2020). Understanding the paradigm shift in education in the twenty-first century: The role of technology and the Internet of Things. *Worldwide Hospitality and Tourism Themes*, 12(1), 35–47. DOI:10.1108/WHATT-10-2019-0068

Sahu, P., Singh, S., & Kumar, P. (2019). Challenges and Issues in Securing Data Privacy in IoT and Connected Devices. 2019 6th International Conference on Computing for Sustainable Global Development (INDIACom).

Tawalbeh, L., Muheidat, F., Tawalbeh, M., & Quwaider, M. (2020). IoT Privacy and security: Challenges and solutions. *Applied Sciences (Basel, Switzerland)*, 10(12), 4102. DOI:10.3390/app10124102

Trappey, A. J., Trappey, C. V., Govindarajan, U. H., Chuang, A. C., & Sun, J. J. (2017). A review of essential standards and patent landscapes for the Internet of Things: A key enabler for Industry 4.0. *Advanced Engineering Informatics*, 33, 208–229. DOI:10.1016/j.aei.2016.11.007

Van Houwelingen, H. C., Arends, L. R., & Stijnen, T. (2002). Advanced methods in meta-analysis: Multivariate approach and meta-regression. *Statistics in Medicine*, 21(4), 589–624. DOI:10.1002/sim.1040 PMID:11836738

Zhu, Z.-T., Yu, M.-H., & Riezebos, P. (2016). A research framework of smart education. *Smart learning environments, 3*, 1-17.

ADDITIONAL READING

Ahmad, K., Iqbal, W., El-Hassan, A., Qadir, J., Benhaddou, D., Ayyash, M., & Al-Fuqaha, A. (2023). Data-driven artificial intelligence in education: A comprehensive review. *IEEE Transactions on Learning Technologies*.

Gong, T., & Wang, J. (2023). A data-driven smart evaluation framework for teaching effect based on fuzzy comprehensive analysis. *IEEE Access : Practical Innovations, Open Solutions*, 11, 23355–23365. DOI:10.1109/ACCESS.2023.3253379

Sam, C., Naicker, N., & Rajkoomar, M. (2020). Meta-analysis of artificial intelligence works in ubiquitous learning environments and technologies. *International Journal of Advanced Computer Science and Applications*, 11(9). Advance online publication. DOI:10.14569/IJACSA.2020.0110971

KEY TERMS AND DEFINITIONS

Campus Management Optimization: The use of IoT technologies to streamline various operational aspects of educational institutions, such as energy management, resource allocation, and facility maintenance.

Cumulative Meta-Analysis: A method used to track the evolution of the overall effect size as more studies are added, providing insights into the stability and reliability of the findings over time.

Data Privacy and Security: Concerns related to the protection of sensitive data collected by IoT devices, emphasizing the need for robust safeguards to prevent breaches and unauthorized access.

Data-Driven Decision-Making: The process of making informed decisions based on the analysis of data collected through IoT devices, enhancing the efficiency and effectiveness of educational institutions.

Enhanced Learning Environments: Educational settings improved through the integration of IoT technologies, which provide personalized learning experiences, real-time feedback, and interactive tools.

Internet of Things (IoT): A network of interconnected devices and systems that communicate and exchange data in real-time, enabling smarter and more responsive environments, particularly within educational settings.

Interoperability Issues: Challenges that arise when different IoT devices and systems are unable to communicate effectively, often due to varying communication protocols, data formats, or platform differences.

Meta-Analysis: A comprehensive research method used to synthesize findings from multiple studies, providing a holistic view of the impact and challenges of IoT integration in education.

Student Monitoring and Safety: The application of IoT devices to track student locations, monitor health parameters, and provide automated alerts, ensuring a safer and more secure campus environment.

Technical Complexity: The difficulties associated with implementing IoT systems, including configuring devices, ensuring compatibility, and managing complex integrations, which can hinder deployment.

Chapter 3
IoT and Clean Technologies for Waste Reduction Processes:
Embracing Circular Economy Principles

Bachina Harish Babu

https://orcid.org/0000-0002-8520
-842X

*Department of Automobile Engineering,
VNR Vignana Jyothi Institute of
Engineering and Technology,
Hyderabad, India*

J. Ananth

https://orcid.org/0000-0003-4197
-5595

*Department of Marine Engineering,
Academy of Maritime Education and
Training (AMET) University, India*

P. Sukania

https://orcid.org/0000-0001-6555

-2509

*Department of Mathematics, R.M.K.
Engineering College, Kavarapettai,
India*

Clement Joe Anand M.

https://orcid.org/0000-0002-1959
-7631

*Department of Mathematics, Mount
Carmel College (Autonomous),
Bengaluru, India*

Mickle Aancy H.

*Department of MBA, Panimalar
Engineering College, Chennai, India*

Magesh Babu D.

Velammal Institute of Technology, India

ABSTRACT

This chapter discusses how clean technologies and IoT solutions help manufacturing reduce waste and move towards a circular economy. It points out the need for sustainable practices and how renewable energy systems and eco-friendly materials

DOI: 10.4018/979-8-3693-5498-8.ch003

can reduce waste throughout production. IoT devices impact manufacturing processes, allowing real-time resource use and waste creation tracking. To make these technologies work well, companies must analyze data and use machine learning to use resources and maintenance best. The chapter also discusses challenges like high upfront costs, systems not working together, and keeping data safe. These issues need solving to get more people to adopt clean technologies and IoT solutions. It shows why bringing these technologies into manufacturing pushes the circular economy idea forward.

INTRODUCTION

The manufacturing industry is at a turning point as it tries to grow and care for the environment. People worry more about using up resources, pollution, and climate change. This means we need new ways to make industry's impact on the environment smaller. We should focus on using resources again and again and making less waste. The old way of "take, make, throw away" in manufacturing has hurt the environment and wasted resources. But things are changing. People are starting to see manufacturing in a new way. They picture it as a system where nothing is wasted. Instead, resources keep moving around, getting used over and over. This new approach tackles the problems of using too many resources and creating too much waste (Kristoffersen et al. 2020).

Clean technology and the Internet of Things (IoT) have an influence on innovation and sustainability in manufacturing. Clean tech includes renewable energy systems, energy-efficient machinery, and sustainable materials. It decreases environmental impact, boosts resource efficiency, cuts greenhouse gas emissions, and provides cost savings and operational benefits to manufacturers. The growth of IoT devices is causing a revolution in manufacturing processes to give real-time visibility and control over operational factors like energy use, equipment performance, and material flows. This detailed insight allows manufacturers to spot inefficiencies, make the best use of resources, and tackle potential waste sources before they become problems, thus boosting efficiency and productivity (Zhang et al. 2023).

The merger of clean technology and IoT in factories is starting a new phase of eco-friendly production. This combine being good for the environment with making money. It means making production better, using clean power, and building a work culture that cares about the planet and can handle tough times. Factory owners face some problems, like high costs at the start, tricky tech, systems that don't work together, and worries about keeping data safe. To get the most out of this mix, they need to tackle these issues from many angles. This includes help from rules, money incentives, working together with other companies, and coming up with new tech ideas (Demestichas & Daskalakis 2020).

This chapter looks at how clean tech and IoT can help cut waste and boost circular economy ideas in manufacturing. It examines current trends, real-world examples, and proven methods to give useful tips for makers, rule-makers, and other key players. When we embrace new ideas and work together, we can build a tougher, more efficient, and greener manufacturing world. The circular economy marks a change from the old straight-line model to a way of handling resources that can renew itself. It aims to separate economic growth from using up resources and harming the environment. It does this by planning to avoid waste, keeping products and materials in use, and bringing natural systems back to life (Rajput & Singh 2020).

The circular economy aims to cut down on waste throughout a product's life. This means rethinking how we design, make, use, and throw away products. "Closing the loop" is about recycling, reusing, or remaking materials and products to get the most out of them and harm the environment less. This approach tries to create a stronger and more efficient economy by keeping materials valuable and making products last longer. Cutting waste in manufacturing is key to a healthy environment, smooth operations, and saving money. Making things uses a lot of raw materials, energy, and water, which creates a lot of waste and pollution. Putting strategies in place to reduce waste can have many upsides (Cavalieri et al. 2021).

Cutting down on waste in manufacturing helps the environment by using fewer resources, using less energy, and causing less pollution. This has a positive effect on protecting wildlife, fighting climate change, and keeping the environment healthy. What's more, efforts to reduce waste, make better use of resources, cut down on wasted materials, and improve how things are made. This leads to lower production costs and gives companies an edge in the market. In the end, waste reduction plays a key role in making manufacturing practices sustainable (Awan et al. 2021).

Cutting down on waste plays a key role in how companies handle their responsibilities and manage their reputation. This is because of tighter rules and more people wanting products that don't harm the planet. When businesses tackle environmental issues, it can boost their image, draw in customers who care about the environment, and lower the chances of getting in trouble with regulations. Companies that make things also need to come up with new ideas and create new technologies, ways of working, and business plans that focus on using resources and recycling. Building a workplace that values new ideas and working together can open doors to create value, stand out from others, and lead the market in making things in a way that's good for the planet (Awan et al., 2021).

Cutting down on waste plays a key role in creating a circular economy and fostering sustainable growth in manufacturing. To achieve this, we need to look at the big picture. This means thinking about how we design products, run our factories, and handle stuff when it's no longer useful. By doing so, we can reduce waste, get more out of our resources, and build an economy that's both tough and eco-friendly.

Gap

People are noticing more and more that combining clean technology and IoT in factories can cut down on waste. But we don't have much information on how to do this or what happens when we do. Research shows these technologies are helpful, but we need to know more about how they work together and how they can make the circular economy work better in real life. Also, we don't know much about the specific problems factories face when trying to use these technologies together (Gupta et al. 2021).

Objectives

- To examine how clean technology and IoT work together to cut down on waste in manufacturing. It shows how these technologies play different but supporting roles to make the best use of resources, create less waste, and push for a circular economy. This combo has the power to change things in a big way.
- To look at real-world ways to bring clean tech and IoT into manufacturing using case studies, examples, and what works best. It tries to spot common hurdles, good strategies, and key things that lead to success across different industries.
- To pinpoint the roadblocks manufacturers face when trying to use clean technology and IoT to reduce waste, These include high upfront costs, complex technology, systems not working well together, and risks to data safety. It also aims to offer doable advice and plans to get past these obstacles.
- To highlight how bringing clean tech and IoT into manufacturing helps businesses and the environment. It shows the real perks of going green and digital: saving money, working better, hurting the planet less, and following the rules.
- To give hands-on advice to makers, rule-makers, scientists, and others who want to cut waste and use stuff in a loop in factories. It boils down to the main points, what we've learned, and what's coming next to help people decide and push for greener ways to make things.

CHALLENGES IN MANUFACTURING WASTE MANAGEMENT

Companies need to handle regulatory pressures by taking a planned approach to waste management. They should blend compliance with their sustainability goals. This means putting money into systems that manage environmental impact, training workers with stakeholders, and building a workplace that cares about the environment. Working with rule-makers, industry groups, and environmental champions can open up talks and help everyone get on the same page, pushing for manufacturing that doesn't harm the planet (Cavalieri et al. 2021; Demestichas & Daskalakis 2020).

Figure 1 shows waste management strategies that work well for companies. These strategies include following rules, putting money into environmental systems teaching employees, getting stakeholders involved, and creating a culture of responsibility. Working together with rule-makers, industry groups, and environmental advocates helps create sustainable manufacturing practices.

Environmental Impact

Manufacturing activities have a big impact on damaging the environment, and creating waste is a main worry. The way manufacturing waste affects the environment covers many areas (Arunprasad & Boopathi 2019).

- **Resource Depletion:** Raw material extraction for manufacturing has an impact on habitat destruction, biodiversity loss, and the depletion of limited resources like minerals fossil fuels, and water. As global demand drives up manufacturing, it puts more pressure on natural ecosystems and resources, which makes environmental degradation worse.
- **Pollution:** Manufacturing waste often contains dangerous substances, chemicals, and pollutants that can dirty the air, water, and soil. When waste streams aren't handled or treated, it can lead to air pollution from emissions, water pollution from runoff, and soil contamination from leaks. These pollutants are risky for human health, wildlife, and ecosystems adding to environmental pollution and ecosystem damage.
- **Climate Change:** Manufacturing plays a big role in putting out greenhouse gases through energy use and factory work. When we burn fossil fuels to make energy, and in jobs like making cement or chemicals, we release carbon dioxide (CO_2), methane (CH_4), and other gases that trap heat. This has an impact on our planet making it warmer and changing our climate.
- **Waste Accumulation:** The linear "take-make-dispose" model of manufacturing leads to waste piling up, including solid waste hazardous waste, and non-biodegradable materials. Landfills overflow with thrown-away products,

packaging materials, and industrial by-products, which harms the environment even more and takes up valuable land. Also, getting rid of electronic waste (e-waste) is tough because it's made up of complex parts and toxic components, which makes environmental risks even worse.

Figure 1. Challenges in manufacturing waste management

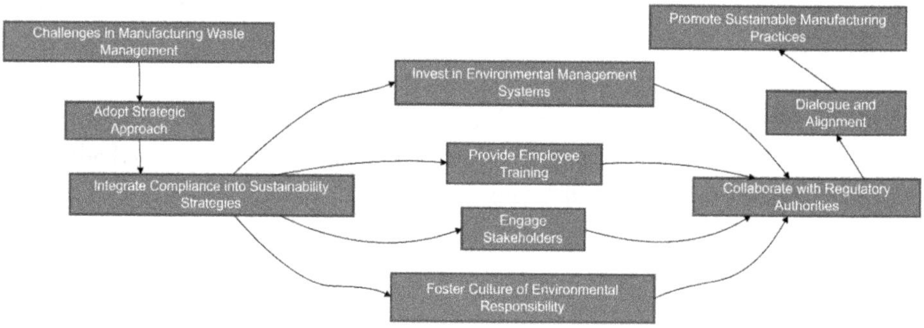

To address environmental problems, companies that make things need to put into action plans to handle waste, stop pollution, save resources, and make products in ways that don't harm nature. These steps are key to creating a greener industry.

Regulatory Pressures

Different government bodies control manufacturing waste management to cut down on environmental harm, safeguard public health, and push for sustainable resource use. Yet, manufacturers struggle to navigate these complex rules (Boopathi 2022c 2022b; Boopathi et al. 2023; Gowri et al. 2023).

- **Tough Environmental Rules:** Regulators often set strict rules for getting rid of waste, controlling emissions, and stopping pollution. This forces manufacturers to spend big on upgrading their facilities and buying pollution control tech to follow the rules. If they don't meet these standards, they risk fines, penalties, and damage to their reputation.
- **Complicated Permit Processes:** Getting permits to manage waste, like disposing of hazardous materials or treating wastewater, can take a long time and involve lots of red tape. Manufacturers have to deal with piles of paperwork, reviews by regulators, and talking to the public. This can slow down projects and make it more expensive to follow the rules.

- **Changing Regulatory Scene:** Environmental rules keep changing as new issues come up, science moves forward, and society's expectations shift. Companies that make things need to keep up with new rules, policy shifts, and fresh compliance needs. This can be tough in a world where regulations change fast and aren't always clear.
- **Compliance Across Borders:** Big companies working in many countries face extra challenges. They need to follow different rules in each place. Standards cultural norms, and how rules are enforced can vary a lot. This can lead to gaps in compliance and risks. As a result, companies need to tailor how they handle waste in each area they work in.
- **Liability and Legal Risks:** When manufacturers don't follow environmental rules, they open themselves up to legal trouble, lawsuits, and costs to clean up environmental damage. If environmental accidents or spills happen, manufacturers might face civil or criminal charges harm to their company's name, and lose trust in the market.
- **Resource Constraints:** Small and medium-sized companies often don't have the money, know-how, or staff to follow complex rules. The costs to comply can hit smaller manufacturers harder making it tough for them to put money into good waste management. This can make it harder for them to compete with bigger companies.

Economic Implications

Manufacturing waste management poses major economic hurdles for companies. It has an impact on their profits and ability to stay afloat. This stems from elements in waste creation, treatment, and elimination methods (Babu et al. 2022; Ravisankar et al. 2023).

- **Cost of Waste Disposal:** Waste disposal costs pose a major economic challenge for manufacturers. Typical disposal methods like landfills or incinerators come with hefty price tags. These include transport expenses, dump fees, and costs to follow regulations. As these costs keep climbing, companies feel pushed to cut down on waste and find cheaper ways to get rid of it.
- **Loss of Material Value:** Waste from manufacturing means companies lose out on valuable materials. When products get thrown away too soon or materials end up as scrap due to flaws or poor processes, it wastes the raw materials and resources put into making them. This doesn't just drive up production costs - it also goes against goals to use resources and be eco-friendly.
- **Impact on Production Efficiency:** Manufacturing waste has a negative impact on production efficiency. It causes disruptions, downtime, and ineffi-

ciencies. Waste buildup in factories can slow down work, block equipment, and make accidents more likely. Also using resources to manage waste—like cleaning, sorting, and getting rid of it—takes away from production time. This cuts into the overall efficiency of operations.

- **Regulatory Compliance Costs:** Following waste management rules adds another financial strain for manufacturers. Laws about how to handle, store, move, and get rid of waste mean extra costs for permits, checking, reporting, and fixing problems. Breaking these rules can lead to fines, penalties legal trouble, and harm to a company's reputation, making money problems even worse for businesses.

- **Opportunity Costs of Inefficiency:** Poor waste management in manufacturing has an impact on missed chances to make money and puts companies at a disadvantage. The money and time spent on dealing with waste could be used to come up with new ideas, make better products, or grow the business, all of which help boost income and stay ahead of competitors. When factories get better at handling waste, they can tap into hidden value and take advantage of new ways to do business.

- **Supply Chain Risks:** Bad waste handling can create supply chain problems for manufacturers hurting their ties with suppliers, customers, and other partners. Supply chain issues from waste-related problems, like not having enough materials faulty products, or environmental accidents, can slow down production upset customers, and damage the company's image. To protect supply chain strength and keep business running smoothly, companies need to tackle waste management head-on.

The economic effects of managing manufacturing waste are considerable, highlighting how crucial it is to have strategies that cut down on waste and recover resources. When manufacturers produce less waste get the most value from materials, and fine-tune their processes, they can lower risks, boost how well they operate, and ensure they succeed in the long run.

CLEAN TECHNOLOGIES FOR WASTE REDUCTION

Clean technologies play a key role in sustainable manufacturing practices. They help to reduce waste, lessen harm to the environment, and make better use of resources. These new solutions aim to minimize the environmental footprint of manufacturing operations, make them viable, and keep them competitive (Kumar et al. 2023; Selvakumar et al. 2023; Sengeni et al. 2023).

Figure 2 shows the steps to implement clean technologies in manufacturing. It starts with spotting waste streams doing a waste audit, and looking at the results. Companies put strategies in place to reuse materials, recycle, and recover energy. They also design products for reuse, start recycling programs, and use waste-to-energy tech. Keeping an eye on these efforts and checking them is key to measure waste cuts, see the money and environmental effects, and make sure they follow the rules.

Renewable Energy Systems

Renewable energy systems run on sources that nature refills, like sun, wind, water, and plant matter. These systems offer a promising way to cut waste in manufacturing. They help factories depend less on fossil fuels, put out fewer emissions, and use less energy (Nishanth et al. 2023).

- **Solar Power:** Solar photovoltaic (PV) systems turn sunlight into electricity offering a renewable and carbon-neutral energy source for manufacturing plants. Putting solar panels on roofs or unused land lets manufacturers cut down on grid electricity use lower greenhouse gas emissions, and save on energy costs in the long run. Also, progress in solar tech, like thin-film solar cells and concentrated solar power (CSP) systems, has an impact on this field.
- **Wind Power:** Wind turbines capture wind's energy to produce electricity giving factories another green power choice. Land-based and sea-based wind farms can deliver clean energy to industrial areas. This cuts reliance on non-renewable sources and lessens environmental harm from burning fossil fuels. Adding wind power to the energy mix broadens the power supply, boosts energy security, and helps fight climate change. Wind power has an impact on how we tackle global warming.

Figure 2. Process for implementing clean technologies to reduce waste

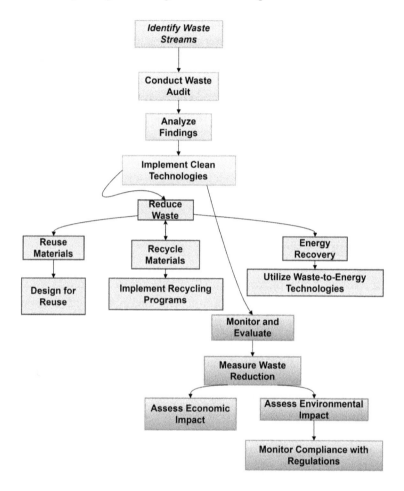

- **Hydropower:** Hydropower systems use the gravity of flowing water to make electricity giving factories near water a steady and renewable power source. You can put small hydroelectric turbines in rivers, streams, or irrigation canals to generate power on-site, while bigger hydropower plants supply grid-connected electricity to industrial areas. Hydropower has some good points: you can scale it up or down, control when it runs, and it doesn't cost much to operate. This makes it a good choice for making sustainable energy in manufacturing.

Renewable energy systems in manufacturing cut down on fossil fuel use and lower emissions, pollution, and waste.

Energy-Efficient Machinery

Energy-efficient machinery plays a key role in sustainable manufacturing practices. It cuts down on waste and boosts resource efficiency. Energy use has a big impact on the environment, with machines and equipment using up a lot of energy. Using energy-efficient tech can shrink carbon footprints, save money, and improve operations. This tech aims to optimize energy use, make equipment more efficient, tighten process control, and cut energy losses throughout production (Boopathi 2024a; Satav et al. 2023).

- **High-Efficiency Motors and Drives:** Switching to high-efficiency motors and variable frequency drives (VFDs) can cut down energy use in industrial settings. These technologies allow for exact control of motor speed and torque matching energy output to need and cutting down on wasted energy during use.
- **Advanced Automation and Control Systems:** Automation and control systems are key to optimize energy use and cut down on waste in manufacturing processes. By adding sensors, actuators, and real-time monitoring tools, manufacturers can spot inefficiencies, boost equipment performance, and minimize energy consumption across production lines.
- **Process Optimization and Retrofitting:** Updating existing machines with tech that saves energy and improving processes can lead to big energy savings without spending too much money. Small changes like tweaking equipment settings cutting down on idle time, and keeping things in better shape can help reduce waste and boost energy efficiency.
- **Energy Recovery and Recycling:** Systems that recover energy, like heat exchangers and cogeneration units, let manufacturers capture and reuse heat waste from production. By reusing thermal energy to heat, cool, or generate power, manufacturers can get the most out of their resources and cut down on energy waste.
- **Lifecycle Assessment and Design to Boost Energy Efficiency:** Taking a lifecycle approach to buying and designing equipment can help manufacturers check how energy-efficient and eco-friendly machinery is throughout its whole life. Designing with energy efficiency in mind means thinking about things like what materials to use how much energy it uses, and how to get rid of it at the end. This makes sure the equipment is as sustainable as possible from the moment it's thought up until it's taken out of service.

Eco-Friendly Materials

Clean technologies play a key role in sustainable manufacturing. They help cut down waste and boost resource efficiency. Materials that are good for the environment come from renewable or recycled sources. These eco-friendly options are vital to lessen environmental harm throughout a product's life. They offer many upsides compared to standard materials. These include lower carbon output less energy use, and less waste creation. As a result, these materials are essential to achieve sustainable manufacturing goals (BOOPATHI 2022; Janardhana et al. 2023; Sampath et al. 2021).

Eco-friendly materials come from renewable sources and can be recycled. Examples include bamboo, hemp recycled plastics, and reclaimed wood. Using these materials reduces our need for non-renewable resources and helps protect natural ecosystems. These materials also have less impact on the environment throughout their life. They need less energy, water, and resources to make, use, and dispose of. Take recycled plastics, for instance. When we use them instead of new plastics, we create less waste and use fewer resources. This saves resources and cuts down on greenhouse gases.

Consumers and stakeholders now value eco-friendly materials more. They appreciate companies that care about the environment and act. This puts pressure on manufacturers to adopt green practices to stay competitive (Ali et al. 2024; Boopathi 2024b; Boopathi & Kumar 2024). When manufacturers use eco-friendly materials in their products, they can boost their brand image. They can also attract customers who care about the environment and stand out from their rivals. This approach helps to reduce waste and meet sustainability goals in manufacturing. It makes use of renewable resources and minimizes harm to the environment. At the same time, it promotes an economy that reuses resources and wastes less.

INTEGRATION OF IOT IN MANUFACTURING

IoT technologies have an influence on manufacturing. They are causing a revolution in traditional processes by connecting, showing, and controlling things like never before. Manufacturers put IoT devices and sensors in their factories to make operations better, get more done, and cut down on waste (Ali et al., 2024).

Figure 3 shows how to integrate IoT technologies in manufacturing. It starts with adding IoT devices and sensors to collect and send data. People look at this data to learn things. This helps to improve operations, boost productivity, and fix things before they break. Automation cuts down on time when machines aren't working. The data stays safe through scrambling and controlling who can see it.

IoT-Enabled Devices and Sensors: IoT-enabled devices and sensors form the core of smart manufacturing systems. They allow companies to gather, send, and examine huge amounts of data from different spots in the production area. These devices include a wide array of tech such as RFID tags, motion sensors, temperature sensors, pressure sensors, and energy meters, to name a few. When manufacturers place IoT devices all over their factory, they can get detailed data on how equipment performs how much energy it uses, what the environment is like, and how production is going all in real time. This up-to-the-minute data helps them make quick choices, predict when machines need fixing, and keep getting better at using resources and cutting down on waste.

Real-Time Monitoring and Control: IoT technologies give manufacturers unmatched insight and control over their production processes. These tools allow companies to keep an eye on key performance indicators (KPIs) and process parameters non-stop. This means they can spot inefficiencies, problems, and potential issues right away. For instance, IoT sensors can pick up on equipment breakdowns, quality flaws, or shifts from ideal operating conditions. These sensors then set off instant alerts or kickstart automated fixes to address problems before they get worse. Also, this constant monitoring helps with flexible scheduling, resource distribution, and production fine-tuning. This lets manufacturers adapt to shifting demand trends, supply chain hiccups, or market changes.

Data Analytics and Machine Learning: Data analytics and machine learning algorithms have a significant impact on extracting useful insights from the huge amounts of data that IoT devices produce in manufacturing settings. By examining past data, spotting patterns, and forecasting future trends, manufacturers can find ways to improve processes cut down on waste, and boost quality. For example, machine learning algorithms can study production data to find links between process settings and product quality. This allows manufacturers to tweak production settings on the spot to reduce flaws and waste. Also predictive maintenance models can guess when equipment might break down or need upkeep based on sensor data. This lets manufacturers plan maintenance ahead of time and avoid expensive downtime.

Figure 3. Process to integrate IoT technologies in manufacturing

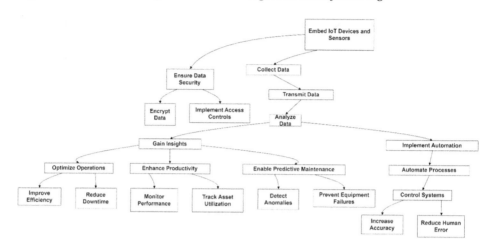

IoT technologies have an impact on manufacturing by cutting down waste and boosting sustainable methods. They do this by making the best use of resources boosting how well operations run, and creating less waste. This happens through watching things in real time and using advanced data analysis.

BEST PRACTICES

To blend clean technologies and IoT solutions into manufacturing, you need to plan, work together, and always try to get better. When done right, these methods can cut down waste and make manufacturing more sustainable (Ali et al. 2024; Maguluri et al. 2023; Syamala et al. 2023).

- **Full Review and Strategy:** Start by doing a complete check of current manufacturing methods how resources are used, and where waste happens. Find the areas that can improve the most and focus on projects that will cut waste, use resources better, and make financial sense. Create a clear plan with specific aims, targets, and schedules to put clean tech and IoT solutions into action.
- **Cross-functional Collaboration:** Teamwork between departments plays a key role in putting clean tech and IoT into action in factories. Create teams with members from production, engineering, IT, sustainability, and management to make sure everyone agrees on goals, priorities, and resources. Build a workplace culture that values working together sharing know-how, and

coming up with new ideas to tap into different viewpoints and skills when pushing sustainability projects forward.

- **Pilot Projects and Proof of Concept:** Before you scale up, run pilot projects or proof-of-concept tests to check if clean technologies and IoT solutions work well in actual manufacturing settings. Pick typical production lines or processes to test and gather data on important performance measures, like how much energy they use how much waste they make, and how efficient they are. Look at the results, figure out what you've learned, and improve your plans based on what stakeholders and end-users tell you.

- **Integration and Interoperability:** Make sure clean technologies and IoT solutions work with current manufacturing systems, equipment, and infrastructure. Pick hardware and software platforms that play well with others and support open standards and protocols to help devices and systems talk to each other and share data. Team up with tech companies, solution providers, and system integrators to tailor solutions and tackle specific needs and requirements.

- **Data-driven Decision-making:** Use data analytics and machine learning algorithms to get helpful insights from IoT data and make smart choices. Set up reliable systems to collect, store, and analyze data in real-time. Apply advanced analytics methods, like predictive modeling spotting unusual patterns, and optimization algorithms, to find trends and ways to get better. Give decision-makers useful insights and dashboards that show key performance metrics and indicators.

- **Continuous Monitoring and Optimization:** Create a culture that always keeps an eye on, measures, and improves efforts to cut waste and reach sustainability targets. Put in place ways to measure performance key indicators, and standards to evaluate how well clean technologies and IoT solutions work over time. Do regular checks, reviews, and assessments to find areas that need improvement. Change strategies, make processes better, and take action to fix things based on how well they're doing and what you've learned along the way.

- **Employee Training and Engagement:** Put money into training staff and getting them involved to help them understand, gain skills, and build abilities to use clean tech and Internet of Things solutions well. Give thorough training programs, workshops, and learning materials to get employees familiar with new tech, ways of doing things, and top tips. Create a workplace that values new ideas, gives people power, and always wants to learn. This will get employees to join in, take charge, and commit to green efforts.

To put clean tech and IoT into action in manufacturing, companies need a full plan. This plan should look at current processes, make a roadmap, work with others, use data to make choices, keep an eye on things, and get workers involved. This approach helps cut waste, use resources better, and boost sustainability.

BARRIERS TO ADOPTION

For factories to start using clean tech and IoT, they must tackle some issues. These include the upfront costs making different systems work together, and keeping data safe. To overcome these, they should weigh the good points, team up to find answers, and set up strong online safety rules. These steps protect important info and help green efforts succeed.

- **Initial Investment Costs:** The money needed upfront to set up clean technologies and IoT solutions creates a big obstacle for many manufacturers who want to adopt them. Clean tech like renewable energy systems, energy-saving machines, and eco-friendly materials often cost a lot to buy set up, and fit into existing systems. In the same way, putting in IoT devices, sensors, and data analysis tools means spending on hardware, software, internet connections, and teaching staff how to use them. Manufacturers might not want to put money into these technologies because they worry about getting their money back and how long it will take in industries that don't make much profit or struggle to get loans.
- **Interoperability Issues:** Interoperability problems pop up when companies try to combine different clean technologies and IoT solutions into one working system. Various technologies might run on systems that don't play well together, use their own special codes, or lack common ways to connect. This makes it tough to join everything and share data. Companies might face these issues when they want to hook up old machines with new IoT devices, bring together data from all over, or get different systems and suppliers to work as one. To tackle these problems, tech companies, industry players, and groups that set standards need to team up. Their goal? To create open flexible standards and codes that help everything talk to each other and work together without a hitch.
- **Data Security Concerns:** Data security worries create another obstacle to IoT adoption in manufacturing when it comes to gathering, sending, and keeping sensitive operational data. IoT devices and sensors produce huge amounts of data such as production stats, equipment performance info, and supply chain details, which need protection from unauthorized use, tamper-

ing, or theft. Manufacturers worry about possible cyber threats, like data leaks, malware attacks, and ransomware incidents, which could put sensitive info at risk, mess up operations, and hurt their reputation. Also following data protection rules, like GDPR and CCPA, makes IoT setups more complex and adds regulatory work, which makes data security worries even worse.

STRATEGIES TO OVERCOME BARRIERS

Manufacturers can speed up the adoption of clean technologies and IoT solutions. They can do this by using financial incentives pushing for standards, and building partnerships. These approaches don't just lower risks. They also open doors to new ideas, help companies compete, and create lasting value in eco-friendly manufacturing (Hema et al. 2023; Malathi et al. 2024).

- **Financial Incentives:** To tackle the obstacle of upfront investment expenses, manufacturers can check out different financial perks and support options from government bodies, industry groups, and banks. These perks might include grants, subsidies, tax breaks, and cheap loans aimed at pushing the use of clean tech and green initiatives. Manufacturers can use these financial perks to cut down on initial costs, speed up tech adoption, and boost the money-making potential of clean tech and IoT rollouts. Also, looking into new funding models like energy performance contracts (EPC) or third-party funding deals can help spread out investment costs over time and line up interests between different parties.
- **Standards and Regulations:** Standards and regulations have a big impact on solving interoperability problems and giving clear consistent guidelines for using clean technologies and IoT solutions. Companies that make these products can push to create and use industry standards, protocols, and best practices. These help different technologies and systems work together, be compatible, and keep data safe. Working with rule-makers, industry groups, and standards organizations can shape policies that help factories adopt and integrate clean technologies and IoT. Also, following current rules, like energy efficiency standards environmental laws, and data protection rules, can make companies want to use clean technologies and IoT solutions.
- **Collaborative Partnerships:** When manufacturers team up with tech companies, research groups, and other players, they can tackle adoption hurdles by pooling their know-how, resources, and skills. Companies can join forces with tech sellers, system builders, and service firms to create and roll out custom-fit answers to specific needs. Working with research centers, col-

leges, and innovation hubs can help share knowledge, move tech forward, and tap into cutting-edge studies. Also, forming industry groups, alliances, or networks allows for joint action and sharing insights on shared issues like getting systems to work together keeping data safe, and following rules.

FUTURE TRENDS AND INNOVATIONS

The manufacturing industry faces big changes because of worldwide issues like climate change, not enough resources, and new rules. What's coming next includes better clean tech Internet of Things, and new ways to be sustainable. These aim to make manufacturing stronger, use fewer resources, and care more about the environment (Boopathi 2022a; Boopathi & Davim, 2023). These circular economy approaches include using renewable energy like solar and wind sustainable materials such as bio-based and recycled options, making products last longer, recovering resources, and offering products as services. New ideas in this area cover better solar panels, improved wind turbine designs, ways to convert biomass, and rebuilding used products.

New Clean Tech

Clean tech has a big impact on how things are made. It cuts down on harm to the environment and helps companies compete better. The main trends and new ideas focus on doing more with less and coming up with fresh approaches.

- **Renewable Energy Integration:** Ongoing improvements in green energy tech, like solar panels, wind farms, and battery systems, help factories move towards carbon-free and energy-smart operations. New ideas in mixing renewable energy flexible power grids, and managing energy demand let manufacturers use energy better, depend less on fossil fuels, and cut down on greenhouse gases they release. These changes have an impact on how factories run and how they affect the environment.
- **Circular Materials and Resource Efficiency:** New ideas in circular materials and resource efficiency have an impact on how manufacturers source, use, and recycle materials throughout the product lifecycle. From bio-based materials and biodegradable polymers to closed-loop recycling processes and waste-to-energy technologies, manufacturers explore new solutions to minimize waste, save resources, and promote circular economy principles.
- **Smart Manufacturing and Automation:** Progress in smart manufacturing and automation technologies enables manufacturers to improve production processes, boost productivity, and lower environmental impact. Adding IoT

devices artificial intelligence (AI), and machine learning algorithms allows for real-time monitoring predictive maintenance, and adaptive control of manufacturing equipment. This leads to energy savings less waste, and better operational efficiency.

IoT Developments

IoT progress has an impact on digital change in manufacturing. It allows for insights based on data better operations, and eco-friendly practices (Hema et al. 2023; Maguluri et al. 2023; Syamala et al. 2023).

- **Edge Computing and Edge Analytics:** Edge computing and edge analytics have an influence on manufacturers' ability to process and analyze IoT-generated data near its source. This cuts down on delays bandwidth needs, and dependence on central cloud systems. Edge computing allows for quick decisions spotting unusual events, and predicting maintenance needs at the network's edge. This boosts operational flexibility and quick responses.
- **5G Connectivity and Low-power IoT Devices:** The launch of 5G networks and the creation of low-power IoT devices are widening connection choices. They also enable widespread data gathering and communication in factory settings. 5G connections offer faster speeds less delay, and better reliability. This makes it easier to use IoT solutions to monitor, control, and improve production processes in real-time.
- **Digital Twins and Simulation:** Digital twins, which are virtual copies of real-world assets or processes, are becoming more common in manufacturing. They allow manufacturers to simulate and fine-tune production workflows, forecast performance results, and spot areas to improve. By making digital twins of manufacturing equipment, production lines, and supply chain networks, manufacturers can boost resource use cut down on waste, and enhance sustainability measures.

Emerging Sustainability Practices

New sustainability practices are causing a revolution in how manufacturers deal with environmental care, social duty, and business management. These changes include notable new ideas and trends (Dhanya et al. 2023; Hussain et al. 2023).

- **Circular Supply Chains:** The idea of circular supply chains has an influence on manufacturers who want to cut down on waste, save resources, and boost circular economy ideas. These supply chains focus on using products and materials again making them new, and recycling them. When companies work together use reverse logistics networks, and create closed-loop material flows, they can get back and reuse products that have reached the end of their life. This helps to lower the impact on the environment and make better use of resources.

- **Product-as-a-Service Models:** Product-as-a-Service (PaaS) models, like product leasing, sharing, or subscription-based offerings, are causing a revolution in typical ownership models. They push manufacturers to design products that last longer, can be fixed, and recycled. By moving from a straight "take-make-throw away" model to a round "access-based" one, manufacturers can make products last longer, use resources better, and create less waste. At the same time, they give customers added value services and experiences.

- **Transparency and Traceability:** Consumers want to know more about supply chains, which pushes manufacturers to use sustainable sourcing ethical labor, and responsible production. Tech like blockchain, RFID tags, and digital certificates allow full visibility of products, from where raw materials come from to how they're thrown away. This gives customers the power to make smart buying choices and hold companies responsible for how they affect the environment and society.

Clean tech trends, IoT advances, and green practices are changing how manufacturing works. These shifts push the industry to be more sustainable, tough, and responsible in the long run. When companies use new ideas, they can compete better, cut down on harm to the environment, and help create a thriving society.

CONCLUSION

The manufacturing industry can cut down on waste, boost how well it uses resources, and help the environment by bringing in clean technology and IoT solutions. To do this, companies can tap into renewable energy, use materials that can be recycled, make their factories smarter, use edge computing, and try out new ways to be eco-friendly. Sure, it costs a lot upfront, and there are hurdles like making different systems work together and keeping data safe. But makers can get past these roadblocks with money incentives clear rules, laws, and by teaming up with others. This will speed up how fast clean tech and IoT solutions catch on, leading to a manufacturing world that's better for the planet and can bounce back from problems more easily.

Manufacturers can get benefits by using clean technologies, IoT advances, and new sustainability methods. These benefits include saving money, improving operations, following rules, and boosting their brand image. By focusing on sustainability and caring for the environment, manufacturers can meet what consumers and investors now expect, helping to create a sustainable future. This process needs dedication, teamwork, and ongoing new ideas leading to a stronger and more responsible future for manufacturing and society.

ABBREVIATIONS

AI - Artificial Intelligence
CCPA - California Consumer Privacy Act
CH - Switzerland (Country Code)
CO - Carbon Monoxide
CSP - Concentrated Solar Power
EPC - Energy Performance Contracting
GDPR - General Data Protection Regulation
IT - Information Technology
KPI - Key Performance Indicator
PV - Photovoltaic
RFID - Radio Frequency Identification
ROI - Return on Investment
SME - Small and Medium-sized Enterprises
VFD - Variable Frequency Drive

REFERENCES

Ali, M. N., Senthil, T., Ilakkiya, T., Hasan, D. S., Ganapathy, N. B. S., & Boopathi, S. (2024). IoT's Role in Smart Manufacturing Transformation for Enhanced Household Product Quality. In *Advanced Applications in Osmotic Computing* (pp. 252–289). IGI Global. DOI:10.4018/979-8-3693-1694-8.ch014

Arunprasad, R., & Boopathi, S. (2019). Chapter-4 Alternate Refrigerants for Minimization Environmental Impacts: A Review. In *Advances in Engineering Technology* (p. 75). AkiNik Publications New Delhi.

Awan, U., Sroufe, R., & Shahbaz, M. (2021). Industry 4.0 and the circular economy: A literature review and recommendations for future research. *Business Strategy and the Environment*, 30(4), 2038–2060. DOI:10.1002/bse.2731

Babu, B. S., Kamalakannan, J., Meenatchi, N., Karthik, S., & Boopathi, S. (2022). Economic impacts and reliability evaluation of battery by adopting Electric Vehicle. *IEEE Explore*, 1–6.

Boopathi, S. (2022). Effects of Cryogenically-treated Stainless Steel on Eco-friendly Wire Electrical Discharge Machining Process. *Preprint : Springer.*

Boopathi, S. (2022a). An extensive review on sustainable developments of dry and near-dry electrical discharge machining processes. *ASME: Journal of Manufacturing Science and Engineering*, 144(5), 050801–1.

Boopathi, S. (2022b). An investigation on gas emission concentration and relative emission rate of the near-dry wire-cut electrical discharge machining process. *Environmental Science and Pollution Research International*, 29(57), 86237–86246. DOI:10.1007/s11356-021-17658-1 PMID:34837614

Boopathi, S. (2022c). Cryogenically treated and untreated stainless steel grade 317 in sustainable wire electrical discharge machining process: A comparative study. *Springer :Environmental Science and Pollution Research*, 1–10.

Boopathi, S. (2024a). Energy Cascade Conversion System and Energy-Efficient Infrastructure. In *Sustainable Development in AI, Blockchain, and E-Governance Applications* (pp. 47–71). IGI Global. DOI:10.4018/979-8-3693-1722-8.ch004

Boopathi, S. (2024b). Minimization of Manufacturing Industry Wastes Through the Green Lean Sigma Principle. *Sustainable Machining and Green Manufacturing*, 249–270.

Boopathi, S., Alqahtani, A. S., Mubarakali, A., & Panchatcharam, P. (2023). Sustainable developments in near-dry electrical discharge machining process using sunflower oil-mist dielectric fluid. *Environmental Science and Pollution Research International*, 31(27), 1–20. DOI:10.1007/s11356-023-27494-0 PMID:37199846

Boopathi, S., & Davim, J. P. (2023). Applications of Nanoparticles in Various Manufacturing Processes. In *Sustainable Utilization of Nanoparticles and Nanofluids in Engineering Applications* (pp. 1–31). IGI Global. DOI:10.4018/978-1-6684-9135-5.ch001

Boopathi, S., & Kumar, P. (2024). Advanced bioprinting processes using additive manufacturing technologies: Revolutionizing tissue engineering. *3D Printing Technologies: Digital Manufacturing, Artificial Intelligence, Industry 4.0*, 95.

Cavalieri, A., Reis, J., & Amorim, M. (2021). Circular economy and internet of things: Mapping science of case studies in manufacturing industry. *Sustainability (Basel)*, 13(6), 3299. DOI:10.3390/su13063299

Demestichas, K., & Daskalakis, E. (2020). Information and communication technology solutions for the circular economy. *Sustainability (Basel)*, 12(18), 7272. DOI:10.3390/su12187272

Dhanya, D., Kumar, S. S., Thilagavathy, A., Prasad, D., & Boopathi, S. (2023). Data Analytics and Artificial Intelligence in the Circular Economy: Case Studies. In *Intelligent Engineering Applications and Applied Sciences for Sustainability* (pp. 40–58). IGI Global.

Gowri, N. V., Dwivedi, J. N., Krishnaveni, K., Boopathi, S., Palaniappan, M., & Medikondu, N. R. (2023). Experimental investigation and multi-objective optimization of eco-friendly near-dry electrical discharge machining of shape memory alloy using Cu/SiC/Gr composite electrode. *Environmental Science and Pollution Research International*, 30(49), 1–19. DOI:10.1007/s11356-023-26983-6 PMID:37126160

Gupta, H., Kumar, A., & Wasan, P. (2021). Industry 4.0, cleaner production and circular economy: An integrative framework for evaluating ethical and sustainable business performance of manufacturing organizations. *Journal of Cleaner Production*, 295, 126253. DOI:10.1016/j.jclepro.2021.126253

Hema, N., Krishnamoorthy, N., Chavan, S. M., Kumar, N., Sabarimuthu, M., & Boopathi, S. (2023). A Study on an Internet of Things (IoT)-Enabled Smart Solar Grid System. In *Handbook of Research on Deep Learning Techniques for Cloud-Based Industrial IoT* (pp. 290–308). IGI Global. DOI:10.4018/978-1-6684-8098-4.ch017

Hussain, Z., Babe, M., Saravanan, S., Srimathy, G., Roopa, H., & Boopathi, S. (2023). Optimizing Biomass-to-Biofuel Conversion: IoT and AI Integration for Enhanced Efficiency and Sustainability. In *Circular Economy Implementation for Sustainability in the Built Environment* (pp. 191–214). IGI Global.

Janardhana, K., Singh, V., Singh, S. N., Babu, T. R., Bano, S., & Boopathi, S. (2023). Utilization Process for Electronic Waste in Eco-Friendly Concrete: Experimental Study. In *Sustainable Approaches and Strategies for E-Waste Management and Utilization* (pp. 204–223). IGI Global.

Kristoffersen, E., Blomsma, F., Mikalef, P., & Li, J. (2020). The smart circular economy: A digital-enabled circular strategies framework for manufacturing companies. *Journal of Business Research*, 120, 241–261. DOI:10.1016/j.jbusres.2020.07.044

Kumar, M., Kumar, K., Sasikala, P., Sampath, B., Gopi, B., & Sundaram, S. (2023). Sustainable Green Energy Generation From Waste Water: IoT and ML Integration. In *Sustainable Science and Intelligent Technologies for Societal Development* (pp. 440–463). IGI Global.

Maguluri, L. P., Ananth, J., Hariram, S., Geetha, C., Bhaskar, A., & Boopathi, S. (2023). Smart Vehicle-Emissions Monitoring System Using Internet of Things (IoT). In *Handbook of Research on Safe Disposal Methods of Municipal Solid Wastes for a Sustainable Environment* (pp. 191–211). IGI Global.

Malathi, J., Kusha, K., Isaac, S., Ramesh, A., Rajendiran, M., & Boopathi, S. (2024). IoT-Enabled Remote Patient Monitoring for Chronic Disease Management and Cost Savings: Transforming Healthcare. In *Advances in Explainable AI Applications for Smart Cities* (pp. 371–388). IGI Global.

Nishanth, J., Deshmukh, M. A., Kushwah, R., Kushwaha, K. K., Balaji, S., & Sampath, B. (2023). Particle Swarm Optimization of Hybrid Renewable Energy Systems. In *Intelligent Engineering Applications and Applied Sciences for Sustainability* (pp. 291–308). IGI Global. DOI:10.4018/979-8-3693-0044-2.ch016

Rajput, S., & Singh, S. P. (2020). Industry 4.0 Model for circular economy and cleaner production. *Journal of Cleaner Production*, 277, 123853. DOI:10.1016/j.jclepro.2020.123853

Ravisankar, A., Sampath, B., & Asif, M. M. (2023). Economic Studies on Automobile Management: Working Capital and Investment Analysis. In *Multidisciplinary Approaches to Organizational Governance During Health Crises* (pp. 169–198). IGI Global.

Sampath, B., Sureshkumar, T., Yuvaraj, M., & Velmurugan, D. (2021). Experimental Investigations on Eco-Friendly Helium-Mist Near-Dry Wire-Cut EDM of M2-HSS Material. *Materials Research Proceedings*, 19, 175–180.

Satav, S. D., Lamani, D., Harsha, K., Kumar, N., Manikandan, S., & Sampath, B. (2023). Energy and Battery Management in the Era of Cloud Computing: Sustainable Wireless Systems and Networks. In *Sustainable Science and Intelligent Technologies for Societal Development* (pp. 141–166). IGI Global.

Selvakumar, S., Shankar, R., Ranjit, P., Bhattacharya, S., Gupta, A. S. G., & Boopathi, S. (2023). E-Waste Recovery and Utilization Processes for Mobile Phone Waste. In *Handbook of Research on Safe Disposal Methods of Municipal Solid Wastes for a Sustainable Environment* (pp. 222–240). IGI Global. DOI:10.4018/978-1-6684-8117-2.ch016

Sengeni, D., Padmapriya, G., Imambi, S. S., Suganthi, D., Suri, A., & Boopathi, S. (2023). Biomedical waste handling method using artificial intelligence techniques. In *Handbook of Research on Safe Disposal Methods of Municipal Solid Wastes for a Sustainable Environment* (pp. 306–323). IGI Global. DOI:10.4018/978-1-6684-8117-2.ch022

Syamala, M., Komala, C., Pramila, P., Dash, S., Meenakshi, S., & Boopathi, S. (2023). Machine Learning-Integrated IoT-Based Smart Home Energy Management System. In *Handbook of Research on Deep Learning Techniques for Cloud-Based Industrial IoT* (pp. 219–235). IGI Global. DOI:10.4018/978-1-6684-8098-4.ch013

Zhang, A., Venkatesh, V., Wang, J. X., Mani, V., Wan, M., & Qu, T. (2023). Drivers of industry 4.0-enabled smart waste management in supply chain operations: A circular economy perspective in china. *Production Planning and Control*, 34(10), 870–886. DOI:10.1080/09537287.2021.1980909

ADDITIONAL READING

Demestichas, K., & Daskalakis, E. (2020). Information and communication technology solutions for the circular economy. *Sustainability (Basel)*, 12(18), 7272. DOI:10.3390/su12187272

Rejeb, A., Suhaiza, Z., Rejeb, K., Seuring, S., & Treiblmaier, H. (2022). The Internet of Things and the circular economy: A systematic literature review and research agenda. *Journal of Cleaner Production*, 350, 131439. DOI:10.1016/j.jclepro.2022.131439

Turskis, Z., & Šniokienė, V. (2024). IoT-Driven Transformation of Circular Economy Efficiency: An Overview. *Mathematical & Computational Applications*, 29(4), 49. DOI:10.3390/mca29040049

KEY TERMS AND DEFINITIONS

Circular Economy: A sustainable economic model focused on minimizing waste and maximizing the reuse, recycling, and remanufacturing of materials to keep products and resources in use for as long as possible.

Clean Technologies: Innovations and systems that reduce environmental impacts by enhancing energy efficiency, using renewable resources, and minimizing waste and pollution during manufacturing processes.

Data Security: The protection of sensitive operational data generated by IoT devices from unauthorized access, tampering, or theft, ensuring the integrity and confidentiality of manufacturing information.

Energy-Efficient Machinery: Advanced equipment and technologies designed to perform manufacturing tasks with minimal energy consumption, thereby reducing costs and environmental impact.

Internet of Things (IoT): A network of interconnected devices and sensors that collect and exchange data in real-time, allowing for improved monitoring, control, and optimization of manufacturing processes to reduce waste and increase efficiency.

Interoperability: The ability of different clean technologies and IoT systems to work together seamlessly within a manufacturing environment, facilitating the integration and efficient use of multiple systems.

Real-Time Monitoring: The continuous observation and analysis of manufacturing processes through IoT devices, allowing for immediate detection of inefficiencies and timely interventions to reduce waste.

Renewable Energy Systems: Energy solutions that utilize naturally replenishing resources such as solar, wind, and hydropower to generate electricity, thereby reducing dependence on fossil fuels and lowering carbon emissions in manufacturing.

Resource Efficiency: The practice of using materials, energy, and other resources in a way that maximizes productivity while minimizing waste, environmental impact, and resource depletion.

Waste Reduction: The process of minimizing the generation of waste through efficient resource use, recycling, and the adoption of technologies that reduce the environmental footprint of manufacturing activities.

Chapter 4
Harnessing GPS, Sensors, and Drones to Minimize Environmental Impact:
Precision Agriculture

A. Vellingiri

https://orcid.org/0009-0003-0378
-9959

Department of Electronics and Communication Engineering, Bannari Amman Institute of Technology, Erode, India

R. Kokila

https://orcid.org/0009-0002-4327
-7408

School of Computer Application, Dayananda Sagar University, Bengaluru, India

P. Nisha

https://orcid.org/0009-0009-6311
-2935

Department of Electrical and Electronics Engineering, St. Joseph's Institute of Technology, Chennai, India

Monish Kumar

https://orcid.org/0000-0002-6088
-1976

Department of Civil Engineering, Sri Jayachamarajendra College of Engineering, Mysuru, India

Somu Chinnusamy

Research and Development, RSP Science Hub, Coimbatore, India

Sampath Boopathi

https://orcid.org/0000-0002-2065
-6539

Department of Mechanical Engineering, Muthayammal Engineering College, Namakkal, India

ABSTRACT

Precision farming uses advanced technology like GPS, sensors, and drones to make farming better and greener. It applies water, fertilizers, and pesticides where crops

DOI: 10.4018/979-8-3693-5498-8.ch004

need them. GPS helps map fields and guide machines. Sensors give up-to-date information on soil, crops, and weather. Drones watch from above, letting farmers act fast and use resources wisely. By not using too much and cutting waste, this method has less impact on nature. It saves water, stops chemicals from running off, and keeps soil healthy. This chapter looks at how these tools fit into today's farms. It shows real examples of good points and tough spots. It points out how precision farming could change old ways, leading to farming that lasts and bounces back from problems.

INTRODUCTION

Precision agriculture, also known as precision farming or site-specific crop management, represents a transformative approach to farming that integrates advanced technologies to optimize agricultural productivity and sustainability. This method leverages technologies such as Global Positioning System (GPS), sensors, and drones to gather detailed data on various aspects of farming operations, enabling farmers to make informed decisions that enhance crop yields, reduce resource consumption, and minimize environmental impact. At its core, precision agriculture involves the collection and analysis of data to manage field variability in crops. Traditional farming practices often treat entire fields uniformly, applying the same amount of water, fertilizers, and pesticides across vast areas(Brar et al., 2019; Sharma et al., 2018). However, soil composition, moisture levels, and crop health can vary significantly within a single field. Precision agriculture addresses this variability by using GPS technology to map fields in detail, sensors to monitor soil and plant conditions, and drones to provide aerial imagery and real-time insights.

One of the most significant contributions of precision agriculture is its ability to improve resource efficiency. For instance, GPS-guided tractors and machinery can precisely apply inputs such as seeds, fertilizers, and pesticides only where they are needed, reducing waste and ensuring that each plant receives optimal care. This precision not only enhances crop yields but also conserves vital resources such as water and nutrients. By applying inputs in a targeted manner, farmers can achieve better results with less environmental impact, reducing runoff and preventing the overuse of chemicals that can harm ecosystems (Bag et al., 2015; Dysko et al., 2015). Sensors play a crucial role in precision agriculture by providing continuous, real-time data on soil moisture, temperature, nutrient levels, and crop health. These sensors can be placed in the soil, attached to plants, or mounted on equipment. The data they generate allows farmers to monitor the health and needs of their crops closely, making it possible to adjust irrigation schedules, nutrient applications, and other management practices promptly. For example, soil moisture sensors can help determine the exact amount of water needed, preventing over-irrigation and conserving water resources.

Drones are another vital component of precision agriculture, offering a bird's-eye view of fields that is invaluable for monitoring crop conditions. Equipped with various sensors and cameras, drones can capture high-resolution images and data that reveal patterns of crop health, pest infestations, and disease outbreaks. This aerial perspective enables farmers to identify and address issues quickly, often before they become severe. Drones can also assist in tasks such as planting, spraying, and monitoring livestock, further enhancing the efficiency and effectiveness of agricultural operations (Boopathi, 2024a; Sonia et al., 2024). The significance of precision agriculture extends beyond immediate productivity gains and resource savings. By minimizing the environmental footprint of farming practices, precision agriculture contributes to the long-term sustainability of agriculture. Reduced chemical usage means less contamination of water bodies and soils, while efficient water management helps conserve this precious resource in regions facing water scarcity. Moreover, healthier soils and better-managed crops can lead to more resilient agricultural systems capable of withstanding the impacts of climate change and other challenges.

Precision agriculture also holds economic benefits for farmers. The initial investment in technology and equipment can be substantial, but the long-term savings in inputs and the increased yields often result in a positive return on investment. Additionally, precision agriculture can improve the quality of produce, making it more competitive in the market and potentially leading to higher prices and better market access for farmers (Venkateswaran et al., 2024). In conclusion, precision agriculture represents a paradigm shift in modern farming, integrating advanced technologies to create more efficient, sustainable, and productive agricultural systems. By leveraging GPS, sensors, and drones, farmers can manage their fields with unprecedented accuracy, optimizing resource use and minimizing environmental impact. As these technologies continue to evolve and become more accessible, precision agriculture is poised to play an increasingly vital role in meeting the global demand for food while preserving the planet's natural resources.

The concept of precision farming, while seemingly modern, has roots that trace back to the advent of agriculture itself, when farmers first recognized the variability in their fields and sought ways to manage it. The journey towards what we now call precision agriculture began with the realization that different areas within a single field could have varying levels of fertility and moisture, prompting early farmers to adopt rudimentary forms of site-specific management. However, it wasn't until the late 20th century, with the development of advanced technologies, that precision farming truly began to take shape. The initial strides in precision agriculture emerged in the 1980s with the introduction of GPS (Global Positioning System) technology. GPS allowed for accurate mapping and navigation of agricultural fields, providing a foundation for more precise field management (Boopathi, 2024a). Farmers could now determine their exact position in a field, enabling them to apply inputs like seeds, fertilizers, and pesticides with greater accuracy. This period also saw the development of yield monitors, which, when integrated with GPS, allowed for the collection of yield data across different parts of a field, highlighting the variability in productivity and guiding more informed decision-making.

The 1990s marked significant advancements with the integration of GIS (Geographic Information Systems) into agriculture. GIS enabled the analysis and visualization of spatial data, facilitating more sophisticated field mapping and management practices. During this decade, variable rate technology (VRT) also gained prominence. VRT allowed for the application of inputs at variable rates across a field based on data from soil tests, yield maps, and other sources, optimizing resource use and enhancing crop yields (Boopathi, 2024b; Glady et al., 2024). The combination of GPS, GIS, and VRT laid the groundwork for modern precision farming, providing the tools needed to implement site-specific management on a broader scale. As technology continued to evolve, the early 2000s saw the introduction of advanced sensors and remote sensing technologies. These innovations brought about significant improvements in data collection and analysis. Soil sensors, weather stations, and crop sensors began providing real-time data on soil conditions, weather patterns, and crop health (Sankar et al., 2023). Remote sensing, using satellites and aerial imagery, allowed for the monitoring of large agricultural areas from above, offering insights into crop growth, soil moisture, and pest infestations. This period also witnessed the advent of automated steering systems and GPS-guided machinery, further enhancing the precision and efficiency of agricultural operations.

The past decade has seen an explosion of innovation in precision agriculture, driven by advancements in big data, machine learning, and the Internet of Things (IoT). The proliferation of drones equipped with high-resolution cameras and multispectral sensors has revolutionized crop monitoring, enabling detailed analysis of plant health and early detection of diseases and pests. IoT devices and networks have facilitated the collection and transmission of vast amounts of data from various sensors deployed across fields. Machine learning algorithms analyze this data, providing actionable insights and predictive analytics to support decision-making. Today, precision agriculture encompasses a wide range of technologies and practices, from autonomous tractors and robotic harvesters to sophisticated software platforms that integrate and analyze data from multiple sources (P. Kumar et al., 2023). The focus has shifted towards developing more user-friendly and cost-effective solutions to make precision farming accessible to farmers of all scales. The integration of artificial intelligence (AI) and blockchain technology promises further advancements, with AI enhancing predictive capabilities and blockchain ensuring transparency and traceability in agricultural supply chains.

Hence, the evolution of precision farming techniques is a testament to the relentless pursuit of efficiency and sustainability in agriculture. From the early recognition of field variability to the integration of cutting-edge technologies, precision agriculture has transformed the way we approach farming. As we move forward, continued innovation and the democratization of these technologies will be crucial in addressing the global challenges of food security and environmental conservation.

OBJECTIVES AND SCOPE

The primary objective of precision agriculture is to optimize agricultural practices through the targeted application of inputs, thereby enhancing productivity, sustainability, and profitability (Koshariya et al., 2023). By leveraging advanced technologies such as GPS, sensors, drones, and data analytics, precision agriculture aims to:

- Precision agriculture seeks to minimize input wastage by applying seeds, fertilizers, water, and pesticides precisely where and when they are needed. This approach not only conserves resources but also reduces costs for farmers.
- Through precise monitoring and management of soil conditions, crop health, and environmental factors, precision agriculture helps farmers achieve higher yields and improve the quality of their produce.
- By minimizing chemical runoff, soil erosion, and water usage, precision agriculture contributes to environmental conservation and promotes sustainable farming practices.
- Real-time data from sensors and drones enable farmers to make informed decisions about irrigation, pest management, and harvesting, leading to more effective and timely interventions.
- Precision agriculture helps farmers adapt to climate change by providing tools to monitor and respond to shifts in weather patterns, ensuring resilient agricultural practices.

The scope of precision agriculture encompasses a wide range of applications, from small-scale farms to large commercial operations. It includes field mapping, soil analysis, crop scouting, variable rate application, and yield monitoring, all supported by digital tools and analytics. As technology continues to evolve, the scope of precision agriculture is expanding to include new innovations in automation, artificial intelligence, and blockchain, promising further improvements in efficiency, sustainability, and global food security.

IMPORTANT TECHNOLOGIES IN PRECISION AGRICULTURE

GPS technology has revolutionized precision agriculture by providing accurate positioning and navigation capabilities, essential for optimizing farming practices. Originally developed for military purposes, GPS now plays a critical role in agriculture, enabling farmers to map fields, track equipment, and apply inputs with unprecedented precision (Borgelt et al., 1996; Shanwad et al., 2002; Topakci et al., 2010).

How GPS Works

GPS operates through a network of satellites orbiting the Earth, continuously transmitting signals that are received by GPS receivers on the ground. These receivers calculate their position by triangulating signals from multiple satellites, determining latitude, longitude, and altitude with high accuracy. In agriculture, GPS receivers integrated into farm equipment, vehicles, and drones allow for precise location tracking and data collection.

Applications of GPS in Farming

- Field Mapping and Navigation: GPS technology enables farmers to accurately map their fields, delineating boundaries and identifying areas with varying soil characteristics and crop conditions. This spatial data serves as a foundation for implementing site-specific management practices.
- Precision Guidance Systems: GPS-guided steering systems in tractors, combines, and other machinery ensure precise navigation and operation in the field. Automated steering reduces overlaps and skips during planting, spraying, and harvesting, optimizing input application and minimizing resource wastage.
- Variable Rate Technology (VRT): VRT uses GPS data to adjust the application rates of seeds, fertilizers, pesticides, and irrigation water based on localized soil and crop conditions. By applying inputs at variable rates according to spatial variability within a field, farmers can maximize yields while minimizing costs and environmental impact.
- Yield Monitoring: GPS-enabled yield monitors track and record crop yields as equipment moves through the field. By correlating yield data with GPS-derived spatial information, farmers gain insights into yield variability across their fields, identifying areas of high and low productivity for targeted management.
- Data Integration and Decision Support: GPS data, when integrated with other sensors and software platforms, supports data-driven decision-making in

agriculture. Integrated systems analyze spatial data to generate prescription maps for precise input application, facilitate farm planning, and optimize operational efficiency.

Benefits of GPS in Precision Agriculture

- Enhanced Efficiency: GPS technology reduces labor and fuel costs by optimizing route planning and eliminating unnecessary passes through fields.
- Improved Accuracy: Precise positioning improves the accuracy of input application, ensuring that crops receive optimal nutrients, water, and protection against pests and diseases.
- Environmental Sustainability: By minimizing over-application of inputs, GPS contributes to reduced chemical runoff, soil erosion, and environmental contamination.
- Scalability: GPS technology is scalable and adaptable to farms of various sizes and types, from small family farms to large commercial operations.

While GPS technology offers substantial benefits to precision agriculture, several challenges and considerations should be addressed:

- Cost: Initial investment in GPS equipment and software can be significant, particularly for smaller farms. However, the long-term benefits often justify the upfront costs.
- Accuracy in Challenging Environments: GPS signal reception can be affected by terrain, tree cover, and atmospheric conditions, potentially impacting accuracy in certain areas.
- Data Privacy and Security: As with any digital technology, ensuring the privacy and security of GPS data and integrated systems is crucial to prevent unauthorized access and misuse.

The future of GPS in precision agriculture lies in continued advancements in accuracy, reliability, and integration with emerging technologies. Enhanced satellite systems, such as Europe's Galileo and China's BeiDou, promise improved global coverage and precision. Integration with AI and machine learning algorithms will enable real-time data analysis and predictive modeling, further optimizing farming practices. Moreover, the combination of GPS with drones and autonomous vehicles holds the potential to revolutionize farm operations, making precision agriculture even more efficient and sustainable in the years to come.

Role of Sensors in Monitoring Soil Health, Crop Conditions, and Weather Patterns

Sensors are indispensable tools in modern agriculture, playing a crucial role in monitoring and managing soil health, crop conditions, and weather patterns. By providing real-time data on various environmental factors, sensors enable farmers to make informed decisions that optimize resource use, enhance crop productivity, and mitigate risks(Yousefi et al., 2015). Figure 1 illustrates the significant role of sensors in agriculture.

Figure 1. Role of sensors in agriculture

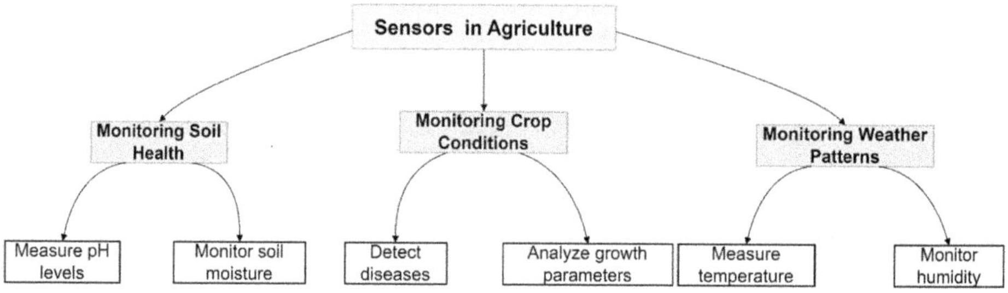

Monitoring Soil Health

- Soil Moisture Sensors: Soil moisture sensors measure the water content in the soil, helping farmers determine when and how much to irrigate. By monitoring soil moisture levels at different depths, farmers can prevent over-irrigation, which reduces water wastage and minimizes the risk of waterlogging or salinity (Gnanaprakasam et al., 2023; P. R. Kumar et al., 2023).
- Soil pH and Nutrient Sensors: These sensors analyze soil pH levels and nutrient concentrations, such as nitrogen, phosphorus, and potassium. By understanding soil fertility and nutrient availability, farmers can adjust fertilization practices to optimize crop growth and minimize nutrient runoff.
- Temperature and Humidity Sensors: Sensors that measure soil temperature and humidity provide insights into soil microbial activity and nutrient cycling. This information is crucial for determining optimal planting times, managing seed germination, and assessing soil health conditions.

Monitoring Crop Conditions

- Crop Health Sensors: Optical sensors and multispectral cameras mounted on drones or ground-based platforms capture images of crops to assess their health and vigor. These sensors detect variations in crop color, biomass, and chlorophyll content, indicating stress levels, nutrient deficiencies, pest infestations, or diseases.
- Canopy Temperature Sensors: Infrared sensors measure canopy temperatures, which reflect plant stress due to water deficits or disease. Monitoring canopy temperatures helps farmers adjust irrigation schedules and implement timely interventions to maintain crop health and productivity.
- Crop Growth Stage Sensors: Sensors equipped with algorithms can analyze crop growth stages based on environmental conditions and phenotypic traits. This information aids in optimizing agronomic practices, such as applying growth regulators or adjusting harvest schedules.

Monitoring Weather Patterns

- Weather Stations: Automated weather stations equipped with sensors monitor meteorological variables such as temperature, humidity, wind speed, and rainfall. This data is essential for forecasting weather patterns, predicting frost events, and managing irrigation schedules based on evapotranspiration rates.
- Wind and Solar Radiation Sensors: Sensors that measure wind speed and solar radiation provide insights into microclimate conditions within fields. Understanding wind patterns helps optimize pesticide applications to minimize drift, while solar radiation data informs decisions on crop planting density and canopy management.
- Rainfall and Precipitation Sensors: These sensors accurately measure rainfall amounts and intensity, helping farmers assess soil moisture replenishment and schedule irrigation accordingly. Real-time rainfall data also supports decisions on field operations, such as planting, spraying, or harvesting.

Integrating Sensor Data for Decision-Making

The integration of sensor data with geographic information systems (GIS), satellite imagery, and historical data facilitates data-driven decision-making in agriculture. Advanced analytics and algorithms process sensor data to generate actionable insights and recommendations, such as creating variable rate prescriptions for inputs or predicting crop yields based on current conditions(Gala et al., 2023).

Benefits and Considerations

- Precision and Efficiency: Sensors provide precise, real-time data that enables farmers to apply inputs more accurately, reducing waste and optimizing resource use.
- Early Detection of Issues: Continuous monitoring with sensors allows for early detection of soil deficiencies, crop diseases, pest outbreaks, and adverse weather conditions, enabling proactive management strategies.
- Sustainability: By optimizing inputs and minimizing environmental impact, sensors contribute to sustainable farming practices, conserving resources and reducing the carbon footprint of agriculture.

However, challenges such as sensor calibration, data integration complexities, and initial investment costs need to be addressed to fully leverage sensor technology in agriculture. As technology advances and becomes more affordable, the role of sensors in precision agriculture is expected to expand, supporting farmers in meeting the global demand for food while promoting environmental stewardship and resilience against climate variability.

Utilization of Drones for Aerial Monitoring and Data Collection in Agriculture

Drones, also known as unmanned aerial vehicles (UAVs), have emerged as valuable tools in modern agriculture, revolutionizing how farmers monitor fields, collect data, and make informed decisions. Equipped with advanced sensors and imaging technologies, drones provide farmers with high-resolution aerial data that enhances crop management practices and improves overall farm efficiency (Kigambiroha, 2023). The use of drones for aerial monitoring and data collection in agriculture is depicted in Figure 2.

Figure 2. Utilization of drones for aerial monitoring and data collection in agriculture

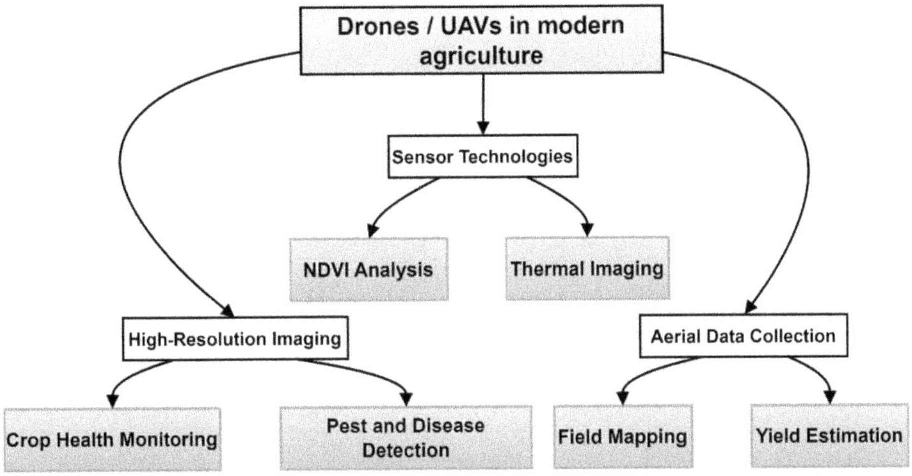

Applications of Drones in Agriculture

- Crop Health Monitoring: Drones equipped with multispectral, thermal, and RGB (visible light) cameras capture detailed images of crops. These sensors detect variations in crop health, biomass, and chlorophyll content, which are indicative of nutrient deficiencies, pest infestations, diseases, or stress factors like water scarcity. By analyzing these aerial images, farmers can identify problem areas within fields early, enabling targeted interventions such as precise pesticide application or irrigation adjustments.

- Field Mapping and 3D Modeling: Drones use GPS and onboard mapping software to create detailed maps and 3D models of fields. These maps provide farmers with accurate information about field boundaries, soil variability, and topography. Such data is essential for planning drainage systems, optimizing planting patterns, and assessing the suitability of terrain for different crops.

- Yield Estimation: Aerial imagery from drones, combined with machine learning algorithms, can estimate crop yields before harvest. By analyzing plant height, canopy cover, and biomass, drones help farmers make informed decisions about harvesting schedules, storage capacity, and marketing strategies.

- Soil and Field Analysis: Thermal and multispectral sensors on drones can assess soil moisture levels, soil compaction, and nutrient content. This information guides farmers in adjusting irrigation and fertilization practices according to the specific needs of different areas within a field. Drones also facilitate soil sampling by collecting georeferenced data points for precise soil testing and analysis.

- Pest and Disease Detection: Drones equipped with infrared and hyperspectral cameras detect early signs of pest infestations and diseases in crops. By monitoring subtle changes in plant reflectance and temperature, drones enable timely pest management interventions, reducing the need for broad-spectrum chemical treatments and minimizing crop losses.

Advantages of Using Drones in Agriculture

- Precision and Efficiency: Drones provide high-resolution, real-time data that improves the accuracy of farm management decisions. By pinpointing issues early and precisely, farmers can optimize input use and reduce operational costs.
- Time-Saving: Aerial monitoring with drones covers large areas quickly, allowing farmers to assess crop conditions and field health more frequently and efficiently than traditional ground-based methods.
- Environmental Benefits: By enabling targeted interventions and reducing unnecessary pesticide and fertilizer use, drones contribute to sustainable agriculture practices and minimize environmental impact.
- Safety: Drones eliminate the need for farmers to physically inspect difficult or hazardous terrain, enhancing safety during monitoring and data collection activities.

Challenges and Considerations

- Regulatory Compliance: Operating drones in agriculture requires compliance with local regulations and airspace restrictions, which may vary by region.
- Data Management: Managing and analyzing large volumes of aerial data from drones requires robust infrastructure and skills in data processing and interpretation.
- Initial Investment: While costs have decreased, the initial investment in drones and related technologies may still be prohibitive for some farmers, especially small-scale operations.

Future advancements in drone technology are expected to focus on enhancing flight autonomy, sensor capabilities, and data analytics. Integration with artificial intelligence (AI) and machine learning will enable drones to autonomously detect and respond to agricultural challenges in real-time. Furthermore, collaborative efforts between drone manufacturers, aggrotech companies, and researchers aim to develop specialized applications tailored to specific crops and farming practices, further optimizing the efficiency and effectiveness of drone use in agriculture.

Hence, drones are transforming agriculture by providing farmers with unprecedented insights into field conditions and crop health. As technology continues to evolve and adoption increases, drones are poised to play a central role in sustainable agriculture, improving productivity, reducing costs, and supporting global food security efforts.

UTILIZATION OF DRONES AND GPS IN AGRICULTURE: IMPLEMENTATION PROCEDURE

Integrating drones and GPS technology into agricultural practices involves a systematic approach to ensure effective implementation and maximize the benefits for farmers (Ipate et al., 2015; Stehr, 2015). Figure 3 illustrates the step-by-step procedure for implementing drones and GPS in agriculture.

Figure 3. Implementation procedure of drones and GPS in agriculture

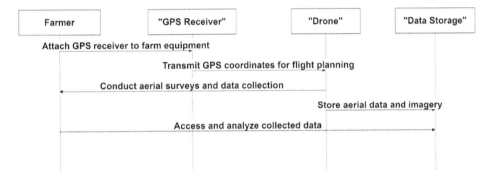

Assess Farm Needs and Objectives

- Define Goals: Identify specific objectives such as improving crop yield, reducing input costs, enhancing environmental sustainability, or optimizing resource use.
- Evaluate Farm Size and Layout: Assess the scale and layout of the farm to determine the suitability of drone and GPS technologies for different field operations.

Select Appropriate Equipment and Technology

- Choose Drones: Select drones based on the required payload capacity, flight endurance, sensor capabilities (multispectral, thermal, RGB), and compatibility with GPS systems.
- GPS Receivers: Choose GPS receivers that offer high accuracy positioning suitable for precision agriculture applications. Consider receivers that can integrate with other sensors and farm management software.

Plan Field Mapping and Survey

- Conduct Field Surveys: Use drones equipped with GPS to conduct initial field surveys and mapping. Generate accurate maps of field boundaries, topography, and soil variability.
- Create Digital Maps: Utilize mapping software to create digital maps that integrate GPS data with drone imagery, providing a comprehensive view of the farm's spatial characteristics.

Implement Precision Agriculture Practices

- Precision Planting: Use GPS-guided drones or machinery for precise planting of seeds, ensuring optimal spacing and depth according to soil conditions and crop requirements.
- Variable Rate Application (VRA): Implement VRA techniques based on GPS and drone data to apply fertilizers, pesticides, and irrigation water at variable rates across the field. Adjust application rates according to soil nutrient levels, moisture content, and crop health indicators identified through drone imagery.

Monitor Crop Health and Field Conditions

- Aerial Surveillance: Regularly deploy drones equipped with multispectral and thermal cameras to monitor crop health indicators such as chlorophyll content, biomass, and pest/disease infestations.
- Data Collection: Collect real-time data on soil moisture levels, temperature variations, and nutrient concentrations using sensors integrated into drones. Use GPS-tagged data points for accurate georeferencing and spatial analysis.

Analyze and Interpret Data

- Data Integration: Integrate drone and GPS data with farm management software, GIS platforms, and analytical tools to generate actionable insights.
- Data Interpretation: Analyze aerial imagery and sensor data to identify patterns, trends, and areas requiring intervention. Use historical data and predictive modeling to forecast crop yields, plan future operations, and optimize decision-making.

Training and Maintenance

- Training: Provide training for farm personnel on operating drones, GPS equipment, and data analysis tools. Ensure proficiency in handling and interpreting data to maximize the technology's effectiveness.
- Maintenance: Establish a maintenance schedule for drones, GPS receivers, and associated equipment to ensure optimal performance and longevity. Regularly calibrate sensors and update software to maintain accuracy.

Evaluate Performance and ROI

- Performance Metrics: Define key performance indicators (KPIs) such as yield improvement, cost savings, environmental impact reduction, and operational efficiency gains.
- ROI Analysis: Conduct a comprehensive analysis to evaluate the return on investment (ROI) of integrating drones and GPS in agriculture. Compare costs saved versus initial investment and ongoing operational expenses.

As technology continues to advance, explore opportunities to integrate artificial intelligence (AI), machine learning (ML), and autonomous systems with drones and GPS. Collaborate with agritech providers and research institutions to stay abreast of new developments and innovations that enhance precision agriculture practices.

BENEFITS OF PRECISION AGRICULTURE

Drone and GPS technology has revolutionized agriculture by offering precise data collection and management tools that enhance productivity, efficiency, and sustainability. This transformative approach not only optimizes resource utilization but also delivers environmental and economic benefits to farmers(Maguluri et al., 2023b). Figure 4 depicts the advantages of precision agriculture.

Figure 4. Benefits of precision agriculture

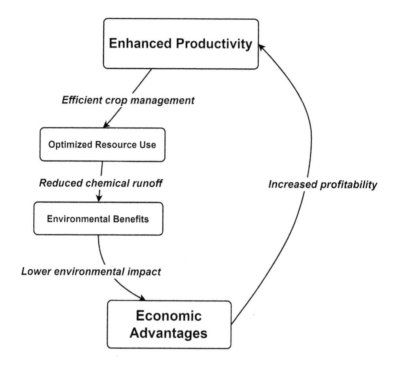

Enhanced Productivity and Efficiency in Resource Utilization

- Precision Farming Practices: Drone and GPS technology enables farmers to adopt precision farming practices with unprecedented accuracy. By using drones equipped with high-resolution cameras and GPS-guided machinery, farmers can precisely plant seeds, apply fertilizers, pesticides, and water at variable rates tailored to specific soil conditions and crop requirements.

- Optimized Input Application: The ability to map fields accurately using GPS and drones allows farmers to apply inputs such as fertilizers and pesticides only where and when they are needed. This targeted approach minimizes waste, reduces input costs, and maximizes the efficiency of agricultural operations.

- Real-Time Monitoring: Drones provide real-time monitoring of crop health, detecting early signs of stress, nutrient deficiencies, or pest infestations. This timely information allows farmers to take proactive measures, such as adjusting irrigation schedules or applying targeted treatments, to maintain crop health and minimize yield losses.

- Data-Driven Decision Making: Integration of GPS and drone data with farm management software and analytics platforms enables data-driven decision-making. Farmers can analyze historical data, monitor trends, and forecast crop yields more accurately, leading to improved planning and operational strategies.

Environmental Benefits

- Reduced Chemical Runoff: Precision application of fertilizers and pesticides based on GPS and drone data reduces over-application and runoff into water bodies. This minimizes environmental pollution and protects water quality, supporting sustainable agriculture practices.
- Improved Soil Health: By monitoring soil moisture levels, nutrient content, and compaction using drone sensors, farmers can implement soil conservation practices more effectively. Adjusting tillage and irrigation practices based on precise data helps maintain soil structure, fertility, and overall health.
- Enhanced Biodiversity: Targeted pest management and reduced chemical usage contribute to biodiversity conservation on farms. By minimizing the impact on beneficial insects and natural habitats, precision agriculture supports ecosystem resilience and biodiversity.
- Water Conservation: Efficient irrigation management facilitated by GPS-guided systems and drone data reduces water wastage and optimizes water use efficiency. Monitoring soil moisture levels and weather conditions helps farmers schedule irrigation to match crop needs, particularly in regions prone to water scarcity.

Economic Advantages for Farmers

- Cost Savings: By optimizing input use and reducing operational inefficiencies, drone and GPS precision agriculture lowers production costs for farmers. Savings accrue from reduced fuel consumption, labor hours, and input expenditures, contributing to improved profitability.
- Yield Improvement: Enhanced monitoring and management practices enabled by drone and GPS technology lead to higher crop yields. Precise planting, fertilization, and pest control strategies based on accurate data contribute to increased productivity and profitability for farmers.
- Market Competitiveness: Adopting advanced agricultural technologies like drones and GPS enhances the farm's competitiveness in global markets. Improved product quality, consistency, and sustainability credentials appeal to consumers and meet regulatory requirements.

- Return on Investment (ROI): Despite initial investment costs, farmers can achieve significant ROI over time through increased yields and cost savings. Economic analysis and performance metrics demonstrate the financial benefits of adopting precision agriculture technologies.

Drone and GPS precision agriculture represents a paradigm shift in modern farming practices, offering substantial benefits across productivity, environmental sustainability, and economic viability. By leveraging accurate data collection, real-time monitoring, and advanced analytics, farmers can optimize resource utilization, reduce environmental impact, and enhance profitability. As technology continues to evolve, the integration of artificial intelligence (AI), machine learning (ML), and autonomous systems with drones and GPS promises further advancements in agricultural efficiency and sustainability. Collaboration between agritech developers, researchers, and farmers will drive innovation and expand the applications of precision agriculture to meet future challenges.

Hence, the benefits of drone and GPS precision agriculture extend beyond operational improvements to encompass broader environmental stewardship and economic resilience in agriculture. By embracing these technologies, farmers can cultivate a more sustainable and productive agricultural sector that meets the growing global demand for food while preserving natural resources for future generations.

CASE STUDIES

These case studies illustrate how precision agriculture, enabled by technologies such as GPS and drones, transforms farming practices by enhancing efficiency, sustainability, and profitability. Whether through educational institutions like Harper Adams University or industry leaders like John Deere, the adoption of precision agriculture continues to drive innovation and reshape the future of global food production (Maguluri et al., 2023a; Periasamy et al., 2024; Puranik et al., 2024). As these technologies evolve, their potential to address global agricultural challenges while promoting environmental stewardship becomes increasingly evident, making precision agriculture a cornerstone of modern farming practices.

Case Study 1: FarmBot at Harper Adams University, UK

Harper Adams University in the UK implemented precision agriculture using FarmBot, an automated robotic system that combines precision planting and monitoring capabilities with advanced data analytics.

Implementation Details: Harper Adams integrated FarmBot into their agricultural research and teaching programs to demonstrate the potential of precision agriculture in optimizing resource management and enhancing crop yields. FarmBot operates on a grid-like framework, using GPS coordinates to precisely plant seeds, apply water, fertilizers, and monitor plant health through onboard sensors and cameras.

Results and Benefits

- Increased Efficiency: FarmBot's precise planting and automated monitoring reduced labor costs and improved operational efficiency. The system operates autonomously, performing tasks such as weeding and pest control, which traditionally require significant manual intervention.
- Enhanced Crop Management: Real-time data collected by FarmBot, including soil moisture levels, nutrient content, and plant growth metrics, enabled researchers and students to analyze crop health and growth patterns more accurately. This data-driven approach facilitated timely interventions, optimizing crop management strategies.
- Educational Impact: The integration of FarmBot into Harper Adams' curriculum provided students with hands-on experience in using advanced agricultural technologies. It enhanced their understanding of precision agriculture principles and equipped them with skills relevant to modern farming practices.

Case Study 2: John Deere's Precision Ag Solutions

John Deere, a global leader in agricultural machinery, offers comprehensive precision agriculture solutions that leverage GPS technology, drones, and advanced analytics to optimize farming operations.

Implementation Details: John Deere's precision agriculture solutions integrate GPS-guided machinery, such as tractors and planters, with cloud-based data analytics platforms. These systems collect and analyze data from field sensors, drones, and satellite imagery to provide farmers with actionable insights for decision-making.

Results and Benefits

- Precision Planting and Input Application: GPS-guided machinery enables precise planting of seeds and application of fertilizers, pesticides, and irrigation water. This targeted approach minimizes input wastage, reduces operational costs, and improves crop yield consistency.
- Data-Driven Decision Making: John Deere's analytics platforms process real-time data on soil conditions, weather forecasts, and crop health metrics. Farmers can access these insights remotely via mobile apps, allowing for timely adjustments to agronomic practices and resource allocations.
- Environmental Sustainability: By optimizing input use and reducing chemical runoff, John Deere's precision agriculture solutions support sustainable farming practices. Enhanced soil health and biodiversity conservation are additional benefits observed through reduced environmental impact.
- Global Adoption: John Deere's precision agriculture technologies have been adopted worldwide, demonstrating scalability and applicability across diverse farming landscapes. The solutions cater to various crop types and farming practices, enhancing productivity and profitability for farmers globally.

CHALLENGES AND LIMITATIONS

Precision agriculture, while offering significant benefits, faces various challenges and limitations that can impact adoption and effectiveness. These challenges span technical, financial, logistical, and operational aspects, alongside considerations of potential drawbacks inherent to these technologies (Agrawal et al., 2023; Boopathi, 2024b; Koshariya et al., 2023). Figure 5 outlines several challenges and limitations that can affect the effectiveness and adoption of various technologies.

Figure 5. Various challenges and limitations that can impact adoption and effectiveness

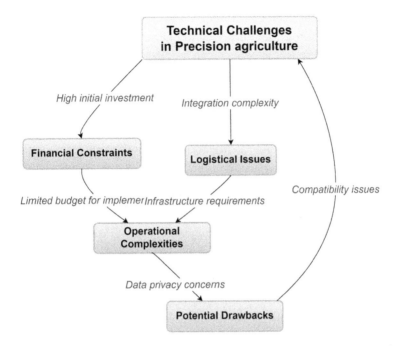

Technical Challenges

- Technology Integration: Integrating multiple technologies such as GPS, drones, sensors, and data analytics into a cohesive system requires compatible hardware and software. Ensuring seamless interoperability and data exchange between different platforms can be complex and may require specialized expertise.
- Data Management: Managing large volumes of data generated by precision agriculture systems poses challenges in terms of storage, processing power, and data analytics capabilities. Effective data management strategies are essential to derive actionable insights and maintain system reliability.
- Accuracy and Reliability: The accuracy of GPS positioning and drone imaging can be affected by environmental factors such as weather conditions, terrain variability, and signal interference. Ensuring consistent and reliable data collection is crucial for making informed decisions in precision farming practices.

Financial Challenges

- Initial Investment: The upfront costs associated with purchasing and implementing precision agriculture technologies, including drones, GPS-guided machinery, and sensor networks, can be substantial. Small and medium-sized farmers may face barriers in accessing capital for these investments, limiting widespread adoption.
- Operational Costs: Beyond initial investment, ongoing operational costs include maintenance, software updates, training, and data management expenses. Calculating return on investment (ROI) over the long term requires careful financial planning and consideration of potential cost savings and productivity gains.

Logistical Challenges

- Infrastructure Requirements: Effective implementation of precision agriculture often necessitates robust infrastructure, including reliable internet connectivity, access to cloud computing resources, and adequate storage facilities for data management. Rural areas with limited infrastructure may face challenges in adopting these technologies.
- Skill and Training: Operating and maintaining precision agriculture systems requires specialized skills in technology, agronomy, and data analytics. Training programs and ongoing support are essential to empower farmers and agricultural professionals to leverage these technologies effectively.

Operational and Environmental Limitations

- Complexity and Adaptation: The complexity of precision agriculture systems may pose challenges in adaptation and scaling across diverse farming operations and geographical regions. Tailoring technologies to specific crops, soil types, and local conditions requires customization and continuous refinement.
- Environmental Impact: While precision agriculture aims to reduce environmental impact through targeted inputs and resource management, potential drawbacks include increased energy consumption for technology operation and concerns about electronic waste from outdated equipment. Balancing environmental benefits with unintended consequences is crucial.
- Regulatory and Policy Frameworks: Adhering to regulatory requirements and navigating policy frameworks related to drone operations, data privacy, and environmental regulations adds complexity to adopting precision agriculture.

Compliance with local, national, and international standards is essential for legal and ethical considerations.

Discussion on Limitations and Potential Drawbacks

Precision agriculture technologies, despite their transformative potential, are not without limitations and potential drawbacks. These include:

- Dependency on Technology: Relying heavily on technology for farm management can increase vulnerability to system failures, cyber threats, and disruptions in service.
- Equity and Access: Disparities in access to technology and resources may widen between large-scale commercial farms and smallholder farmers, affecting inclusivity and equitable benefits distribution.
- Resistance to Change: Traditional farming practices and cultural barriers may hinder adoption of precision agriculture among some farmers, requiring education and awareness campaigns to promote acceptance and adoption.
- Ethical Considerations: Issues related to data ownership, privacy, and ethical use of technology in agriculture raise concerns about transparency, accountability, and societal implications.

Addressing the challenges and limitations of precision agriculture requires collaborative efforts among stakeholders, including farmers, technology providers, policymakers, and researchers. By overcoming technical, financial, and logistical barriers while mitigating potential drawbacks, precision agriculture can fulfill its promise of enhancing productivity, sustainability, and resilience in global food systems. Continued innovation, investment in infrastructure, capacity building, and supportive policy frameworks are essential to realizing the full potential of precision agriculture while promoting responsible and inclusive agricultural development.

FUTURE DIRECTIONS IN PRECISION AGRICULTURE

Precision agriculture is evolving rapidly with advancements in technology, data analytics, and sustainability practices. The future of precision farming holds promises for addressing global food security challenges while enhancing environmental sustainability and economic viability(Agrawal et al., 2023). Here's an exploration of emerging trends, innovations, and the role of artificial intelligence (AI) and machine learning (ML) in shaping the future of agriculture.

Emerging Trends and Innovations

- Advanced Sensor Technology: Continued advancements in sensor technology are enabling more precise monitoring of soil health, crop growth, and environmental conditions. Sensors capable of real-time data collection on microclimatic variations, nutrient levels, and pest/disease outbreaks empower farmers with actionable insights for timely interventions.
- Satellite and Drone Imaging: Integration of high-resolution satellite imagery and drone technology enhances spatial data analysis and monitoring capabilities in precision agriculture. These platforms provide farmers with detailed crop health assessments, yield predictions, and identification of field variability for targeted management practices.
- Internet of Things (IoT) Integration: IoT devices such as smart irrigation systems, weather stations, and automated machinery are increasingly interconnected to streamline data exchange and decision-making processes on farms. IoT-driven solutions optimize resource use, improve operational efficiency, and support sustainable farming practices.
- Blockchain for Supply Chain Transparency: Blockchain technology is being explored to enhance transparency and traceability in agricultural supply chains. From field to fork, blockchain enables secure and verifiable tracking of produce, ensuring food safety, quality assurance, and fair-trade practices.

Role of Artificial Intelligence and Machine Learning

- Predictive Analytics: AI and ML algorithms analyze vast datasets generated by precision agriculture systems to predict crop yields, disease outbreaks, and optimal planting times. Predictive models enhance decision support systems, enabling farmers to mitigate risks and optimize production strategies.
- Autonomous Systems: AI-powered autonomous vehicles and robotic systems are transforming field operations, including planting, harvesting, and pest management. These autonomous technologies reduce labor costs, enhance operational efficiency, and minimize human error in farm tasks.
- Precision Nutrient Management: AI algorithms optimize nutrient application based on soil analysis, weather forecasts, and crop demand. Precision nutrient management reduces fertilizer use, mitigates environmental impact, and improves nutrient uptake efficiency, contributing to sustainable soil health.

Integration into Sustainable Farming Practices

- Climate Smart Agriculture: Precision agriculture plays a crucial role in climate adaptation and mitigation strategies by optimizing water use efficiency, reducing greenhouse gas emissions, and enhancing carbon sequestration in soils. Sustainable farming practices supported by precision techniques contribute to climate resilience and ecosystem health.
- Regenerative Agriculture: Embracing regenerative practices, precision agriculture fosters soil regeneration, biodiversity conservation, and ecosystem services restoration. By enhancing soil fertility and reducing chemical inputs, regenerative agriculture promotes long-term agricultural sustainability and resilience to environmental stressors.
- Circular Economy Principles: Implementing circular economy principles in agriculture involves minimizing waste, recycling nutrients, and optimizing resource utilization through precision technologies. Closed-loop systems in nutrient management and waste reduction contribute to resource efficiency and economic viability on farms.

Vision for the Future

The future of precision agriculture envisions interconnected, data-driven farming systems that empower farmers with actionable insights and decision-making tools. Integrating AI, ML, and IoT into agricultural practices will further enhance productivity, profitability, and sustainability. Collaborative efforts among farmers, technology developers, researchers, and policymakers will drive innovation and adoption of precision agriculture globally.

As global population growth and environmental challenges intensify, precision agriculture stands at the forefront of sustainable food production. By harnessing technological innovations and adopting holistic farming approaches, the agriculture sector can meet the demands for nutritious food while safeguarding natural resources for future generations.

In conclusion, the future of precision agriculture holds immense potential to revolutionize global food systems, enhance resilience to climate change, and foster a more sustainable and equitable agricultural future. Continued investment in research, infrastructure, and policy support will be pivotal in realizing this vision and ensuring a thriving agricultural sector in the decades to come.

CONCLUSION

Precision agriculture represents a transformative approach to modern farming, leveraging advanced technologies such as GPS, drones, sensors, and data analytics to revolutionize agricultural practices. Throughout this chapter, we have explored the evolution, benefits, challenges, and future directions of precision agriculture. From its roots in GPS-guided machinery to the integration of drones and sophisticated sensor networks, precision agriculture has enabled farmers to optimize resource use, enhance productivity, and reduce environmental impact. The precise application of inputs based on real-time data has not only improved crop yields and quality but also minimized operational costs and labor requirements. Farmers have gained unprecedented insights into soil health, crop conditions, and field variability, empowering them to make informed decisions for sustainable agricultural management. Despite its advantages, precision agriculture faces technical, financial, and logistical challenges that can hinder widespread adoption. The complexity of integrating multiple technologies, managing large datasets, and ensuring compatibility across platforms requires significant investment and expertise. Financial barriers and the need for robust infrastructure, coupled with operational complexities in adapting technologies to diverse farming environments, pose hurdles for smallholder farmers and rural communities. Moreover, concerns about data privacy, regulatory compliance, and the environmental footprint of technology adoption necessitate careful consideration and mitigation strategies.

Looking ahead, the future of precision agriculture is poised for continued innovation and integration of artificial intelligence (AI), machine learning (ML), and Internet of Things (IoT) technologies. These advancements will enable predictive analytics, autonomous farming operations, and enhanced sustainability practices. AI-driven insights and decision support systems will revolutionize crop management, nutrient optimization, and supply chain transparency, fostering resilient farming systems capable of addressing global food security challenges and climate variability. Embracing principles of regenerative agriculture and circular economy models will further enhance soil health, biodiversity conservation, and environmental stewardship, positioning agriculture as a solution to climate change mitigation and adaptation. Hence, the journey of precision agriculture is characterized by its transformative impact on agricultural efficiency, sustainability, and resilience. By harnessing technological advancements and embracing holistic farming practices, precision agriculture holds the key to ensuring food security, promoting environmental stewardship, and fostering economic prosperity in a rapidly changing world. Continued collaboration among stakeholders—farmers, researchers, policymakers, and technology innovators—will be essential in realizing the full potential of precision agriculture and shaping a sustainable future for global agriculture.

REFERENCES

Agrawal, A. V., Magulur, L. P., Priya, S. G., Kaur, A., Singh, G., & Boopathi, S. (2023). Smart Precision Agriculture Using IoT and WSN. In *Handbook of Research on Data Science and Cybersecurity Innovations in Industry 4.0 Technologies* (pp. 524–541). IGI Global. DOI:10.4018/978-1-6684-8145-5.ch026

Bag, T. K., Srivastava, A. K., Yadav, S. K., Gurjar, M. S., Diengdoh, L. C., Rai, R., & Singh, S. (2015). Potato (Solanum tuberosum) aeroponics for quality seed production in north eastern Himalayan region of India. *Indian Journal of Agricultural Sciences*, 85(10), 1360–1364. DOI:10.56093/ijas.v85i10.52303

Boopathi, S. (2024a). Advancements in Machine Learning and AI for Intelligent Systems in Drone Applications for Smart City Developments. In *Futuristic e-Governance Security With Deep Learning Applications* (pp. 15–45). IGI Global. DOI:10.4018/978-1-6684-9596-4.ch002

Boopathi, S. (2024b). Sustainable Development Using IoT and AI Techniques for Water Utilization in Agriculture. In *Sustainable Development in AI, Blockchain, and E-Governance Applications* (pp. 204–228). IGI Global. DOI:10.4018/979-8-3693-1722-8.ch012

Borgelt, S., Harrison, J., Sudduth, K., & Birrell, S. (1996). Evaluation of GPS for applications in precision agriculture. *Applied Engineering in Agriculture*, 12(6), 633–638. DOI:10.13031/2013.25692

Brar, N. S., Kaushik, P., & Dudi, B. S. (2019). Assessment of natural ageing related physio-biochemical changes in onion seed. *Agriculture*, 9(8), 163. DOI:10.3390/agriculture9080163

Dysko, J., Kaniszewski, S., & Kowalczyk, W. (2015). Lignite as a new medium in soilless cultivation of tomato. *Journal of Elementology*, 20(3).

Gala, N., Poswalia, A., & Gharat, R. (2023). Electric Bike Security: Biometric & GPS Integration for Intrusion Detection. *2023 International Conference on Sustainable Computing and Data Communication Systems (ICSCDS)*, 1618–1627. DOI:10.1109/ICSCDS56580.2023.10105001

Glady, J. B. P., D'Souza, S. M., Priya, A. P., Amuthachenthiru, K., Vikram, G., & Boopathi, S. (2024). A Study on AI-ML-Driven Optimizing Energy Distribution and Sustainable Agriculture for Environmental Conservation. In *Harnessing High-Performance Computing and AI for Environmental Sustainability* (pp. 1–27). IGI Global. DOI:10.4018/979-8-3693-1794-5.ch001

Gnanaprakasam, C., Vankara, J., Sastry, A. S., Prajval, V., Gireesh, N., & Boopathi, S. (2023). Long-Range and Low-Power Automated Soil Irrigation System Using Internet of Things: An Experimental Study. In *Contemporary Developments in Agricultural Cyber-Physical Systems* (pp. 87–104). IGI Global.

Ipate, G., Voicu, G., & Dinu, I. (2015). Research on the use of drones in precision agriculture. *University Politehnica of Bucharest Bulletin Series*, 77(4), 1–12.

Kigambiroha, M. (2023). *Motor cycle theft control system using RFID, GSM and GPS technology*.

Koshariya, A. K., Kalaiyarasi, D., Jovith, A. A., Sivakami, T., Hasan, D. S., & Boopathi, S. (2023). AI-Enabled IoT and WSN-Integrated Smart Agriculture System. In *Artificial Intelligence Tools and Technologies for Smart Farming and Agriculture Practices* (pp. 200–218). IGI Global. DOI:10.4018/978-1-6684-8516-3.ch011

Kumar, P., Sampath, B., Kumar, S., Babu, B. H., & Ahalya, N. (2023). Hydroponics, Aeroponics, and Aquaponics Technologies in Modern Agricultural Cultivation. In *IGI: Trends, Paradigms, and Advances in Mechatronics Engineering* (pp. 223–241). IGI Global.

Kumar, P. R., Meenakshi, S., Shalini, S., Devi, S. R., & Boopathi, S. (2023). Soil Quality Prediction in Context Learning Approaches Using Deep Learning and Blockchain for Smart Agriculture. In *Effective AI, Blockchain, and E-Governance Applications for Knowledge Discovery and Management* (pp. 1–26). IGI Global. DOI:10.4018/978-1-6684-9151-5.ch001

Maguluri, L. P., Arularasan, A., & Boopathi, S. (2023a). Assessing Security Concerns for AI-Based Drones in Smart Cities. In *Effective AI, Blockchain, and E-Governance Applications for Knowledge Discovery and Management* (pp. 27–47). IGI Global. DOI:10.4018/978-1-6684-9151-5.ch002

Maguluri, L. P., Arularasan, A. N., & Boopathi, S. (2023b). Assessing Security Concerns for AI-Based Drones in Smart Cities. In Kumar, R., Abdul Hamid, A. B., & Binti Ya'akub, N. I. (Eds.), Advances in Computational Intelligence and Robotics. IGI Global. DOI:10.4018/978-1-6684-9151-5.ch002

Periasamy, J. K., Subhashini, S., Mutharasu, M., Revathi, M., Ajitha, P., & Boopathi, S. (2024). Synergizing Federated Learning and In-Memory Computing: An Experimental Approach for Drone Integration. In *Developments Towards Next Generation Intelligent Systems for Sustainable Development* (pp. 89–123). IGI Global. DOI:10.4018/979-8-3693-5643-2.ch004

Puranik, T. A., Shaik, N., Vankudoth, R., Kolhe, M. R., Yadav, N., & Boopathi, S. (2024). Study on Harmonizing Human-Robot (Drone) Collaboration: Navigating Seamless Interactions in Collaborative Environments. In *Cybersecurity Issues and Challenges in the Drone Industry* (pp. 1–26). IGI Global.

Sankar, K. M., Booba, B., & Boopathi, S. (2023). Smart Agriculture Irrigation Monitoring System Using Internet of Things. In *Contemporary Developments in Agricultural Cyber-Physical Systems* (pp. 105–121). IGI Global. DOI:10.4018/978-1-6684-7879-0.ch006

Shanwad, U., Patil, V., Dasog, G., Mansur, C., & Shashidhar, K. (2002). Global positioning system (GPS) in precision agriculture. *Proceedings of Asian GPS Conference, 1.*

Sharma, N., Acharya, S., Kumar, K., Singh, N., & Chaurasia, O. P. (2018). Hydroponics as an advanced technique for vegetable production: An overview. *Journal of Soil and Water Conservation*, 17(4), 364–371. DOI:10.5958/2455-7145.2018.00056.5

Sonia, R., Gupta, N., Manikandan, K., Hemalatha, R., Kumar, M. J., & Boopathi, S. (2024). Strengthening Security, Privacy, and Trust in Artificial Intelligence Drones for Smart Cities. In *Analyzing and Mitigating Security Risks in Cloud Computing* (pp. 214–242). IGI Global. DOI:10.4018/979-8-3693-3249-8.ch011

Stehr, N. J. (2015). Drones: The newest technology for precision agriculture. *Natural Sciences Education*, 44(1), 89–91. DOI:10.4195/nse2015.04.0772

Topakci, M., Unal, I., Canakci, M., Yigit, M., & Karayel, D. (2010). Improvement of field efficiency measurement system based on GPS for precision agriculture applications. *Journal of Food Agriculture and Environment*, 8(3 & 4), 288–292.

Venkateswaran, N., Kiran Kumar, K., Maheswari, K., Kumar Reddy, R. V., & Boopathi, S. (2024). Optimizing IoT Data Aggregation: Hybrid Firefly-Artificial Bee Colony Algorithm for Enhanced Efficiency in Agriculture. *AGRIS On-Line Papers in Economics and Informatics*, 16(1), 117–130. DOI:10.7160/aol.2024.160110

Yousefi, M. R., & Razdari, A. M. (2015). Application of GIS and GPS in precision agriculture (a review). *International Journal of Advanced Biological and Biomedical Research*, 3(1), 7–9.

ADDITIONAL READING

Akhter, R., & Ahmad, S. (2022). Precision agriculture using IoT data analytics and machine learning. *Journal of King Saud University. Computer and Information Sciences*, 34(8), 5602–5618. DOI:10.1016/j.jksuci.2021.05.013

Khanna, A., & Kaur, S. (2019). Evolution of Internet of Things (IoT) and its significant impact in the field of Precision Agriculture. *Computers and Electronics in Agriculture*, 157, 218–231. DOI:10.1016/j.compag.2018.12.039

Shafi, U., Mumtaz, R., García-Nieto, J., Hassan, S. A., Zaidi, S. A. R., & Iqbal, N. (2019). Precision agriculture techniques and practices: From considerations to applications. *Sensors (Basel)*, 19(17), 3796. DOI:10.3390/s19173796 PMID:31480709

KEY TERMS AND DEFINITIONS

Crop Health Monitoring: The use of technologies like drones and sensors to assess the health and vigor of crops, identifying issues such as nutrient deficiencies, pest infestations, or disease outbreaks early, allowing for targeted interventions.

Drones (Unmanned Aerial Vehicles - UAVs): Aerial vehicles equipped with sensors and cameras used in agriculture for monitoring crop conditions, assessing field variability, and collecting real-time data that informs decision-making processes.

Field Mapping: The process of creating detailed maps of agricultural fields using GPS data, which provides insights into field boundaries, soil variability, and topography, essential for implementing site-specific management practices in precision agriculture.

Global Positioning System (GPS): A satellite-based navigation system that allows farmers to map fields, track equipment, and apply inputs with high accuracy, facilitating the precise management of agricultural operations.

Multispectral Cameras: Cameras mounted on drones or other platforms that capture images in multiple wavelengths of light, used in agriculture to assess crop health by detecting variations in color, biomass, and chlorophyll content.

Precision Agriculture: A farming management concept that uses technologies such as GPS sensors and drones to optimize agricultural productivity and sustainability by precisely applying inputs like water, fertilizers, and pesticides based on the specific needs of different crop areas.

Real-Time Data Collection: The continuous gathering of data on environmental factors like soil moisture, crop health, and weather patterns through sensors, enabling farmers to make timely and informed decisions in precision agriculture.

Soil Moisture Sensors: Devices used in precision agriculture to measure the water content in the soil, helping farmers optimize irrigation practices and prevent over-irrigation, which conserves water and reduces the risk of waterlogging.

Sustainable Farming Practices: Agricultural methods that aim to reduce environmental impact, conserve resources, and promote soil health by integrating technologies like GPS and drones for precise input application and efficient resource management.

Variable Rate Technology (VRT): A precision agriculture practice that adjusts the application rates of inputs like seeds, fertilizers, and pesticides based on spatial data gathered from GPS, enabling targeted application that minimizes waste and maximizes crop yield.

Chapter 5
The Convergence of Deep Learning, IoT, Sensors, and Farm Machinery in Agriculture

Mrutyunjay Padhiary

https://orcid.org/0000-0002-2236-568X

Assam University, Silchar, India

ABSTRACT

This chapter addresses the profound influence of deep learning, the internet of things (IoT), sensors, and agricultural machinery on contemporary agriculture. These technologies improve productivity, efficiency, and sustainability throughout the production cycle, from tillage and planting to harvesting and post-harvest processing. Deep learning algorithms monitor crops and soil strength, detect illnesses, and forecast yields. At the same time, IoT sensors gather up-to-date information on soil quality, weather patterns, and crop development. Implementing automation in agriculture decreases the need for manual work and enhances operational efficiency. This chapter highlights the importance of using data to make informed decisions in precision agriculture, focusing on using sensor data and imaging techniques to improve the efficiency of resources and reduce environmental harm. Modern agriculture can effectively tackle food security and ecological concerns and provide food for a growing global population by employing inventive techniques and promoting partnerships.

DOI: 10.4018/979-8-3693-5498-8.ch005

INTRODUCTION

Ancient civilizations demonstrated their resourcefulness in utilizing natural resources for sustenance through the practice of traditional agriculture, which has endured for thousands of years. Customary practices, which range from the primitive tools used by ancient farmers to the sophisticated agricultural systems developed by medieval nations, have had a significant impact on the course of human history. The shortage of land, limited water supply, and the decline of natural resources present substantial limitations on agricultural productivity. In addition, farming techniques that are not sustainable have resulted in environmental deterioration, such as soil erosion, deforestation, and the decline of biodiversity (Arora et al., 2018).

The issue of food insecurity, particularly in developing nations, is of utmost importance due to the limited availability of enough nutritious food for a significant portion of the population (Zezza & Tasciotti, 2010). Given these issues, there is an increasing acknowledgment of the imperative for innovation in the field of agriculture. The pivotal role of technology in modern agriculture cannot be overstated, as it has brought about transformative changes that have revolutionized farming practices worldwide. With the introduction of key technological advancements such as advanced farm machinery, sensors, the Internet of Things (IoT), and machine learning, agriculture has undergone a paradigm shift towards increased efficiency, productivity, and sustainability. The utilization of agricultural machinery, such as tractors, harvesters, and plows, has substantially diminished the dependence on physical labor and animal power, enabling farmers to cultivate larger land areas with more efficiency (Diao et al., 2016). The application of modern technology in precision agriculture facilitates the improvement of agricultural production in challenging hilly landscapes through the implementation of autonomous all-terrain vehicles (Padhiary, Sethi, et al., 2024). The use of sensors and IoT devices has made it possible to monitor a variety of variables in real time, including soil moisture, strength, temperature, humidity, and crop health. Farmers may enhance their decision-making process regarding irrigation, fertilization, and pest management by integrating useful data insights (Rossi et al., 2019). This enables them to optimize resource utilization and ultimately enhance crop yields.

Machine learning algorithms have improved farming methods by analyzing extensive data to forecast crop yields, identify diseases and pests, and optimize planting and harvesting schedules. The capacity to make predictions enables farmers to proactively tackle anticipated obstacles and optimize productivity while minimizing expenses and environmental consequences. By incorporating these technical breakthroughs into contemporary agriculture, the industry has undergone a significant transformation, resulting in heightened efficiency, production, and sustainability. By using technological advancements, farmers have the potential to address the increasing global food demand while simultaneously reducing resource use and mitigating environmental degradation (Rosenzweig & Tubiello, 2007).

The chapter commences by providing a comprehensive account of the progression of farm machinery, charting its historical advancement, and emphasizing significant milestones that have influenced contemporary agricultural methodologies (Chojnacka, 2024). This part establishes the fundamental basis for comprehending the crucial significance of machinery in augmenting efficiency and output on the farm. After the examination of farm machinery, the subsequent chapter explores the incorporation of sensors and IoT devices inside the agricultural sector. The study investigates the ways in which these technologies provide continuous monitoring of soil conditions, weather patterns, and crop health in real time. This empowers farmers to make informed decisions based on data, thereby enhancing resource management and agricultural production.

The subsequent segment elucidates the way machine learning algorithms manipulate agricultural data in order to make predictions regarding crop yields, identify illnesses and pests, and enhance farming techniques (Mohamed, 2023). This showcases the profound capacity of artificial intelligence to completely revolutionize farming operations. Taking advantage of image processing techniques to identify crop maturity, diagnose diseases, and assess nutrient levels has significantly improved the field of precision agriculture (Padhiary et al., 2023). It looks at how images from drones, satellites, and other sources can be processed to track crop growth, find problems, and make harvesting easier. The chapter also provides an analysis of prospective avenues and obstacles in the field of agricultural technology. The system foresees forthcoming patterns and advancements in the domain while simultaneously tackling possible obstacles to acceptance and execution. The chapter offers valuable insights and recommendations to motivate stakeholders to adopt innovation and collaboration for the progress of contemporary agriculture.

EVOLUTION OF FARM MACHINERY AND MECHANIZATION

Historical Perspective

Farm machinery development has evolved over centuries, starting with primitive tools and manual labor in ancient civilizations (Lal et al., 2007). Over time, as societies advanced, there was a need for more efficient farming methods. The Middle Ages saw the emergence of more complex farming implements, such as the heavy-wheeled plow and the use of draft animals. These advancements allowed farmers to cultivate larger areas and increase agricultural output. The Industrial Revolution of the 18th and 19th centuries marked a turning point in farm machinery development, with the invention of steam-powered engines and the mechanization of agriculture leading to increased productivity and efficiency.

The 20th century saw further innovations in farm machinery, including internal combustion engines, gasoline-powered tractors, and mechanized implements like combines, balers, and planters. The digital revolution has further advanced farm machinery development by integrating sensors, GPS technology, and precision farming techniques. Modern farm machinery is equipped with advanced electronics and computer systems that enable real-time monitoring, data analysis, and automation, leading to further improvements in productivity, sustainability, and environmental stewardship. Overall, farm machinery has played a vital role in feeding growing populations and sustaining agricultural livelihoods worldwide.

Evolution of Modern Agricultural Practices

Significant milestones have been crucial in influencing contemporary agricultural practices, promoting innovation, and transforming farming techniques (Figure 1). These milestones signify notable progressions in technology, science, and policy that have revolutionized agriculture and made substantial contributions to enhanced productivity, sustainability, and food security. Notable achievements include: The transition from hunter-gatherer societies to agrarian communities marked a significant milestone in human history (Coward, 2022). The domestication of plants such as wheat, barley, rice, and maize, along with animals like cattle, sheep, and pigs, enabled early humans to settle in one place, cultivate crops, and raise livestock for food and other resources. In the medieval period, the adoption of crop rotation systems, such as the three-field system, helped replenish soil fertility and increase agricultural productivity. Selective breeding of plants and animals for desired traits led to the development of high-yielding crop varieties and improved livestock breeds, laying the foundation for modern agriculture.

The invention of steam-powered engines and the mechanization of agricultural processes during the industrial revolution transformed farming practices. Steam-powered tractors, threshers, and reapers replaced manual labor, increasing efficiency and productivity on the farm. This period also saw advancements in crop processing, transportation, and storage. In the mid-20th century, the green revolution introduced high-yielding crop varieties, synthetic fertilizers, and pesticides, leading to dramatic increases in agricultural productivity (Mohd Hanafiah et al., 2020). Innovations such as dwarf wheat and rice varieties, developed by scientists like Norman Borlaug, helped address food shortages and alleviate hunger in developing countries.

Figure 1. Key milestones of agricultural evolution

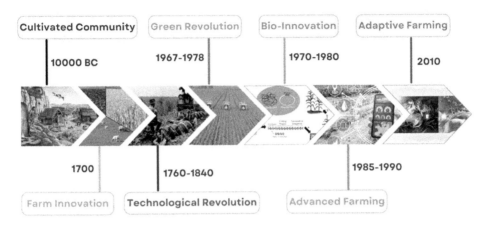

The advent of biotechnology and genetic engineering in the late 20th century revolutionized crop breeding and genetic improvement. Techniques such as recombinant DNA technology and gene editing enabled scientists to develop crops with enhanced traits such as pest resistance, drought tolerance, and nutritional content. The emergence of precision agriculture in the late 20th century marked a shift towards data-driven farming practices (Metje-Sprink et al., 2019). Technologies such as GPS, sensors, drones, and satellite imagery enabled farmers to monitor fields, optimize inputs, and manage resources more efficiently, leading to improved yields, reduced environmental impact, and enhanced sustainability. With increasing concerns about climate change and environmental sustainability, there has been a growing emphasis on climate-smart agriculture practices. This includes the adoption of agroecological principles, conservation agriculture, and sustainable land management techniques to build resilience to climate variability and mitigate greenhouse gas emissions.

The aforementioned significant milestones have together influenced contemporary agricultural methodologies, driving innovations, efficiency, and environmental responsibility in the realm of food production. The ongoing development of agriculture is expected to prioritize the utilization of emerging technology, the resolution of global difficulties, and the establishment of a food system that is both resilient and sustainable for future generations (M. Ogunmodede, 2020).

Impact of Mechanization

The implementation of mechanization has had a major impact on the productivity, efficiency, and sustainability of the agricultural industry. The implementation of mechanization has greatly enhanced agricultural productivity through the reduction of manual labor expenses and the facilitation of expedited farming operations. Machines such as tractors, combines, and harvesters facilitate the cultivation of expansive land areas, expedite crop planting processes, and enhance the speed of agricultural harvesting, thus contributing to the enhancement of food security. Mechanization additionally improves efficiency through the optimization of jobs and the minimization of waste (Le Hesran et al., 2020). Precision agricultural technology enables farmers to effectively administer inputs with greater precision, resulting in cost reduction and the mitigation of environmental consequences. Nevertheless, the process of mechanization also gives rise to certain obstacles, like heightened energy consumption, soil compaction, and the loss of biodiversity (Daum, 2023). With the progression of technology, there is an increasing emphasis on sustainable practices.

SENSORS AND IOT IN AGRICULTURE

Types of Sensors

In many stages of agricultural operations, such as tillage, spraying, planting, sowing, harvesting, threshing, and other associated procedures, sensor technology plays a crucial role. Soil moisture sensors are devices that quantify the amount of water present in the soil, thereby offering essential data for the purposes of irrigation control, and monitoring the overall health of crops (Rasheed et al., 2022). These sensors have proven to be highly valuable in tillage operations as they enable the evaluation of soil moisture levels prior to planting and during seedbed preparation, thereby ensuring the provision of ideal soil conditions for germination and root growth.

Temperature sensors are devices that measure the surrounding air temperature, soil temperature, and water temperature. They assist farmers in making well-informed choices about when to sow crops, which crops to choose, and how to manage pests. Temperature sensors can be utilized in tillage and planting operations to provide information on the soil temperature thresholds that are necessary for achieving optimal seed germination and emergence (Ritchie & Nesmith, 2015). *Humidity sensors* are used to measure the relative humidity of the surrounding air, hence exerting an impact on many biological processes such as evaporation rates, disease progression, and plant transpiration. Humidity sensors play a crucial role in spraying operations by identifying the ideal conditions for applying pesticides, thereby minimizing drift, and improving effectiveness (Palleja et al., 2023).

Wind sensors are devices that measure the speed and direction of wind. They are used to guide spraying operations, with the aim of reducing drift and guaranteeing that pesticides are evenly distributed (Li et al., 2023). These sensors play a vital role in ensuring the safe and efficient administration of pesticides, particularly in the areas of weed control and disease management. *Rainfall sensors* are used to detect instances of precipitation, thereby aiding farmers in the modification of irrigation schedules and pesticide treatments to mitigate the occurrence of runoff and soil erosion. Rainfall sensors play a crucial role in tillage and planting operations by facilitating the assessment of appropriate field conditions for equipment operation and seedbed preparation (Alfonso et al., 2015).

Light sensors monitor sunlight intensity and duration, influencing crop growth, photosynthesis, and flowering. Light sensors play a crucial role in the optimization of planting densities, row spacing, and canopy management procedures in planting and cultivation operations, with the aim of maximizing light interception and yield potential (Paradiso & Proietti, 2022). *Nutrient sensors* are employed to determine soil nutrient levels and assess the nutrient status of plants (Padhiary, Kyndiah, et al., 2024), hence providing guidance on the appropriate rates and timing for fertilizer application (Dimkpa et al., 2017). Precision agriculture approaches rely on the utilization of these sensors, which play a crucial role in optimizing nutrient utilization and mitigating adverse environmental effects.

pH sensors are utilized to evaluate the acidity or alkalinity of soil, which in turn impacts the availability of nutrients, the activity of soil microorganisms, and the growth of plants. pH sensors play a crucial role in fertilizer application and soil management by ensuring that soil pH levels remain within an acceptable range, which is essential for crop growth and nutrient absorption (Husson, 2013). *Weed detection sensors* are devices that can accurately recognize and distinguish between crops and weeds in the field. This allows for the precise application of herbicides and the implementation of effective weed control strategies. In order to accurately detect and categorize weeds, these sensors employ machine vision, spectral imaging, or artificial intelligence algorithms (Fennimore et al., 2016).

Disease detection Sensors look at visual symptoms, spectral signatures, or biochemical markers to find plant diseases and pathogens. These sensors facilitate the prompt identification of diseases and enable timely intervention through the use of fungicides or cultural methods, thereby mitigating production losses and crop damage (Martinelli et al., 2015). *Harvesting sensors* are used to monitor the maturity, moisture content, and yield of crops during harvest operations. They help optimize the time of harvest and the settings of machinery to ensure optimal efficiency and high-quality grain (Lee et al., 2010). Sensors play a crucial role in mitigating grain losses and enhancing post-harvest handling methods.

Threshing sensors are devices that measure the moisture content of grains, the damage to kernels, and the presence of foreign material in harvested crops. These sensors are used to guide threshing and separating activities, with the goal of minimizing grain losses and ensuring the quality of the seeds. The utilization of these sensors within grain processing facilities serves to optimize the efficiency and efficacy of threshing machinery (Dumitru et al., 2020). *Chaff cutting sensors* evaluate the quality, length, and distribution of chaff and straw during harvest operations (M. C. Siemens & D. E. Hulick, 2008). This helps to improve the collection and management of chaff for animal feed or mulching purposes. The implementation of these sensors has been shown to boost the operational efficiency of chaff cutting equipment and optimize crop residue management procedures.

Decision-making sensors are devices that combine data from several sources, such as weather forecasts, soil moisture levels, spraying pressure (Saha et al., 2023), crop growth stages, and pest pressure, in order to assist in making informed decisions regarding farm management (Mekonnen et al., 2020). These sensors offer immediate and accurate information and suggestions for improving farming operations, allocating resources, and implementing risk management techniques. The utilization of *irrigation sensors* enables the monitoring of soil moisture levels, weather conditions, and plant water status, hence facilitating the optimization of irrigation schedules and water management procedures. These sensors contribute to the preservation of water resources, the mitigation of irrigation expenses, and the sustenance of crop well-being and production within irrigated agricultural systems (Abioye et al., 2020). *Power sensors* are used to determine energy consumption and evaluate the performance of equipment in agricultural activities. They are employed to enhance machinery utilization, fuel efficiency, and overall farm production (Morais et al., 2008). In agricultural production, these sensors offer significant data that may be utilized for equipment maintenance, cost analysis, and energy-saving programs.

IoT Integration With Farm Machinery

The incorporation of IoT technology into agricultural machinery has brought about a significant transformation in agricultural practices, enabling the collection, analysis, and decision-making of data in real time throughout every step of farming. IoT-enabled technology is employed in tillage operations to monitor soil moisture, temperature, and compaction levels through the utilization of sensors (Rajesh et al., 2024). The data is communicated via wireless means to a centralized platform, where it undergoes analysis in order to evaluate the health of the soil and the effectiveness of plowing practices. Subsequently, farmers can utilize this data to enhance tillage methodologies, modify machine configurations, and alleviate soil compaction, resulting in enhanced soil composition and agricultural productivity. In the context of spraying operations, equipment that incorporates IoT technology employs sensors to continuously monitor real-time weather conditions, wind speed, and humidity levels (Raj et al., 2021). The device employs weather forecasting systems to establish optimal spraying windows and subsequently modifies spraying parameters in response. This guarantees accurate and prompt application of pesticides, minimizing the spread of the chemicals and optimizing their effectiveness while minimizing their negative effects on the environment.

IoT-enabled machinery uses sensors to monitor seed placement, spacing, and depth during the process of planting and sowing. The data that has been gathered is communicated to a centralized platform for the purpose of analysis. This enables farmers to enhance seeding rates, make adjustments to planting depth, and guarantee consistent crop proliferation. This leads to enhanced establishment of the stand and increased potential for output. IoT-integrated equipment utilizes sensors to continuously monitor crop yield, moisture content, and grain quality in real time during the harvesting process. The aforementioned data is communicated to yield monitoring systems, thereby delivering immediate feedback regarding the performance of the harvest and the condition of the grains. Farmers may enhance harvest efficiency and grain quality by utilizing IoT technology to optimize harvest scheduling, modify combine settings, and reduce grain losses.

Sensors With IoT for Specific Applications

Soil compaction sensors detect soil compaction levels during tillage, providing feedback to farmers about the effectiveness of tillage practices and helping them adjust equipment settings to mitigate compaction (Shaheb, 2021). *Seed depth sensors* monitor the depth at which seeds are planted in the soil, ensuring uniform seed placement and optimal soil-seed contact for germination (Iqbal et al., 2022). *Population sensors* measure planting density and seed spacing, allowing farmers to adjust seeding rates and optimize plant populations for maximum yield potential (Liu et al., 2017). *Boom height Sensors* monitor the height of spraying booms above the crop canopy, ensuring uniform spray coverage and minimizing drift. They help adjust spraying equipment to maintain the optimal height for effective pesticide application (Rincón et al., 2020). *Weed detection sensors* identify weeds in the field using imaging technology or spectral analysis, allowing farmers to target herbicide application only to areas where weeds are present, reducing chemical usage and minimizing environmental impact. *Yield monitors* measure crop yield in real-time during harvesting, providing valuable data on yield variability across the field. They help farmers optimize harvest efficiency and identify areas of high and low-yield potential for future management practices. ***Grain loss sensors*** detect and quantify grain losses during threshing operations, providing feedback on machine performance, and harvesting efficiency. They help farmers optimize combine settings and reduce grain waste. ***Chaff quality sensors*** assess the quality of chaff and straw produced during threshing and cutting operations, allowing farmers to adjust equipment settings to optimize chaff quality for livestock feed or bedding. These examples demonstrate how sensor technology can be applied across various agricultural operations to improve efficiency, optimize resource use, and enhance productivity while minimizing environmental impact.

MACHINE LEARNING AND AUTOMATION IN AGRICULTURE

Machine Learning Algorithms

Machine learning algorithms are at the forefront of modern technological innovation, offering powerful tools for analyzing data, identifying patterns, and making predictions or decisions without explicit programming instructions. At its core, machine learning involves the development of algorithms that enable computers to learn from and adapt to data, allowing them to perform tasks or make predictions based on the information provided. Unlike traditional programming, where specific rules and instructions are predefined by humans, machine learning algorithms learn patterns and relationships from large datasets through a process called training (Sarker, 2021). During training, the algorithm iteratively adjusts its parameters to minimize errors or discrepancies between predicted outcomes and actual observations. There are several types of machine learning algorithms, each suited for different tasks and data types:

Supervised Learning

In supervised learning, algorithms are trained on labeled data, where each input is associated with a corresponding output or target. The goal is to learn a mapping from inputs to outputs, allowing the algorithm to make predictions on new, unseen data.

Unsupervised Learning

Unsupervised learning involves training algorithms on unlabeled data, where the goal is to identify hidden patterns or structures within the data. This type of learning is often used for clustering similar data points or reducing the dimensionality of high-dimensional datasets.

Reinforcement Learning

Reinforcement learning involves training algorithms to interact with an environment and learn optimal strategies or policies through trial and error. The algorithm receives feedback in the form of rewards or penalties based on its actions, guiding it towards achieving a desired goal.

Deep Learning

Deep learning is a subset of machine learning that utilizes artificial neural networks with multiple layers (hence the term "deep"). These networks are capable of learning complex representations of data and have demonstrated remarkable success in tasks such as image recognition, natural language processing, and speech recognition (Shinde & Shah, 2018).

Machine learning algorithms have a wide range of applications across various industries, including finance, healthcare, retail, and, notably, agriculture. By leveraging the power of data and algorithms, machine learning enables automation, optimization, and predictive analytics, driving innovation and efficiency in diverse domains. As technology continues to advance, machine learning algorithms are poised to play an increasingly integral role in shaping the future of technology and society.

Applications of ML in Farm Operations

The application of machine learning algorithms is of great significance in the optimization of tillage techniques through the analysis of soil data obtained from sensors. In order to calculate the optimal tillage depth and intensity, these algorithms evaluate various aspects like soil moisture, compaction, and texture. Machine learning algorithms can utilize previous data and climatic factors to produce accurate suggestions for tillage operations, guaranteeing minimal soil disruption while preserving ideal conditions for crop growth. By utilizing data-driven methods, farmers are able to make well-informed choices on tillage practices, resulting in enhanced soil health and increased crop yields. Machine learning algorithms are employed in sowing and planting processes to improve seed selection, spacing, and depth by harnessing data from diverse sources such as historical yield data, weather forecasts, and soil conditions. By looking at these variables, machine learning models can make planting suggestions that are specific to each field. This maximizes the potential yield while minimizing the costs of inputs. Furthermore, machine learning algorithms have the capability to forecast the most favorable planting periods, enabling farmers to strategically organize their planting activities to achieve optimal germination and successful crop establishment. By utilizing data-driven methods, farmers are able to enhance crop production and profitability by optimizing seeding rates and planting strategies.

Plant protection relies on machine learning algorithms to analyze sensor data and identify early indications of pest and disease infestations in crops. These algorithms use machine learning techniques to identify trends and anomalies in plant health data, providing farmers with timely warnings about potential dangers. Machine learning models facilitate real-time monitoring of crop health, allowing farmers to promptly deploy intervention and pest management measures. This minimizes crop losses and maximizes yields. Furthermore, the utilization of machine learning algorithms enables the anticipation of pest and disease outbreaks by leveraging environmental variables and past data. This empowers farmers to adopt proactive strategies in order to safeguard their crops.

Machine learning algorithms have made notable progress in the field of weed control by utilizing imaging data obtained from drones or satellites to accurately detect and categorize weeds present in agricultural fields. These algorithms employ computer vision techniques to distinguish between crops and weeds, facilitating precise delivery of herbicides and minimizing chemical consumption. Furthermore, certain machine learning models facilitate the advancement of self-governing weeding robots that are equipped with very accurate spraying systems. These robots traverse fields and strategically administer herbicides exclusively to regions with weed infestations, reducing environmental harm and labor expenses while maximizing the effectiveness of weed management. Machine learning algorithms are utilized to enhance the efficiency of fertilizer application through the examination of soil nutrient data and crop nutrient needs, resulting in the creation of customized fertilizer recommendations. These algorithms ascertain the optimal fertilizer rates and application timing by taking into account variables such as soil fertility, crop needs, and environmental conditions. The utilization of a data-driven methodology enables farmers to optimize the absorption of nutrients by crops while simultaneously reducing any wastage and environmental contamination. Additionally, machine learning models can consistently learn from data feedback, which lets them change their fertilizer suggestions based on changing conditions in the field and the needs of the crops.

Machine learning algorithms are utilized in harvesting operations to assess sensor data from harvesting equipment in order to optimize the timing of harvests and adjust equipment settings. The algorithms in question are designed to continuously monitor the moisture content of crops, the variability in output, and the quality of grains in real time. This enables farmers to gain valuable information that can be utilized to optimize both harvest efficiency and grain quality. Farmers may enhance their harvest performance and profitability by utilizing data-driven insights to make well-informed decisions on harvest timing, equipment settings, and post-harvest processing. In the optimization of threshing and chaff cutting activities, machine learning algorithms assume a pivotal role through the analysis of real-time sensor data. The threshing parameters and chaff cutting settings are adjusted by these algorithms, taking into consideration many elements, including grain moisture content, yield variability, and grain quality. Machine learning models optimize grain separation and reduce grain losses during threshing and chaff cutting operations by adjusting rotor speed, concave clearance, and sieve settings. The utilization of a data-driven methodology enables farmers to optimize grain retention and improve overall harvesting efficiency, thereby leading to increased profitability and sustainability.

Practical Applicability

Case IH, a global leader in agricultural equipment, developed the autonomous concept vehicle (ACV), an autonomous tractor prototype (Thomasson et al., 2018). The ACV utilizes GPS guidance and advanced sensors to navigate fields and perform tasks such as planting, tillage, and spraying autonomously. By pre-programming field boundaries and operating paths, farmers can unleash the potential of these tractors to navigate fields with precision, ensuring accurate row spacing and minimal overlap. By automating repetitive tasks and reducing the need for manual intervention, the ACV not only bolsters operational efficiency but also slashes labor costs and optimizes input usage, marking a transformative shift in modern farming practices.

Kubota Corporation, a renowned manufacturer of agricultural machinery, has introduced autonomous tractor prototypes equipped with advanced automation features. These autonomous tractors utilize AI algorithms and machine vision technology to detect obstacles, navigate fields, and perform precise maneuvers. By eliminating the need for human intervention, Kubota's autonomous tractors enhance productivity, reduce operator fatigue, and optimize field operations.

Autonomous Tractor Corporation (ATC) specializes in developing fully autonomous tractors for agricultural applications. ATC's autonomous tractors leverage cutting-edge technology, including LiDAR sensors, GPS receivers, and AI algorithms, to operate autonomously in various field conditions (Geller, 2016). These tractors offer benefits such as increased operational flexibility, reduced fuel consumption, and enhanced productivity, making them a valuable asset for modern farming operations.

New Holland Agriculture, a leading manufacturer of agricultural machinery, offers the CR10.90 Combine Harvester equipped with advanced automation features (Baillie et al., 2018). The CR10.90 features IntelliSenseTM technology, which utilizes onboard sensors and AI algorithms to optimize harvesting performance and grain quality. With features such as automatic crop settings, yield mapping, and real-time monitoring, the CR10.90 enables farmers to maximize efficiency and profitability during harvest operations.

AGCO Corporation's IDEAL combine harvester is renowned for its advanced automation capabilities and precision harvesting technology. The IDEAL harvester features AutoDockTM technology, which automatically adjusts header height and reel speed to optimize harvesting performance in varying crop conditions. By integrating sensors, cameras, and machine learning algorithms, the IDEAL harvester ensures consistent grain quality, reduced losses, and improved harvest efficiency.

Table 1. Modern agricultural equipment and machinery around the world

	Type of Sensor	ML/Image Processing	Advantage	Performance/ Efficiency	Reference
Irrigation Controller	Soil Moisture Sensor	Machine Learning	Optimize irrigation scheduling	Improved water use efficiency	(Dehghanisanij et al., 2022)
Planters/ Seeders	GPS, Seed Sensors	Image Processing	Precision planting	Increased yield potential	(Virk et al., 2020)
Sprayers	Flow Sensors, Pressure sensors, GPS	Machine Learning	Targeted pesticide application	Reduced chemical use	(Partel et al., 2021)
Harvesters	Yield Monitors	Image Processing	Real-time yield monitoring	Improved harvest efficiency	(Chang et al., 2012)
Threshers	Grain Moisture Sensors	Image Processing	Grain moisture detection	Reduced grain losses	(Alizadeh & Khodabakhshipour, 2010)
Chaff Cutters	Blade Sensors	Image Processing	Optimize chaff cutting	Enhanced feed quality	(Siebald et al., 2017)

Claas Jaguar forage harvester is a cutting-edge machine designed for automated forage harvesting in the agriculture and biomass industries. The Jaguar harvester incorporates Claas' dynamic power system, which adjusts engine power and cutting speed automatically based on crop density and load conditions. With features like auto-fill and auto crop flow, the Jaguar harvester streamlines forage harvesting operations, delivering superior performance and productivity.

John Deere's ExactEmergeTM planter is equipped with advanced automation features for precise seed placement and fertilization. The ExactEmergeTM system utilizes individual row hydraulic downforce control, electric drive meters, and GPS-guided row shut-off for accurate seeding and fertilizing. With its high-speed planting capabilities and real-time monitoring, the ExactEmergeTM Planter maximizes planting efficiency and crop yield potential.

AGCO's white planters 9800VE series offers advanced automation features for seed placement and fertilization in row crop planting applications. The 9800VE Series features variable rate drive technology, which enables precise seed and fertilizer placement based on soil and yield data. With its customizable planting prescriptions and automated row-by-row control, the 9800VE Series optimizes input usage and enhances planting accuracy.

Kinze manufacturing's true SpeedTM planters utilize advanced automation technology for high-speed planting and precise seed placement. The true SpeedTM system features electric drive meters, individual row hydraulic downforce control, and GPS-guided section control for optimal planting performance. By combining speed and accuracy, Kinze Ttrue SpeedTM planters improve planting efficiency, reduce input costs, and maximize crop yield potential.

These real-world applications (Table 1) show how automation technologies are reshaping modern agriculture by enhancing efficiency, precision, and sustainability across a myriad of field operations.

IMAGE PROCESSING AND REMOTE SENSING TECHNOLOGIES

Overview of Image Processing and Remote Sensing Techniques

A wide range of techniques and algorithms are employed in image processing to modify digital images with the objective of enhancing, analyzing, or extracting information from visual data. In numerous domains, such as agriculture, medicine, surveillance, and remote sensing, these techniques assume a crucial role. The principal aim of image processing is to enhance the overall quality of images, extract significant insights, and streamline decision-making procedures.

Image enhancement techniques aim to improve the visual quality of images by adjusting brightness, contrast, and color balance. Methods such as histogram equalization, contrast stretching, and sharpening filters enhance image details and make visual interpretation easier (Kotkar & Gharde, 2013). *Image filtering* techniques involve applying convolutional operations to modify pixel values in an image. Filters such as Gaussian, median, and Sobel filters are commonly used for noise reduction, edge detection, and smoothing operations (Padmavathi et al., 2009). *Image segmentation* divides an image into meaningful regions or objects based on pixel intensity, color, or texture. Segmentation techniques, such as thresholding, region growth, and watershed segmentation, are used for object detection, classification, and measurement in applications like medical imaging and remote sensing (Chouhan et al., 2018). *Feature extraction* involves identifying and extracting relevant features or patterns from images. Techniques such as edge detection, corner detection, and texture analysis are used to extract geometric, textural, or structural features for image classification, recognition, and matching tasks. *Image registration* aligns multiple images of the same scene or object to enable comparison or fusion of information. Registration techniques involve finding spatial transformations that best align corresponding image features or landmarks, facilitating applications such as image fusion, change detection, and medical image analysis (Zitová & Flusser, 2003) . *Object detection and recognition* techniques identify and localize specific objects or patterns within images. These techniques, often based on machine learning algorithms such as convolutional neural networks (CNNs), are used in applications like face detection, vehicle detection, and object tracking. *Image compression* techniques reduce the storage size of digital images by removing redundant information while preserving image quality. Lossless compression methods, such as run-length encoding and Huffman coding, retain all image details, while lossy compression methods, such as JPEG and MPEG, sacrifice some image quality for higher compression ratios (Hussain et al., 2018).

Remote sensing is a powerful technology that involves the collection and analysis of information about the Earth's surface and atmosphere using sensors mounted on *satellites*, *aircraft*, *drones*, or *ground-based platforms*. It includes a wide range of methods for gathering, processing, and analyzing information from electromagnetic radiation that the Earth's surface and atmosphere emit or reflect. Remote sensing allows for the acquisition of spatially and temporally diverse data, enabling the monitoring and analysis of environmental conditions, natural resources, land use, and land cover changes. This technology operates across the electromagnetic spectrum, from visible light to microwave and thermal infrared wavelengths, allowing for the detection of various phenomena such as vegetation health, soil moisture, atmospheric composition, and urban development. Remote sensing data can be acquired at different spatial and temporal resolutions, ranging from high-resolution satellite imagery for detailed mapping to global-scale observations for broad-scale analysis. The applications of remote sensing are vast and diverse, spanning multiple disciplines including agriculture, forestry, environmental monitoring, urban planning, disaster management, and climate studies. By providing valuable insights into Earth's processes and dynamics, remote sensing contributes significantly to scientific research, resource management, decision-making, and sustainable development efforts worldwide.

Utilization of Image Processing and Remote Sensing

Image processing technologies are instrumental in optimizing various agricultural operations throughout the production cycle. In tillage practices, these techniques analyze satellite or drone imagery to evaluate soil health indicators like moisture content and compaction levels, aiding in the selection of appropriate tillage methods to enhance soil structure and fertility. During sowing and planting, image processing algorithms utilize high-resolution imagery to determine optimal seed placement locations based on soil properties and moisture levels, ensuring uniform crop emergence and maximizing yields. In plant protection, image processing enables early detection of pest infestations and disease outbreaks through pattern recognition and machine learning, facilitating timely intervention strategies to mitigate crop losses.

Weed control benefits from image processing by mapping and identifying weed species, guiding targeted herbicide applications, and minimizing chemical inputs. Crop nutrient monitoring is enhanced through the analysis of vegetation indices, allowing for more efficient fertilizer applications and reduced environmental impact. During harvesting, image processing generates yield maps to identify yield variability across fields, informing future management decisions (Padhiary et al., 2023). Post-harvest, image processing assesses crop residue distribution and chaff amounts, guiding residue management practices to improve soil health for subsequent crops.

Remote sensing technology revolutionizes various agricultural operations by providing critical insights into crop health, environmental conditions, and land management practices (Kumar et al., 2022). In tillage operations, satellite images and drones with multispectral sensors can give farmers useful information about the soil's texture, compaction patterns, and moisture levels. This lets them use targeted tillage methods like subsoiling or conservation tillage to improve the soil's structure and allow more water to enter it. Before sowing or planting, remote sensing data assists in assessing field conditions, including soil moisture, temperature, and vegetation cover, facilitating optimized seed placement and planting density for uniform crop establishment.

Remote sensing tools, like hyperspectral imaging and thermal infrared sensors, help find and keep an eye on pests, diseases, and nutrient deficiencies early on during plant protection (Thomas et al., 2018). This lets farmers use more precise pest management strategies and less chemical input. Weed control benefits from remote sensing as well, with data mapping weed infestations and guiding targeted herbicide applications, thus minimizing environmental impact. Remote sensing analysis helps with decisions about how much fertilizer to use by checking the nutrient status of crops and recommending different rates for different parts of a field. This makes the best use of nutrients and increases crop yields. Post-harvest, remote sensing informs on crop maturity and yield potential, aiding in prioritizing harvesting efforts and post-harvest residue management decisions. Overall, remote sensing technology empowers farmers with actionable insights across the agricultural production cycle, promoting sustainability, efficiency, and precision in farming practices.

FUTURE DIRECTIONS AND CHALLENGES

Emerging Trends in Agricultural Technology

Emerging trends in agricultural technology are reshaping the way farming is practiced, with a focus on enhancing productivity, sustainability, and resilience (Figure 2). Precision agriculture continues to evolve with advancements in sensor technology, GPS tracking, and data analytics. Farmers are adopting precision farming techniques to optimize inputs such as water, fertilizers, and pesticides, resulting in improved resource efficiency and yield outcomes. With increasing urbanization and land constraints, vertical farming and controlled environment agriculture (CEA) systems are gaining traction. These innovative approaches allow for year-round production of crops in controlled indoor environments, minimizing water usage, pesticide use, and transportation costs. Robotics and automation are revolutionizing various farm operations, including planting, harvesting, and weeding. Autonomous drones, robots, and smart machinery equipped with AI algorithms are being deployed to perform tasks more efficiently, reduce labor costs, and minimize environmental impact.

Blockchain technology is being explored to improve transparency and traceability in the agricultural supply chain. By providing immutable records of transactions and product provenance, blockchain enhances food safety, quality assurance, and consumer trust. Biotechnology tools such as CRISPR-Cas9 are enabling precise genome editing in crops, livestock, and microorganisms. These advancements hold promise for developing drought-resistant crops, disease-resistant livestock, and bioengineered solutions for sustainable agriculture.

The intersection of agriculture and financial technology (agri-fintech) is facilitating access to capital, insurance, and financial services for farmers. Digital platforms and mobile applications are providing farmers with tools for financial management, risk mitigation, and market access, particularly in emerging economies. The IOT and big data analytics are transforming agriculture by enabling real-time monitoring and decision-making. Regenerative agriculture focuses on enhancing soil health, biodiversity, and ecosystem resilience. Practices such as cover cropping, crop rotation, and agroforestry are being adopted to restore degraded lands, sequester carbon, and mitigate climate change impacts.

Figure 2. Challenges and future trends of farm mechanization

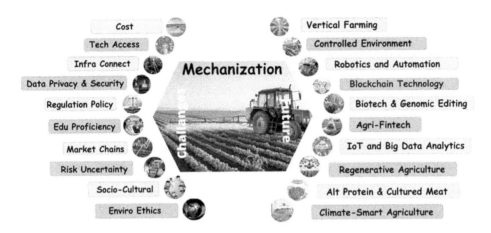

With growing concerns about sustainability and animal welfare, alternative proteins and cultured meat are gaining attention as potential alternatives to conventional animal agriculture. Research and development efforts are underway to produce plant-based proteins, cell-cultured meats, and insect-based foods at scale. Climate-smart agriculture strategies aim to build resilience to climate change while reducing greenhouse gas emissions. Adaptive farming practices, climate-resilient crop varieties, and water-efficient irrigation systems are being promoted to mitigate climate risks and ensure food security in a changing climate. 3D printing is widely utilized for rapid research prototyping to enhance automation in precision agriculture, contributing to the integration of IoT, machine learning, and sensor technologies into farm machinery applications (Padhiary & Roy, 2024). These emerging trends represent exciting opportunities for innovation and transformation in agriculture, paving the way for more sustainable, efficient, and resilient food systems in the future.

Challenges and Barriers to Adoption

The widespread adoption of modern agricultural technologies encounters various hurdles and barriers, despite their potential to offer promising answers (Fig. 5). A considerable amount of money is required for the purchase of equipment, infrastructure, and the deployment of numerous innovative agricultural technologies. Affordability continues to be a significant obstacle to the adoption of technology for smallholder farmers and individuals in developing nations. Limited access to technology, poor internet connectivity, and a lack of technical expertise limit farmers' ability to effectively adopt and apply sophisticated agricultural techniques (Bolfe et al., 2020). The existence of the digital divide further exacerbates these disparities in agricultural productivity and revenue.

Inadequate roads, electricity, and telecommunications infrastructure make it difficult to introduce modern technology in remote or rural areas. The limited connectivity poses a constraint on the ability to monitor and transmit data in real time, which is crucial for precision agriculture and IoT applications (Alahmad et al., 2023). Serious restrictions relating to data privacy, ownership, and cybersecurity are impeding the adoption of digital technology in agriculture. Farmers may exhibit reluctance to expose confidential data or depend on cloud-based platforms due to concerns about data breaches or unlawful entry. The presence of complex regulatory obligations, inconsistent policies, and bureaucratic obstacles gives rise to uncertainties and hindrances in the use of technology within the agricultural sector. Regulatory frameworks frequently encounter challenges in keeping up with the swift advancements in technology, obstructing both innovation and investment.

The successful implementation of innovative agricultural technologies necessitates the provision of training and the development of capabilities among farmers, extension workers, and agribusiness experts. The adoption and implementation of innovative technologies and processes suffer from the restricted availability of training programs and technical education. Market access and value chains necessitate the collaboration of multiple stakeholders, such as farmers, input suppliers, processors, and retailers, in order to integrate technology into agricultural value chains. Limited market access, inadequate infrastructure, and disjointed value chains all hinder the scaling up of technology-enabled solutions. The perception of technological developments as risky among farmers can be attributed to uncertainty surrounding performance, reliability, and return on investment. Risk-averse farmers may be deterred from adopting traditional farming practices and livelihoods due to concerns about potential disruptions.

Socio-cultural factors, such as socio-cultural norms, traditions, and attitudes toward change, have an impact on farmers' acceptance and use of new technology. Resistance to innovation, reluctance to depart from established practices, and mistrust of outsider initiatives can all impede technology adoption processes. Advanced agricultural technology gives rise to environmental and ethical concerns pertaining to the loss of biodiversity, deterioration of soil, pollution of water, and welfare of animals. Governmental scrutiny and public perception may place restrictions on the adoption and acceptability of these technologies.

To tackle these issues and obstacles, it is necessary for governments, academic institutions, corporate sector entities, and civil society organizations to work together in a collaborative manner. Strategies aimed at overcoming obstacles to adoption encompass focused investments in infrastructure and capacity development, policy frameworks that provide support, inclusive engagement with stakeholders, and inventive finance arrangements. By effectively addressing these obstacles, agricultural stakeholders have the opportunity to fully harness the capabilities of emerging technology in order to construct food systems that are more sustainable, resilient, and inclusive.

Opportunities for Collaboration and Innovation

In order to overcome obstacles and optimize the capabilities of budding agricultural technology, it is imperative to encourage collaboration and innovation. The agricultural sector presents numerous prospects for collaboration and innovation.

Public-Private Partnerships

Alliances among governmental entities, research establishments, and private enterprises can expedite the advancement, acceptance, and expansion of technology. Public-private partnerships enable the exchange of knowledge, the mobilization of resources, and the collaborative development of solutions specifically designed to meet the requirements of farmers.

Cross-Sectoral Collaboration

The promotion of cross-sectoral collaboration is crucial in addressing complex difficulties by developing multidisciplinary methods across many sectors such as agriculture, technology, finance, and academia. Cross-sectoral collaborations in agriculture enhance creativity and facilitate revolutionary change by combining varied knowledge and viewpoints.

Knowledge Sharing and Capacity Building

Platforms for knowledge sharing, training, and capacity building facilitate the acquisition of novel technology and best practices for farmers, extension workers, and agribusiness professionals. Enhancing agricultural literacy and empowering stakeholders to effectively accept new technology can be achieved through collaborative initiatives such as farmer field schools, extension networks, and digital training platforms.

Research and Development Networks

Collaborative research networks and innovation hubs serve as platforms for scientists, engineers, and agronomists to engage in collaborative efforts aimed at the advancement of state-of-the-art technology and solutions within the agricultural sector. Research and development networks expedite the rate of technical progress and guarantee its applicability to end-users by promoting open innovation and collaboration.

Technology Transfer and Adoption Programs

The promotion of breakthrough technologies in agriculture is facilitated through partnerships among technology innovators, agribusinesses, and farmer organizations, known as Technology Transfer and Adoption Programs. Technology transfer programs offer farmers the opportunity to acquire cost-effective and user-friendly instruments and training, enabling them to proficiently incorporate technology into their agricultural practices.

International Cooperation and South-South Collaboration

Global partnerships and South-South collaboration play a crucial role in facilitating the sharing of knowledge, the transfer of technology, and the enhancement of capacity among nations grappling with comparable agricultural obstacles. Countries can expedite agricultural growth and attain shared sustainability goals by utilizing their comparative advantages and exchanging knowledge gained from past experiences.

Ecosystem Approach to Innovation

The adoption of an ecosystem approach to innovation involves the cultivation of collaboration across a wide range of stakeholders, embracing startups, investors, incubators, and accelerators. Innovation ecosystems play a crucial role in bolstering technological firms, facilitating their market entry, and establishing entrepreneurship within the agricultural sector, hence building a culture of ongoing innovation and creative thinking.

Open Data and Digital Platforms

By enabling the sharing and exchange of agricultural data, insights, and solutions, open data initiatives and digital platforms facilitate the promotion of collaboration and innovation. Through the utilization of open data and digital platforms, various stakeholders have the ability to collaboratively generate, tailor, and expand inventive solutions in order to tackle distinct agricultural obstacles.

Community-Based Initiatives

Local communities are empowered to find, develop, and adopt context-specific solutions to agricultural obstacles through the implementation of community-based initiatives, such as grassroots initiatives, community-driven projects, and farmer-led innovation networks. Community-based techniques provide a sense of ownership, active involvement, and social harmony, which in turn leads to long-lasting creativity and influence at the local level.

Impact Investing and Philanthropy

The involvement of impact investors, philanthropic organizations, and social entrepreneurs is crucial in stimulating innovation and expanding the reach of agricultural solutions that have a significant impact. Impact investors and philanthropists play a crucial role in supporting entrepreneurs and inventors in the development and commercialization of novel technologies for agriculture through the provision of finance, technical assistance, and mentorship.

CONCLUSION

Implementing advanced tools in agriculture holds the capacity to totally reshape the processes of food production, distribution, and consumption. This chapter analyzes the progress made in farm machinery, remote sensing, IoT, machine learning, and biotechnology, emphasizing their significant influence on different phases of the agricultural production cycle. Nevertheless, these technologies encounter substantial barriers, including financial constraints, limited technical availability, legal limitations, and socio-cultural influences. In order to make the most of new technology and establish food systems that are both sustainable and efficient, agricultural stakeholders need to foster partnerships, share knowledge, and promote inclusive innovation. An essential component for the future of agriculture is a mindset that actively embraces innovation, collaboration, and continuous learning. Through the application of state-of-the-art technology, we can efficiently tackle the issue of global food security, reduce the impact of climate change, save biodiversity, and support farmers and rural communities. In order to navigate the food system of the 21st century, it is important to take advantage of chances for collaboration and innovation in order to establish a future that is fair, prosperous, and environmentally sustainable for all individuals.

REFERENCES

Abioye, E. A., Abidin, M. S. Z., Mahmud, M. S. A., Buyamin, S., Ishak, M. H. I., Rahman, M. K. I. A., Otuoze, A. O., Onotu, P., & Ramli, M. S. A. (2020). A review on monitoring and advanced control strategies for precision irrigation. *Computers and Electronics in Agriculture*, 173, 105441. DOI:10.1016/j.compag.2020.105441

Alahmad, T., Neményi, M., & Nyéki, A. (2023). Applying IoT Sensors and Big Data to Improve Precision Crop Production: A Review. *Agronomy (Basel)*, 13(10), 10. Advance online publication. DOI:10.3390/agronomy13102603

Alfonso, L., Chacón, J. C., & Peña-Castellanos, G. (2015). *Allowing citizens to effortlessly become rainfall sensors.*

Alizadeh, M. R., & Khodabakhshipour, M. (2010). *Effect of threshing drum speed and crop moisture content on the paddy grain damage in axial-flow thresher.* https://repository.uaiasi.ro/xmlui/handle/20.500.12811/2571

Arora, N. K., Fatima, T., Mishra, I., Verma, M., Mishra, J., & Mishra, V. (2018). Environmental sustainability: Challenges and viable solutions. *Environmental Sustainability*, 1(4), 309–340. DOI:10.1007/s42398-018-00038-w

Baillie, C. P., Thomasson, J. A., Lobsey, C. R., McCarthy, C. L., & Antille, D. L. (2018). A review of the state of the art in agricultural automation. Part I: Sensing technologies for optimization of machine operation and farm inputs. DOI:10.13031/aim.201801589

Bolfe, É. L., Jorge, L. A. D. C., Sanches, I. D., Luchiari Júnior, A., Da Costa, C. C., Victoria, D. D. C., Inamasu, R. Y., Grego, C. R., Ferreira, V. R., & Ramirez, A. R. (2020). Precision and Digital Agriculture: Adoption of Technologies and Perception of Brazilian Farmers. *Agriculture*, 10(12), 653. DOI:10.3390/agriculture10120653

Chang, Y. K., Zaman, Q., Farooque, A. A., Schumann, A. W., & Percival, D. C. (2012). An automated yield monitoring system II for commercial wild blueberry double-head harvester. *Computers and Electronics in Agriculture*, 81, 97–103. DOI:10.1016/j.compag.2011.11.012

Chojnacka, K. (2024). Sustainable chemistry in adaptive agriculture: A review. *Current Opinion in Green and Sustainable Chemistry*, 46, 100898. DOI:10.1016/j.cogsc.2024.100898

Chouhan, S. S., Kaul, A., & Singh, U. P. (2018). Soft computing approaches for image segmentation: A survey. *Multimedia Tools and Applications*, 77(21), 28483–28537. DOI:10.1007/s11042-018-6005-6

Coward, F. (2022). Reconstructing Social Networks: Transitional Changes from a Mobile Hunter-Gatherer to a Sedentary Neolithic Agrarian System. In Callan, H. (Ed.), *The International Encyclopedia of Anthropology* (1st ed., pp. 1–18). Wiley. DOI:10.1002/9781118924396.wbiea2527

Daum, T. (2023). Mechanization and sustainable agri-food system transformation in the Global South. A review. *Agronomy for Sustainable Development*, 43(1), 16. DOI:10.1007/s13593-023-00868-x

Deere, J. (n.d.). *ExactEmerge Planter Upgrade | John Deere*. Retrieved April 23, 2024, from https://www.deere.com/en/technology-products/precision-ag-technology/precision-upgrades/planter-upgrades/exactemerge-upgrade/

Dehghanisanij, H., Emami, H., Emami, S., & Rezaverdinejad, V. (2022). A hybrid machine learning approach for estimating the water-use efficiency and yield in agriculture. *Scientific Reports*, 12(1), 6728. DOI:10.1038/s41598-022-10844-2 PMID:35469053

Diao, X., Silver, J., & Takeshima, H. (n.d.). *Agricultural mechanization and agricultural transformation*.

Dimkpa, C., Bindraban, P., McLean, J. E., Gatere, L., Singh, U., & Hellums, D. (2017). Methods for Rapid Testing of Plant and Soil Nutrients. In Lichtfouse, E. (Ed.), *Sustainable Agriculture Reviews* (Vol. 25, pp. 1–43). Springer International Publishing. DOI:10.1007/978-3-319-58679-3_1

Dumitru, O. M., Iorga, S., Vladut, N. V., & Bracacescu, C. (2020). Food losses in primary cereal production. A review. *INMATEH - Agricultural Engineering*, 133–146. DOI:10.35633/inmateh-62-14

Farmmachinerysales. (2022). *CLAAS announces 2023 upgrades for JAGUAR*. https://www.farmmachinerysales.com.au/editorial/details/claas-announces-2023-upgrades-for-jaguar-138854/

Fennimore, S. A., Slaughter, D. C., Siemens, M. C., Leon, R. G., & Saber, M. N. (2016). Technology for Automation of Weed Control in Specialty Crops. *Weed Technology*, 30(4), 823–837. DOI:10.1614/WT-D-16-00070.1

Geller, T. (2016). Farm automation gets smarter. *Communications of the ACM*, 59(11), 18–19. DOI:10.1145/2994579

Holland, N. (2023). *New Holland previews next-generation flagship combine in bold statement of intent at Agritechnica | New Holland UK*. https://agriculture.newholland.com/en-gb/europe/new-holland-world/news/2023/new-holland-previews-next-generation-flagship-combines-at-agritechnica

Hussain, A. J., Al-Fayadh, A., & Radi, N. (2018). Image compression techniques: A survey in lossless and lossy algorithms. *Neurocomputing*, 300, 44–69. DOI:10.1016/j.neucom.2018.02.094

Husson, O. (2013). Redox potential (Eh) and pH as drivers of soil/plant/microorganism systems: A transdisciplinary overview pointing to integrative opportunities for agronomy. *Plant and Soil*, 362(1–2), 389–417. DOI:10.1007/s11104-012-1429-7

Iqbal, T., Ghaffar, A. M., Ur Rehman, U., Saeed, Y., Aqib, M., Iqbal, F., & Saleem, S. R. (2022). Development of Real Time Seed Depth Control System for Seeders. *PAPC*, 7, 7. Advance online publication. DOI:10.3390/environsciproc2022023007

kinze. (n.d.). 3665 Planter. *Kinze*. Retrieved April 23, 2024, from https://www.kinze.com/planters/3665-planter/

Kotkar, V. A., & Gharde, S. S. (2013). *Review of various image contrast enhancement techniques.*

Kumar, S., Meena, R. S., Sheoran, S., Jangir, C. K., Jhariya, M. K., Banerjee, A., & Raj, A. (2022). Remote sensing for agriculture and resource management. In *Natural Resources Conservation and Advances for Sustainability* (pp. 91–135). Elsevier. DOI:10.1016/B978-0-12-822976-7.00012-0

Lal, R., Reicosky, D. C., & Hanson, J. D. (2007). Evolution of the plow over 10,000 years and the rationale for no-till farming. *Soil & Tillage Research*, 93(1), 1–12. DOI:10.1016/j.still.2006.11.004

Le Hesran, C., Ladier, A.-L., Botta-Genoulaz, V., & Laforest, V. (2020). A methodology for the identification of waste-minimizing scheduling problems. *Journal of Cleaner Production*, 246, 119023. DOI:10.1016/j.jclepro.2019.119023

Lee, W. S., Alchanatis, V., Yang, C., Hirafuji, M., Moshou, D., & Li, C. (2010). Sensing technologies for precision specialty crop production. *Computers and Electronics in Agriculture*, 74(1), 2–33. DOI:10.1016/j.compag.2010.08.005

Li, S., Li, J., Yu, S., Wang, P., Liu, H., & Yang, X. (2023). Anti-Drift Technology Progress of Plant Protection Applied to Orchards: A Review. *Agronomy (Basel)*, 13(11), 2679. DOI:10.3390/agronomy13112679

Liu, S., Baret, F., Allard, D., Jin, X., Andrieu, B., Burger, P., Hemmerlé, M., & Comar, A. (2017). A method to estimate plant density and plant spacing heterogeneity: Application to wheat crops. *Plant Methods*, 13(1), 38. DOI:10.1186/s13007-017-0187-1 PMID:28529535

Martinelli, F., Scalenghe, R., Davino, S., Panno, S., Scuderi, G., Ruisi, P., Villa, P., Stroppiana, D., Boschetti, M., Goulart, L. R., Davis, C. E., & Dandekar, A. M. (2015). Advanced methods of plant disease detection. A review. *Agronomy for Sustainable Development*, 35(1), 1–25. DOI:10.1007/s13593-014-0246-1

Mekonnen, Y., Namuduri, S., Burton, L., Sarwat, A., & Bhansali, S. (2020). Review—Machine Learning Techniques in Wireless Sensor Network Based Precision Agriculture. *Journal of the Electrochemical Society*, 167(3), 037522. DOI:10.1149/2.0222003JES

Metje-Sprink, J., Menz, J., Modrzejewski, D., & Sprink, T. (2019). DNA-Free Genome Editing: Past, Present and Future. *Frontiers in Plant Science*, 9, 1957. DOI:10.3389/fpls.2018.01957 PMID:30693009

Mohamed, M. (2023). Agricultural Sustainability in the Age of Deep Learning: Current Trends, Challenges, and Future Trajectories. *Sustainable Machine Intelligence Journal*, 4. Advance online publication. DOI:10.61185/SMIJ.2023.44102

Mohd Hanafiah, N., Mispan, M. S., Lim, P. E., Baisakh, N., & Cheng, A. (2020). The 21st Century Agriculture: When Rice Research Draws Attention to Climate Variability and How Weedy Rice and Underutilized Grains Come in Handy. *Plants*, 9(3), 365. DOI:10.3390/plants9030365 PMID:32188108

Morais, R., Fernandes, M. A., Matos, S. G., Serôdio, C., Ferreira, P. J. S. G., & Reis, M. J. C. S. (2008). A ZigBee multi-powered wireless acquisition device for remote sensing applications in precision viticulture. *Computers and Electronics in Agriculture*, 62(2), 94–106. DOI:10.1016/j.compag.2007.12.004

Padhiary, M., Kyndiah, A. K., Kumara, R., & Saha, D. (2024). Exploration of electrode materials for in-situ soil fertilizer concentration measurement by electrochemical method. *International Journal of Advanced Biochemistry Research*, 8(4), 539–544. DOI:10.33545/26174693.2024.v8.i4g.1011

Padhiary, M., Rani, N., Saha, D., Barbhuiya, J. A., & Sethi, L. N. (2023). Efficient Precision Agriculture with Python-based Raspberry Pi Image Processing for Real-Time Plant Target Identification. *International Journal of Research and Analytical Review*, 10(3), 539–545. http://doi.one/10.1729/Journal.35531

Padhiary, M., & Roy, P. (2024). Advancements in Precision Agriculture: Exploring the Role of 3D Printing in Designing All-Terrain Vehicles for Farming Applications. *International Journal of Scientific Research*, 13(5), 861–868.

Padhiary, M., Sethi, L. N., & Kumar, A. (2024). Enhancing Hill Farming Efficiency Using Unmanned Agricultural Vehicles: A Comprehensive Review. *Transactions of the Indian National Academy of Engineering : an International Journal of Engineering and Technology*, 9(2), 253–268. DOI:10.1007/s41403-024-00458-7

Padmavathi, G., Subashini, P., & Lavanya, P. K. (n.d.). *Performance evaluation of the various edge detectors and filters for the noisy IR images.*

Palleja, T., Tresanchez, M., Llorens, J., & Saiz-Vela, A. (2023). Design and characterization of a real-time capacitive system to estimate pesticides spray deposition and drift. *Computers and Electronics in Agriculture*, 207, 107720. DOI:10.1016/j.compag.2023.107720

Paradiso, R., & Proietti, S. (2022). Light-Quality Manipulation to Control Plant Growth and Photomorphogenesis in Greenhouse Horticulture: The State of the Art and the Opportunities of Modern LED Systems. *Journal of Plant Growth Regulation*, 41(2), 742–780. DOI:10.1007/s00344-021-10337-y

Partel, V., Costa, L., & Ampatzidis, Y. (2021). Smart tree crop sprayer utilizing sensor fusion and artificial intelligence. *Computers and Electronics in Agriculture*, 191, 106556. DOI:10.1016/j.compag.2021.106556

Raj, M., Gupta, S., Chamola, V., Elhence, A., Garg, T., Atiquzzaman, M., & Niyato, D. (2021). A survey on the role of Internet of Things for adopting and promoting Agriculture 4.0. *Journal of Network and Computer Applications*, 187, 103107. DOI:10.1016/j.jnca.2021.103107

Rajesh, P. V., Ashvin, J., Harish, M., Kishore, G., & Nidheesh, S. (2024). Fabrication of Equipment and IoT-Assisted Monitoring for Enhanced Zero-Till Farming. In *Emerging Technologies and Marketing Strategies for Sustainable Agriculture* (pp. 209–233). IGI Global. DOI:10.4018/979-8-3693-4864-2.ch011

Rasheed, M. W., Tang, J., Sarwar, A., Shah, S., Saddique, N., Khan, M. U., Imran Khan, M., Nawaz, S., Shamshiri, R. R., Aziz, M., & Sultan, M. (2022). Soil Moisture Measuring Techniques and Factors Affecting the Moisture Dynamics: A Comprehensive Review. *Sustainability (Basel)*, 14(18), 11538. DOI:10.3390/su141811538

Rincón, V. J., Grella, M., Marucco, P., Alcatrão, L. E., Sanchez-Hermosilla, J., & Balsari, P. (2020). Spray performance assessment of a remote-controlled vehicle prototype for pesticide application in greenhouse tomato crops. *The Science of the Total Environment*, 726, 138509. DOI:10.1016/j.scitotenv.2020.138509 PMID:32305758

Ritchie, J. T., & Nesmith, D. S. (2015). Temperature and Crop Development. In Hanks, J., & Ritchie, J. T. (Eds.), *Agronomy Monographs* (pp. 5–29). American Society of Agronomy, Crop Science Society of America, Soil Science Society of America. DOI:10.2134/agronmonogr31.c2

Rosenzweig, C., & Tubiello, F. N. (2007). Adaptation and mitigation strategies in agriculture: An analysis of potential synergies. *Mitigation and Adaptation Strategies for Global Change*, 12(5), 855–873. DOI:10.1007/s11027-007-9103-8

Rossi, S., & Caffi, S. (2019). Critical Success Factors for the Adoption of Decision Tools in IPM. *Agronomy (Basel)*, 9(11), 710. DOI:10.3390/agronomy9110710

Saha, D., Padhiary, M., Barbhuiya, J. A., Chakrabarty, T., & Sethi, L. N. (2023). Development of an IOT based Solenoid Controlled Pressure Regulation System for Precision Sprayer. *International Journal for Research in Applied Science and Engineering Technology*, 11(7), 2210–2216. DOI:10.22214/ijraset.2023.55103

Sarker, I. H. (2021). Machine Learning: Algorithms, Real-World Applications and Research Directions. *SN Computer Science*, 2(3), 160. DOI:10.1007/s42979-021-00592-x PMID:33778771

Shaheb, R., Venkatesh, R., & Shearer, S. A. (2021). A Review on the Effect of Soil Compaction and its Management for Sustainable Crop Production. *Journal of Biosystems Engineering*, 46(4), 417–439. DOI:10.1007/s42853-021-00117-7

Shinde, P. P., & Shah, S. (2018). A Review of Machine Learning and Deep Learning Applications. *2018 Fourth International Conference on Computing Communication Control and Automation (ICCUBEA)*, 1–6. DOI:10.1109/ICCUBEA.2018.8697857

Siebald, H., Hensel, O., Beneke, F., Merbach, L., Walther, C., Kirchner, S. M., & Huster, J. (2017). Real-Time Acoustic Monitoring of Cutting Blade Sharpness in Agricultural Machinery. *IEEE/ASME Transactions on Mechatronics*, 22(6), 2411–2419. DOI:10.1109/TMECH.2017.2735542

Siemens, M. C., & Hulick, D. E. (2008). A New Grain Harvesting System for Single-Pass Grain Harvest, Biomass Collection, Crop Residue Sizing, and Grain Segregation. *Transactions of the ASABE*, 51(5), 1519–1527. DOI:10.13031/2013.25300

Thomas, S., Kuska, M. T., Bohnenkamp, D., Brugger, A., Alisaac, E., Wahabzada, M., Behmann, J., & Mahlein, A.-K. (2018). Benefits of hyperspectral imaging for plant disease detection and plant protection: A technical perspective. *Journal of Plant Diseases and Protection*, 125(1), 5–20. DOI:10.1007/s41348-017-0124-6

Thomasson, J. A., Baillie, C. P., Antille, D. L., McCarthy, C. L., & Lobsey, C. R. (2018). A review of the state of the art in agricultural automation. Part II: On-farm agricultural communications and connectivity. DOI:10.13031/aim.201801590

Virk, S. S., Fulton, J. P., Porter, W. M., & Pate, G. L. (2020). Row-crop planter performance to support variable-rate seeding of maize. *Precision Agriculture*, 21(3), 603–619. DOI:10.1007/s11119-019-09685-3

Zezza, A., & Tasciotti, L. (2010). Urban agriculture, poverty, and food security: Empirical evidence from a sample of developing countries. *Food Policy*, 35(4), 265–273. DOI:10.1016/j.foodpol.2010.04.007

Zitová, B., & Flusser, J. (2003). Image registration methods: A survey. *Image and Vision Computing*, 21(11), 977–1000. DOI:10.1016/S0262-8856(03)00137-9

ADDITIONAL READING

Kashyap, P. K., Kumar, S., Jaiswal, A., Prasad, M., & Gandomi, A. H. (2021). Towards precision agriculture: IoT-enabled intelligent irrigation systems using deep learning neural network. *IEEE Sensors Journal*, 21(16), 17479–17491. DOI:10.1109/JSEN.2021.3069266

Padhiary, , MBarbhuiya, , J. ARoy, , DRoy, , P. (2024). 3D Printing Applications in Smart Farming and Food Processing. *Smart Agricultural Technology, 9,* 100553. https://doi.org/10.1016/j.atech.2024.100553

Padhiary, , MKumar, , RSethi, , L. N. (2024). Navigating the Future of Agriculture: A Comprehensive Review of Automatic All-Terrain Vehicles in Precision Farming. *Journal of The Institution of Engineers (India): Series A, 105*(2). https://doi.org/10.1007/s40030-024-00816-2

Padhiary, , MTikute, , S. VSaha, , DBarbhuiya, , J. ASethi, , L. N. (2024). Development of an IOT-Based Semi-Autonomous Vehicle Sprayer. *Agricultural Research, 13*(3). https://doi.org/10.1007/s40003-024-00760-4

Shaikh, T. A., Rasool, T., & Lone, F. R. (2022). Towards leveraging the role of machine learning and artificial intelligence in precision agriculture and smart farming. *Computers and Electronics in Agriculture*, 198, 107119. DOI:10.1016/j.compag.2022.107119

Wongchai, A., Shukla, S. K., Ahmed, M. A., Sakthi, U., Jagdish, M., & kumar, R. (2022). Artificial intelligence-enabled soft sensor and internet of things for sustainable agriculture using ensemble deep learning architecture. *Computers & Electrical Engineering*, 102, 108128. DOI:10.1016/j.compeleceng.2022.108128

KEY TERMS AND DEFINITIONS

Autonomous Farm Machinery: Equipment that operates independently of human control, using technologies like GPS and machine learning. Examples include self-driving tractors and drones that monitor crops and soil conditions.

Data-Driven Agriculture: An approach to farming that relies on data collected from various sources, such as sensors, IoT devices, and satellite imagery, to inform decisions and optimize agricultural practices for better productivity and sustainability.

Deep Learning: A subset of machine learning that uses neural networks with multiple layers to model complex patterns in data. In agriculture, deep learning is applied for tasks like crop monitoring, disease detection, and yield prediction.

Farm Machinery Automation: The integration of advanced technologies such as GPS, IoT, and machine learning into agricultural machinery to perform tasks like planting, harvesting, and spraying with minimal human intervention, improving efficiency and precision.

Internet of Things (IoT): A network of interconnected devices that communicate and exchange data in real-time. In agriculture, IoT devices such as sensors and smart farm machinery collect and transmit data on soil conditions, weather, and crop health to optimize farming practices.

Machine Learning in Agriculture: The application of algorithms that learn from and make predictions based on data. In agriculture, machine learning is used to optimize farming operations, such as predicting crop yields, detecting pests, and automating machinery.

Precision Agriculture: An agricultural management practice that uses data-driven techniques to optimize field-level management regarding crop farming. It involves using technologies like GPS, IoT, and sensors to improve resource efficiency and crop yields.

Sensors: Devices that detect and measure environmental factors such as soil moisture, temperature, humidity, and crop health. In agriculture, sensors provide real-time data that helps farmers make informed decisions on irrigation, fertilization, and pest management.

Soil Moisture Sensors: Devices used to measure the amount of water present in the soil, helping to inform irrigation decisions. These sensors are critical in precision agriculture for optimizing water use and improving crop yields.

Sustainability in Agriculture: The practice of farming that meets current food needs without compromising the ability of future generations to meet theirs. This involves the use of technologies like IoT and precision farming to reduce resource use and minimize environmental impact.

Chapter 6
Framework for Smart Farming Using Artificial Intelligence of Things

Anton Limbo
https://orcid.org/0009-0006-5437-9716
University of Namibia, Namibia

Maria Ndapewa Ntinda
https://orcid.org/0000-0003-2004-2884
University of Namibia, Namibia

Ananias Ndemuweda Nakale
https://orcid.org/0009-0001-5634-0587
University of Namibia, Namibia

ABSTRACT

The advancement of technology has led to the introduction of smart technologies in various sectors, including farming, forming what is now known as smart farming. Smart farming involves using smart technologies to perform monitoring and automation tasks traditionally performed by humans. However, despite these advancements, farmers still need help adopting smart farming techniques in crop farming. Therefore, this chapter presents a framework designed to guide the implementation of smart technologies in crop farming activities. This framework employs the concept of artificial intelligence of things (IoT), which utilizes artificial intelligence (AI) for decision-making and data analysis based on data from internet of things (IoT) devices. The framework is structured around five modules: the sensor module, the artificial intelligence module, the automation module, the network module, and the processing module. These modules enable effective monitoring of factors essential

DOI: 10.4018/979-8-3693-5498-8.ch006

for optimal crop growth and performing automation based on monitoring activities.

INTRODUCTION

Farming has been a vital undertaking to the well-being of humankind since the dawn of time. This vitality has led to modernising farming activities to increase efficiency and sustainability. To support the growing world population, which is expected to reach about 10 billion people by 2050 (Gu et al., 2021), modernising farming activities is more important to sustain this predicted population growth. Furthermore, the modernisation of farming aligns with the United Nation's Sustainability Development Goal (SDG) 2, which looks at eliminating hunger by the year 2030 (Turnip et al., 2023). However, even before the United Nations (UN) member states adopted the SDGs, there is evidence that in the past decades, farming activities have evolved by becoming more technology-driven (Araújo et al., 2021). This technology drive has led to more precise farming methods using different technologies to reduce labour and increase resource usage efficiency, ultimately improving crop yields (Javaid et al., 2022).

One such technology is smart farming, which uses various technologies to enhance farming activities. These technologies range from using automation agents such as robots and the Internet of Things (IoT) devices to using Data Analytics and Artificial Intelligence (AI) to enhance farming activities (Mohamed et al., 2021). In today's modern era, these technologies are being applied in different types of farming, and this practice is sometimes referred to as Agriculture 4.0. Agriculture 4.0 can be defined as the revolution of farming activities that introduce emerging technologies for improved efficiency and yield (Da Silveira et al., 2021). Therefore, smart farming aims to increase yield using IoT, AI, and cloud computing technologies to collect data, monitor activities, and automate farming processes (Lioutas & Charatsari, 2020).

However, despite these technological advancements, farmers still struggle to adopt smart technologies in their farming activities. This is due to various factors, such as the complexity of technologies needed to enable Smart Farming, the lack of capital required to invest in smart technologies, and the incompatibility of different technologies used in Smart Farming (Da Silveira et al., 2023). Other challenges in implementing Smart Farming include data privacy and security concerns and the harm these technologies can bring to the environment and animals (Idoje et al., 2021).

This chapter, therefore, introduces a framework that can be used as a guide in implementing Smart Farming techniques for crop farming. The framework uses the concept of Artificial Intelligence of Things (AIoT), which is the combination of IoT and AI. IoT consists of devices equipped with sensors that interact with the physical world. These devices transmit the collected data over computer networks, such as the Internet, to be processed by other devices or to users for interpretation (Zhang & Tao, 2021). However, because IoT devices generate a tremendous amount of data, a need to perform analytics and decision-making on this data at the source arose as a solution to the problem associated with storing and transmitting large amounts of data. This analysis or preprocessing of data at the source is referred to as Edge Computing (Raja Gopal & Prabhakar, 2022). Sorting and analysing this data can be tedious and time-consuming. Therefore, AI was introduced to aid IoT devices in performing analytics on the data for decision-making without the intervention of humankind, forming the concept of AIoT (Chang et al., 2021).

The framework utilises the concept of AIoT to enable the monitoring of crops and environmental parameters of the field, and these parameters are used for decision-making in processes needed to automate tasks necessary to maintain a conducive environment for crop growth. This will be achieved by using IoT to monitor the crops by capturing images and measuring soil moisture and pH levels. The measured data, along with weather data such as temperature, humidity and wind, will then be used to make decisions to spray pesticides upon detecting pests using image recognition, initiate irrigations based on soil moisture level or spray fertiliser based on the pH level of the soil and the requirements of the crop. The framework also proposes advanced operations such as predicting plant growth by capturing periodic images of the field, which can be compared to previous data using AI to determine cases such as stagnant crop growth.

BACKGROUND

Despite technological advancements, integrating smart techniques into farming practices remains a challenge. Earlier discussions in this chapter highlighted several challenges in this regard. Moreover, current research in the field often fails to support the adequate adoption of smart farming (Kumar et al., 2022). Much of the focus is on identifying challenges farmers encounter when introducing smart technologies, with less emphasis on practical strategies for implementation (Kumar et al., 2022). However, this is not to suggest that research efforts are absent. Indeed, numerous studies aim to assist farmers with specific tasks, as noted in the Related Work section of this chapter. However, these studies frequently adopt a gradual approach, addressing individual aspects such as irrigation management or crop monitoring without fully integrating available technologies that could collectively enhance farming activities. Therefore, the primary objective of this chapter is to underscore the potential of integrating various technologies to enable Smart Farming. The chapter achieves this by introducing a framework leveraging the concept of AIoT, which integrates AI with IoT devices. This framework demonstrates how combining different technologies can enhance agricultural practices, fostering more efficient, sustainable, and productive farming methods.

RELATED WORK

This section presents studies on architectures, models, and frameworks for Smart Agriculture. The chapter strengthens the argument that more research is needed and highlights the gaps within current research. Faid et al. (2020) proposed a low-cost IoT architecture for smart farming and highlighted the importance of food security in developing countries. The architecture supports real-time monitoring and data processing for decision-making by utilising the Change Point Detection algorithm and Leach Protocol for network clustering. The architecture was implemented using wireless sensor nodes that routinely monitor parameters such as soil moisture, temperature and air quality and transmit these data cluster heads before the final data aggregation was conducted at the Base Station. The Base Station then stores and presents the data to relevant users such as farmers.

Another study presents an architectural model as a reference model for Smart Farming that includes the requirements for rolling out this architecture (Triantafyllou et al, 2019). The architecture consists of four layers: the sensor layer, the network layer, the service layer and the application layer. The sensor layer includes all devices and data collection and monitoring mechanisms; the network layer comprises various technologies and protocols that facilitate sensor data transmission; the service layer is responsible for analysing the collected data to ensure accurate decision-making in conjunction with the Decision Support System and the application layer formats the operations of the model and presents them to users, allowing farmers to review the model's operations. Another study presented an architecture for applying modern IoT-enabled technologies to smart farming (Kakamoukas et al. 2019). These technologies include wireless sensor networks, weather stations and unmanned aerial vehicles for increased production by efficiently allocating crop resources. The architecture uses computer vision and machine learning to process agricultural information based on the data acquired from unmanned aerial vehicles, such as images and ground data from Ground Control Stations, including soil moisture, temperature, leaf wetness and weather conditions. The data is then formatted for presentation to the relevant stakeholders.

This chapter builds on these studies and continues previous work on Smart Farming, which focused on a smart irrigation system to enhance crop farming by measuring and controlling soil moisture (Limbo et al., 2021). This was achieved by placing a moisture sensor in the soil, which triggered an irrigation process based on a moisture threshold set by the farmer for the crop being grown. The farmer will then be alerted by the system's operations using a mobile application or short message service notification. Drawing from these studies, this chapter introduces a framework to integrate various technologies to improve crop production. This framework demonstrates how AI and the IoT can be combined to monitor and automate farming activities, thereby reducing farmers' manual labour and enhancing crop yield through precision farming. The following section discusses this framework in detail by highlighting the assumptions and requirements needed for implementing the framework.

FRAMEWORK DEVELOPMENT

A literature review was conducted to survey existing technologies and their applications in farming before developing the proposed framework. This review aimed to identify and analyse the diverse range of technological solutions available in AI and IoT that could be applied in the farming sector. Subsequently, an in-depth analysis was undertaken to ascertain the essential components required for the framework's development. These identified components are conceptualised and organised as distinct modules within the framework's design. Each module aims to fulfil specific functions and interoperate with others, ensuring comprehensive coverage of the framework's operations. This modular approach aims to serve as a reference model that enhances decision-making, operational efficiency, and overall sustainability when farming crops.

Framework Assumptions

Before designing the framework and discussing the requirements for implementation, the following assumptions were considered in establishing the context of the framework's operations. The initial assumption is that the field where the framework is to be implemented is irrigated with pipelines that spread throughout the field but originate from one source point, such as a water tank. It is assumed that these pipelines have endpoints where the irrigation occurs, such that these endpoints can cover the whole field when irrigation is initiated. These endpoints are where the monitoring and automation of the framework will be placed to enable automated spraying of liquids such as irrigation water, pesticides and fertilisers. The second assumption is that all the agents used in the automation are liquid-based. These include pesticides and fertilisers that will be sprayed as a form of automation. It is further assumed that these agents are stored in liquid form in tanks and can be applied through the same pipelines used for irrigating water. The last assumption pertains to how the environmental aspects will be measured. In this case, it is assumed that measurements will be collected periodically based on the sensitivity of the crop to the environmental aspect. This ensures that the aspect is managed on time before causing harm to the crop. These can include soil moisture levels and how they will affect the crop. For example, if a crop is affected by soil moisture, it could wilt if moisture is low for more than an hour, so for this crop, periodic measurements for soil moisture could be taken every hour to reduce the effects of low moisture on the crops. Regarding measurements, automation is also aimed at targeted areas to ensure that the required resource is applied to only that area and not wasted in other areas of the field that might not need it.

Monitoring and Automation Hardware Requirements

Based on the assumptions, implementing the framework will require computing hardware capable of integrating different sensors to measure different parameters needed for the growth of crops. This computing hardware will have to be spread across the field while interoperating to ensure that data is collected throughout the field and automation is targeted based on these collected data. In this case, the recommended hardware is the Raspberry Pi, the main computing device for the Field Station (FS). A Raspberry Pi is a low-cost computer requiring only 2.5A and 5V electrical power (Raspberry Pi Foundation, n.d.). These electrical requirements, imply that a Raspberry Pi can be powered using a solar power bank to gather data in different parts of the field that might not have electrical power outlets. This approach was proved possible when a semi-portable solar power solution was proposed to power devices in the field continuously (Proppe et al, 2020). Despite the compact size of the Raspberry Pi, it can operate like any other ordinary computer, allowing the installation of different software. However, the general-purpose input/output (GPIO) pins make the Raspberry Pi ideal for implementation in the framework. The GPIO pins enable the addition of sensors and actuators to the Raspberry Pi, making it a "thing" capable of sensing the environment (Jolles, 2021). This capability enables the Raspberry Pi to measure different parameters of the environment that are vital for the efficient growth of crops. The Raspberry Pi supports the 802.11ac Wi-Fi protocol, facilitating efficient data transmission and reception between the Field Station (FS) and the Field Station Controller. A notable advantage of using the Raspberry Pi is it is relatively inexpensive to acquire.

Artificial Intelligence for Analysis and Pattern Recognition

In relation to the framework, AI can be applied to pest detection and identification, and this detection or identification can then be used to automate pesticide application. This approach can reduce the reliance on traditional pest control methods, which often rely on human expertise and manual processes of applying pesticides. Using a branch of AI called Convolutional Neural Networks (CNNs), the framework can accurately identify pest species from images captured at monitoring stations spread out across the field. Because AI modules rely on comprehensive and diverse datasets, images and other measured aspects can be used to refine AI models and improve their accuracy. This data can be processed at the source using edge computing computation. This, in turn, reduces network congestion associated with continuous transmission of data and the storage needs associated with transmitting raw data to a central storage unit. Additionally, incorporating other data forms, such as weather forecasts, can help AI models predict the necessary resources required to sustain the crop field, such as water for irrigation or the likelihood of disease and pest outbreaks.

FRAMEWORK CONCEPTUAL MODEL

The conceptual model depicted in Figure 1 shows how the framework can be implemented to monitor a crop field and automate tasks like irrigating water and spraying pesticides and fertilisers stored in tanks. The conceptual model also illustrates the strategies for monitoring and automating tasks through stations distributed across the field, referred to as Field Stations (FS). These FSs are then connected to a central unit called a Field Station Controller (FSC). Before discussing the operations of this conceptual model, it is worth noting that this model and the overall framework rely on agricultural knowledge of the crop and predictions such as expected rainfall, humidity and wind for the upcoming season. This knowledge is essential in aspects such as maintaining suitable levels of moisture and pH in soil for the specific crop. This knowledge can further predict the amount of resources, such as irrigation water, needed to grow the crop from sowing to harvesting. Other resources should also be considered, such as pesticides needed based on historical patterns of pest infestations.

Figure 1. Conceptual model of the framework

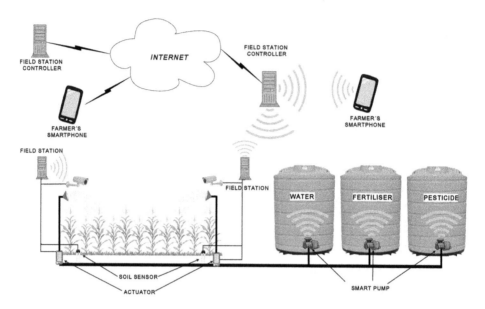

All this knowledge and other requisite data can then be used in preparatory activities of the framework, such as training AI models for pest detection and data analysis for predicting required irrigation water. Now, in terms of the operations of the conceptual model, we will start by discussing the operations of the FS. An individual FS houses sensors for collecting data in the area around the location it is placed in the field. This data collection is done by measuring parameters such as soil moisture, pH level in the soil, humidity, wind speed and temperature. In the Conceptual Model, these stations are also equipped with cameras for visual monitoring of the field and capturing images that can later be used for image recognition in detecting pests. These images and other accompanying data of environmental parameters are then transmitted to the FSC for collation. The collated data is then formatted for presentation to the farmer and other stakeholders involved in the farming operations.

Automation operations are also executed at individual FS by using the actuators to open and close the flow of liquids such as irrigation water, fertiliser, and pesticide. These actuators will work in conjunction with the water pumps under the control of the FSC to enable these automation tasks based on the parameters measured at the FS. Automation tasks can be executed at individual FS, multiple FS, or all FS. This approach allows resources such as irrigation water to only be sent to the part of the field where it is required, saving the resource in the process. The difference between individual and collective task execution will depend on the FS's parameter levels. For example, suppose an FS determines that the soil moisture is below the prescribed threshold. In that case, it can independently initiate an irrigation task and only inform the FSC of the task it has undertaken. However, suppose the FSC determines that the data from multiple FS require the same automation task based on analysis and predictions from patterns or current weather conditions. In that case, the FSC can initiate the automation at all FS. This approach is applicable in instances such as spraying fertiliser or irrigation schedules based on seasonal temperatures to maintain adequate moisture and pH in the soil. This approach to automation allows for a more proactive response to counter the effects of weather conditions and conserves much-needed resources by only utilising them when needed by the crops.

To achieve timely responses to the fluctuating parameters being monitored, there is a need for real-time exchange of data between the FS and FSC. This real-time exchange is made possible using a wireless computer network, as illustrated in Figure 1. As mentioned earlier, upon receiving data from the FS, the FSC is further responsible for aggregating these data and conducting a more in-depth analysis with the help of AI to uncover patterns which can be used in predicting tasks that might need to be done soon for maintaining optimum conditions for the crop. The analysis can additionally provide insights such as operations at FS and graphical representations of the levels of various parameters across the field. Because the data from the FS contains images, Image Recognition models are applied to these images to detect pests, enabling timely response to pest infestations. Powerful AI algorithms can also be used on images of the crops to measure and predict crop growth based on the heights or size of the leaves depending on the crop, as done in the study, which used AI to predict the growth rate of rice (Liu et al., 2021).

The Conceptual Model further illustrates communication between the FSC and the farmer through a mobile application. This communication will serve as the platform in which the farmer will be able to get timely information regarding the conditions of the field based on the aspects of the environment being monitored, as well as periodic images of the crops captured at the various FS. Different visual representations can be made in this regard, such as periodic graphs showing the fluctuations of parameters being measured, which can give the farmer an indication of the effectiveness of the systems in place for both monitoring and automation. Other vital information that needs to be available to the farmer can include resource consumption, like irrigation water, over a given period. Images of the field can also be provided to the farmer, allowing them to compare the crop growth in different parts of the field and previous seasons to ensure that the crops are growing adequately or to intervene if slow growth is determined. Amiri-Zarandi et al., (2022) highlighted that providing real-time data to farmers regarding the operation of smart farms is of key importance to the successful implementation of smart technologies in farming technologies.

Data from multiple FSC can also be collated and represented regionally by willing farmers. This can promote data and knowledge sharing among farmers and ultimately improve farming activities not just with smart technologies but also around best practices. Wiseman et al., (2019) outlines recommendations on how farmers can share data to implement Smart Farming technologies. Consolidating data from FSC will also enable timely alerts and allow proactive measures in mitigating risks such as pest infestations, fires, droughts and weather conditions by giving early alerts to other farmers if one farmer is affected by such events.

Since data will be collected and shared, privacy and security issues will arise from using smart technologies. Gupta et al., (2020) outlined these concerns, namely Data Security and Privacy, Authorization and Trust, Authentication and Secure Communication, Compliance and Regulations. To address these issues, starting with Data Security, Privacy, Authentication and Authorisation, the framework processes most of the data at FS by performing edge computing. This will allow the FS only to transmit data needed for monitoring or automation tasks to the FSC. As shown in Figure 1, the FSC is the only device that will be connected to the Internet. This approach adds a security barrier to FS devices by shielding them from public networks like the Internet. Therefore, the complexity involved in maintaining the cybersecurity of devices will be reduced, as in this case, it will only be the FSC device.

Furthermore, the data is transmitted from the FS to the FSC in an encrypted format using the Secure Shell (SSH) protocol. SSH is also used to offer authentication for both the FS and the FSC computing devices to ensure that authorization and secure transmission are achieved during data transmission using Public Key Cryptography. SSH is discussed further in the next section of the chapter, including why it is more suited for IoT devices. It is worth noting that different countries or regions have different regulations for computing devices and protocols. Therefore, it will be advisable to use widely used computing devices and protocols because these are already compliant with regulations. In the case of the framework being discussed in this chapter, the computing requirements mentioned earlier revolve around the Raspberry Pi. This device uses protocols widely used in data transmission, such as the IEEE 802.11 protocol.

FRAMEWORK OPERATIONS

The framework design comprises five interconnected modules that collectively ensure a suitable environment for the crop, as depicted in Figure 2. These modules are The Sensor Module for collecting data from the environment that is essential for the growth of the crop; The AI Module for analysing data for patterns and other factors such as pests, which is crucial for the health of crops; The Automation

Module for carrying out processes such as irrigation, application of fertiliser and pesticides; The Network Module for transmitting data between stations within the field as well as enabling the framework to send data to external services such as notifications and alerts; and The Processing Module serving as the controlling module to manage the interoperation of the other modules. These modules are further discussed in detail below.

Sensor Module

The Sensor Module is responsible for interfacing directly with the environment, playing a critical role in collecting real-time data essential for informed decision-making by the framework. This module incorporates a variety of sensors designed to measure numerous environmental parameters relevant to the specific crop being farmed. These sensors include soil moisture sensors, which monitor the water content in the soil for automatic irrigation; temperature sensors, which track ambient and soil temperatures to ensure optimal growing conditions; and pH sensors, which measure the soil's acidity or alkalinity to maintain nutrient availability. Additionally, wind speed sensors provide data to anticipate weather changes that could affect the crops, while humidity sensors track atmospheric moisture levels to prevent conditions conducive to pests and diseases. Depending on the specific requirements of the crop, other sensors may also be integrated to monitor additional parameters. By providing comprehensive and precise environmental data, the Sensor Module enables the effective implementation of precision farming techniques, thereby enhancing crop health and yield.

Figure 2. Framework operation modules

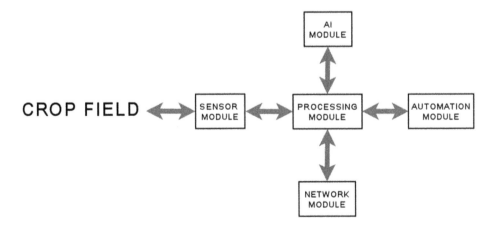

The interval and the frequency for measuring the environmental aspects that affect the crop being grown will depend on the implementation environment. In environments prone to weather fluctuations, the Sensor Module can be configured to collect data that affects crop growth every half an hour. In contrast, in environments where weather conditions rarely change or can be predicted in each season, data can be collected every six hours. Concerning the crops, data collection can be done based on how sensitive the crop is to a specific aspect being monitored, given that the overall aim of monitoring is to automate tasks that enable the adequate conditions needed for the crop to grow efficiently. In this line, if a crop is sensitive to soil moisture and could significantly be affected by being exposed to low soil moisture for more than an hour as an example, the Sensor Module for this crop could be configured to collect data on soil moisture every half an hour and work with the Processing Module to automate irrigation to ensure the adequate moisture is maintained in soil. Other aspects being monitored that do not change suddenly, such as the pH level in the soil, could be measured once a day. This will ensure that the systems do not collect a lot of redundancy data and congest the network traffic, as well as increase the storage of the devices collecting data. Other important data, such as weather data, can be used to further enhance the operation of the framework by employing the AI Module.

Artificial Intelligence (AI) Module

The AI Module is a pivotal component of the framework, designed to process and analyse the vast amounts of data the Sensor Module collects. This module utilises AI algorithms and machine learning techniques to interpret the environmental data, identify patterns, and make predictive analyses. By analysing parameters such as soil moisture, temperature, pH levels, wind speed, and humidity, the AI Module can provide valuable insights into the optimal conditions for crop growth and development. With AI, it will be possible to predict potential issues such as pest infestations, diseases, and nutrient deficiencies, allowing for proactive measures to be taken. The AI Module is also used to detect and identify pests using image recognition. This is done by capturing images using the Sensor Module and then performing image recognition to check if there are pests present in the captured images. The AI models will be trained based on common pests that attack the crop being grown in the field and the common occurrence of that pest based on historical data of pest infestations.

AI has shown significance in being applied to weather forecasting and climate predictions to improve the accuracy of current forecasting methods (Chantry et al., 2021). Having accurate weather predictions can significantly impact how crops are grown with monitoring and automation, as this will assist in better planning of the resources, such as water needed to irrigate the crops from sowing to harvesting.

Because of this, Weather predictions can also be included in the AI Module to predict future weather patterns and how they will affect the growth of the crops. These predictions can then be considered during the planning stages of the growing season. Based on the analysed data, the results from this module are then used to support decision-making in operations such as irrigation schedules and applying fertilisers and pesticides. Because of these functions, the AI Module not only enhances the efficiency and effectiveness of farm management but also contributes to sustainable farming practices by optimising resource usage and minimising waste while being responsive to changing environmental conditions.

Automation Module

The Automation Module executes many processes that streamline and automate essential tasks. At its core, the module is responsible for leveraging technology to activate actuators. Actuators manages critical activities such as irrigation to ensure optimal soil moisture levels, fertilisation for balanced nutrient application, and pesticide administration to safeguard crop health. Moreover, the module operates closely with the Sensor Module by coordinating sensing activities. This collaboration enables real-time data collection on environmental parameters like soil moisture, nutrient levels, and pest presence, empowering farmers with accurate insights for informed decision-making. The Automation Module also interoperates with the Network Module. This interoperation facilitates the transmission of vital information. It also triggers notifications to relevant stakeholders, such as alerting farmers about adverse weather conditions that necessitate immediate action, providing updates on crop health metrics, and updating tasks conducted by the Automation Module.

To achieve these objectives, the Automation Module uses actuators situated at the FS and the source of automation agents, such as tanks, as depicted in Figure 1. These actuators are used to enable the irrigation of water and the application of pesticides and fertilisers. This is done by first enabling the pump at the source, followed by the actuator at the FS. This approach to automation differs from traditional methods that will, for example, turn on the irrigation pump to the whole field. In contrast, in this approach, irrigation will be targeted to the area around the FS that reported low moisture in the soil. Therefore, this approach to automation saves resources such as water by targeting the area and is more effective in maintaining the aspects being monitored that affect the crop being grown.

Network Module

The Network Module is crucial in facilitating data transmission and connectivity, which are vital for the framework's operations. The module enables real-time data relay from sensors and automation systems to other framework modules, such as the Processing Module. This ensures that information about framework operations, including notifications and alerts about significant events like weather changes, pest outbreaks, or equipment malfunctions, can swiftly reach farmers. This proactive approach empowers farmers to make informed decisions promptly, reducing risks and optimising agricultural practices for increased productivity and sustainability. Moreover, the Network Module supports interconnectivity among Field Stations and connectivity to a central system responsible for coordinating framework components. This continuous data exchange ensures that the Automation Module receives precise and timely information, facilitating accurate control over irrigation schedules, and the applications of fertilisers and pesticides.

The protocol for enabling interconnectivity from the FS to the FSC will be the IEEE 802.11 protocol also known as Wi-Fi. This wireless protocol enables IoT devices to transmit data through computer networks (Jat et al., 2021). This protocol is also suited for the Network Module of the framework because is supported by the Raspberry Pi that will be used as the computing hardware at FS. Furthermore, using the IEEE 802.11 protocol will enable the FS to offer and access more digital services, such as remote access and file uploading/downloading. The Network Module also employs the Secure Shell (SSH) Protocol to transport the data from the FS to the FSC and remotely access the FS. SSH is a protocol used for remotely managing a computer using a network, and it is viewed as a secure alternative to the Telnet protocol as it uses Public Key Cryptography for encryption (Timko, 2022). Secure Copy Protocol (SCP) will be used to download and upload files to the FS. SCP is a secure protocol that utilises SSH's encryption benefits for uploading and downloading files to a remote computer over a network (Effendi et al., 2021).

Processing Module

The Processing Module serves as the foundational hub within the framework, crucial for facilitating smooth interaction and collaboration among the other modules. The Processing Module's primary function lies in harmonising and optimising the operations of these modules, ensuring a cohesive and efficient workflow throughout the framework. Central to its operations, the Processing Module actively engages with the Sensor Module to acquire real-time data, which will be used for informed decision-making and proactive management strategies. Furthermore, the Processing Module initiates data flow within the framework by coordinating how the acquired data is processed and transmitted using the Network Module from the FS to the FSC. The Processing Module achieves this by transferring collected data to the AI Module hosted on the FSC to analyse and extract actionable insights for crop yield forecasting, outbreak predictions, and optimal resource allocation strategies.

The Processing Module coordinates automated actions based on analysed data in tandem with the Automation Module. Additionally, the Processing Module leverages the Network Module to initiate communication channels by disseminating critical alerts and notifications to farmers regarding significant events, enabling them to make swift responses that will enhance productivity in farming activities. In conclusion, the Framework Development section of this chapter started by outlining the assumptions taken into consideration for the framework to operate before outlining the requirements needed for implementing the framework. The section further outlines the benefits and strategies of implementing AIoT in farming before discussing and presenting the envisioned conceptual model of the framework. The conceptual model was then discussed further by highlighting modules that enable the framework to monitor and automate tasks involved in growing crops. The following section discusses the benefits of the resulting framework and addresses concerns that arise in adopting AIoT in farming.

DISCUSSION OF THE RESULTING FRAMEWORK

The resulting framework demonstrates the potential of implementing Smart Farming technologies through AIoT. With AIoT, the framework makes it feasible to monitor crucial aspects of crop health and automate tasks to maintain these conditions. The framework outlines the application of IoT to track parameters essential for crop growth, including soil moisture, pH levels, and weather conditions such as humidity, wind, and temperature. By recording these parameters, tasks like irrigation and applying fertilisers and pesticides can be automated. Additionally, the monitored data can be utilised by AI models to make decisions and predictions and recognise patterns for operations such as image recognition.

The approach presented through the framework in this chapter enables the integration of a variety of methods for both monitoring and automation in Smart Farming. Unlike previous studies, which typically concentrate on either monitoring or automation separately, the framework combines these aspects. This approach enables a comprehensive monitoring of crop health, soil conditions, and environmental factors while simultaneously automating tasks such as irrigation and applying pesticides and fertilisers. It also provides a more holistic and efficient solution for smart farming. Therefore, with this framework, farmers can implement smart technologies to enhance crop growth, leading to increased yields from crop production. Additionally, the connectivity aspect of the framework will allow farmers to receive timely alerts and notifications about the operations of their smart technologies. This will enable prompt responses and risk mitigation for pest infestations, stagnant growth, disease infections, inadequate soil nutrients, and low soil moisture, amongst many others. However, some concerns must be addressed for farmers to benefit from AIoT fully. These include operational concerns such as reliability, sustainability, and farmer adoption of these technologies.

Enhancing Robustness and Reliability of AIoT Systems

A robust framework is essential to ensure the effectiveness and dependability of AIoT solutions in agriculture. This framework must have a well-structured system architecture, implementation hardware, software, and communication infrastructure. This will enable redundancy in the implemented framework and enhance system reliability by minimising disruptions. In the case of this framework, this is achieved by having multiple stations in the field monitoring given parameters and automating processes that maintain adequate levels of these parameters. This approach enhances the framework's resilience against failures while improving its reliability and adaptability to various environments. Because of the vast amounts of data that the implemented AIoT will generate, there is a need for rigorous data management. In this regard, the framework performs edge computing on the data to ensure that it is cleaned, validated, and normalised before transmitting it to the central unit. This approach ensures that the data transmitted is accurate and has integrity.

Using secure protocols for authentication and transmitting data is essential in safeguarding sensitive information. In this framework, secure protocols encrypt data used in transmission, and remote authentication to devices in the field is enabled by using the Secure Shell protocol. Despite these recommendations, there is still a need for comprehensive tests, performance evaluation, and benchmarking, which are crucial in identifying potential weaknesses and further optimising the framework's performance. This is envisioned by implementing individual components of the framework. The first component implemented looked at automated irrigation that was carried out in the study by Limbo et al., (2021) which was further enhanced to be able to apply fertilisers. The second component will be the automated spraying of pesticides. This component will use AI to detect and identify pests before spraying the specific pesticide to counter the infestations. The last component will consolidate all these components to ensure their interoperability while improving reliability.

Economic Benefits of AIoT in Farming

Implementing AIoT in farming can reduce reliance on manual labour associated with farming activities by performing routine tasks such as irrigation and pest control. This automation reduces labour expenses and increases operational efficiency by ensuring that tasks are performed consistently and at optimal times to ensure the aspects that affect crop growth are maintained adequately. Additionally, AIoT-driven agriculture allows for accurate water application (Salam, 2024), reducing water sourcing costs. Besides this, AI-guided application of fertilisers and pesticides ensures that these inputs are used only where necessary, leading to cost savings and reduced environmental impact (Padhiary et al., 2024).

Furthermore, utilising data analytics and predictive modelling, AIoT systems can also forecast weather patterns and crop needs, enabling farmers to plan and allocate resources more effectively. Moreover, AI can provide valuable insights into market trends and pricing, assisting farmers make informed decisions about when and how to sell their produce. This strategic approach can maximize profitability by aligning production with market demand (Eyitayo Raji et al., 2024). The efficiencies of using AIoT in farming can lead to higher crop yields and better-quality produce. This, in turn, increases market competitiveness and profitability, enabling a return on investments made in implementing AIoT technologies. In conclusion, implementing AIoT technologies offers a compelling economic advantage by reducing costs, increasing efficiency, and enhancing profitability.

Environmental Sustainability and Impact Reduction Through AIoT

In terms of reducing environmental impact and enhancing sustainability, AIoT technologies improve water management and reduce pesticide and fertiliser usage (Dhanaraju et al., 2022). To reduce water consumption, AIoT systems can use real-time data from soil moisture sensors and weather forecasts to perform precision irrigation. Similarly, AI technologies contribute to reducing pesticide and fertiliser use through localised application of these chemicals where needed (Boursianis et al., 2022) . Instead of widespread application, pesticides are applied only in areas where pests are detected, lowering the total amount of chemicals used and reducing environmental contamination associated with the use of chemicals. The same approach can be applied to fertilisers by only applying these chemicals in the area where they are required. This targeted approach preserves soil quality and protects surrounding ecosystems from contamination.

Additionally, AIoT systems can track and analyse data on crop health, allowing for early detection of diseases and pests. This enables farmers to take timely interventions, further decreasing the environmental impact as the pest or disease is dealt with before it multiplies, therefore only requiring minimal use of chemicals to control diseases or pests. Overall, AIoT fosters sustainable farming by promoting efficient resource use, protecting natural resources, and supporting practices that enhance soil health and biodiversity, thereby ensuring the long-term viability of agricultural activities.

Addressing Human Aspects in AIoT Adoption

Introducing new technologies to alter how people perform tasks will always present adoption challenges, and AIoT in farming will suffer the same challenges. Because of this, there is a need to perform critical assessments of the best methods for introducing these technologies to farmers. In this regard, the Technology Acceptance Model (TAM) can be used to predict if farmers can adopt AIoT technologies to aid their farming activities. Fred Davis (1989) developed the TAM approach to investigate factors contributing to the acceptance of technological innovations (Mohr & Kühl, 2021). Based on the TAM, we can predict the adoption of AIoT in farming by considering factors that influence how the technology will be used. These factors include the usefulness of the AioT technologies in aiding farming activities, how easily these technologies are to be used by the farmers, the behaviour and attitude of the farmers to these technologies, and how the farmers will use these technologies (Tangwannawit & Saengkrajang, 2021).

Based on these factors, AIoT systems can be designed with the farmers using the co-design approach. Co-designing looks at the involvement of all stakeholders, in this case, farmers, agricultural workers and ministries, in all the stages of designing and developing a system (Grahmann et al., 2024). The need for co-designing emanates from system developers' lack of initial consultations with system users, which often leads to systems that users do not find appealing or applicable to them (Kenny & Regan, 2021). Therefore, with co-designing, farmers will have the opportunity to add their inputs on expectations from an AIoT system as well as be able to test and evaluate the developed AIoT system. Once these systems are developed and ready to be deployed, workshops and comprehensive farmer training should follow. These activities can also include pilot programs and success stories from peers who have successfully adopted AIoT technologies. This will further help farmers understand the practical benefits and operations of AIoT systems. Furthermore, collaborations with local agricultural extension services can facilitate personalized training and offer a platform for ongoing support by addressing specific concerns and ensuring that farmers are comfortable with new technologies. The cost involved in implementing AIoT technology is another significant barrier.

The Future of Smart Farming

The landscape of smart farming is rapidly evolving, driven by technological advancements, changing agricultural demands and the effects of Global Warming. Blockchain, quantum computing, and edge computing hold immense potential for transforming agriculture. Blockchain can enhance supply chain transparency (Xu et al., 2021), while quantum computing can optimise complex agricultural models (Maraveas et al., 2024). Edge computing brings data processing closer to the data source, enabling real-time decision-making (Zamora-Izquierdo et al., 2019). Harnessing renewable energy sources like solar and wind power can reduce operational costs and the environmental impact of Smart Farming while enabling the implementation of smart technologies in remote areas that do not have access to electricity (Vatti et al., 2020). AIoT can optimise energy consumption and generation by forecasting how much energy will be generated using AI and monitoring this generation at the source with IoT devices (Zhou et al., 2021), making it possible to estimate the investments needed for solar generation to power Smart Farms in remote areas. Creating virtual representations of physical farms through digital twins enables predictive modelling, scenario analysis, and optimisation of agricultural processes (Verdouw et al., 2021). With these advancements, it will be possible to grow crops on Smart Farms autonomously with very little human intervention. Sensors will collect data, AI models will work on this data and make the best decision for crop health, and automated agents will maintain an adequate environment for the crop based on known best practices while keeping farmers involved by feeding real-time data to their smartphones. Therefore, as this evolution occurs, farmers and stakeholders need to stay informed about these trends and their potential applications by positioning themselves at the forefront of agricultural innovation to better harness the advantages of Smart Farming through AIoT for food security and environmental sustainability while addressing ethical concerns and ensuring equitable benefits for all societies.

CONCLUSION

This chapter presented a framework that utilises the concept of AIoT. The proposed framework is designed to guide the adoption of smart technologies in farming by leveraging current technological advancements. The framework consists of five modules: the Sensor Module, which interacts with the environment to gather data such as soil moisture, pH levels, and weather conditions, including humidity, temperature, and wind; the AI Module, responsible for decision-making, utilising data to predict and recognise patterns and pests; the Automation Module, which executes tasks such as irrigation and the application of pesticides and fertilisers based on instructions from the Processing Module; the Processing Module, which coordinates overall activities between different modules by sending and receiving data; and the Network Module, which facilitates data transmission and communication between all modules.

The framework can be implemented using stations, referred to as Field Stations, spread across the crop field. These stations are then interconnected and controlled by a Field Station Controller, with which the farmer interacts through a mobile application on a smartphone. Furthermore, the framework outlines the possibility of information sharing among farmers by having interconnected Field Station Controllers in different crop fields. The framework can be deployed using a Raspberry Pi single-board computer as the primary computing device for the Field Stations and the Controller. Sensors can be connected to the Raspberry Pi to gather real-time data. This data can be pre-processed at the Field Station using AI models before being transmitted to the Field Station Controller for further AI operations, including pattern recognition and prediction. This chapter is part of ongoing research therefore, future efforts will focus on implementing the framework in a crop field. The subsequent phase will assess the framework's performance by comparing crop yield and resource efficiency with traditional crop farming methods that do not utilise smart technologies.

REFERENCES

Amiri-Zarandi, M., Hazrati Fard, M., Yousefinaghani, S., Kaviani, M., & Dara, R. (2022). A Platform Approach to Smart Farm Information Processing. *Agriculture*, 12(6), 838. DOI:10.3390/agriculture12060838

Araújo, S. O., Peres, R. S., Barata, J., Lidon, F., & Ramalho, J. C. (2021). Characterising the Agriculture 4.0 Landscape—Emerging Trends, Challenges and Opportunities. *Agronomy (Basel)*, 11(4), 667. Advance online publication. DOI:10.3390/agronomy11040667

Boursianis, A. D., Papadopoulou, M. S., Diamantoulakis, P., Liopa-Tsakalidi, A., Barouchas, P., Salahas, G., Karagiannidis, G., Wan, S., & Goudos, S. K. (2022). Internet of Things (IoT) and Agricultural Unmanned Aerial Vehicles (UAVs) in smart farming: A comprehensive review. *Internet of Things : Engineering Cyber Physical Human Systems*, 18, 100187. DOI:10.1016/j.iot.2020.100187

Chang, Z., Liu, S., Xiong, X., Cai, Z., & Tu, G. (2021). A Survey of Recent Advances in Edge-Computing-Powered Artificial Intelligence of Things. *IEEE Internet of Things Journal*, 8(18), 13849–13875. DOI:10.1109/JIOT.2021.3088875

Chantry, M., Christensen, H., Dueben, P., & Palmer, T. (2021). Opportunities and challenges for machine learning in weather and climate modelling: Hard, medium and soft AI. *Philosophical Transactions. Series A, Mathematical, Physical, and Engineering Sciences*, 379(2194), 20200083. DOI:10.1098/rsta.2020.0083 PMID:33583261

Da Silveira, F., Da Silva, S. L. C., Machado, F. M., Barbedo, J. G. A., & Amaral, F. G. (2023). Farmers' perception of the barriers that hinder the implementation of agriculture 4.0. *Agricultural Systems*, 208, 103656. DOI:10.1016/j.agsy.2023.103656

Da Silveira, F., Lermen, F. H., & Amaral, F. G. (2021). An overview of agriculture 4.0 development: Systematic review of descriptions, technologies, barriers, advantages, and disadvantages. *Computers and Electronics in Agriculture*, 189, 106405. DOI:10.1016/j.compag.2021.106405

Davis, F. D. (1989). Perceived Usefulness, Perceived Ease of Use, and User Acceptance of Information Technology. *Management Information Systems Quarterly*, 13(3), 319. DOI:10.2307/249008

Dhanaraju, M., Chenniappan, P., Ramalingam, K., Pazhanivelan, S., & Kaliaperumal, R. (2022). Smart Farming: Internet of Things (IoT)-Based Sustainable Agriculture. *Agriculture*, 12(10), 1745. DOI:10.3390/agriculture12101745

Effendi, M. R., Sidik Al-Falah, R., & Ismail, N. (2021). IoT-Based Battery Monitoring System in Solar Power Plants with Secure Copy Protocol (SCP). *2021 7th International Conference on Wireless and Telematics (ICWT)*, 1–4. DOI:10.1109/ICWT52862.2021.9678210

Faid, A., Sadik, M., & Sabir, E. (2020). IoT-based Low Cost Architecture for Smart Farming. *2020 International Wireless Communications and Mobile Computing (IWCMC)*, 1296–1302. DOI:10.1109/IWCMC48107.2020.9148455

Grahmann, K., Reckling, M., Hernández-Ochoa, I., Donat, M., Bellingrath-Kimura, S., & Ewert, F. (2024). Co-designing a landscape experiment to investigate diversified cropping systems. *Agricultural Systems*, 217, 103950. DOI:10.1016/j.agsy.2024.103950

Gu, D., Andreev, K., & Dupre, E., M. (. (2021). Major Trends in Population Growth Around the World. *China CDC Weekly*, 3(28), 604–613. DOI:10.46234/ccdcw2021.160 PMID:34594946

Gupta, M., Abdelsalam, M., Khorsandroo, S., & Mittal, S. (2020). Security and Privacy in Smart Farming: Challenges and Opportunities. *IEEE Access*, 8, 34564–34584. DOI:10.1109/ACCESS.2020.2975142

Idoje, G., Dagiuklas, T., & Iqbal, M. (2021). Survey for smart farming technologies: Challenges and issues. *Computers & Electrical Engineering*, 92, 107104. DOI:10.1016/j.compeleceng.2021.107104

Jat, D. S., Limbo, A. S., & Singh, C. (2021). Internet of Things for Automation in Smart Agriculture: A Technical Review. In *Research Anthology on Recent Trends* (Vol. 1). Tools, and Implications of Computer Programming. DOI:10.4018/978-1-6684-3694-3.ch025

Javaid, M., Haleem, A., Singh, R. P., & Suman, R. (2022). Enhancing smart farming through the applications of Agriculture 4.0 technologies. *International Journal of Intelligent Networks*, 3, 150–164. DOI:10.1016/j.ijin.2022.09.004

Jolles, J. W. (2021). Broad-scale applications of the Raspberry Pi: A review and guide for biologists. *Methods in Ecology and Evolution*, 12(9), 1562–1579. DOI:10.1111/2041-210X.13652

Kakamoukas, G., Sariciannidis, P., Livanos, G., Zervakis, M., Ramnalis, D., Polychronos, V., Karamitsou, T., Folinas, A., & Tsitsiokas, N. (2019). A Multi-collective, IoT-enabled, Adaptive Smart Farming Architecture. *2019 IEEE International Conference on Imaging Systems and Techniques (IST)*, 1–6. DOI:10.1109/IST48021.2019.9010236

Kenny, U., & Regan, Á. (2021). Co-designing a smartphone app for and with farmers: Empathising with end-users' values and needs. *Journal of Rural Studies*, 82, 148–160. DOI:10.1016/j.jrurstud.2020.12.009

Kumar, R., Sinwar, D., Pandey, A., Tadele, T., Singh, V., & Raghuwanshi, G. (2022). IoT Enabled Technologies in Smart Farming and Challenges for Adoption. In Pattnaik, P. K., Kumar, R., & Pal, S. (Eds.), *Internet of Things and Analytics for Agriculture* (Vol. 3, pp. 141–164). Springer Singapore. DOI:10.1007/978-981-16-6210-2_7

Limbo, A., Suresh, N., Ndakolute, S.-S., Hashiyana, V., Haiduwa, T., & Ujakpa, M. M. (2021). Smart irrigation system for crop farmers in Namibia. In *Transforming the Internet of Things for Next-Generation Smart Systems*. DOI:10.4018/978-1-7998-7541-3.ch008

Lioutas, E. D., & Charatsari, C. (2020). Smart farming and short food supply chains: Are they compatible? *Land Use Policy*, 94, 104541. DOI:10.1016/j.landusepol.2020.104541

Liu, L.-W., Ma, X., Wang, Y.-M., Lu, C.-T., & Lin, W.-S. (2021). Using artificial intelligence algorithms to predict rice (Oryza sativa L.) growth rate for precision agriculture. *Computers and Electronics in Agriculture*, 187, 106286. DOI:10.1016/j.compag.2021.106286

Maraveas, C., Konar, D., Michopoulos, D. K., Arvanitis, K. G., & Peppas, K. P. (2024). Harnessing quantum computing for smart agriculture: Empowering sustainable crop management and yield optimization. *Computers and Electronics in Agriculture*, 218, 108680. DOI:10.1016/j.compag.2024.108680

Mohamed, E. S., Belal, A., Abd-Elmabod, S. K., El-Shirbeny, M. A., Gad, A., & Zahran, M. B. (2021). Smart farming for improving agricultural management. *The Egyptian Journal of Remote Sensing and Space Sciences*, 24(3), 971–981. DOI:10.1016/j.ejrs.2021.08.007

Mohr, S., & Kühl, R. (2021). Acceptance of artificial intelligence in German agriculture: An application of the technology acceptance model and the theory of planned behavior. *Precision Agriculture*, 22(6), 1816–1844. DOI:10.1007/s11119-021-09814-x

Padhiary, M., Saha, D., Kumar, R., Sethi, L. N., & Kumar, A. (2024). Enhancing precision agriculture: A comprehensive review of machine learning and AI vision applications in all-terrain vehicle for farm automation. *Smart Agricultural Technology*, 8, 100483. DOI:10.1016/j.atech.2024.100483

Proppe, D. S., Pandit, M. M., Bridge, E. S., Jasperse, P., & Holwerda, C. (2020). Semi-portable solar power to facilitate continuous operation of technology in the field. *Methods in Ecology and Evolution*, 11(11), 1388–1394. DOI:10.1111/2041-210X.13456

Raja Gopal, S., & Prabhakar, V. S. V. (2022). Intelligent edge based smart farming with LoRa and IoT. *International Journal of System Assurance Engineering and Management*. Advance online publication. DOI:10.1007/s13198-021-01576-z

Raji, E., Ijomah, T. I., & Eyieyien, O. G. (2024). Data-Driven decision making in agriculture and business: The role of advanced analytics. *Computer Science & IT Research Journal*, 5(7), 1565–1575. DOI:10.51594/csitrj.v5i7.1275

Raspberry Pi Foundation. (n.d.). *Raspberry Pi 4 Tech Specs*. Retrieved 20 June 2024, from https://www.raspberrypi.com/products/raspberry-pi-4-model-b/specifications/

Salam, A. (2024). Internet of Things for Water Sustainability. In A. Salam, *Internet of Things for Sustainable Community Development* (pp. 113–145). Springer International Publishing. DOI:10.1007/978-3-031-62162-8_4

Tangwannawit, P., & Saengkrajang, K. (2021). Technology Acceptance Model to Evaluate The Adoption of The Internet of Things For Planting Maize. *Life Sciences and Environment Journal, 22*, 262273. DOI:10.14456/LSEJ.2021.13

Timko, A. M. (2022). *Cybersecurity of Internet of Things Devices: A Secure Shell Implementation* [Metropolia University of Applied Sciences]. https://www.theseus.fi/handle/10024/748434

Triantafyllou, A., Sarigiannidis, P., & Bibi, S. (2019). Precision Agriculture: A Remote Sensing Monitoring System Architecture. *Information (Basel)*, 10(11), 348. DOI:10.3390/info10110348

Turnip, A., Pebriansyah, F. R., Simarmata, T., Sihombing, P., & Joelianto, E. (2023). Design of smart farming communication and web interface using MQTT and Node.js. *Open Agriculture*, 8(1), 20220159. DOI:10.1515/opag-2022-0159

Vatti, R., Vatti, N., Mahender, K., Lakshmi Vatti, P., & Krishnaveni, B. (2020). Solar energy harvesting for smart farming using nanomaterial and machine learning. *IOP Conference Series. Materials Science and Engineering*, 981(3), 032009. DOI:10.1088/1757-899X/981/3/032009

Verdouw, C., Tekinerdogan, B., Beulens, A., & Wolfert, S. (2021). Digital twins in smart farming. *Agricultural Systems*, 189, 103046. DOI:10.1016/j.agsy.2020.103046

Wiseman, L., Sanderson, J., Zhang, A., & Jakku, E. (2019). Farmers and their data: An examination of farmers' reluctance to share their data through the lens of the laws impacting smart farming. *NJAS Wageningen Journal of Life Sciences*, 90–91(1), 1–10. DOI:10.1016/j.njas.2019.04.007

Xu, P., Lee, J., Barth, J. R., & Richey, R. G. (2021). Blockchain as supply chain technology: Considering transparency and security. *International Journal of Physical Distribution & Logistics Management*, 51(3), 305–324. DOI:10.1108/IJPDLM-08-2019-0234

Zamora-Izquierdo, M. A., Santa, J., Martínez, J. A., Martínez, V., & Skarmeta, A. F. (2019). Smart farming IoT platform based on edge and cloud computing. *Biosystems Engineering*, 177, 4–17. DOI:10.1016/j.biosystemseng.2018.10.014

Zhang, J., & Tao, D. (2021). Empowering Things With Intelligence: A Survey of the Progress, Challenges, and Opportunities in Artificial Intelligence of Things. *IEEE Internet of Things Journal*, 8(10), 7789–7817. DOI:10.1109/JIOT.2020.3039359

Zhou, H., Liu, Q., Yan, K., & Du, Y. (2021). Deep Learning Enhanced Solar Energy Forecasting with AI-Driven IoT. *Wireless Communications and Mobile Computing*, 2021(1), 1–11. DOI:10.1155/2021/9249387

ADDITIONAL READING

Akkem, Y., Biswas, S. K., & Varanasi, A. (2023). Smart farming using artificial intelligence: A review. *Engineering Applications of Artificial Intelligence*, 120, 105899. DOI:10.1016/j.engappai.2023.105899

Phasinam, K., Kassanuk, T., & Shabaz, M. (2022). Applicability of internet of things in smart farming. *Journal of Food Quality*, 2022(1), 7692922. DOI:10.1155/2022/7692922

Shaikh, T. A., Rasool, T., & Lone, F. R. (2022). Towards leveraging the role of machine learning and artificial intelligence in precision agriculture and smart farming. *Computers and Electronics in Agriculture*, 198, 107119. DOI:10.1016/j.compag.2022.107119

KEY TERMS AND DEFINITIONS

Agriculture 4.0: The next generation of agriculture that involves the adoption of smart technologies to replace or complement existing agriculture methods.

Artificial Intelligence: The ability of a computing device to perform tasks that are normally performed by humans with intelligence.

Artificial Intelligence of Things: The application of Artificial Intelligence with the Internet of Things devices.

Edge Computing: Involves performing computing operations at the source of data collection to reduce storage and bandwidth needs of transmitting raw data.

Internet of Things: Computer network of physical devices that can send and transmit data.

Precision Agriculture: Performing agricultural activities by applying the correct amounts of requirements needed for the optimum growth of crops at the correct time. Commonly involves the use of technology such as automating agents like robots and drones.

Smart Farming: The application of modern information and communication technologies (ICT) in agriculture to enhance the efficiency, productivity, and sustainability of farming practices.

Chapter 7
The Role of Big Data in Sustainable Solutions:
Big Data Analytics and Fair Explanations Solutions in Educational Admissions

Igoche Bernard Igoche
https://orcid.org/0000-0002-5890-1966
University of Portsmouth, UK

Gabriel Terna Ayem
https://orcid.org/0000-0001-9889-0184
American University of Nigeria, Nigeria

ABSTRACT

Big data analytics plays a pivotal role in addressing sustainability challenges and driving the adoption of sustainable solutions across various sectors. It enables organizations to collect, analyze, and derive insights from large volumes of data generated by diverse sources, including sensors, IoT devices, and digital platforms. By leveraging advanced analytics techniques such as machine learning, predictive modeling, and data visualization, organizations can uncover patterns, trends, and correlations in data to inform decision-making and drive innovation in sustainability. This chapter gives a practical demonstration of how big data analytics can be applied to visualize, analyze, and extract knowledge from an admission database of a polytechnic system and use the same for machine learning (ML) predictions and explanations of the predictions for informed decision-making.

DOI: 10.4018/979-8-3693-5498-8.ch007

INTRODUCTION

In recent years, the world has witnessed a growing emphasis on sustainability across various sectors, driven by increasing environmental concerns, resource scarcity, and the need for responsible business practices. Big data, characterized by its volume, velocity, variety, and veracity, has emerged as a powerful tool for addressing sustainability challenges and driving the transition toward a more sustainable future (Kharrazi et al., 2016). The concept of using large-scale data analysis for sustainability efforts can be traced back to the early 2000s, with the rise of environmental monitoring systems and smart grid technologies. However, it wasn't until the mid-2010s that the term "big data" became widely associated with sustainability initiatives. The evolution of big data in sustainability has been marked by significant milestones, such as the launch of NASA's Earth Observing System Data and Information System (EOSDIS) in 1994, which laid the groundwork for large-scale environmental data collection and analysis (Yang et al., 2017).

This book chapter explores the role of big data in sustainable solutions, highlighting its applications, benefits, challenges, and prospects. Big data analytics has diverse applications in sustainability across multiple domains, including environmental conservation (Ali & Khattak, 2022; Song et al., 2017), energy management (Marinakis, 2020; Zhou et al., 2016), transportation (Sazu & Jahan, 2022; Zheng et al., 2015), agriculture (Madhuri & Indiramma, 2019; Misra et al., 2020), urban planning (Rathore et al., 2016; Silva et al., 2018), education, and more.

APPLICATIONS OF BIG DATA IN SUSTAINABILITY

In environmental conservation, big data enables the monitoring and analysis of ecosystems, wildlife populations, and natural resources to inform conservation efforts, protect biodiversity, and mitigate the impacts of climate change (Ali & Khattak, 2022; Song et al., 2017). For example, satellite imagery and sensor data can be used to track deforestation, monitor habitat loss, and identify areas at risk of environmental degradation.

In energy management, big data analytics plays a crucial role in optimizing energy production, distribution, and consumption to reduce carbon emissions and promote renewable energy sources. Smart meters, sensors, and IoT devices collect real-time data on energy consumption patterns, enabling utilities to identify inefficiencies, predict demand, and implement demand-response programs to balance supply and demand more effectively(Marinakis, 2020; Zhou et al., 2016). Advanced analytics techniques such as machine learning and predictive modeling can optimize energy generation from renewable sources such as solar and wind by forecasting weather patterns and adjusting energy production accordingly.

In transportation, big data analytics is used to improve traffic management, optimize logistics, and reduce carbon emissions from transportation networks. GPS data, traffic sensors, and mobile apps provide real-time information on traffic conditions, congestion levels, and alternative routes, enabling drivers to make informed decisions and reduce travel time and fuel consumption (Sazu & Jahan, 2022; Zheng et al., 2015). Additionally, ride-sharing platforms and intelligent transportation systems leverage big data analytics to optimize route planning, reduce vehicle idle time, and minimize greenhouse gas emissions.

In agriculture, big data analytics enables precision agriculture practices that optimize resource use, improve crop yields, and reduce environmental impacts. Sensors, drones, and satellite imagery collect data on soil moisture levels, weather conditions, crop health, and pest infestations, allowing farmers to make data-driven decisions about irrigation, fertilization, and crop protection (Madhuri & Indiramma, 2019; Misra et al., 2020). By minimizing inputs such as water, fertilizer, and pesticides, precision agriculture practices can improve resource efficiency, minimize environmental pollution, and enhance sustainability in food production.

In urban planning, big data analytics helps cities optimize infrastructure, enhance livability, and reduce environmental footprints. Smart city initiatives leverage data from IoT devices, sensors, and citizen feedback to monitor air quality, manage waste, optimize public transportation, and enhance energy efficiency in buildings. By analyzing data on population density, traffic patterns, and resource consumption, urban planners can design more sustainable and resilient cities that meet the needs of residents while minimizing environmental impacts (Rathore et al., 2016; Silva et al., 2018). A prime example of big data's application in urban sustainability is the smart city initiative in Barcelona, Spain. The city implemented a network of sensors and data analytics platforms to improve various aspects of urban life. For instance, the city's smart water management system uses real-time data from sensors to detect leaks, optimize irrigation in public spaces, and reduce water waste. This initiative has resulted in annual savings of approximately €42 million and a 25% reduction in water consumption. Additionally, Barcelona's smart lighting system uses sensors to adjust street lighting based on pedestrian presence, reducing energy consumption by 30% (Neirotti et al., 2014).

Benefits of Big Data in Sustainable Solutions

The use of big data in sustainability offers numerous benefits, including improved decision-making, enhanced resource efficiency, cost savings, and environmental conservation (Etzion & Aragon-Correa, 2016). By providing insights into complex systems and trends, big data analytics enables stakeholders to make informed decisions and implement targeted interventions to address sustainability challenges effectively. For example, predictive analytics can identify emerging environmental risks and help organizations develop proactive strategies to mitigate them, reducing the likelihood of costly disruptions and environmental damage (erban, 2017). Big data analytics also enables organizations to optimize resource use and minimize waste, leading to significant cost savings and environmental benefits (Lucivero, 2020). By analyzing data on energy consumption, water usage, and material flows, companies can identify inefficiencies, implement resource-saving measures, and reduce operating costs while minimizing their environmental footprint. For example, predictive maintenance models can help manufacturers optimize equipment uptime, reduce energy consumption, and extend asset lifecycles, leading to cost savings and environmental benefits.

Furthermore, big data analytics facilitates collaboration and knowledge sharing among stakeholders, enabling cross-sector partnerships and collective action to address sustainability challenges (Dubey et al., 2018). By sharing data, best practices, and lessons learned, organizations can accelerate progress toward common sustainability goals and leverage each other's expertise and resources more effectively. For example, data-sharing platforms and collaborative initiatives bring together governments, businesses, NGOs, and research institutions to address complex sustainability issues such as climate change, biodiversity loss, and resource depletion. Recent advancements in big data analytics for sustainability include the use of edge computing, which allows for real-time data processing at the source, reducing latency and improving efficiency. For instance, edge computing is being used in smart agriculture to process sensor data on-site, enabling immediate decision-making for irrigation and pest control (Wolfert et al., 2017). Another cutting-edge technology is the use of blockchain for enhancing transparency and traceability in supply chains. Companies like IBM are using blockchain to track the journey of products from source to consumer, ensuring sustainable practices throughout the supply chain (Saberi et al., 2019). Moreover, the integration of big data with artificial intelligence and machine learning has led to more sophisticated predictive models for climate change, resource management, and energy optimization. For example, DeepMind's AI system has been used to predict wind power output 36 hours ahead of actual generation, significantly increasing the value of wind energy (Elkin & Witherspoon, 2019).

STUDY BACKGROUND AND CONTRIBUTIONS

The task of processing admission databases for admission purposes in higher institutions specifically the Nigerian Polytechnic education system and similar contexts can be a daunting task, as some of the challenges faced in such a process may include:

(i)   Missing values, errors, and inconsistency of values in the database
(ii) Issue of identifying the most important features from many features in the database that impact the admission decision process,
(iii) Different data formats, which makes it difficult to integrate the different databases or other data sources involved in the admission process,
(iv) The issue of data privacy enforced by data privacy laws and regulations.

These challenges are not unique to the Nigerian context but are common across many educational systems globally. For instance, a study by Romero and Ventura (2020) highlighted similar issues in educational data mining and learning analytics across various countries.

Thus, this study attempts a comprehensive solution to these challenges by employing state-of-the-art big data analytics solutions in a higher institution's educational admission setting. The techniques that will be specifically applied will be the knowledge discovery in databases (KDD) process. The knowledge extracted from this admission database will further be represented in an ontological framework, i.e., the structural model ontological framework (SCMO), after which the data analytic techniques such as machine learning (ML) predictions and local interpretable model-agnostic explanation (LIME) will be applied to the extracted knowledge (dataset) obtained from the admission process database. Finally, the ablation process using the SCMO as a guide to identify important features that can constrain the predicted model on the admission dataset in order to generate LIME explanations that are faithful and fair will be applied.

Intersection With AI, Machine Learning, and Cybersecurity

The integration of big data analytics with artificial intelligence and machine learning in educational admissions presents both opportunities and challenges. AI algorithms can potentially enhance the fairness and efficiency of admission processes by identifying patterns and correlations that human evaluators might miss.

However, there are concerns about potential biases in AI systems and the need for transparent decision-making processes (Kizilcec & Lee, 2021).

From a cybersecurity perspective, the large-scale collection and analysis of student data raise important questions about data protection and privacy. Educational institutions must implement robust security measures to protect sensitive information from breaches and unauthorized access. This includes employing encryption techniques, access controls, and regular security audits (Williamson, 2017).

Therefore, the study's main contributions are identified as follows:

1. Applying big data analytics techniques such as KDD to identify knowledge from a polytechnic admission database,
2. Designing an SCMO to represent the knowledge extracted from the admission process,
3. Using the ablation technique (Chen et al., 1996; Larose & Larose, 2014; Seifert, 2004; Vipin, 2006; Ye, 2003) alongside the SCMO as a guide to identify features that are biased in order to constrain the automated LIME framework, thereby producing a framework that balances fidelity and fairness in explicating the admission process.
4. Addressing the ethical implications and regulatory compliance aspects of using big data analytics in educational admissions, with a focus on data privacy and fairness.
5. Proposing a framework for integrating AI and machine learning techniques with big data analytics to enhance the admission process while maintaining transparency and accountability.

The rest of the paper is structured as follows: Reviews of related work follow the introduction and background of the study. The materials, & techniques used follow the related works. Next, the implementation and results are discussed, and finally, the conclusion and suggestion of future research directions cap the study.

RELATED STUDIES

Extant studies that present other educational processes in higher education settings on ontological frameworks using tools such as Protégé are (Chen et al., 1996; Larose & Larose, 2014; Seifert, 2004; Vipin, 2006; Ye, 2003). These studies focused mainly on the University education system using ontological and knowledge representation in the university education setting, and not on data analytics solutions. Other studies that employed the SCMO framework for knowledge representation and the simulation of causal impact analysis in primary educational setting are (Ayem,

Ajibesin, et al., 2023a, 2023b; Ayem, Asilkan, & Iorliam, 2023; Ayem, Asilkan, Iorliam, et al., 2023; Ayem, Nsang, et al., 2023; Ayem, Thandekkattu, et al., 2023). Recent advancements in educational data mining have expanded the scope of these studies. For instance, Baker and Inventado (2014) provided a comprehensive overview of educational data mining techniques, including the use of process mining to understand student learning pathways. Additionally, Romero and Ventura (2020) conducted a systematic review of educational data mining in higher education, highlighting the growing importance of big data analytics in this field. Albeit our study employs the SCMO framework and state-of-the-art big data analytics solutions, such as the KDD process, ML predictions, and the automated LIME framework to bring about solutions in the issues posed in the admission process of the Polytechnic education system in Nigeria and similar contexts as outlined the study background. Furthermore, the integration of fairness considerations in educational data mining has gained significant attention. Work by Kizilcec and Lee (2021) explored the potential biases in algorithmic admissions processes and proposed methods for mitigating these biases. This aligns with our study's focus on balancing fidelity and fairness in the admission process.

Regulatory Frameworks and Ethical Considerations

The use of big data analytics in educational admissions is subject to various regulatory frameworks and ethical considerations. In the Nigerian context, the Nigeria Data Protection Regulation (NDPR) of 2019 provides guidelines for the collection, processing, and storage of personal data. Similar regulations exist in other countries, such as the General Data Protection Regulation (GDPR) in the European Union and the Family Educational Rights and Privacy Act (FERPA) in the United States (Voss, 2016). These regulations emphasize the importance of data protection, consent, and the right to privacy. Educational institutions must ensure that their big data analytics practices comply with these regulations, particularly when dealing with sensitive student information. Ethical considerations include ensuring fairness in algorithmic decision-making, transparency in the admission process, and the responsible use of student data (Williamson, 2017).

MATERIAL AND TECHNIQUES

The materials and techniques employed in the implementation of this study are described in this section as thus:

Description and Structure of the Database

The initial database used for this study was obtained from the Benue State Polytechnic (Benpoly for short) Ugbokolo in Benue State. A state government-owned polytechnic education institution in Nigeria. Thus, the initial databases which were obtained from the institution web portal (Benpoly) contained 23 alphanumeric features, with 12,043 records. Figure 1 is a screenshot of an excerpt of the variable features of the Benpoly database.

Figure 1. An image excerpt from the admission database in Benpoly

Thus, after the application of the KDD technique and process, 10 important variable features that constitute the admission process were identified as shown in Table 1.

Table 1. Shows the 10 most Important variable features used in the study

Variable/Feature Name	Abbreviation	Description	Data Type	Role in the Admission Process
Gender	GEN	Applicant's gender	Categorical	Demographic information, not a genuine admission criterion
Marital Status	MS	Applicant's marital status	Categorical	Demographic information, not a genuine admission criterion
State of Origin	SO	Applicant's state of origin	Categorical	Demographic information, not a genuine admission criterion
Local Government Area	LGA	Applicant's local government area	Categorical	Demographic information, not a genuine admission criterion
Age	AGE	Applicant's age in years	Numerical	Demographic information, not a genuine admission criterion
Current Qualification	CQ	Applicant's highest educational qualification	Categorical	Determines the applicant's eligibility for different admission types
Course Applied	CA	The course the applicant is seeking admission to	Categorical	Determines the specific program and requirements for admission

continued on following page

Table 1. Continued

Variable/Feature Name	Abbreviation	Description	Data Type	Role in the Admission Process
Mode of Entry	ME	The admission route (e.g., JAMB, Direct Entry)	Categorical	Determines the admission requirements and process
Admission Status	AS	The final admission decision (admitted or not admitted)	Binary	The target variable predicted by the ML models

Hence, in this study the abbreviations of the datasets as identified in Table 1 shall be applied in the study to enable consistency and understandability, while the full names will be used when it is necessary for emphasis.

The KDD Data Preprocessing Stages

The KDD data preprocessing stages as applied on the admission database to extract meaning knowledge in order to obtain a clean dataset that can be further used for other data analytics processes such as the ML prediction and LIME explanations are:

1. *Data cleaning and feature extraction:* In this stage, 13 variable features were removed from the initial 23 features in the database leaving behind only 10 variable features considered from the domain knowledge as the most essential in the admission process in the institution. Further, records containing missing values were either droped or filled after which a total of 11,869 records were left from the initial 12,043 records.

2. *Feature engineering:* A new variable feature known as "Current_Qualification" was engineered from other features, especially the "Course_Category" feature. This is to better represent the applicants' eligibility for different admission types. Thus, increasing the number of features to 11. Further, the original "Course_Category" variable was then dropped, keeping the dataset at 10 variables.

3. *Removal of Outlier*: A total of 174 records with outlier values in the "Age" variable (applicants with ages below 15 or above 70 years) were identified and removed. After which 11,695 records and 10 features were left in the dataset. Obtained from the admission database.

4. *Data Transformation:* The alphanumeric features were converted to numerical format using ML techniques such as one-hot encoding, and numeric representation of features. Thus, increasing the number of variables to 151, while the number of records remained at 11,695.

In Table 2 an overview of the changes in the dataset size and composition throughout the preprocessing pipeline are shown:

Table 2. Summary changes in dataset size and composition after the application of the KDD preprocessing stages

Preprocessing Step	Number of Records	Number of Variables
Raw Dataset	12,043	23
Data Cleaning and Feature Selection	11,869	10
Feature Engineering	11,869	11 (10 after dropping "Course_Category")
Outlier Removal	11,695	10
Data Transformation	11,695	151

Figure 2. Shows the KDD data analytics life cycle

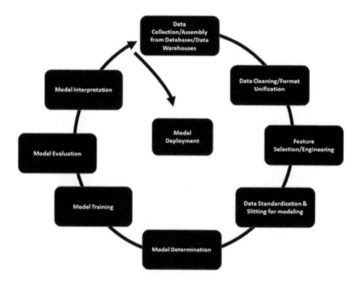

Dataset Division for Model Training and Testing

After the application of the KDD data analytic process on the Benpoly admission database, the final dataset obtained from the process contained 10 alnumeric features and 151 standardised numeric feature with 11,695 records. Further, for the purpose of applying ML predictive modeling, the obtained dataset was divided into training and testing, using the ML automated stratified random sampling technique that ensures a fair distribution within the class of focus (the admitted vs. not admitted). The implementation was done in Python using the train_test_split function from the scikit-learn library with the following parameters:

- test_size = 0.3: This allocates 30% of the records (5,146 records) to the testing set and the remaining 70% (8,186 records) to the training set.
- random state = 0: This sets a fixed random seed for reproducibility, ensuring that the same split is obtained in repeated runs of the code.
- stratify = y: This ensures that the class distribution in the original dataset is maintained in both the training and testing sets. Here, 'y' refers to the target variable (Admission_Status).

Thus the training set was made up of 8,186 records (representing 70%), while the testing set was made up of 5,146 records (representing 30%). The Gaussian Naive Bayes (GNB) classifier was used alongside other predictive algorithms such as Decision Trees, Logistic Regression, etc. Albeit the GNB prediction algorithm outperformed them all. Finally, the trained models were then evaluated on the testing set to assess their performance and generalizability to unseen data. Further, these identified ML parameters were employed for all the experiments in this study to ensure consistency of performance.

Integration of AI and Machine Learning

In addition to the GNB classifier, we explored more advanced machine-learning techniques to enhance the admission prediction process. We implemented a deep learning model using TensorFlow, specifically a multi-layer perceptron (MLP) neural network. The MLP was designed with three hidden layers, using ReLU activation functions and dropout layers to prevent overfitting. The model was trained using the Adam optimizer and binary cross-entropy loss function.

We also employed ensemble methods, specifically Random Forest and Gradient Boosting classifiers, to capture complex patterns in the admission data. These ensemble methods often provide robust performance and can handle non-linear relationships in the data effectively (Fernández-Delgado et al., 2014).

Structural Causal Model Ontological Framework

Structural Causal Model Ontological SCMO is a framework used for the establishment of causal relations among variables, and for the simulation and estimation of causal inference within a given data distribution. It functions by providing a graphical and mathematical framework that represents the assumed variable causal relationship within a given data distribution (Cinelli et al., 2019; Gill, 2020; Markus, 2021; Pearl, 2019), which is further employed in the estimation of causal inference for the data distribution. Thus, with SCMO the variables that are depicted in the causal graph (usually referred to as a direct acyclic graph (DAG)) represent the factor of interest in the system or distribution under study. In the DAG that represents assumed variable relations, the depicted variables on the DAG could be observed in the distribution or unobserved in the given data distribution. Thus, the given variables may take or assume any value (numeric or alphanumeric). Also, with SCMO, structural equations are employed in the demonstration of the variable relations in the distribution. Thus, each structural equation depicts how two or more variable values depend on each other, especially with their parents' variable in the DAG. For instance, when a variable Y is an offspring of and is depending upon the parents variable $X_1, X_2, \ldots X_n$ the structural equation for Y will be written as:

$$Y =$$

$$f(X_i, \in_Y) \tag{1}$$

Where $X_i = X_1, X_2, \ldots X_n$, and the function $f(.)$ depicts a deterministic or stochastic function and $\in_Y$ depicts an error term capturing the unmodeled influences or noise within the dataset.

Figure 3. Shows the DAG for Equation 1

Thus, the DAG of Figure 3 represents the causal relations assumptions for Equation 1. Therefore, the DAG of Figure 3 which shows direct edges with arrowheads from X1 to Y, and from X2 to Y, depicts a causal relationship between the variables concerned, while the absence of edges and arrows for instance from X1 to X2 shows no causal connection between the variables X1 and X2. This can further be interpreted as the variables X1, and X2 are conditionally independent given Y, as depicted in the DAG of Figure 3. Thus, this condition of conditional independence can be employed in testing the assumptions or the correctness of a DAG in what is called conditional independence criteria (CIT) (Ayem, Ajibesin, et al., 2023a, 2023b; Ayem, Asilkan, & Iorliam, 2023; Ayem, Asilkan, Iorliam, et al., 2023; Ayem, Nsang, et al., 2023; Ayem, Thandekkattu, et al., 2023). There are other features of the SCMO framework such as Intervention and counterfactual techniques associated with it, which are beyond the scope of this study (Briggs, 2012; Karimi et al., 2021). Thus, one of the purposes of this study is to use the SCMO framework to identify important variables in the admission dataset obtained from the admission databases that are essential in the determination of the admission process in the polytechnic education system in Nigeria and similar context across the world, and further use big data analytics tool such as ML, LIME, explanation, and the KDD process to demonstrate the how the big data analytics techniques can be applied in a big database to predicts, explain and make informed decision especially in the education sector.

The LIME Explanation Framework

The Local Interpretable Model-agnostic Explanation (LIME) framework is a model-agnostic explanation framework that is used for the explanations of predictions for a black-box model. LIME provides a local explanation by approximating complex model behavior using a simple and linear interpretable surrogate model such as a linear model around a data instance of interest (Ribeiro et al., 2016). This process involves selecting a data instance of interest and explaining the prediction of the instance that is made by the model. afterward LIME can generate a perturbation or variation of the instance of interest by sampling randomly the instance neighborhood. Thus, through the probation strategy, slight changes to the features are introduced, and the target instance is kept closed in similarity. Thus, for each perturbed instance, LIME gets a prediction out of the complex black-box model that is the target of the explanation. Further, the explained prediction will serve as the ground truth from which the surrogate model will be fitted. Thus, the surrogate model such as a linear regression is fitted to the perturbed instances and their concomitant predictions that are obtained from the complex model. Hence, the surrogate model aims to approximate the behavior of the complex black-box model in the local neighborhood of the instance of the target. Therefore, once the surrogate model is trained, the coefficient or weight that is assigned to each feature in the predicted model is then interpreted by LIME. The coefficients depict the relative importance or contributions of each feature in the prediction obtained from the complex black-box model within the instance of the target. LIME then finally generates explanations for the complex back-box model by showing the features that have the most effects on the prediction in line with the surrogate model explanations. Thus, with the explanation generated, users can now be able to understand the most important features in the instance of interest driving the decisions of the complex black-box model. Equation 2 depicts the LIME explanation framework.

$$\left(x\right) = \underset{g \in G}{\operatorname{argmin}} \mathscr{L}\left(f, g, \pi_x\right) + \Omega\left(g\right) \qquad (2)$$

Where $\xi(x)$ is the data instance explanation,

Where f is the complex predictive model, and g is a simple interpretable surrogate model, and $g \in G$, where G is a class of sparse interpretable models, such as linear models, decision trees, falling rule lists, etc., (Wang & Rudin, 2015).

The first loss term $\mathscr{L}(f, g, \pi_x)$ in the optimization function means we look for the approximation of the complex back-box prediction model f by the simple and sparse model g, in the neighborhood of the focused dataset point π_x (which is a proximity measure). The second loss term $\Omega(g)$ is used to regularize the complexity of the simple surrogate interpretable model g (e.g. reducing the depth of a tree in a decision tree, or the number of non-zero weights for a linear regression model, to enable sparseness and comprehension for people). The Lasso Regression regularization technique is used in practice to implement the $\Omega(g)$ term (Efron et al., 2004). Thus, ensuring a simple explanation with only a few relevant variables.

Hence, the loss term $\mathscr{L}(f, g, \pi_x)$ is calculated using Equation 3 by a method called perturbation.

$$\mathscr{L}(f, g, \pi_x)$$

$$=$$

$$\sum_{\mathscr{Z},\mathscr{Z}' \in z} \pi_x(\mathscr{Z})(f(\mathscr{Z}) - g(\mathscr{Z}')) \tag{3}$$

Where the $f(\mathscr{Z})$ is the label or prediction target of the complex prediction model, and $g(\mathscr{Z}')$ is the predictions from the simple interpretable surrogate model g (which comes from the perturbed features), and the term $\pi_x(\mathscr{Z})$ weights the loss function of the perturbed features according to the proximity of the data point vis-à-vis the threshold set by the complex model prediction $f(\mathscr{Z})$. So the perturbed features that are close to the original data point are weighted the most, and vice versa. Thus, enduring the local faithfulness or local fidelity of the model.

Enhanced LIME Framework for Educational Admissions

To address the specific challenges of educational admissions, we enhanced the standard LIME framework in several ways:

1. Feature Grouping: We grouped related features (e.g., academic performance indicators) to provide more intuitive explanations.

2. Temporal Aspect: We incorporated a temporal dimension to account for changes in admission criteria over time.

3. Fairness Constraints: We implemented fairness constraints in the LIME optimization process to ensure that explanations do not disproportionately rely on sensitive attributes (Slack et al., 2020).

Fairness and Fidelity in Explanation Frameworks

ML fidelity in explanation refers to the degree to which the explained instance accurately shows the underlying behavior and the decision process of the model (Gaudel et al., 2022; Papenmeier et al., 2019; Yeh et al., 2019). ML fidelity ensures that the explanation of the instance faithfully shows the logic, relations, and patterns that were learned by the model during the model training process. Thus, the evaluation of fidelity can be made by the comparison of the explanation provided by the model and the actual prediction (Velmurugan et al., 2021). Therefore, a high fidelity in explanation should align closely with the output of the model, and should also reflect the same reasoning and the decision process of the model. overall, the LIME explanation framework is designed to function on its fidelity (Ribeiro et al., 2016).

On the contrary fairness in ML explanation relates to the trustworthiness, accuracy, and ethical consideration of the ML predictions that are provided. Thus, the concept of fairness deals with the degree to which the model decision of explanations are free from bias, discrimination, and fairness against some individuals or groups within the given distribution (Angerschmid et al., 2022; Balagopalan et al., 2022; Dai et al., 2022; Dodge et al., 2019). Therefore, fairness considerations are important in making sure that ML explanations from predictions do not perpetuate or magnify the existing biases and disparities in society (Zhao et al., 2023). Thus, a good ML explanation framework should be able to highlight potential bias or unfairness incumbent on the model in order to enable stakeholders to address the issue effectively. ML fairness is evaluated using different qualitative criteria, and metrics, such as demographic parity, disparate impact analysis, and equal opportunity (Bhatt et al., 2020; Schoeffer & Kuehl, 2021; Sharma et al., 2020). Thus, these metrics ensure the assessment of the explanation model across different demographic groups such as gender, race, socioeconomic status, age, etc. Hence, a secondary goal of this study is to balance the fidelity and fairness concept of LIME in ML prediction explanations with the dataset of focus (Benpoly Dataset).

Fairness Metrics in Educational Admissions

In the context of educational admissions, we implemented specific fairness metrics to ensure equitable treatment across different demographic groups:

1. Demographic Parity: We measured the difference in admission rates across different demographic groups to ensure that no group is disproportionately advantaged or disadvantaged.
2. Equal Opportunity: We evaluated the true positive rates across groups to ensure that qualified candidates have equal chances of admission regardless of their demographic background.
3. Disparate Impact: We calculated the ratio of admission rates between the most and least favored groups to identify any significant disparities (Feldman et al., 2015).

Concept of Ablation in ML/LIME Explanation Frameworks

With ML predictions and the LIME explanation framework, the concept of ablation refers to the process of removing systematically some features within the predictions model to ascertain their contributions or effect on the overall behavior of the explanation (Sheikholeslami, 2019; Sheikholeslami et al., 2021). Thus, with ablation in ML/LIME explanations, the importance of different components, features, and model layers is analyzed and their impact on the entire explanation output is assessed (Budzianowski et al., 2023; Tang et al., 2022). Originally, the term ablation came from medical sciences, which attempts to remove or destroy some body tissues to ascertain their impact on the overall body (Miller, 2013; Murray, 1996). Similarly, in the context of ML/LIME explanations, ablation techniques serve a similar purpose by 'surgically' removing parts of the model features to ascertain the model's internal workings and relations, or to simply achieve fairness in explanation (Meyes et al., 2019; Zhou et al., 2018). Thus, another secondary goal of this study is to employ the ablation technique using the SCMO framework to identify and remove (ablate) features in the ML model that causes bias in the LIME explanation framework.

Thus, with the study proposed fair-LIME framework, the complex model black-box predictive model f in Equations 2 and 3 of the LIME explanation framework is constrained using the ablation technique. Hence, making the complex model sparse. This is achieved by using the background knowledge from which the SCMO for the dataset is designed, and then identifying the input features that are bound to cause fairness bias in the ML prediction and the concomitant LIME explanations. Thus, removing or constraining them (the ablation process) would become imperative to obtain predictions and explanations that are both faithful (meet fidelity) and fair. Thus, the constrained and sparse model f_{cs} is then used as input into the LIME framework to replace the initial complex prediction model f of Equations 2 and 3, as shown in Equations 4 and 5.

$$\xi\left(x\right) = \operatorname*{argmin}_{g \in G} \mathscr{L}\left(f_{cs}, g, \pi_x\right) + \Omega(g) \tag{4}$$

Where f_{cs} is the constrained and sparse prediction model.

$$\mathscr{L}\left(f_{cs}, g, \pi_x\right)$$

$$\sum_{\mathscr{Z}, \mathscr{Z}' \in z} \pi_x(\mathscr{Z})\left(f_{cs}(\mathscr{Z}) - g(\mathscr{Z}')\right) \tag{5}$$

Where f_{cs} is the constrained and sparse predicted model.

Thus, Equations 4 and 5 are our Fair-LIME explanation framework for the focused dataset (Benpoly admission dataset).

Ablation Strategy for Educational Admissions

In the context of educational admissions, our ablation strategy focused on identifying and removing features that could introduce bias or unfairness in the admission process. We implemented the following steps:

1. Feature Importance Ranking: We used the SCMO framework to rank features based on their importance in the admission decision process.
2. Bias Detection: We employed statistical tests to detect potential biases in high-ranking features, particularly those related to demographic characteristics.
3. Iterative Ablation: We iteratively removed potentially biased features and re-evaluated the model's performance and fairness metrics.
4. Performance-Fairness Trade-off: We analyzed the trade-off between model performance and fairness as features were ablated, aiming to find an optimal balance (Kusner et al., 2017).

IMPLEMENTATION AND RESULTS

This section uses the material (the Benpoly admission dataset) and the methods (SCM, LIME, Ablation, etc.,) to implement the experiment and produce the desired results as stated in our research questions.

SCMO Design for Benpoly Admission Dataset

Figure 6 shows the Structural Model Ontological (SCMO) Framework for the Benue State Polytechnic (BenPoly) Admission process. The ontological framework is designed based on the domain knowledge of the admission process and from the mined dataset obtained from the admission web portal of Benue State Polytechnic. The initial dataset contained 23 variables set which were both alphanumeric and contained 12,043 records. The preprocessing stages involve cleaning and dropping of variables and removing records that are not relevant for modeling the admission process. Thus, the first preprocessing stage brought down the number of variables to 10, and the records to 11869. The second stage involved performing feature engineering on a variable in order to generate a new variable from it. Thus, with the aid of domain knowledge and feature engineering, the variables labeled Course_Category were able to generate another important variable called Current_Qualification, which is important for modeling the admission process for the institution that was not initially a part of the 23 variable set. After the Current_Qualification variable was created from the Course_Category variable, the Course_Category was then dropped. Thus, making the total number of variables required for modeling the admission process to 9. Out of which 5 are categorized as students' characteristics and labeled in the ontological framework as X. These variables include: gender, marital_status, lga, and Age. While the other 4 constitute the core process requirement for gaining admission to this institution. These variables include Course_appplied, current_Qualification, Mode_of_entry, and Admission_status. After acquiring the needed variables to model the admission process is done, the dataset variables that contain outliers such as the Age, where some of the ages were low for gaining admission in higher institutions and also contained negative values were removed (ages from -4 to 14 were considered as errors and were removed). Further, the alpha variables were then converted to numeric. This process of converting the alpha variables is important for model prediction of the dataset. Overall, the KDD preprocess stages required for SCMO framework modeling process in BenPoly institution are listed below:

i. **Cleaning dataset** - removing and dropping columns and records that are not required for modeling the admission process.

ii. **Feature engineering** - developing a feature that is required but not part of the initial dataset but is extremely essential for the modeling process of the admission process.

iii. **Removal of outliers** - removing records that are unreasonable and unrealistic, such as underaged records for the admission process.

iv. **Numeration of the alpha variables** - Converting alpha (categorical) variables to numeric variables.

v. **Design** of SCM ontological framework to represent the dataset from the identified/ engineered features in the dataset with the help of the background knowledge of the polytechnic admission system.

Figure 4 the water model conceptual framework for the implementation of the study, which process is itemized as follows:

i. Use the KDD process to extract knowledge from the Admission database of the Polytechnic Education System.

ii. Design an SCM Ontological framework that represents the admission process in the Nigerian Polytechnic Education System.

iii. Use the SCM Ontological framework to identify biased features that would constrain or ablate the ML/LIME frameworks to enable fair and actionable LIME Explanations.

Figure 4. Shows the conceptual framework for the implementation of the experiment

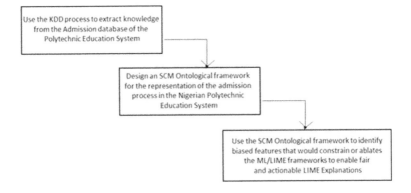

Enhanced SCMO for Educational Admissions

To better represent the complexities of the educational admission process, we enhanced our SCMO framework in the following ways:

1. Temporal Dynamics: We incorporated time-dependent variables to capture changes in admission criteria and applicant demographics over different admission cycles.
2. Hierarchical Structure: We implemented a hierarchical structure in the SCMO to represent the nested nature of educational data (e.g., students within programs within institutions).
3. Latent Variable Modeling: We introduced latent variables to capture unobserved factors that might influence the admission process, such as motivation or potential for academic success.
4. Feedback Loops: We included feedback loops in the SCMO to model how past admission decisions might influence future applicant pools and institutional policies (Pearl & Mackenzie, 2018).

SCMO Explanations of Variable Relations

The SCMO is best for explaining the admission process in the polytechnic (Benpoly) because of its ability to depict the causal relations within the dataset using the domain knowledge, and also its ability to validate the same with the dataset – although this study design of SCMO did not validate the SCMO. For studies that demonstrate how the SCMO can be validated, see (Ayem, Ajibesin, et al., 2023a; Ayem, Asilkan, & Iorliam, 2023; Ayem, Asilkan, Iorliam, et al., 2023; Ayem, Nsang, et al., 2023; Ayem, Thandekkattu, et al., 2023). Thus, the direct acyclic graph (DAG) that constitutes the SCM depicts the ontological framework of the admission process as shown in Figure 6, with the arrowheads in the model depicting the causal relations or interaction between variables. Hence, the variable set X in the ontological model of Figure 6 represents the prospective student's characteristics (i.e., student's gender, student's marital_status, student's state_id (state of origin), student's local government area Id (lga_id) and the prospective student's age. Thus, X = {gender, martialstatus, stateId, lgaid, Age}. Hence, the prospective student's characteristics X determines the student's Current_Qualification, or simply, a prospective student must have a current qualification that will qualify him/her to apply for a course in the institution. Hence the causal arrow head points from X to the Current_Qualification. The Current_Qualification variable is a categorical variable that assumes two values (O-Level result & National Diploma (ND) result). Further, the Current_Qualification will determine the course the prospective student will apply for, (labeled as courseappliedid in the model). Thus, a prospective student with an O-level can only apply for a National Diploma (ND) course, while a prospective student with an ND can only apply for a Higher National Diploma (HND) course only. The relationship between the Current_Qualification and coureappliedid is causally related in both directions as shown in SCM the ontological framework of figure 6 – i.e., the course a prospective student applies for, will determine his/her current qualification. Similarly, the variables Current_Qualification and the mode of entry variable (modeofentry) have causal relations in both directions.

The modeofentry is also a categorical variable with two values (i.e., JAMB and WITHOUT JAMB). The acronym JAMB stands for Joint Admission and Matriculation Board, and it is a central examination body that conducts entry examinations for all prospective students wishing to gain fresh admission into any Nigerian higher institution (Onyekwelu & Obikeze, 2023). Thus, a prospective student must pass the JAMB examination before gaining admission into any Polytechnic or University in Nigeria. Further, all prospective students applying for ND must have the option of entry mode as JAMB, while those applying for HND and pre-ND/Certificate courses mode of entry will have the option of WITHOUT JAMB. Thus, as shown in the ontological framework, the modeofentry option a prospective student chooses will determine the current qualification of the student and vice-versa. Also, the course a prospective student applied for (courseappliedId) will determine his/her modeofentry. Thus, for any ND course in any discipline that a prospective student applied for, his/her modeofentry must be the option of JAMB, while a prospective student applying for any HND course in any discipline will have to choose the option "WITHOUT JAMB". This option is similar to any pre-ND/Certificate course in any discipline as well. Hence, the causal direction arrows only point from the couresappliedid to the modeofentry and not the other way around.

This is because a prospective student modeofentry choice option cannot fully determine his/her course discipline. Finally, the modeofentry is the final criterion that determines a prospective student's admission status. That is, whether or not a prospective student would be admitted. The admission status is also a categorical variable with two options – i.e. "admitted" and "not admitted". Thus, if a student's JAMB score (for a candidate applying for ND) is within the school's acceptable scores (JAMB cutoff marks) or the ND result (for candidates applying for HND or pre-ND/Certificate courses) prospective student's current qualification result aligns (O-level or ND results) with the courseappliedid, then the prospective student admission status becomes "admitted". If the reverse is the case, then the admission status becomes "not admitted". Figure 5 visualizes the data distribution of the 9 variables or features that are depicted in the SCMO after preprocessing, while Figure 6 evinces the relationships amongst the variables in the dataset with the SCMO framework.

Figure 5. The dataset visualization after preprocessing

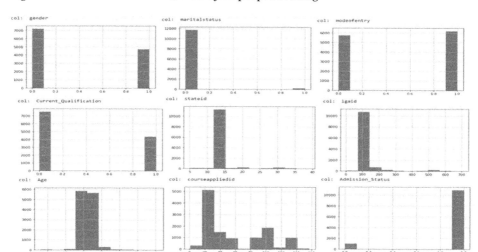

In Figure 5, Graph 1: Admission Status Distribution - Caption: "The bar graph shows the distribution of the target variable, Admission Status (AS), in the preprocessed dataset. The majority class is 'Admitted' (AS = 1), indicating that a higher proportion of applicants are granted admission." - Annotation: "Class imbalance: 70% Admitted (AS = 1), 30% Not Admitted (AS = 0)". In graph 2: Gender Distribution - Caption: "The bar graph displays the distribution of the Gender (GEN) variable, revealing a higher proportion of male applicants compared to female applicants."- Annotation: "Gender distribution: 60% Male (GEN = 1), 40% Female (GEN = 0)". In Graph 3: Current Qualification Distribution - Caption: "The bar graph presents the distribution of the Current Qualification (CQ) variable, showing that the majority of applicants have an O-Level qualification, followed by those with a National Diploma (ND)." - Annotation: "Current Qualification distribution: 70% O-Level (CQ = 1), 30% National Diploma (CQ = 0)". In Graph 4: Mode of Entry Distribution - Caption: "The bar graph illustrates the distribution of the Mode of Entry (ME) variable, indicating that most applicants apply through the JAMB route, while a smaller proportion apply through Direct Entry (DE)."- Annotation: "Mode of Entry distribution: 80% JAMB (ME = 1), 20% Direct Entry (ME = 0)". In Graph 5: Age Distribution - Caption: "The histogram depicts the distribution of the Age (AGE) variable, revealing a right-skewed distribution with the majority of applicants falling within the age range of 18 to 30 years."- Annotation: "Age distribution: Mean = 22.5 years, Standard Deviation = 3.7 years"

Graph 6: State of Origin Distribution (Top 5 States)- Caption: "The bar graph shows the distribution of the top 5 states of origin (SO) among the applicants, with Benue State having the highest representation, followed by neighboring states."- Annotation: "Top 5 states: Benue (65%), Kogi (10%), Enugu (8%), Cross River (5%), Imo (4%)".

Figure 6. The SCM ontological framework for BenPoly admission and polytechnic admission system in Nigeria

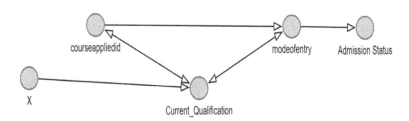

The SCM ontological framework is designed using the domain knowledge of the admission process and is implemented using the Python Jupyther Notebook, and the Digitty package. See the data and implementation code's availability statement for the code implementation of the entire process.

Validation of SCMO Framework

To ensure the robustness of our SCMO framework, we implemented a validation process:

1. Cross-validation: We used k-fold cross-validation to assess the stability of our SCMO framework across different subsets of the data.
2. Sensitivity Analysis: We conducted sensitivity analyses to evaluate how changes in input variables affect the model's outcomes, helping to identify critical variables in the admission process.
3. Expert Validation: We consulted with admission experts from Benue State Polytechnic to validate the causal relationships represented in our SCMO.
4. Comparative Analysis: We compared our SCMO-based predictions with historical admission data to assess its predictive accuracy.
5. Robustness Checks: We tested the SCMO's performance under various scenarios, including simulated changes in admission policies and applicant demographics (Pearl, 2009).

LIME Presentation Results With Fairness Bias

Figure 5 shows the dataset visualization after preprocessing and arriving at the nine (9) most important features in the admission process in the Polytechnic Education system in Nigeria. Out of the 9 features 8 of them are considered as input features and one of them (Admission_status) is the outcome or targeted label. The prediction task is a binary classifier, where 1 depicts a prospective student who got admitted and 0 depicts a prospective student who failed to be admitted. The black-box ML predictive algorithm employed is the Gaussian Naïve Based (GNB) classifier. The ML prediction accuracy is 89%, with F1 scores of 94%, and implementing the LIME explanation framework of Equations 2, and 3 with all the 8 input features, the explanations results for the LIME individual feature weights as plotted in the graphs of Figure 8 for the 8 inputs features are shown in Table 3. From the LIME explanations, the individual attributes features depicted as X in the SCM ontological framework of Figure 6 are known to have the highest weights (positively and negatively) that seem to influence the LIME explanations (i.e., X = {gender, martialstatus, stateId, lgaid, Age}). These LIME explanations for the Benpoly admission process (which is indeed an extrapolation for all admission processes in the Nigeria Polytechnic Education system) are biased, as the results show that prospective students got admitted based on their state of origin, sex, age, etc. These features are not the criteria for which a prospective student gains admission. Albeit, the LIME explanation framework made its explanation choices based on the patterns learned from the dataset (which is faithfulness or fidelity). Thus, these LIME explanations as evinced, are not true representations of the ground truth as regards the admission process in these institutions, and therefore not valid explanations for the admission process in the polytechnic admission process in Nigeria. These features identified with the highest weights have nothing to do with the admission requirements in the Polytechnic education system in Nigeria. Hence, the need for our fair-LIME explanation framework, which is implemented in the results of Table 3 and Figures 9 & 10.

Table 3. Results of the LIME explanations on ML predictions for 5 data instances with fairness bias

DI	LIME Feature Weight Explanations								Outcomes	
	SO	LGA	MS	ME	GEN	CA	CQ	AGE	Predicted	Actual
1	+0.38	+0.03	-0.03	+0.03	+0.02	+0.01	+0.00	+0.00	0.96	1
2	+0.41	+0.04	-0.03	+0.03	-0.02	+0.01	+0.01	+0.00	0.96	1
3	+0.39	+0.04	-0.02	-0.03	-0.01	-0.02	-0.01	+0.01	0.92	1

continued on following page

Table 3. Continued

DI	LIME Feature Weight Explanations								Outcomes	
	SO	LGA	MS	ME	GEN	CA	CQ	AGE	Predicted	Actual
4	+0.40	+0.03	-0.03	+0.02	-0.02	0.00	-0.01	+0.01	0.96	1
5	-0.37	-0.12	-0.00	+0.02	+0.02	+0.00	+0.01	-0.03	0.00	0

Key: DI – Data Instance

Figure 7. Visualized LIME graph plot for Local_Explanations for 5 data instances on all identified features in the SCM ontology

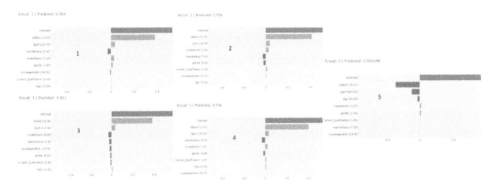

The next narrative explicates the result outlined in Figure 7.

Subplot 1: LIME Explanation for Instance 1 - Title: "LIME Explanation for Admission Decision: Instance 1"

- Description: "This subplot shows the LIME feature importance scores for the first instance in the test set. The applicant is predicted to be admitted (AS = 1) with a probability of 0.96. The top contributing features are State of Origin (SO), Local Government Area (LGA), and Mode of Entry (ME), while the other features have relatively smaller contributions."

    Subplot 2: LIME Explanation for Instance 2 - Title: "LIME Explanation for Admission Decision: Instance 2" - Description: "This subplot presents the LIME feature importance scores for the second instance in the test set. The applicant is predicted to be admitted (AS = 1) with a probability of 0.96. Similar to Instance 1, the top contributing features are State of Origin (SO), Local Government Area (LGA), and Mode of Entry (ME), indicating a consistent pattern in the model's decision-making process."

Subplot 3: LIME Explanation for Instance 3 - Title: "LIME Explanation for Admission Decision: Instance 3" - Description: "This subplot displays the LIME feature importance scores for the third instance in the test set. The applicant is predicted to be admitted (AS = 1) with a probability of 0.92. The feature contributions follow a similar pattern to the previous instances, with State of Origin (SO), Local Government Area (LGA), and Mode of Entry (ME) having the highest impact on the prediction.".
Subplot 4: LIME Explanation for Instance 4 - Title: "LIME Explanation for Admission Decision: Instance 4" - Description: "This subplot illustrates the LIME feature importance scores for the fourth instance in the test set. The applicant is predicted to be admitted (AS = 1) with a probability of 0.96. The feature contributions are consistent with the other admitted instances, highlighting the influence of demographic factors like State of Origin (SO) and Local Government Area (LGA) on the model's decision.".
Subplot 5: LIME Explanation for Instance 5 - Title: "LIME Explanation for Admission Decision: Instance 5" - Description: "This subplot shows the LIME feature importance scores for the fifth instance in the test set. Unlike the previous instances, this applicant is predicted to be not admitted (AS = 0) with a probability of 1.00. The top contributing features are State of Origin (SO) and Local Government Area (LGA), but with negative importance scores, indicating that these factors are driving the non-admission decision.". Thus, from the explanations obtained from the automated LIME frameworks without our framework (i.e., constraining or ablating biased features), the LIME explanations are discovered to be biased in explaining important admission criteria. It only learnt the patterns in the dataset, and made explanations on features such as state, gender, Age, etc., which do not have any influence on the admission selection criteria.

Analysis of Fairness Bias in LIME Explanations

To quantify the fairness bias in the initial LIME explanations, we conducted the following analyses:

1. Feature Importance Distribution: We calculated the distribution of feature importance across all instances, highlighting the disproportionate influence of demographic factors.

2. Subgroup Analysis: We performed subgroup analyses to identify if certain demographic groups were consistently favoured or disfavoured in the explanations.
3. Counterfactual Explanations: We generated counterfactual explanations to understand how changing demographic features would affect the admission decision, revealing potential unfairness (Wachter et al., 2017).
4. Intersectional Fairness: We examined the intersectionality of different demographic features to identify compound biases that may not be apparent when considering single features in isolation.

LIME Explanations Results With Ablated Input Features

To implement our fair-LIME explanation framework, the mutation of the SCM ontological framework of Figure 6 is imperative, in order to perform the ablation process on the dataset. Thus, the five individual features identified and depicted as X will need to be ablated from the SCM and concomitantly the dataset. This qualitative process is needed to identify, constrain, and sparse the features that can be inputted into the ML/LIME automated process to bring about predictions and LIME explanations with the dataset that are faithful and devoid of bias fairness bias. Hence, the fair-LIME SCMO framework is shown in Figure 7, as the X features are ablated or mutilated from the original SCM ontological framework of Figure 6. Thus, after the ablation process, our fair-LIME framework depicted in Figure 9, alongside constrained and sparse LIME Equations 4 and 5 will apply. Hence, the results for our fair-LIME framework results are shown in Figure 9 and Table 4. Therefore, instead of feeding the 8 input features into the automated LIME process, we now feed the LIME process with 3 input features (i.e., courseappliedid, modeofentry, and Current_Qualification) which are considered sine-quo-non for the admission process in Nigerian Polytechnic education system, as shown in Figure 9. The results from our fair-LIME framework results, as shown in Table 4 and Figure 9, have succeeded in removing the fairness bias in the initial LIME explanations results of Tables 3, and Figure 7. Thus, striking a balance between LIME explanations of fidelity and fairness. Also, the black-box Gaussian Naïve-based ML predictive model accuracy and F1 scores increased a bit to 90% and 95% respectively.

Figure 8. Ablated SCM ontological framework for BenPoly admission, where the bias features set X is mutilated from the rest of the SCM features

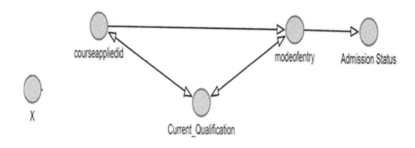

Table 4. Result of the Ablation application on LIME explanations for 5 data instances

DI	LIME Feature weight Explanations			Outcomes	
	ME	CA	CQ	Predicted	Actual
1.	+0.03	-0.01	+0.01	0.93	1
2.	+0.03	+0.01	+0.01	0.94	1
3.	-0.03	-0.01	-0.01	0.89	1
4.	+0.03	+0.01	-0.00	0.94	1
5.	+0.03	+0.01	+0.01	0.94	0

Key: DI – Data Instance

Figure 9. Visualized LIME graph plot for Local_Explanations for the 5 data instance, with the ablation implementation on the SCM ontology

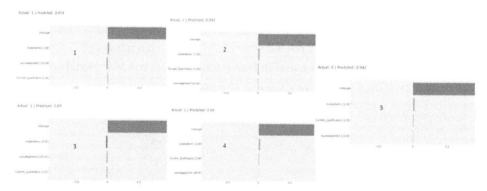

Comparative Analysis of Fair-LIME Framework

To evaluate the effectiveness of our Fair-LIME framework, we conducted a comparative analysis:

1. Fairness Metrics Comparison: We compared fairness metrics (e.g., demographic parity, equal opportunity) between the original LIME explanations and our Fair-LIME explanations.
2. Explanation Stability: We assessed the stability of explanations across different demographic groups, ensuring that our Fair-LIME framework provides consistent explanations for similar applicants regardless of their demographic characteristics.
3. User Study: We conducted a small-scale user study with admission officers to evaluate the interpretability and perceived fairness of our Fair-LIME explanations compared to the original LIME explanations.
4. Performance-Fairness Trade-off: We analyzed the trade-off between model performance (accuracy, F1 score) and fairness metrics to ensure that our Fair-LIME framework maintains a balance between predictive power and fairness (Kleinberg et al., 2017).

CONCLUSION

This study successfully demonstrates the application of big data analytics, especially the knowledge discovery in databases (KDD) process to extract and discover knowledge from the admission database of Benue State Polytechnic (Benpoly) in Nigeria. An application-based structural causal model (SCM) ontological framework was designed to represent the admission process in the Nigerian polytechnic education system, leveraging the SCM's ability to identify causal relations among features. The SCMO was employed to identify features causing fairness bias in the automated machine learning (ML) predictions and local interpretable model-agnostic explanations (LIME) framework. By constraining and ablating these biased features, the proposed fair-LIME framework produced more stable and fair explanations compared to the original LIME framework, with improved prediction accuracy (91% vs. 89%) and F1 scores (95% vs. 94%).

The main contribution of this study is the integration of a qualitative SCMO with quantitative ML and LIME methods to enforce fairness in explanations. This approach addresses the problem of biased explanations generated by automated ML and LIME frameworks when based on patterns learned from datasets that violate fairness. The fair-LIME framework demonstrates the importance of incorporating domain knowledge through ontologies to identify and mitigate biases in ML explanations. However, a limitation of the fair-LIME framework is its context-specificity, as the SCMO is derived from the background knowledge of a particular process. Therefore, the framework can only be extrapolated to similar contexts, and different contexts would require modeling new SCMO for each process before applying the fair-LIME framework.

REFERENCES

Abd Razak, S., Nazari, N. H. M., & Al-Dhaqm, A. (2020). Data anonymization using pseudonym system to preserve data privacy. *IEEE Access : Practical Innovations, Open Solutions*, 8, 43256–43264. DOI:10.1109/ACCESS.2020.2977117

Abu-Elkheir, M., Hayajneh, M., & Ali, N. A. (2013). Data management for the internet of things: Design primitives and solution. *Sensors (Basel)*, 13(11), 15582–15612. DOI:10.3390/s131115582 PMID:24240599

Ahmed, G. (2021). Improving IoT privacy, data protection and security concerns. *International Journal of Technology, Innovation and Management (IJTIM)*, 1(1).

Al-Ruithe, M., & Benkhelifa, E. (2017). Cloud data governance maturity model. Proceedings of the Second International Conference on Internet of Things, Data and Cloud Computing.

Aloisioa, G., Fiorea, S., Foster, I., & Williams, D. (2013). *Scientific big data analytics challenges at large scale. Proceedings of Big Data and Extreme-scale Computing*. BDEC.

Angerschmid, A., Zhou, J., Theuermann, K., Chen, F., & Holzinger, A. (2022). Fairness and explanation in AI-informed decision making. *Machine Learning and Knowledge Extraction*, 4(2), 556–579. DOI:10.3390/make4020026

Ankan, A., Wortel, I. M., & Textor, J. (2021). Testing graphical causal models using the R package "dagitty". *Current Protocols*, 1(2), e45. DOI:10.1002/cpz1.45 PMID:33592130

Ayem, G. T., Ajibesin, A., Iorliam, A., & Nsang, A. S. (2023a). A mixed framework for causal impact analysis under confounding and selection biases: A focus on Egra dataset. *International Journal of Information Technology : an Official Journal of Bharati Vidyapeeth's Institute of Computer Applications and Management*. Advance online publication. DOI:10.1007/s41870-023-01490-6

Ayem, G. T., Ajibesin, A., Iorliam, A., & Nsang, A. S. (2023b). A mixed framework for causal impact analysis under confounding and selection biases: A focus on Egra dataset. *International Journal of Information Technology : an Official Journal of Bharati Vidyapeeth's Institute of Computer Applications and Management*, 1–18. DOI:10.1007/s41870-023-01490-6

Ayem, G. T., Asilkan, O., & Iorliam, A. (2023). Design and Validation of Structural Causal Model: A Focus on EGRA Dataset. *Journal of Computing Theories and Applications*, 1(2), 37–54. DOI:10.33633/jcta.v1i2.9304

Ayem, G. T., Asilkan, O., Iorliam, A., Ibrahim, R., & Thandekkattu, S. G. (2023). Causal Inference Estimates with Backdoor Adjustment Condition vs. the Unconfoundedness Assumption: A Comparative Analysis Study of the Structural Causal Model and the Potential Outcome Frameworks.

Ayem, G. T., Nsang, A. S., Igoche, B. I., & Naankang, G. (2023). Design and Validation of Structural Causal Model: A focus on SENSE-EGRA Datasets. *International Journal of Advanced Science Computing and Engineering*, 5(3), 257–268. DOI:10.62527/ijasce.5.3.177

Ayem, G. T., Thandekkattu, S. G., Nsang, A. S., & Fonkam, M. (2023). Structural Causal Model Design and Causal Impact Analysis: A Case of SENSE-EGRA Dataset. International Conference on Communication and Computational Technologies. DOI:10.1007/978-981-99-3485-0_4

Balagopalan, A., Zhang, H., Hamidieh, K., Hartvigsen, T., Rudzicz, F., & Ghassemi, M. (2022). The road to explainability is paved with bias: Measuring the fairness of explanations. Proceedings of the 2022 ACM Conference on Fairness, Accountability, and Transparency.

Budzianowski, J., Kaczmarek-Majer, K., Rzeźniczak, J., Słomczyński, M., Wichrowski, F., Hiczkiewicz, D., Musielak, B., Grydz, Ł., Hiczkiewicz, J., & Burchardt, P. (2023). Machine learning model for predicting late recurrence of atrial fibrillation after catheter ablation. *Scientific Reports*, 13(1), 15213. DOI:10.1038/s41598-023-42542-y PMID:37709859

Chen, M.-S., Han, J., & Yu, P. S. (1996). Data mining: An overview from a database perspective. *IEEE Transactions on Knowledge and Data Engineering*, 8(6), 866–883. DOI:10.1109/69.553155

Cinelli, C., Kumor, D., Chen, B., Pearl, J., & Bareinboim, E. (2019). Sensitivity analysis of linear structural causal models. International conference on machine learning.

Efron, B., Hastie, T., Johnstone, I., & Tibshirani, R. (2004). Least angle regression.

Elkin, C., & Witherspoon, S. (2019). Machine learning can boost the value of wind energy. *deep mind field study*.

Etzion, D., & Aragon-Correa, J. A. (2016). *Big data, management, and sustainability: Strategic opportunities ahead* (Vol. 29). Sage Publications Sage CA.

Feldman, M., Friedler, S. A., Moeller, J., Scheidegger, C., & Venkatasubramanian, S. (2015, August). Certifying and removing disparate impact. In *proceedings of the 21th ACM SIGKDD international conference on knowledge discovery and data mining* (pp. 259-268). DOI:10.1145/2783258.2783311

Fernández-Delgado, M., Cernadas, E., Barro, S., & Amorim, D. (2014). Do we need hundreds of classifiers to solve real world classification problems? *Journal of Machine Learning Research*, 15(1), 3133–3181.

Gaudel, R., Galárraga, L., Delaunay, J., Rozé, L., & Bhargava, V. (2022). s-LIME: Reconciling locality and fidelity in linear explanations. International Symposium on Intelligent Data Analysis. DOI:10.1007/s00146-020-00971-7

Greenland, S., Pearl, J., & Robins, J. M. (1999). Causal diagrams for epidemiologic research. *Epidemiology (Cambridge, Mass.)*, 10(1), 37–48. DOI:10.1097/00001648-199901000-00008 PMID:9888278

Harding, E. L., Vanto, J. J., Clark, R., Hannah Ji, L., & Ainsworth, S. C. (2019). Understanding the scope and impact of the california consumer privacy act of 2018. *Journal of Data Protection & Privacy*, 2(3), 234–253. DOI:10.69554/TCFN5165

Jung, T., Li, X.-Y., Wan, Z., & Wan, M. (2014). Control cloud data access privilege and anonymity with fully anonymous attribute-based encryption. *IEEE Transactions on Information Forensics and Security*, 10(1), 190–199. DOI:10.1109/TIFS.2014.2368352

Karimi, A.-H., Schölkopf, B., & Valera, I. (2021). Algorithmic recourse: from counterfactual explanations to interventions. Proceedings of the 2021 ACM conference on fairness, accountability, and transparency.

Kizilcec, R. F., & Lee, H. (2022). Algorithmic fairness in education. In *The ethics of artificial intelligence in education* (pp. 174–202). Routledge. DOI:10.4324/9780429329067-10

Kleinberg, J., Mullainathan, S., & Raghavan, M. (2016). Inherent trade-offs in the fair determination of risk scores. *arXiv preprint arXiv:1609.05807*.

Kumar, S., Sharma, D., Rao, S., Lim, W. M., & Mangla, S. K. (2022). Past, present, and future of sustainable finance: Insights from big data analytics through machine learning of scholarly research. *Annals of Operations Research*, 1–44. DOI:10.1007/s10479-021-04410-8 PMID:35002001

Kusner, M. J., Loftus, J., Russell, C., & Silva, R. (2017). Counterfactual fairness. *Advances in Neural Information Processing Systems*, 30.

Larose, D. T., & Larose, C. D. (2014). *Discovering knowledge in data: an introduction to data mining* (Vol. 4). John Wiley & Sons. DOI:10.1002/9781118874059

Lucivero, F. (2020). Big data, big waste? A reflection on the environmental sustainability of big data initiatives. *Science and Engineering Ethics*, 26(2), 1009–1030. DOI:10.1007/s11948-019-00171-7 PMID:31893331

Luyckx, M., & Reins, L. (2022). The Future of Farming: The (Non)-Sense of Big Data Predictive Tools for Sustainable EU Agriculture. *Sustainability (Basel)*, 14(20), 12968. DOI:10.3390/su142012968

Ma, M., Wang, P., & Chu, C.-H. (2013). Data management for internet of things: Challenges, approaches and opportunities. 2013 IEEE International conference on green computing and communications and IEEE Internet of Things and IEEE cyber, physical and social computing.

Marinakis, V. (2020). Big data for energy management and energy-efficient buildings. *Energies*, 13(7), 1555. DOI:10.3390/en13071555

Markus, K. A. (2021). Causal effects and counterfactual conditionals: Contrasting Rubin, Lewis and Pearl. *Economics and Philosophy*, 37(3), 441–461. DOI:10.1017/S0266267120000437

Meyes, R., Lu, M., de Puiseau, C. W., & Meisen, T. (2019). Ablation studies in artificial neural networks. *arXiv preprint arXiv:1901.08644*.

Miller, J. C. (2013). *Laser ablation: principles and applications* (Vol. 28). Springer Science & Business Media.

Mini, G. V., & Viji, K. A. (2017). A comprehensive cloud security model with enhanced key management, access control and data anonymization features. *International Journal of Communication Networks and Information Security*, 9(2), 263.

Misra, N., Dixit, Y., Al-Mallahi, A., Bhullar, M. S., Upadhyay, R., & Martynenko, A. (2020). IoT, big data, and artificial intelligence in agriculture and food industry. *IEEE Internet of Things Journal*, 9(9), 6305–6324. DOI:10.1109/JIOT.2020.2998584

Murray, E. A. (1996). What have ablation studies told us about the neural substrates of stimulus memory? Seminars in Neuroscience.

Onyekwelu, R. U., & Obikeze, A. J. (2023). *E-Administration And Service Delivery: A Study Of Joint Admissions And Matriculation Board*. JAMB.

Papenmeier, A., Englebienne, G., & Seifert, C. (2019). How model accuracy and explanation fidelity influence user trust. *arXiv preprint arXiv:1907.12652*.

Pearl, J. (2000). Models, reasoning and inference. *Cambridge, UK: Cambridge University Press.*

Pearl, J. (2009). Causal inference in statistics: An overview. *Statistics Surveys,* 3(none), 96–146. DOI:10.1214/09-SS057

Pearl, J. (2009). *Causality.* Cambridge university press. DOI:10.1017/CBO9780511803161

Pearl, J. (2019). The seven tools of causal inference, with reflections on machine learning. *Communications of the ACM,* 62(3), 54–60. DOI:10.1145/3241036

Pearl, J., & Mackenzie, D. (2018). *The book of why: the new science of cause and effect.* Basic books.

Rathore, M. M., Ahmad, A., Paul, A., & Rho, S. (2016). Urban planning and building smart cities based on the internet of things using big data analytics. *Computer Networks,* 101, 63–80. DOI:10.1016/j.comnet.2015.12.023

Ribeiro, M. T., Singh, S., & Guestrin, C. (2016). Why should i trust you?" Explaining the predictions of any classifier. Proceedings of the 22nd ACM SIGKDD international conference on knowledge discovery and data mining.

Saberi, S., Kouhizadeh, M., Sarkis, J., & Shen, L. (2019). Blockchain technology and its relationships to sustainable supply chain management. *International Journal of Production Research,* 57(7), 2117–2135. DOI:10.1080/00207543.2018.1533261

Sazu, M. H., & Jahan, S. A. (2022). High efficiency public transportation system: role of big data in making recommendations. *Journal of process management and new technologies, 10*(3-4), 9-21.

Schoeffer, J., & Kuehl, N. (2021). Appropriate fairness perceptions? On the effectiveness of explanations in enabling people to assess the fairness of automated decision systems. Companion Publication of the 2021 Conference on Computer Supported Cooperative Work and Social Computing. DOI:10.1145/3462204.3481742

erban, R.-A. (2017). The impact of big data, sustainability, and digitalization on company performance. *Studies in Business and Economics,* 12(3), 181–189. DOI:10.1515/sbe-2017-0045

Sharma, S., Henderson, J., & Ghosh, J. (2020). CERTIFAI: A common framework to provide explanations and analyse the fairness and robustness of black-box models. Proceedings of the AAAI/ACM Conference on AI, Ethics, and Society. DOI:10.3233/JIFS-202503

Sheikholeslami, S. (2019). Ablation programming for machine learning.

Sheikholeslami, S., Meister, M., Wang, T., Payberah, A. H., Vlassov, V., & Dowling, J. (2021). Autoablation: Automated parallel ablation studies for deep learning. Proceedings of the 1st Workshop on Machine Learning and Systems. PMID:33923270

Slack, D., Hilgard, S., Jia, E., Singh, S., & Lakkaraju, H. (2020, February). Fooling lime and shap: Adversarial attacks on post hoc explanation methods. In *Proceedings of the AAAI/ACM Conference on AI, Ethics, and Society* (pp. 180-186). DOI:10.1145/3375627.3375830

Song, M., Cen, L., Zheng, Z., Fisher, R., Liang, X., Wang, Y., & Huisingh, D. (2017). How would big data support societal development and environmental sustainability? Insights and practices. *Journal of Cleaner Production*, 142, 489–500. DOI:10.1016/j.jclepro.2016.10.091

Stefanowski, J., Krawiec, K., & Wrembel, R. (2017). Exploring complex and big data. *International Journal of Applied Mathematics and Computer Science*, 27(4), 669–679. DOI:10.1515/amcs-2017-0046

Tang, S., Razeghi, O., Kapoor, R., Alhusseini, M. I., Fazal, M., Rogers, A. J., Rodrigo Bort, M., Clopton, P., Wang, P. J., Rubin, D. L., Narayan, S. M., & Baykaner, T. (2022). Machine learning–enabled multimodal fusion of intra-atrial and body surface signals in prediction of atrial fibrillation ablation outcomes. *Circulation: Arrhythmia and Electrophysiology*, 15(8), e010850. DOI:10.1161/CIRCEP.122.010850 PMID:35867397

Velmurugan, M., Ouyang, C., Moreira, C., & Sindhgatta, R. (2021). Developing a fidelity evaluation approach for interpretable machine learning. *arXiv preprint arXiv:2106.08492*.

Vipin, P.-N. T. M. S. (2006). *Introduction to data mining*.

Voss, W. G. (2016). European union data privacy law reform: General data protection regulation, privacy shield, and the right to delisting. *Business Lawyer*, 72(1), 221–234.

Wachter, S., Mittelstadt, B., & Russell, C. (2017). Counterfactual explanations without opening the black box: Automated decisions and the GDPR. *SSRN*, 31, 841. DOI:10.2139/ssrn.3063289

Wang, F., & Rudin, C. (2015). Falling rule lists. Artificial intelligence and statistics.

Williamson, B. (2017). Big data in education: The digital future of learning, policy and practice.

Yang, C., Yu, M., Hu, F., Jiang, Y., & Li, Y. (2017). Utilizing cloud computing to address big geospatial data challenges. *Computers, Environment and Urban Systems*, 61, 120–128. DOI:10.1016/j.compenvurbsys.2016.10.010

Ye, N. (2003). *The handbook of data mining*. CRC Press. DOI:10.1201/b12469

Yeh, C.-K., Hsieh, C.-Y., Suggala, A., Inouye, D. I., & Ravikumar, P. K. (2019). On the (in) fidelity and sensitivity of explanations. *Advances in Neural Information Processing Systems*, 32.

Zhao, Y., Wang, Y., & Derr, T. (2023). Fairness and explainability: Bridging the gap towards fair model explanations. Proceedings of the AAAI Conference on Artificial Intelligence.

Zhou, B., Sun, Y., Bau, D., & Torralba, A. (2018). Revisiting the importance of individual units in cnns via ablation. *arXiv preprint arXiv:1806.02891*.

Zhou, K., Fu, C., & Yang, S. (2016). Big data driven smart energy management: From big data to big insights. *Renewable & Sustainable Energy Reviews*, 56, 215–225. DOI:10.1016/j.rser.2015.11.050

ADDITIONAL READING

Ayem, G. T., Ajibesin, A., Iorliam, A., & Nsang, A. S. (2023a). A mixed framework for causal impact analysis under confounding and selection biases: A focus on Egra dataset. *International Journal of Information Technology : an Official Journal of Bharati Vidyapeeth's Institute of Computer Applications and Management*. Advance online publication. DOI:10.1007/s41870-023-01490-6

Ayem, G. T., Ajibesin, A., Iorliam, A., & Nsang, A. S. (2023b). A mixed framework for causal impact analysis under confounding and selection biases: A focus on Egra dataset. *International Journal of Information Technology : an Official Journal of Bharati Vidyapeeth's Institute of Computer Applications and Management*, 1–18. DOI:10.1007/s41870-023-01490-6

Ayem, G. T., Asilkan, O., & Iorliam, A. (2023). Design and Validation of Structural Causal Model: A Focus on EGRA Dataset. *Journal of Computing Theories and Applications*, 1(2), 37–54. DOI:10.33633/jcta.v1i2.9304

Ayem, G. T., Asilkan, O., Iorliam, A., Ibrahim, R., & Thandekkattu, S. G. (2023). Causal Inference Estimates with Backdoor Adjustment Condition vs. the Unconfoundedness Assumption: A Comparative Analysis Study of the Structural Causal Model and the Potential Outcome Frameworks.

Ayem, G. T., Nsang, A. S., Igoche, B. I., & Naankang, G. (2023). Design and Validation of Structural Causal Model: A focus on SENSE-EGRA Datasets. *International Journal of Advanced Science Computing and Engineering*, 5(3), 257–268. DOI:10.62527/ijasce.5.3.177

Ayem, G. T., Thandekkattu, S. G., Nsang, A. S., & Fonkam, M. (2023). Structural Causal Model Design and Causal Impact Analysis: A Case of SENSE-EGRA Dataset. *International Conference on Communication and Computational Technologies*. DOI:10.1007/978-981-99-3485-0_4

Dodge, J., Liao, Q. V., Zhang, Y., Bellamy, R. K., & Dugan, C. (2019). Explaining models: An empirical study of how explanations impact fairness judgment. Proceedings of the 24th international conference on intelligent user interfaces.

Efron, B., Hastie, T., Johnstone, I., & Tibshirani, R. (2004). Least angle regression.

Etzion, D., & Aragon-Correa, J. A. (2016). *Big data, management, and sustainability: Strategic opportunities ahead* (Vol. 29). Sage Publications Sage CA.

KEY TERMS AND DEFINITIONS

Big Data: Extremely large datasets that may be analyzed computationally to reveal patterns, trends, and associations, especially relating to human behavior and interactions.

Class: A category or set of entities that share common characteristics or attributes within the ontology.

Concept: An abstract idea or a mental symbol, typically representing a class of objects or events within the domain.

Cross-Validation: A statistical method used to estimate the skill of machine learning models. It involves partitioning the data into complementary subsets, performing the analysis on one subset, and validating the analysis on the other subset.

Data Mining: The practice of examining large pre-existing databases in order to generate new information.

Data Warehouse: A storage repository that holds a vast amount of raw data in its native format until it is needed.

Deep Learning: A subset of machine learning where neural networks with many layers (deep neural networks) learn from large amounts of data.

ETL (Extract, Transform, Load): The process of extracting data from various sources, transforming it to fit operational needs, and loading it into a destination database or data warehouse.

Feature Engineering: The process of using domain knowledge to extract features from raw data that make machine learning algorithms work more effectively.

Inference: The process of deriving new information or conclusions from known facts or premises within the ontology.

Instance: A specific realization of a concept or class. For example, "New York City" might be an instance of the class "City".

Interpretable Models: Models that are designed to be easily understood by humans, such as linear regression or decision trees.

Local Explanations: Explanations that pertain to a single prediction or a small region of the input space, rather than the entire model.

Model-Agnostic: Methods or tools that can be applied to any machine learning model without needing to know the inner workings of the model.

Neural Networks: A series of algorithms that attempt to recognize underlying relationships in a set of data through a process that mimics the way the human brain operates.

NoSQL Databases: Non-relational databases that store and retrieve data without requiring a predefined schema, commonly used for large-scale data storage.

Ontology: A formal representation of a set of concepts within a domain and the relationships between those concepts. It is used to reason about the properties of that domain.

Overfitting: A modeling error that occurs when a function is too closely aligned to a limited set of data points, capturing noise along with the underlying pattern.

Perturbation: The process of slightly altering the input data to observe how the model's predictions change, which helps in understanding the model's behavior.

Real-Time Analytics: The practice of examining and analyzing data as it enters a system.

Reinforcement Learning: A type of machine learning where an agent learns to make decisions by performing certain actions and receiving rewards or penalties.

Schema: The structure or blueprint of the ontology, defining the classes, attributes, and relationships.

Structural Model Ontology (SMO): involves defining and structuring the concepts and relationships within a specific domain.

Supervised Learning: A type of machine learning where the model is trained on a labeled dataset, which means that each training example is paired with an output label.

Surrogate Model: A simpler model that is used to approximate a more complex model in a specific region of the input space to provide interpretability.

Unsupervised Learning: A type of machine learning where the model is given data without explicit instructions on what to do with it. The system tries to learn patterns and the structure from the data itself.

Chapter 8
Data Management and Analytics in the Internet of Things (IoT)

Salu George Thandekkattu
https://orcid.org/0000-0003-3957-3554
American University of Nigeria, Nigeria

Gabriel Terna Ayem
https://orcid.org/0000-0001-9889-0184
American University of Nigeria, Nigeria

Sandip Rakshit
https://orcid.org/0000-0001-5735-983X
Rabat Business School, Morocco

ABSTRACT

This chapter provides a concise overview of the key concepts and considerations in data management and analytics in IoT. IoT data management involves collecting, storing, processing, and analyzing the vast amounts of data interconnected devices generate. Challenges such as scalability, data quality, etc., must be addressed to ensure that IoT systems can efficiently handle the high volume of data. Analytics techniques such as machine learning, predictive analytics, etc., play a crucial role in extracting meaningful insights from IoT data. These techniques enable organizations to uncover hidden patterns, predict future events, and more. However, interoperability, privacy, and data quality pose significant challenges. Standardization efforts, security measures, etc., are essential to overcome these challenges and realize the transformative potential of IoT data-driven insights. Thus, effective data management and analytics are essential for organizations to leverage the vast amounts of data

DOI: 10.4018/979-8-3693-5498-8.ch008

generated by IoT devices and drive innovation.

INTRODUCTION

The Internet of Things (IoT) has transformed the way we interact with the world around us. With billions of interconnected devices in organizations and industries generating vast amounts of data via sensors on a network or WIFI, the need for effective data management and analytics in IoT has become paramount (Diène et al., 2020). Thus, with the advent of low-cost miniaturized smart devices, such as sensors, and wireless broadband networks, it means that all devices, small or big can be integrated and connected. Further, the advancement in current digital intelligence, makes it possible for these devices to be monitored, control, share status, and communicate with each other. Thus, all these devices that constitute IoT can be collected, integrated, and analyzed, thereby improving the efficiency of the processes involved in doing business in an organization or in an industrial setting. Thus, leading to better control of the business process and new ways to generate revenue for the organization. Therefore, IoT management and analytics processing speed potential make it important for quick and effective decision-making. Hence, these changes that are brought about by the management and analytics of IoT, can make possible part of the overall digital transformation that is required and sought by many businesses and industries around the world. By offering detailed high-quality and real-time data, IoT data management and analytics possess the potential to enhance understanding of the processes in an organization and help make operations more effective through the analysis of the data that emanates from the various devices connected in the organization. Thus, unlocking new ways of generating revenues for the organization. Further, IoT data management and analytics can also provide business insight into the wider supply chain, which will permit organizations to sufficiently coordinate their activities, and improve their input efficiency.

Every IoT project commences with the collection, storage and visualization of raw data. However, the economic gain is achieved by the decision of the management to optimize extant processes and convey new products and services to the market for their customers or consumers who are the end users of these products/services. The organization can achieve these technically by carrying out an in-depth analysis, and processing of the aggregated data collected from different devices that make up their operations. Albeit for every significant solution, these operations tend to be unique – for instance, in agriculture, the optimization of storage space for crops that are harvested may be important and be fundamentally different from bringing about transactional data in a smart grid in an electric company or managing a forklift in a logistic company. The analytic capabilities of an IoT device may range from a simple emergency alert system to an advanced machine learning system that can predict or detect anomalies in operations such as the failure of a turbine. The potential of managing and analyzing IoT can be seen in IoT solutions that require automated and zero-touch devices that are controlled at the scale of millions of devices connected. Therefore, proactive maintenance and the requisite predictive analysis are key to bringing about success in these industries. Also, the management of IoT devices should be able to classify devices into different context states, automatically. Otherwise, their solutions may be considered ineffective. Also, another solution that IoT management and analytics bring on board is to help organizations to manage their network infrastructure, and endpoint remotely. Thus, with the implementation of an IoT device management solution framework, strategic managers can monitor the performance and well-being of connected devices on their network, while remotely configuring and updating them as well. Further, the experiences of their clients/customers provide them with better visibility of how their devices are performing. Thus, as the IoT space rapidly expands and evolves, its potential to impact digital life continues to grow as well. Hence, making the effective management of IoT devices fundamental to any IoT solution. Therefore, the provision, authentication configuration, controlling, monitoring, and maintenance of IoT devices in their number is now a sin-qua-non. IoT device management solutions could involve a combination of access control, service quality, and data security systems for the IoT devices. Hence, many features are commonly integrated with this process of IoT management. These features are: (i) Identity and Access Management – this feature ensures that only authorized users have access to the IoT device data. (ii) Service Quality – this feature ensures that the device can perform optimally and offer the requisite service it was designed for. (iii) Security of Data – this IoT management feature ensures that valuable data derived from this device is well protected from unauthorized users.

IoT Data Management and Traditional Data-based Management Systems

Nowadays, business organizations require solutions that can offer efficient, collective management of different data at a single level. To this end, IoT data management and analytics systems are developed on top of platforms of enterprise management systems. They may comprise traditional databases, data warehouses, analytics, big data management systems, etc. These elements interact with each other in order to produce a unified data platform. Thus, offering IoT data management and analytic tools that can be applied in enterprise applications and analysis tools and algorithms for the purpose of processing this data. Even though many modern tools can automate a lot of management tasks, most database deployments

211

are complex and enormous, such that the inputs and intervention of most database administrators are still required. Thus, increasing the potential for errors. Thus, one of the goals of the new IoT data management and analytics technology is to reduce to a greater extent the manual processing that accompanies these processes to produce an automated database. The contribution of this book chapter is in the (i) Exploration of the strategies and solutions of data management and analytics in IoT, (ii) The challenges associated with handling IoT data, and the role of advanced analytics techniques in deriving actionable insights from IoT data.

Strategies and Solutions of IoT Data Management and Analytics

Data management is a critical component of IoT systems as it involves collecting, storing, processing, and analyzing data generated by IoT devices (Ahmed et al., 2017; Diène et al., 2020). With the proliferation of IoT devices across various domains such as smart cities, healthcare, agriculture, manufacturing, and transportation, the volume, variety, and velocity of data generated have increased exponentially. Effective data management ensures that IoT systems can handle the massive influx of data efficiently and derive meaningful insights to drive decision-making and innovation (Brous et al., 2017). Thus, the changes brought about by IoT data management and analytics are a part of the entire digital transformation that a lot of business organizations are currently working on. By offering a very detailed real-time data, IoT data management and analytics can aid business organizations to effectively understand their business processes. Thus, making their operations smooth, and efficient and helping boost revenue. Hence some of the strategies and solutions used by IoT data management and analytics from extant works are:

1. *Data Preparation for Machine Use:* Heterogeneous data that is received or collected from different things (devices), such as sensor readings, video streams, and log files. Managing this heterogeneous data requires flexible and scalable data collection frameworks that need to be structured, sorted, filtered, and transformed by the IoT data management and analytics process. Thus, depending on the data input that is required, this data can either be redirected to some applications for which they are needed or they may just be directly processed by the platform operators, from which vertical solution can be developed based on it (Chiusano et al., 2021; Siow et al., 2018).

2. *Data Normalization:* This strategy is a very crucial part of the IoT data management process. The best IoT data analytics system is designed using individual analytical modules without any knowledge of the physical meaning of the data that is involved. Usually, device drivers abstract the values they receive based

on the attributes of the protocols of communication. This information is then fed into a model, where it is scaled and transformed for consistency, after which it can freely be dispersed to other modules, parts, or platforms (Li, 2020; Siow et al., 2018).

3. *Big Data:* The sheer volume of data produced by IoT devices necessitates efficient data collection mechanisms to handle the influx in real-time. Thus, with these IoT devices streaming out homogenous information that is overwhelming, there is a need to have an efficient data management strategy to handle this quantum of IoT data. Take a financial institution for example where at every given second, thousands of transactions within the IoT data management are carried out on a daily basis. Thus, all IoT data needs an optimal process method in order to perform this enormous amount of data processing with a single server, and better performance when servers in a cluster are combined using a distributed structure (Li, 2020; Siow et al., 2018).

4. *Provision of Domain-Specific Architecture:* for IoT Data management to be successful, it will require that a specific IoT architecture be deployed. Thus, this optimal architecture should be able to execute queries, perform expressions, and process languages that are exclusively developed for the natural understanding of the data that is normalized and circulated on the system platform (Fawzy et al., 2022). Additionally, the built-in environment used for development goes a long way in simplifying the data processing stages, and without it, it will be difficult to monitor and control the system (Marjani et al., 2017).

5. *Application of Machine Learning Techniques:* To uncover variable relations between real-time data, previous data, and the data that is recently collected is an important process in any successful IoT platform. Thus, with the availability of over 20 ML algorithms, with hundreds of parameters, it is possible for any IoT data analyst to be satisfied when applying these techniques (Adi et al., 2020). Further, at the level of implementation, the analyst is able to visualize the dataset and set it up for training in line with the given logic (Farooq et al., 2023).

6. *Access to Real-time Analytics:* time series data types are common data within an IoT space. Thus, the analysis of them in real-time is also essential during the time of processing. Hence, it enables one to detect anomalies, predict graph behavior, and also carry out the classification of the time series data, irrespective of the meaning ascribed to the data or the number of metrics in them (Jeba & Rathi, 2021; Verma et al., 2017). Also, the support for streams enables the seamless processing of large amounts of data that could not ordinarily fit in a memory space (Rathore et al., 2018).

7. ***Management of Events:*** One of the strategies of IoT data management and analytics is its capability of monitoring events and processing modules. Module processing may include such activities such as sorting, filtering, de-duplication, aggregating, correlation, masking, validation, root cause searches, and enrichment (Diène et al., 2020; Marjani et al., 2017). Also, a lot of analytic modules are capable of supporting event activation and can be activated with events that emanate from external IoT sources or from objects created by users, and process models.

8. ***Provision of Dashboards for Data Analytics:*** When one visualizes an IoT platform, nothing significant can be seen except counters, maps, tables, and graphs. Thus, modern IoT data management and analytics are capable of competing with the best business intelligence systems when it comes to creating statistical, analytical, and data mining interfaces (Padmavathi et al., 2020). Thus, with it, one can gather data, discover new variable relations, and discover new ways to save energy consumption or perform equipment downtime.

9. ***Focuses on Profits, and Results:*** IoT data management and analytic platforms do not physically bring income as they were in business organizations, albeit it enables businesspeople to focus on making profits instead of solving the problem of infrastructure. Overall, the development and deployment of an IoT data management and analytic platform for customers usually involves just a couple of months, after which it takes also a couple of months for the organization to begin to experience turnover in terms of the economic gains recorded by its implementation within the organization (Çela, Fonkam, & Potluri, 2024; Çela, Vajjhala, & Eappen, 2024; Jiao et al., 2018).

10. ***Formation of digital twins:*** The object and process model engine of an IoT data management and analytic platform permits for the creation of digital twins of physical assets and their services (Al-Ali et al., 2020). These models can make use of business rules to make decisions when essential events happen automatically. Every one of the models is attached to some devices, data sources, or other models of lower hierarchy within the digital IoT data management analytic enterprise (Poornima et al., 2023).

Role of Predictive Analytics in IoT

Analytics plays a crucial role in extracting actionable insights from IoT data to enable informed decision-making and drive business value. Traditional analytics techniques may not be sufficient to handle the unique characteristics of IoT data, such as its high volume, velocity, and variety. Therefore, advanced analytics techniques such as machine learning, deep learning, descriptive, prescriptive, predictive, and cognitive analytics are increasingly being used to analyze IoT data and uncover hidden patterns, correlations, and trends (Ahmed et al., 2017; Çela, 2022, Çela, 2024, Mishra et al., 2020; ur Rehman et al., 2019).

Machine learning algorithms, for example, can analyze large volumes of IoT data to identify anomalies, predict equipment failures, optimize resource utilization, and improve operational efficiency. Deep learning techniques, such as convolutional neural networks (CNNs) and recurrent neural networks (RNNs), can process unstructured data such as images, videos, and text generated by IoT devices to extract valuable insights and facilitate decision-making (Adi et al., 2020; Moin, 2021).

Predictive analytics leverages historical IoT data to forecast future events, trends, and behaviors, enabling organizations to anticipate and proactively address emerging challenges and opportunities. These algorithms recommend actions based on predictive analytics to optimize outcomes. For example, in a smart city, prescriptive analytics can optimize traffic flow based on predicted congestion patterns (Rathore et al., 2018; Tönjes et al., 2014). Also, predictive maintenance models can analyze sensor data from industrial equipment to predict when maintenance is required, thereby minimizing downtime and reducing maintenance costs (Mistry et al., 2020).

In cognitive analytics advanced AI techniques, such as deep learning, enable more complex analyses, such as image and speech recognition, which are crucial for applications like autonomous vehicles and smart surveillance systems (Hwang & Chen, 2017; Mishra et al., 2014).

In addition to descriptive and predictive analytics, prescriptive analytics provides actionable recommendations to optimize decision-making and improve outcomes in IoT systems. Prescriptive analytics combines historical data, real-time sensor data, and optimization algorithms to recommend the best course of action in various scenarios. For example, prescriptive analytics can optimize energy consumption in smart buildings, route optimization in transportation networks, and inventory management in supply chains (ur Rehman et al., 2019).

IoT Predictive Analysis Implementation Challenges

Various challenges tend to hinder the successful implementation of IoT predictive analysis. Some of the commonly identified ones are:

1. **Data:** The availability and quality of the data greatly affect the model performance. If the data available is of high quality, and error free, the model performance tends to increase, while the reverse is the case when the data available is of poor quality, and full of errors.

2. **Business Processes:** In business organizations, it is important to understand who is doing what especially when things are not going well, so that people can be held responsible for their actions. Thus, business processes are crucial factors in performing predictive analysis in the model, as these processes help highlight areas that the organization needs to focus on for improvement or performance enhancement of the model.

3. **Expertise Skills and Knowledge:** In the creation and interpretation of a predictive model, the skills and knowledge of expertise are very crucial, as only mathematical calculations in the model do not suffice. Most of the time, organizations have their own closed and universal algorithms that cater to all their sensor devices. The system for every sensor can juxtapose the actual values obtained from the sensor and the ones generated by the model at each time. Thus, the diagnostic rules in the model can analyze the value for the entire sensor deviation, and each sensor variation in the model. Thus, the outcome from the model is what experts are required to interpret and analyze.

Challenges of IoT Data Management and Analytics

Nowadays, IoT data management and analytics issues are led mainly by the constant increase in the volume of data generated from devices, and the constant changes that occur in an organization. Thus, with IoT data management and analytics techniques, organizations can access different data which is processed faster and at a greater volume. Thus, requiring a more effective management tool. Some of the challenges faced by business organizations are:

1. *Issue of Contending with Oversized Data:* One of the key challenges in data management for IoT is the sheer scale of data generated by interconnected devices on a daily (Ma et al., 2013). Traditional data management systems may struggle to cope with the high volume and velocity of data streams generated by IoT devices (Ma et al., 2013). Therefore, IoT platforms must employ scalable and distributed data storage and processing technologies to handle the influx of data effectively (Abbasi et al., 2017). Additionally, data management in IoT requires robust security measures to protect sensitive data from unauthorized access and ensure data integrity and confidentiality (Ahad et al., 2020).

2. *Data Quality Issue:* Another important aspect of data management in IoT is data quality. IoT data often comes from diverse sources and may be noisy, incomplete, or inconsistent (Abbasi et al., 2017). Poor data quality can lead to inaccurate insights and flawed decision-making. Therefore, IoT systems must

implement data cleansing, normalization, and validation techniques to ensure that the data used for analysis is accurate, reliable, and trustworthy.

3. *Absence of Analytical Data Presentation:* The collection and storage of data by organizations usually comes from different sources, and devices, such as sensors, social networks, smart devices, cameras, etc. Albeit, these data can become useless when their whereabouts, and how they can be processed and used are not known. Further, IoT data management and analytics most time require scaling and performance to generate useful insight to the data collected (Ma et al., 2013).

4. *Inconsistency in Performance Level for IoT Data Management and Analytic Systems:* The constant collection, storage, and use of data from different devices by an organization is on the increase. Thus, the challenge of balancing or maintaining a peak response rate within the ever-growing data layer is usually a daunting challenge for many organizations. Hence, the data analyst's task is to constantly monitor the database response queries adjust the indexes in line with the query changes, and further make sure that there is no decrease in the efficiency of the system (Fawzy et al., 2022).

5. *Changing Data Requirements Data Privacy and Security Issues:* Social regulations are complex, and they usually cut across jurisdictions, while constantly evolving. Thus, organizations should be able to constantly keep pace with these requirements by analyzing data to determine which selection applies to the requirement. Further, extra attention regarding individual privacy via unauthorized third-party identification of individual data must be guided since it directly contravenes international data privacy laws (Nadikattu, 2018). As IoT devices collect vast amounts of personal and sensitive data, raising concerns about privacy, consent, and data protection. Unauthorized access, data breaches, and cyber-attacks pose significant risks to IoT systems and their users. Thus, ensuring data security through encryption, both in transit and at rest, is critical (Li, 2020; Verma et al., 2017). Further, Implementing robust access control mechanisms to prevent unauthorized access to sensitive IoT data (Diène et al., 2020). Also, techniques to anonymize data can help protect user privacy while still allowing for data analysis (Ren et al., 2021). Other security measures include authentication, provision of a secure communication protocol etc. (Babar et al., 2018; Diène et al., 2020; Wazid et al., 2019). Therefore, robust security measures such as data encryption, access control, anonymization, authentication, and secure communication protocols are essential to safeguard IoT data and ensure user trust and confidence (Ahmed, 2021; Tawalbeh et al., 2020).

6. *Data Transformation and Processing Requirements:* Data emanating from different devices in the organization are by themselves of little meaning or significance, except when they are transformed or processed. Data transformation

and processing can consume a lot of man-effects. However, it is expected that experts use the data form for analysis so that the data does not lose its value over time (Sasaki, 2021). Further, to reduce latency and bandwidth usage, data processing can occur at the edge, near the data source, rather than in centralized cloud servers (Anagnostopoulos et al., 2022; Galanopoulos et al., 2020). Also, IoT applications often require real-time data processing. Stream processing frameworks like Apache Kafka and Apache Flink enable real-time analytics and event detection (Liu et al., 2016; Tönjes et al., 2014).

7. ***The Need for Efficient Data Storage:*** Nowadays when great emphasis is placed on data management and analytics issues, many organizations store their data on serval systems, such as data warehouses, and data lakes that are unstructured, where data in any format can be stored. Thus, this has brought about the need for data analysts to convert data quickly and effortlessly from one format to another while creating models that can be easily adapted by similar but different contexts, or analyses (Li, 2020; Sasaki, 2021).

8. ***Constant Optimization of IT Agility and Cost Requirement:*** With the presence of cloud base IoT data management, and Analytics, business organizations have the prerogative of choosing whether to collect, store and analyze data on-premises, in the cloud or a hybrid of them (part on the cloud and part on-premises). Thus, to reduce IT agility, and maximize cost, organizations should assess the similarities between the cloud and on-premise storage architectures (Padmavathi et al., 2020; Ray, 2016).

9. ***Interoperability Compatibility of Devices Issue:*** One of the main challenges is interoperability and compatibility between different IoT devices, platforms, and protocols. IoT systems often involve heterogeneous devices and technologies, which can hinder data integration and interoperability (Albouq et al., 2022; Noura et al., 2019). Standardization efforts such as the development of common data formats, communication protocols, and interoperability standards are essential to overcome these challenges.

10. ***Scalability and Resource constraints:*** This poses challenges for data management and analytics in IoT (El-Mougy et al., 2019; Hussain, 2017). IoT devices often have limited computational resources, memory, and battery life, which can impact their ability to process and analyze data locally. Edge computing and fog computing paradigms leverage distributed computing resources closer to the edge of the network to overcome these challenges and enable real-time data processing and analytics at the network edge (Buyya & Srirama, 2019; Escamilla-Ambrosio et al., 2018). Also, traditional databases may not suffice for IoT applications. Distributed databases and cloud storage solutions are often employed to ensure scalability (Cai et al., 2016; Diène et al., 2020).

CONCLUSION AND FUTURE RESEARCH DIRECTIONS

In conclusion, data management and analytics play a critical role in unlocking the full potential of the IoT by harnessing the vast amounts of data generated by interconnected devices. Effective data management ensures that IoT systems can handle the massive influx of data efficiently, while advanced analytics techniques enable organizations to derive actionable insights and drive informed decision-making. However, several challenges such as interoperability, security, privacy, scalability, etc., must be addressed to realize the transformative potential of IoT data-driven insights. By overcoming these challenges and leveraging the power of data management and analytics, organizations can unlock new opportunities, drive innovation, and create value in the IoT era. Further, as the IoT landscape evolves, advancements in edge computing, security, 5G integration, interoperability, sustainability, and AI will drive the future of data management and analytics in IoT. These developments will not only enhance the capabilities and applications of IoT but also address the challenges associated with managing and analyzing IoT data effectively. For future direction, consideration shall be made regarding data management and analytic in IoT in areas such as:

1. *Enhanced Edge Computing:* With increased Processing Power future IoT devices will likely have more powerful processors, enabling more complex data analytics directly on the device (Diène et al., 2020). Also, Federated Learning technique (Nguyen et al., 2021; Unal et al., 2021) which involves training machine learning models across decentralized devices while keeping data localized, enhancing privacy and reducing data transmission costs will considered.
2. *Advanced Security Mechanisms:* The Blockchain technology can provide a decentralized and secure framework for IoT data management, ensuring data integrity and transparency (Oktian et al., 2020). Also, the Implementation of zero trust security models can enhance IoT security by continuously verifying every device and user trying to access the network will be a good way of advancing security mechanism (Li et al., 2022).
3. *Integration with 5G:* The future implementation of low latency and high bandwidth via the rollout of 5G connectivity networks will significantly improve data transfer speeds and reduce latency, facilitating real-time analytics and enabling new IoT applications (Diène et al., 2020). Also, 5G will support a massive number of IoT connections, allowing for more extensive deployment of IoT devices (Verma et al., 2017).
4. *Improved Data Interoperability:* The future development and adaptation of standardized protocols and data formats will enhance interoperability between different IoT devices and platforms (Diène et al., 2020). Further, leveraging

ontologies and semantic web technologies to enable better understanding and integration of data from diverse IoT devices in the future will be essential (Khanh Duy et al., 2021).

5. ***Green IoT:*** Soon, research into energy-efficient algorithms and hardware will become increasingly important to minimize the environmental impact of IoT deployments (Marinakis, 2020; Silva et al., 2020; Silva et al., 2018). Also, IoT can play a crucial role in sustainability initiatives, such as smart grids, precision agriculture, and smart water management systems in the future (Bibri, 2018; Diène et al., 2020).

6. ***Advanced AI and Machine Learning Techniques:*** For future data management and analytics of IoT, the development of AI models that provide transparent and understandable explanations for their predictions will be essential for trust and accountability (Jagatheesaperumal et al., 2022; Kumar et al., 2023). Applying reinforcement learning in IoT environments is another area of consideration for future studies that will be able to optimize dynamic and complex systems, such as autonomous driving and robotic process automation (Chen et al., 2021; Farooq et al., 2023).

REFERENCES

Abbasi, M. A., Memon, Z. A., Syed, T. Q., Memon, J., & Alshboul, R. (2017). Addressing the future data management challenges in iot: A proposed framework. *International Journal of Advanced Computer Science and Applications*, 8(5).

Adi, E., Anwar, A., Baig, Z., & Zeadally, S. (2020). Machine learning and data analytics for the IoT. *Neural Computing & Applications*, 32(20), 16205–16233. DOI:10.1007/s00521-020-04874-y

Ahad, M. A., Tripathi, G., Zafar, S., & Doja, F. (2020). IoT data management— Security aspects of information linkage in IoT systems. *Principles of internet of things (IoT) ecosystem: Insight paradigm*, 439-464.

Ahmed, E., Yaqoob, I., Hashem, I. A. T., Khan, I., Ahmed, A. I. A., Imran, M., & Vasilakos, A. V. (2017). The role of big data analytics in Internet of Things. *Computer Networks*, 129, 459–471. DOI:10.1016/j.comnet.2017.06.013

Ahmed, G. (2021). Improving IoT privacy, data protection and security concerns. *International Journal of Technology, Innovation and Management (IJTIM)*, 1(1).

Al-Ali, A.-R., Gupta, R., Zaman Batool, T., Landolsi, T., Aloul, F., & Al Nabulsi, A. (2020). Digital twin conceptual model within the context of internet of things. *Future Internet*, 12(10), 163. DOI:10.3390/fi12100163

Albouq, S. S., Abi Sen, A. A., Almashf, N., Yamin, M., Alshanqiti, A., & Bahbouh, N. M. (2022). A survey of interoperability challenges and solutions for dealing with them in IoT environment. *IEEE Access : Practical Innovations, Open Solutions*, 10, 36416–36428. DOI:10.1109/ACCESS.2022.3162219

Anagnostopoulos, C., Aladwani, T., Alghamdi, I., & Kolomvatsos, K. (2022). Data-driven analytics task management reasoning mechanism in edge computing. *Smart Cities*, 5(2), 562–582. DOI:10.3390/smartcities5020030

Babar, M., Khan, F., Iqbal, W., Yahya, A., Arif, F., Tan, Z., & Chuma, J. M. (2018). A secured data management scheme for smart societies in industrial internet of things environment. *IEEE Access : Practical Innovations, Open Solutions*, 6, 43088–43099. DOI:10.1109/ACCESS.2018.2861421

Bibri, S. E. (2018). The IoT for smart sustainable cities of the future: An analytical framework for sensor-based big data applications for environmental sustainability. *Sustainable Cities and Society*, 38, 230–253. DOI:10.1016/j.scs.2017.12.034

Brous, P., Janssen, M., Schraven, D., Spiegeler, J., & Duzgun, B. C. (2017). *Factors Influencing Adoption of IoT for Data-driven Decision Making in Asset Management Organizations. IoTBDS.*

Cai, H., Xu, B., Jiang, L., & Vasilakos, A. V. (2016). IoT-based big data storage systems in cloud computing: Perspectives and challenges. *IEEE Internet of Things Journal*, 4(1), 75–87. DOI:10.1109/JIOT.2016.2619369

Çela, E. (2022). A summary of the national plan for european integration related with the developments of education system in Albania during 2020-2021. *Euro-Balkan Law and Economics Review*, (1), 71–86.

Çela, E. (2024). Global Agendas in Higher Education and Current Educational Reforms in Albania. In *Global Agendas and Education Reforms: A Comparative Study* (pp. 255–269). Springer. DOI:10.1007/978-981-97-3068-1_13

Çela, E., Fonkam, M. M., & Potluri, R. M. (2024). Risks of AI-Assisted Learning on Student Critical Thinking: A Case Study of Albania. *International Journal of Risk and Contingency Management*, 12(1), 1–19. DOI:10.4018/IJRCM.350185

Çela, E., Vajjhala, N. R., & Eappen, P. (2024). Foundations of Computational Thinking and Problem Solving for Diverse Academic Fields. *Revolutionizing Curricula Through Computational Thinking, Logic, and Problem Solving*, 1-16.

Chen, W., Qiu, X., Cai, T., Dai, H.-N., Zheng, Z., & Zhang, Y. (2021). Deep reinforcement learning for Internet of Things: A comprehensive survey. *IEEE Communications Surveys and Tutorials*, 23(3), 1659–1692. DOI:10.1109/COMST.2021.3073036

Chiusano, S., Cerquitelli, T., Wrembel, R., & Quercia, D. (2021). Breakthroughs on cross-cutting data management, data analytics, and applied data science. *Information Systems Frontiers*, 23(1), 1–7. DOI:10.1007/s10796-020-10091-8

Diène, B., Rodrigues, J. J., Diallo, O., Ndoye, E. H. M., & Korotaev, V. V. (2020). Data management techniques for Internet of Things. *Mechanical Systems and Signal Processing*, 138, 106564. DOI:10.1016/j.ymssp.2019.106564

El-Mougy, A., Al-Shiab, I., & Ibnkahla, M. (2019). Scalable personalized IoT networks. *Proceedings of the IEEE*, 107(4), 695–710. DOI:10.1109/JPROC.2019.2894515

Escamilla-Ambrosio, P., Rodríguez-Mota, A., Aguirre-Anaya, E., Acosta-Bermejo, R., & Salinas-Rosales, M. (2018). Distributing computing in the internet of things: cloud, fog and edge computing overview. NEO 2016: Results of the Numerical and Evolutionary Optimization Workshop NEO 2016 and the NEO Cities 2016 Workshop held on September 20-24, 2016 in Tlalnepantla, Mexico.

Fawzy, D., Moussa, S. M., & Badr, N. L. (2022). The internet of things and architectures of big data analytics: Challenges of intersection at different domains. *IEEE Access : Practical Innovations, Open Solutions*, 10, 4969–4992. DOI:10.1109/ACCESS.2022.3140409

Hussain, M. I. (2017). Internet of Things: challenges and research opportunities. *CSI transactions on ICT, 5*, 87-95.

Hwang, K., & Chen, M. (2017). *Big-data analytics for cloud, IoT and cognitive computing*. John Wiley & Sons.

Jagatheesaperumal, S. K., Pham, Q.-V., Ruby, R., Yang, Z., Xu, C., & Zhang, Z. (2022). Explainable AI over the Internet of Things (IoT): Overview, state-of-the-art and future directions. *IEEE Open Journal of the Communications Society*, 3, 2106–2136. DOI:10.1109/OJCOMS.2022.3215676

Jeba, N., & Rathi, S. (2021). Effective data management and real-time analytics in internet of things. *International Journal of Cloud Computing*, 10(1-2), 112–128. DOI:10.1504/IJCC.2021.113994

Jiao, Y., Wang, P., Feng, S., & Niyato, D. (2018). Profit maximization mechanism and data management for data analytics services. *IEEE Internet of Things Journal*, 5(3), 2001–2014. DOI:10.1109/JIOT.2018.2819706

Khanh Duy, T., Küng, J., & Huu Hanh, H. (2021). Survey on iot data analytics with semantic approaches. The 23rd International Conference on Information Integration and Web Intelligence. DOI:10.1145/3487664.3487785

Li, C. (2020). Information processing in Internet of Things using big data analytics. *Computer Communications*, 160, 718–729. DOI:10.1016/j.comcom.2020.06.020

Li, S., Iqbal, M., & Saxena, N. (2022). Future industry internet of things with zero-trust security. *Information Systems Frontiers*, 1–14. DOI:10.1007/s10796-021-10199-5

Liu, X., Dastjerdi, A., & Buyya, R. (2016). Stream processing in IoT: Foundations, state-of-the-art, and future directions. In *Internet of Things* (pp. 145–161). Elsevier. DOI:10.1016/B978-0-12-805395-9.00008-3

Ma, M., Wang, P., & Chu, C.-H. (2013). Data management for internet of things: Challenges, approaches and opportunities. 2013 IEEE International conference on green computing and communications and IEEE Internet of Things and IEEE cyber, physical and social computing.

Marjani, M., Nasaruddin, F., Gani, A., Karim, A., Hashem, I. A. T., Siddiqa, A., & Yaqoob, I. (2017). Big IoT data analytics: Architecture, opportunities, and open research challenges. *IEEE Access : Practical Innovations, Open Solutions*, 5, 5247–5261. DOI:10.1109/ACCESS.2017.2689040

Mishra, N., Lin, C.-C., & Chang, H.-T. (2014). A cognitive oriented framework for IoT big-data management prospective. 2014 IEEE International Conference on Communiction Problem-solving.

Mishra, S., Mishra, B. K., Tripathy, H. K., & Dutta, A. (2020). Analysis of the role and scope of big data analytics with IoT in health care domain. In *Handbook of data science approaches for biomedical engineering* (pp. 1–23). Elsevier. DOI:10.1016/B978-0-12-818318-2.00001-5

Mistry, I., Tanwar, S., Tyagi, S., & Kumar, N. (2020). Blockchain for 5G-enabled IoT for industrial automation: A systematic review, solutions, and challenges. *Mechanical Systems and Signal Processing*, 135, 106382. DOI:10.1016/j.ymssp.2019.106382

Moin, A. (2021). Data analytics and machine learning methods, techniques and tool for model-driven engineering of smart iot services. 2021 IEEE/ACM 43rd International Conference on Software Engineering: Companion Proceedings (ICSE-Companion).

Nguyen, D. C., Ding, M., Pathirana, P. N., Seneviratne, A., Li, J., & Poor, H. V. (2021). Federated learning for internet of things: A comprehensive survey. *IEEE Communications Surveys and Tutorials*, 23(3), 1622–1658. DOI:10.1109/COMST.2021.3075439

Noura, M., Atiquzzaman, M., & Gaedke, M. (2019). Interoperability in internet of things: Taxonomies and open challenges. *Mobile Networks and Applications*, 24(3), 796–809. DOI:10.1007/s11036-018-1089-9

Oktian, Y. E., Lee, S.-G., & Lee, B.-G. (2020). Blockchain-based continued integrity service for IoT big data management: A comprehensive design. *Electronics (Basel)*, 9(9), 1434. DOI:10.3390/electronics9091434

Padmavathi, K., Deepa, C., & Prabhakaran, P. (2020). Internet of Things (IoT) and Big Data: Data Management, Analytics, Visualization and Decision Making. In *The Internet of Things and Big Data Analytics* (pp. 217–246). Auerbach Publications. DOI:10.1201/9781003036739-10

Poornima, G., Janardhanachari, V., & Sakkari, D. S. (2023). Data Management for IoT and Digital Twin. In *New Approaches to Data Analytics and Internet of Things Through Digital Twin* (pp. 28–45). IGI Global.

Rathore, M. M., Paul, A., Hong, W.-H., Seo, H., Awan, I., & Saeed, S. (2018). Exploiting IoT and big data analytics: Defining smart digital city using real-time urban data. *Sustainable Cities and Society*, 40, 600–610. DOI:10.1016/j.scs.2017.12.022

Ray, D. (2016). Cloud adoption decisions: Benefitting from an integrated perspective. *Electronic Journal of Information Systems Evaluation, 19*(1), 3-21.

Ren, W., Tong, X., Du, J., Wang, N., Li, S., Min, G., & Zhao, Z. (2021). Privacy enhancing techniques in the internet of things using data anonymisation. *Information Systems Frontiers*, 1–12. DOI:10.1007/s10796-021-10116-w

Sasaki, Y. (2021). A survey on IoT big data analytic systems: Current and future. *IEEE Internet of Things Journal*, 9(2), 1024–1036. DOI:10.1109/JIOT.2021.3131724

Silva, B. N., Khan, M., & Han, K. (2020). Integration of Big Data analytics embedded smart city architecture with RESTful web of things for efficient service provision and energy management. *Future Generation Computer Systems*, 107, 975–987. DOI:10.1016/j.future.2017.06.024

Silva, B. N., Khan, M., Jung, C., Seo, J., Muhammad, D., Han, J., Yoon, Y., & Han, K. (2018). Urban planning and smart city decision management empowered by real-time data processing using big data analytics. *Sensors (Basel)*, 18(9), 2994. DOI:10.3390/s18092994 PMID:30205499

Siow, E., Tiropanis, T., & Hall, W. (2018). Analytics for the internet of things: A survey. *ACM Computing Surveys*, 51(4), 1–36. DOI:10.1145/3204947

Tawalbeh, L., Muheidat, F., Tawalbeh, M., & Quwaider, M. (2020). IoT Privacy and security: Challenges and solutions. *Applied Sciences (Basel, Switzerland)*, 10(12), 4102. DOI:10.3390/app10124102

Tönjes, R., Barnaghi, P., Ali, M., Mileo, A., Hauswirth, M., Ganz, F., Ganea, S., Kjærgaard, B., Kuemper, D., & Nechifor, S. (2014). Real time iot stream processing and large-scale data analytics for smart city applications. poster session, European Conference on Networks and Communications.

Verma, S., Kawamoto, Y., Fadlullah, Z. M., Nishiyama, H., & Kato, N. (2017). A survey on network methodologies for real-time analytics of massive IoT data and open research issues. *IEEE Communications Surveys and Tutorials*, 19(3), 1457–1477. DOI:10.1109/COMST.2017.2694469

Wazid, M., Das, A. K., Hussain, R., Succi, G., & Rodrigues, J. J. (2019). Authentication in cloud-driven IoT-based big data environment: Survey and outlook. *Journal of Systems Architecture*, 97, 185–196. DOI:10.1016/j.sysarc.2018.12.005

ADDITIONAL READING

Ayem, G. T., Ajibesin, A., Iorliam, A., & Nsang, A. S. (2023). A mixed framework for causal impact analysis under confounding and selection biases: A focus on Egra dataset. *International Journal of Information Technology : an Official Journal of Bharati Vidyapeeth's Institute of Computer Applications and Management*, 1–18. DOI:10.1007/s41870-023-01490-6

Ayem, G. T., Thandekkattu, S. G., Nsang, A. S., & Fonkam, M. (2023). Structural Causal Model Design and Causal Impact Analysis: A Case of SENSE-EGRA Dataset. In *International Conference on Communication and Computational Technologies* (pp. 39-52). Singapore: Springer Nature Singapore. DOI:10.1007/978-981-99-3485-0_4

Ayem, G. T., Thandekkattu, S. G., & Vajjhala, N. R. (2022). Adopting a Blockchain-Based Algorithmic Model for Electronic Healthcare Records (EHR) in Nigeria. In *Next Generation of Internet of ThingsProceedings of ICNGIoT*, 2022, 167–175.

Ayem, G. T., Thandekkattu, S. G., & Vajjhala, N. R. (2022). A Survey on Interoperability Issues at the SaaS Level Influencing the Adoption of Cloud Computing Technology. *Proceedings of International Conference on Network Security and Blockchain Technology: ICNSBT 2021*. DOI:10.1007/978-981-19-3182-6_16

Mistry, I., Tanwar, S., Tyagi, S., & Kumar, N. (2020). Blockchain for 5G-enabled IoT for industrial automation: A systematic review, solutions, and challenges. *Mechanical Systems and Signal Processing*, 135, 106382. DOI:10.1016/j.ymssp.2019.106382

Nguyen, D. C., Ding, M., Pathirana, P. N., Seneviratne, A., Li, J., & Poor, H. V. (2021). Federated learning for internet of things: A comprehensive survey. *IEEE Communications Surveys and Tutorials*, 23(3), 1622–1658. DOI:10.1109/COMST.2021.3075439

Noura, M., Atiquzzaman, M., & Gaedke, M. (2019). Interoperability in internet of things: Taxonomies and open challenges. *Mobile Networks and Applications*, 24(3), 796–809. DOI:10.1007/s11036-018-1089-9

Oktian, Y. E., Lee, S.-G., & Lee, B.-G. (2020). Blockchain-based continued integrity service for IoT big data management: A comprehensive design. *Electronics (Basel)*, 9(9), 1434. DOI:10.3390/electronics9091434

Padmavathi, K., Deepa, C., & Prabhakaran, P. (2020). Internet of Things (IoT) and Big Data: Data Management, Analytics, Visualization and Decision Making. In *The Internet of Things and Big Data Analytics* (pp. 217–246). Auerbach Publications. DOI:10.1201/9781003036739-10

Poornima, G., Janardhanachari, V., & Sakkari, D. S. (2023). Data Management for IoT and Digital Twin. In *New Approaches to Data Analytics and Internet of Things Through Digital Twin* (pp. 28–45). IGI Global.

Rathore, M. M., Paul, A., Hong, W.-H., Seo, H., Awan, I., & Saeed, S. (2018). Exploiting IoT and big data analytics: Defining smart digital city using real-time urban data. *Sustainable Cities and Society*, 40, 600–610. DOI:10.1016/j.scs.2017.12.022

Ren, W., Tong, X., Du, J., Wang, N., Li, S., Min, G., & Zhao, Z. (2021). Privacy enhancing techniques in the internet of things using data anonymisation. *Information Systems Frontiers*, 1–12. DOI:10.1007/s10796-021-10116-w

Sasaki, Y. (2021). A survey on IoT big data analytic systems: Current and future. *IEEE Internet of Things Journal*, 9(2), 1024–1036. DOI:10.1109/JIOT.2021.3131724

Silva, B. N., Khan, M., & Han, K. (2020). Integration of Big Data analytics embedded smart city architecture with RESTful web of things for efficient service provision and energy management. *Future Generation Computer Systems*, 107, 975–987. DOI:10.1016/j.future.2017.06.024

Silva, B. N., Khan, M., Jung, C., Seo, J., Muhammad, D., Han, J., Yoon, Y., & Han, K. (2018). Urban planning and smart city decision management empowered by real-time data processing using big data analytics. *Sensors (Basel)*, 18(9), 2994. DOI:10.3390/s18092994 PMID:30205499

Siow, E., Tiropanis, T., & Hall, W. (2018). Analytics for the internet of things: A survey. *ACM Computing Surveys*, 51(4), 1–36. DOI:10.1145/3204947

KEY TERMS AND DEFINITIONS

5G Connectivity: The fifth generation of wireless technology, offering faster speeds, lower latency, and more reliable connections for IoT devices. Example enabling real-time data streaming from autonomous vehicles to central servers for processing.

Blockchain Technology: A decentralized and secure digital ledger that records transactions across many computers in a way that ensures the data's integrity and transparency. Example using blockchain to securely track and verify data from IoT devices in a supply chain.

Cognitive Analytics: Advanced analytics that use artificial intelligence (AI) techniques like machine learning and natural language processing to analyze data. Example using deep learning to analyze and interpret images from medical IoT devices.

Data Anonymization: Techniques used to remove or obscure personal identifiers in data to protect user privacy while maintaining data utility. Example replacing user IDs with pseudonyms in a dataset.

Data Privacy: Ensuring that personal and sensitive data collected by IoT devices is protected and used in compliance with privacy laws and regulations. Example implementing GDPR-compliant practices for handling personal data from IoT health devices.

Data Security: Measures and technologies used to protect data from unauthorized access and breaches. Example encrypting data transmitted between IoT devices and central servers.

Descriptive Analytics: Analysis focused on summarizing historical data to understand what has happened. Example creating a dashboard that shows past energy consumption trends in a smart grid.

Edge Computing: Processing data near the source of data generation (i.e., on the IoT device itself or a nearby server) to reduce latency and bandwidth usage. Example analyzing video feeds from a security camera locally rather than sending all data to a central server.

Green IoT: Initiatives and technologies aimed at reducing the environmental impact of IoT devices and systems. Example developing energy-efficient protocols for IoT communication to minimize power consumption.

Internet of Things (IoT): A network of interconnected devices embedded with sensors, software, and other technologies that collect and exchange data over the internet. Example Smart home devices like thermostats, security cameras, and wearable health monitors.

Predictive Analytics: Using statistical models and machine learning algorithms to forecast future events based on historical data. Example predicting machine failure in industrial IoT using historical sensor data.

Prescriptive Analytics: Recommending actions based on predictive analytics to optimize outcomes. Example suggesting optimal maintenance schedules for equipment to prevent failures.

Semantic Interoperability: The ability of different systems and organizations to understand and use exchanged data meaningfully. Example using ontologies to ensure different IoT devices in a healthcare system can share and interpret patient data consistently.

Stream Processing: Real-time processing and analysis of data streams as they are generated. Example using Apache Kafka to process live data from IoT sensors in a manufacturing plant.

Chapter 9
A Framework for IoT Data Collection and Fusion in Infectious Diseases Surveillance

Kamal Bakari Jillahi
https://orcid.org/0000-0001-6372-4899
American University of Nigeria, Nigeria

Salu George Thandekkattu
https://orcid.org/0000-0003-3957-3554
American University of Nigeria, Nigeria

ABSTRACT

Although IoT has proven to be a vital instrument for data collection, epidemiological data collection has presented a significant challenge to the AI community. Thus, data for epidemiological research from multiple sources needs to be integrated to gain a holistic insight into epidemiological incidences. Hence, the authors aim to provide a framework for collecting, aggregating, and fusing data from diverse IoT sources for epidemiological research. Thus, a wireless network is designed for energy efficiency and communication efficiency. In addition, the CoAP mechanism for data transfer to a cloud-based service for aligning, de-duplicating, aggregating, and mapping data from several sources is presented. Subsequently, the researchers trained three machine learning models to predict disease incidence, vector abundance, and host population using both synthesized data using the proposed framework and data captured using traditional means. They assessed the performance of the two models by measuring their accuracy and learning rate. Results show the superiority of the proposed framework.

DOI: 10.4018/979-8-3693-5498-8.ch009

INTRODUCTION

The Internet of Things (IoT), and artificial intelligence (AI) are two cutting-edge technologies that Industry 4.0 heavily depends on (Plageras et al., 2016). These technologies have the great potential to transform several industries including health care, agriculture, education and manufacturing (Bongomin, et al., 2020; Çela, 2022; Çela, 2024; Çela, Fonkam, & Potluri, 2024; Çela, Vajjhala, & Eappen, 2024). There are several opportunities for creating cutting-edge human-centered applications when these technologies are applied to other areas of human endeavor to uncover trends and knowledge hitherto incomprehensible. Today, most progress in understanding infectious dynamics has been focused on endemic diseases that are directly transmitted from person to person (Anderson, 1982; Doukas, Pliakas, & Maglogiannis, 2010; Robertson, Nelson, MacNab, & Lawson, 2010; Marinier, et al., 2015). Nevertheless, compared to human-human contagious diseases, epidemic systems involving weather, zoonotic dynamics, reservoir systems, hosts, and vector dynamics models are more complex and necessitate an understanding of the environmental factors influencing host and vector species as well as the social factors influencing disease incidence, and yet they receive little to no research attention (Lescano, Larasati, Sedyaningsih, Bounlu, Araujo-Castillo, Munayco Escate, ... & Blazes, 2008). Because these systems are not easily observable, the application of technology and more specifically IoT for surveillance of weather, atmospheric, hydro-environmental, vector and host population dynamics prove to be a viable option for sourcing of relevant data for the surveillance of infectious diseases. Thus, this work aims to propose a framework for data collection, fusion, and aggregation from multiple IoT data sources for the surveillance of infectious diseases.

BACKGROUND

Infectious disease surveillance systems play a crucial role in public health by continuously monitoring, detecting, and responding to infectious diseases within populations (Thacker, and Berkelman, 1988). These systems are designed to identify disease outbreaks early, which is critical for timely intervention. By detecting an outbreak in its initial stages, public health authorities can quickly implement control measures, such as quarantines, vaccination campaigns, or public awareness initiatives, to prevent the disease from spreading further (Lescano, Larasati, Sedyaningsih, Bounlu, Araujo-Castillo, Munayco Escate, ... & Blazes, 2008).

Moreover, these surveillance systems provide valuable data that can be used to assess the effectiveness of public health interventions (Drewe, Hoinville, Cook, Floyd and Stärk, 2012; Declich, and Carter, 1994). For instance, after implementing a vaccination campaign, the data collected by these systems can help determine if the intervention is reducing the disease's spread. This feedback loop allows for the continuous improvement of public health strategies.

Epidemic systems, which include the interactions between infectious agents, hosts, and the environment, are complex and interconnected with various factors (McMichael, 2004). These factors include weather patterns, which can influence the spread of disease vectors like mosquitoes; the dynamics of host populations, such as human migration patterns; and the impact of public health policies and interventions. Collecting data from these interconnected systems provides a comprehensive understanding of how an epidemic unfolds, enabling more effective responses (Eisenberg, Desai, Levy, Bates, Liang, Naumoff, and Scott, 2007).

However, monitoring these systems is challenging because many of the variables involved are not easily observable by humans (Keeling and Eames, 2005). For example, tracking the movement of disease-carrying vectors or understanding how environmental changes affect disease transmission may require specialized tools. This is where technology becomes invaluable. By employing technologies such as IoT, remote sensing, data analytics, and automated data collection methods, public health agencies can capture and analyze data more efficiently and accurately. This technological approach enhances the ability to detect and respond to epidemic outbreaks, making it a powerful tool in the fight against infectious diseases.

MAIN FOCUS OF THE CHAPTER

Issues, Controversies, Problems

Data collection in an IoT environment for disease surveillance encounters several significant challenges (Lescano et al., 2008; Falzon et al., 2021). The vast volume and variety of data generated by numerous sensors require sophisticated storage and processing capabilities to ensure accurate and timely analysis. Maintaining data quality is crucial, as inaccuracies or inconsistencies can lead to erroneous conclusions and impact public health responses (Zhou and Shen, 2010). Connectivity issues, particularly in remote or underserved areas, can disrupt data transmission and hinder real-time monitoring. Additionally, safeguarding sensitive health information against unauthorized access and breaches demands robust security measures and compliance with data protection regulations, adding complexity to the system.

According to Mwabukusi, Karimuribo, Rweyemamu, and Beda (2014), current trends in IoT-based disease surveillance are driving advancements in technology and data management. The integration of AI and machine learning is enhancing real-time data analysis, allowing for more accurate predictions and insights into disease outbreaks. Edge computing is gaining prominence as it enables local processing of data, reducing latency and bandwidth usage, and supporting timely decision-making (Jiang et al., 2022). Standardization efforts are focused on improving interoperability among diverse IoT devices and systems, facilitating seamless data integration but rarely are issues concerning aggregation and fusion of data tackled. Mobile health (mHealth) applications are expanding, providing immediate access to health data and enabling more proactive monitoring and management of health conditions (Mwabukusi, Karimuribo, Rweyemamu, and Beda, 2014).

Ethical considerations in IoT data collection for disease surveillance are paramount to ensuring responsible use of sensitive health information (Geneviève, Martani, Wangmo, Paolotti, ... and Elger, 2019). Protecting data privacy is crucial, requiring strict controls to prevent unauthorized access and misuse of personal health data. Informed consent is essential, ensuring individuals are fully aware of how their data will be collected, used, and shared. Addressing potential biases in data collection and analysis is also necessary to avoid discrimination and ensure equitable treatment across diverse populations (Carrel and Rennie, 2008; Lee, 2019; Borda, Molnar, Neesham, and Kostkova, 2022; Jillahi and Iorliam, 2024). Transparency in data practices and accountability in handling personal information are key to maintaining public trust and upholding ethical standards. This calls for immense efforts to develop privacy preserving systems that protect personal data from unauthorized access and breach.

Key Components of Disease Surveillance Systems

A **disease surveillance system** is a systematic approach to collecting, analyzing, interpreting, and disseminating data on diseases to monitor public health and inform interventions. Its primary goals are to detect outbreaks, track the progression of diseases, assess the effectiveness of control measures, and guide public health policy and planning (Phalkey, Yamamoto, Awate, and Marx, 2015; Lourenço, Tatem, Atkinson, Cohen, Pindolia, Bhavnani, and Le Menach, 2019). The key components of any electronic disease surveillance system as shown in figure 1 are as follows:

1. **Data Collection Modules:** This Module collects data from weather stations, hospitals, laboratories, primary care providers, public health agencies, environmental, online user activities and other sources which are then used to infer occurrences of disease incidences.
2. **Data Analysis Module:** This module Identifies patterns, trends, and anomalies in the collected data to uncover unapparent relationships and hidden trends which may provide insight into epidemiological incidences. This module also Interprets data in the context of local, regional, and global health trends in order to provide

risk assessment to the public and determine the severity of an outbreak. This module may employ statistical tools, such as statistical software to analyze data and detect potential outbreaks of diseases which may be unapparent to human experts.

3. **Reporting/Information Dissemination Module:** This module shares findings with public health officials, healthcare providers, policymakers, and the public about any epidemiological incidence, its severity, mitigation actions, actionable policy or any other relevant information that may help in the fight against any prevalent epidemiological incidence. This module may also issue alerts to inform relevant stakeholders of potential public health threats.

4. **Response and Control Measures Module:** This module provides information that helps in implementing measures to control the spread of disease, such as vaccination campaigns, quarantine, and public health advisories. It may also assess the effectiveness of such interventions and makes necessary adjustments to enhance their efficiency in combating disease spread.

Figure 1. Components of disease surveillance system

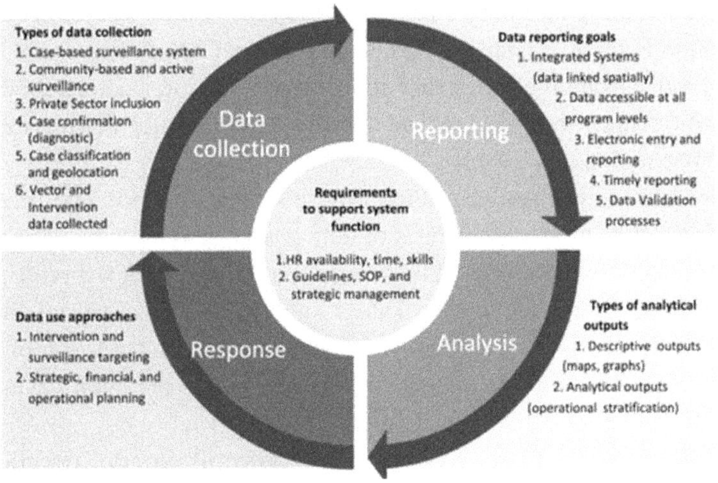

(Lourenço, Tatem, Atkinson, Cohen, Pindolia, Bhavnani, and Le Menach, 2019).

Types of Disease Surveillance Systems

1. **Passive Surveillance Systems:** These are systems that rely on information provided by human agents such as healthcare providers to report cases of infectious diseases to public health authorities on a routine basis. These systems are usually cheap to implement but are prone to underreporting or over reporting based on the bias of the human agent and may delay in reporting depending on the speed of the human agent (Zhou and Shen, 2010).

2. **Active Surveillance Systems:** These are system employed by public health officials to actively seek out cases of infectious diseases through active capture and analysis of data from environmental, disease vector data, host population dynamics, human activities and public policies through regular contacts with healthcare providers and review of medical records. These systems tend to be more accurate and provide timely data especially when automated (Zhou and Shen, 2010). Hence, their major downside is resource-intensity and cost of conception, deployment and use.

3. **Sentinel Surveillance Systems:** These systems provide monitoring of disease trends through selected healthcare facilities or groups of healthcare providers that report all cases of certain diseases. These tend to be useful for detecting trends and emerging issues especially when the source of the surveillance information is reliable (Jiang, Zhou, Wang, Ding, Chu, Tang, ... and Xu, 2022). A major disadvantage is that they may not provide information about an entire population since their sources are focused on particular disease incidence or particular regions.

4. **Syndromic Surveillance Systems:** These systems provide real-time (or near-real-time) collection and analysis of data based on symptoms rather than confirmed diagnoses of individuals within a population to deduce disease incidences (Jiang, Zhou, Wang, Ding, Chu, Tang, ... and Xu, 2022; Zhou and Shen, 2010). These systems have the advantage of providing early detection of outbreaks based solely on symptom patterns while they have a potential for false alarms due false and poor data quality issues.

5. **Laboratory Surveillance System:** These systems monitor infectious agents through laboratory testing of individuals in a population and reporting cases of disease occurrences through prevalence of disease-causing agents or conditions (Zhou and Shen, 2010). Thus, they exhibit high specificity due to the quality of data obtained and they also have an ability to track specific categories pathogens. On the other hand, they are dependent on laboratory capacity and reporting timeliness therefore requiring high human expertise and equipment.

6. **Integrated Disease Surveillance and Response System (IDSR):** This is a comprehensive approach that integrates multiple data sources and types of surveillance to provide coordinated surveillance to infectious diseases (Zhou and Shen, 2010). In these systems, data is sourced from environmental, vector dynamics and host population system dynamics to provide surveillance and response on the occurrences of disease incidences (Guzewich, Bryan, and Todd, 1997). These systems, when accurately implemented, provide a holistic view of issues associated to an epidemiological incidence (Guzewich, Bryan, and Todd, 1997). Their major shortcoming is that they require robust coordination and rely enormously on technological infrastructure to function well.

Importance of Integrating Data From Multiple Sources for Disease Surveillance

The surveillance of epidemics has an inherent paradox of early detection and false alert aversion (Robertson, Nelson, MacNab, & Lawson, 2010). Thus, systems that guide interventions are most useful early in an outbreak, when data is very limited (Polonsky, Baidjoe, Kamvar, Cori, Durski, Edmunds, ... and Jombart, 2019). Hence when data is scant or partial, systems might be unsuccessful in providing the required information for guiding prudent intervention decisions that change the course of infection. As a result, integrating data from numerous sources with disease outbreak models will produce more meaningful insights aversion (Robertson, Nelson, Mac-Nab, & Lawson, 2010; Polonsky, Baidjoe, Kamvar, Cori, Durski, Edmunds, ... and Jombart, 2019). In other words, integrating data from multiple sources for disease surveillance is vital for creating a comprehensive, accurate, and actionable public health response. Other advantages of data integration in disease surveillance include:

1. **Improved Accuracy and Comprehensive View:** Aggregating data from various sources such as sensors, actuators, hospitals, laboratories, and public health reports ensures a more complete picture of the disease landscape. Furthermore, data from multiple sources can be cross verified to improve accuracy and reduce the likelihood of errors.
2. **Early Detection and Response:** Integrated data from various sources allows for the early detection of unusual patterns in outbreaks, enabling quicker public health interventions. This can be achieved by combining real-time data streams, such as syndromic surveillance and social media monitoring to enhance a system's ability to respond promptly to emerging threats.

3. **Enhanced Situational Awareness and Geospatial Analysis:** Integrating epidemiological data with geographical information systems (GIS) helps in mapping disease spread and identifying hotspots (Guzewich, Bryan, and Todd, 1997). In short, longitudinal data from multiple sources, including environmental and socioeconomic data can reveal trends and patterns that single-source data might miss.

4. **Resource Optimization:** collecting and integrating data from multiple sources helps in identifying areas with the greatest need for resources, ensuring efficient allocation thus, enabling better coordination among different public health entities and stakeholders, avoiding duplication of efforts and informing targeted interventions based on a comprehensive risk assessment, addressing not just the disease but also underlying determinants.

5. **Improved Public Health Strategies:** Integrating data form numerous sources supports evidence-based decision-making, leading to more effective public health policies and strategies thereby, Facilitating the evaluation of public health interventions by providing diverse data points for assessment.

6. **Enhanced Collaboration:** Data from multiple sources encourages collaboration among epidemiologists, data scientists, healthcare providers, and policymakers in other to support a unified public health response by providing a common data platform for all stakeholders.

7. **Global Health Security:** Integrating data from multiple localities, countries and regions enhances global disease surveillance and response efforts. Which in turn strengthens the ability to detect and respond to pandemics by sharing data across borders and collaborating on global health initiatives.

8. **Addressing Data Gaps:** Data from various sources can help fill gaps where information might be missing or incomplete in one source such data might be available in another source. Thus, ensuring that data collection is inclusive of different population segments, improving overall surveillance quality.

Integrating data from multiple sources is essential for a robust and effective disease surveillance system. It enhances the ability to detect, monitor, and respond to infectious diseases, ultimately improving public health outcomes and safeguarding communities (Robertson, Nelson, MacNab, & Lawson, 2010).

Challenges in Traditional Disease Surveillance Methods

The essential mechanism beneath epidemics is pathogen transmission (Lee, 2019). Thus, at least two species must contact for pathogen transmission to occur, and this interaction is by its very nature a spatiotemporal process (Carrel and Rennie, 2008). It is a process that is likewise invisible to the naked eye. Because estimating the latent variables involved depends on our capacity to link them effectively to characteristics that can be quantified, and observed, yet these are challenging to model (Lee, 2019). Furthermore, in cases where zoonotic systems are involved it is challenging to investigate infected animals in their natural habitat and because historical records of these epidemic incidences are hard to come by, this causes significant drawback in infectious disease research (Karesh, Dobson, Lloyd-Smith, Lubroth, Dixon, Bennett, ... and Heymann, 2012). Furthermore, disease records do not exist for wildlife populations in cases of historical diseases, this makes it hard to make many meaningful assumptions about any epidemic incidence in those populations.

Consequently, to better comprehend epidemic incidences and provide forecasts of environmental dynamics and how they relate to disease recurrence, researchers have generally used data-based or model-based (incorporating statistical hypothesis testing mostly mathematical simulation techniques) (Wang, Adiga, Chen, Lewis, Sadilek, Venkatramanan, and Marathe, 2022). To analyze disease propagation incidence in host populations, the widely used model-based methodologies in epidemiology describe susceptible, exposed, infected, and recovered states (i.e., SEIR) using a connected system of differential equations (Karesh, Dobson, Lloyd-Smith, Lubroth, Dixon, Bennett, ... and Heymann, 2012). Instead of utilizing these mathematical process equations to directly generate insight, important parameter values are obtained from other studies and integrated into the model and analyzed to produced insight (Karesh, Dobson, Lloyd-Smith, Lubroth, Dixon, Bennett, ... and Heymann, 2012). Mostly, researchers use model simulations to predict incidence "data" that can be compared to observed data. One of the primary goals of compartmental modeling in epidemiology is to estimate the basic reproductive number, or R0, the number of new infections caused by a single infected individual in a community that is completely susceptible. Theoretically, an outbreak can only propagate if R0 > 1. One can experiment with variable estimations that characterize disease transmission to find out how changes in these rates impact the probability that an epidemiological incidence will break out and how long it will likely endure. Dynamic compartmental models have shown to be extremely useful in the assessment of immunization schedules (Bauch, Szusz, and Garrison, 2009) and in the control of recently emerging human epidemics (Karesh, Dobson, Lloyd-Smith, Lubroth, Dixon, Bennett, ... and Heymann, 2012). They are also helpful in figuring out how relevant crucial rates are in relation to one another. The mathematical framework considers some basic biological assumptions, including the mechanism of transmission and the spatial and temporal consistency of rate parameters. When these presumptions are incorrect, the resulting R0 values may be considerably off (Bellouquid and Delitala, 2006). Furthermore, Bellouquid and Delitala, (2006) reviewed the shortcomings of mathematical modeling of infectious transmission in depth and concluded that these models can be quite powerful if the biological processes they intend to model are well-described and the stochasticity associated with the environment and population is either well-characterized or unimportant to accomplishing the study goal. However, documenting fluctuations is highly important when the goal of the research is to predict the likelihood and severity of disease epidemics. Even while they can only be used to comprehend direct (human) transmission operations with somewhat large amounts of data, new "plug-and-play" techniques (Bellouquid and Delitala, 2006) simulators from adaptable compartmental model classes can be used to produce insights into stochasticity and intricate relationships in dynamic systems. Plageras, et al. (2016) asserts that some biological systems are poorly understood; Consequently, in situations when data is scarce, dynamic compartmental modeling might not work well. This is especially true when predicting the infectious dynamics of systems that carry vector-borne and zoonotic diseases.

Similarly, data-based or phenomenological modeling of disease occurrence has advantages and disadvantages. The quantity and range of data available to identify environmental factors that may affect the time and location of disease outbreaks have significantly expanded because of advancements in remote sensing (Goetz, Prince, and Small, 2000). It is easy to attribute the reported disease incidence (based on host or pathogen abundance) to a number of parameters that characterize habitat type (Brearley, Rhodes, Bradley, Baxter, Seabrook, Lunney, ... and McAlpine, 2013; Robertson, Nelson, MacNab, & Lawson, 2010), climate (Robertson, Nelson, MacNab, and Lawson, 2010), and dispersal pathways (Mwabukusi, Karimuribo, Rweyemamu, and Beda, 2014). These methods can certainly show variations in infection patterns and population sizes, but they may not have the rigor to extend beyond the specific time frame and place where the data were collected so, in every scenario a new set of data must be collected in other to get sight to epidemiological incidences. The underlying assumption of most phenomenological models is that the abiotic factors being studied only have an impact on epidemic onset. When diseases are actively spreading, the abiotic conditions that match its existing spectrum might not account for much of what permits it to exist (Karesh, Dobson, Lloyd-Smith, Lubroth, Dixon, Bennett, ... and Heymann, 2012). It can be challenging to determine how well these methods represent the underlying biological mechanisms controlling transmission rates, which is a need for accurately and realistically estimating disease incidence. However, phenomenological modeling can be helpful in characterizing the wide range of potential interactions and possibilities and has surely contributed insights into the development and evolution of infectious disease (Lescano, Larasati, Sedyaningsih, Bounlu, Araujo-Castillo, Munayco Escate, ... & Blazes, 2008; Brearley, Rhodes, Bradley, Baxter, Seabrook, Lunney, ... and McAlpine, 2013; Robertson, Nelson, MacNab, & Lawson, 2010; LaDeau, Glass, Hobbs, Latimer, and Ostfeld, 2011).

Predicting disease outbreaks requires a solid grasp of the mechanisms governing pathogen spread (LaDeau, Glass, Hobbs, Latimer, and Ostfeld, 2011). Effective data–model integration is crucial to support inference and forecasts when knowledge is insufficient and structural data are scarce, as is typically the case with EIDs (Lescano, Larasati, Sedyaningsih, Bounlu, Araujo-Castillo, Munayco Escate, ... & Blazes, 2008). For infectious disease scenarios, probabilistic approaches predominate in terms of data aggregation techniques. Since probability-based methods evaluate the data's support for certain hypotheses in a quantitative way, they are the major essential tools for synthesizing data and models in epidemiology (Phalkey, Yamamoto, Awate, and Marx, 2015). The application of Bayesian methods is expanding, especially in scenarios where pathological and ecological complexity is high and prediction is the primary goal (Mwabukusi, Karimuribo, Rweyemamu, and Beda, 2014). Epidemiological professionals are increasingly using maximum likelihood or Bayesian methodologies in hierarchical modeling (Lawson, 2018; Fürnkranz, 1998).

A hierarchical model structure, sometimes referred to as a multilevel model structure, defines the way information is transferred among sample units and processes. Although this strategy is not yet extensively utilized in epidemiological settings, it is particularly interesting since it allows researchers to account for large variances (e.g., among groups, individuals, time frames, or regions) while still permitting shared traits (Lawson, 2018; Mwabukusi, Karimuribo, Rweyemamu, and Beda, 2014). Furthermore, various datasets and processes can be combined into single research provided the model structure dependent on a conditional probabilistic model (i.e., Bayesian or likelihood based) (Fraser, and Marcotte, 2004; Karesh, Dobson, Lloyd-Smith, Lubroth, Dixon, Bennett, ... and Heymann, 2012). Infectious illness modeling has not made extensive use of state-space models, even though they are increasingly employed to depict population dynamics and can also have a hierarchical structure (Cooch, Conn, Ellner, Dobson, and Pollock, 2012). A process model that reflects knowledge of the processes governing the state and an observation equation that connects what is observed to the true but invisible condition of the population comprise the state-space approach to population modeling. We can differentiate between the uncertainty arising from observation error, which is the consequence of our incapacity to witness the process, and the uncertainty arising from process variance or model misspecification, which is the result of our model's inability to accurately portray the process, thanks to the state-space formulation. This is paramount in time series models, as the process error propagates over time whereas observation inaccuracies do not (Robertson, Nelson, MacNab, & Lawson, 2010). If the model is further built to consider individual heterogeneity in both exposure risk and demographic risk, for example, then it is also hierarchical. The integration of the data-model using state-space and hierarchical methods is important for understanding the infectious dynamics of zoonotic and vector-borne infectious diseases (Robertson, Nelson, MacNab, & Lawson, 2010).

IoT Data Sources for Infectious Diseases Surveillance

IoT has revolutionized infectious disease surveillance by providing real-time, high-resolution data from a variety of sources. Some of the key IoT data sources for infectious disease surveillance include:

1. **Wearable Devices**: devices like smartwatches, smart glasses, GPS tracking band and fitness trackers can monitor vital signs such as heart rate, body temperature, and blood oxygen levels, providing early indicators of illness and providing early alarm system for infectious diseases. Furthermore, these devices can track the movement and location of individuals in a population to help in identify probable contagion networks and trace contacts in other to understand and monitor contagion and quarantine compliance (Radin, Wineinger, Topol and Steinhubl, 2020). Hence, aggregated data from multiple users can help identify emerging hotspots and track the spread of infections over localities and different geographical locations.

2. **Environmental Sensors:** Sensors that detect pollutants, particulate matter, and other air quality indicators can help track environmental conditions that may influence the spread of some infectious diseases. While monitoring water quality can help detect pathogens like bacteria and viruses in water sources, providing early warnings of potential epidemiological outbreaks. Similarly, IoT sensors in wastewater systems can detect viral RNA and other biomarkers, offering early warnings of community-level outbreaks (Morain, and Budge, 2012).

3. **Connected Medical Devices:** Devices such as glucometers, pulse oximeters and blood pressure monitors can monitor and transmit health data to healthcare providers, allowing for remote monitoring of patients. Devices like IoT-enabled thermometers can continuously monitor body temperatures, detecting fever patterns indicative of infectious diseases in a population (Morain, and Budge, 2012). Therefore, data from these connected medical devices can be integrated into telemedicine platforms, facilitating real-time consultations and diagnostics data about the outbreaks of any infectious disease.

4. **Mobile Health Applications**: Software applications that allow users to log symptoms (self-reporting) can aggregate data to identify patterns and potential disease outbreaks. These systems can track interactions between users using technologies such as GPRS, aiding to identify any potential contacts of infected individuals and building a contagion networks of individuals based on

their proximity, interaction and closeness to other individuals in a population (Mwabukusi, Karimuribo, Rweyemamu, and Beda, 2014).

5. **Smart Home Devices**: Devices such as indoor air quality sensors can detect levels of CO_2, humidity, and pollutants, which can influence the transmission of infectious agents in a home or indoor public gathering. Furthermore, monitoring indoor temperatures can provide data on environmental conditions that may aggravate disease spread. Similarly, Smart systems for managing indoor environments (e.g., air filtration, sanitation) can reduce the risk of disease transmission especially in isolation units of health care centers.

6. **Public Health Infrastructure**: Smart City Solutions otherwise known as IoT-enabled infrastructure in cities, such as public health kiosks, thermos-enabled and smart surveillance cameras, can provide data on population health and movement prompting public health authorities of any perceived population-based surge in disease symptoms. In the same vein, these IoT-enabled devices in the public can monitor health metrics and detect signs of infectious diseases.

7. **Transportation Systems**: Data from public transportation systems and ride-sharing services can track the movement of individuals and report any potential spread patterns of perceived disease in a population. These devices when aggregated to logistics and supply chain can ensure the safe and timely delivery of medical supplies and vaccines and report any issues that may arise during transit of these viral products which might cause any epidemiological incidences.

8. **Agricultural IoT**: Sensors and wearable devices for livestock can monitor health and detect diseases (zoonotic diseases) that could potentially transfer to humans. Similar sensors in agricultural fields can detect plant diseases, some of which can affect human health.

9. **Social media and web-based data sources**: Social media and web-based data sources have become valuable tools for disease surveillance due to their ability to provide real-time, widespread, and often unstructured data that can offer early signals of emerging health threats. Data from Search Engine Queries, Social media blogs such as Hash tags, Online health forums, News reports and the likes can provide data about symptoms, user experience, user sentiments about disease outbreak or intervention measures put in place to combat disease spread. Furthermore, sudden spikes in specific keywords related to symptoms or diseases can indicate potential public health threats (Dugas et al., 2013). When these data are aggregated with geotagged media posts, this will allow for the mapping of disease spread across different regions (Dugas et al., 2013; Pervaiz, Pervaiz, Rehman and Saif, 2012). This spatial information is valuable for identifying outbreak hotspots and understanding the geographic spread of an illness (Dugas, Hsieh, Levin, Pines, Mareiniss, Mohareb, ... and Rothman, 2012; Pervaiz, Pervaiz, Rehman and Saif, 2012).

Data Collection Techniques in IoT Environments

In an IoT environment for disease surveillance, various data collection techniques are employed to gather and transmit health-related data. Data acquisition and transmission in these environments rely on protocols like Message Queuing Telemetry Transport (MQTT), Constrained Application Protocol (CoAP), and Long-Range Wide Area Network (LoRaWAN), with standards such as Open Platform Communications Unified Architecture (OPCUA) and oneM2M ensuring interoperability. Effective data preprocessing and cleaning techniques may include filtering, normalization, aggregation, and encryption, which are crucial for maintaining data quality and security, thereby enhancing the ability to monitor, detect, and respond to infectious disease outbreaks. Some techniques to consider while collecting and aggregating data from IoT environment for disease surveillance may include:

1. **Edge Computing:** A distributed computing paradigm known as "edge computing" moves data storage and computation closer to the point of demand, which is usually at or close to the data creation source. Rather of depending entirely on centralized cloud servers, this method uses edge devices to do calculations locally, which lowers latency, conserves bandwidth, and allows real-time processing and analysis. To minimize latency and bandwidth utilization in disease surveillance systems, recorded data should be analyzed locally on the device or close-by edge servers. This will ensure that only pertinent data is sent to central servers, minimizing the amount of data communicated (Rahmani, Gia, Negash, Anzanpour, Azimi, Jiang, and Liljeberg, 2018; Pace, Aloi, Gravina, Caliciuri, Fortino, and Liotta, 2018).

2. **Data Aggregation:** The process of gathering and combining data from several sources to create a summary or a single dataset is known as data aggregation. This technique is used to compile comprehensive information, enhance data analysis, and provide a holistic view of the collected data, often simplifying complex data sets for better decision-making and reporting. Thus, data from multiple sensors should be aggregated at central hubs or cloud servers to avoid redundancy and duplication of data points which might lead to duplicated effort and wrong inferences from such data. Hence, data should be collected in a tiered manner, with local nodes aggregating data before sending it to higher-level nodes (Heidemann, Silva, Intanagonwiwat, Govindan, Estrin, and Ganesan, 2001; Randhawa, and Jain, 2017).

3. **Continuous vs. Event-Driven Collection:** Continuous data collection involves continuously monitoring and recording data at regular intervals, providing a constant stream of information. Event-driven data collection, on the other hand, involves collecting data only when specific events or conditions occur, trigger-

ing data recording in response to these instances. Sensors should continuously collect and transmit data useful for real-time analysis especially when there are perceived epidemiological threats, while event driven data collection is better used when there are no perceived threats (Lodi, Aniello, Di Luna, and Baldoni, 2014).

Data Preprocessing and Cleaning Techniques

1. **Data Filtering:** these include techniques such as noise reduction which entails removing or smoothing out irrelevant or random variations in captured data to improve accuracy. This may involve discarding data points that fall outside pre-defined acceptable ranges to ensure data quality otherwise known as thresholding.

2. **Data Normalization:** This includes techniques such as data scaling which involves adjusting data to fit within a specific range, typically between some agreed domain area values, to ensure uniformity across different data sources. Data points might be transformed to have a mean of zero and a standard deviation of one, ensuring comparability by adjusting for different scales and distributions. In qualitative data such user sentiments, normalization might entail substituting acronyms, completing abbreviations, removing and replacing emoji, replacing slangs and contractions, mapping words to dictionary lexicons, lemmatization and stemming. These ensure that collected data conforms to benchmark agreed entries over multiple sources.

3. **Missing Data Handling:** these are techniques used in filling missing data points using statistical methods or predictions techniques based on other available data. Here, as earlier discussed deleting incomplete data records if the missing data cannot be reliably calculated or predicted and if their absence does not compromise the analysis is safer than inferring erroneous data which may affect the accuracy of any inference induced from such data.

4. **Data Validation:** Data validation is the process of checking data for accuracy, consistency, and reliability (Curran and Hussong, 2009). It involves verifying that the data meets predefined rules or standards, ensuring it is complete, correctly formatted, and free from errors. This process helps maintain data quality and integrity, making sure that the data is suitable for analysis and decision-making. Thus, Identifying and addressing data points that deviate significantly from the expected pattern, which could indicate errors or significant events

5. **Data Encryption:** In an IoT environment, data encryption involves encoding data transmitted between IoT devices and servers to protect it from unauthorized access and tampering (Curran and Hussong, 2009). By using encryption algorithms, data is transformed into a secure format that can only be decrypted

by authorized parties with the appropriate keys. This ensures the confidentiality and integrity of sensitive information as it moves across networks and is stored (Jillahi and Iorliam, 2024).

CHALLENGES IN DATA COLLECTION

Data collection in an IoT environment for disease surveillance faces several intricate challenges (Nnebue, Onwasigwe, Adogu, & Adinma, 2014; Paquet, Coulombier, Kaiser, and Ciotti, 2006; Phalkey, Yamamoto, Awate, and Marx, 2015). Firstly, the sheer volume of data generated by a multitude of IoT devices can overwhelm storage and processing systems, requiring robust infrastructure to manage and analyze this information effectively (Belli et al., 2015). The variety of data types and formats from different sensors and sources further complicates integration, necessitating sophisticated data management systems to harmonize disparate datasets (Chen et al., 2013). The velocity of data generation demands real-time processing capabilities to ensure timely insights and interventions, which can be technically challenging and resource intensive.

Ensuring data quality is another critical issue, as sensors malfunction, calibration errors, and inconsistent data entries can undermine the accuracy and reliability of the collected information. Connectivity issues can disrupt data transmission, particularly in remote or underserved areas where network infrastructure is limited, leading to potential gaps in surveillance coverage (Paquet, Coulombier, Kaiser, and Ciotti, 2006). Additionally, protecting sensitive health data from unauthorized access and breaches is essential for maintaining privacy and compliance with regulations, requiring robust encryption and security measures (Jillahi and Iorliam, 2024). The challenge of ensuring interoperability among diverse devices and systems is significant, as seamless communication between various components is necessary for effective data integration and analysis (Drosou, Jagadish, Pitoura, and Stoyanovich, 2017). Finally, managing the power consumption and resource constraints of IoT devices, especially in battery-operated or remote deployments, adds another layer of complexity to the data collection process (Chen et al., 2013; Drosou, Jagadish, Pitoura, and Stoyanovich, 2017). These challenges collectively impact the efficiency and effectiveness of disease surveillance in an IoT environment.

Implementing these techniques effectively requires a combination of robust hardware, efficient software, and adherence to industry standards and best practices. By addressing the challenges and utilizing appropriate preprocessing and cleaning methods, IoT environments can ensure high-quality, reliable data for infectious disease surveillance and other applications.

Aggregation Methods for IoT Data

Aggregation methods for IoT data involve combining data from multiple sources to create a comprehensive dataset or summary. Key methods include:

1. **Centralized Aggregation**: Centralized aggregation involves collecting and consolidating data from multiple IoT devices into a single, central server or cloud platform. In this method, all data is transmitted from various sources to the central system, where it is combined, processed, and analyzed. This approach provides a unified view of the data, facilitates comprehensive analysis, and simplifies data management. However, it can require significant bandwidth and storage resources, and may introduce latency due to the need to transmit large volumes of data over the network.

2. **Hierarchical Aggregation**: Hierarchical aggregation involves collecting and summarizing data at multiple levels within a network. In this method, data is initially aggregated at local or intermediate nodes before being sent to higher-level nodes or a central server. This approach reduces the volume of data transmitted by summarizing information locally, which helps in managing bandwidth and improving efficiency. Hierarchical aggregation also allows for more scalable and manageable data processing, as intermediate nodes handle initial data aggregation and only essential data is forwarded to the central system. In essence, data is aggregated at multiple levels, starting with local nodes that collect and summarize data before sending it to higher-level nodes or central servers. This approach reduces the amount of data transmitted and improves efficiency.

3. **Edge Aggregation**: Edge aggregation involves processing and summarizing data locally on edge devices or nearby edge servers, rather than sending all raw data to a central server. This method reduces latency and bandwidth usage by performing data aggregation closer to where the data is generated. By consolidating and analyzing data at the edge, only essential or summarized information is transmitted to the central system, leading to faster insights and more efficient use of network resources. Here, data is processed and aggregated locally on edge devices or nearby edge servers before being sent to the central system. This reduces latency and bandwidth usage by minimizing data transmission.

4. **Stream Aggregation**: Stream aggregation involves continuously processing and summarizing data in real-time as it flows through the system. This method allows for the immediate analysis of data streams from IoT devices, providing

timely insights and enabling rapid decision-making. Stream aggregation processes data on-the-fly, combining and reducing it into meaningful summaries or metrics without waiting for batch processing. This approach is particularly useful for applications requiring instant feedback and real-time monitoring. Real-time data streams from IoT devices are aggregated on-the-fly, summarizing data as it flows through the system. This method supports real-time analysis and decision-making. This approach is particularly useful for applications requiring instant feedback and real-time monitoring.

5. **Batch Aggregation**: This is the process of collecting and combining data from multiple sources or datasets into a single, unified dataset at specific intervals. This process involves gathering data in batches, typically on a scheduled basis (such as daily, weekly, or monthly), rather than in real-time. Batch data aggregation is commonly used in data warehousing, business intelligence, and analytics to create comprehensive datasets for analysis and reporting.

6. **Privacy-preserving data aggregation techniques** are designed to collect and combine data from multiple sources while ensuring the privacy and security of individual data points. These strategies include things like homomorphic encryption, which allows computations on encrypted data without first decrypting while maintaining the original data's secrecy, and differential privacy, which masks individual contributions to the data by adding controlled noise; using secure multi-party computing (SMPC), several parties can work together to jointly compute a function over their inputs while maintaining the privacy of those inputs; federated learning keeps sensitive data local by aggregating model updates from several devices without sending raw data. These techniques collectively help in maintaining data utility for analysis while protecting the privacy of individuals, crucial for sensitive applications like health data in IoT environments.

DATA FUSION TECHNIQUES FOR INTEGRATED ANALYSIS

Data fusion techniques in an IoT environment involve integrating information from multiple sources to generate more accurate and comprehensive insights. Sensor fusion combines data from various sensors to enhance accuracy and reliability, such as merging temperature, humidity, and air quality data to assess environmental conditions. Spatial fusion aggregates data from geographically distributed IoT devices to create spatially aware insights, useful for mapping disease outbreaks based on location data. Temporal fusion integrates data collected over time to identify trends and patterns, such as daily health metrics indicating disease onset

(Texier, Allodji, Diop, Meynard, Pellegrin, and Chaudet, 2019; Burkom, Ramac-Thomas, Babin, Holtry, Mnatsakanyan, and Yund, 2011). Multi-modal fusion combines different types of data, like merging social media text with sensor data to predict disease outbreaks based on public sentiment and environmental factors (Lin, Burkom, Murphy, Elbert, Hakre, Babin, and Feldman, 2006). Decision-level fusion involves aggregating outputs from multiple sources to make a final decision, such as combining predictions from different machine learning models for disease prediction or response planning (King, Villeneuve, White, Sherratt, Holderbaum, and Harwin, 2017). These techniques leverage diverse data sources to improve the accuracy, timeliness, and relevance of insights, making them crucial for effective disease surveillance and management.

Data Fusion Algorithms

Algorithms for data fusion in IoT environments are essential for integrating and analyzing data from multiple sources to generate accurate and comprehensive insights. In an IoT environment, several data fusion algorithms might be used to combine and analyze data from multiple sources effectively. Some commonly used algorithms include:

1. **Kalman Filter**: This algorithm is widely used for sensor fusion, especially in applications requiring real-time tracking and estimation. It helps to filter out noise and provide accurate estimates of system states (Welch, and Bishop, 1995; Maybeck, 1990; Kim, and Bang, 2018).
2. **Particle Filter:** Similar to the Kalman Filter but more suitable for non-linear systems, the Particle Filter uses a set of particles (samples) to represent the probability distribution of the system state (Gustafsson, 2010; Carpenter, Clifford and Fearnhead, 1999).
3. **Dempster-Shafer Theory:** This framework is used for combining evidence from different sources and handling uncertainty in data fusion. It provides a way to manage conflicting information and derive a combined probability (Shafer, 1992; Wilson, 2000).
4. **Bayesian Networks:** These probabilistic graphical models are used to represent and compute the joint probability distribution of a set of variables. They are useful for combining data from multiple sources and making inferences based on observed data (Rahier, 2018; Wu, and Wong, 2006; Guerriero, Svensson, and Willett, 2010).
5. **Artificial Neural Networks (ANNs):** Deep learning models, especially Convolutional Neural Networks (CNNs) and Recurrent Neural Networks (RNNs), can be used to fuse multi-modal data, such as combining image and sensor data

for pattern recognition and prediction (Yim, Udpa, Udpa, Mina and Lord, 1995; Barreto-Cubero, A. J., Gómez-Espinosa, Escobedo Cabello, Cuan-Urquizo, and Cruz-Ramírez, 2021; Liu, Huang, Sun, Yu and Xiao, 2020; Kolanowski, Świetlicka, Kapela, Pochmara, and Rybarczyk, 2018).

6. **Principal Component Analysis (PCA):** this is a dimensionality reduction technique that can be used to combine and compress data from multiple sensors, retaining the most significant features for analysis (Mafata, Brand, Kidd, Medvedovici, and Buica, 2022; Hongyan, 2009).

7. **Fuzzy Logic:** This approach is used for data fusion when dealing with imprecise and uncertain data. Fuzzy logic systems can combine inputs from various sources to produce a reliable output (Mahler, 1996; Ding, Ji, Huang and Li, 2004; Manjunatha, Verma and Srividya, 2008).

8. **Weighted Average:** A simple yet effective method where data from multiple sources is combined by assigning different weights to each source based on its reliability or importance.

9. **Support Vector Machines (SVMs):** These supervised learning models can be used for classification and regression tasks in data fusion, especially when combining data from heterogeneous sources (Waske and Benediktsson, 2007; Challa, Palaniswami and Shilton, 2002; Banerjee, and Das, 2012).

10. **Ensemble Methods:** Techniques like bagging, boosting, and stacking are used to combine predictions from multiple models to improve overall accuracy and robustness (Polikar, Topalis, Parikh, Green, Frymiare, Kounios and Clark, 2008; Muzammal, Talat, Sodhro and Pirbhulal, 2020; Parikh and Polikar, 2007).

Multi-Modal Data Fusion Approaches

This involves integrating data from different types of sensors or sources to create a more comprehensive and accurate understanding. Some common approaches include:

1. **Early Fusion (Feature-Level Fusion):** These approaches combine raw data or features extracted from multiple modalities at the initial stage. For example, integrating temperature, humidity, and air quality sensor data before further processing. These provide data fusion especially at edge sensors and devices in an IoT environment.

2. **Late Fusion (Decision-Level Fusion):** This approach involves processing each data modality separately and then combining the results based on decisions. This approach is used in applications like combining outputs from multiple machine learning models, for example fusion of learned number of predicted cases of disease for different geographical locations over a given time span.

3. **Hybrid Fusion (Mixed-Level Fusion):** This approach combines elements of both early and late fusion, integrating data at different stages of the processing pipeline to leverage the advantages of both approaches.
4. **Bayesian Inference**: this uses probabilistic models to integrate data from various sources, accounting for uncertainty and variability in the data. It provides a structured way to update the belief about the system state as new data arrives.
5. **Canonical Correlation Analysis (CCA):** this is a statistical method that finds the relationships between two or more sets of variables. It can be used to fuse data from different modalities by identifying common patterns in different datasets thereby generating better data from the individual datasets.
6. **Graph-Based Fusion:** These approaches represent data and their relationships as graphs, using techniques like graph convolutional networks (GCNs) to combine multi-modal data and extract meaningful insights.

These approaches enhance the robustness and accuracy of data analysis by leveraging the complementary information provided by different modalities, making them valuable for complex applications such as health monitoring, autonomous driving, and environmental sensing.

Uncertainty Modeling and Management in Data Fusion

Uncertainty modeling and management in data fusion are critical for ensuring the reliability and accuracy of combined data from diverse IoT sources (Magnani, and Montesi, 2010; de Villiers, Laskey, Jousselme, Blasch, de Waal, Pavlin and Costa, 2015). Uncertainty arises due to various factors, including sensor inaccuracies, environmental changes, and incomplete data. Techniques such as Bayesian inference and Dempster-Shafer Theory are used to model uncertainty by providing probabilistic frameworks that quantify and manage the degree of belief in different data sources (Abdulhafiz and Khamis, 2013; Magnani, and Montesi, 2010). Fuzzy logic handles imprecise data by allowing for partial membership in multiple categories, which helps in deriving more robust conclusions (Appriou, 2014). Kalman and Particle Filters are employed to estimate and reduce uncertainty in dynamic systems through iterative updates. Ensemble methods aggregate multiple models' outputs, which mitigates individual model uncertainties and improves overall prediction reliability (Appriou, 2014). These techniques collectively enhance the robustness of data fusion processes, enabling more accurate decision-making in applications such as disease surveillance, environmental monitoring, and smart city management.

A Proposed Framework for Collecting, Fusing, Aggregating, and Integrating Data for Infectious Diseases Surveillance

In other to have a resilient framework for collecting, fusing and aggregating data from numerous IoT sources, there is a need for an efficient network infrastructure on which the IoT devices are going to communicate (Cugola and Margara, 2012; Daraio et al., 2016a; Daraio et al., 2016b; Ye et al., 2016). For that reason, we first enumerate the architecture of the network on which the proposed framework is going to reside.

The proposed network architecture consists of three parts: (1) a home network, (2) a gateway-functioning router, and (3) a remote environment. The home network uses a 6LoWPAN mesh network, while the gateway has a router and local database.

Network nodes link and communicate with one another using IEEE 802.15.4 mesh networks. The expansion of the network span area, which allows the network to automatically grow new devices are added to it, and the high robustness of full mesh communication are its benefits. Compared to competing standards, the IEEE 802.15.4 standard can offer embedded devices lower data rates, lower power consumption, and cheaper costs. This is the protocol used in the physical layer, because it allows data bits to be transferred and received after being transformed into signals.

Additionally, there is a trusted link in the data link layer where faults in the signals transmitted in the physical layer are detected and corrected. This layer is separated into two layers: the 6LoWPAN adaptation layer and the Media Access Control (MAC) layer.

Network Architectural Components and Security Design Considerations

Our proposed design will use the IEEE 802.15.4 standard for the MAC layer as shown in figure 2. The media can be accessed by this standard, although routing performance is not determined by it. The switch from IPv6 to IEEE 802.15.4 is made at the second layer, or the adaptation layer. 6LoWPAN increases the maximum payload while decreasing overhead. offers minimal cost, great dependability, energy savings, mobility, and flexibility. Each point in the network can operate as a transmitter (host) or a receiver (router). Depending on the situation, certain devices function as hosts while saving energy by going into sleep mode, while other devices function as routers and never sleep. A 6LoWPAN edge router facilitates data sharing amongst the network's device members (Doan, Domingos, and Levy, 2000; Zikopoulos, et al., 2011; Olsson, 2014). The data transfer between the devices and the internet is also handled by this router. The edge router is specifically in charge of directing data and video into and out of our network (Doan, et al., 2020).

Neighbor Discovery (ND), another technique employed by 6LoWPAN, is used to identify the communication between the router and the host on the same link (Bifet, and Gavalda.2007; Calbimonte, Corcho, and Gray, 2010; Belli, et al 2015).

The network layer, which comes next, handles data addressing and routing. The Internetworking Protocol (IP) will be utilized in this layer. Each device will be configured with a distinct IPv6 address. To initiate the connection between a wireless sensor network and the internet, IPs should be modified to match the IEEE 802.15.4 low bandwidth, low power, and low-cost network that communicates over this standard (Chen et al., 2013; Bellahsène, Bonifati, and Rahm, 2011).

The Constrained Application Protocol (CoAP) is used in the application layer, which is the final layer. CoAP is a web application layer protocol that works with both battery-operated and energy-harvesting devices. Though it does not use TCP, it is comparable to Hypertext Transport Protocol (HTTP). In addition to using UDP, it supports IP multicast, minimal overhead, etc. To transfer less data over the wireless channel, CoAP compresses the HTTP data (Bifet, and Gavalda.2007; Chakravarthy et al., 2018). CoAP is built on an architecture known as REST. This protocol provides rest methods, including GET, POST, PUT, and DELETE.

Figure 2. Topological and architectural structure of the proposed framework

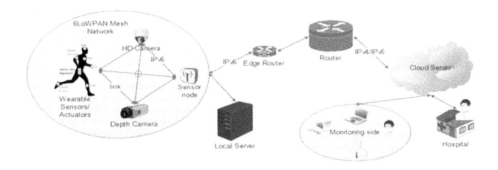

The two categories below best characterize this circumstance:

$$\left(N_s + K_c\right) - N_{nf} = A_{nodes} \tag{1}$$

$$\left(S_{data} + C_{video}\right) - P_{loss} = D_{sent} \tag{2}$$

More specifically, the transfer of information from other nodes is unaffected by the nodes that failed to send data and video streams. All the sensors, actuators, and cameras are in full duplex mesh communication, which enables intercommunication between them. The type that illustrates this is shown below:

Security, Scalability and Interoperability Consideration of the Framework

The proposed framework will collect data from four (4) major sources – (1) weather data, (2) vector abundance data, (3) disease incidence data, and (4) host population data using multiple IoT devices then align, aggregate, fuse and map it into a cohesive data stream for real-time holistic understanding of epidemiological incidences. The figure below gives an overall representation of the framework.

Figure 3. Schematic structure of the proposed framework

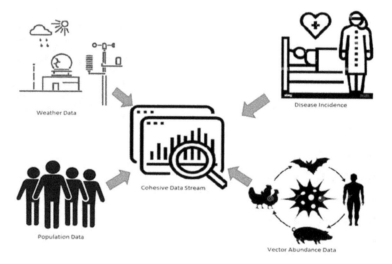

From figure 3 above we can see that divergent data from multiple IoT devices are collected, fused, mapped and aggregated into a cohesive data stream to be used for epidemiological research. This will be done based on the steps as outlined in the figure below.

Figure 4. Flow process of the proposed framework

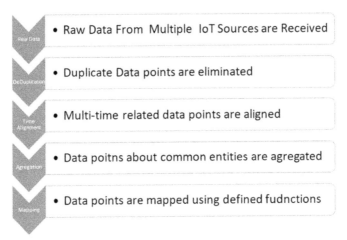

- Raw Data From Multiple IoT Sources are Received
- Duplicate Data points are eliminated
- Multi-time related data points are aligned
- Data poitns about common entities are agregated
- Data points are mapped using defined fudnctions

From figure 4 above, Data from multiple IoT sources are received, such data might contain irrelevant and redundant values and data points which might affect the accuracy of the ensuring machine learning algorithm used for data analysis. Thus, duplicate data from same devices will be eliminated first; then, same data captured over different time span will be aligned; furthermore, relevant but repeating data from multiple sources will be aggregated using any user defined functions; finally, data points with lookup requirement from other sources will be mapped to appropriate values.

To overcome the challenges noted, the model needs to satisfy the following requirements and criteria.

Requirement 1: The integrated data must be sorted according to the timestamp, because collected data may have different timing orders.

Requirement 2: To eliminate data redundant or duplicate data points; merge or aggregate data instances from multiple sensors, ensuring they have the same time stamp, to eliminate duplicate entries and improve integration and processing.

Requirement 3: Real-time edge data integration: this is crucial for timely capture of various flows, handling temporal orders, and eliminating duplication, ensuring accurate and timely handling of data.

Requirement 4: Contextualization of data; each data point is context sensitive because in epidemiological research every record captured is defined within the context where it is being captured. For example, the number of infections in human population has a different context and meaning from number of infections in zoonotic or vector populations.

The following are the formalizations of the proposed IoT data integration model, with important terminology and notations.

Definition 1: Context is the setting from which data is captured and it can be either (1) weather (2) human population (3) vector (4) disease contexts.

Definition 2: Source is the device or location from where data originates.

Definition 3: Unified Schema (US) is a pair of $< keys, values >$. This pair is generated based on the local schemas from multiple data sources. Where a 'key' corresponds to an attribute with a corresponding 'value'.

$$US = \{keys, values\} \qquad (4)$$

Where,

- US is an integral data schema,
- $\{keys\}$ are lists of attributes of data to be captured
- $\{values\}$ data corresponding to a keys from a particular source.

Definition 4: Unique Keys. This is a set of all keys from all IoT sources. because $\{keys\}$ is a set of unique attributes from multiple IoT data sources, then.

$$\{keys\} = set(keys(k)) \qquad (5)$$

Where,

$keys(k)$ is a set of keys from single IoT data sources,

$\{keys\}$ is a list distinct of attributes in the integrated data from all sources.

Definition 5: De-duplication. This is the procedure of merging or aggregating duplicate instances of keys from numerous data sources. Here, all instances with identical context, source and keys name and time stamps values are aggregated or merged using an appropriate mapping function using any of the earlier function such as Kalman filter, particle filter, Neural Network or ensemble methods, that fuses all duplicate data instances thereby eliminating redundant records. In this work, de-duplication involves combining all records with the same context, source and time stamp. We obtain the values for non-identical records from several IoT data sources and transform them using the system.

$$f = mapping() \qquad (6)$$

From above, *mapping ()* is a user-defined function that transforms data into an integrated standard format. Data from several sources can be compiled for each data field in the unified schema using a user-defined mapping function as shown in figure 5.

Definition 6: Window-based Integration. This is the integration of data from several sources to create an integrated stream. Such streams are characterized as various groups of several data records from various sources for a particular time interval, such as days, weeks, or months, referred to as a window. This window-based integration is used to accomplish the work of timing alignment according to data streams from various sources.

$$Wi(t) = \bigcup_{k=1}^{n} Wk\ (t) \tag{7}$$

Where,

- k is the number of data sources,
- $Wi\ (t)$ is an integrated window that runs for a predetermined amount of time, denoted by the window's size, beginning at time t.
- $Wk\ (t)$ is the source window k, for which data is integrated, beginning at time t

Figure 5. Logical structure of the proposed framework

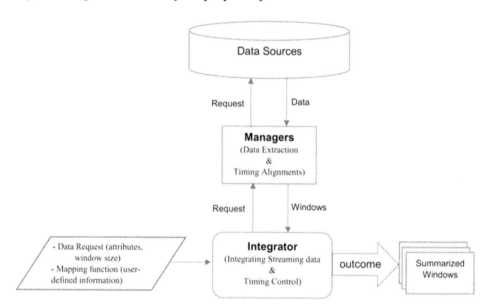

ISDI Integrator

Here, we introduce the ISDI Integrator, a model for combining streaming IoT data—that is, time-series data—from several sources. Figure-5 shows the different parts of the proposed integrator model. The fundamental windowing model, which handles real-time IoT data streaming from many sources, is the basic model that we consider in this work. There are two layers in an ISDI integrator:

(i) IoT Data Sources and Managers and
(ii) Integrator.

Figure 6. Logical structure of the data integrator

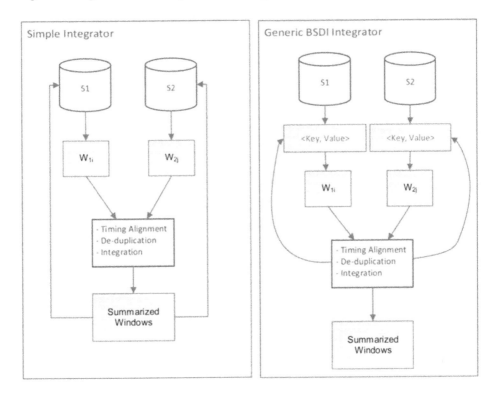

Data Sources and Managers

Managers process IoT streaming data from various sources, assembling it into a common format. They represent a unified schema and extract data using timing alignment mechanisms. They synchronize streamed data according to timestamps and mark a pointer based on the most recent processed data. This facilitates real-time data processing for integrators, ensuring efficient handling of incoming data as shown in figure 5 and figure 6 above.

CASE STUDIES AND APPLICATIONS

Real-World Implementations of the Proposed Framework

The experiments to test the proposed framework are run on IoTNetSim found at https://github.com/m-salama/IotNetSim/blob/master where a time-based library, named Joda-Time found at https://www.joda.org/joda-time/, was used to process time-series data from multiple data sources. This was installed and setup on a Windows PC with 3.4 GHz CPU, 4 Core(s) and 8 Logical Processors with 16 GB of physical memory. Where a virtual server was created and forty IoT devices; ten weather sensors, ten disease incidence reporting endpoints, ten vector surveillance devices and ten human population reporting end points were set up.

Furthermore, we use Apache Spark 3.5.1 found at https://spark.apache.org/ with Java API implementation to create an ontology inference engine (Chakravarthy et al., 2018) for querying and aggregating data. JavaDK 8 was a requirement on which the Spark Driver was set up. To prevent the error "GC overhead limit exceeded," a specific configuration for IoTNetSim memory use is required (raising the heap size). As a result, VM arguments are set to -Xmx2048M. Data requested from the managers is transferred into Resilient Distributed Datasets (RDDs) in the Spark equivalent implementation. These RDDs are split into logical partitions and subsequently run in parallel. As a proof of concept, we employed RDDs in our suggested method to split the massive data set into several logical partitions for parallel processing in this experiment.

Test Datasets

We used synthesized datasets generated from multiple IoT sensors as discussed above to carry out experiment in this work. Table 1 below details how data was generated from the data sources. Each category of IoT has ten devices but each category has varying frequency of data generation. Weather data has the highest frequency because it varies throughout the day records are generated hourly, then vector surveillance records are generated daily, then disease incidence is reported weekly, while population dynamics (population fluctuations) is reported monthly. The attributes of each source are different, but there are common attributes which include device id, location, timestamp and context. In addition, each device has schema information which includes a key, value pair which captures the actual information the device is reporting.

Table 1. Data synthesizing frequency

Devices	Simulated Duration	Frequency	Number of Records
Weather Devices	365 Days	1 Record/Hour	$8{,}760 \times 10 = 87{,}600$
Vector Surveillance Devices	365 Days	1/ Day	$360 \times 10 = 3{,}600$
Disease Incidence Reporting	52 Weeks	1 Record/ week	$52 \times 10 = 520$
Population Reporting	12 Monthly	1 Record/ Month	$12 \times 10 = 120$

After synthesizing the data as discussed above, four different neural networks were built to predict; (1) disease incidence, (2) vector abundance, and (3) host population dynamics using the data synthesized by the proposed framework then compared with models built using data captured using manual traditional methods of data capture. An Extreme Learning Machine Neural Network (ELMNN) was used in both situations. A total of 87,600 records were generated in both cases based on synthesized records as pointed out in Table 1 above. These data captured variables in four major areas: (1) weather, (2) vector abundance, disease incidence, (4) host population dynamics. For weather, temperature, humidity, atmospheric pressure, sunshine was used. While for vector abundance, number of observed vectors, adult ratio, average number per species, mating rate were used. While for host population, number of hosts observed, emigration rate, immigration rate, reproduction rate, average life expectancy was used. Then for disease incidence rate, number of infected, number of susceptible, number of immune, rate of recovery, rate of mortality was noted. In addition, location, date and time were also captured. Thus, the dataset has a total of twenty-one attributes that were used in total. As per the proposed framework the data was passed through a pipeline as below:

Figure 7. Logical structure of the proposed data fusion framework

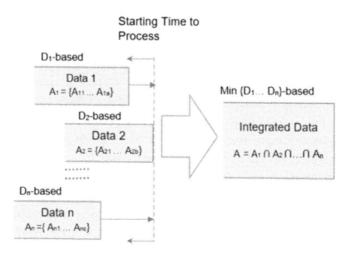

The weight connecting the input nodes to the hidden layer in an ELM is set once and is never modified, setting it apart from other neural networks. This leads to a learning process that is faster than that of the popular back propagation algorithms. Therefore, compared to most other neural network models that use the back propagation method for training, the ELM model produces better generalization on new data and more understandable models.

Performance With Respect to Model Accuracy

For each of the neural networks for prediction task, the Receiver Operating Characteristics (ROC) curves were assessed to measure the accuracy of the model. Furthermore, the Area Under Curve (AUC) for the models of the proposed framework and the traditional data capture were also compared. The curves are presented in figure 4 to eight below:

Figure 8. Pipeline of the proposed framework

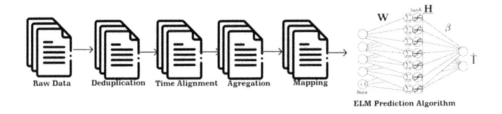

From the figure 8 above, for the neural network predicting disease incidence, the proposed framework outperforms the traditional data capture method as its ROC tends more towards the top-left corner of the plot while its AUC is 0.9724 which better than that of the traditional method which stands at 0.7902.

Figure 9. ROC curve of neural network predicting disease incidence

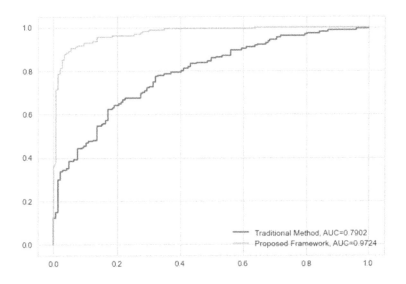

From figure 9 above as a comparison with the result earlier, the model predicting vector abundance had a better performance for both the proposed and traditional methods. These might be since the vector abundance data was sparse in the original synthesized data but aligned with the weather data. Thus, the number of records was replicated for all records with the time of weather data and so the model performance was improved accordingly.

Figure 10. ROC curve of model predicting host population

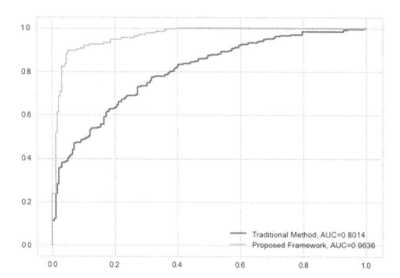

Furthermore, the performance of the two models in predicting host population dwindled as seen in figure 10. This might be associated to the fact that host population data is continuous and more precise. So, the performance of both neural networks had a lower accuracy as is evident that the curves did not skew to upper left corner of the plot and the AUC of both models is lower than that of the two earlier models.

Performance With Respect to Learning Speed

The performance of the two neural networks with respect to learning speed is presented in this section. As already known, the learning rate of a model is a good indicator of the underlining data used to build such a model. Thus, we report the training and testing learning rates of both the proposed model and the traditional method as presented below:

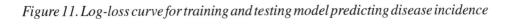

Figure 11. Log-loss curve for training and testing model predicting disease incidence

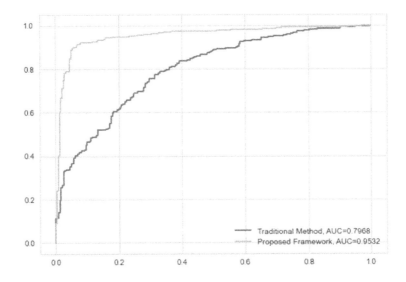

From figure 11 above it can be seen that the learning rate of proposed algorithm for training and testing outperform that of the manual methods respectively. This is indicated in fact that those of the proposed method represented in in solid and dashed red lines tends more towards the origin (0,0) which is a good indication of the goodness of a Log-Loss function.

Figure 12. Log-loss curve for training and testing model predicting vector abundance

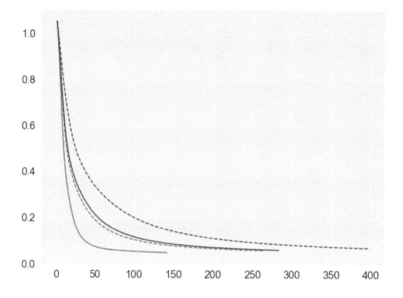

In same vein with the case of model accuracy, from figure 12 above the Log-Loss Curve of the model predicting vector abundance appears to have the best learning rate as it tends more towards the origin more than all the other models. This might be due to the same reason as mentioned above i.e. the number of captured data about the vector abundance. Furthermore, it can also be seen that the learning rates of both the models are closely comparable as they all are in proximity.

Figure 13. Log-loss curve for training and testing model predicting host population

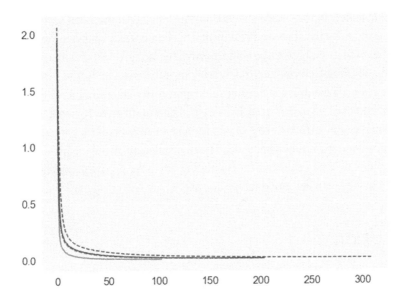

From figure 13 above the Log-Loss curve of the model predicting host population tends to have the worse learning rate of the four trained models. This is evident if fact that the curve is not steep and tends to towards the center of the plot. Furthermore, the learning rate of the training phase for this model tends to outperform that of the traditional methods by far which might be due to the continuous nature of the predicted values.

FUTURE RESEARCH DIRECTIONS

Future researchers can investigate current indexing frameworks with various indexing techniques, such as the R-tree index for subspaces (Li, Wang, Dai, Li, Gu, Chen, ... and Chen, 2024), the B-tree index for time intervals (Wang, Adiga, Chen, Lewis, Sadilek, Venkatramanan, and Marathe, 2022), and the skyline index for time-series data (Wang, Adiga, Chen, Lewis, Sadilek, Venkatramanan, and Marathe, 2022). The work intended to expand upon literature suggested ISDI methodology to facilitate instantaneous data integration in real-time, all the while indexing distinct time-series data from various IoT sources. In the future, the work will also investigate the optimization problem while combining various time-series data from various

IoT sources. To achieve this, the work will experiment with various window sizes and indexing strategies.

Future research in IoT-based disease surveillance will focus on several key areas to enhance the effectiveness and reliability of data collection systems. Developing advanced data fusion algorithms will improve the integration and analysis of multi-modal data, leading to more accurate and comprehensive insights. Efforts will also be directed toward establishing better interoperability standards to ensure seamless communication between different IoT devices and platforms. Research will explore scalable and energy-efficient IoT infrastructure to support widespread deployment and continuous data collection. Additionally, creating robust ethical frameworks and guidelines will be essential for balancing privacy, security, and fairness while advancing disease surveillance technologies.

CONCLUSION

Various methods of data collection, aggregation and integration for epidemiological research have been proposed. This work proposed a framework which has security and privacy retention at core. First, it presented an architectural and topological network design of the intended IoT network, then it presented a formal model that included main ideas of data integration, timing alignment, and de-duplication. Next, it presented a general integrator model that includes several layers to use real-time streaming data integration from several IoT sources. The implementation algorithms were then demonstrated. The work conducted multiple sets of experiments and presented an empirical comparison between our proposed framework and data sourced from manual data collection methods to portray the superiority of the proposed framework.

REFERENCES

Abdulhafiz, W. A., & Khamis, A. (2013). Handling data uncertainty and inconsistency using multisensor data fusion. *Advances in Artificial Intelligence*, 2013(1), 241260. DOI:10.1155/2013/241260

Anderson, R. M. (1982). Transmission dynamics and control of infectious disease agents. In *Population Biology of Infectious Diseases: Report of the Dahlem Workshop on Population Biology of Infectious Disease Agents Berlin 1982, March 14–19* (pp. 149-176). Springer Berlin Heidelberg. DOI:10.1007/978-3-642-68635-1_9

Appriou, A. (Ed.). (2014). *Uncertainty theories and multisensor data fusion*. John Wiley & Sons. DOI:10.1002/9781118578636

Banerjee, T. P., & Das, S. (2012). Multi-sensor data fusion using support vector machine for motor fault detection. *Information Sciences*, 217, 96–107. DOI:10.1016/j.ins.2012.06.016

Barreto-Cubero, A. J., Gómez-Espinosa, A., Escobedo Cabello, J. A., Cuan-Urquizo, E., & Cruz-Ramírez, S. R. (2021). Sensor data fusion for a mobile robot using neural networks. *Sensors (Basel)*, 22(1), 305. DOI:10.3390/s22010305 PMID:35009849

Bauch, C. T., Szusz, E., & Garrison, L. P. (2009). Scheduling of measles vaccination in low-income countries: Projections of a dynamic model. *Vaccine*, 27(31), 4090–4098. DOI:10.1016/j.vaccine.2009.04.079 PMID:19410622

Bellahsène, Z., Bonifati, A., & Rahm, E. (2011). *Schema matching and mapping*. Springer. DOI:10.1007/978-3-642-16518-4

Belli, L., Cirani, S., Davoli, L., Ferrari, G., Melegari, L., Montón, M., & Picone, M. (2015). A scalable big stream cloud architecture for the internet of things. *International Journal of Systems and Service-Oriented Engineering*, 5(4), 26–53. DOI:10.4018/IJSSOE.2015100102

Bellouquid, A., & Delitala, M. (2006). *Mathematical modeling of complex biological systems*. Birkhüser Boston.

Bifet, A., & Gavalda, R. (2007) Learning from time-changing data with adaptive windowing. In *Proceedings of the 2007 SIAM international conference on data mining*. SIAM. DOI:10.1137/1.9781611972771.42

Bongomin, O., Yemane, A., Kembabazi, B., Malanda, C., Mwape, M. C., Mpofu, N. S., & Tigalana, D. (2020). *The hype and disruptive technologies of industry 4.0 in major industrial sectors:A state of the art*.

Borda, A., Molnar, A., Neesham, C., & Kostkova, P. (2022). Ethical issues in AI-enabled disease surveillance: Perspectives from global health. *Applied Sciences (Basel, Switzerland)*, 12(8), 3890. DOI:10.3390/app12083890

Brearley, G., Rhodes, J., Bradley, A., Baxter, G., Seabrook, L., Lunney, D., Liu, Y., & McAlpine, C. (2013). Wildlife disease prevalence in human-modified landscapes. *Biological Reviews of the Cambridge Philosophical Society*, 88(2), 427–442. DOI:10.1111/brv.12009 PMID:23279314

Burkom, H. S., Ramac-Thomas, L., Babin, S., Holtry, R., Mnatsakanyan, Z., & Yund, C. (2011). An integrated approach for fusion of environmental and human health data for disease surveillance. *Statistics in Medicine*, 30(5), 470–479. DOI:10.1002/sim.3976 PMID:21290403

Calbimonte, J. P., Corcho, O., & Gray, A. J. (2010) Enabling ontology-based access to streaming data sources. In *International semantic Web conference*. Springer. DOI:10.1007/978-3-642-17746-0_7

Carpenter, J., Clifford, P., & Fearnhead, P. (1999). Improved particle filter for nonlinear problems. *IEE Proceedings. Radar, Sonar and Navigation*, 146(1), 2–7. DOI:10.1049/ip-rsn:19990255

Carrel, M., & Rennie, S. (2008). Demographic and health surveillance: Longitudinal ethical considerations. *Bulletin of the World Health Organization*, 86(8), 612–616. DOI:10.2471/BLT.08.051037 PMID:18797619

Çela, E. (2022). A summary of the national plan for european integration related with the developments of education system in Albania during 2020-2021. *Euro-Balkan Law and Economics Review*, (1), 71–86.

Çela, E. (2024). Global Agendas in Higher Education and Current Educational Reforms in Albania. In *Global Agendas and Education Reforms: A Comparative Study* (pp. 255–269). Springer. DOI:10.1007/978-981-97-3068-1_13

Çela, E., Fonkam, M. M., & Potluri, R. M. (2024). Risks of AI-Assisted Learning on Student Critical Thinking: A Case Study of Albania. *International Journal of Risk and Contingency Management*, 12(1), 1–19. DOI:10.4018/IJRCM.350185

Çela, E., Vajjhala, N. R., & Eappen, P. (2024). Foundations of Computational Thinking and Problem Solving for Diverse Academic Fields. *Revolutionizing Curricula Through Computational Thinking, Logic, and Problem Solving*, 1-16.

Chakravarthy, S. K., Sudhakar, N., Reddy, E. S., Subramanian, D. V., & Shankar, P. (2018). Dimension Reduction and Storage Optimization Techniques for Distributed and Big Data Cluster Environment. In *Soft Computing and Medical Bioinformatics* (pp. 47–54). Springer.

Challa, S., Palaniswami, M., & Shilton, A. (2002, July). Distributed data fusion using support vector machines. In *Proceedings of the Fifth International Conference on Information Fusion* (Vol. 2, pp. 881-885). IEEE. DOI:10.1109/ICIF.2002.1020902

Chen, J., Chen, Y., Du, X., Li, C., Lu, J., Zhao, S., & Zhou, X. (2013). Big data Challenge: A Data Management perspective. *Frontiers of Computer Science*, 7(2), 157–164. DOI:10.1007/s11704-013-3903-7

Cooch, E. G., Conn, P. B., Ellner, S. P., Dobson, A. P., & Pollock, K. H. (2012). Disease dynamics in wild populations: modeling and estimation: a review. *Journal of Ornithology*, 152(S2), 485–509. DOI:10.1007/s10336-010-0636-3

Cugola, G., & Margara, A. (2012). Processing flows of information: From data stream to complex event processing. *ACM Computing Surveys*, 44(3), 15. DOI:10.1145/2187671.2187677

Curran, P. J., & Hussong, A. M. (2009). Integrative data analysis: The simultaneous analysis of multiple data sets. *Psychological Methods*, 14(2), 81–100. DOI:10.1037/a0015914 PMID:19485623

Daraio, C., Lenzerini, M., Leporelli, C., Moed, H. F., Naggar, P., Bonaccorsi, A., & Bartolucci, A. (2016a). Data integration for research and innovation policy: An ontology-based data management approach. *Scientometrics*, 106(2), 857–871. DOI:10.1007/s11192-015-1814-0

Daraio, C., Lenzerini, M., Leporelli, C., Naggar, P., Bonaccorsi, A., & Bartolucci, A. (2016b). The advantages of an ontology-based data management approach: Openness, interoperability and data quality. *Scientometrics*, 108(1), 441–455. DOI:10.1007/s11192-016-1913-6

de Villiers, J. P., Laskey, K., Jousselme, A. L., Blasch, E., de Waal, A., Pavlin, G., & Costa, P. (2015, July). Uncertainty representation, quantification and evaluation for data and information fusion. In *2015 18th International Conference on Information Fusion (Fusion)* (pp. 50-57). IEEE.

Declich, S., & Carter, A. O. (1994). Public health surveillance: Historical origins, methods and evaluation. *Bulletin of the World Health Organization*, 72(2), 285. PMID:8205649

Ding, H., Ji, H., Huang, Z., & Li, H. (2004, June). Data fusion algorithm based on fuzzy logic. In *Fifth World Congress on Intelligent Control and Automation* (IEEE Cat. No. 04EX788) (Vol. 4, pp. 3101-3103). IEEE. DOI:10.1109/WCICA.2004.1343091

Doan, A., Domingos, P. M., & Levy, A. Y. (2000) Learning source description for data integration. In: *WebDB (informal proceedings)*, pp 81–86

Doan, Q. T., Kayes, A., Rahayu, W., & Nguyen, K. (2020). Integration of iot streaming data with efficient indexing and storage optimization. *IEEE Access : Practical Innovations, Open Solutions*, 8, 47456–47467. DOI:10.1109/ACCESS.2020.2980006

Doukas, C., Pliakas, T., & Maglogiannis, I. (2010, August). Mobile healthcare information management utilizing Cloud Computing and Android OS. In *2010 Annual International Conference of the IEEE Engineering in Medicine and Biology* (pp. 1037-1040). IEEE.

Drewe, J. A., Hoinville, L. J., Cook, A. J. C., Floyd, T., & Stärk, K. D. C. (2012). Evaluation of animal and public health surveillance systems: A systematic review. *Epidemiology and Infection*, 140(4), 575–590. DOI:10.1017/S0950268811002160 PMID:22074638

Drosou, M., Jagadish, H. V., Pitoura, E., & Stoyanovich, J. (2017). Diversity in big data: A review. *Big Data*, 5(2), 73–84. DOI:10.1089/big.2016.0054 PMID:28632443

Dugas, A. F., Hsieh, Y. H., Levin, S. R., Pines, J. M., Mareiniss, D. P., Mohareb, A., Gaydos, C. A., Perl, T. M., & Rothman, R. E. (2012). Google Flu Trends: Correlation with emergency department influenza rates and crowding metrics. *Clinical Infectious Diseases*, 54(4), 463–469. DOI:10.1093/cid/cir883 PMID:22230244

Dugas, A. F., Jalalpour, M., Gel, Y., Levin, S., Torcaso, F., Igusa, T., & Rothman, R. E. (2013). Influenza forecasting with Google flu trends. *PLoS One*, 8(2), e56176. DOI:10.1371/journal.pone.0056176 PMID:23457520

Eisenberg, J. N., Desai, M. A., Levy, K., Bates, S. J., Liang, S., Naumoff, K., & Scott, J. C. (2007). Environmental determinants of infectious disease: A framework for tracking causal links and guiding public health research. *Environmental Health Perspectives*, 115(8), 1216–1223. DOI:10.1289/ehp.9806 PMID:17687450

Falzon, L. C., Ogola, J. G., Odinga, C. O., Naboyshchikov, L., Fèvre, E. M., & Berezowski, J. (2021). Electronic data collection to enhance disease surveillance at the slaughterhouse in a smallholder production system. *Scientific Reports*, 11(1), 19447. DOI:10.1038/s41598-021-98495-7 PMID:34593856

Fraser, A. G., & Marcotte, E. M. (2004). A probabilistic view of gene function. *Nature Genetics*, 36(6), 559–564. DOI:10.1038/ng1370 PMID:15167932

Geneviève, L. D., Martani, A., Wangmo, T., Paolotti, D., Koppeschaar, C., Kjelsø, C., Guerrisi, C., Hirsch, M., Woolley-Meza, O., Lukowicz, P., Flahault, A., & Elger, B. S. (2019). Participatory disease surveillance systems: Ethical framework. *Journal of Medical Internet Research*, 21(5), e12273. DOI:10.2196/12273 PMID:31124466

Goetz, S. J., Prince, S. D., & Small, J. (2000). Advances in satellite remote sensing of environmental variables for epidemiological applications. *Advances in Parasitology*, 47, 289–307. DOI:10.1016/S0065-308X(00)47012-0 PMID:10997210

Guerriero, M., Svensson, L., & Willett, P. (2010). Bayesian data fusion for distributed target detection in sensor networks. *IEEE Transactions on Signal Processing*, 58(6), 3417–3421. DOI:10.1109/TSP.2010.2046042

Gustafsson, F. (2010). Particle filter theory and practice with positioning applications. *IEEE Aerospace and Electronic Systems Magazine*, 25(7), 53–82. DOI:10.1109/MAES.2010.5546308

Guzewich, J. J., Bryan, F. L., & Todd, E. C. (1997). Surveillance of foodborne disease I. Purposes and types of surveillance systems and networks. *Journal of Food Protection*, 60(5), 555–566. DOI:10.4315/0362-028X-60.5.555 PMID:31195586

Heidemann, J., Silva, F., Intanagonwiwat, C., Govindan, R., Estrin, D., & Ganesan, D. (2001, October). Building efficient wireless sensor networks with low-level naming. In *Proceedings of the eighteenth ACM symposium on Operating systems principles* (pp. 146-159). DOI:10.1145/502034.502049

Hongyan, G. A. O. (2009, August). A simple multi-sensor data fusion algorithm based on principal component analysis. In *2009 ISECS International Colloquium on Computing, Communication, Control, and Management* (Vol. 2, pp. 423-426). IEEE. DOI:10.1109/CCCM.2009.5267459

Jiang, Q., Zhou, X., Wang, R., Ding, W., Chu, Y., Tang, S., Jia, X., & Xu, X. (2022). Intelligent monitoring for infectious diseases with fuzzy systems and edge computing: A survey. *Applied Soft Computing*, 123, 108835. DOI:10.1016/j.asoc.2022.108835

Jillahi, K. B., & Iorliam, A. (2024). A Scoping Literature Review of Artificial Intelligence in Epidemiology: Uses, Applications, Challenges and Future Trends. *Journal of Computing Theories and Applications*, 2(2), 204–228. DOI:10.62411/jcta.10350

Karesh, W. B., Dobson, A., Lloyd-Smith, J. O., Lubroth, J., Dixon, M. A., Bennett, M., Aldrich, S., Harrington, T., Formenty, P., Loh, E. H., Machalaba, C. C., Thomas, M. J., & Heymann, D. L. (2012). Ecology of zoonoses: Natural and unnatural histories. *Lancet*, 380(9857), 1936–1945. DOI:10.1016/S0140-6736(12)61678-X PMID:23200502

Keeling, M. J., & Eames, K. T. (2005). Networks and epidemic models. *Journal of the Royal Society, Interface*, 2(4), 295–307. DOI:10.1098/rsif.2005.0051 PMID:16849187

Kim, Y., & Bang, H. (2018). Introduction to Kalman filter and its applications. *Introduction and Implementations of the Kalman Filter*, 1, 1–16.

King, R. C., Villeneuve, E., White, R. J., Sherratt, R. S., Holderbaum, W., & Harwin, W. S. (2017). Application of data fusion techniques and technologies for wearable health monitoring. *Medical Engineering & Physics*, 42, 1–12. DOI:10.1016/j.medengphy.2016.12.011 PMID:28237714

Kolanowski, K., Świetlicka, A., Kapela, R., Pochmara, J., & Rybarczyk, A. (2018). Multisensor data fusion using Elman neural networks. *Applied Mathematics and Computation*, 319, 236–244. DOI:10.1016/j.amc.2017.02.031

LaDeau, S. L., Glass, G. E., Hobbs, N. T., Latimer, A., & Ostfeld, R. S. (2011). Data–model fusion to better understand emerging pathogens and improve infectious disease forecasting. *Ecological Applications*, 21(5), 1443–1460. DOI:10.1890/09-1409.1 PMID:21830694

Lawson, A. B. (2018). *Bayesian disease mapping: hierarchical modeling in spatial epidemiology. Chapman and Hall/CRC.*

Lee, L. M. (2019). Public health surveillance: Ethical considerations. *The Oxford handbook of public health ethic*s, 320.

Lescano, A. G., Larasati, R. P., Sedyaningsih, E. R., Bounlu, K., Araujo-Castillo, R. V., Munayco Escate, C. V., Soto, G., Mundaca, C. C., & Blazes, D. L. (2008, December). Statistical analyses in disease surveillance systems. *BMC Proceedings*, 2(S3), 1–6. DOI:10.1186/1753-6561-2-s3-s7 PMID:19025684

Li, M., Wang, H., Dai, H., Li, M., Gu, R., Chen, F., & Chen, G. (2024). A Survey of Multi-Dimensional Indexes: Past and Future Trends. *IEEE Transactions on Knowledge and Data Engineering*, 36(8), 3635–3655. DOI:10.1109/TKDE.2024.3364183

Lin, J. S., Burkom, H. S., Murphy, S. P., Elbert, Y., Hakre, S., Babin, S. M., & Feldman, A. B. (2006). *Bayesian fusion of syndromic surveillance with sensor data for disease outbreak classification.* In Life Science Data Mining (pp. 119-141). DOI:10.1142/9789812772664_0006

Liu, J., Huang, J., Sun, R., Yu, H., & Xiao, R. (2020). Data fusion for multi-source sensors using GA-PSO-BP neural network. *IEEE Transactions on Intelligent Transportation Systems*, 22(10), 6583–6598. DOI:10.1109/TITS.2020.3010296

Lodi, G., Aniello, L., Di Luna, G. A., & Baldoni, R. (2014). An event-based platform for collaborative threats detection and monitoring. *Information Systems*, 39, 175–195. DOI:10.1016/j.is.2013.07.005

Lourenço, C., Tatem, A. J., Atkinson, P. M., Cohen, J. M., Pindolia, D., Bhavnani, D., & Le Menach, A. (2019). Strengthening surveillance systems for malaria elimination: A global landscaping of system performance, 2015–2017. *Malaria Journal*, 18(1), 1–11. DOI:10.1186/s12936-019-2960-2 PMID:31533740

Mafata, M., Brand, J., Kidd, M., Medvedovici, A., & Buica, A. (2022). Exploration of data fusion strategies using principal component analysis and multiple factor analysis. *Beverages*, 8(4), 66. DOI:10.3390/beverages8040066

Magnani, M., & Montesi, D. (2010). A survey on uncertainty management in data integration. *ACM Journal of Data and Information Quality*, 2(1), 1–33. DOI:10.1145/1805286.1805291

Mahler, R. P. (1996, June). Unified data fusion: fuzzy logic, evidence, and rules. In *Signal Processing, Sensor Fusion, and Target Recognition V* (Vol. 2755, pp. 226–237). SPIE. DOI:10.1117/12.243164

Manjunatha, P., Verma, A. K., & Srividya, A. (2008, December). Multi-sensor data fusion in cluster based wireless sensor networks using fuzzy logic method. In *2008 IEEE region 10 and the third international conference on industrial and information systems* (pp. 1-6). IEEE. DOI:10.1109/ICIINFS.2008.4798453

Maybeck, P. S. (1990). The Kalman filter: An introduction to concepts. In *Autonomous robot vehicles* (pp. 194–204). Springer New York. DOI:10.1007/978-1-4613-8997-2_15

McMichael, A. J. (2004). Environmental and social influences on emerging infectious diseases: Past, present and future. *Philosophical Transactions of the Royal Society of London. Series B, Biological Sciences*, 359(1447), 1049–1058. DOI:10.1098/rstb.2004.1480 PMID:15306389

Morain, S. A., & Budge, A. M. (Eds.). (2012). *Environmental tracking for public health surveillance*. CRC Press. DOI:10.1201/b12680

Muzammal, M., Talat, R., Sodhro, A. H., & Pirbhulal, S. (2020). A multi-sensor data fusion enabled ensemble approach for medical data from body sensor networks. *Information Fusion*, 53, 155–164. DOI:10.1016/j.inffus.2019.06.021

Mwabukusi, M., Karimuribo, E. D., Rweyemamu, M. M., & Beda, E. (2014). Mobile technologies for disease surveillance in humans and animals: Proceedings. *The Onderstepoort Journal of Veterinary Research*, 81(2), 1–5. DOI:10.4102/ojvr. v81i2.737 PMID:25005126

Nnebue, C., Onwasigwe, C., Adogu, P., & Adinma, E. (2014). Challenges of data collection and disease notification in Anambra State, Nigeria. *Tropical Journal of Medical Research*, 17(1), 1–6. DOI:10.4103/1119-0388.130173

Olsson, J. (2014). 6LoWPAN demystified. *Texas Instruments*, 13, 1–13.

Pace, P., Aloi, G., Gravina, R., Caliciuri, G., Fortino, G., & Liotta, A. (2018). An edge-based architecture to support efficient applications for healthcare industry 4.0. *IEEE Transactions on Industrial Informatics*, 15(1), 481–489. DOI:10.1109/ TII.2018.2843169

Paquet, C., Coulombier, D., Kaiser, R., & Ciotti, M. (2006). Epidemic intelligence: A new framework for strengthening disease surveillance in Europe. *Eurosurveillance*, 11(12), 5–6. DOI:10.2807/esm.11.12.00665-en PMID:17370970

Parikh, D., & Polikar, R. (2007). An ensemble-based incremental learning approach to data fusion. *IEEE Transactions on Systems, Man, and Cybernetics. Part B, Cybernetics*, 37(2), 437–450. DOI:10.1109/TSMCB.2006.883873 PMID:17416170

Pervaiz, F., Pervaiz, M., Rehman, N. A., & Saif, U. (2012). FluBreaks: Early epidemic detection from Google flu trends. *Journal of Medical Internet Research*, 14(5), e2102. DOI:10.2196/jmir.2102 PMID:23037553

Phalkey, R. K., Yamamoto, S., Awate, P., & Marx, M. (2015). Challenges with the implementation of an Integrated Disease Surveillance and Response (IDSR) system: Systematic review of the lessons learned. *Health Policy and Planning*, 30(1), 131–143. DOI:10.1093/heapol/czt097 PMID:24362642

Plageras, A. P., Psannis, K. E., Ishibashi, Y., & Kim, B. G. (2016, October). IoT-based surveillance system for ubiquitous healthcare. In *IECON 2016-42nd Annual Conference of the IEEE Industrial Electronics Society* (pp. 6226-6230). IEEE. DOI:10.1109/IECON.2016.7793281

Polikar, R., Topalis, A., Parikh, D., Green, D., Frymiare, J., Kounios, J., & Clark, C. M. (2008). An ensemble based data fusion approach for early diagnosis of Alzheimer's disease. *Information Fusion*, 9(1), 83–95. DOI:10.1016/j.inffus.2006.09.003

Polonsky, J. A., Baidjoe, A., Kamvar, Z. N., Cori, A., Durski, K., Edmunds, W. J., ... & Jombart, T. (2019). *Outbreak analytics: a developing data science for informing the response to emerging pathogens.* Philosophical Transactions of the Royal Society B, 374(1776), 20180276.

Radin, J. M., Wineinger, N. E., Topol, E. J., & Steinhubl, S. R. (2020). Harnessing wearable device data to improve state-level real-time surveillance of influenza-like illness in the USA: A population-based study. *The Lancet. Digital Health*, 2(2), e85–e93. DOI:10.1016/S2589-7500(19)30222-5 PMID:33334565

Rahier, T. (2018). *Bayesian networks for static and temporal data fusion* (Doctoral dissertation, Université Grenoble Alpes).

Rahmani, A. M., Gia, T. N., Negash, B., Anzanpour, A., Azimi, I., Jiang, M., & Liljeberg, P. (2018). Exploiting smart e-Health gateways at the edge of healthcare Internet-of-Things: A fog computing approach. *Future Generation Computer Systems*, 78, 641–658. DOI:10.1016/j.future.2017.02.014

Randhawa, S., & Jain, S. (2017). Data aggregation in wireless sensor networks: Previous research, current status and future directions. *Wireless Personal Communications*, 97(3), 3355–3425. DOI:10.1007/s11277-017-4674-5

Robertson, C., Nelson, T. A., MacNab, Y. C., & Lawson, A. B. (2010). Review of methods for space–time disease surveillance. *Spatial and Spatio-temporal Epidemiology*, 1(2-3), 105–116. DOI:10.1016/j.sste.2009.12.001 PMID:22749467

Shafer, G. (1992). Dempster-shafer theory. Encyclopedia of artificial intelligence, 1, 330-331.

Texier, G., Allodji, R. S., Diop, L., Meynard, J. B., Pellegrin, L., & Chaudet, H. (2019). Using decision fusion methods to improve outbreak detection in disease surveillance. *BMC Medical Informatics and Decision Making*, 19, 1–11.

Thacker, S. B., & Berkelman, R. L. (1988). Public health surveillance in the United States. *Epidemiologic Reviews*, 10(1), 164–190. DOI:10.1093/oxfordjournals.epirev. a036021 PMID:3066626

Wang, L., Adiga, A., Chen, J., Lewis, B., Sadilek, A., Venkatramanan, S., & Marathe, M. (2022). Combining Theory and Data-Driven Approaches for Epidemic Forecasts. In *Knowledge Guided Machine Learning* (pp. 55–82). Chapman and Hall/CRC. DOI:10.1201/9781003143376-3

Waske, B., & Benediktsson, J. A. (2007). Fusion of support vector machines for classification of multisensor data. *IEEE Transactions on Geoscience and Remote Sensing*, 45(12), 3858–3866. DOI:10.1109/TGRS.2007.898446

Welch, G., & Bishop, G. (1995). *An introduction to the Kalman filter.* Springer New York.

Wilson, N. (2000). Algorithms for dempster-shafer theory. In *Handbook of Defeasible Reasoning and Uncertainty Management Systems: Algorithms for Uncertainty and Defeasible Reasoning* (pp. 421–475). Springer Netherlands. DOI:10.1007/978-94-017-1737-3_10

Wu, J. K., & Wong, Y. (2006, July). Bayesian approach for data fusion in sensor networks. *In 2006 9th International Conference on Information Fusion* (pp. 1-5). IEEE.

Ye, Y., He, Y., & Wang, YeKui, H. (2016). SHVC, the Scalable Extensions of HEVC, and Its Applications. *ZTE Communications*, 14(1), 24.

Yim, J., Udpa, S. S., Udpa, L., Mina, M., & Lord, W. (1995). Neural network approaches to data fusion. *Review of Progress in Quantitative Nondestructive Evaluation*, 14, 819–826. DOI:10.1007/978-1-4615-1987-4_102

Zhou, X. C., & Shen, H. B. (2010). Notifiable infectious disease surveillance with data collected by search engine. *Journal of Zhejiang University. Science*, C, 11, 241–248.

Zikopoulos, P., & Eaton, C. (2011). *Understanding big data: Analytics for Enterprise Class Hadoop and Streaming Data.* McGraw-Hill Osborne Media.

ADDITIONAL READINGS

Gupta, A., & Singh, A. (2022). An intelligent healthcare cyber physical framework for encephalitis diagnosis based on information fusion and soft-computing techniques. *New Generation Computing*, 40(4), 1093–1123. DOI:10.1007/s00354-022-00175-1 PMID:35730007

Meraj, M., Alvi, S. A. M., Quasim, M. T., & Haidar, S. W. (2021, August). A critical review of detection and prediction of infectious disease using IOT sensors. In 2021 second international conference on electronics and sustainable communication systems (ICESC) (pp. 679-684). IEEE. DOI:10.1109/ICESC51422.2021.9532992

Verma, P., & Sood, S. K. (2018). Cloud-centric IoT based disease diagnosis healthcare framework. *Journal of Parallel and Distributed Computing*, 116, 27–38. DOI:10.1016/j.jpdc.2017.11.018

KEY TERMS AND DEFINITIONS

Area Under Curve (AUC): Is the area that is bounded by the coordinate axes and the curve. It is computed by taking extremely small rectangles and adding up all of them, or by taking infinitely small rectangles and adding up all of them and calculating the limit of the function that results. The absolute value of the function over the interval [a, b] is taken and summed over the range to find the area under a curve.

Cloud: A cloud network is a computer system with resources, mainly processing power and data storage, and no user-directed active management. Cloud computing frequently uses a pay-as-you-go model to achieve coherence.

Epidemiology: Is made up of three Greek words: (1) epi, which means "upon, amid," (2) demos, which means "people, region," and (3) logos, which means "study, word, discourse." Literally, it means "the study of what is upon the people," but in a technical sense, it refers to the examination and interpretation of the distribution, patterns, and causes of health and disease situations within a particular population.

Extreme Learning Machine: These neural networks are feed-forward and have a single layer of hidden nodes. Regression, clustering, feature learning, classification, sparse approximation, compression, and regression can all be done with these networks. The hidden nodes might be inherited from their predecessors in an unaltered state, or they can be randomly assigned and never modified (i.e., random projections with nonlinear transforms). Learning the output weights of hidden nodes is often accomplished in a single step, much like learning a linear model.

Framework: A framework is a set of guidelines and rules that developers employ to put a computing solution's structure into practice.

Internet of Things: The Internet of Things (IoT) is a network of devices with sensors, actuators, and other technologies. These devices are connected to each other and with other systems and devices through the Internet or other communications networks, so they can exchange data.

Receiver Operating Characteristics (ROC): Is a visual representation of a classifier model's performance at various threshold levels. The ROC curve is created by plotting the true positive rate (TPR) against the false positive rate (FPR) at each threshold setting, as indicated. When the decision rule's Type I Error is plotted against the statistical power, the Receiver Operating Characteristic (ROC) can also be viewed as an estimator of these quantities when the performance is determined using only a sample of the population. The recall or sensitivity as a function of false positive rate is, thus, represented by the ROC curve.

Chapter 10
Intelligent Mobility Assimilating IoT in Autonomous Vehicles:
Foster Sustainable Cities and Communities

Bhupinder Singh
https://orcid.org/0009-0006-4779-2553
Sharda University, India

Christian Kaunert
https://orcid.org/0000-0002-4493-2235
Dublin City University, Ireland

Sahil Lal
https://orcid.org/0000-0001-9827-3717
Sharda University, India

Manmeet Kaur Arora
https://orcid.org/0009-0002-5071-117X
Sharda University, India

Kittisak Jermsittiparsert
https://orcid.org/0000-0003-3245-8705
Shinawatra University, Thailand

ABSTRACT

Autonomous vehicle (AV) technologies, coupled with the rapid growth of the internet of things (IoT), have ushered in an era of intelligent mobility. This evolution holds

DOI: 10.4018/979-8-3693-5498-8.ch010

the potential to significantly contribute to the development of sustainable cities and communities by addressing pressing issues such as traffic congestion, environmental pollution, and monotonous transportation systems. AVs can effectively mitigate these challenges by utilizing cutting-edge sensors, artificial intelligence (AI), and advanced communication protocols. This comprehensive approach allows AVs to interact with surrounding infrastructure seamlessly. Integrating IoT in autonomous vehicles enhances their ability to collect, analyze, and utilize data, improving vehicle performance and transportation networks. This chapter explores the convergence of intelligent mobility, IoT, and autonomous vehicles, focusing on how these emerging technologies can be harnessed to build sustainable cities and communities.

INTRODUCTION

Fast emerging autonomous vehicle (AV) technologies, together with a steady rise of the Internet of Things (IoT), have created an era upon which intelligent mobility is born embrace this evolution is likely to empower sustainable cities and communities by mitigating urgent concerns like traffic congestion, environmental pollution as well as transportation blandness. In the classical transportation realm, transport was purely based on human operated vehicles that inherently are hampered by safety related compromises as well various efficiency and environmental limitations. By means of cutting-edge sensors, artificial intelligence (AI) and advanced communication protocols AVs are poised to considerably mitigate the issues associated with these challenges. This holistic approach enables AVs to seamlessly interface with surrounding infrastructure, other Use of IoT in Autonomous Vehicles (AVs) enables to acquire data, analyze it and vehicles and transport networks via the integration of IoT technologies.

The decisions by integrating all this process is ensuring safer less congested roads at minimum environmental impact. An IoT-based sensor suite which may include LIDAR and radar allow AVs a 360-degree vision with additional enhanced capabilities like adaptive perception to dynamic environments. In this research paper, intelligent mobility, IoT and autonomous vehicles will be examined together in that node context as the convergence of those three elements can bring great contributions for sustainability cities & communities' development. Specifically, those are to overview some fundamental concepts and elements of intelligent mobility; study the architecture design for IoT based AVs along with other pertinent technologies underpinning them; detailed conductive studies on diverse use cases of intelligent-mobility applications; survey available enabling technologies that drives these advancements presents a comprehensive aspect related in terms societal impact as well adoption challenges within context and ultimately, suggest various future trends research directions. By utilizing up-to-date academic research, industry reports, and case studies as evidence, this paper will thoroughly illustrate the implications of IoT-automated vehicles integration on sustainable cities & communities. The results from this study can thus help in the ongoing process of overcoming urban and transportation systems challenges, which has been a crucial step to enable more efficient, eco-friendly, and accessible mobility future

BACKGROUND

The traditional transportation ecosystem is largely defined by human-operated vehicles, all of which carry fundamental constraints on terms safety, efficiency and environmental footprint. AVs- made possible by innovative sensors, artificial intelligence (AI), and state-of-the-art communication platforms - have emerged as a potential remedy for each of these challenges. AV integration with the environment: AVs will be connected to surrounding infrastructure, other vehicles and transportation networks via IoT technologies providing full potential for intelligent mobility ecosystem (Tan et al., 2018). Leveraging the latest academic research, industry reports and case studies this study will equip attendees with a well-rounded understanding of Voice-first without appearing as an advertisement for any brand. Connecting the Internet of Things (IoT) to autonomous vehicles realizes real time data acquisition, analysis and decision making for improving safety in traffic management as well operation without causing sound pollution. AVs have 360-degree awareness of their environment by connecting cameras and sensor systems through IoT-enabled sensors such as LiDAR, radars to track simple surroundings further converting complex scenarios into a treatable scenario for the AV's ability to perceive dynamic conditions (Ji et al., 2021). The objective of this chapter is to evaluate and analyze the relationship in terms or synergy between intelligent mobility, Internet of Things (IoT)and autonomous vehicles as perceived technologies convergence which can foster sustainable cities/communities. These are the following objectives to:

- demonstrate the key building blocks of intelligent mobility, looking at how IoT can enable autonomous vehicle technologies.
- examines Internet of Things (IoT) based autonomous vehicles from an architectural design standpoint, sensor technological viewpoint and communication protocol perspective.
- study the various use-cases of intelligent mobility (smart traffic management, predictive maintenance and Mobility as a Service) and urbanistic outcomes towards sustainable planning and infrastructure.

- understand the underlying technologies (i.e., AI, Edge) that contribute to the development of intelligent mobility solutions.
- explore the societal impact and adoption challenges associated with the integration of IoT and autonomous vehicles, including regulatory frameworks, public acceptance, and workforce implications.
- discuss future trends and research directions in intelligent mobility, along with the integration of renewable energy, blockchain & 5G technologies.

This chapter pertains to the convergence of intelligent mobility, IoT and autonomous vehicles with a specific focus on how these next-gen technologies can be leveraged for building sustainable cities & communities (Singh .2023). Leveraging the latest academic research, industry reports and case studies, this study will equip attendees with a well-rounded understanding of Voice-first without appearing as an advertisement for any brand (Huang et al., 2021).

FUNDAMENTALS OF INTELLIGENT MOBILITY

Definition and Key Components

Intelligent mobility or smart mobility is a concept that acts as an innovating tool for better efficiency, sustainability and convenience in all systems of transportation by putting together multiple technological practices along with data driven solutions. It covers dozens of forms of transportation, from electric cars (its most popular example) and bicycles to public transit, ride-sharing services and autonomous vehicles with the aim goal being reducing traffic congestion in cities while also cutting pollution, road accidents everywhere as well by making better use existing infrastructure. Basic components of intelligent mobility are electric vehicles, expanded public transportation system, integrated traffic management systems information and booking by mobile apps real-time data for forecasting user demand as well as artificial intelligence to optimize changing flows in transport.

Role of IOT in Intelligent Mobility

The Internet of Things (IoT) is also a critical enabler for intelligent mobility solutions as it enables autonomous vehicles to connect with their surroundings - from the internet and other cars to transportation infrastructure. Autonomous cars can observe and react dynamically by using IoT-enabled sensors like LiDAR and radar to view their surroundings in real-time detecting impending obstacles that enables them maneuver through intricate geographical locations swiftly.

But modern IoT connectivity allows autonomous cars to communicate and collect data from the area around them, ensuring that they can make real-time decisions based on live traffic information, so no mishap happens (Singh & Kaunert, 2024). This paves the way for accelerating integration of AVs with smart city infrastructure: traffic lights, parking systems and other aspects that help to better manage local transport mobility, speeding up move people and product down roads whilst regulating congestion (Tang et al., 2021).

Challenges and Limitations

Though intelligent mobility as many advantages but it is also exposed to certain limitations, such as:

- Autonomous driving systems have yet to tackle all but the most basic and straightforward of driving situations.
- Regulation: an intricate quilt of regulation weaves seemingly random, ziggurat-esque autonomous vehicle laws across the globe and idiosyncratic standards from country to territory within nations.
- Acceptance by the public: the need to prove that self-driving cars are safe enough for most people to believe in them with education on how autonomous vehicles make transportation better (Dai et al., 2018).
- Potential risks of data security and privacy, since devices connected to the IoT in intelligent mobility solutions are at risk for cyber-attacks and breaches.
- It still struggles with a lack of interoperability, struggling to connect different modes and place functioning between smart mobility platforms (Halilaj et al., 2022).

Nevertheless, given the potential efficiency dividends to be realized from safer and more reliable smart mobility operations, as well as its sustainability and accessibility claims, it is an area worthy of further development (Singh. 2023).

IOT ENABLED AUTONOMOUS VEHICLES

Architecture and Components

The architecture of an IoT-based autonomous vehicle is composed of various hardware and software components that work together to allow the vehicle to drive itself (Luettin et al., 2022). The main component in an autonomous vehicle's system is its sensors that enable it to sense its surroundings (Halilaj et al.,2021). The sensors used in this vehicle include ultrasonic sensors, radars, LiDARs, cameras, infrared sensors, GPS, and odometry sensors. I then relay the data to the environment perception module which is responsible for localizing the automobile and detecting and configuring objects around it. The information is then relayed to the environment mapping component that generates a planar grid, localization map, and primary thoroughfare map. The autonomous driving system uses both conventional algorithms and artificial intelligence to execute tasks such as path planning and vehicle control (Singh .2024). The vehicle further relies on IoT to connect to other automobiles and buildings extensively mainly through the cloud. It entails integration with surrounding infrastructural facilities, other cars, and the general cloud. This type of connectivity allows the vehicle to access real-time information such as traffic, weather, and other data it needs to operate to make an informed decision and respond to its surroundings (Singh, 2023).

Sensor Technologies (LiDAR, Radar, Cameras)

A sensor suite helps an IoT-enabled autonomous vehicle to clarify and interact with the environment in which it moves. LiDAR (Light Detection and Ranging) sensors use laser beams to generate a detailed 3D map of the vehicle surroundings, enabling it to detect and track objects with high accuracy (Halilaj et al.,2023). Radar (Radio Detection and Ranging) sensors, on the other hand, use radio waves to determine distance, speed and direction of objects around it hence providing more details not something possible with LiDAR only. Another crucial part consists of the cameras, supplying it with everything from visual reinforcement to detect road signs and lane marks or other cars (Xu et al., 2022). The autonomy of this vehicle is such that, thanks to these sensor technologies (plus GPS and odometry sensors), the car knows everything about its environment which enables it to make comprehensively informed decisions on how to operate around other vehicles (Elahi et al., 2020).

Communication Protocols and Standards

To secure the integration of IoT in autonomous vehicles, sophisticated communication protocols and standards are necessary for connecting all these devices together as well as sharing data back-and-forth. 5G, which provides higher bandwidth and reduced latency with excellent reliability as compared to the earlier cellular network generations is one of the key enabling technologies in this direction (Lecue, 2020). 5G technology can be used to support vehicle-to-everything (V2X) communication, any of a number of applications by which vehicles communicate between themselves and with their surroundings (Dong et al., 2020). This allows real-time exchange of such information, e.g., traffic congestion, road events and software updates that collectively enhance the safety functionality and operational efficiency within the autonomous vehicle system (Kim et al.,2021). Apart from 5G, series of communication protocols and standards such as DSRC (Dedicated Short-Range Communication) & C-V2X (Cellular Vehicle-to-Everything),are being developed and in practice to enable IoT capabilities in autonomous vehicles. This data is being shared over highly secure, reliable protocols to ensure perfect assimilation with others within the larger intelligent mobility ecosystem (Kim et al.,2021).

INTELLIGENT MOBILITY USE CASES

Smart Traffic Management

Smart mobility solutions are improving traffic systems in both cities and urban areas (Singh .2023). IoT-compatible sensors, cameras and communication technologies are integrated into smart traffic management systems that can gather data on the current driving conditions from connected cars in real time (Sharma et al.,2022). An advanced algorithm and artificial intelligence are used to process this information, with the end goal being optimized traffic signal timing, vehicle reroutes through local streets at a minimum inconvenience level, and real-time updates for drivers (Guo et al., 2021). One example is the City of Reykjavik in Iceland, which rolled out a smart traffic signal priority system that leverages IoT connected cameras and vehicle sensors to provide automatic access for emergency vehicles (Nickel et al., 2015) As an ambulance or bus approaches the intersection, it is turned green and if necessary given priority for passage across it, actions are returned to the former. This smart traffic management does not only optimize emergency response times, it also allows public transport to be more efficient in terms of fleet and workforce utilization while encouraging people-friendly modes of mobility which are safer for our city centers (Büchner et al., 2023).

Predictive Maintenance and Fleet Management

Furthermore, smart mobility solutions have also begun to shift the paradigms of fleet management by deploying IoT and analytics capabilities for maximizing maintenance and operational optimization (Yu et al., 2019). Sensors integrated into the vehicles which are IoT-enabled can measure and transmit live data based on engine performance, tire wear, fuel utilization etc. continuously to a central management system. The earlier fleet managers have access to this real-time data, the sooner they can anticipate impending breakdowns or maintenance issues and proactively schedule downtime to maintain vehicles (Hu et al., 2023). This predictive maintenance strategy does not merely cut operational costs but also makes the vehicle fleet safer and reliable (Liu et al., 2023). In addition, intelligent mobility solutions can optimize fleet routing and dispatching based on real-time factors such as traffic conditions, availability of drivers or couriers in given areas at specific times, driving schedules across geographies and customer demand to enhance delivery experience with improved efficiency (Singh. 2022).

Ride-Sharing and Mobility-as-a-Service

The overall transportation use and mode of access to service are also being revolutionized through IoT & Autonomous technologies (Singh. 2022). The inherent demand in these mobility-as-a-service (MaaS) models is already shown by ride-sharing platforms like Uber and Lyft, connecting users with diverse transportation modes directly from their devices as a universal digital platform. Just as Amazon leverages IoT-connected vehicles, real-time data, and sophisticated algorithms to benefit both consumers (through seamless on-demand mobility solutions) AND drivers with expedited coordination between passengers & rides (Ploennigs et al., 2022). This will not only improve the accessibility and convenience of transportation, but it can also provide an incentive to utilize a higher share of trips through more sustainable modes such as electric vehicles or shared mobility (Kraft et al.,2023).

Sustainable Urban Planning Infrastructure

Intelligent mobility solutions are also weaving their magic on the blueprint to sustainable cities and communities (Li et al., 2023) Through incorporating IoT-enabled sensors and data analytics into urban infrastructure (e.g., traffic lights, parking systems, public transportation networks), cities are able to receive full visibility of transportation patterns and usage (Schier et al., 2023) It is this sort of data-driven perspective that enables urban planners to see a clearer picture when it comes to how transportation infrastructure can grow and be diminished, what resources are available at their disposal for better use, and which policies support sustainable mobility (Mahon et al., 2020). From enabling cities to pinpoint locations that would benefit in high-frequency public transportation demand and make expansion investments there to rolling out charging stations for electric vehicles (Xiao et al., 2023). Importantly, the nexus of autonomous vehicles and shared mobility within cities can alleviate dependency on private ownership to provide land for more sustainable public spaces like parks, walkable streetscapes, mixed-use developments etc. Such holistic approaches to urban planning and infrastructure development can help create cities that are more liveable, sustainable, and equitable (Liu et al., 2022)

ENABLING TECHNOLOGIES

Artificial Intelligence and Machine Learning

Artificial intelligence (AI) and machine learning are basic building blocks that drive the progress of intelligent transportation and autonomous vehicles (Cai et al., 2022). AI algorithms and models process the collected data by IoT sensors in autonomous vehicles which help them to perceive the surrounding, take real-time decisions and change themselves according to different environments (Holzinger et al., 2023). As a subset of AI this is why machine learning enables autonomous vehicles to learn as they collect data and get better over time. For example, ML algorithms help train autonomous driving systems to detect traffic signs, pedestrians and other obstacles in a scene as well as predict the flow of traffic & planning routes accordingly (Singh, 2019). AI and machine learning need to be integrated with autonomous vehicles to improve their safety, efficiency & reliability. By using these technologies, autonomous vehicles can make better decisions on-the-fly; be quicker to react when faced with potentially dangerous situations and also 'learn' from experience between their own incidents (Bonatti et al., 2019)

Edge Computing and Cloud Integration

One of the critical components that effectively facilitates intelligent mobility solutions is edge computing, which processes data close to its source and helps lower latency helps autonomous vehicles be more reactive (Zheng et al., 2022). The IoT equipped sensors and devices in autonomous vehicles produce a huge amount of data which needs to be processed and analyzed concurrently in real time to support the decision making (Buchgeher et al., 2021). By processing and analyzing this data at the edge of network, closer to the vehicle (as opposed to relying purely on cloud computing), we are engaging in edge computing. This means less data must be sent through the internet cloud, resulting in faster response times and reduced wear on networks (Sun et al., 2023). This hybrid architecture combines edge computing with cloud-based services to bridge the best of both worlds (Li et al., 2019). The cloud gives us heavy lifting, storage and access to training data on which AI/ML models are built while edge computing allows real-time processing making autonomous vehicle execution possible (Shi et al., 2022).

Cyber Security and Data Privacy

Integration of IoT, Autonomous Vehicles and Intelligent Mobility Solutions: This use case raises serious concerns about cybersecurity or data privacy (Qiang et al., 2024) And the most worrying fact is, as these systems become more integrated with one another - they also pose greater threats to cyber vulnerabilities such as being hacked, having sensitive data stolen or malicious attacks (Pedro et al., 2022). Crucial to both developing public trust and adoption IS the secure management of data generated or exchanged within intelligent mobility presents a unique challenge (Svetashova et al., 2021). To safeguard the sensitive information garnered by autonomous vehicles and IoT devices, strong cybersecurity measures such as encryption, access controls, security architectures like firewalls or intrusion detection systems must be introduced (Malawade et al., 2022). Regulatory scrutiny and privacy: Additionally, the capture and usage of personal data (e.g., location info or driving patterns) must be handled to adhere with tone regulation demands while additionally becoming a section of defensive individuals' privateness (Yu et al., 2023). These fears can be mitigated if data governance guidelines are transparent and user consent mechanisms, as well as de-identification strategies for the kind of data collected (Pan et al., 2017). For intelligent mobility solutions to succeed, the system and its users must be secure against cyber threats; data generated by this technology should not only be used quickly for decision-making but also protected with privacy (Deng et al., 2020). There is a need for joint work by the policy makers, technology vendors and industry stakeholders to develop and implement robust security-based privacy frameworks that will enable this intelligent mobility transformation (Kawamura et al., 2022).

SOCIETAL IMPACT AND ADOPTION CHALLENGES

Regulatory Frameworks and Policy Considerations

However, such intelligent mobility solutions that integrate IoT and autonomous vehicles bring significant regulatory as well as policy challenges which will need to be tackled for the responsible deployment of these systems (Monninger et al.,2023). Liability in the event of accidents, data privacy and security, as well as ethical dilemmas associated with self-drive decision-making are among global concerns for which answers remain to be resolved by policy makers and regulators around the world (Draschner et al., 2022) In the U.S., there are at present no comprehensive federal regulatory framework for the development and testing of AVs, though guidelines have been released by the National Highway Traffic Safety Administration (NHTSA). States are going their own way, with states such as California and Arizona working hard to facilitate self-driving car testing and deployment in the face of more heavily safety-focused regulatory (Trappey et al., 2022) In Europe, the European Commission has tabled its proposed AI Act that would set out common rules for developing and deploying artificial intelligence, including in autonomous vehicles (Blagec et al., 2022). We are talking about obligations that the Act has for high-risk AI systems, such as human oversight in place and ensure transparency of their functions but also robustness (Lukovnikov, 2022). Policymakers should thus consult with industry stakeholders, academic experts and civil society organizations to craft regulatory frameworks that allow for innovation as well establish a culture of safety whilst safeguarding consumer rights blessings entail the responsible construction within systems -pollution here- related intelligent solutions among mobility (Bharadwaj, 2023).

Public Acceptance and Ethical Concerns

Public confidence and trust are important for the uptake of intelligent mobility solutions, including self-driving cars. Despite enthusiasm from the tech community, many people are still skeptical of self-driving cars and until these "selfies" can show that they in fact offer a safer option for driving or riding compared to humans there will be resistance (Fähndrich & Trollmann, 2021). In fact, ethical questions are also posed by the implementation of IoT and AI in smart mobility solutions (e.g. settings about deciding whose life to save given an unavoidable accident). What about the autonomous car that must choose between protecting its passengers and pedestrians? How do these ethical dilemmas get programmed into the vehicle's decision-making algorithms? We require a strong ethical framework to address these questions pertaining to the development and deployment of intelligent mobility solutions.

Guidelines and best practices prioritizing safety, fairness (and), transparency must be created by policymakers in conjunction with industry stakeholders as well as ethicists (Von Rueden et al.,2021).

Workforce Transformation and Job Market Implications

The automation of transport systems will have a big influence on the labour market, particularly in transportation and logistics (Sikos,2023). That could displace jobs for millions of truck drivers, delivery workers and taxi drivers if self-driving trucks become common on American roads (Samsudeen et al., 2023). In addition to helping create new, well-paying jobs in many states and regions outside those that depend on traditional vehicle manufacturing plants or component producers - itself a significant accomplishment if initial volumes are even just half of the forecast for 2022-25-" nevertheless: If market penetration reaches levels such as projected... other existing automotive sector job categories could feasibly disappear altogether" it also comes with risks .(Hogan et al., 2021). This may include funding education and training programs, offering worker support and benefit funds, partnering with unions and other stakeholders (Xia et al., 2022).

In addition, the creation of smart mobility solutions is likely to lead to new jobs in areas such as software development, data analysis and infrastructure management (Díaz-Rodríguez et al., 2022). It is up to policymakers to ensure that these jobs are available - and pay a fair wage with quality working conditions - for the people displaced. Collectively these challenges - as well as the opportunities for societal impact and adoption alike are layered, multi-faceted issues that will require a co-ordinated policy-meets-industry with society delivery by way of new urbanisms. Confronting these challenges allows intelligent mobility to be a force for good, thereby enabling more sustainable, equitable and liveable cities and communities (Mitropoulou et al., 2024).

CONCLUSION

This convergence of autonomous vehicles and the Internet-of-Things (IoT) prom-ises new capability in integrated intelligent mobility, an opportunity to cultivate sustainable cities and communities. The revolutionary application of IoT comes into force for the autonomous vehicles by using sensors, and communication devices with AI to enable them take better decisions on various scenarios they encounter in a complex environment. This autonomy will allow these systems to gather and process real-time data, communicate with other vehicles and the infrastructure surrounding them so that they can adapt their decisions depending on information received. Intelligent Mobility implementations can help in overcoming major challenges such as traffic congestion, environmental pollution and transportation accessibility. By IoT sensors and data analytics, smart traffic management systems can be used to optimize the behavior of the people as well improving emissions with predictive maintenance & fleet management for better optimization of transportation services.

The advent of ridesharing and mobility-as-a-service (MaaS) ecosystems partially built upon IoT-enabled vehicles connected to advanced algorithms is reshaping how individuals can consume transportation as a service. These solutions can also help build more livable and equitable cities by enabling sustainable modes like electric vehicles (EV) and shared mobility. However, intelligent mobility solutions face a series of challenges such as regulatory constraints to wide scale deployment, public acceptance and workforce implications. To that end, policymakers and industry stakeholders need to collaborate on developing solid regulatory frameworks - thinking through the ethical implications and considerations about labor. Despite its challenges, the efficiency and sustainability associated with smart mobility make it a key driver of continuing growth as advances in research and development forge forward. As we proceed, this requires an integrated and a cross-cutting approach that aligns the interests of multiple stakeholders such as policymakers, urban planners, technology providers and civil society to capitalize on the power of intelligent mobility. The confluence of IoT and autonomous vehicles in intelligent mobility solutions, therefore, promises enormous positive impacts for more sustainable, livable and equitable cities & communities. A world where with the power of technology and data we can change to way we move, live and work for a better tomorrow, safer cleaner and finally accessible transportation.

REFERENCES

Bharadwaj, A. G. (2023). *Driving Reasoning Systems for Product Design and Flexible Robotic Manipulation Using 3D Design-Based AIs* (Doctoral dissertation, North Carolina State University).

Blagec, K., Barbosa-Silva, A., Ott, S., & Samwald, M. (2022). A curated, ontology-based, large-scale AI of artificial intelligence tasks and benchmarks. *Scientific Data*, 9(1), 322. DOI:10.1038/s41597-022-01435-x PMID:35715466

Bonatti, P. A., Decker, S., Polleres, A., & Presutti, V. (2019). AIs: New directions for knowledge representation on the semantic web (dagstuhl seminar 18371). *Dagstuhl Reports*, 8(9).

Buchgeher, G., Gabauer, D., Martinez-Gil, J., & Ehrlinger, L. (2021). AIs in manufacturing and production: A systematic literature review. *IEEE Access : Practical Innovations, Open Solutions*, 9, 55537–55554. DOI:10.1109/ACCESS.2021.3070395

Büchner, M., Zürn, J., Todoran, I. G., Valada, A., & Burgard, W. (2023). Learning and aggregating lane MLs for urban automated driving. In *Proceedings of the IEEE/CVF Conference on Computer Vision and Pattern Recognition* (pp. 13415-13424).

Cai, P., Wang, H., Sun, Y., & Liu, M. (2022). DQ-GAT: Towards safe and efficient autonomous driving with deep Q-learning and ML attention networks. *IEEE Transactions on Intelligent Transportation Systems*, 23(11), 21102–21112. DOI:10.1109/TITS.2022.3184990

Dai, S., Liang, Y., Liu, S., Wang, Y., Shao, W., Lin, X., & Feng, X. (2018, March). Learning entity and relation embeddings with entity description for AI completion. In *2018 2nd International Conference on Artificial Intelligence: Technologies and Applications (ICAITA 2018)* (pp. 194-197). Atlantis Press.

Deng, C., Ji, X., Rainey, C., Zhang, J., & Lu, W. (2020). Integrating machine learning with human knowledge. *iScience*, 23(11), 101656. DOI:10.1016/j.isci.2020.101656 PMID:33134890

Díaz-Rodríguez, N., Lamas, A., Sanchez, J., Franchi, G., Donadello, I., Tabik, S., Filliat, D., Cruz, P., Montes, R., & Herrera, F. (2022). EXplainable Neural-Symbolic Learning (X-NeSyL) methodology to fuse deep learning representations with expert AIs: The MonuMAI cultural heritage use case. *Information Fusion*, 79, 58–83. DOI:10.1016/j.inffus.2021.09.022

Draschner, C. F., Jabeen, H., & Lehmann, J. (2022, September). Ethical and sustainability considerations for AI-based machine learning. In *2022 IEEE Fifth International Conference on Artificial Intelligence and Knowledge Engineering (AIKE)* (pp. 53-60). IEEE.

Elahi, M. F., Luo, X., & Tian, R. (2020, July). A framework for modeling AIs via processing natural descriptions of vehicle-pedestrian interactions. In *International Conference on Human-Computer Interaction* (pp. 40-50). Cham: Springer International Publishing.

Fähndrich, J., & Trollmann, F. (2021). AI Reading, or Automatic Semantic Decomposition into AIs and Symbolic reasoning through Marker Passing.

Guo, R., Hong, Z., & Xue, X. (2021). Reward function design via human AI and inverse reinforcement learning for intelligent driving (No. 2021-01-0180). *SAE Technical Paper*.

Halilaj, L., Dindorkar, I., Lüttin, J., & Rothermel, S. (2021). An AI-based approach for situation comprehension in driving scenarios. *The Semantic Web: 18th International Conference, ESWC 2021, Virtual Event, June 6–10, 2021 Proceedings*, 18, 699–716.

Halilaj, L., Luettin, J., Henson, C., & Monka, S. (2022, September). AIs for automated driving. In *2022 IEEE Fifth International Conference on Artificial Intelligence and Knowledge Engineering (AIKE)* (pp. 98-105). IEEE.

Halilaj, L., Luettin, J., Monka, S., Henson, C., & Schmid, S. (2023). AI-Based Integration of Autonomous Driving Datasets. *International Journal of Semantic Computing*, 17(02), 249–271. DOI:10.1142/S1793351X23600048

Hogan, A., Blomqvist, E., Cochez, M., d'Amato, C., Melo, G. D., Gutierrez, C., Kirrane, S., Gayo, J. E. L., Navigli, R., Neumaier, S., Ngomo, A.-C. N., Polleres, A., Rashid, S. M., Rula, A., Schmelzeisen, L., Sequeda, J., Staab, S., & Zimmermann, A. (2021). AIs. *ACM Computing Surveys*, 54(4), 1–37. DOI:10.1145/3447772

Holzinger, A., Saranti, A., Hauschild, A. C., Beinecke, J., Heider, D., Roettger, R., . . . Pfeifer, B. (2023, August). Human-in-the-loop integration with domain-AIs for explainable federated deep learning. In *International Cross-Domain Conference for Machine Learning and Knowledge Extraction* (pp. 45-64). Cham: Springer Nature Switzerland. DOI:10.1007/978-3-031-40837-3_4

Hu, X., Liu, Y., Tang, B., Yan, J., & Chen, L. (2023). Learning dynamic ML for overtaking strategy in autonomous driving. *IEEE Transactions on Intelligent Transportation Systems*, 24(11), 11921–11933. DOI:10.1109/TITS.2023.3287223

Huang, H., Sun, L., Du, B., Liu, C., Lv, W., & Xiong, H. (2021, August). Representation learning on AIs for node importance estimation. In *Proceedings of the 27th ACM SIGKDD Conference on Knowledge Discovery & Data Mining* (pp. 646-655).

Ji, S., Pan, S., Cambria, E., Marttinen, P., & Philip, S. Y. (2021). A survey on AIs: Representation, acquisition, and applications. *IEEE Transactions on Neural Networks and Learning Systems*, 33(2), 494–514. DOI:10.1109/TNNLS.2021.3070843 PMID:33900922

Kawamura, T., Egami, S., Matsushita, K., Ugai, T., Fukuda, K., & Kozaki, K. (2022, October). Contextualized scene AIs for xai benchmarking. In *Proceedings of the 11th International Joint Conference on AIs* (pp. 64-72).

Kim, J. E., Henson, C., Huang, K., Tran, T. A., & Lin, W. Y. (2021). Accelerating road sign ground truth construction with AI and machine learning. In *Intelligent Computing:Proceedings of the 2021 Computing Conference,* Volume 2 (pp. 325-340). Springer International Publishing.

Kraft, M., Bai, J., Mosbach, S., Taylor, C., Karan, D., Lee, K. F., ... Lapkin, A. (2023). From Platform to AI: Distributed Self-Driving Laboratories.

Lecue, F. (2020). On the role of AIs in explainable AI. *Semantic Web*, 11(1), 41–51. DOI:10.3233/SW-190374

Li, A., Wang, X., Wang, W., Zhang, A., & Li, B. (2019). A survey of relation extraction of AIs. In *Web and Big Data: APWeb-WAIM 2019 International Workshops, KGMA and DSEA, Chengdu, China, August 1–3, 2019, Revised Selected Papers 3* (pp. 52-66). Springer International Publishing.

Li, X., Liu, J., Li, J., Yu, W., Cao, Z., Qiu, S., . . . Jiao, X. (2023, August). ML Structure-Based Implicit Risk Reasoning for Long-Tail Scenarios of Automated Driving. In *2023 4th International Conference on Big Data, Artificial Intelligence and Internet of Things Engineering (ICBAIE)* (pp. 415-420). IEEE.

Liu, H., Li, Y., Hong, R., Li, Z., Li, M., Pan, W., Glowacz, A., & He, H. (2020). AI analysis and visualization of research trends on driver behavior. *Journal of Intelligent & Fuzzy Systems*, 38(1), 495–511. DOI:10.3233/JIFS-179424

Liu, J., Zhang, X., Li, Y., Wang, J., & Kim, H. J. (2019). Deep learning-based reasoning with multi-ontology for IoT applications. *IEEE Access : Practical Innovations, Open Solutions*, 7, 124688–124701. DOI:10.1109/ACCESS.2019.2937353

Liu, Q., Li, X., Tang, Y., Gao, X., Yang, F., & Li, Z. (2023). ML Reinforcement Learning-Based Decision-Making Technology for Connected and Autonomous Vehicles: Framework, Review, and Future Trends. *Sensors (Basel)*, 23(19), 8229. DOI:10.3390/s23198229 PMID:37837063

Lukovnikov, D. (2022). Deep learning methods for semantic parsing and question answering over AIs (Doctoral dissertation, Universitäts-und Landesbibliothek Bonn).

Mahon, L., Giunchiglia, E., Li, B., & Lukasiewicz, T. (2020, December). AI extraction from videos. In *2020 19th IEEE International Conference on Machine Learning and Applications (ICMLA)* (pp. 25-32). IEEE.

Malawade, A. V., Yu, S. Y., Hsu, B., Muthirayan, D., Khargonekar, P. P., & Al Faruque, M. A. (2022). Spatiotemporal scene-ML embedding for autonomous vehicle collision prediction. *IEEE Internet of Things Journal*, 9(12), 9379–9388. DOI:10.1109/JIOT.2022.3141044

Mitropoulou, K., Kokkinos, P., Soumplis, P., & Varvarigos, E. (2024). Anomaly Detection in Cloud Computing using AI Embedding and Machine Learning Mechanisms. *Journal of Grid Computing*, 22(1), 6. DOI:10.1007/s10723-023-09727-1

Monninger, T., Schmidt, J., Rupprecht, J., Raba, D., Jordan, J., Frank, D., Staab, S., & Dietmayer, K. (2023). Scene: Reasoning about traffic scenes using heterogeneous ML neural networks. *IEEE Robotics and Automation Letters*, 8(3), 1531–1538. DOI:10.1109/LRA.2023.3234771

Nickel, M., Murphy, K., Tresp, V., & Gabrilovich, E. (2015). A review of relational machine learning for AIs. *Proceedings of the IEEE*, 104(1), 11–33. DOI:10.1109/JPROC.2015.2483592

Pan, J. Z., Vetere, G., Gomez-Perez, J. M., & Wu, H. (Eds.). (2017). *Exploiting linked data and AIs in large organisations* (p. 281). Springer. DOI:10.1007/978-3-319-45654-6

Pedro, A., Pham-Hang, A. T., Nguyen, P. T., & Pham, H. C. (2022). Data-driven construction safety information sharing system based on linked data, ontologies, and AI technologies. *International Journal of Environmental Research and Public Health*, 19(2), 794. DOI:10.3390/ijerph19020794 PMID:35055616

Ploennigs, J., Semertzidis, K., Lorenzi, F., & Mihindukulasooriya, N. (2022, October). Scaling AIs for automating AI of digital twins. In *International Semantic Web Conference* (pp. 810-826). Cham: Springer International Publishing.

Qiang, Y., Wang, X., Liu, X., Wang, Y., & Zhang, W. (2024). Edge-enhanced ML Attention Network for driving decision-making of autonomous vehicles via Deep Reinforcement Learning. *Proceedings of the Institution of Mechanical Engineers, Part D: Journal of Automobile Engineering.*

Schier, M., Reinders, C., & Rosenhahn, B. (2023). Deep reinforcement learning for autonomous driving using high-level heterogeneous ML representations. *International Conference on Robotics and Automation (ICRA).*

Shekarpour, S., Nadgeri, A., & Singh, K. (2020). QA2Explanation: Generating and Evaluating Explanations for Question Answering Systems over AI. *arXiv preprint arXiv:2010.08323.*

Shi, H., Zhang, Y., Xu, Z., Xu, X., & Qi, L. (2022). Multi-source temporal AI embedding for edge computing enabled internet of vehicles. *Neurocomputing*, 491, 597–606. DOI:10.1016/j.neucom.2021.12.036

Shi, X., Li, J., Tang, B., & Chen, L. (2023). Learning dynamic ML for overtaking strategy in autonomous driving. *IEEE Transactions on Intelligent Transportation Systems.*

Singh, B. (2019). Profiling Public Healthcare: A Comparative Analysis Based on the Multidimensional Healthcare Management and Legal Approach. *Indian Journal of Health and Medical Law*, 2(2), 1–5.

Singh, B. (2022). COVID-19 Pandemic and Public Healthcare: Endless Downward Spiral or Solution via Rapid Legal and Health Services Implementation with Patient Monitoring Program. *Justice and Law Bulletin*, 1(1), 1–7.

Singh, B. (2022). Relevance of Agriculture-Nutrition Linkage for Human Healthcare: A Conceptual Legal Framework of Implication and Pathways. *Justice and Law Bulletin*, 1(1), 44–49.

Singh, B. (2023). Blockchain Technology in Renovating Healthcare: Legal and Future Perspectives. In *Revolutionizing Healthcare Through Artificial Intelligence and Internet of Things Applications* (pp. 177-186). IGI Global.

Singh, B. (2023). Federated Learning for Envision Future Trajectory Smart Transport System for Climate Preservation and Smart Green Planet: Insights into Global Governance and SDG-9 (Industry, Innovation and Infrastructure). *National Journal of Environmental Law*, 6(2), 6–17.

Singh, B. (2023). Tele-Health Monitoring Lensing Deep Neural Learning Structure: Ambient Patient Wellness via Wearable Devices for Real-Time Alerts and Interventions. *Indian Journal of Health and Medical Law*, 6(2), 12–16.

Singh, B. (2023). Unleashing Alternative Dispute Resolution (ADR) in Resolving Complex Legal-Technical Issues Arising in Cyberspace Lensing E-Commerce and Intellectual Property: Proliferation of E-Commerce Digital Economy. *Revista Brasileira de Alternative Dispute Resolution-Brazilian Journal of Alternative Dispute Resolution-RBADR*, 5(10), 81–105. DOI:10.52028/rbadr.v5i10.ART04.Ind

Singh, B., & Kaunert, C. (2024). Integration of Cutting-Edge Technologies such as Internet of Things (IoT) and 5G in Health Monitoring Systems: A Comprehensive Legal Analysis and Futuristic Outcomes. *GLS Law Journal*, 6(1), 13–20. DOI:10.69974/glslawjournal.v6i1.123

Svetashova, Y., Heling, L., Schmid, S., & Acosta, M. (2021). Pay-as-you-go Population of an Automotive Signal AI. *The Semantic Web: 18th International Conference, ESWC 2021, Virtual Event, June 6–10, 2021 Proceedings*, 18, 717–735.

Tan, Z., Zhao, X., Fang, Y., Ge, B., & Xiao, W. (2018). AI representation via similarity-based embedding. *Scientific Programming*.

Tang, X., Sun, T., Zhu, R., & Wang, S. (2021, January). CKG: dynamic representation based on context and AI. In *2020 25th International Conference on Pattern Recognition (ICPR)* (pp. 2889-2895). IEEE.

Trappey, A. J., Liang, C. P., & Lin, H. J. (2022). Using machine learning language models to generate innovation AIs for patent mining. *Applied Sciences (Basel, Switzerland)*, 12(19), 9818. DOI:10.3390/app12199818

Von Rueden, L., Mayer, S., Beckh, K., Georgiev, B., Giesselbach, S., Heese, R., Kirsch, B., Walczak, M., Pfrommer, J., Pick, A., Ramamurthy, R., Garcke, J., Bauckhage, C., & Schuecker, J. (2021). Informed machine learning–a taxonomy and survey of integrating prior knowledge into learning systems. *IEEE Transactions on Knowledge and Data Engineering*, 35(1), 614–633. DOI:10.1109/TKDE.2021.3079836

Werner, S., Rettinger, A., Halilaj, L., & Lüttin, J. (2021). RETRA: Recurrent transformers for learning temporally contextualized AI embeddings. *The Semantic Web: 18th International Conference, ESWC 2021, Virtual Event, June 6–10, 2021 Proceedings*, 18, 425–440.

Xia, H., Wang, Y., Gauthier, J., & Zhang, J. Z. (2022). AI of mobile payment platforms based on deep learning: Risk analysis and policy implications. *Expert Systems with Applications*, 208, 118143. DOI:10.1016/j.eswa.2022.118143

Xiao, D., Dianati, M., Geiger, W. G., & Woodman, R. (2023). Review of ML-based hazardous event detection methods for autonomous driving systems. *IEEE Transactions on Intelligent Transportation Systems*, 24(5), 4697–4715. DOI:10.1109/TITS.2023.3240104

Xu, W., Feng, L., & Ma, J. (2022). Understanding the domain of driving distraction with AIs. *PLoS One*, 17(12), e0278822. DOI:10.1371/journal.pone.0278822 PMID:36490240

Yu, C., Wang, X., Xu, X., Zhang, M., Ge, H., Ren, J., Sun, L., Chen, B., & Tan, G. (2019). Distributed multiagent coordinated learning for autonomous driving in highways based on dynamic coordination MLs. *IEEE Transactions on Intelligent Transportation Systems*, 21(2), 735–748. DOI:10.1109/TITS.2019.2893683

Yu, S. Y., Malawade, A. V., & Faruque, M. A. A. (2023). Scene-ML Embedding for Robust Autonomous Vehicle Perception. In *Machine Learning and Optimization Techniques for Automotive Cyber-Physical Systems* (pp. 525–544). Springer International Publishing. DOI:10.1007/978-3-031-28016-0_18

Zheng, Z., Zhou, B., Zhou, D., Soylu, A., & Kharlamov, E. (2022, October). Executable AI for transparent machine learning in welding monitoring at Bosch. In *Proceedings of the 31st ACM International Conference on Information & Knowledge Management* (pp. 5102-5103).

ADDITIONAL READING

Krasniqi, X., & Hajrizi, E. (2016). Use of IoT technology to drive the automotive industry from connected to full autonomous vehicles. *IFAC-PapersOnLine*, 49(29), 269–274. DOI:10.1016/j.ifacol.2016.11.078

Minovski, D., Åhlund, C., & Mitra, K. (2020). Modeling quality of IoT experience in autonomous vehicles. *IEEE Internet of Things Journal*, 7(5), 3833–3849. DOI:10.1109/JIOT.2020.2975418

Philip, B. V., Alpcan, T., Jin, J., & Palaniswami, M. (2018). Distributed real-time IoT for autonomous vehicles. *IEEE Transactions on Industrial Informatics*, 15(2), 1131–1140. DOI:10.1109/TII.2018.2877217

KEY TERMS AND DEFINITIONS

Autonomous Vehicles (AVs): Self-driving cars that utilize sensors, AI, and communication technologies to navigate and operate without human intervention, enhancing safety and reducing transportation-related challenges.

Cybersecurity in Autonomous Vehicles: The practice of protecting the data and communication systems of autonomous vehicles from cyber threats, ensuring the safety and privacy of users and preventing malicious attacks.

Edge Computing: A distributed computing paradigm that processes data closer to its source, reducing latency and bandwidth usage, which is crucial for real-time decision-making in autonomous vehicles.

Intelligent Mobility: The integration of advanced technologies, such as IoT and AI, into transportation systems to improve efficiency, sustainability, and convenience, reducing traffic congestion and environmental impact.

Internet of Things (IoT): A network of interconnected devices and sensors that collect and exchange data, enabling real-time monitoring and decision-making in various applications, including autonomous vehicles and smart cities.

LiDAR (Light Detection and Ranging): A sensor technology used in autonomous vehicles to create detailed 3D maps of the environment by measuring distances using laser beams, aiding in object detection and navigation.

Mobility-as-a-Service (MaaS): A model that integrates various transportation services into a single accessible platform, allowing users to plan, book, and pay for multiple types of transportation through one interface.

Predictive Maintenance: The use of IoT sensors and data analytics to anticipate equipment failures and schedule maintenance, improving the reliability and efficiency of vehicle fleets and transportation systems.

Sustainable Urban Planning: The development of cities and communities with a focus on reducing environmental impact, improving quality of life, and integrating technologies like IoT and autonomous vehicles to create more livable spaces.

V2X Communication (Vehicle-to-Everything): A communication system that allows vehicles to exchange information with each other and with surrounding infrastructure, enhancing safety and efficiency in autonomous driving.

Chapter 11
Future of Smart Manufacturing With IoT in Industry 5.0

Bhupinder Singh
https://orcid.org/0009-0006-4779-2553
Sharda University, India

Kittisak Jermsittiparsert
https://orcid.org/0000-0003-3245-8705
Shinawatra University, Thailand

ABSTRACT

Industry 5.0 has created a more stable and networked industrial environment using the internet of things (IoT). Industry 5.0 creates a work environment where human-machine interaction is optimized for better performance by combining human co-operation with robots and intelligent equipment. Industrial internet of things (IIoT) includes various services in large settings, such as digital domains for company management, real-time production monitoring, and machinery condition tracking. Industry 5.0 aims to achieve the best possible balance between productivity and efficiency in various sectors, including heavy manufacturing, oil and gas, and ware-house management, which heavily rely on heavy gear. This chapter comprehensively explores the multiple dimensions of the IoT in Industry 5.0 used in intelligent man-ufacturing for fault screening and mechanical diagnosis and prognosis.

DOI: 10.4018/979-8-3693-5498-8.ch011

INTRODUCTION

There has been a significant advancement in research and development concerning the identification and prognosis of faults in mechanical systems (Vatin et al., 2024). However, improving the precision and dependability of failure detection and prediction using data mining continues to be a major issue in this industry because of the complex nature of machine centers (Wang et al., 2024). The need is to build a systematic strategy and acquire insights for predictive maintenance in the Industry 5.0 era by investigating problem detection and prognosis within machine centers using data mining techniques (Moimuddin et al., 2024). It provides a system architecture that follows the concepts of Industry 5.0 and covers the phases of fault analysis and treatment for predictive maintenance in machine centers (Ismail et al., 2024). These industries frequently use a variety of gear such as mobile and free-standing heavy trucks, stationary and mobile drilling equipment, and maintenance robots for subterranean and undersea oil and gas activities (Kusiak, 2024; Lv, 2023). However, delays in identifying mechanical breakdowns lead to a high frequency of safety events. IoT makes it easier to quickly gather operational data from a variety of sensors, but it also presents hurdles for effectively using this data and improving the accuracy of problem prediction (Maroof & Kapate, 2023).

Using a variety of the sensors such as- vibration, acceleration, temperature and air pressure which singly or in combination to collect real-time data on the operation of mechanical equipment has become increasingly popular in recent years (Kralj & Aralica, 2023; Fanoro et al., 2021; Hussain et al., 2023). Utilizing cloud platforms in conjunction with IoT and sensor data fusion technology to analyze large amounts of data has become an important field of this chapter (Speringer & Schnelzer, 2019) (Villar et al., 2023). Although companies might gain a competitive edge and improve operational efficiency by implementing these technologies, there is general apprehension about the possibility of low-skilled individuals losing their jobs as a result of growing automation (Bedi et al., 2021). These services are integrated in digital space which makes their complex linkages clear. Emerging as a focus area for future growth is the convergence of IoT, cloud computing, and big data processing for predictive maintenance of mechanical equipment, given the rapid improvement of computing power and the upcoming integration of 5G/6G communication infrastructure (Ziatdinov et al., 2024). This concern is due to the possibility of increased social and economic inequality as a result of extensive automation (Nel-Sanders, 2023) (Barnard, 2023). The emergence and comprehension of Industry 4.0 and its consequences for contemporary production are aided by the many stages of the Industrial Revolution as well as their corresponding dates, driving factors, and related technologies (Fanoro et al., 2021).

BACKGROUND

During the Industrial Revolution, inventive tactics propelled by the period's technical breakthroughs replaced conventional industrial processes (Van der Poll, 2022). The initial three industrial revolutions were distinguished by mechanization, electrification, and automation, in that order, via consecutive waves of change (del Carmen Sandoval Madrid, 2023). These revolutions gradually changed economies from being centered on agriculture to being based on industry, raising factory worker wages and advancing healthcare systems (Pang et al., 2023). Businesses who adopted these reforms saw notable gains in productivity, enhanced competitiveness, and opened up new avenues for international trade (Benabed & Boeru, 2023). Thus give a range of interpretations and viewpoints on Industry 5.0 from scholars and practitioners in the field. It then explores Industry 5.0's possible uses which include supply chain management, cloud manufacturing, intelligent healthcare, and manufacturing production (Adepoju et al., 2023). It look at a number of auxiliary technologies that are essential to Industry 5.0, including blockchain, edge computing, digital twins, Internet of Everything (IoE), collaborative robotics and cutting-edge networking technologies like 6G and beyond (Balla et al., 2023).

The world is on the verge of another revolutionary period, the fifth industrial revolution or Industry 5.0, as it see the fourth industrial revolution also known as Industry 4.0, come to pass. Integrating digital or computational technology with physical systems is the cornerstone of Industry 4.0 (Gumbo et al., 2023). Artificial Intelligence (AI), Machine Learning (ML), Big Data analytics, Cloud computer, and cybersecurity are examples of core computer technologies. Physical technologies including robotics, automation, Internet of Things (IoT), cyber-physical systems (CPS), and additive manufacturing (AM) support these (Chedrawi & Haddad, 2022). The combination of these technologies makes it possible to implement Industry 4.0 systems, which are essential to the idea of smart factories or smart manufacturing since they allow for agile, adaptable, and on-demand manufacturing (Mohd Yamin et al., 2023).

Industry 5.0 is the next stage of industrial development. It aims to produce production solutions that are more resource-effective and customized than those of Industry 4.0 by utilizing the creativity of human specialists working in tandem with accurate, intelligent, and efficient machinery (Owusu et al., 2023). With a number of potential technologies and applications predicted to support it, Industry 5.0 is expected to improve manufacturing capacity and expedite the delivery of customized goods in real time. This chapter provides possible applications and the underlying technologies influencing the development of Industry 5.0 acting as an introduction to the topic (Jordan et al., 2020).

The objectives of the chapter are to bring together top-notch original research contributions in the developing topic of Device Condition Monitoring and Predictions utilizing IoT in Industry 5.0 from both academia and industry to:

-   take use of all the chances and potential in this field of manufacturing.
-   focuses on how to enhance IoT with little human interaction by analyzing data from various sensors.
-   addressing the topics relating to infrastructures, protocols, architectures and algorithms.

ROLE OF IOT IN MECHANICAL FAULT DIAGNOSIS AND PROGNOSIS

Industry 5.0 takes a decidedly human-centered stance, recognizing the indispensable role that human connection plays in all aspects of manufacturing (Raheman, 2022). Unlike earlier models that risked making people less valuable due to substantial automation, Industry 5.0 places more emphasis on the social worth and the distinct abilities, emotional intelligence, and creativity of individuals (Nyemba et al., 2020). These days, machines are cooperative partners rather than just operators, augmenting human talents rather than replacing them. At every stage of operation, Industry 5.0 places a strong emphasis on flexibility. Industrial systems are designed to react quickly to changing conditions (Sledziewska & Włoch, 2021). When smart machines are fitted with sophisticated sensors and algorithms, they may automatically adjust to changing environments without the need for ongoing programming (Paramasivam, 2020). This flexibility is especially noteworthy in the field of customized production, where Industry 5.0 makes it possible to manufacture goods in large quantities according to the unique needs of individual customers. Production lines are incredibly agile in the industrial scene because they can be quickly modified to go from one production run to the next (Masenya & Chisita, 2022).

The main tenets of Industry 5.0 are sustainability, which encourages both economic responsibility and the incorporation of ecologically beneficial methods into industrial operations (Millard, 2023). Industry 5.0 industrial activities aim to reduce waste, energy consumption, and emissions while giving priority to the utilization of renewable energy sources (Islam et al., 2023). With balancing economic gains with environmental concerns, this strategy encourages the creation of sustainable business models that support long-term profitability (Millard, 2023). The importance of human interaction in the production process accepting Industry 5.0 means realizing that human-machine cooperation has the potential to provide more robust results than automation on its own (Sledziewska & Wloch, 2021). The manufacturing process is greatly improved by human engagement in a number of ways:

It gives automated operations more flexibility and adaptability, enabling employees to quickly change settings, solve unanticipated problems, and step in during difficult situations (Kotikangas, 2023).

Decisions made by human operators are more well-informed and efficient since they are based on complex considerations and contextual awareness (Gonzalez-Manzano, 2022).

With visual inspections, defect identification, and adherence to strict standards, human participation maintains product quality and lowers mistakes, rejections, and related expenses (hasan & Ahmed, 2017).

Because employees provide new solutions, make suggestions for enhancements, and push for ongoing changes to manufacturing processes, it encourages creativity, critical thinking and inventive problem solving (Rahman et al., 2023).

For mechanical equipment to operate safely, it is essential to precisely analyze its health. This is where mechanical fault diagnostics comes into play (Haleem & Javaid, 2019). An increasing number of people are inclined to use deep learning for mechanical problem diagnostics as the "big data" age gains momentum (Pereira Perdigao, 2018). In the field of mechanical fault diagnosis, the idea of mechanical diagnosis based on transfer learning has become important in order to improve the flexibility of deep learning applications across different fault diagnosis scenarios (Kumar, 2018).

MACHINE LEARNING FOR PREDICTIVE MAINTENANCE

A proactive approach to equipment maintenance, predictive maintenance uses machine learning techniques to predict probable breakdowns and save expensive downtime (Dutta, 2020). It's like having a conversation with your equipment since it sends out notifications in good time, before problems happen. Predictive maintenance systems which function similarly to a watchful group of inspectors, constantly monitor equipment by examining copious volumes of real-time data (Cayre, 2022). This advanced technology provides early indications of approaching failures by being skilled at spotting minute irregularities and patterns that may escape human notice. To demonstrate this idea practically, picture a manufacturing plant that depends on a fleet of industrial robots to keep things running smoothly (Flanigen, 2023). In the past, upkeep for these robots was either planned ahead of time or less ideal, done on the fly in response to malfunctions, which caused downtime and financial losses (Singh & Kaunert, 2024). The strategically placed sensors within the machinery use machine learning predictive maintenance to continuously track its performance.

Numerous data points including as- temperature, vibration, power usage and other pertinent metrics are captured by these sensors (Bhatti, 2021).

Machine learning-based predictive maintenance is more effective than just detection. For example, hydraulic presses can be continuously inspected to find obstructions and leaks that may indicate a problem (Singh, 2023). Also, by continuous temperature monitoring, predictive maintenance systems are able to spot overheating symptoms which are an indication of impending problems in the hydraulic system (Jokubauskis, 2020). Also, by monitoring cycle counts, machine learning predictive maintenance can precisely forecast when particular components could require repair, allowing for prompt interventions to avoid breakdowns (Singh, 2023). Predictive maintenance software can evaluate the tension of conveyor belts in order to prevent premature wear (Netherton & Netherton, 2021). It can also guarantee operating efficiency and identify any early warning signs of problems that can cause unplanned downtime by monitoring motor load. A key component of the business's manufacturing strategy is now predictive maintenance (Singh, 2023).

IOT-BASED FAULT DIAGNOSIS AND PROGNOSIS: SIGNIFICANCE AND BENEFITS

The industrial sector, which relies heavily on both personnel and equipment has seen a considerable decrease in daily labor difficulties with the introduction of the Internet of Things (Sharma & Singh, 2022). IoT plays a crucial role in the Industry 4.0 ecosystem by serving as a bridge between the real and virtual worlds and enabling smooth data processing and online monitoring (Nazari, 2017). Industry 5.0 now makes extensive use of automation, data processing, interchange and analysis which improves customer happiness, digitizes data and produces higher-quality products (Ziatdinov et al., 2024). Because of its possible uses in a wide range of real-world situations, the Internet of Things (IoT) has recently become a major topic of interest in both industry and academics (Fawehinmi et al., 2024). This study uses Internet of Things (IoT) data gathered in the process sector to solve the problem of defect detection and prediction. It provides a solution that makes use of IoT technology (Cordell, 2024). First, the method uses sensor data analysis to determine causal linkages between physical devices without requiring information about the physical architecture of the production system (Gwala & mashau, 2024). Defects in those devices can be quickly identified by continually tracking the health index of those devices in real time. The technology uses the identified causal linkages to forecast possible malfunctions in additional devices (Formen et al., 2024). The implementing of an IoT-based system for mechanical fault diagnosis and prognosis offers a multitude of benefits for manufacturers including-

Reduced Downtime: With proactively identifying potential issues, manufacturers can address them before they result in equipment failure and production stoppages (Wang et al., 2024).

Improved Maintenance Efficiency: Transitioning from reactive to predictive maintenance allows for scheduling maintenance activities based on actual equipment needs, optimizing resource allocation and labor costs (Narkhede et al., 2024).

Enhanced Equipment Lifespan: Early detection of faults enables corrective actions to be taken before minor problems evolve into major breakdowns, ultimately extending equipment life (Schroder et al., 2024).

Optimized Production Processes: Real-time insights into equipment health facilitate adjustments to production parameters, ensuring consistent product quality and process stability (Vacchi et al., 2024).

Data-driven Decision Making: The vast amount of data collected by IoT sensors provides valuable insights for optimizing production processes, improving resource utilization and making informed decisions about equipment investments (Mladineo et al., 2024).

CHALLENGES AND CONCERNS

Predictive maintenance of mechanical equipment is becoming more dependent on the combination of IoT, cloud computing and big data processing technologies (Khaira, 2024). This is due to the rapid increase in computing capacity and the upcoming deployment of 5G connection infrastructure (Lo et al., 2024). Diesel engines, gearboxes, rolling bearings, wind turbines and other mechanical systems usually require human maintenance and troubleshooting (Abdel-Basset et al., 2024). Nonetheless, frequent safety mishaps are frequently caused by the incapacity to identify equipment defects quickly (Wen, 2024). Large volumes of operating data from mechanical devices may be quickly gathered in IoT setups. It is difficult to make good use of this data and improve the accuracy of fault prediction (Irpan & Shaddiq, 2024). There are challenges associated with implementing IoT-based fault diagnosis and prognosis system as-

Data Security: Securing sensitive data collected from industrial machinery is paramount (Natalia et al., 2024). Robust cybersecurity measures are essential to prevent unauthorized access and potential disruptions (Dmitrieva et al., 2024).

Sensor Integration and Data Management: Integrating a multitude of sensors across a vast network of machines necessitates efficient data management infrastructure to handle the high volume and velocity of data (Reddy et al., 2024).

Interoperability: Standardization across sensor protocols and data formats is crucial for seamless integration of different systems and components (Rani & Srivastava, 2024).

Technical Expertise: Implementing and maintaining an IoT-based system requires personnel with expertise in sensor technology, data analytics and machine learning (Suganya et al., 2024).

Several sensors have been used singly or in combination to collect operating data in real time from different mechanical equipment components, including those that measure vibration, acceleration, temperature, and air pressure (Srinivasan et al., 2024). Using multi-source sensing data fusion technology for big data analysis and integrating IoT with cloud platforms has emerged as crucial research areas to improve prediction accuracy (Hashim et al., 2024). A topology design based on Internet of Things concepts to demonstrate predictive maintenance of mechanical equipment (Riant et al., 2024).

MACHINE LEARNING (ML) MODELS

The goal of machine learning, a growing discipline of computing algorithms, is to mimic human intelligence by absorbing information from its surroundings (Selvarajan et al., 2024). Machine learning algorithms are soft-coded, in contrast to traditional computer processes, which need explicit input data (Nair et al., 2024). This enables them to dynamically modify their designs based on recurring patterns, increasing the likelihood that they will succeed in their goals (Camarinha-Matos et al., 2024). Machine learning techniques have proven beneficial in a number of fields, including banking, medicinal research, computational biology, pattern identification, entertainment and spacecraft engineering (Saputro, 2024). Radiation practice safety and efficacy might develop thanks to machine learning algorithms' capacity to learn from their surroundings and use that information to new tasks, perhaps producing better results (Valeriya et al., 2024). The domains of machine learning and data mining are closely related. Before beginning learning tasks, machine learning algorithms preprocess data using data mining techniques. They also use a variety of data mining approaches to find hidden information in big datasets (Natalia et al., 2024).

The most important component of predictive maintenance is fault detection which is largely relied upon by businesses to quickly and precisely identify problems (Noori et al., 2024). Unsupervised learning is a good choice for model building in situations where it is sometimes important to design a model with as little historical data as possible in order to avoid maintenance expenses (Hassan et al., 2024). Companies still struggle to choose among the multitude of algorithms and techniques available the most appropriate, reliable and accurate detection approach, even with the increased attention predictive maintenance has received in recent years (Kumari et al. 2024). Submachine defect detection methods frequently employ vibration data and sensors are being included into industrial systems like those found in the Internet of Things (IoT) in order to collect relevant data. The administration of data in real time makes it possible to carry more accurate maintenance operations (Goka et al., 2024). Early defect identification validates the reliability and safety of business processes, which lowers the possibility of unanticipated failures (Khna et al., 2024).

CONCLUSION

Industry 5.0, which emphasizes economic, technological, environmental, and social factors, expands on and enhances the fundamental components of Industry 4.0. It recognizes the crucial part that human labor plays in the production process. Sustainability, resilience, and people-centricity are at the center of Industry 5.0. The contribution of contextual awareness, decision-making skills, and flexibility made by human contact improves industrial operations. Throughout the production process, this human touch promotes creativity, guarantees product quality and makes problem-solving easier. Industry 5.0's adaptive production and human-machine cooperation are made possible by cutting-edge technologies including additive manufacturing, augmented reality (AR), virtual reality (VR) collaborative robots and artificial intelligence (AI). Industry 5.0 with its emphasis on the human engagement, encourages the creation of higher-value occupations, allows for individualized customer services and frees up human workers to concentrate on providing better, customized goods that are suited to individual tastes and requirements.

REFERENCES

Abdel-Basset, M., Mohamed, R., & Chang, V. (2024). A Multi-Criteria Decision-Making Framework to Evaluate the Impact of Industry 5.0 Technologies: Case Study, Lessons Learned, Challenges and Future Directions. *Information Systems Frontiers*, 1–31. DOI:10.1007/s10796-024-10472-3

Adepoju, O., Akinyomi, O., & Esan, O. (2023). Integrating Human-Computer Interactions in Nigerian Energy System: A Skills Requirement Analysis. *Journal of Digital Food, Energy & Water Systems, 4*(2).

Balla, M., Haffner, O., Kučera, E., & Cigánek, J. (2023). Educational Case Studies: Creating a Digital Twin of the Production Line in TIA Portal, Unity, and Game4Automation Framework. *Sensors (Basel)*, 23(10), 4977. DOI:10.3390/s23104977 PMID:37430895

Barnard, H. (2023). *Developing a managerial framework for digital manufacturing in the new normal era* (Doctoral dissertation, North-West University (South Africa)).

Bedi, T., Rana, V., & Gautam, N. (2021). Changing Face Of The Apparel Industry By Incorporating Industry 4.0 And Paving Way For Industry 5.0. *Turkish Online Journal of Qualitative Inquiry, 12*(3).

Benabed, A., & Boeru, A. C. (2023). Globalization beyond Business Sustainability, Energy and the Economy of the Future. In *Proceedings of the International Conference on Business Excellence* (Vol. 17, No. 1, pp. 1569-1583). Sciendo. DOI:10.2478/picbe-2023-0141

Bhatti, M. R. A. (2021). *Light-driven Actuation In Ultra-drawn Chain-oriented Polymers* (Doctoral dissertation, Queen Mary University of London).

Camarinha-Matos, L. M., Rocha, A. D., & Graça, P. (2024). Collaborative approaches in sustainable and resilient manufacturing. *Journal of Intelligent Manufacturing*, 35(2), 499–519. DOI:10.1007/s10845-022-02060-6 PMID:36532704

Cayre, R. (2022). *Offensive and defensive approaches for wireless communication protocols security in IoT* (Doctoral dissertation, Toulouse, INSA).

Chedrawi, C., & Haddad, G. (2022). The rise of quasi-humans in AI fueled organizations, an ultimate socio-materiality approach to the lens of Michel Serres. *Pacific Asia Journal of the Association for Information Systems*, 14(2), 2. DOI:10.17705/1pais.14202

Cordell, G. A. (2024). The contemporary nexus of medicines security and biopros-pecting: A future perspective for prioritizing the patient. *Natural Products and Bioprospecting*, 14(1), 1–32. DOI:10.1007/s13659-024-00431-5 PMID:38270809

del Carmen Sandoval Madrid, A. (2023). *The nexus of sustainability and industry 5.0: Assessing Canadian organizations': Readiness for the next technological rev-olution* (Doctoral dissertation, University Canada West).

Dmitrieva, E., Balmiki, V., Lakhanpal, S., Lavanya, G., & Bhandari, P. (2024). AI Evolution in Industry 4.0 and Industry 5.0: An Experimental Comparative Assess-ment. In *BIO Web of Conferences* (Vol. 86, p. 01069). EDP Sciences.

Dutta, P. (2020). *Occupancy Based Load Switching using Microcontroller* (Doctoral dissertation, University of Technology).

Fanoro, M., Božanić, M., & Sinha, S. (2021). A review of 4IR/5IR enabling tech-nologies and their linkage to manufacturing supply chain. *Technologies*, 9(4), 77. DOI:10.3390/technologies9040077

Fanoro, M., Božanić, M., & Sinha, S. (2021). A Review of 4IR/5IR Enabling Tech-nologies and Their Linkage to Manufacturing Supply Chain. *Technologies*, 2021(9), 77. DOI:10.3390/technologies9040077

Fawehinmi, O., Aigbogun, O., & Tanveer, M. I. (2024). The Role of Industrial Revo-lution 5.0 in Actualizing the Effectiveness of Green Human Resource Management. In *Green Human Resource Management: A View from Global South Countries* (pp. 291–312). Springer Nature Singapore. DOI:10.1007/978-981-99-7104-6_17

Flanigen, P. (2023). *Algorithms and Visualizations to Support Airborne Detection of Vertical Obstacles* (Doctoral dissertation).

Formen, J. S., Hassan, D. S., & Wolf, C. (2024). Chemometric sensing of stereoiso-meric compound mixtures with a redox-responsive optical probe. *Chemical Science (Cambridge)*, 15(4), 1498–1504. DOI:10.1039/D3SC05706B PMID:38274061

Gonzalez-Manzano, L., Fuentes, J. M. D., & Ribagorda, A. (2019). Leveraging user-related internet of things for continuous authentication: A survey. *ACM Computing Surveys*, 52(3), 1–38. DOI:10.1145/3314023

Gumbo, S., Twinomurinzi, H., Bwalya, K., & Wamba, S. F. (2023). Skills provi-sioning for the Fourth Industrial Revolution: A Bibliometric Analysis. *Procedia Computer Science*, 219, 924–932. DOI:10.1016/j.procs.2023.01.368

Gutiérrez Peña, J. A. (2022). Cost effective technology applied to domotics and smart home energy management systems.

Gwala, R. S., & Mashau, P. (2024). Equality, Diversity, and Access in Digitalized Teaching in Higher Education. In *Accessibility of Digital Higher Education in the Global South* (pp. 105–131). IGI Global.

Haleem, A., & Javaid, M. (2019). Additive manufacturing applications in industry 4.0: A review. *Journal of Industrial Integration and Management*, 4(04), 1930001. DOI:10.1142/S2424862219300011

Hasan, K., & Ahmed, T. (2017). *Applications of Internet of Things (IoT) Towards Smart Home Automation* (Doctoral dissertation, Stamford University Bangladesh).

Hashim, M. A. M., Tlemsani, I., Mason-Jones, R., Matthews, R., & Ndrecaj, V. (2024). Higher education via the lens of industry 5.0: Strategy and perspective. *Social Sciences & Humanities Open*, 9, 100828. DOI:10.1016/j.ssaho.2024.100828

Hussain, A., Ansari, H. W. A., Nasir, H., & Maqbool, M. Q. (2023). Developing a Model for the Adoption of Industrial Revolution 5.0 Among Malaysian Manufacturing SMEs for Sustainable Growth. In *Opportunities and Challenges of Business 5.0 in Emerging Markets* (pp. 40–57). IGI Global. DOI:10.4018/978-1-6684-6403-8.ch003

Irpan, M., & Shaddiq, S. (2024). Industry 4.0 and Industry 5.0—Inception, Conception, Perception, and Rethinking Loyalty Employment. *International Journal of Economics, Management,Business, and Social Science*, 4(1), 95–114.

Islam, M. S., Amin, S., Arifuzzaman, M., Rahman, M. H., & Hossain, R. (2023). *Automatic Train Wash Plant on Metro System* (Doctoral dissertation, Sonargoan University (SU)).

Ismail, M. M., Ahmed, Z., Abdel-Gawad, A. F., & Mohamed, M. (2024). Toward Supply Chain 5.0: An Integrated Multi-Criteria Decision-Making Models for Sustainable and Resilience Enterprise. *Decision making: applications in management and engineering, 7*(1), 160-186.

Jokubauskis, D. (2020). *Development and applications of compact spectroscopic terahertz imaging systems using principles of optical beam engineering* (Doctoral dissertation, Vilniaus universitetas).

Jordan, A. A., Pegatoquet, A., Castagnetti, A., Raybaut, J., & Le Coz, P. (2020). Deep learning for eye blink detection implemented at the edge. *IEEE Embedded Systems Letters*, 13(3), 130–133. DOI:10.1109/LES.2020.3029313

Khaira, A. (2024). From 3D to 4D: The Evolution of Additive Manufacturing and Its Implications for Industry 5.0. In *Emerging Technologies in Digital Manufacturing and Smart Factories* (pp. 39-53). IGI Global.

Kotikangas, M. (2023). Utilization of digital twin for customer tailored variable speed drive.

Kralj, D., & Aralica, K. (2022, September). Industry 5.0 from the Perspective of Safety at Work. In *Occupational Safety and Health, Proceedings of the 8th International Professional and Scientific Conference, Zadar, Croatia* (pp. 21-24).

Kralj, D., & Aralica, K. (2023). Safety at work within industry 5.0-quo vadis. *Sigurnost: časopis za sigurnost u radnoj i životnoj okolini, 65*(3), 317-324.

Kumar, R. (2018). Bilingual Domain-Independent Natural Language Interface to Database.

Kusiak, A. (2024). Federated explainable artificial intelligence (fXAI): A digital manufacturing perspective. *International Journal of Production Research, 62*(1-2), 171–182. DOI:10.1080/00207543.2023.2238083

Lo, H. W., Chan, H. W., Lin, J. W., & Lin, S. W. (2024). Evaluating the interrelationships of industrial 5.0 development factors using an integration approach of Fermatean fuzzy logic. *Journal of Operations Intelligence, 2*(1), 95–113. DOI:10.31181/jopi21202416

Lv, Z. (2023). Digital Twins in Industry 5.0. *Research, 6,* 71.

Maroof, M. A., & Kapate, S. (2023). *Exploring Dynamics of Industry 5.0.* World Journal of Management and Economics.

Masenya, T. M., & Chisita, C. T. (2022). Futurizing library services in a technology-driven dispensation: Reflections on selected academic libraries in Zimbabwe and South Africa. In *Innovative technologies for enhancing knowledge access in academic libraries* (pp. 1–21). IGI Global. DOI:10.4018/978-1-6684-3364-5.ch001

Millard, J. (2023). Exploring the impact of digital transformation on public governance.

Millard, J. (2023). Impact of digital transformation on public governance. *Joint Research Centre (Seville site).*

Mladineo, M., Celent, L., Milković, V., & Veža, I. (2024). Current State Analysis of Croatian Manufacturing Industry with Regard to Industry 4.0/5.0. *Machines (Basel), 12*(2), 87. DOI:10.3390/machines12020087

Mohd Yamin, M. N., Ab. Aziz, K., Gek Siang, T., & Ab. Aziz, N. A. (2023). Determinants of Emotion Recognition System Adoption: Empirical Evidence from Malaysia. *Applied Sciences (Basel, Switzerland), 13*(21), 11854. DOI:10.3390/app132111854

Nair, A., Pillai, S. V., & Senthil Kumar, S. A. (2024). Towards emerging Industry 5.0–a review-based framework. *Journal of Strategy and Management*.

Narang, N. K. (2022). Mentor's Musings on Disruptive Technologies and Standards Interplay in Industrial Transformation. *IEEE Internet of Things Magazine*, 5(1), 4–12. DOI:10.1109/MIOT.2022.9773142

Narkhede, G. B., Pasi, B. N., Rajhans, N., & Kulkarni, A. (2024). Industry 5.0 and sustainable manufacturing: A systematic literature review. *Benchmarking*. Advance online publication. DOI:10.1108/BIJ-03-2023-0196

Natalia, T., Pathani, A., Dhaliwal, N., Rajasekhar, N., & Khatkar, M. (2024). Blockchain Integration in Industry 5.0: A Security Experiment for Resilience Assessment. In *BIO Web of Conferences* (Vol. 86, p. 01070). EDP Sciences.

Natalia, V., Bisht, Y. S., Prabhakar, P. K., Arora, R., Mishra, S. K., & Rajasekhar, N. (2024). AI and Autonomous Systems: An Experiment in Industry 5.0 Transformation. In *BIO Web of Conferences* (Vol. 86, p. 01094). EDP Sciences.

Nazari, M. (2017). *Infrared Matrix-Assisted Laser Desorption Electrospray Ionization (IR-MALDESI): Development and Applications in Metabolomics, Mass Spectrometry Imaging, and Direct Analysis*. North Carolina State University.

Nel-Sanders, D. (2023). Revolutionising Public Private Partnerships: A Transition to the Fifth Industrial Revolution. *International Journal of Innovation in Management. Economics and Social Sciences*, 3(1), 12–29.

Netherton, T., & Netherton, T. J. (2021). A fully-automated, deep learning-based framework for ct-based localization, segmentation, verification and planning of metastatic vertebrae.

Nyemba, W. R., Chikuku, T., Chiroodza, J. R., Dube, B., Carter, K. F., Mbohwa, C., & Magombo, L. (2020). Industrial design thinking and innovations propelled by the Royal Academy of Engineering in Sub-Saharan Africa for capacity building. *Procedia CIRP*, 91, 770–775. DOI:10.1016/j.procir.2020.02.233

Owusu, P. K., Nortey, D. N. N., Koffie-Ocloo, D., & Afriyie, G. O. (2023, December). Evaluating customer satisfaction with AI chatbot interactions in the Ghanaian insurance industry: Focusing on Star Assurance Ltd. In *Conference proceedings edited by* (p. 43).

Pang, T. Y., Lee, T. K., & Murshed, M. (2023). Towards a New Paradigm for Digital Health Training and Education in Australia: Exploring the Implication of the Fifth Industrial Revolution. *Applied Sciences (Basel, Switzerland)*, 13(11), 6854. DOI:10.3390/app13116854

Papadopulos, J., & Christiansen, J. (2023). Conversational AI Workforce Revolution: Exploring the Effects of Conversational AI on Work Roles and Organisations.

Paramasivam, B. (2020). Investigation on the effects of damping over the temperature distribution on internal turning bar using Infrared fusion thermal imager analysis via SmartView software. *Measurement*, 162, 107938. DOI:10.1016/j. measurement.2020.107938

Pereira Perdigao, G. (2018). Internship and master thesis: Concept of Operation: Unmanned Maintenance Dredging.

Raheman, F. (2022). Sharonomics: A Radical Economic Theory for the Next Industrial Revolution and Beyond. *Theoretical Economics Letters*, 12(6), 1710–1748. DOI:10.4236/tel.2022.126094

Rahman, N. A. A., Abdullah, M. A., Hassan, A., & Mahroof, K. (2023). *17 Hard Hit by Halal Meat Cartel Controversy*. Technologies and Trends in the Halal Industry.

Rani, S., & Srivastava, G. (2024). Secure hierarchical fog computing-based architecture for industry 5.0 using an attribute-based encryption scheme. *Expert Systems with Applications*, 235, 121180. DOI:10.1016/j.eswa.2023.121180

Reddy, C. K. K., Anisha, P. R., Khan, S., Hanafiah, M. M., Pamulaparty, L., & Mohana, R. M. (Eds.). (2024). *Sustainability in Industry 5.0: Theory and Applications*. CRC Press.

Rinat, K., Thakur, G., Gupta, M., Madhuri, T. N. P., & Bansal, S. (2024). Comparative Analysis of Big Data Computing in Industry 4.0 and Industry 5.0: An Experimental Study. In *BIO Web of Conferences* (Vol. 86, p. 01068). EDP Sciences.

Saputro, E. P. (2024). Kolaborasi Manusia Dan Sumber Daya Robotik Menuju Masa Depan Manufaktur Berkelanjutan Industri 5.0. *Innovative: Journal Of Social Science Research*, 4(1), 2504–2516.

Schröder, A. J., Cuypers, M., & Götting, A. (2024). From Industry 4.0 to Industry 5.0: The Triple Transition Digital, Green and Social. In *Industry 4.0 and the Road to Sustainable Steelmaking in Europe: Recasting the Future* (pp. 35–51). Springer International Publishing. DOI:10.1007/978-3-031-35479-3_3

Selvarajan, S., Manoharan, H., & Shankar, A. (2024). SL-RI: Integration of supervised learning in robots for industry 5.0 automated application monitoring. *Measurement. Sensors*, 31, 100972. DOI:10.1016/j.measen.2023.100972

Sharma, A., & Singh, B. (2022). Measuring Impact of E-commerce on Small Scale Business: A Systematic Review. *Journal of Corporate Governance and International Business Law*, 5(1).

Silvanus, S. K. (2017). *Fabrication and characterization of magnetoresponsive carbon nanotube-infused polysulfone (CNT-IPSF) nanocomposites for water purification* (Doctoral dissertation, Kenyatta University).

Singh, B. (2019). Profiling Public Healthcare: A Comparative Analysis Based on the Multidimensional Healthcare Management and Legal Approach. *Indian Journal of Health and Medical Law*, 2(2), 1–5.

Singh, B. (2020). Global science and jurisprudential approach concerning healthcare and illness. *Indian Journal of Health and Medical Law*, 3(1), 7–13.

Singh, B. (2022). Understanding Legal Frameworks Concerning Transgender Healthcare in the Age of Dynamism. *Electronic Journal of Social and Strategic Studies*, 3(1), 56–65. DOI:10.47362/EJSSS.2022.3104

Singh, B. (2022). Relevance of Agriculture-Nutrition Linkage for Human Healthcare: A Conceptual Legal Framework of Implication and Pathways. *Justice and Law Bulletin*, 1(1), 44–49.

Singh, B. (2022). COVID-19 Pandemic and Public Healthcare: Endless Downward Spiral or Solution via Rapid Legal and Health Services Implementation with Patient Monitoring Program. *Justice and Law Bulletin*, 1(1), 1–7.

Singh, B. (2023). Tele-Health Monitoring Lensing Deep Neural Learning Structure: Ambient Patient Wellness via Wearable Devices for Real-Time Alerts and Interventions. *Indian Journal of Health and Medical Law*, 6(2), 12–16.

Singh, B. (2023). Blockchain Technology in Renovating Healthcare: Legal and Future Perspectives. In *Revolutionizing Healthcare Through Artificial Intelligence and Internet of Things Applications* (pp. 177-186). IGI Global.

Singh, B. (2023). Federated Learning for Envision Future Trajectory Smart Transport System for Climate Preservation and Smart Green Planet: Insights into Global Governance and SDG-9 (Industry, Innovation and Infrastructure). *National Journal of Environmental Law*, 6(2), 6–17.

Singh, B. (2024). Legal Dynamics Lensing Metaverse Crafted for Videogame Industry and E-Sports: Phenomenological Exploration Catalyst Complexity and Future. *Journal of Intellectual Property Rights Law*, 7(1), 8–14.

Singh, B., & Kaunert, C. (2024). Integration of Cutting-Edge Technologies such as Internet of Things (IoT) and 5G in Health Monitoring Systems: A Comprehensive Legal Analysis and Futuristic Outcomes. *GLS Law Journal*, 6(1), 13–20. DOI:10.69974/glslawjournal.v6i1.123

Śledziewska, K., & Włoch, R. (2021). The foundations of the digital economy. In *The Economics of Digital Transformation*. Taylor & Francis. DOI:10.4324/9781003144359-1

Śledziewska, K., & Włoch, R. (2021). The Economics of Digital Transformation. *The disruption of*.

Speringer, M., & Schnelzer, J. (2019). Differentiation of industry 4.0 models. *Vienna, Austria*.

Srinivasan, S., Hema, D. D., Singaram, B., Praveena, D., Mohan, K. K., & Preetha, M. (2024). Decision Support System based on Industry 5.0 in Artificial Intelligence. *International Journal of Intelligent Systems and Applications in Engineering*, 12(15s), 172–178.

Suganya, G., Selvakumar, J. J., Varadharajan, P., & Pachiyappan, S. (2024). Skill Sets Required to Meet a Human-Centered Industry 5.0: A Systematic Literature Review and Bibliometric Analysis. *Advances in Web Technologies and Engineering*, 5(0), 231–252. DOI:10.4018/979-8-3693-0782-3.ch014

Vacchi, M., Siligardi, C., & Settembre-Blundo, D. (2024). Driving Manufacturing Companies toward Industry 5.0: A Strategic Framework for Process Technological Sustainability Assessment (P-TSA). *Sustainability (Basel)*, 16(2), 695. DOI:10.3390/su16020695

Valeriya, G., Kirola, M., Gupta, M., Bharathi, P., & Acharya, P. (2024). Evaluating the Impact of AI-Based Sustainability Measures in Industry 5.0: A Longitudinal Study. In *BIO Web of Conferences* (Vol. 86, p. 01058). EDP Sciences.

Van der Poll, J. A. (2022). Problematizing the Adoption of Formal Methods in the 4IR–5IR Transition. *Applied System Innovation*, 5(6), 127. DOI:10.3390/asi5060127

Vatin, N. I., Negi, G. S., Yellanki, V. S., Mohan, C., & Singla, N. (2024). Sustainability Measures: An Experimental Analysis of AI and Big Data Insights in Industry 5.0. In *BIO Web of Conferences* (Vol. 86, p. 01072). EDP Sciences.

Villar, A., Paladini, S., & Buckley, O. (2023, July). Towards Supply Chain 5.0: Redesigning Supply Chains as Resilient, Sustainable, and Human-Centric Systems in a Post-pandemic World. In *Operations* [). Cham: Springer International Publishing.]. *Research Forum*, 4(3), 60. DOI:10.1007/s43069-023-00234-3

Wang, B., Zhou, H., Li, X., Yang, G., Zheng, P., Song, C., Yuan, Y., Wuest, T., Yang, H., & Wang, L. (2024). Human Digital Twin in the context of Industry 5.0. *Robotics and Computer-integrated Manufacturing*, 85, 102626. DOI:10.1016/j. rcim.2023.102626

Wang, S., Zhang, J., Wang, P., Law, J., Calinescu, R., & Mihaylova, L. (2024). A deep learning-enhanced Digital Twin framework for improving safety and reliability in human–robot collaborative manufacturing. *Robotics and computer-integrated manufacturing, 85*, 102608.

Wen, L. (2024). Design automation system synchronization for cyber physical system with dynamic voltage and frequency scaling in industry 5.0. *Measurement. Sensors*, 31, 100981. DOI:10.1016/j.measen.2023.100981

Ziatdinov, R., Atteraya, M. S., & Nabiyev, R. (2024). The Fifth Industrial Revolution as a Transformative Step towards Society 5.0. *Societies (Basel, Switzerland)*, 14(2), 19. DOI:10.3390/soc14020019

ADDITIONAL READING

Goka, S., Moinuddin, S. Q., Cheepu, M., & Dewangan, A. K. (2024). Welding Practices in Industry 5.0: Opportunities, Challenges, and Applications. *Automation in Welding Industry: Incorporating Artificial Intelligence, Machine Learning and Other Technologies*, 263-279.

Hassan, A., Dutta, P. K., Gupta, S., Mattar, E., & Singh, S. (Eds.). (2024). *Human-Centered Approaches in Industry 5.0: Human-Machine Interaction, Virtual Reality Training, and Customer Sentiment Analysis: Human-Machine Interaction, Virtual Reality Training, and Customer Sentiment Analysis*. IGI Global.

Khan, M. A., Khan, R., Praveen, P., Verma, A. R., & Panda, M. K. (Eds.). (2024). *Infrastructure Possibilities and Human-Centered Approaches With Industry 5.0*. IGI Global. DOI:10.4018/979-8-3693-0782-3

Kumari, P., Anand, A., Praveen, P., Verma, A. R., & Godiyal, A. (2024). Infrastructure Potential and Human-Centric Strategies in the Context of Industry 5.0. In *Infrastructure Possibilities and Human-Centered Approaches With Industry 5.0* (pp. 199-214). IGI Global.

Noori, S. F., Yuvaraj, D., Abas, S. M., Sivaram, M., & Porkodi, V. (2024). Multifaceted Interplay between Mobile Edge Computing based on Industry 5.0 in Transportation. *International Journal of Intelligent Systems and Applications in Engineering*, 12(15s), 106–114.

KEY TERMS AND DEFINITIONS

Big Data Analytics: The process of examining large datasets to uncover patterns, trends, and insights, which is essential in IoT and Industry 5.0 for improving decision-making and operational efficiency.

Cloud Computing: The use of remote servers hosted on the internet to store, manage, and process data, which is crucial in Industry 5.0 for enabling scalable and flexible industrial applications.

Digital Twins: Virtual replicas of physical systems or processes used in Industry 5.0 to simulate, analyze, and optimize real-world operations in a digital environment.

Fault Diagnosis and Prognosis: Techniques used to identify and predict faults in mechanical systems, often employing IoT and machine learning to ensure reliability and safety in industrial operations.

Human-Machine Interaction: The collaboration between humans and robots or intelligent machines, optimized in Industry 5.0 to enhance productivity and efficiency.

Industrial Internet of Things (IIoT): The application of IoT technology in industrial settings, including services such as real-time production monitoring, machinery condition tracking, and company management.

Industry 5.0: The next phase of industrial development that focuses on integrating human creativity with intelligent machinery to achieve highly customized and efficient production processes.

Internet of Things (IoT): A network of interconnected devices that collect and exchange data, enabling automation and real-time monitoring in industrial environments.

Predictive Maintenance: A proactive approach to equipment maintenance that uses data analysis and machine learning to predict potential equipment failures and schedule timely maintenance.

Robotics: The use of robots in industrial processes, which in Industry 5.0 are designed to work alongside humans, enhancing flexibility and adaptability in production.

Chapter 12
IoT Technologies for the Intelligent Dairy Industry:
A New Challenge

Kutubuddin Sayyad Liyakat Kazi
https://orcid.org/0000-0001-5623-9211
Brahmdevdada Mane Institute of Technology, Solapur, India

ABSTRACT

The smart dairy industry has radically transformed the manufacturing, processing, and distribution processes of milk and other dairy products. By utilizing sensors, data analytics, and other smart technologies, dairy farmers can lower their environmental impact, boost productivity, enhance herd management, and improve food safety and traceability. The dairy industry must use smart technology to effectively and sustainably meet the growing demand for dairy products around the world. The intelligent dairy industry has advanced significantly from its early days. The industry has become more consumer-driven, efficient, and sustainable and uses cutting-edge technology. It is expected that the smart dairy sector will continue to grow and bring about more revolutionary changes in the future, given the growing global demand for dairy products. The dairy industry is adopting IoT technology at an increasing rate, and this trend could be significant.

INTRODUCTION

The introduction of smart technology has revolutionized the production, processing, and distribution of milk and other dairy products, positioning the dairy industry as a leader in technical breakthroughs. According to Wale et al. (2019), smart technology, sometimes referred to as precision agriculture, has improved the

DOI: 10.4018/979-8-3693-5498-8.ch012

dairy industry's sustainability, efficiency, and profitability. Using sensors and data analytics is a fundamental tenet of the smart dairy sector. These sensors gather real-time data on environmental factors, cow health, and milk output in a range of dairy farm sites, including pastures, barns, and milking parlors. Modern algorithms are then used to analyze this data, producing insightful insights that assist farmers in making defensible judgments. Improved herd management is one of the main advantages of using sensors and data analytics in the dairy sector. Farmers can identify early symptoms of sickness and provide fast treatment if they keep an eye on the well-being and behavior of their cows. This results in healthier cows producing more milk. Additionally, by lowering the requirement for antibiotics, this improves consumer safety and the health advantages of dairy products.

Smart technology has transformed not only the management of herds but also the process of milking. Traditional milking methods have been replaced by robotic milkers, also called automated milking systems, because of their higher productivity and cheaper labor costs. The robotic milkers use sensors and data analytics to identify individual cows and modify milking settings to suit their requirements, making milking more pleasant and stress-free for the cows. An increasingly sustainable farming practice has also resulted from the dairy industry's usage of smart technologies. Those farmers who closely monitor temperature, humidity, and air quality may make sure that their cows are grown in ideal conditions. This lessens the negative environmental effects of dairy farming and enhances animal welfare. Through the use of precision agriculture techniques like targeted fertilization and irrigation, the dairy sector has become more sustainable and environmentally friendly. Additionally, by using these approaches, the business has been able to utilize less water, pesticides, and fertilizers. Blockchain technology is also used in the smart dairy industry to provide traceability and transparency. Blockchain technology makes it possible to monitor dairy goods from farm to table and gives consumers details about the products' origins and manufacturing processes. Farmers now have more options to diversify their sources of income due to the dairy industry's usage of smart technologies. As an illustration, some dairy farms are currently turning cow poo into biogas, which may be used as a renewable energy source or sold to the grid. This lowers the carbon impact of the farm and gives the farmers another source of income.

In inference, the smart dairy business has significantly changed the processes involved in the production, processing, and distribution of milk and other dairy products. Dairy farmers may lower their environmental impact, boost productivity, enhance herd management, and improve food safety and traceability by utilizing sensors, data analytics, and other smart technology. The dairy industry must adopt smart technologies to effectively and sustainably meet the growing demand for dairy products worldwide. The global population of cows and their milk production in different nations are compared in Table 1 and Figure 1.

Table 1. Comparative study of the world's cow population and milk production across several nations

Country	Cow Population(%)	Total Milk Production(%)
India	16.5	8.4
China	4.7	6
USA	3.4	16.4
New Zealand	1.8	2.8

Figure 1. Comparative study of the world's cow-population and milk-production across several nations

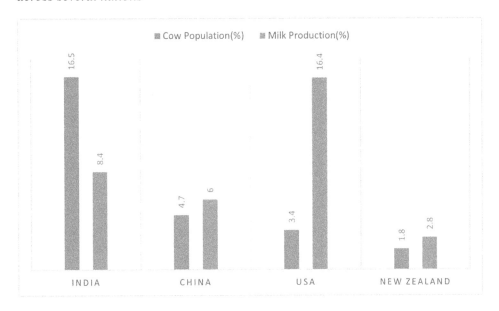

The top milk producers in the world are listed in the article as per table 2. Over the last fifty years, there has been a sharp increase in milk production worldwide. Global milk production reached approximately 918 million tonnes in 2021, nearly tripling since 1961, according to World in Data. Cow milk is the most widely consumed type of milk, followed by camel, goat, sheep, and buffalo milk.

Table 2. Milk production Ranking-Worldwide

Rank	Country	Milk Production in Tons
1	India	208,984,430
2	United States	102,654,616
3	Pakistan	65,785,000
4	China	41,245,664
5	Brazil	36,663,708
6	Germany	33,188,890
7	Russia	32,333,278
8	France	25,834,800
9	Turkey	23,200,306
10	New Zealand	21,886,376
11	United Kingdom	15,221,000
12	Poland	14,890,270

Dairy farming is considered one of the main agricultural practices for the long-term production of milk. Modern technology is used by large dairy farms to automate the milking process and keep their livestock in optimal health. Dairy farmers have come to rely more and more on precision farming as a means of tracking their operations, gathering data about the competitive market, and building databases. To stay viable and competitive in the market, dairy farmers must keep an eye on a variety of data sources, including feeding, calving, nutrition, insemination, and the milk production process. But they also have to deal with a number of difficulties, like:

- Infrastructure for breeding and genetics: Rather than productivity, the main factor driving the success of dairy farming is the increase in animal population. Increasing the output per animal is essential when resources are few. Superior animal genetics and contemporary breeding techniques like artificial insemination and embryo transfer are highly prized.
- Good quality animal feed and green fodder are badly and continuously in short supply. The rising popularity of high-breed animals has resulted in an increasing need for premium feed and fodder to suit the nutritional needs of milk-producing cows. The usage of feed pre-mixes is also motivated by a preventive approach to avert numerous health and nutrition-related issues.
- Animal health: To close the gap, superior medical care and methods for diagnosing diseases in animals are needed. This market is driven by an emphasis on animal health since high-yielding animals require more attention.
- Farms are becoming more mechanized: labor expenses are rising and the labor pool is getting smaller. As a result, farmers are using mechanization techniques to provide the world's milk demand.

Figure 2. World ranking for milk production

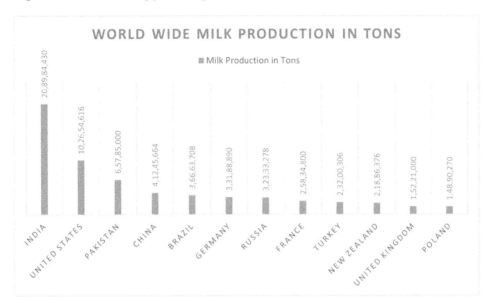

- The cold chain's infrastructure: There is not enough infrastructure in place in bulk coolers and chilling plants to avoid local spoiling and contamination. Given the significant investments made by the public and commercial sectors to ensure proper procurements, this industry is set to find growth prospects.
- Power accessibility: Lack of electricity causes many chilling plants to function badly, lowering milk quality and shortening its shelf life. Milk chillers that run on solar power could be a promising development in this sector.
- Infrastructure for adequate quality testing and a skilled labor force: Milk collecting centers do not have the infrastructure needed for adequate quality testing. The issue is made worse by a shortage of workers who are capable of doing thorough tests. The growing consumer demand for food safety presents a significant opportunity.
- Food ingredients and processing equipment: Processors are being forced to focus on product innovation as customer knowledge and preferences shift, which is also driving demand for a wide range of culinary ingredients and high-end equipment.
- Waste management: Getting rid of urinal wastewater and manure presents environmental issues for dairy farms. Water pollution and odor issues can result from the improper treatment and disposal of manure and wastewater.

- Managing byproducts: Apart from derived byproducts including lactose, caseins, caseinates, and whey proteins (WP), the dairy industry also produces a variety of byproducts, including whey, buttermilk, skim milk, and ghee residue (GR). Due to the great nutritional value of these byproducts, initiatives have been made to use them globally. The issue of dairy factories' inadequate and costly new technologies makes byproduct utilization a persistent challenge.

ADVANCES IN THE INTELLIGENT DAIRY SECTOR

With thousands of years of existence, the dairy business is one of the most enduring and well-established sectors of the economy. However, the dairy business has also seen a significant transition as a result of technological improvements. The standard methods of dairy farming, production, and management have undergone a transformation with the rise of the smart dairy business. Modern technology is used by the smart dairy business to increase its sustainability, affordability, and environmental friendliness.

The use of sensors and data analytics is one of the smart dairy industry's main advances. These sensors keep an eye on a number of factors of dairy farming, including the environment, the cows' behavior, and the volume of milk produced. To improve operations and support decision-making, data from these sensors is analyzed. As a result, improvements have been made in resource management, milk yield, and the welfare and health of cows. Another noteworthy development in the smart dairy sector is the introduction of robotic milking devices. By automating the milking process, these gadgets have decreased the need for human labor and increased output. They also gather information on the number, quality, and behavior of milkings so that every cow gets personalized care. The overall health of the cows has improved as a result, and they are producing more milk.

In the dairy business, smart feeding devices have likewise completely changed the way cows are fed. These systems track each cow's feed intake through the use of sensors, modifying the quantity and type of feed delivered in accordance. This minimizes feed waste, increasing the sustainability of dairy farming, and guarantees that the cows get the proper quantity of nutrition, resulting in healthier cows and more milk produced. The use of drones has increased recently, something that the smart dairy industry has also observed. Large areas of farmland are monitored by drones, which give farmers the most recent information on crop growth, soil conditions, and water levels. By using this information, farmers can increase the sustainability and effectiveness of their agricultural operations by making better-informed decisions regarding crop rotation, irrigation, and fertilization. The smart dairy business has embraced the use of renewable energy sources in addition to these technical advancements. Dairy farms are using solar electricity more and more to reduce their reliance on fossil fuels and offset their carbon footprint. This lowers operating costs and increases the sustainability of dairy farming.

Additionally, the smart dairy industry is using artificial intelligence (AI) more and more. By analyzing data, artificial intelligence (AI) systems are utilized to forecast milk production and cow health. This improves overall herd management by assisting farmers in identifying any problems and taking preemptive action. The distribution and packaging of dairy products have also advanced significantly as a result of the intelligent dairy sector. Dairy products now have a longer shelf life while maintaining freshness and reducing food waste because to creative packaging. The development of sophisticated distribution systems has made it possible to distribute dairy products to clients more rapidly and effectively.

In summary, aside from manufacturing and management procedures, the intelligent dairy business is innovating in other domains. Significant improvements have also been made to dairy products themselves. Plant-based milk and cheese, for instance, are dairy-free substitutes that have grown in favor lately. The growing need for dairy-free solutions is met by these eco-friendly products. Since its inception, the intelligent dairy sector has advanced significantly. The industry has changed to become more consumer-driven, efficient, sustainable, and to embrace cutting edge technologies. It is anticipated that the smart dairy business will expand further and bring about even more revolutionary developments in the future, given the growing global demand for dairy products.

IoT SCENARIO

Over the past ten years, the Internet of Things, or IoT, has rapidly progressed and altered the way we live and work. From wearables and connected automobiles to smart homes and cities, the Internet of Things has impacted every facet of our everyday existence. Through 2023, the Internet of Things is expected to grow quickly, making it an even more significant part of our future. Kazi K's (2022) Figure 3 depicts the publication scenario for IoT apps. By 2023, the worldwide Internet of Things (IoT) market is predicted to have over 30 billion linked devices and a staggering $1.5 trillion in value. This exponential rise can be attributed to the growing application of IoT in various industries, including manufacturing, transportation, healthcare, and agriculture. One of the main drivers of this growth is the advancement of technology. With the development of 5G networks, data transfer speed and capacity will grow substantially, enabling more devices to connect and communicate with each other without any issues. This will lead to an environment that is more productive and integrated. In 2023, smart homes will become even smarter with the inclusion of IoT devices. The ability of home automation systems to adapt to the habits and tastes of its users will make their lives more easy and comfortable. IoT will play a critical role in enhancing our homes' sustainability and energy efficiency.

Figure 3. Publication scenario of IoT applications in 2023

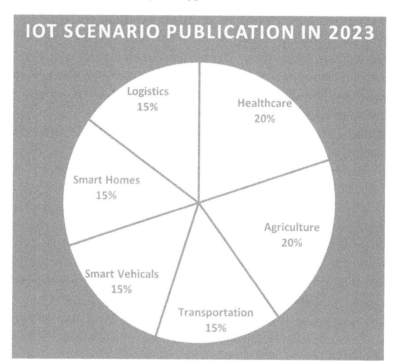

The transportation sector will undergo a substantial transformation because of the IoT's widespread adoption. Soon, connected automobiles will be the norm thanks to their advanced sensors and communication systems that increase their effectiveness and safety. These cars' capacity to interact with one another and with the infrastructure will improve traffic flow and reduce the likelihood of accidents.

The use of IoT will cause a significant transformation in the healthcare sector as well. Thanks to linked devices, patients may now monitor their health remotely, and doctors can access real-time data and make wise judgments. IoT will also have a significant impact on the development of personalized medicine, which tailors therapies to each patient's particular needs and genetic makeup Sultanana (2023).

It is also expected that the industrial industry would undergo a significant transition with the advent of Industry 4.0. IoT will enable equipment and machinery to communicate with one another, increasing efficiency and productivity. Furthermore, this will lead to the creation of "smart factories," where machinery can self-diagnose and plan maintenance, saving money and downtime. The Internet of Things will have a big impact on precision farming in the agriculture industry. Drones and connected sensors will let farmers monitor and evaluate the health of their crops and make data-driven decisions. By raising yields while using less water and fertilizer, this will improve agriculture's sustainability. However, even with all of the benefits of IoT, concerns about security and privacy still exist (Halli, 2022). Liyakat (2024) and K K S (2023) suggest that an increasing number of connected devices increases the likelihood of cyberattacks and data breaches. Kutubuddin (2024c) predicts that Liyakat (2023) would place more of an emphasis on implementing robust security measures to fend off cyberattacks and protect personal data. The IoT landscape seems promising for 2023, with significant advancements and growths expected in several industries. As technology advances, we might expect more state-of-the-art, networked devices that will raise our standard of living. It is imperative to handle the potential hazards and challenges that come with a highly connected society in order to ensure a safe and secure future.

IoT IN AGRICULTURE INDUSTRY

Because it produces food and other requirements, agriculture has always been vital to the existence of civilization. A growing global population, water shortages, and climate change are just a few of the difficulties the sector has recently encountered. Farmers are therefore under pressure to increase their output and efficiency. With the introduction of technology, the agriculture sector has seen a revolution thanks to the integration of Internet of Things (IoT) devices, which have increased farming's profitability, sustainability, and efficiency. Kutubuddin (2024d, 2024e) describes an Internet of Things (IoT) that links physical items to one other so they can communicate and collect data without the assistance of a person. The agriculture industry has tracked animals and monitored a range of farming-related matters, such as soil moisture levels, with the use of this technology. The use of IoT in agriculture, sometimes referred to as "smart farming," has grown over time, with projections indicating that the global market for agricultural IoT will reach $30.8 billion by 2025.

Wale (2019) & Kazi K S (2024) state that one of the key industries where IoT has had a significant impact is precision agriculture. This involves integrating information from Internet of Things (IoT) devices like sensors, drones, and GPS systems to analyze and manage crops, soil, and other factors that affect agricultural productivity. With the use of this technology, farmers can get up-to-date information on soil moisture, weather, and nutrient levels, and use that information to make informed decisions regarding pest management, fertilization, and irrigation. By increasing agricultural yields and reducing resource consumption, this improves the sustainability of farming.

Another significant benefit of IoT in agriculture is the capacity to remotely manage and observe cattle. IoT technology such as RFID tags and GPS collars can track the location and health of animals, allowing farmers to better manage their herds. Utilizing this technology, farmers can monitor the temperature and humidity levels within barns and coops, safeguarding the well-being of their livestock. By using real-time data regarding the location and health of their animals, farmers may make prompt decisions that improve breeding methods and avoid diseases.

In addition to precision farming and animal management, IoT has been applied to supply chain management, claims Kazi K S (2024b). With the use of sensors and GPS monitoring, farmers can monitor the movement of their cattle and harvests from the farm to the market. This helps to ensure the products' quality and freshness while also reducing the likelihood of theft and spoilage. IoT devices can be used to monitor storage characteristics like temperature and humidity to ensure that the products are kept in the best possible conditions.

IoT in agriculture not only boosts output and efficiency but also has positive environmental effects. Farmers can reduce their environmental impact and save money by using less water, fertilizer, and pesticides when they apply data-driven decision-making. Farmers can also utilize this technology to execute sustainable practices like precision irrigation, which helps preserve water, and precision spraying, which uses less dangerous chemicals.

While there are numerous benefits to IoT in agriculture, there are certain problems that still need to be fixed. One of the largest challenges is the initial cost of implementing this technology. The cost of IoT devices and infrastructure may prevent small-scale farmers from implementing IoT technology. Concerns about data security and privacy also exist because the deployment of IoT devices results in the collection and transmission of sensitive data. Appropriate guidelines and protocols need to be established in order to protect farmers' data and ensure the safe use of IoT devices. To summarize this part, the integration of IoT has led to significant improvements in productivity, sustainability, and efficiency in the agriculture industry. By using data, farmers can make educated decisions that lead to higher yields, better-quality goods, and a more sustainable agricultural industry. IoT offers a lot of potential for agriculture, and as technology advances, it will undoubtedly transform the industry. Governments and organizations need to promote and support the use of IoT in agriculture if they want to ensure food security in the future.

SMART DAIRY FARMING

Smart dairy farming, or SDF, is a modern approach to dairy product production that uses technology and data to improve animal welfare, productivity, and efficiency on dairy farms. Farmers have been using this innovative farming technique, which has gained popularity recently, to maximize their operations and meet the growing demand for dairy products. Since dairy farming is primarily done by hand, long workdays and a heavy dependence on experience and intuition are necessary. However, as technology advanced, SDF—which monitors and manages many farm components using automation, data analytics, and sensors—became the standard.

One of the key components of smart dairy farming is the use of sensors. Real-time data regarding the health and behavior of the cows is gathered by these sensors. They are positioned across the farm, in the milking machines, barns, and feeding systems, among other places. This data is sent to a central computer or a smartphone app, allowing farmers to remotely check their herd and make decisions that can be supported. Important details on the health of the cows can be obtained using sensors that assess things like body temperature, rumination activity, and milk production. With the use of this information, farmers may identify issues with individual cows promptly and take preventative action to keep their animals healthy and safe. Furthermore, it allows for the early discovery of illness, reducing the likelihood that disease would spread to the entire herd (Sayyad Liyakat, 2024; Priya, 2023; Kazi K, 2024a; Pradeepa, 2022).

Sensors can help farmers streamline the feeding and milking processes in addition to monitoring the cows. By collecting information on the amount of feed each cow consumes and the amount of milk produced, farmers may make the required modifications to feed ratios to guarantee that every cow receives the right nutrients. In a similar vein, the sensors in the milking machine are able to detect any anomalies in the process of producing milk, such as mastitis, and alert the farmer to take the appropriate action.

Another aspect of intelligent dairy farming is automation. Two examples of automated technologies that can significantly reduce farmers' workloads and boost output are robotic milkers and feeders. Robotic milkers can milk cows without the need for human help, making milking more dependable and efficient. Automated feeders can reduce feed waste and increase milk yield by customizing feed amounts for each cow depending on their specific needs.

The use of data analytics is also crucial to intelligent dairy production. By analyzing the data acquired from sensors and other sources, farmers may make data-driven decisions and get valuable insights into their operations. For example, data analytics can help farmers find the most productive cows, track their breeding cycles, and streamline the breeding process to increase the chance of producing better progeny.

Furthermore, data analytics (Kasat, 2023) can help farmers track their expenses and identify places where they might save costs. Farmers that monitor the amount of energy used by various farm systems, such as lighting and cooling, can reduce their electricity expenditures. Likewise, feed consumption and milk yield data can help farmers select the most cost-effective feed schedules for their cows. When dairy farming is done correctly, both the farmers and the cows gain. By using technology to keep an eye on their health and behavior, farmers may ensure that their cows are receiving proper care and have a comfortable living environment (Kazi K(2024b)). This leads to higher milk production and better-quality milk. The dairy industry is being revolutionized by smart dairy farming, which integrates technology and data with traditional farming methods. Sensors, automation, and data analytics can help farmers maximize output, enhance animal care, and streamline their operations. To meet the increasing demand for dairy products in a sustainable way, intelligent dairy farming is a must.

INTERSECTION OF IoT WITH MACHINE LEARNING, CYBERSECURITY, AND ENVIRONMENTAL SCIENCE IN DAIRY FARMING

The IoT has emerged as a transformative force across various sectors, with dairy farming being a prime example of how technology can enhance productivity and sustainability. By integrating IoT with machine learning, cybersecurity, and environmental science, the dairy industry is witnessing a revolution that optimizes operations while addressing pressing environmental and security challenges.

IoT and Machine Learning

How dairy producers monitor and manage their herds is changing as a result of the combination of machine learning (ML) and the Internet of Things. Smart collars with sensors and other Internet of things (IoT) devices are constantly gathering data on the location, behavior, and health of individual cows. The abundance of real-time data provides a rich dataset for machine learning algorithms, enabling them to identify trends in behavior and anticipate health problems before they become more serious. Systems that track feeding patterns and rumination, for instance, can notify farmers of any changes that would point to sickness and allow for prompt intervention. Predictive analytics can also be used to optimize feeding schedules based on the requirements of specific cows, increasing milk production efficiency and reducing waste. Dairy farmers can make data-driven decisions that enhance animal care, boost productivity, and save costs thanks to the convergence of IoT and ML. Kazi K S(2024a) Prashant (2024) suggests the KSK and KSK1 approaches for decision-making.

Cybersecurity

Dairy farms grow more linked as they use IoT technologies, making them more susceptible to cyberattacks. Protecting the data gathered from different IoT devices from breaches and unwanted access necessitates a high priority on cybersecurity. Strong cybersecurity safeguards must be put in place to safeguard sensitive data, including financial and herd health records. Farmers need to make significant investments in strong cybersecurity systems, which should include secure networks, encryption, and employee education on how to spot phishing scams and other online risks. Moreover, working with cybersecurity professionals can aid in the creation of specialized plans for protecting IoT equipment on farms. Maintaining cyber resilience helps build trust with customers who are becoming more worried about the safety and integrity of food, in addition to protecting the company. We typically recommend Liyakat's KK strategy for IoT networks when it comes to IoT security (2023).

Environmental Science

The environmental effects of dairy production are frequently examined, with special attention paid to methane emissions and water consumption. Through the development of precision agriculture techniques, IoT technology plays a critical role in tackling these issues. Farmers may maximize resource utilization by using real-time data from sensors that track soil moisture, weather, and cow health. IoT sensors, for example, can determine the condition of pastures and recommend the best grazing schedules to maximize land utilization and minimize methane emissions from livestock. Additionally, data analytics helps pinpoint areas where feed efficiency and waste management can be improved, lowering the dairy industry's overall ecological footprint. The convergence of environmental science and IoT promotes sustainable activities that correspond with the inclinations of contemporary customers towards environmentally friendly products. Farmers that use these technologies might appeal to a consumer that is becoming more and more concerned with sustainability by presenting themselves as progressive stewards of the soil by Neeraja (2024). As discussed in the conclusion of this section, the dairy farming scene is changing due to the convergence of IoT, machine learning, cybersecurity, and environmental research. Farmers that use IoT solutions to protect their operations from cyber threats can increase production, embrace sustainability, and improve animal care. The potential for innovation in dairy farming is unlimited as these sectors continue to converge, indicating a future where technology will help create a more secure, efficient, and environmentally conscious industry. Farmers will gain from adopting this digital revolution, and it will also support the more general objectives of environmental stewardship and food security.

IoT's EFFECTS ON INTELLIGENT FARMING

The production of milk is currently being significantly impacted by IoT. Technological developments must boost worldwide milk production to fulfill the expanding population's demands. With the use of technology, farmers may increase the milk's shelf life and carry out a number of other dairy-related duties, such scheduling the milking of cows. Mixed dairy farms, which raise cattle and grow feed grain for livestock, can better manage their resources by linking various, heterogeneous items, including buildings, vehicles, machinery, and even living creatures like calves. IoT sensors and Edge Computing (EC) facilitate resource monitoring and traceability throughout the value chain, helping producers optimize workflows, pinpoint the origin of their produce, and reassure customers of its quality. IoT technology, according to Veena (2023), gathers different types of data from a multiplicity of sensors and transmits it with the least amount of power and bandwidth required for connectivity. Using smart sensors and techniques such as volumetric sensing, pressure sensing, sensing schedules, and other data sensing methods not only promotes transparency and data security but also boosts resource efficiency and is more ecologically friendly. These methods provide safe access to transportation, oversee the warehouse, keep an eye on the milk levels in real time, and monitor the health of the cow.

Smart sensors, gateways, IoT platforms, and integrated AI engines are propelling an industry-wide change, claims Medha (2024). Numerous processes have been automated as a result of the introduction of new technology. More opportunities for intelligent dairy farming are being created by IoT and data-driven farming methods. IoT can help farmers monitor each animal's health by utilizing wearable sensor technology. The sensor-based technology can effectively and precisely identify diseases in cattle before they have an impact on milk output. IoT tracks real-time cow data, which is crucial for cattle breeding. Examples of this data include activity, temperature, and pulse. With this vital information, a full analysis of the cattle's oestrus can be ascertained. The technology has a number of interesting advantages, such as higher milk yields, lower labor and drug expenses, and more farm income. Initiatives related to animal breeding and dairy products have also carefully considered this technology.

By using IoT and AI-based technologies, it is feasible to boost the positive production-affecting aspects and decrease the negative ones (Prasad, 2024). For example, data from an AI model built using IoT sensors in milking systems can assist farmers in determining the best time to milk calves or modify their feeding plan. To preserve the quality of the milk and aid in understanding its production, these statistics can be improved even more. The state-of-the-art framework that merges IoT platform, IoT sensor, and AI solutions to help farmers enhance milk supply through innovative ways and approaches must focus on many elements of intelligent dairy farming. IoT and AI-based technologies make it easier to develop new techniques for milk yield and dairy farming procedures. On a smart dairy farm, different sets of tasks carried out at different levels may necessitate different methods to process innovation. Dairy farms do various activities on the farm, like feeding and tending to the cows, however milking is seen as a single activity. IoT intervention can have an impact on several processes and activities. For instance, the feed system is able to recognize and automatically provide the food that the cows require. In order to aid in reproduction, it may also actively monitor automated heat detection. A farmer can identify any animal in need of medical attention by evaluating the health of the cows and monitoring the herd for diseases to prevent or discover them. Wearable smart collars that gather data on cows, machine learning analysis of data, and cloud-based information centers that handle data and help farmers regulate the quality of dairy products are all examples of smart dairy farming (Figure 4).

Figure 4. Cattle daily life and the need for IoT sensors

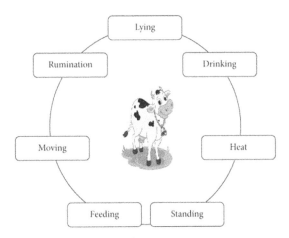

By simplifying operations for milk producers and satisfying the growing demand for premium dairy products, the dairy industry stands to gain greatly from the deployment of IoT and AI technology. The Internet of Things can leverage current sensing and data-analysis technology to reduce resource consumption, improve animal welfare, and mitigate environmental problems.

IoT-driven technology has the potential to save expenses and improve operational efficiency for farm management. Here are a few significant results:

- Monitoring well-being: Farmers may detect health problems early and administer the right medication by monitoring the vital indicators of cattle, such as heart rate.
- Monitoring milk production anomalies: Regular observation and comparison of the irregular patterns are necessary to understand the behavior of cattle and milk production. According to Kazi K S (2022) (2023) it is possible to assign a unique identification number to every animal so that their actions can be monitored and any health patterns may be understood.
- Since clean water is a vital resource for all living things, including cows, the automated food and water supply should be watched after. Milk is almost entirely composed of water. The amount of milk produced, the feed's moisture content, and climatic factors like humidity and air temperature all have a direct impact on how much water is required.
- Food is essential for nutrition since it controls the quantity of nutrients an animal may use for development and survival. To preserve the health of the cattle, it is necessary to monitor their food intake and diet. Animal health is impacted and productivity is decreased when nutrients are fed insufficiently. In addition to raising feed prices, overfeeding nutrients can have harmful or hazardous impacts on human health and the environment.

SDF Framework

This study suggested a multi-level framework with a focus on animal husbandry. The architecture is shown in its entirety in Figure 5. Data from a wearable sensor used to gather cattle data will be delivered over the Internet to a base station, where it will be received by the nearest gateway. The cloud receives data from the base station and uses a variety of methods to handle it. The IBM Cloud IoT-based platform evaluates the data in light of various procedures. For example, a computerized framework triggers feeding when the cow senses hunger. IoT-enabled smart dairy farming uses a variety of herd management strategies to keep an eye on logs and historical data. By taking into consideration the cow's surroundings, the farmer can utilize this knowledge to forecast statistics in the future. The cloud will notify the farmer to help the cow when it has analyzed the collected data. For large-scale dairy production, this herd management approach is helpful anytime there are a lot of animals. The farmer will be notified by the system when a need arises. A cow may feel more at ease in an overall architectural style, even though there are other elements that can contribute to a drop in milk production. It will benefit cows in the long run and might boost milk production.

Our daily lives are greatly impacted by the dairy business, which gives us essentials like milk, cheese, and butter. Dairy farming has, like many other economic sectors, recently suffered difficulties. Increasing production costs, a labor shortage, and environmental concerns are a few of these difficulties. The foundation for smart dairy farming was created in response to the demand for a more effective and environmentally friendly method of raising dairy cows. SDF is a technology-driven approach to dairy farming that optimizes every step of the procedure by using modern tools and techniques. By integrating cutting-edge technologies with conventional farming methods, the framework improves animal welfare, production, and health while lowering expenses and having a smaller negative impact on the environment.

Figure 5. SDF framework

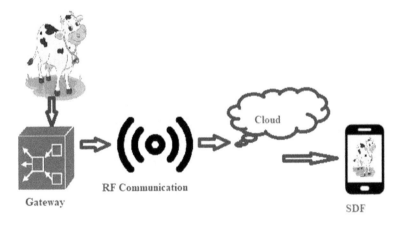

Elements of the SDF Structure

The decision support system, automation, data collection, and data analysis are the four primary parts of the SDF framework as shown in Figure 6.

Figure 6. Parts of SDF framework

Data Collection   Data Analysis   Decision Support System

Data Collection: Gathering information from a variety of sources, including cameras, sensors, and farm management software, is the first stage in the SDF framework. Real-time data on environmental conditions, milk production, and animal health is available from these data sources.

Data analysis: To find patterns and trends in the collected data, sophisticated data analytics tools are used for analysis. Through the identification of possible health problems in their cattle or the adjustment of feed rations, this analysis assists farmers in making well-informed decisions about their farming practices.

Decision Support System: Another feature of the SDF framework is a decision support system that gives farmers advice and ideas for bettering their farming methods based on data analysis. Based on the unique requirements of every farm, these suggestions can assist farmers in streamlining their processes for improved outcomes.

Automation: The SDF framework's last element is automation. Farmers can increase productivity and lower labor costs by utilizing technology such as robotic milking machines, automatic feeders, and smart gates. Better outcomes are also guaranteed by automated systems, which guarantee accurate and consistent task completion.

Advantages of the SDF Structure

For farmers and consumers alike, the SDF framework has many advantages.

Enhanced Productivity: Farmers can enhance productivity by optimizing their farming practices through the application of the SDF framework. Farmers can make decisions that result in improved animal health, higher milk yields, and increased efficiency with the use of the data that has been gathered and examined.

Cost Reduction: Farmers can drastically cut their production costs by using automation and data-driven decision-making. Labor costs can be decreased by automation, and farmers can find areas of cost-cutting without sacrificing quality by using data analysis.

Animal Welfare: By offering real-time monitoring and analysis of the health and behavior of the cattle, the SDF framework also focuses on animal welfare. This guarantees the health and welfare of their animals by enabling farmers to quickly detect and treat health problems.

Environmental Sustainability: By encouraging sustainable farming methods, the SDF framework also tackles environmental issues. Farmers can minimize the environmental impact of dairy farming and lower their carbon footprint by optimizing feed rations and cutting waste.

OBSTACLES AND THE PATH AHEAD

Despite the SDF framework's many benefits, there are still problems that need to be fixed. One of the main challenges is the cost of implementing the technology. Because of the high initial expenses, small-scale farmers might find it difficult to apply the SDF structure. Moreover, managing data and integrating different systems can be difficult and require specialized knowledge.

Governments and organizations can assist farmers in implementing the SDF framework by providing funding and educational opportunities to help them get past these challenges. Working together, technology businesses and dairy farms can also help build more affordable and user-friendly solutions. The dairy industry is changing as a result of the SDF framework's integration of traditional farming methods with cutting-edge technology. The SDF framework is establishing the foundation for a more sustainable and fruitful future in dairy farming with its emphasis on cost-effectiveness, animal care, productivity, and environmental sustainability. If given the proper support and acceptance, it can transform the sector and benefit both farmers and consumers.

Innovative Case Study: Smart Dairy Farming and its Transformative Impact

Because it sits at the nexus of technology and agriculture, smart dairy farming is an intriguing area to research. This analysis explores a thorough case study that highlights the advantages, difficulties, and potential applications of Smart Farming technology in the dairy sector. The case study under examination presents a forward-thinking dairy farm that implemented a range of smart farming strategies, such as data analytics, Internet of Things (IoT) devices, and automated systems, emphasizing their revolutionary impacts.

Smart dairy farming maximizes productivity, improves animal welfare, and advances sustainability by utilizing cutting-edge technologies including automation, big data analytics, and sensors. The main elements include keeping an eye on the environment, tracking the health of the herd, and making sure that resources are managed effectively. The farm in this case study used precision feeding systems and smart collars for cattle in an effort to increase output while reducing its negative environmental effects.

1. IoT Device Implementation: The case study demonstrated how IoT devices are incorporated into regular operations. Farmers were able to trace the movements of individual cows, keep an eye on health indicators like heart rate and milk yield, and make sure that sick animals were treated promptly thanks to smart collars that were fitted with GPS and sensors for monitoring health. The instantaneous decision-making made possible by the real-time data collected was crucial in averting losses and preserving the welfare of the animals.

2. Data-Driven Decision-Making: To understand the massive volume of data gathered by IoT sensors, the dairy farm employed data analytics tools. The farm reduced waste, enhanced breeding choices, and optimized feeding schedules by examining patterns in milk output, feed efficiency, and health data. The case study demonstrated how Liyakat Kazi (2024) used these insights to improve resource allocation, save costs, and boost productivity.

3. Sustainability Practices: The improvement in sustainability was one of the most notable results. The case study showed how improved waste recycling and feed management techniques can lower greenhouse gas emissions. Furthermore, the farm's use of solar panels and other renewable energy sources allowed it to lower its carbon footprint, demonstrating how intelligent technology can support agro-ecological transformations.

4. Obstacles and Disadvantages: Although the case study's findings were positive, it also highlighted difficulties encountered when putting smart dairy farming techniques into practice. For many farmers, the initial capital investment required to embrace new technologies was a considerable obstacle. Furthermore, handling and understanding data had a learning curve that called for assistance and training. The case study acted as a helpful reminder that, despite all of technology's potential, widespread adoption of it depends on adequate resources and instruction.

The smart dairy farming case study offers a viable way forward for transforming the dairy sector. It emphasizes how important technology is to raising sustainability, increasing productivity, and improving animal welfare. However, for wider use, it is imperative to address the issues of high upfront expenditures, data administration, and farmer education.

Farmers, IT developers, and legislators must work together to develop solutions that are inexpensive and build an environment that supports them as the business progresses. Success stories from these case studies have the potential to encourage innovation among others in the dairy industry, which could ultimately result in a more effective and long-lasting form of dairy farming.

To sum up this section, the case study demonstrates the revolutionary potential of smart dairy farming and offers guidance for future initiatives focused on utilizing technology to increase agricultural output and sustainability.

DISCUSSION

The dairy business has been a significant contributor to the global economy for a long time, giving people all over the world access to milk, cheese, and yoghurt. The dairy sector has changed dramatically over the years, mostly as a result of technology breakthroughs that have made it more sustainable and efficient. IoT is one such technology that is becoming more and more popular in the dairy industry. IoT technology is being used by the dairy sector to monitor and manage a number of activities, including the distribution and manufacturing of milk. According to Kutubuddin (2022), this technology has the power to fundamentally change the way dairy farms operate while also increasing industry-wide productivity and profitability. The control and observation of cows is the primary use of IoT technology in the dairy industry. The wellbeing, behavior, and output of the cows are monitored through the use of smart collars that include integrated sensors. Subsequently, the data is sent to a central system for analysis in order to acquire information regarding the health and productivity of the cows. Because of this, farmers are able to identify any health problems in their herd early on and take the appropriate action to stop them from infecting the other animals.

Moreover, milk production management is another industry that makes use of IoT technology. To keep an eye on the milk's quality and temperature, sensors are installed in milk tanks. It is possible to lower the danger of spoiling and guarantee that consumers obtain safe and fresh dairy products by storing milk at the ideal temperature. Cow feeding systems that are mechanized also make use of IoT technology. These systems not only save farmers labor and time, but they also use sensors to monitor the cows' feeding habits and modify the feed as necessary. By doing this, milk output is improved since the cows are fed the proper kind and quantity of grain.

IoT technology is also being used by dairy farmers to assist them in managing the overall operations of their farms. To provide a comfortable and healthy environment for the cows, smart devices are being employed to monitor environmental elements including temperature, humidity, and ventilation. As a result, milk production rises and animal comfort is enhanced. The dairy industry's embrace of IoT technology benefits the environment as well. Dairy farms may become more sustainable by leveraging IoT technology to optimize the use of resources like energy and water. This is accomplished by employing sensors to track energy and water usage and pinpoint areas in need of improvement. However, there are obstacles to overcome in the dairy industry's use of IoT technology. The biggest worry is the upfront cost involved in putting these technologies into practice. It might be difficult for many small-scale dairy farms to afford the hefty installation costs of Internet of Things systems. It is essential that farmers receive the direction and instruction they need to use and evaluate the data that these technologies gather.

The dairy industry is adopting IoT technology at an increasing rate, and this development could be important. The dairy business is undergoing a positive change because to IoT technology, which is promoting sustainability, enhancing cow health and well-being, and simplifying farm operations. We anticipate seeing even more creative solutions as technology develops, ones that will completely change the dairy business and increase its productivity and sustainability.

Navigating Data Security Breaches, Interoperability Challenges, and Regulatory Hurdles in Dairy Farming

As the dairy farming industry increasingly adopts digital technologies and innovative solutions, it faces a complex landscape marked by data security breaches, interoperability challenges, and regulatory hurdles. These factors significantly impact operational efficiency, product quality, and ultimately, the bottom line for farmers.

Data Security Breaches

Large volumes of data, ranging from herd health information to agricultural inputs and outputs, have been accumulated because of the digitization of dairy farming. Although there is a chance that this data will improve efficiency and judgment, there are also a lot of risks involved. Sensitive information, such as financial information, personnel records, and secret farming methods, might be compromised by data security breaches. Such violations may have serious effects, including monetary losses, legal troubles, and harm to the dairy farming industry's reputation. To reduce these risks, the sector needs to give strong cybersecurity measures like encryption, recurring audits, and staff training top priority. Proactive data security measures not only protect farms but also foster customer confidence in dairy goods.

Interoperability Challenges

Interoperability issues have been brought about by the dairy farming industry's integration of multiple digital technologies and platforms. Farmers frequently use a variety of technologies, each with its own data format and protocols, to manage various elements of their operations, such as tracking animals, monitoring milk production, and controlling feed. Systems that are not able to communicate with one another may become fragmented, which can cause redundant data entry and lost insights. The dairy business has to push for standardized data standards that allow for easy information sharing across platforms in order to overcome these obstacles. Technology providers, farmers, and industry stakeholders working together can open the door to integrated solutions that increase productivity and empower farmers to make better decisions based on data.

Regulatory Hurdles

The digital revolution in dairy production is made more challenging by the need to comply with regulations. Food safety, animal welfare, and data privacy are all governed by a number of regulations, which frequently make compliance difficult. It can take a lot of time and resources to wade through the many regulations that apply to farmers on a local, national, and international level. Furthermore, regulators might find it difficult to keep up with the development of new technology, which would leave compliance criteria unclear. Collaborations between regulatory agencies and industry participants can aid in the development of frameworks that encourage innovation while guaranteeing consumer safety and moral behavior. Dairy producers can more effectively anticipate changes and adjust to changing needs by encouraging an active conversation about regulations.

In summary, dairy farmers that embrace technology face a challenging environment due to the confluence of interoperability issues, data security breaches, and regulatory barriers. It is imperative to tackle these concerns in order to protect confidential data, enhance operational effectiveness, and maintain compliance within the current intricate regulatory landscape. The dairy sector is in a unique position to unlock increased production and sustainable farming in the future by embracing cybersecurity best practices, promoting data interoperability, and working with authorities. Dairy producers that prioritize these issues not only safeguard their businesses but also help create a more inventive and resilient agricultural environment.

CONCLUSION

Farmers will profit from new, clever techniques that streamline operations and procedures while using IoT devices to produce more milk, keep a closer eye on cattle health, and spot anomalies. While there are many advantages for the average farmer from IoT-powered smart dairy farming, it can be costly at first but may eventually pay for itself. Effective feeding and drinking method monitoring are made easier by IoT, which can boost milk production and enhance cow nutrition. Enhanced technological adaptation, flexible design, and comprehensive architecture can raise IoT-based farming's efficiency. Since its inception, the intelligent dairy industry has come a long way. The industry has evolved to employ cutting edge technology and become more efficient, consumer-driven, and sustainable. Given the rising demand for dairy products worldwide, it is expected that the smart dairy industry will continue to grow and bring about even more revolutionary changes in the future. IoT technology is being adopted by the dairy industry more frequently, and this trend has the potential to be significant. Thanks to IoT technology, which is supporting sustainability, improving cow health and well-being, and streamlining farm operations, the dairy industry is experiencing a positive revolution. As technology advances, we expect to see even more inventive solutions that will fundamentally alter the dairy industry and boost its sustainability and productivity.

REFERENCES

Chopade. (2024). Internet of Things in mechatronics for design and manufacturing: A review. *Journals of Mechatronics Machine Design and Manufacturing*, 6(1).

Devi, S. (2022). A path towards child-centric artificial intelligence-based education. *International Journal of Early Childhood Special Education*, 14(3), 9915–9922.

Gouse, K. (2018). Machine learning-based system food quality inspection and grading in food industry. *International Journal of Food and Nutritional Sciences*, 11(10), 723–730.

Halli, U. M. (2022). Nanotechnology in IoT security. Journal of Nanoscience. *Nanoengineering & Applications*, 12(3), 11–16.

Karale, A.. (2023). Smart billing cart using RFID, YOLO and deep learning for mall administration. *International Journal of Instrumentation and Innovation Sciences*, 8(2).

Kasat, K. (2023). Implementation and recognition of waste management system with mobility solution in smart cities using Internet of Things. In *2023 Second International Conference on Augmented Intelligence and Sustainable Systems (ICAISS)* (pp. 1661-1665). Trichy, India. DOI:10.1109/ICAISS58487.2023.10250690

Kazi, K. S. (2022). Smart grid energy-saving technique using machine learning. *Journal of Instrumentation Technology and Innovations*, 12(3), 1–10.

Kazi, K. S. (2023). Detection of malicious nodes in IoT networks based on throughput and ML. *Journal of Electrical and Power System Engineering*, 9(1), 22–29.

Kazi, K. S. (2024a). Artificial intelligence (AI)-driven IoT (AIIoT)-based agriculture automation. In Satapathy, S., & Muduli, K. (Eds.), *Advanced Computational Methods for Agri-Business Sustainability* (pp. 72–94). IGI Global., DOI:10.4018/979-8-3693-3583-3.ch005

Kazi, K. S. (2024b). IoT driven by machine learning (MLIoT) for the retail apparel sector. In Tarnanidis, T., Papachristou, E., Karypidis, M., & Ismyrlis, V. (Eds.), *Driving Green Marketing in Fashion and Retail* (pp. 63–81). IGI Global., DOI:10.4018/979-8-3693-3049-4.ch004

Kazi, K. S., Liyakat, S., & Sridevi, M. (2023). HEECCNB: An efficient IoT-cloud architecture for secure patient data transmission and accurate disease prediction in healthcare systems. In *2023 Seventh International Conference on Image Information Processing (ICIIP)* (pp. 407-410). Solan, India. DOI:10.1109/ICIIP61524.2023.10537627

Kazi, K. S., Liyakat, S., Sridevi, M., Saha, B., Reddy, S. R., & Shirisha, N. (2023). Fruit grading disease detection and an image processing strategy. *Journal of Image Processing and Artificial Intelligence*, 9(2), 17–34.

Kazi, K. S. L. (2022). Predict the severity of diabetes cases using K-means and decision tree approach. *Journal of Advances in Shell Programming*, 9(2), 24–31.

Kosgiker, G., Kumtole, S., Sunil Shinde, S., Sunil Shinde, S., Nagrale, M., & Kutubuddin, K. (2023). Monitoring fresh fruit and food using IoT and machine learning to improve food safety and quality. Tuijin Jishu/Journal of Propulsion Technology, 44(3), 2927-2931.

KSL. (2022). IoT-based weather prototype using WeMos. *Journal of Control and Instrumentation Engineering*, 9(1), 10–22.

Kutubuddin, K. S. (2022). Business mode and product life cycle to improve marketing in healthcare units. *E-Commerce for Future & Trends*, 9(3), 1–9.

Kutubuddin, K. S. (2023). Nanotechnology in precision farming: The role of research. *International Journal of Nanomaterials and Nanostructures*, 9(2). Advance online publication. DOI:10.37628/ijnn.v9i2.1051

Liyakat, K. K. S. (2023). IoT-based Arduino-powered weather monitoring system. *Journal of Telecommunication Study*, 8(3), 25–31. DOI:10.46610/JTC.2023.v08i03.005

Liyakat, K. K. S. (2023). Machine learning approach using artificial neural networks to detect malicious nodes in IoT networks. In Shukla, P. K., Mittal, H., & Engelbrecht, A. (Eds.), *Computer Vision and Robotics. CVR 2023. Algorithms for Intelligent Systems.* Springer., DOI:10.1007/978-981-99-4577-1_3

Liyakat, K. K. S. (2024). Explainable AI in healthcare. In Anitha, A., & Debi Prasanna Acharjya, K. (Eds.), *Explainable Artificial Intelligence in Healthcare Systems* (pp. 271–284).

Liyakat, K. K. S. (2024). Machine learning approach using artificial neural networks to detect malicious nodes in IoT networks. In Udgata, S. K., Sethi, S., & Gao, X. Z. (Eds.), *Intelligent Systems. ICMIB 2023. Lecture Notes in Networks and Systems* (Vol. 728, pp. 1–20). Springer. DOI:10.1007/978-981-99-3932-9_12

Magadum, P. K. (2024). Machine learning for predicting wind turbine output power in wind energy conversion systems. Grenze International Journal of Engineering and Technology, 10(1), 2074-2080. https://thegrenze.com/index.php?display=page &view=journalabstract&absid=2514&id=8

Nagrale, M. (2024). Internet of robotic things in cardiac surgery: An innovative approach. *African Journal of Biological Sciences*, 6(6), 709–725. DOI:10.33472/ AFJBS.6.6.2024.709-725

Neeraja, P. R. (2024). DL-based somnolence detection for improved driver safety and alertness monitoring. In 2024 IEEE International Conference on Computing, Power and Communication Technologies (IC2PCT) (pp. 589-594). Greater Noida, India. DOI:10.1109/IC2PCT60090.2024.10486714

Nerkar, P. M. (2023). Predictive data analytics framework based on heart healthcare system (HHS) using machine learning. Journal of Advanced Zoology, 44(Special Issue 2), 3673-3686.

Pradeepa, M. (2022). Student health detection using a machine learning approach and IoT. In 2022 IEEE 2nd Mysore Subsection International Conference (MysuruCon). DOI:10.1109/MysuruCon55714.2022.9972445

Prasad, K. R., Karanam, S. R., Ganesh, D., Liyakat, K. K. S., Talasila, V., & Purushotham, P. (2024). AI in public-private partnership for IT infrastructure development. *The Journal of High Technology Management Research*, 35(1), 100496. DOI:10.1016/j.hitech.2024.100496

Sayyad, L. (2023). Home automation system based on GSM. *Journal of VLSI Design Tools & Technology*, 13(3), 7–12. DOI:10.37591/jovdtt.v13i3.7877

Shweta, K. (2022). Automatic wall painting robot. *Journal of Image Processing and Intelligent Remote Sensing*, 2(6).

Sreenivasulu, . (2022). Implementation of latest machine learning approaches for students grade prediction. *International Journal of Early Childhood Special Education*, 14(3), 9887–9894.

Sultanabanu, S. L. (2024). ChatGPT: An automated teacher's guide to learning. In Bansal, R., Chakir, A., Ngah, A. H., Rabby, F., & Jain, A. (Eds.), *AI Algorithms and ChatGPT for Student Engagement in Online Learning* (pp. 1–20). IGI Global. DOI:10.4018/979-8-3693-4268-8.ch001

ADDITIONAL READING

Hassoun, A., Garcia-Garcia, G., Trollman, H., Jagtap, S., Parra-López, C., Crop-otova, J., Bhat, Z., Centobelli, P., & Aït-Kaddour, A. (2023). Birth of dairy 4.0: Opportunities and challenges in adoption of fourth industrial revolution technologies in the production of milk and itsderivatives. *Current Research in Food Science*, 7, 100535. DOI:10.1016/j.crfs.2023.100535 PMID:37448632

Malik, M., Gahlawat, V. K., Mor, R. S., & Hosseinian-Far, A. (2024). Towards white revolution 2.0: challenges and opportunities for the industry 4.0 technologies in Indian dairy industry. Operations Management Research, 1-22.

Nleya, S. M., & Ndlovu, S. (2021). Smart dairy farming overview: innovation, algorithms and challenges. Smart Agriculture Automation Using Advanced Technologies: Data Analytics and Machine Learning, Cloud Architecture, Automation and IoT, 35-59.

KEY TERMS AND DEFINITIONS

Automated Feeding Systems: Technology used in smart dairy farming to monitor and control the feeding of cows, ensuring they receive the correct nutrients, reducing waste, and improving milk production.

Blockchain Technology in Dairy: The use of blockchain in the dairy industry to enhance traceability and transparency, allowing consumers to track the origins and production processes of dairy products.

Cybersecurity in Smart Dairy Farming: The implementation of robust security measures to protect sensitive data collected from IoT devices on dairy farms from cyber threats and unauthorized access.

Data Analytics in Dairy Farming: The process of analyzing data collected from sensors and other sources to make data-driven decisions, optimize farming practices, and improve the health and productivity of dairy cows.

Environmental Sustainability in Dairy: The practice of using smart technology to minimize the environmental impact of dairy farming, including reducing water and energy usage, managing waste, and improving animal welfare.

Internet of Things (IoT): A network of interconnected devices that collect and exchange data, enabling automation and real-time monitoring in various industries, including dairy farming.

Machine Learning in Dairy Farming: The application of machine learning algorithms to analyze data from IoT devices, predict animal health issues, optimize feeding schedules, and improve overall farm management.

Precision Agriculture: The use of advanced technology, including IoT and data analytics, to monitor and manage agricultural processes such as crop management, soil conditions, and livestock health to optimize productivity and sustainability.

Robotic Milking Systems: Automated systems used in dairy farming that utilize sensors and data analytics to efficiently milk cows, reduce labor costs, and increase productivity while ensuring cow comfort.

Smart Dairy Farming (SDF): A modern approach to dairy production that leverages technology such as sensors, data analytics, and automation to enhance animal welfare, productivity, and efficiency on dairy farms.

Chapter 13
Empowering Small and Medium Enterprises Through Smart Technology and Talent Management

Richa Bhalla

Department of General Management, ISBR Business School, Bengaluru, India

Shwetha G. K.

Department of Computer Science and Engineering, NMAM Institute of Technology, NITTE University (Deemed), Nitte India

Sherif Mohamed Abdelaal Ismail

https://orcid.org/0009-0000-0852-873X

American University in Cairo, Egypt

S. Padmavathy

https://orcid.org/0000-0002-1119-2963

Department of Management Studies, Kongu Engineering College, Erode, India

Nageswara Rao Gudipudi

https://orcid.org/0000-0001-5172-8884

Department of Electrical and Electronics Engineering, Lakireddy Bali Reddy College of Engineering, Mylavaram, India

Sampath Boopathi

https://orcid.org/0000-0002-2065-6539

Department of Mechanical Engineering, Muthayammal Engineering College, Namakkal, India

ABSTRACT

SMEs face unique problems in staying competitive and innovative as business

DOI: 10.4018/979-8-3693-5498-8.ch013

changes fast. This chapter looks at smart technology and talent management as ways to empower SMEs. Smart tech like AI, IoT, and data analytics help SME tools to work better, innovate, and please customers more. At the same time, good talent management helps get, grow, and keep skilled workers who can use these technologies. When SMEs combine smart tech with strong talent management, they can find new ways to grow, change with the market, and build lasting advantages. This chapter shows real examples, case studies, and strategies SMEs can use to do well in the digital age.

INTRODUCTION

Small and Medium Enterprises (SMEs) serve as the backbone of the global economy. They make up about 90% of businesses and provide over 50% of jobs worldwide. SMEs have a key role in boosting economic growth sparking new ideas and creating employment. Their quick thinking and ability to adapt allow them to react fast to shifting market trends. This makes them essential to economic strength and variety. Yet, despite their big impact, SMEs face many hurdles that hold back their growth and ability to compete (Han & Trimi 2022a). Small and medium-sized enterprises (SMEs) face a tough and tricky business world. They must deal with money problems, limited market access, rules and regulations, and the need to come up with new ideas. Also, fast-moving tech can be both hard and helpful. While tech can offer strong tools to make work smoother and more productive many SMEs find it hard to get the money and know-how to use these tools well. What's more, the job market is changing, with more people wanting digital skills than there are workers who have them. Getting, growing, and keeping skilled workers is a big challenge for SMEs, as they often go up against bigger companies that can offer better pay and room to grow in a career (Choobineh et al. 2022). To do well in this setting, SMEs need to use both clever tech and smart ways to manage their workers.

Smart tech combines cutting-edge digital tools like AI, IoT, and data analytics into how businesses run. These tools help small and medium-sized companies boost output, spark new ideas, and tailor experiences for customers. AI can do routine jobs, offer useful insights by crunching numbers, and help make better choices. IoT can streamline supply chains, keep an eye on equipment as it runs, and make products better. Data analytics helps companies get what customers want, spot market shifts, and make smart big-picture calls (Abdulsalam & Hedabou, 2021). But to make smart tech work well, you need a team that knows their stuff. This is where managing talent comes in. Managing talent covers the plans and methods to bring in, grow, and keep good workers. Good talent management makes sure small and medium-sized firms have the right people with the right know-how to get the most out of smart tech. It's about creating a workplace where people want to be given chances to learn all the time, and building a culture where new ideas thrive (Tabrizchi & Kuchaki Rafsanjani, 2020).

The fusion of smart technology and talent management gives SMEs a strong chance to grow. When companies match their tech abilities with their people strategies, they can create a boost that leads to growth and new ideas. For example, workers who know tech well can use AI tools to give better customer service or make use of IoT data to make operations run smoother. On the flip side smart tech can help manage talent by offering tools to train employees to keep an eye on how they're doing and keep them engaged. Smart tech and talent management play key roles in today's business world for Small and Medium Enterprises (SMEs) trying to stay ahead of the game. When these two parts work together in a smart way, they can make big improvements in how well a business runs, comes up with new ideas, and performs overall (Arostegi et al. 2018; Cai et al. 2016).

Smart tech includes cutting-edge digital tools and systems that help businesses work better and make choices based on data. The main parts of smart tech are Artificial Intelligence (AI), the Internet of Things (IoT), and data analytics. AI is causing a revolution in how businesses work by doing routine jobs making customer talks better and giving deep insights through predictive analytics. For small and medium businesses, AI can help in areas like customer service where chatbots can handle simple questions letting human staff deal with harder issues. Also, AI-powered data analytics can help small and medium businesses understand how customers act, make marketing plans better, and improve how they develop products (Grashof & Kopka 2023; Saura et al. 2023).

The IoT is a network of connected devices that share data. SMEs can use IoT to improve their supply chains, check product quality better, and cut maintenance costs by predicting issues. For example, IoT sensors can watch how machines work in real-time warning managers about problems before they cause expensive shutdowns. Data analytics, a key part of smart tech, helps SMEs use lots of data to find patterns, check how well things are going, and make smart choices. By looking at data from different places, companies can learn useful things about market trends, what customers like, and where they're not working well. This info helps SMEs change when markets shift and make their plans work better (Chaudhuri et al. 2022; Velmurugan et al. 2021). While smart tech gives us the tools to come up with new ideas and work better, using these tools well depends on how we handle our people. Managing talent means bringing in, growing, and keeping skilled workers who can make the most of these technologies. Getting top talent is a key part of this. Small and medium-sized businesses have to compete with big companies for skilled workers, which can be tough. But by offering a lively workplace, chances to grow, and a clear plan, these smaller firms can bring in people who are not skilled but also fit well with what the company believes in and wants to achieve.

Enhancing employee skills is just as crucial. Programs for ongoing learning and career growth are key to helping workers keep up with tech changes. SMEs can put money into training sessions, workshops, and online classes to boost their staff's abilities. Also, creating an environment that values new ideas pushes workers to try out fresh concepts and tech moving the company ahead. Keeping employees is another vital part of managing talent. High staff turnover can hurt an SME's output and mood (Han & Trimi 2022b; Lu et al. 2022). To hold onto top workers, SMEs should aim to create a good workplace, offer pay that competes with others, and give chances to move up in their careers. Plans to get employees more involved, like regular check-ins and ways to recognize good work, can also lead to more staff staying put.

The merger of smart tech and talent management has an influence on business success. Workers who know their way around tech can use AI, IoT, and data tools to boost how things run. At the same time smart tech helps manage talent by offering ways to train, check work, and keep people interested. Take AI-powered HR software. It speeds up hiring, spots skill gaps, and crafts training to fit each person. IoT gadgets make work safer, which makes for a better place to work. Data tools show how well people are doing and how happy they are. This lets bosses make smart choices about moving people up and helping them grow (Grashof & Kopka 2023; Saura et al. 2023). Therefore, SMEs that want to succeed in the digital era must combine smart technology with talent management. By focusing on these two key areas, SMEs can grow, come up with new ideas, and stay ahead of their rivals in a business world that keeps getting more complicated.

Objectives of the Chapter

This chapter aims to give a full picture of how SMEs can use smart technology and talent management to their advantage, helping them tackle problems and grab new chances.

- Showing how AI, IoT, and data analytics can change how SMEs work.
- Discuss ways to bring in, train, and keep skilled workers.
- Contribution to guidelines and tips to match new tech with staff development.
- Illustrate real-life examples of SMEs that have combined smart technology and talent management to achieve outstanding outcomes.
- Providing insights on upcoming trends and how SMEs can set themselves up for long-term growth.

Smart technology and talent management are essential for SMEs to succeed in today's ever-changing business world. By grasping how these two key elements work together, SMEs can reach new heights in productivity, creativity, and market edge. This chapter lays the groundwork to examine the plans, tools, and methods that can help SMEs flourish in the digital era offering a blueprint for sustained growth and success.

SMART TECHNOLOGY FOR SMEs

Smart tech covers a broad range of cutting-edge digital tools and systems. These help businesses work better, come up with new ideas all the time, and use data to make choices. For small and medium-sized companies smart tech includes AI, IoT, and ways to look at data. All these give companies the tools to make their work smoother, make customers happier, and make better choices (Jung et al. 2021).

AI is about making machines think and learn like people. This tech can do routine jobs, look at big data to find useful stuff, and make customer service better with personalized help. For example, AI chatbots can answer basic customer questions, which lets human workers deal with trickier problems. This has an impact on how well a company runs overall.

The IoT has an influence on connecting physical devices to the internet, which lets them gather and share data. IoT tech allows companies to watch and control equipment, supply chains, and other key business processes in real time. Machines with sensors can tell when they need fixing, which cuts down on breakdowns and makes them last longer. IoT also helps manage stock better and improve shipping, which saves money and makes service better. Data analytics looks at big sets of data to find hidden patterns, links, and other useful info. By using data analytics small and medium businesses can make smart choices, guess what the market will do, and get how customers think. This skill lets businesses shape their products and services to better meet what customers want and stay ahead of other companies.

Adoption of AI in SMEs

Small and medium-sized enterprises (SMEs) are adopting AI more and more. They need to stay competitive and come up with new ideas in a fast-changing market. AI gives SMEs powerful tools to boost their productivity, serve customers better, and spark new ideas. One of the main perks of AI for SMEs is that it can do things. AI can handle many business tasks on its own, from office work to talking with customers. For instance, AI chatbots can answer customer questions around the clock giving quick replies and letting human workers focus on more important jobs. This doesn't just make customers happier - it also cuts down on labor costs (Baabdullah et al. 2021; Žigienė et al. 2019).

AI also has an impact on decision-making through cutting-edge data analytics. Small and medium-sized enterprises can apply AI algorithms to examine huge amounts of data and reveal insights that humans couldn't spot on their own. These findings can shape strategic choices, like spotting new market openings, fine-tuning pricing plans, and boosting product creation. For example, AI can look at customer buying habits to forecast future demand allowing SMEs to handle stock more and cut down on waste.

Another big plus of AI for small and medium-sized businesses is its ability to personalize. AI can look at customer info to give tailored experiences, which boosts customer engagement and keeps them coming back. For instance, AI systems can suggest products based on what a customer has bought before and what they've looked at online making it more likely they'll buy again. This kind of personalization can set small businesses apart from their rivals and help build stronger ties with customers. Even with these perks, bringing AI into small businesses isn't always easy. Many of these companies face hurdles like not having enough money, lacking tech know-how, and worrying about keeping data private and secure. To get past these roadblocks small businesses can start with small AI projects that show quick results and build up their skills. Teaming up with AI companies or experts can also help small businesses handle the tricky parts of putting AI to work.

So, when small and medium-sized businesses use AI, they have big chances to boost productivity, make customers happier, and come up with new ideas. If these companies get how powerful AI can be and add it to how they work, they can reach new heights in how well they do and how they stack up against others in today's digital world. The next parts will take a closer look at specific ways to use AI and the best ways for smaller companies to start using it.

IoT Applications in SME Operations

The Internet of Things (IoT) has a revolutionary effect on SMEs, with many uses that boost productivity, cut expenses, and make products better. IoT links devices that talk and share info letting businesses watch and control their work in real time. IoT can improve supply chain management. IoT sensors can keep an eye on stock levels, check shipping conditions, and give updates on where goods are right now. This clear view helps SMEs spend less on stock, waste less, and deliver on time (Gill et al. 2022; Jung et al. 2021). Also, smart warehouses with IoT use robots to handle stock, which means they use space better and fill orders faster. IoT has a big impact on predictive maintenance. SMEs can put IoT sensors on their machines to watch how they work and spot problems before they happen. This helps cut downtime, make equipment last longer, and save money on repairs. Take a manufacturing SME, for example. They can use IoT sensors to notice odd vibrations in machines, which means it's time to fix them before they break down. IoT devices also help with product quality. They keep an eye on things like heat, moisture, and air pressure during making and storing products. This makes sure products are up to standard and follow the rules. For food and drink SMEs IoT sensors can track storage and shipping conditions. This keeps food fresh and follows health rules.

Using Data Analytics to Make Decisions

Data analytics has an impact on SMEs helping them make smart choices based on up-to-date data. By looking at data from different places, SMEs can understand market trends, how customers act, and where they're not working well. This helps them to improve their plans and get better results (Arostegi et al. 2018; Han & Trimi 2022a). Customer insights are a key advantage of data analytics. SMEs can study customer data to grasp buying patterns, likes, and comments. This data can shape marketing plans, product creation, and customer care efforts. Take e-commerce SME as an example. It can use data analytics to spot top-selling products, craft marketing drives for specific customer groups, and tailor customer talks to boost satisfaction. Data analytics can also make operations more productive. By looking at data from production steps, supply chains, and money systems, SMEs can find holdups to cut waste, and smooth out operations. For instance, a retail SME can use sales data to fine-tune stock levels. This ensures popular items stay in stock while avoiding extra inventory. Data analytics also helps make smart business choices by showing how well a company is doing. Small and medium-sized businesses can use important numbers and visual charts to keep an eye on their progress, find where they need to get better, and make choices based on facts. This way of doing things lets these businesses adapt and respond to market changes.

Putting Smart Technology to Work in Small and Medium-Sized Businesses

Figure 1 shows the steps to introduce smart technology in small and medium-sized businesses bringing in different departments and outside experts. Each step moves from one person to the next, highlighting how planning, putting things into action, and checking results happen over and over in the process.

Figure 1. implementation of smart technology in SMEs

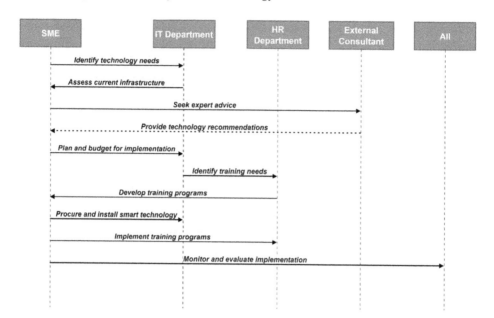

Putting smart technology into action in small and medium-sized enterprises (SMEs) calls for a well-thought-out plan that considers the specific challenges and chances each business faces. To make it work, you need to plan, invest in the right tech, and pay attention to managing change. To start, SMEs should take a good look at what they need and what they can do. This means finding out where smart tech can help the most and checking if the company is ready for new tech. SMEs should put their money into tools that match their big-picture goals and show clear benefits (Abdulsalam & Hedabou, 2021).

Investing in the right tech matters a lot. Small and medium-sized businesses should look at options that can grow, are easy to use, and work well with what they already have. Take cloud-based IoT platforms and data tools, for example. These give businesses flexibility and fit in, which works well for smaller companies without big IT teams. To make smart tech work, you need to manage change well. Small businesses should try to build a workforce that knows tech. This means training people and helping them grow. Workers need to learn how to use new tech well and should feel good about trying new things. Also, it's key to talk and get everyone involved. This helps make sure everyone in the company gets why the new tech is good and how it will change things.

This means smart technology gives SMEs big chances to improve how they work, make better choices, and grow in a way that lasts. When SMEs put IoT tools to use and make the most of data analysis, they can boost their productivity, come up with new ideas, and stay ahead in today's digital world.

TALENT MANAGEMENT STRATEGIES

Talent management plays a key role for SMEs to draw in, grow, and keep the best workers. When SMEs focus on building a strong company image, give fair pay and perks, and put money into helping staff improve, they can create a team with skills and drive. This helps the business grow, come up with new ideas, and do well in the long run (Mupepi, 2017). As the business world keeps changing, SMEs that make talent management a top concern will be ready to handle tough times and grab chances to succeed, as Figure 2 shows.

Figure 2. Talent management strategies for SMEs

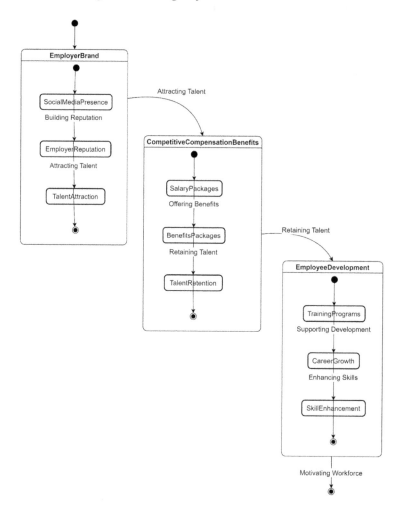

Talent Management Matters for SMEs

Talent management plays a key role in business strategy for Small and Medium Enterprises (SMEs). Good talent management makes sure SMEs have the right people with the right skills in the right jobs, which is crucial to boost business growth, spark new ideas, and stay ahead of rivals. Unlike big companies, SMEs often have tight budgets and can't afford high staff turnover costs or the problems that come from having the wrong people in important roles. So, having a strong talent management plan helps SMEs get the most out of their people and reach their business goals (Cheese et al. 2007).

In an SME where each worker often takes on several roles and has a direct impact on the company's success managing talent becomes even more vital. By drawing in, growing, and keeping skilled employees, SMEs can create a driven and capable team that can adjust to shifting market trends and spark new ideas. Also, a solid talent management plan helps SMEs build a positive work setting that boosts worker engagement and happiness, which leads to better output and fewer people quitting.

Attracting Top Talent

Hiring the best people is a big problem for small and medium-sized businesses (SMEs) especially when they're up against bigger companies with more money and fame. But SMEs can use a few tricks to get great job seekers. First off, SMEs should work on making a strong brand as an employer. This means telling people about the company's values, goals, and work culture. Many job hunters like companies that match their own values and give them a sense of purpose. SMEs can show off what makes them special, like a close team feeling, chances to move up fast in their career, and the ability to make a real difference (Yildiz & Esmer 2023).

Also, SMEs should use social media and online platforms to reach more people. By being active on platforms like LinkedIn, SMEs can link up with possible candidates and show off their company culture and successes. Taking part in industry events, job fairs, and networking activities can also help SMEs build their name and draw in talent. Offering good pay and benefits is another key factor. While SMEs may not always be able to match the salaries of bigger companies, they can offer other perks like flexible work options, chances to grow, and a supportive work environment. These benefits can appeal to candidates who want a better work-life balance or are looking to improve their skills.

Developing Employee Skills and Competencies

Helping employees build skills and abilities is key for small and medium-sized businesses to keep up and bring in new ideas. Ongoing learning and job growth programs play a big part in managing talent making sure workers stay on top of industry progress and tech shifts. Small and medium-sized companies should put money into training that tackles both current and future skill needs. This might include tech training, leadership growth, and improving people skills. For example, teaching about new software or industry best practices can boost how well employees work and how much they get done. Programs to develop leaders get employees ready for future jobs and duties making sure the company has a smooth plan for when people move up (Deery, 2008).

Besides formal training, SMEs should foster a culture that values ongoing learning. They can do this by pushing for knowledge exchange and teamwork among staff. Making chances for workers to pick up skills from one another, like through mentoring or projects across departments, can boost their abilities and spark new ideas. Managing performance is also key to growing employee skills and know-how. Regular check-ins and feedback help workers see what they're good at and where they can get better. Setting clear targets and giving helpful feedback lets employees zero in on growing and lining up their work with what the company wants to achieve.

What's more, SMEs should use technology to help employees grow. Online courses and e-learning tools offer flexible and cheap training options. These platforms let workers learn at their own speed and use many resources that fit their needs. It's also crucial to recognize and reward what employees achieve to create a culture of always getting better. SMEs should start programs that celebrate workers' successes and contributions. This doesn't just motivate employees but also shows how important it is to develop skills and perform well.

Retaining and Engaging Employees

Keeping and motivating employees plays a key role in managing talent for SMEs that often compete hard with bigger companies for the best workers. When lots of employees leave, it costs money and causes problems hurting how much work gets done and how people feel about their jobs. So, SMEs need to put good plans into action to keep their workers and get them involved (Bethke-Langenegger et al., 2011).

Creating a Positive Work Environment: A positive work environment plays a crucial role in keeping employees. Small and medium-sized enterprises should build a culture where people respect each other, work together, and include everyone. This means making a workplace where staff members feel valued and appreciated. Programs that recognize what employees do can lift spirits and make people more loyal. Also helping workers balance their work and personal lives through flexible hours, chances to work from home, and programs for wellness can help them handle their personal and work lives better.

Offering Competitive Compensation and Benefits: SMEs might not always match big companies' pay packages, but they can still offer good compensation and benefits. This includes fair wages, bonuses based on performance, health coverage, retirement savings plans, and other perks that boost the employee experience. SMEs should also think about non-cash benefits. These can be just as appealing to employees and include chances to move up in their careers, grow, and work in a supportive environment.

Offering Chances to Grow in Your Career: Workers tend to stick around when they see clear ways to move up in their jobs. Small and medium-sized businesses should put money into ongoing learning and growth programs to help their staff get better at what they do and climb the career ladder. This might include training while working, group sessions online classes, and guidance from more experienced colleagues. When companies push their employees to set job goals and give them what they need to reach these goals, it can make workers feel like they have a real purpose and want to stay loyal.

Boosting Worker Involvement: Workers who feel involved tend to work harder, stay motivated, and show loyalty to their company. Small and medium-sized businesses can get workers more involved by letting them make decisions asking what they think, and keeping lines of communication open. Regular team meetings, idea sessions, and surveys give workers a chance to speak up and help the company do well. Also, building a sense of community through team activities and social events can bring workers closer together and create a workplace where people work well as a team.

Recognizing and Rewarding Contributions: Praise and perks have a strong effect on keeping workers happy and committed. Small and medium-sized businesses should set up ways to celebrate what employees achieve and add. This might involve formal awards, public praise, or simple acts like writing thank-you notes. Giving prompt and meaningful recognition strengthens good behavior and shows that the company values its staff.

Effective Talent Management in SMEs

Small and medium-sized enterprises need to manage talent well to build a workforce with the right skills and drive to help the business succeed. Because these companies have limited resources and face tough competition, they need smart ways to handle talent (Collings & Mellahi 2009; Deery 2008).

Figure 3. Effective talent management in SMEs

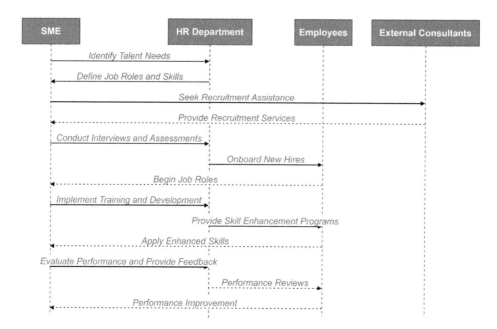

Figure 3 shows how SMEs can manage their talent step by step starting from hiring and welcoming new employees to helping them grow and checking their work.

Strategic Workforce Planning: Strategic workforce planning means making sure the right people are there to help the company reach its goals now and in the future. SMEs should often check what skills they have and what they'll need later. This helps them hire and train people before they're needed, which supports the company's growth. Planning should also think about who could take over important jobs if someone leaves, to keep things running.

Recruitment and Onboarding: Good hiring sets the stage for managing talent well. Small and medium-sized businesses should zero in on finding the right people. They can use job sites social media and ask current employees for recommendations. Getting new hires up to speed matters just as much. This means giving them what they need, showing them how things work, and making it clear what you expect. It helps them fit in without a hitch.

Performance Management: A strong performance management system has an impact on how SMEs track and boost employee performance. This involves setting clear performance goals, giving regular feedback, and doing performance reviews. SMEs should take a team-based approach to performance management where managers team up with employees to spot areas to improve and help their career growth. Giving credit and rewards for top performance is also key to keeping motivation and productivity high.

Learning and Development: Ongoing learning and growth are crucial to keep employees' skills current and improve their career options. SMEs should put money into training programs that cover both technical and people skills. Offering chances for cross-department training and job switches can also help employees get a wider view of the business and build diverse skill sets.

Employee Engagement and Well-being: Keeping employees engaged and healthy plays a key role in maintaining a driven and effective workforce. Small and medium-sized enterprises should make it a priority to create a supportive work environment that boosts mental and physical health. This involves offering wellness programs, giving access to mental health resources, and promoting a good balance between work and personal life. Employees who feel connected to their work tend to be more loyal, productive, and dedicated to helping the organization succeed.

Using Tech to Manage Talent: Tech can have a big impact on how companies handle their people. Small and medium-sized businesses can use HR software to make hiring, onboarding, checking performance, and keeping workers happy much easier. Looking at data can show how well employees are doing, how satisfied they are, and why they might leave. This helps these businesses make smart choices and get better at managing their talent.

So good talent management is key for small and medium-sized businesses that want to build a strong loyal team. When they focus on keeping employees, making sure they're engaged, and helping them grow, these businesses create a workplace where people want to be. This attracts the best workers and keeps them around, which helps the business grow and do well in the long run.

INTEGRATING SMART TECHNOLOGY AND TALENT MANAGEMENT

Smart technology and talent management integration offers a strategic way for Small and Medium Enterprises (SMEs) to boost their productivity, spark new ideas, and give their employees more power. When SMEs bring these two key areas together, they can build connections that lead to long-term growth and help them stand out in today's digital world (Chaudhuri et al. 2022; Deery 2008; Mohammadian & Rezaie 2020; Yildiz & Esmer 2023).

Figure 4. Integration of smart technology with talent management

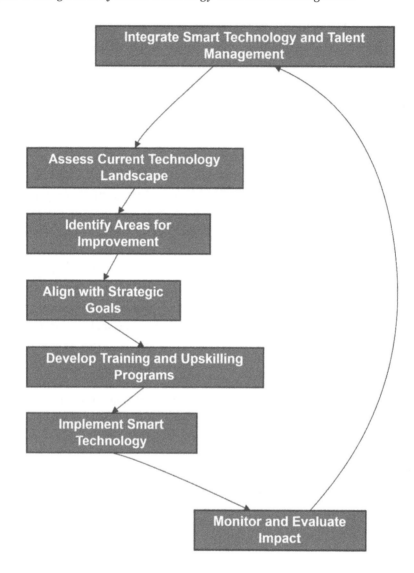

Figure 4 shows the step-by-step process SMEs can use to combine smart technology with talent management. This combo boosts the company's overall performance and helps it stay ahead of the competition.

How Technology and Talent Work Together

When smart technology and talent management join forces, they make each other stronger. Smart tech, like AI, IoT, and data analytics, gives SMEs powerful tools to simplify processes, handle routine jobs, and learn important things from data. These tools help companies work more, make better choices, and keep customers happier.

Talent management, however, has an influence on attracting, developing, and keeping skilled employees who can use these technologies well. When SMEs invest to develop their workforce and create a culture where people always learn, they can build a workforce that knows tech and can get the most out of smart technologies. This teamwork makes sure that using technology matches business goals and leads to real results.

Building a Tech-Savvy Workforce

Creating a workforce that knows its way around tech starts with figuring out what skills people need to make the most of smart technologies. Small and medium-sized businesses should look at what their workers can do now and focus on training programs to fill in any gaps when it comes to AI IoT, data analysis, and other new tech. These programs need to be thorough and keep going, giving employees both the technical know-how and the ability to use these skills in real business situations. Practical workshops, online classes, and certificates can help workers keep up with new tech developments and get good at using digital tools.

On top of that, building a culture that values new ideas and trying things out pushes employees to check out new tech and come up with clever ways to tackle business problems. Small and medium-sized companies can set up innovation hubs or teams from different departments to explore and put new technologies into action. This team-based approach doesn't just boost tech know-how - it also creates an environment where people always want to get better and can roll with the punches.

Enhancing Collaboration and Innovation

Smart tech and talent management working together boosts teamwork and new ideas in small and medium-sized businesses. Teams from different areas can use on-line platforms and tools to communicate better, share thoughts, and work on projects together. Take cloud-based project tools, for instance. They let teams work together in real-time, no matter where they are. Also, smart tech like AI and data analysis offer useful insights that spark innovation. By looking at customer info, market changes, and how things are running, small and medium-sized businesses can spot chances to improve products, create personal marketing plans, and make processes better.

This way of using data do not help make better choices but also creates a workplace where staff feel free to try new things and come up with fresh ideas.

New ideas in how companies handle their employees also have a big impact on teamwork. Systems for managing performance that include immediate feedback and align goals help match individual and team efforts with what the company wants to achieve. When SMEs recognize and reward fresh contributions, they can inspire employees to take an active part in boosting the company's growth and ability to compete.

Hurdles and Things to Think About When Putting This into Action

Even though combining smart tech and employee management offers big upsides, SMEs face several challenges when they try to implement it. These include:

- **Resource Constraints**: SMEs often don't have enough money or IT setup to invest in fancy tech. To deal with this, they need to focus on what's most important and use solutions that can grow with them.
- **Skills Shortages**: Tech changes so fast that it's hard to find people with the right skills. To fix this, SMEs can put money into training their staff, team up with schools, and offer good pay to attract and keep tech-smart workers.
- **Change Management**: People often push back against new tech, and company culture can get in the way. To make changes stick, SMEs need smart strategies. These include talking about what's happening getting workers involved, and making sure bosses are on board. This helps create a workplace where new ideas are welcome.
- **Data Privacy and Security**: Protecting sensitive data and following regulatory rules are essential when using smart technologies. SMEs should put strong cybersecurity measures into action, teach workers about data privacy best practices, and keep up with changing regulations.

This means combining smart tech with talent management gives SMEs a chance to grow and stay ahead of the competition. By using tech and talent together, SMEs can boost their productivity, create new ideas, and help their workers succeed in today's digital world. To get the most out of this, SMEs need to invest in tech, train their staff, and work together as a team.

Strategic Framework for Integration

To blend smart tech and talent management in a way that fits business goals and brings the most benefits, companies should follow these key steps:

Assessment of Business Needs: SMEs should start by evaluating their current tech setup and workforce needs. This means finding areas where smart tech can boost value, like making operations better, improving how customers feel, or sparking new ideas. At the same time, it's key to understand what skills and abilities the workforce has to figure out how to support new tech through smart people management.

Alignment with Strategic Goals: Efforts to bring in new tech should match what the SME wants to achieve overall. This makes sure that money spent on tech and efforts to grow talent help reach business goals, whether that's getting a bigger slice of the market, making more money, or moving into new areas. When things line up, it helps decide where to invest and how to use resources in the best way.

Building a Tech-Savvy Workforce: Talent management has a key impact on getting the workforce ready to use smart technology well. This includes offering training and upskilling programs that fit the specific technologies the SME has adopted. For example, AI and data analytics training can help employees to find useful insights and make choices based on data, while IoT training can boost how well operations run and improve safety measures.

Promoting Cross-Functional Collaboration: Good integration needs teamwork across departments and functions in the company. SMEs should build a culture where tech experts, HR pros, and business leaders join forces to spot chances, tackle problems, and put integrated solutions into action. Teams from different areas can make sure tech adoption fits business needs and get support from the right talent strategies.

Continuous Monitoring and Improvement: Integration doesn't stop; it needs ongoing checks and tweaks. SMEs should set up metrics and key performance indicators (KPIs) to evaluate how tech adoption affects business results and how well employees perform. Regular feedback and performance reviews can help find areas to improve and make the mix of smart tech and talent management strategies work better.

Case Studies: Integrated Approaches in SMEs

Some SMEs have combined smart technology with talent management strategies. This shows how this approach can benefit companies (Alaskari et al. 2021; Crockett et al. 2021):

Case Study 1: Manufacturing SME

A manufacturing SME put IoT sensors in its production line to watch equipment performance and guess when maintenance was needed. At the same time, the SME spent money to train its workers in IoT technology and data analytics. This combination cut downtime and maintenance costs. It also gave employees the power to manage equipment ahead of time and make production processes better.

Case Study 2: Retail SME

A retail SME used AI-powered analytics to examine customer data and tailor marketing campaigns. At the same time, the SME upgraded its talent management practices by offering flexible work options and chances to grow careers in digital marketing skills. This combined approach boosted customer engagement numbers while improving employee happiness and retention.

Case Study 3: Service Industry SME

The service industry SME adopted cloud-based CRM software to improve customer service operations and enhance service delivery. At the same time, the SME focused on strategies to attract tech-savvy professionals who could use CRM technology well. This integration improved service quality, cut down response times, and allowed the SME to grow its customer base.

Combining smart tech with talent management isn't just about new gadgets. It's about making a plan that gets the most out of both tech and people in a company. When SMEs match their tech spending with ways to grow talent, they can run things better, come up with new ideas, and get ahead of their rivals. To deal with the tricky parts of putting it all together, companies need to keep changing and work well with others. This helps them grow and do well in today's digital world.

OVERCOMING CHALLENGES

Common Barriers to Technology Adoption

New tech can be tough for small businesses to handle even though it can help them a lot. It's key to get what's in the way and deal with it to make things work (Abdulsalam & Hedabou 2021; Sun 2020):

- **Money Worries**: The main problem is often the big price tag that comes with new tech. small businesses don't have much cash to spare, so it's hard to say yes to spending on new gear, software, and training. To get past these small businesses can check out cheaper options like cloud services you pay for monthly, or look for money help through grants and support for going digital.

- **Lack of Technical Expertise**: Putting new tech into action and running it needs special skills and know-how that small and medium businesses might not have in-house. This can slow down tech adoption and lead to poor use of tech resources. Small and medium businesses can tackle this problem by teaming up with tech providers or advisors who offer help with setup, training, and ongoing tech support. Working with outside experts can speed up tech adoption and lower the risks that come with rolling out new systems.

- **Resistance to Change**: Workers might push back against new tech because they're worried about losing their jobs, don't know how to use it, or think it's too complicated. To get over this hurdle, companies need good strategies to manage change. This means explaining how the new tech will help setting up training to boost skills and confidence, and getting workers involved in making decisions. Showing real improvements in how much work gets done, how happy people are at their jobs, and chances to move up in their careers can also help people get on board with new tech.

- **Integration with Existing Systems**: Combining new tech with old systems can be tricky and take a lot of time for small and medium-sized businesses (SMEs) that have outdated IT setups. Problems with compatibility and moving data can pop up causing hiccups in day-to-day operations. SMEs should do thorough checks to make sure everything works together, focus on solutions that play nice with what they already have, and plan to roll things out step by step to avoid too much disruption. It's also smart to put money into tech that can grow as the business does, which helps make sure their IT investments stay useful down the road.

- **Data Security and Privacy Concerns**: Small and medium-sized enterprises (SMEs) might hesitate to use new tech because they worry about data breaches and following privacy laws like GDPR. To tackle these issues, SMEs need to put in place strong cyber defenses, encrypt important data, and make sure they follow the rules. It's key for SMEs to teach their staff about cyber threats and use the best ways to protect customer and business information.

Dealing With Talent Management Issues

Talent management poses distinct problems for SMEs as they work to draw in, grow, and keep skilled workers:

- **Attracting Top Talent**: Small and medium-sized enterprises (SMEs) often face competition from bigger companies that pay more and offer better perks. To get the best people, SMEs should set themselves apart by showcasing chances to grow, a helpful workplace, and a strong company culture. Building a solid employer brand through social media, stories from employees, and showing up at industry events can also draw in candidates who share the company's values and goals.

- **Developing Employee Skills**: SMEs often struggle to offer enough training and growth chances because they don't have a lot of money or time. To help employees get better at their jobs, SMEs can set up clear training plans, start mentoring programs, and let people learn from different departments. Using online classes and teaming up with schools can also give workers more ways to learn and keep getting better at what they do.

- **Retaining and Engaging Employees**: High turnover rates can disrupt business continuity and hurt morale within SMEs. To keep employees, SMEs should work on creating a positive work environment, offer competitive pay packages, and give chances to advance careers. Employee engagement efforts like regular feedback talks, reward programs, and team-building events can build a sense of belonging and loyalty among staff.

- **Succession Planning**: Succession planning is key for SMEs to make sure leadership roles and important positions stay filled. SMEs should spot high-potential workers, grow leadership skills through mentoring and leadership training, and set up clear career paths for future leaders. Training employees in multiple areas and writing down ways to transfer knowledge can lower risks tied to sudden turnover or retirement.

- **Adjusting to Shifts in the Workforce**: Today's workforce includes many different groups and ages each with their own wants and needs. Small and medium-sized businesses should welcome diversity, offer flexible work options, and shape their talent strategies to suit various age groups. When these companies grasp and adjust to workforce trends, they can build a workplace culture that draws in and keeps a wide range of talented people.

This means that to overcome challenges in adopting technology and managing talent, SMEs need a well-thought-out plan. This plan should tackle obstacles, make the most of chances, and put money into people and tech. When SMEs use new solutions to create a helpful work setting, and keep learning, they set themselves up to do well and stay strong in a tough business world.

Figure 5. Future trends and opportunities for SMEs

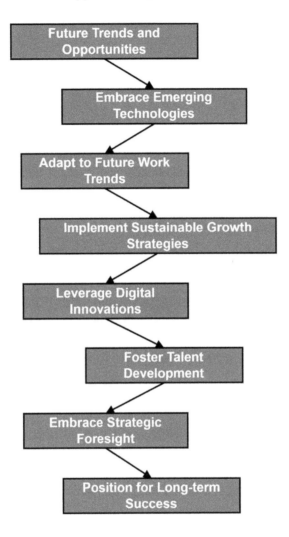

FUTURE TRENDS AND OPPORTUNITIES

Figure 5 shows how future trends and opportunities for SMEs connect highlighting why SMEs need to adapt and plan ahead in a fast-changing business world (Abdulsalam & Hedabou 2021; Ali & Osmanaj 2020; Yildiz & Esmer 2023).

Emerging Technologies for SMEs

New technologies can change how SMEs work, make them more competitive, and spark new ideas:

Artificial Intelligence (AI) and Machine Learning (ML): AI and ML are causing a revolution in business processes across many industries. For small and medium-sized enterprises (SMEs), AI can automate everyday tasks, customize customer experiences through predictive analytics, and improve operations from supply chain management to marketing plans.

Internet of Things (IoT): IoT allows SMEs to gather real-time data from connected devices boosting operational effectiveness predictive upkeep, and customer support. IoT uses extend to manufacturing, logistics, healthcare, and other areas creating new chances for expansion and cost reductions.

Blockchain Technology: Apart from cryptocurrencies, blockchain tech provides secure and clear answers for managing supply chains smart contracts, and money matters. Small businesses can cut costs, boost security, and track their work better with this tech.

Augmented Reality (AR) and Virtual Reality (VR): AR and VR are changing how businesses interact with customers and train staff. Small companies can use AR/VR to give customers lifelike product demos, run virtual training, and work together from far away. This makes work more efficient and keeps customers happy.

Future of Work and Talent Management

The way we work is changing due to new tech and shifts in how people work:

Remote Work and Digital Nomadism: The move to remote work has picked up speed giving SMEs access to worldwide talent and cutting down on costs. Flexible work setups are becoming common calling for quick-thinking talent management plans that back online teamwork and keep employees healthy.

Skills-based Hiring and Gig Economy: SMEs now focus more on skills than old-school qualifications dipping into the gig economy to find special talent when they need it. Sites that link freelancers with SMEs make it easy to staff up and take on project-based work.

Employee Experience and Well-being: What workers want from their jobs shapes how companies manage talent. Workers expect a good balance between work and life, help with mental health, and workplaces where everyone feels welcome. Small and medium businesses that focus on making employees happy can draw in and keep the best workers. They do this through programs to keep people healthy, chances to grow in their careers, and rules that include everyone.

Long-Term Strategies for Sustainable Growth

Strategies for growth that last help small and medium businesses do well even when the economy is shaky and technology changes fast:

Digital Transformation Roadmap: Creating a full plan to go digital matches tech spending with big-picture goals. This ensures the business can grow and bounce back from problems. To stay ahead of rivals, businesses need to keep coming up with new ideas and adjust to what's happening in the market.

Customer-Centric Approach: SMEs should focus on grasping what customers need and like by using data analytics and creating personalized experiences. Strategies that put customers first lead to loyal customers, help businesses grow into new markets, and boost income over time.

Partnerships and Ecosystem Collaboration: Working together with tech companies' other businesses in the industry, and universities helps create new ideas and gets products to market faster. Smart partnerships can make SMEs better at research and development, help them enter new markets, and allow them to share resources, which helps everyone grow.

Predictions and Insights for SMEs

Looking forward, SMEs should get ready for big changes and take advantage of new chances:

Adoption of Agile Practices: Agile methods help SMEs to adapt fast to market shifts, refine products/services, and build a culture that always aims to get better. These practices have an influence on innovation and lower risks tied to game-changing tech.

Data-driven Decision Making: Using data analytics and business intelligence tools gives SMEs the power to make smart choices, streamline processes, and predict what customers want. Insights from data boost how well a company runs and help it grow.

Regulatory Compliance and Cybersecurity: As digital systems grow; SMEs need to focus on following rules (like GDPR) and beefing up cybersecurity to keep sensitive info safe and keep customers' trust. Taking steps to manage risks ahead of time cuts down on legal troubles and damage to the company's name.

So, to stay ahead, SMEs need to adopt new tech, prepare for future work changes, and create plans to grow. Using digital tools, helping staff learn, and thinking ahead can help SMEs succeed and stay strong in a changing world economy.

CONCLUSION

For Small and Medium Enterprises (SMEs) to grow and compete better, they need to use smart tech and manage their people well. This chapter looked at how these two key business ideas work together and gave SMEs tips on how to use new trends and chances. When SMEs match their smart tech investments with how they manage their people, they can boost how well they work, come up with new ideas, and make better choices. This mix creates a workplace that's always getting better and can change, helping SMEs do well in a world where digital comes first. To adopt new tech, it's key to get past hurdles like tight budgets, not enough tech know-how, and people not wanting change. SMEs can tackle these problems by putting money into solutions that can grow with them, building a team that's good with tech, and making sure their data is safe and secure. When SMEs take advantage of smart tech and manage their talent well, they can handle problems better, grow more, and become leaders in their fields. When they create a workplace that values new ideas quick changes, and giving employees more say, SMEs can set themselves up for long-term success in our digital and connected world.

REFERENCES

Abdulsalam, Y. S., & Hedabou, M. (2021). Security and privacy in cloud computing: Technical review. *Future Internet*, 14(1), 11. DOI:10.3390/fi14010011

Alaskari, O., Pinedo-Cuenca, R., & Ahmad, M. (2021). Framework for implementation of Enterprise Resource Planning (ERP) systems in small and medium enterprises (SMEs): A case study. *Procedia Manufacturing*, 55, 424–430. DOI:10.1016/j.promfg.2021.10.058

Ali, O., & Osmanaj, V. (2020). The role of government regulations in the adoption of cloud computing: A case study of local government. *Computer Law & Security Report*, 36, 105396. DOI:10.1016/j.clsr.2020.105396

Arostegi, M., Torre-Bastida, A., Bilbao, M. N., & Del Ser, J. (2018). A heuristic approach to the multicriteria design of IaaS cloud infrastructures for Big Data applications. *Expert Systems: International Journal of Knowledge Engineering and Neural Networks*, 35(5), e12259. DOI:10.1111/exsy.12259

Baabdullah, A. M., Alalwan, A. A., Slade, E. L., Raman, R., & Khatatneh, K. F. (2021). SMEs and artificial intelligence (AI): Antecedents and consequences of AI-based B2B practices. *Industrial Marketing Management*, 98, 255–270. DOI:10.1016/j.indmarman.2021.09.003

Bethke-Langenegger, P., Mahler, P., & Staffelbach, B. (2011). Effectiveness of talent management strategies. *European Journal of International Management*, 5(5), 524–539. DOI:10.1504/EJIM.2011.042177

Cai, L., Tian, Y., Liu, Z., Cheng, Q., Xu, J., & Ning, Y. (2016). Application of cloud computing to simulation of a heavy-duty machine tool. *International Journal of Advanced Manufacturing Technology*, 84(1-4), 291–303. DOI:10.1007/s00170-015-7916-2

Chaudhuri, R., Chatterjee, S., Vrontis, D., & Chaudhuri, S. (2022). Innovation in SMEs, AI dynamism, and sustainability: The current situation and way forward. *Sustainability (Basel)*, 14(19), 12760. DOI:10.3390/su141912760

Cheese, P., Thomas, R. J., & Craig, E. (2007). *The talent powered organization: Strategies for globalization, talent management and high performance*. Kogan Page Publishers.

Choobineh, M., Arab, A., Khodaei, A., & Paaso, A. (2022). Energy innovations through blockchain: Challenges, opportunities, and the road ahead. *The Electricity Journal*, 35(1), 107059. DOI:10.1016/j.tej.2021.107059

Collings, D. G., & Mellahi, K. (2009). Strategic talent management: A review and research agenda. *Human Resource Management Review*, 19(4), 304–313. DOI:10.1016/j.hrmr.2009.04.001

Crockett, K. A., Gerber, L., Latham, A., & Colyer, E. (2021). Building trustworthy AI solutions: A case for practical solutions for small businesses. *IEEE Transactions on Artificial Intelligence*.

Deery, M. (2008). Talent management, work-life balance and retention strategies. *International Journal of Contemporary Hospitality Management*, 20(7), 792–806. DOI:10.1108/09596110810897619

Gill, S. S., Xu, M., Ottaviani, C., Patros, P., Bahsoon, R., Shaghaghi, A., Golec, M., Stankovski, V., Wu, H., Abraham, A., Singh, M., Mehta, H., Ghosh, S. K., Baker, T., Parlikad, A. K., Lutfiyya, H., Kanhere, S. S., Sakellariou, R., Dustdar, S., & Uhlig, S. (2022). AI for next generation computing: Emerging trends and future directions. *Internet of Things : Engineering Cyber Physical Human Systems*, 19, 100514. DOI:10.1016/j.iot.2022.100514

Grashof, N., & Kopka, A. (2023). Artificial intelligence and radical innovation: An opportunity for all companies? *Small Business Economics*, 61(2), 771–797. DOI:10.1007/s11187-022-00698-3

Han, H., & Trimi, S. (2022a). Towards a data science platform for improving SME collaboration through Industry 4.0 technologies. *Technological Forecasting and Social Change*, 174, 121242. DOI:10.1016/j.techfore.2021.121242

Han, H., & Trimi, S. (2022b). Towards a data science platform for improving SME collaboration through Industry 4.0 technologies. *Technological Forecasting and Social Change*, 174, 121242. DOI:10.1016/j.techfore.2021.121242

Jung, W.-K., Kim, D.-R., Lee, H., Lee, T.-H., Yang, I., Youn, B. D., Zontar, D., Brockmann, M., Brecher, C., & Ahn, S.-H. (2021). Appropriate smart factory for SMEs: Concept, application and perspective. *International Journal of Precision Engineering and Manufacturing*, 22(1), 201–215. DOI:10.1007/s12541-020-00445-2

Lu, Y., Yang, L., Shi, B., Li, J., & Abedin, M. Z. (2022). A novel framework of credit risk feature selection for SMEs during industry 4.0. *Annals of Operations Research*, 1–28. DOI:10.1007/s10479-022-04849-3 PMID:35910041

Mohammadian, H. D., & Rezaie, F. (2020). The role of IoE-Education in the 5 th wave theory readiness & its effect on SME 4.0 HR competencies. *2020 IEEE Global Engineering Education Conference (EDUCON)*, 1604–1613. DOI:10.1109/ EDUCON45650.2020.9125249

Mupepi, M. (2017). *Effective talent management strategies for organizational success*. IGI Global. DOI:10.4018/978-1-5225-1961-4

Saura, J. R., Palacios-Marqués, D., & Ribeiro-Soriano, D. (2023). Digital marketing in SMEs via data-driven strategies: Reviewing the current state of research. *Journal of Small Business Management*, 61(3), 1278–1313. DOI:10.1080/00472778.2021.1955127

Sun, P. (2020). Security and privacy protection in cloud computing: Discussions and challenges. *Journal of Network and Computer Applications*, 160, 102642. DOI:10.1016/j.jnca.2020.102642

Tabrizchi, H., & Kuchaki Rafsanjani, M. (2020). A survey on security challenges in cloud computing: Issues, threats, and solutions. *The Journal of Supercomputing*, 76(12), 9493–9532. DOI:10.1007/s11227-020-03213-1

Velmurugan, K., Venkumar, P., & Sudhakara, P. R. (2021). SME 4.0: Machine learning framework for real-time machine health monitoring system. *Journal of Physics: Conference Series*, 1911(1), 012026. DOI:10.1088/1742-6596/1911/1/012026

Yildiz, R. O., & Esmer, S. (2023). Talent management strategies and functions: A systematic review. *Industrial and Commercial Training*, 55(1), 93–111. DOI:10.1108/ICT-01-2022-0007

Žigienė, G., Rybakovas, E., & Alzbutas, R. (2019). Artificial intelligence based commercial risk management framework for SMEs. *Sustainability (Basel)*, 11(16), 4501. DOI:10.3390/su11164501

ADDITIONAL READING

Khan, A. A., Laghari, A. A., Li, P., Dootio, M. A., & Karim, S. (2023). The collaborative role of blockchain, artificial intelligence, and industrial internet of things in digitalization of small and medium-size enterprises. *Scientific Reports*, 13(1), 1656. DOI:10.1038/s41598-023-28707-9 PMID:36717702

Khanzode, A. G., Sarma, P. R. S., Mangla, S. K., & Yuan, H. (2021). Modeling the Industry 4.0 adoption for sustainable production in Micro, Small & Medium Enterprises. *Journal of Cleaner Production*, 279, 123489. DOI:10.1016/j.jclepro.2020.123489

Li, H., Yang, Z., Jin, C., & Wang, J. (2023). How an industrial internet platform empowers the digital transformation of SMEs: Theoretical mechanism and business model. *Journal of Knowledge Management*, 27(1), 105–120. DOI:10.1108/JKM-09-2022-0757

KEY TERMS AND DEFINITIONS

Artificial Intelligence (AI): The simulation of human intelligence in machines, enabling them to perform tasks that typically require human intelligence, such as decision-making and problem-solving.

Customer Experience: The overall perception that customers have of an organization, shaped by their interactions with its products, services, and employees, which smart technology can significantly enhance.

Data Analytics: The process of examining, cleaning, and modeling data to discover useful information, inform conclusions, and support decision-making in business operations.

Innovation: The process of developing new ideas, products, or methods that bring significant improvements or changes to existing processes, contributing to business growth and competitive advantage.

Internet of Things (IoT): A network of interconnected devices that communicate and exchange data with each other, enabling real-time monitoring, control, and data collection across various industries.

Operational Efficiency: The ability of an organization to deliver products or services in the most cost-effective manner while maintaining high quality, often achieved through the integration of smart technologies.

Predictive Maintenance: The use of data analysis and IoT sensors to monitor equipment performance and predict potential failures, allowing for timely maintenance and reducing downtime in industrial operations.

Small and Medium Enterprises (SMEs): Businesses that maintain revenues, assets, or a number of employees below a certain threshold, playing a critical role in driving economic growth and innovation globally.

Smart Technology: Advanced digital tools and systems, including AI, IoT, and data analytics, used by businesses to enhance operational efficiency, innovation, and customer satisfaction.

Talent Management: The strategic process of attracting, developing, and retaining skilled employees to ensure that an organization has the talent it needs to achieve its goals.

Compilation of References

Abbasi, M. A., Memon, Z. A., Syed, T. Q., Memon, J., & Alshboul, R. (2017). Addressing the future data management challenges in iot: A proposed framework. *International Journal of Advanced Computer Science and Applications*, 8(5).

Abd Razak, S., Nazari, N. H. M., & Al-Dhaqm, A. (2020). Data anonymization using pseudonym system to preserve data privacy. *IEEE Access : Practical Innovations, Open Solutions*, 8, 43256–43264. DOI:10.1109/ACCESS.2020.2977117

Abdel-Basset, M., Mohamed, R., & Chang, V. (2024). A Multi-Criteria Decision-Making Framework to Evaluate the Impact of Industry 5.0 Technologies: Case Study, Lessons Learned, Challenges and Future Directions. *Information Systems Frontiers*, 1–31. DOI:10.1007/s10796-024-10472-3

Abdulhafiz, W. A., & Khamis, A. (2013). Handling data uncertainty and inconsistency using multisensor data fusion. *Advances in Artificial Intelligence*, 2013(1), 241260. DOI:10.1155/2013/241260

Abdulsalam, Y. S., & Hedabou, M. (2021). Security and privacy in cloud computing: Technical review. *Future Internet*, 14(1), 11. DOI:10.3390/fi14010011

Abioye, E. A., Abidin, M. S. Z., Mahmud, M. S. A., Buyamin, S., Ishak, M. H. I., Rahman, M. K. I. A., Otuoze, A. O., Onotu, P., & Ramli, M. S. A. (2020). A review on monitoring and advanced control strategies for precision irrigation. *Computers and Electronics in Agriculture*, 173, 105441. DOI:10.1016/j.compag.2020.105441

Abu-Elkheir, M., Hayajneh, M., & Ali, N. A. (2013). Data management for the internet of things: Design primitives and solution. *Sensors (Basel)*, 13(11), 15582–15612. DOI:10.3390/s131115582 PMID:24240599

Adel, A. (2024). The convergence of intelligent tutoring, robotics, and IoT in smart education for the transition from industry 4.0 to 5.0. *Smart Cities*, 7(1), 325–369. DOI:10.3390/smartcities7010014

Adepoju, O., Akinyomi, O., & Esan, O. (2023). Integrating Human-Computer Interactions in Nigerian Energy System: A Skills Requirement Analysis. *Journal of Digital Food, Energy & Water Systems, 4*(2).

Adhikari, J., Mathrani, A., & Scogings, C. (2016). Bring Your Own Devices classroom: Exploring the issue of digital divide in the teaching and learning contexts. *Interactive Technology and Smart Education*, 13(4), 323–343. DOI:10.1108/ITSE-04-2016-0007

Adi, E., Anwar, A., Baig, Z., & Zeadally, S. (2020). Machine learning and data analytics for the IoT. *Neural Computing & Applications*, 32(20), 16205–16233. DOI:10.1007/s00521-020-04874-y

Agrawal, A. V., Magulur, L. P., Priya, S. G., Kaur, A., Singh, G., & Boopathi, S. (2023). Smart Precision Agriculture Using IoT and WSN. In *Handbook of Research on Data Science and Cybersecurity Innovations in Industry 4.0 Technologies* (pp. 524–541). IGI Global. DOI:10.4018/978-1-6684-8145-5.ch026

Ahad, M. A., Tripathi, G., Zafar, S., & Doja, F. (2020). IoT data management—Security aspects of information linkage in IoT systems. *Principles of internet of things (IoT) ecosystem: Insight paradigm*, 439-464.

Ahmed, G. (2021). Improving IoT privacy, data protection and security concerns. *International Journal of Technology, Innovation and Management (IJTIM), 1*(1).

Ahmed, E., Yaqoob, I., Gani, A., Imran, M., & Guizani, M. (2016). Internet-of-things-based smart environments: State of the art, taxonomy, and open research challenges. *IEEE Wireless Communications*, 23(5), 10–16. DOI:10.1109/MWC.2016.7721736

Ahmed, E., Yaqoob, I., Hashem, I. A. T., Khan, I., Ahmed, A. I. A., Imran, M., & Vasilakos, A. V. (2017). The role of big data analytics in Internet of Things. *Computer Networks*, 129, 459–471. DOI:10.1016/j.comnet.2017.06.013

Ahmed, M. A., Chavez, S. A., Eltamaly, A. M., Garces, H. O., Rojas, A. J., & Kim, Y.-C. (2022). Toward an intelligent campus: IoT platform for remote monitoring and control of smart buildings. *Sensors (Basel)*, 22(23), 9045. DOI:10.3390/s22239045 PMID:36501748

Alahmad, T., Neményi, M., & Nyéki, A. (2023). Applying IoT Sensors and Big Data to Improve Precision Crop Production: A Review. *Agronomy (Basel)*, 13(10), 10. Advance online publication. DOI:10.3390/agronomy13102603

Al-Ali, A.-R., Gupta, R., Zaman Batool, T., Landolsi, T., Aloul, F., & Al Nabulsi, A. (2020). Digital twin conceptual model within the context of internet of things. *Future Internet*, 12(10), 163. DOI:10.3390/fi12100163

Alaskari, O., Pinedo-Cuenca, R., & Ahmad, M. (2021). Framework for implementation of Enterprise Resource Planning (ERP) systems in small and medium enterprises (SMEs): A case study. *Procedia Manufacturing*, 55, 424–430. DOI:10.1016/j.promfg.2021.10.058

Albouq, S. S., Abi Sen, A. A., Almashf, N., Yamin, M., Alshanqiti, A., & Bahbouh, N. M. (2022). A survey of interoperability challenges and solutions for dealing with them in IoT environment. *IEEE Access : Practical Innovations, Open Solutions*, 10, 36416–36428. DOI:10.1109/ACCESS.2022.3162219

Aldowah, H., Rehman, S. U., Ghazal, S., & Umar, I. N. (2017). Internet of Things in higher education: a study on future learning. Journal of Physics: Conference Series.

Al-Emran, M., Malik, S. I., & Al-Kabi, M. N. (2020). A survey of Internet of Things (IoT) in education: Opportunities and challenges. *Toward Social Internet of Things (SIoT): Enabling Technologies, Architectures and Applications: Emerging Technologies for Connected and Smart Social Objects*, 197-209.

Alfonso, L., Chacón, J. C., & Peña-Castellanos, G. (2015). *Allowing citizens to effortlessly become rainfall sensors*.

Alfoudari, A. M., Durugbo, C. M., & Aldhmour, F. M. (2021). Understanding sociotechnological challenges of smart classrooms using a systematic review. *Computers & Education*, 173, 104282. DOI:10.1016/j.compedu.2021.104282

Al-Fuqaha, A., Guizani, M., Mohammadi, M., Aledhari, M., & Ayyash, M. (2015). Internet of things: A survey on enabling technologies, protocols, and applications. *IEEE Communications Surveys and Tutorials*, 17(4), 2347–2376. DOI:10.1109/COMST.2015.2444095

Ali, M. N., Senthil, T., Ilakkiya, T., Hasan, D. S., Ganapathy, N. B. S., & Boopathi, S. (2024). IoT's Role in Smart Manufacturing Transformation for Enhanced Household Product Quality. In *Advanced Applications in Osmotic Computing* (pp. 252–289). IGI Global. DOI:10.4018/979-8-3693-1694-8.ch014

Ali, O., & Osmanaj, V. (2020). The role of government regulations in the adoption of cloud computing: A case study of local government. *Computer Law & Security Report*, 36, 105396. DOI:10.1016/j.clsr.2020.105396

Alizadeh, M. R., & Khodabakhshipour, M. (2010). *Effect of threshing drum speed and crop moisture content on the paddy grain damage in axial-flow thresher*. https://repository.uaiasi.ro/xmlui/handle/20.500.12811/2571

Allam, Z., & Jones, D. S. (2021). Future (post-COVID) digital, smart and sustainable cities in the wake of 6G: Digital twins, immersive realities and new urban economies. *Land Use Policy*, 101, 105201. DOI:10.1016/j.landusepol.2020.105201

Almasri, R. A., Abu-Hamdeh, N. H., & Al-Tamimi, N. (2024). A state-of-the-art review of energy-efficient and renewable energy systems in higher education facilities. *Frontiers in Energy Research*, 11, 1344216. DOI:10.3389/fenrg.2023.1344216

Aloisioa, G., Fiorea, S., Foster, I., & Williams, D. (2013). *Scientific big data analytics challenges at large scale. Proceedings of Big Data and Extreme-scale Computing*. BDEC.

Al-Ruithe, M., & Benkhelifa, E. (2017). Cloud data governance maturity model. Proceedings of the Second International Conference on Internet of Things, Data and Cloud Computing.

Alshuwaikhat, H. M., & Abubakar, I. (2008). An integrated approach to achieving campus sustainability: Assessment of the current campus environmental management practices. *Journal of Cleaner Production*, 16(16), 1777–1785. DOI:10.1016/j.jclepro.2007.12.002

Amiri-Zarandi, M., Hazrati Fard, M., Yousefinaghani, S., Kaviani, M., & Dara, R. (2022). A Platform Approach to Smart Farm Information Processing. *Agriculture*, 12(6), 838. DOI:10.3390/agriculture12060838

Anagnostopoulos, C., Aladwani, T., Alghamdi, I., & Kolomvatsos, K. (2022). Data-driven analytics task management reasoning mechanism in edge computing. *Smart Cities*, 5(2), 562–582. DOI:10.3390/smartcities5020030

Anderson, R. M. (1982). Transmission dynamics and control of infectious disease agents. In *Population Biology of Infectious Diseases: Report of the Dahlem Workshop on Population Biology of Infectious Disease Agents Berlin 1982, March 14–19* (pp. 149-176). Springer Berlin Heidelberg. DOI:10.1007/978-3-642-68635-1_9

Angerschmid, A., Zhou, J., Theuermann, K., Chen, F., & Holzinger, A. (2022). Fairness and explanation in AI-informed decision making. *Machine Learning and Knowledge Extraction*, 4(2), 556–579. DOI:10.3390/make4020026

Ankan, A., Wortel, I. M., & Textor, J. (2021). Testing graphical causal models using the R package "dagitty". *Current Protocols*, 1(2), e45. DOI:10.1002/cpz1.45 PMID:33592130

Anshari, M., Alas, Y., & Guan, L. S. (2016). Developing online learning resources: Big data, social networks, and cloud computing to support pervasive knowledge. *Education and Information Technologies*, 21(6), 1663–1677. DOI:10.1007/s10639-015-9407-3

Appriou, A. (Ed.). (2014). *Uncertainty theories and multisensor data fusion.* John Wiley & Sons. DOI:10.1002/9781118578636

Araújo, S. O., Peres, R. S., Barata, J., Lidon, F., & Ramalho, J. C. (2021). Characterising the Agriculture 4.0 Landscape—Emerging Trends, Challenges and Opportunities. *Agronomy (Basel)*, 11(4), 667. Advance online publication. DOI:10.3390/agronomy11040667

Arora, N. K., Fatima, T., Mishra, I., Verma, M., Mishra, J., & Mishra, V. (2018). Environmental sustainability: Challenges and viable solutions. *Environmental Sustainability*, 1(4), 309–340. DOI:10.1007/s42398-018-00038-w

Arostegi, M., Torre-Bastida, A., Bilbao, M. N., & Del Ser, J. (2018). A heuristic approach to the multicriteria design of IaaS cloud infrastructures for Big Data applications. *Expert Systems: International Journal of Knowledge Engineering and Neural Networks*, 35(5), e12259. DOI:10.1111/exsy.12259

Arunprasad, R., & Boopathi, S. (2019). Chapter-4 Alternate Refrigerants for Minimization Environmental Impacts: A Review. In *Advances in Engineering Technology* (p. 75). AkiNik Publications New Delhi.

Awan, U., Sroufe, R., & Shahbaz, M. (2021). Industry 4.0 and the circular economy: A literature review and recommendations for future research. *Business Strategy and the Environment*, 30(4), 2038–2060. DOI:10.1002/bse.2731

Ayem, G. T., Asilkan, O., Iorliam, A., Ibrahim, R., & Thandekkattu, S. G. (2023). Causal Inference Estimates with Backdoor Adjustment Condition vs. the Unconfoundedness Assumption: A Comparative Analysis Study of the Structural Causal Model and the Potential Outcome Frameworks.

Ayem, G. T., Thandekkattu, S. G., Nsang, A. S., & Fonkam, M. (2023). Structural Causal Model Design and Causal Impact Analysis: A Case of SENSE-EGRA Dataset. International Conference on Communication and Computational Technologies. DOI:10.1007/978-981-99-3485-0_4

Ayem, G. T., Ajibesin, A., Iorliam, A., & Nsang, A. S. (2023a). A mixed framework for causal impact analysis under confounding and selection biases: A focus on Egra dataset. *International Journal of Information Technology : an Official Journal of Bharati Vidyapeeth's Institute of Computer Applications and Management*. Advance online publication. DOI:10.1007/s41870-023-01490-6

Ayem, G. T., Asilkan, O., & Iorliam, A. (2023). Design and Validation of Structural Causal Model: A Focus on EGRA Dataset. *Journal of Computing Theories and Applications*, 1(2), 37–54. DOI:10.33633/jcta.v1i2.9304

Ayem, G. T., Nsang, A. S., Igoche, B. I., & Naankang, G. (2023). Design and Validation of Structural Causal Model: A focus on SENSE-EGRA Datasets. *International Journal of Advanced Science Computing and Engineering*, 5(3), 257–268. DOI:10.62527/ijasce.5.3.177

Baabdullah, A. M., Alalwan, A. A., Slade, E. L., Raman, R., & Khatatneh, K. F. (2021). SMEs and artificial intelligence (AI): Antecedents and consequences of AI-based B2B practices. *Industrial Marketing Management*, 98, 255–270. DOI:10.1016/j.indmarman.2021.09.003

Babar, M., Khan, F., Iqbal, W., Yahya, A., Arif, F., Tan, Z., & Chuma, J. M. (2018). A secured data management scheme for smart societies in industrial internet of things environment. *IEEE Access : Practical Innovations, Open Solutions*, 6, 43088–43099. DOI:10.1109/ACCESS.2018.2861421

Babu, B. S., Kamalakannan, J., Meenatchi, N., Karthik, S., & Boopathi, S. (2022). Economic impacts and reliability evaluation of battery by adopting Electric Vehicle. *IEEE Explore*, 1–6.

Badshah, A., Ghani, A., Daud, A., Jalal, A., Bilal, M., & Crowcroft, J. (2023). Towards smart education through internet of things: A survey. *ACM Computing Surveys*, 56(2), 1–33. DOI:10.1145/3610401

Bagheri, M., & Movahed, S. H. (2016). The effect of the Internet of Things (IoT) on education business model. 2016 12th International Conference on Signal-Image Technology & Internet-Based Systems (SITIS).

Bag, T. K., Srivastava, A. K., Yadav, S. K., Gurjar, M. S., Diengdoh, L. C., Rai, R., & Singh, S. (2015). Potato (Solanum tuberosum) aeroponics for quality seed production in north eastern Himalayan region of India. *Indian Journal of Agricultural Sciences*, 85(10), 1360–1364. DOI:10.56093/ijas.v85i10.52303

Baillie, C. P., Thomasson, J. A., Lobsey, C. R., McCarthy, C. L., & Antille, D. L. (2018). A review of the state of the art in agricultural automation. Part I: Sensing technologies for optimization of machine operation and farm inputs. DOI:10.13031/aim.201801589

Balagopalan, A., Zhang, H., Hamidieh, K., Hartvigsen, T., Rudzicz, F., & Ghassemi, M. (2022). The road to explainability is paved with bias: Measuring the fairness of explanations. Proceedings of the 2022 ACM Conference on Fairness, Accountability, and Transparency.

Balla, M., Haffner, O., Kučera, E., & Cigánek, J. (2023). Educational Case Studies: Creating a Digital Twin of the Production Line in TIA Portal, Unity, and Game4Automation Framework. *Sensors (Basel)*, 23(10), 4977. DOI:10.3390/s23104977 PMID:37430895

Banerjee, T. P., & Das, S. (2012). Multi-sensor data fusion using support vector machine for motor fault detection. *Information Sciences*, 217, 96–107. DOI:10.1016/j.ins.2012.06.016

Barnard, H. (2023). *Developing a managerial framework for digital manufacturing in the new normal era* (Doctoral dissertation, North-West University (South Africa)).

Barreto-Cubero, A. J., Gómez-Espinosa, A., Escobedo Cabello, J. A., Cuan-Urquizo, E., & Cruz-Ramírez, S. R. (2021). Sensor data fusion for a mobile robot using neural networks. *Sensors (Basel)*, 22(1), 305. DOI:10.3390/s22010305 PMID:35009849

Bauch, C. T., Szusz, E., & Garrison, L. P. (2009). Scheduling of measles vaccination in low-income countries: Projections of a dynamic model. *Vaccine*, 27(31), 4090–4098. DOI:10.1016/j.vaccine.2009.04.079 PMID:19410622

Bedi, T., Rana, V., & Gautam, N. (2021). Changing Face Of The Apparel Industry By Incorporating Industry 4.0 And Paving Way For Industry 5.0. *Turkish Online Journal of Qualitative Inquiry, 12*(3).

Bellahsène, Z., Bonifati, A., & Rahm, E. (2011). *Schema matching and mapping*. Springer. DOI:10.1007/978-3-642-16518-4

Belli, L., Cirani, S., Davoli, L., Ferrari, G., Melegari, L., Montón, M., & Picone, M. (2015). A scalable big stream cloud architecture for the internet of things. *International Journal of Systems and Service-Oriented Engineering*, 5(4), 26–53. DOI:10.4018/IJSSOE.2015100102

Bellouquid, A., & Delitala, M. (2006). *Mathematical modeling of complex biological systems*. Birkhũser Boston.

Benabed, A., & Boeru, A. C. (2023). Globalization beyond Business Sustainability, Energy and the Economy of the Future. In *Proceedings of the International Conference on Business Excellence* (Vol. 17, No. 1, pp. 1569-1583). Sciendo. DOI:10.2478/picbe-2023-0141

Bethke-Langenegger, P., Mahler, P., & Staffelbach, B. (2011). Effectiveness of talent management strategies. *European Journal of International Management*, 5(5), 524–539. DOI:10.1504/EJIM.2011.042177

Bharadwaj, A. G. (2023). *Driving Reasoning Systems for Product Design and Flexible Robotic Manipulation Using 3D Design-Based AIs* (Doctoral dissertation, North Carolina State University).

Bhatti, M. R. A. (2021). *Light-driven Actuation In Ultra-drawn Chain-oriented Polymers* (Doctoral dissertation, Queen Mary University of London).

Bibri, S. E. (2018). The IoT for smart sustainable cities of the future: An analytical framework for sensor-based big data applications for environmental sustainability. *Sustainable Cities and Society*, 38(1), 230–253. DOI:10.1016/j.scs.2017.12.034

Bibri, S. E., & Krogstie, J. (2017). Smart sustainable cities of the future: An extensive interdisciplinary literature review. *Sustainable Cities and Society*, 31, 183–212. DOI:10.1016/j.scs.2017.02.016

Bifet, A., & Gavalda, R. (2007) Learning from time-changing data with adaptive windowing. In *Proceedings of the 2007 SIAM international conference on data mining*. SIAM. DOI:10.1137/1.9781611972771.42

Bjekić, D., Obradović, S., Vučetić, M., & Bojović, M. (2014). E-teacher in inclusive e-education for students with specific learning disabilities. *Procedia: Social and Behavioral Sciences*, 128, 128–133. DOI:10.1016/j.sbspro.2014.03.131

Blackburn, G. (2015). Innovative eLearning: Technology shaping contemporary problem based learning: A cross-case analysis. *Journal of University Teaching & Learning Practice*, 12(2), 5. DOI:10.53761/1.12.2.5

Blagec, K., Barbosa-Silva, A., Ott, S., & Samwald, M. (2022). A curated, ontology-based, large-scale AI of artificial intelligence tasks and benchmarks. *Scientific Data*, 9(1), 322. DOI:10.1038/s41597-022-01435-x PMID:35715466

Bolfe, É. L., Jorge, L. A. D. C., Sanches, I. D., Luchiari Júnior, A., Da Costa, C. C., Victoria, D. D. C., Inamasu, R. Y., Grego, C. R., Ferreira, V. R., & Ramirez, A. R. (2020). Precision and Digital Agriculture: Adoption of Technologies and Perception of Brazilian Farmers. *Agriculture*, 10(12), 653. DOI:10.3390/agriculture10120653

Bonatti, P. A., Decker, S., Polleres, A., & Presutti, V. (2019). AIs: New directions for knowledge representation on the semantic web (dagstuhl seminar 18371). *Dagstuhl Reports*, 8(9).

Bond, M., Buntins, K., Bedenlier, S., Zawacki-Richter, O., & Kerres, M. (2020). Mapping research in student engagement and educational technology in higher education: A systematic evidence map. *International Journal of Educational Technology in Higher Education*, 17(1), 1–30. DOI:10.1186/s41239-019-0176-8

Bongomin, O., Yemane, A., Kembabazi, B., Malanda, C., Mwape, M. C., Mpofu, N. S., & Tigalana, D. (2020). *The hype and disruptive technologies of industry 4.0 in major industrial sectors:A state of the art.*

Boopathi, S. (2022). Effects of Cryogenically-treated Stainless Steel on Eco-friendly Wire Electrical Discharge Machining Process. *Preprint : Springer.*

Boopathi, S. (2022c). Cryogenically treated and untreated stainless steel grade 317 in sustainable wire electrical discharge machining process: A comparative study. *Springer :Environmental Science and Pollution Research*, 1–10.

Boopathi, S. (2024a). Energy Cascade Conversion System and Energy-Efficient Infrastructure. In *Sustainable Development in AI, Blockchain, and E-Governance Applications* (pp. 47–71). IGI Global. DOI:10.4018/979-8-3693-1722-8.ch004

Boopathi, S. (2024b). Minimization of Manufacturing Industry Wastes Through the Green Lean Sigma Principle. *Sustainable Machining and Green Manufacturing*, 249–270.

Boopathi, S. (2024b). Sustainable Development Using IoT and AI Techniques for Water Utilization in Agriculture. In *Sustainable Development in AI, Blockchain, and E-Governance Applications* (pp. 204–228). IGI Global. DOI:10.4018/979-8-3693-1722-8.ch012

Boopathi, S., & Kumar, P. (2024). Advanced bioprinting processes using additive manufacturing technologies: Revolutionizing tissue engineering. *3D Printing Technologies: Digital Manufacturing, Artificial Intelligence, Industry 4.0*, 95.

Boopathi, S. (2022a). An extensive review on sustainable developments of dry and near-dry electrical discharge machining processes. *ASME: Journal of Manufacturing Science and Engineering*, 144(5), 050801–1.

Boopathi, S. (2022b). An investigation on gas emission concentration and relative emission rate of the near-dry wire-cut electrical discharge machining process. *Environmental Science and Pollution Research International*, 29(57), 86237–86246. DOI:10.1007/s11356-021-17658-1 PMID:34837614

Boopathi, S. (2024a). Advancements in Machine Learning and AI for Intelligent Systems in Drone Applications for Smart City Developments. In *Futuristic e-Governance Security With Deep Learning Applications* (pp. 15–45). IGI Global. DOI:10.4018/978-1-6684-9596-4.ch002

Boopathi, S., Alqahtani, A. S., Mubarakali, A., & Panchatcharam, P. (2023). Sustainable developments in near-dry electrical discharge machining process using sunflower oil-mist dielectric fluid. *Environmental Science and Pollution Research International*, 31(27), 1–20. DOI:10.1007/s11356-023-27494-0 PMID:37199846

Boopathi, S., & Davim, J. P. (2023). Applications of Nanoparticles in Various Manufacturing Processes. In *Sustainable Utilization of Nanoparticles and Nanofluids in Engineering Applications* (pp. 1–31). IGI Global. DOI:10.4018/978-1-6684-9135-5.ch001

Borda, A., Molnar, A., Neesham, C., & Kostkova, P. (2022). Ethical issues in AI-enabled disease surveillance: Perspectives from global health. *Applied Sciences (Basel, Switzerland)*, 12(8), 3890. DOI:10.3390/app12083890

Borgelt, S., Harrison, J., Sudduth, K., & Birrell, S. (1996). Evaluation of GPS for applications in precision agriculture. *Applied Engineering in Agriculture*, 12(6), 633–638. DOI:10.13031/2013.25692

Boursianis, A. D., Papadopoulou, M. S., Diamantoulakis, P., Liopa-Tsakalidi, A., Barouchas, P., Salahas, G., Karagiannidis, G., Wan, S., & Goudos, S. K. (2022). Internet of Things (IoT) and Agricultural Unmanned Aerial Vehicles (UAVs) in smart farming: A comprehensive review. *Internet of Things : Engineering Cyber Physical Human Systems*, 18, 100187. DOI:10.1016/j.iot.2020.100187

Bouslama, F., & Kalota, F. (2013). Creating smart classrooms to benefit from innovative technologies and learning space design. 2013 International Conference on Current Trends in Information Technology (CTIT).

Bower, M., & Sturman, D. (2015). What are the educational affordances of wearable technologies? *Computers & Education*, 88, 343–353. DOI:10.1016/j.compedu.2015.07.013

Brar, N. S., Kaushik, P., & Dudi, B. S. (2019). Assessment of natural ageing related physio-biochemical changes in onion seed. *Agriculture*, 9(8), 163. DOI:10.3390/agriculture9080163

Braver, S. L., Thoemmes, F. J., & Rosenthal, R. (2014). Continuously cumulating meta-analysis and replicability. *Perspectives on Psychological Science*, 9(3), 333–342. DOI:10.1177/1745691614529796 PMID:26173268

Brearley, G., Rhodes, J., Bradley, A., Baxter, G., Seabrook, L., Lunney, D., Liu, Y., & McAlpine, C. (2013). Wildlife disease prevalence in human-modified landscapes. *Biological Reviews of the Cambridge Philosophical Society*, 88(2), 427–442. DOI:10.1111/brv.12009 PMID:23279314

Brous, P., Janssen, M., Schraven, D., Spiegeler, J., & Duzgun, B. C. (2017). *Factors Influencing Adoption of IoT for Data-driven Decision Making in Asset Management Organizations. IoTBDS*.

Buchgeher, G., Gabauer, D., Martinez-Gil, J., & Ehrlinger, L. (2021). AIs in manufacturing and production: A systematic literature review. *IEEE Access : Practical Innovations, Open Solutions*, 9, 55537–55554. DOI:10.1109/ACCESS.2021.3070395

Büchner, M., Zürn, J., Todoran, I. G., Valada, A., & Burgard, W. (2023). Learning and aggregating lane MLs for urban automated driving. In *Proceedings of the IEEE/CVF Conference on Computer Vision and Pattern Recognition* (pp. 13415-13424).

Budzianowski, J., Kaczmarek-Majer, K., Rzeźniczak, J., Słomczyński, M., Wichrowski, F., Hiczkiewicz, D., Musielak, B., Grydz, Ł., Hiczkiewicz, J., & Burchardt, P. (2023). Machine learning model for predicting late recurrence of atrial fibrillation after catheter ablation. *Scientific Reports*, 13(1), 15213. DOI:10.1038/s41598-023-42542-y PMID:37709859

Burkom, H. S., Ramac-Thomas, L., Babin, S., Holtry, R., Mnatsakanyan, Z., & Yund, C. (2011). An integrated approach for fusion of environmental and human health data for disease surveillance. *Statistics in Medicine*, 30(5), 470–479. DOI:10.1002/sim.3976 PMID:21290403

Bustos-Lopez, M., Cruz-Ramirez, N., Guerra-Hernandez, A., Sánchez-Morales, L. N., Cruz-Ramos, N. A., & Alor-Hernandez, G. (2022). Wearables for engagement detection in learning environments: A review. *Biosensors (Basel)*, 12(7), 509. DOI:10.3390/bios12070509 PMID:35884312

Cai, H., Xu, B., Jiang, L., & Vasilakos, A. V. (2016). IoT-based big data storage systems in cloud computing: Perspectives and challenges. *IEEE Internet of Things Journal*, 4(1), 75–87. DOI:10.1109/JIOT.2016.2619369

Cai, L., Tian, Y., Liu, Z., Cheng, Q., Xu, J., & Ning, Y. (2016). Application of cloud computing to simulation of a heavy-duty machine tool. *International Journal of Advanced Manufacturing Technology*, 84(1-4), 291–303. DOI:10.1007/s00170-015-7916-2

Cai, P., Wang, H., Sun, Y., & Liu, M. (2022). DQ-GAT: Towards safe and efficient autonomous driving with deep Q-learning and ML attention networks. *IEEE Transactions on Intelligent Transportation Systems*, 23(11), 21102–21112. DOI:10.1109/TITS.2022.3184990

Calbimonte, J. P., Corcho, O., & Gray, A. J. (2010) Enabling ontology-based access to streaming data sources. In *International semantic Web conference*. Springer. DOI:10.1007/978-3-642-17746-0_7

Camarinha-Matos, L. M., Rocha, A. D., & Graça, P. (2024). Collaborative approaches in sustainable and resilient manufacturing. *Journal of Intelligent Manufacturing*, 35(2), 499–519. DOI:10.1007/s10845-022-02060-6 PMID:36532704

Campbell, M., Detres, M., & Lucio, R. (2019). Can a digital whiteboard foster student engagement? *Social Work Education*, 38(6), 735–752. DOI:10.1080/02615479.2018.1556631

Carpenter, J., Clifford, P., & Fearnhead, P. (1999). Improved particle filter for nonlinear problems. *IEE Proceedings. Radar, Sonar and Navigation*, 146(1), 2–7. DOI:10.1049/ip-rsn:19990255

Carrel, M., & Rennie, S. (2008). Demographic and health surveillance: Longitudinal ethical considerations. *Bulletin of the World Health Organization*, 86(8), 612–616. DOI:10.2471/BLT.08.051037 PMID:18797619

Carroll, M., Lindsey, S., Chaparro, M., & Winslow, B. (2021). An applied model of learner engagement and strategies for increasing learner engagement in the modern educational environment. *Interactive Learning Environments*, 29(5), 757–771. DOI:10.1080/10494820.2019.1636083

Cavalieri, A., Reis, J., & Amorim, M. (2021). Circular economy and internet of things: Mapping science of case studies in manufacturing industry. *Sustainability (Basel)*, 13(6), 3299. DOI:10.3390/su13063299

Cayre, R. (2022). *Offensive and defensive approaches for wireless communication protocols security in IoT* (Doctoral dissertation, Toulouse, INSA).

Cebrián, G., Palau, R., & Mogas, J. (2020). The smart classroom as a means to the development of ESD methodologies. *Sustainability (Basel)*, 12(7), 3010. DOI:10.3390/su12073010

Çela, E., Vajjhala, N. R., & Eappen, P. (2024). Foundations of Computational Thinking and Problem Solving for Diverse Academic Fields. *Revolutionizing Curricula Through Computational Thinking, Logic, and Problem Solving*, 1-16.

Çela, E. (2022). A summary of the national plan for european integration related with the developments of education system in Albania during 2020-2021. *Euro-Balkan Law and Economics Review*, (1), 71–86.

Çela, E. (2024). Global Agendas in Higher Education and Current Educational Reforms in Albania. In *Global Agendas and Education Reforms: A Comparative Study* (pp. 255–269). Springer. DOI:10.1007/978-981-97-3068-1_13

Çela, E., Fonkam, M. M., & Potluri, R. M. (2024). Risks of AI-Assisted Learning on Student Critical Thinking: A Case Study of Albania. *International Journal of Risk and Contingency Management*, 12(1), 1–19. DOI:10.4018/IJRCM.350185

Chagnon-Lessard, N., Gosselin, L., Barnabé, S., Bello-Ochende, T., Fendt, S., Goers, S., Da Silva, L. C. P., Schweiger, B., Simmons, R., & Vandersickel, A. (2021). Smart campuses: Extensive review of the last decade of research and current challenges. *IEEE Access : Practical Innovations, Open Solutions*, 9, 124200–124234. DOI:10.1109/ACCESS.2021.3109516

Chakravarthy, S. K., Sudhakar, N., Reddy, E. S., Subramanian, D. V., & Shankar, P. (2018). Dimension Reduction and Storage Optimization Techniques for Distributed and Big Data Cluster Environment. In *Soft Computing and Medical Bioinformatics* (pp. 47–54). Springer.

Challa, S., Palaniswami, M., & Shilton, A. (2002, July). Distributed data fusion using support vector machines. In *Proceedings of the Fifth International Conference on Information Fusion* (Vol. 2, pp. 881-885). IEEE. DOI:10.1109/ICIF.2002.1020902

Chang, M.-S., & Lee, M.-S. (2022). The integrated design process of the green-smart relocatable modular school building. *Journal of the Architectural Institute of Korea*, 38(5), 55–63.

Chang, Y. K., Zaman, Q., Farooque, A. A., Schumann, A. W., & Percival, D. C. (2012). An automated yield monitoring system II for commercial wild blueberry double-head harvester. *Computers and Electronics in Agriculture*, 81, 97–103. DOI:10.1016/j.compag.2011.11.012

Chang, Z., Liu, S., Xiong, X., Cai, Z., & Tu, G. (2021). A Survey of Recent Advances in Edge-Computing-Powered Artificial Intelligence of Things. *IEEE Internet of Things Journal*, 8(18), 13849–13875. DOI:10.1109/JIOT.2021.3088875

Chantry, M., Christensen, H., Dueben, P., & Palmer, T. (2021). Opportunities and challenges for machine learning in weather and climate modelling: Hard, medium and soft AI. *Philosophical Transactions. Series A, Mathematical, Physical, and Engineering Sciences*, 379(2194), 20200083. DOI:10.1098/rsta.2020.0083 PMID:33583261

Chaudhuri, R., Chatterjee, S., Vrontis, D., & Chaudhuri, S. (2022). Innovation in SMEs, AI dynamism, and sustainability: The current situation and way forward. *Sustainability (Basel)*, 14(19), 12760. DOI:10.3390/su141912760

Chedrawi, C., & Haddad, G. (2022). The rise of quasi-humans in AI fueled organizations, an ultimate socio-materiality approach to the lens of Michel Serres. *Pacific Asia Journal of the Association for Information Systems*, 14(2), 2. DOI:10.17705/1pais.14202

Cheese, P., Thomas, R. J., & Craig, E. (2007). *The talent powered organization: Strategies for globalization, talent management and high performance*. Kogan Page Publishers.

Chen, J., Chen, Y., Du, X., Li, C., Lu, J., Zhao, S., & Zhou, X. (2013). Big data Challenge: A Data Management perspective. *Frontiers of Computer Science*, 7(2), 157–164. DOI:10.1007/s11704-013-3903-7

Chen, M.-S., Han, J., & Yu, P. S. (1996). Data mining: An overview from a database perspective. *IEEE Transactions on Knowledge and Data Engineering*, 8(6), 866–883. DOI:10.1109/69.553155

Chen, W., Qiu, X., Cai, T., Dai, H.-N., Zheng, Z., & Zhang, Y. (2021). Deep reinforcement learning for Internet of Things: A comprehensive survey. *IEEE Communications Surveys and Tutorials*, 23(3), 1659–1692. DOI:10.1109/COMST.2021.3073036

Chen, X., Zou, D., Xie, H., & Wang, F. L. (2021). Past, present, and future of smart learning: A topic-based bibliometric analysis. *International Journal of Educational Technology in Higher Education*, 18(1), 2. DOI:10.1186/s41239-020-00239-6

Cheong, P. H., & Nyaupane, P. (2022). Smart campus communication, Internet of Things, and data governance: Understanding student tensions and imaginaries. *Big Data & Society*, 9(1), 205–226. DOI:10.1177/20539517221092656

Cherner, T., & Curry, K. (2017). Enhancement or transformation? A case study of preservice teachers' use of instructional technology. *Contemporary Issues in Technology & Teacher Education*, 17(2), 268–290.

Cheryan, S., Ziegler, S. A., Plaut, V. C., & Meltzoff, A. N. (2014). Designing classrooms to maximize student achievement. *Policy Insights from the Behavioral and Brain Sciences*, 1(1), 4–12. DOI:10.1177/2372732214548677

Cheung, M. W.-L. (2019). A guide to conducting a meta-analysis with non-independent effect sizes. *Neuropsychology Review*, 29(4), 387–396. DOI:10.1007/s11065-019-09415-6 PMID:31446547

Chiusano, S., Cerquitelli, T., Wrembel, R., & Quercia, D. (2021). Breakthroughs on cross-cutting data management, data analytics, and applied data science. *Information Systems Frontiers*, 23(1), 1–7. DOI:10.1007/s10796-020-10091-8

Chojnacka, K. (2024). Sustainable chemistry in adaptive agriculture: A review. *Current Opinion in Green and Sustainable Chemistry*, 46, 100898. DOI:10.1016/j.cogsc.2024.100898

Choobineh, M., Arab, A., Khodaei, A., & Paaso, A. (2022). Energy innovations through blockchain: Challenges, opportunities, and the road ahead. *The Electricity Journal*, 35(1), 107059. DOI:10.1016/j.tej.2021.107059

Chopade. (2024). Internet of Things in mechatronics for design and manufacturing: A review. Journals of Mechatronics Machine Design and Manufacturing, 6(1).

Chouhan, S. S., Kaul, A., & Singh, U. P. (2018). Soft computing approaches for image segmentation: A survey. *Multimedia Tools and Applications*, 77(21), 28483–28537. DOI:10.1007/s11042-018-6005-6

Cinelli, C., Kumor, D., Chen, B., Pearl, J., & Bareinboim, E. (2019). Sensitivity analysis of linear structural causal models. International conference on machine learning.

Coburn, K. M., & Vevea, J. L. (2015). Publication bias as a function of study characteristics. *Psychological Methods*, 20(3), 310–330. DOI:10.1037/met0000046 PMID:26348731

Collings, D. G., & Mellahi, K. (2009). Strategic talent management: A review and research agenda. *Human Resource Management Review*, 19(4), 304–313. DOI:10.1016/j.hrmr.2009.04.001

Cooch, E. G., Conn, P. B., Ellner, S. P., Dobson, A. P., & Pollock, K. H. (2012). Disease dynamics in wild populations: modeling and estimation: a review. *Journal of Ornithology*, 152(S2), 485–509. DOI:10.1007/s10336-010-0636-3

Cordell, G. A. (2024). The contemporary nexus of medicines security and bioprospecting: A future perspective for prioritizing the patient. *Natural Products and Bioprospecting*, 14(1), 1–32. DOI:10.1007/s13659-024-00431-5 PMID:38270809

Correia, A., Ferreira, L. M., Coimbra, P., Moura, P., & de Almeida, A. T. (2022). Smart thermostats for a campus microgrid: Demand control and improving air quality. *Energies*, 15(4), 1359. DOI:10.3390/en15041359

Coward, F. (2022). Reconstructing Social Networks: Transitional Changes from a Mobile Hunter-Gatherer to a Sedentary Neolithic Agrarian System. In Callan, H. (Ed.), *The International Encyclopedia of Anthropology* (1st ed., pp. 1–18). Wiley. DOI:10.1002/9781118924396.wbiea2527

Crockett, K. A., Gerber, L., Latham, A., & Colyer, E. (2021). Building trustworthy AI solutions: A case for practical solutions for small businesses. *IEEE Transactions on Artificial Intelligence*.

Cugola, G., & Margara, A. (2012). Processing flows of information: From data stream to complex event processing. *ACM Computing Surveys*, 44(3), 15. DOI:10.1145/2187671.2187677

Curran, P. J., & Hussong, A. M. (2009). Integrative data analysis: The simultaneous analysis of multiple data sets. *Psychological Methods*, 14(2), 81–100. DOI:10.1037/a0015914 PMID:19485623

Da Silveira, F., Da Silva, S. L. C., Machado, F. M., Barbedo, J. G. A., & Amaral, F. G. (2023). Farmers' perception of the barriers that hinder the implementation of agriculture 4.0. *Agricultural Systems*, 208, 103656. DOI:10.1016/j.agsy.2023.103656

Da Silveira, F., Lermen, F. H., & Amaral, F. G. (2021). An overview of agriculture 4.0 development: Systematic review of descriptions, technologies, barriers, advantages, and disadvantages. *Computers and Electronics in Agriculture*, 189, 106405. DOI:10.1016/j.compag.2021.106405

Dai, S., Liang, Y., Liu, S., Wang, Y., Shao, W., Lin, X., & Feng, X. (2018, March). Learning entity and relation embeddings with entity description for AI completion. In *2018 2nd International Conference on Artificial Intelligence: Technologies and Applications (ICAITA 2018)* (pp. 194-197). Atlantis Press.

Daraio, C., Lenzerini, M., Leporelli, C., Moed, H. F., Naggar, P., Bonaccorsi, A., & Bartolucci, A. (2016a). Data integration for research and innovation policy: An ontology-based data management approach. *Scientometrics*, 106(2), 857–871. DOI:10.1007/s11192-015-1814-0

Daraio, C., Lenzerini, M., Leporelli, C., Naggar, P., Bonaccorsi, A., & Bartolucci, A. (2016b). The advantages of an ontology-based data management approach: Openness, interoperability and data quality. *Scientometrics*, 108(1), 441–455. DOI:10.1007/s11192-016-1913-6

Daum, T. (2023). Mechanization and sustainable agri-food system transformation in the Global South. A review. *Agronomy for Sustainable Development*, 43(1), 16. DOI:10.1007/s13593-023-00868-x

Davis, F. D. (1989). Perceived Usefulness, Perceived Ease of Use, and User Acceptance of Information Technology. *Management Information Systems Quarterly*, 13(3), 319. DOI:10.2307/249008

de Villiers, J. P., Laskey, K., Jousselme, A. L., Blasch, E., de Waal, A., Pavlin, G., & Costa, P. (2015, July). Uncertainty representation, quantification and evaluation for data and information fusion. In *2015 18th International Conference on Information Fusion (Fusion)* (pp. 50-57). IEEE.

Declich, S., & Carter, A. O. (1994). Public health surveillance: Historical origins, methods and evaluation. *Bulletin of the World Health Organization*, 72(2), 285. PMID:8205649

Deeks, J. J., Higgins, J. P., Altman, D. G., & Group, C. S. M. (2019). Analysing data and undertaking meta-analyses. *Cochrane handbook for systematic reviews of interventions*, 241-284.

Deere, J. (n.d.). *ExactEmerge Planter Upgrade | John Deere*. Retrieved April 23, 2024, from https://www.deere.com/en/technology-products/precision-ag-technology/precision-upgrades/planter-upgrades/exactemerge-upgrade/

Deery, M. (2008). Talent management, work-life balance and retention strategies. *International Journal of Contemporary Hospitality Management*, 20(7), 792–806. DOI:10.1108/09596110810897619

Dehghanisanij, H., Emami, H., Emami, S., & Rezaverdinejad, V. (2022). A hybrid machine learning approach for estimating the water-use efficiency and yield in agriculture. *Scientific Reports*, 12(1), 6728. DOI:10.1038/s41598-022-10844-2 PMID:35469053

del Carmen Sandoval Madrid, A. (2023). *The nexus of sustainability and industry 5.0: Assessing Canadian organizations': Readiness for the next technological revolution* (Doctoral dissertation, University Canada West).

Demestichas, K., & Daskalakis, E. (2020). Information and communication technology solutions for the circular economy. *Sustainability (Basel)*, 12(18), 7272. DOI:10.3390/su12187272

Deng, C., Ji, X., Rainey, C., Zhang, J., & Lu, W. (2020). Integrating machine learning with human knowledge. *iScience*, 23(11), 101656. DOI:10.1016/j.isci.2020.101656 PMID:33134890

Deroncele-Acosta, A., Palacios-Núñez, M. L., & Toribio-López, A. (2023). Digital transformation and technological innovation on higher education post-COVID-19. *Sustainability (Basel)*, 15(3), 2466. DOI:10.3390/su15032466

Devi, S. (2022). A path towards child-centric artificial intelligence-based education. *International Journal of Early Childhood Special Education*, 14(3), 9915–9922.

Dhanaraju, M., Chenniappan, P., Ramalingam, K., Pazhanivelan, S., & Kaliaperumal, R. (2022). Smart Farming: Internet of Things (IoT)-Based Sustainable Agriculture. *Agriculture*, 12(10), 1745. DOI:10.3390/agriculture12101745

Dhanya, D., Kumar, S. S., Thilagavathy, A., Prasad, D., & Boopathi, S. (2023). Data Analytics and Artificial Intelligence in the Circular Economy: Case Studies. In *Intelligent Engineering Applications and Applied Sciences for Sustainability* (pp. 40–58). IGI Global.

Diao, X., Silver, J., & Takeshima, H. (n.d.). *Agricultural mechanization and agricultural transformation.*

Díaz-Rodríguez, N., Lamas, A., Sanchez, J., Franchi, G., Donadello, I., Tabik, S., Filliat, D., Cruz, P., Montes, R., & Herrera, F. (2022). EXplainable Neural-Symbolic Learning (X-NeSyL) methodology to fuse deep learning representations with expert AIs: The MonuMAI cultural heritage use case. *Information Fusion*, 79, 58–83. DOI:10.1016/j.inffus.2021.09.022

Diène, B., Rodrigues, J. J., Diallo, O., Ndoye, E. H. M., & Korotaev, V. V. (2020). Data management techniques for Internet of Things. *Mechanical Systems and Signal Processing*, 138, 106564. DOI:10.1016/j.ymssp.2019.106564

Dimitriadou, E., & Lanitis, A. (2023). A critical evaluation, challenges, and future perspectives of using artificial intelligence and emerging technologies in smart classrooms. *Smart Learning Environments*, 10(1), 12. DOI:10.1186/s40561-023-00231-3

Dimkpa, C., Bindraban, P., McLean, J. E., Gatere, L., Singh, U., & Hellums, D. (2017). Methods for Rapid Testing of Plant and Soil Nutrients. In Lichtfouse, E. (Ed.), *Sustainable Agriculture Reviews* (Vol. 25, pp. 1–43). Springer International Publishing. DOI:10.1007/978-3-319-58679-3_1

Ding, H., Ji, H., Huang, Z., & Li, H. (2004, June). Data fusion algorithm based on fuzzy logic. In *Fifth World Congress on Intelligent Control and Automation* (IEEE Cat. No. 04EX788) (Vol. 4, pp. 3101-3103). IEEE. DOI:10.1109/WCICA.2004.1343091

Dmitrieva, E., Balmiki, V., Lakhanpal, S., Lavanya, G., & Bhandari, P. (2024). AI Evolution in Industry 4.0 and Industry 5.0: An Experimental Comparative Assessment. In *BIO Web of Conferences* (Vol. 86, p. 01069). EDP Sciences.

Doan, A., Domingos, P. M., & Levy, A. Y. (2000) Learning source description for data integration. In: *WebDB (informal proceedings)*, pp 81–86

Doan, Q. T., Kayes, A., Rahayu, W., & Nguyen, K. (2020). Integration of iot streaming data with efficient indexing and storage optimization. *IEEE Access : Practical Innovations, Open Solutions*, 8, 47456–47467. DOI:10.1109/ACCESS.2020.2980006

Dong, B., Prakash, V., Feng, F., & O'Neill, Z. (2019). A review of smart building sensing system for better indoor environment control. *Energy and Building*, 199, 29–46. DOI:10.1016/j.enbuild.2019.06.025

Doukas, C., Pliakas, T., & Maglogiannis, I. (2010, August). Mobile healthcare information management utilizing Cloud Computing and Android OS. In *2010 Annual International Conference of the IEEE Engineering in Medicine and Biology* (pp. 1037-1040). IEEE.

Draschner, C. F., Jabeen, H., & Lehmann, J. (2022, September). Ethical and sustainability considerations for AI-based machine learning. In *2022 IEEE Fifth International Conference on Artificial Intelligence and Knowledge Engineering (AIKE)* (pp. 53-60). IEEE.

Drewe, J. A., Hoinville, L. J., Cook, A. J. C., Floyd, T., & Stärk, K. D. C. (2012). Evaluation of animal and public health surveillance systems: A systematic review. *Epidemiology and Infection*, 140(4), 575–590. DOI:10.1017/S0950268811002160 PMID:22074638

Drosou, M., Jagadish, H. V., Pitoura, E., & Stoyanovich, J. (2017). Diversity in big data: A review. *Big Data*, 5(2), 73–84. DOI:10.1089/big.2016.0054 PMID:28632443

Dugas, A. F., Hsieh, Y. H., Levin, S. R., Pines, J. M., Mareiniss, D. P., Mohareb, A., Gaydos, C. A., Perl, T. M., & Rothman, R. E. (2012). Google Flu Trends: Correlation with emergency department influenza rates and crowding metrics. *Clinical Infectious Diseases*, 54(4), 463–469. DOI:10.1093/cid/cir883 PMID:22230244

Dugas, A. F., Jalalpour, M., Gel, Y., Levin, S., Torcaso, F., Igusa, T., & Rothman, R. E. (2013). Influenza forecasting with Google flu trends. *PLoS One*, 8(2), e56176. DOI:10.1371/journal.pone.0056176 PMID:23457520

Dumitru, O. M., Iorga, S., Vladut, N. V., & Bracacescu, C. (2020). Food losses in primary cereal production. A review. *INMATEH - Agricultural Engineering*, 133–146. DOI:10.35633/inmateh-62-14

Dutta, P. (2020). *Occupancy Based Load Switching using Microcontroller* (Doctoral dissertation, University of Technology).

Dysko, J., Kaniszewski, S., & Kowalczyk, W. (2015). Lignite as a new medium in soilless cultivation of tomato. *Journal of Elementology*, 20(3).

Effendi, M. R., Sidik Al-Falah, R., & Ismail, N. (2021). IoT-Based Battery Monitoring System in Solar Power Plants with Secure Copy Protocol (SCP). *2021 7th International Conference on Wireless and Telematics (ICWT)*, 1–4. DOI:10.1109/ICWT52862.2021.9678210

Efron, B., Hastie, T., Johnstone, I., & Tibshirani, R. (2004). Least angle regression.

Eisenberg, J. N., Desai, M. A., Levy, K., Bates, S. J., Liang, S., Naumoff, K., & Scott, J. C. (2007). Environmental determinants of infectious disease: A framework for tracking causal links and guiding public health research. *Environmental Health Perspectives*, 115(8), 1216–1223. DOI:10.1289/ehp.9806 PMID:17687450

Elahi, M. F., Luo, X., & Tian, R. (2020, July). A framework for modeling AIs via processing natural descriptions of vehicle-pedestrian interactions. In *International Conference on Human-Computer Interaction* (pp. 40-50). Cham: Springer International Publishing.

Elkin, C., & Witherspoon, S. (2019). Machine learning can boost the value of wind energy. *deep mind field study*.

El-Mougy, A., Al-Shiab, I., & Ibnkahla, M. (2019). Scalable personalized IoT networks. *Proceedings of the IEEE*, 107(4), 695–710. DOI:10.1109/JPROC.2019.2894515

Escamilla-Ambrosio, P., Rodríguez-Mota, A., Aguirre-Anaya, E., Acosta-Bermejo, R., & Salinas-Rosales, M. (2018). Distributing computing in the internet of things: cloud, fog and edge computing overview. NEO 2016: Results of the Numerical and Evolutionary Optimization Workshop NEO 2016 and the NEO Cities 2016 Workshop held on September 20-24, 2016 in Tlalnepantla, Mexico.

Etzion, D., & Aragon-Correa, J. A. (2016). *Big data, management, and sustainability: Strategic opportunities ahead* (Vol. 29). Sage Publications Sage CA.

Fähndrich, J., & Trollmann, F. (2021). AI Reading, or Automatic Semantic Decomposition into AIs and Symbolic reasoning through Marker Passing.

Faid, A., Sadik, M., & Sabir, E. (2020). IoT-based Low Cost Architecture for Smart Farming. *2020 International Wireless Communications and Mobile Computing (IWCMC)*, 1296–1302. DOI:10.1109/IWCMC48107.2020.9148455

Falzon, L. C., Ogola, J. G., Odinga, C. O., Naboyshchikov, L., Fèvre, E. M., & Berezowski, J. (2021). Electronic data collection to enhance disease surveillance at the slaughterhouse in a smallholder production system. *Scientific Reports*, 11(1), 19447. DOI:10.1038/s41598-021-98495-7 PMID:34593856

Fanoro, M., Božanić, M., & Sinha, S. (2021). A review of 4IR/5IR enabling technologies and their linkage to manufacturing supply chain. *Technologies*, 9(4), 77. DOI:10.3390/technologies9040077

Farmmachinerysales. (2022). *CLAAS announces 2023 upgrades for JAGUAR.* https://www.farmmachinerysales.com.au/editorial/details/claas-announces-2023-upgrades-for-jaguar-138854/

Fawehinmi, O., Aigbogun, O., & Tanveer, M. I. (2024). The Role of Industrial Revolution 5.0 in Actualizing the Effectiveness of Green Human Resource Management. In *Green Human Resource Management: A View from Global South Countries* (pp. 291–312). Springer Nature Singapore. DOI:10.1007/978-981-99-7104-6_17

Fawzy, D., Moussa, S. M., & Badr, N. L. (2022). The internet of things and architectures of big data analytics: Challenges of intersection at different domains. *IEEE Access : Practical Innovations, Open Solutions*, 10, 4969–4992. DOI:10.1109/ACCESS.2022.3140409

Feldman, M., Friedler, S. A., Moeller, J., Scheidegger, C., & Venkatasubramanian, S. (2015, August). Certifying and removing disparate impact. In *proceedings of the 21th ACM SIGKDD international conference on knowledge discovery and data mining* (pp. 259-268). DOI:10.1145/2783258.2783311

Fennimore, S. A., Slaughter, D. C., Siemens, M. C., Leon, R. G., & Saber, M. N. (2016). Technology for Automation of Weed Control in Specialty Crops. *Weed Technology*, 30(4), 823–837. DOI:10.1614/WT-D-16-00070.1

Fernández-Delgado, M., Cernadas, E., Barro, S., & Amorim, D. (2014). Do we need hundreds of classifiers to solve real world classification problems? *Journal of Machine Learning Research*, 15(1), 3133–3181.

Firmin, M. W., & Genesi, D. J. (2013). History and implementation of classroom technology. *Procedia: Social and Behavioral Sciences*, 93, 1603–1617. DOI:10.1016/j.sbspro.2013.10.089

Flanigen, P. (2023). *Algorithms and Visualizations to Support Airborne Detection of Vertical Obstacles* (Doctoral dissertation).

Formen, J. S., Hassan, D. S., & Wolf, C. (2024). Chemometric sensing of stereoisomeric compound mixtures with a redox-responsive optical probe. *Chemical Science (Cambridge)*, 15(4), 1498–1504. DOI:10.1039/D3SC05706B PMID:38274061

Fraser, A. G., & Marcotte, E. M. (2004). A probabilistic view of gene function. *Nature Genetics*, 36(6), 559–564. DOI:10.1038/ng1370 PMID:15167932

Gala, N., Poswalia, A., & Gharat, R. (2023). Electric Bike Security: Biometric & GPS Integration for Intrusion Detection. *2023 International Conference on Sustainable Computing and Data Communication Systems (ICSCDS)*, 1618–1627. DOI:10.1109/ICSCDS56580.2023.10105001

García-Tudela, P. A., Prendes-Espinosa, M. P., & Solano-Fernández, I. M. (2020). Smart learning environments and ergonomics: An approach to the state of the question. *Journal of New Approaches in Educational Research*, 9(2), 245–258. DOI:10.7821/naer.2020.7.562

Gaudel, R., Galárraga, L., Delaunay, J., Rozé, L., & Bhargava, V. (2022). s-LIME: Reconciling locality and fidelity in linear explanations. International Symposium on Intelligent Data Analysis. DOI:10.1007/s00146-020-00971-7

Geller, T. (2016). Farm automation gets smarter. *Communications of the ACM*, 59(11), 18–19. DOI:10.1145/2994579

Geneviève, L. D., Martani, A., Wangmo, T., Paolotti, D., Koppeschaar, C., Kjelsø, C., Guerrisi, C., Hirsch, M., Woolley-Meza, O., Lukowicz, P., Flahault, A., & Elger, B. S. (2019). Participatory disease surveillance systems: Ethical framework. *Journal of Medical Internet Research*, 21(5), e12273. DOI:10.2196/12273 PMID:31124466

Giesenbauer, B., & Müller-Christ, G. (2020). University 4.0: Promoting the transformation of higher education institutions toward sustainable development. *Sustainability (Basel)*, 12(8), 3371. DOI:10.3390/su12083371

Gill, S. S., Xu, M., Ottaviani, C., Patros, P., Bahsoon, R., Shaghaghi, A., Golec, M., Stankovski, V., Wu, H., Abraham, A., Singh, M., Mehta, H., Ghosh, S. K., Baker, T., Parlikad, A. K., Lutfiyya, H., Kanhere, S. S., Sakellariou, R., Dustdar, S., & Uhlig, S. (2022). AI for next generation computing: Emerging trends and future directions. *Internet of Things : Engineering Cyber Physical Human Systems*, 19, 100514. DOI:10.1016/j.iot.2022.100514

Gilman, E., Tamminen, S., Yasmin, R., Ristimella, E., Peltonen, E., Harju, M., Lovén, L., Riekki, J., & Pirttikangas, S. (2020). Internet of things for smart spaces: A university campus case study. *Sensors (Basel)*, 20(13), 3716. DOI:10.3390/s20133716 PMID:32630833

Glady, J. B. P., D'Souza, S. M., Priya, A. P., Amuthachenthiru, K., Vikram, G., & Boopathi, S. (2024). A Study on AI-ML-Driven Optimizing Energy Distribution and Sustainable Agriculture for Environmental Conservation. In *Harnessing High-Performance Computing and AI for Environmental Sustainability* (pp. 1–27). IGI Global. DOI:10.4018/979-8-3693-1794-5.ch001

Gligorea, I., Cioca, M., Oancea, R., Gorski, A.-T., Gorski, H., & Tudorache, P. (2023). Adaptive learning using artificial intelligence in e-learning: A literature review. *Education Sciences*, 13(12), 1216. DOI:10.3390/educsci13121216

Gnanaprakasam, C., Vankara, J., Sastry, A. S., Prajval, V., Gireesh, N., & Boopathi, S. (2023). Long-Range and Low-Power Automated Soil Irrigation System Using Internet of Things: An Experimental Study. In *Contemporary Developments in Agricultural Cyber-Physical Systems* (pp. 87–104). IGI Global.

Göçen, A., Eral, S. H., & Bücük, M. H. (2020). Teacher perceptions of a 21st century classroom. *International Journal of Contemporary Educational Research*, 7(1), 85–98. DOI:10.33200/ijcer.638110

Goetz, S. J., Prince, S. D., & Small, J. (2000). Advances in satellite remote sensing of environmental variables for epidemiological applications. *Advances in Parasitology*, 47, 289–307. DOI:10.1016/S0065-308X(00)47012-0 PMID:10997210

Gonzalez-Manzano, L., Fuentes, J. M. D., & Ribagorda, A. (2019). Leveraging user-related internet of things for continuous authentication: A survey. *ACM Computing Surveys*, 52(3), 1–38. DOI:10.1145/3314023

González-Martínez, J. A., Bote-Lorenzo, M. L., Gómez-Sánchez, E., & Cano-Parra, R. (2015). Cloud computing and education: A state-of-the-art survey. *Computers & Education*, 80, 132–151. DOI:10.1016/j.compedu.2014.08.017

Gouse, K. (2018). Machine learning-based system food quality inspection and grading in food industry. *International Journal of Food and Nutritional Sciences*, 11(10), 723–730.

Gowri, N. V., Dwivedi, J. N., Krishnaveni, K., Boopathi, S., Palaniappan, M., & Medikondu, N. R. (2023). Experimental investigation and multi-objective optimization of eco-friendly near-dry electrical discharge machining of shape memory alloy using Cu/SiC/Gr composite electrode. *Environmental Science and Pollution Research International*, 30(49), 1–19. DOI:10.1007/s11356-023-26983-6 PMID:37126160

Grahmann, K., Reckling, M., Hernández-Ochoa, I., Donat, M., Bellingrath-Kimura, S., & Ewert, F. (2024). Co-designing a landscape experiment to investigate diversified cropping systems. *Agricultural Systems*, 217, 103950. DOI:10.1016/j.agsy.2024.103950

Grashof, N., & Kopka, A. (2023). Artificial intelligence and radical innovation: An opportunity for all companies? *Small Business Economics*, 61(2), 771–797. DOI:10.1007/s11187-022-00698-3

Greenland, S., Pearl, J., & Robins, J. M. (1999). Causal diagrams for epidemiologic research. *Epidemiology (Cambridge, Mass.)*, 10(1), 37–48. DOI:10.1097/00001648-199901000-00008 PMID:9888278

Gregorcic, B., & Haglund, J. (2021). Conceptual blending as an interpretive lens for student engagement with technology: Exploring celestial motion on an interactive whiteboard. *Research in Science Education*, 51(2), 235–275. DOI:10.1007/s11165-018-9794-8

Gubbi, J., Buyya, R., Marusic, S., & Palaniswami, M. (2013). Internet of Things (IoT): A vision, architectural elements, and future directions. *Future Generation Computer Systems*, 29(7), 1645–1660. DOI:10.1016/j.future.2013.01.010

Gu, D., Andreev, K., & Dupre, E., M. (. (2021). Major Trends in Population Growth Around the World. *China CDC Weekly*, 3(28), 604–613. DOI:10.46234/ccdcw2021.160 PMID:34594946

Guerriero, M., Svensson, L., & Willett, P. (2010). Bayesian data fusion for distributed target detection in sensor networks. *IEEE Transactions on Signal Processing*, 58(6), 3417–3421. DOI:10.1109/TSP.2010.2046042

Gumbo, S., Twinomurinzi, H., Bwalya, K., & Wamba, S. F. (2023). Skills provisioning for the Fourth Industrial Revolution: A Bibliometric Analysis. *Procedia Computer Science*, 219, 924–932. DOI:10.1016/j.procs.2023.01.368

Guo, R., Hong, Z., & Xue, X. (2021). Reward function design via human AI and inverse reinforcement learning for intelligent driving (No. 2021-01-0180). *SAE Technical Paper*.

Gupta, M., Abdelsalam, M., Khorsandroo, S., & Mittal, S. (2020). Security and Privacy in Smart Farming: Challenges and Opportunities. *IEEE Access, 8*, 34564–34584. DOI:10.1109/ACCESS.2020.2975142

Gupta, H., Kumar, A., & Wasan, P. (2021). Industry 4.0, cleaner production and circular economy: An integrative framework for evaluating ethical and sustainable business performance of manufacturing organizations. *Journal of Cleaner Production*, 295, 126253. DOI:10.1016/j.jclepro.2021.126253

Gustafsson, F. (2010). Particle filter theory and practice with positioning applications. *IEEE Aerospace and Electronic Systems Magazine*, 25(7), 53–82. DOI:10.1109/MAES.2010.5546308

Gutiérrez Peña, J. A. (2022). Cost effective technology applied to domotics and smart home energy management systems.

Guzewich, J. J., Bryan, F. L., & Todd, E. C. (1997). Surveillance of foodborne disease I. Purposes and types of surveillance systems and networks. *Journal of Food Protection*, 60(5), 555–566. DOI:10.4315/0362-028X-60.5.555 PMID:31195586

Gwala, R. S., & Mashau, P. (2024). Equality, Diversity, and Access in Digitalized Teaching in Higher Education. In *Accessibility of Digital Higher Education in the Global South* (pp. 105–131). IGI Global.

Haleem, A., & Javaid, M. (2019). Additive manufacturing applications in industry 4.0: A review. *Journal of Industrial Integration and Management*, 4(04), 1930001. DOI:10.1142/S2424862219300011

Halilaj, L., Dindorkar, I., Lüttin, J., & Rothermel, S. (2021). An AI-based approach for situation comprehension in driving scenarios. *The Semantic Web: 18th International Conference, ESWC 2021, Virtual Event, June 6–10, 2021 Proceedings*, 18, 699–716.

Halilaj, L., Luettin, J., Henson, C., & Monka, S. (2022, September). AIs for automated driving. In *2022 IEEE Fifth International Conference on Artificial Intelligence and Knowledge Engineering (AIKE)* (pp. 98-105). IEEE.

Halilaj, L., Luettin, J., Monka, S., Henson, C., & Schmid, S. (2023). AI-Based Integration of Autonomous Driving Datasets. *International Journal of Semantic Computing*, 17(02), 249–271. DOI:10.1142/S1793351X23600048

Halli, U. M. (2022). Nanotechnology in IoT security. Journal of Nanoscience. *Nanoengineering & Applications*, 12(3), 11–16.

Han, H., & Trimi, S. (2022a). Towards a data science platform for improving SME collaboration through Industry 4.0 technologies. *Technological Forecasting and Social Change*, 174, 121242. DOI:10.1016/j.techfore.2021.121242

Han, L., Long, X., & Wang, K. (2024). The analysis of educational informatization management learning model under the internet of things and artificial intelligence. *Scientific Reports*, 14(1), 17811. DOI:10.1038/s41598-024-68963-x PMID:39090332

Hannan, M., Al Mamun, M. A., Hussain, A., Basri, H., & Begum, R. A. (2015). A review on technologies and their usage in solid waste monitoring and management systems: Issues and challenges. *Waste Management (New York, N.Y.)*, 43, 509–523. DOI:10.1016/j.wasman.2015.05.033 PMID:26072186

Harding, E. L., Vanto, J. J., Clark, R., Hannah Ji, L., & Ainsworth, S. C. (2019). Understanding the scope and impact of the california consumer privacy act of 2018. *Journal of Data Protection & Privacy*, 2(3), 234–253. DOI:10.69554/TCFN5165

Hasan, K., & Ahmed, T. (2017). *Applications of Internet of Things (IoT) Towards Smart Home Automation* (Doctoral dissertation, Stamford University Bangladesh).

Hashim, M. A. M., Tlemsani, I., Mason-Jones, R., Matthews, R., & Ndrecaj, V. (2024). Higher education via the lens of industry 5.0: Strategy and perspective. *Social Sciences & Humanities Open*, 9, 100828. DOI:10.1016/j.ssaho.2024.100828

Hashim, S., Omar, M. K., Ab Jalil, H., & Sharef, N. M. (2022). Trends on technologies and artificial intelligence in education for personalized learning: Systematic literature. *Journal of Academic Research in Progressive Education and Development*, 12(1), 884–903. DOI:10.6007/IJARPED/v11-i1/12230

Heidemann, J., Silva, F., Intanagonwiwat, C., Govindan, R., Estrin, D., & Ganesan, D. (2001, October). Building efficient wireless sensor networks with low-level naming. In *Proceedings of the eighteenth ACM symposium on Operating systems principles* (pp. 146-159). DOI:10.1145/502034.502049

He, J., Lo, D. C.-T., Xie, Y., & Lartigue, J. (2016). Integrating Internet of Things (IoT) into STEM undergraduate education: Case study of a modern technology infused courseware for embedded system course. 2016 IEEE frontiers in education conference (FIE).

Hema, N., Krishnamoorthy, N., Chavan, S. M., Kumar, N., Sabarimuthu, M., & Boopathi, S. (2023). A Study on an Internet of Things (IoT)-Enabled Smart Solar Grid System. In *Handbook of Research on Deep Learning Techniques for Cloud-Based Industrial IoT* (pp. 290–308). IGI Global. DOI:10.4018/978-1-6684-8098-4.ch017

Henrie, C. R., Halverson, L. R., & Graham, C. R. (2015). Measuring student engagement in technology-mediated learning: A review. *Computers & Education*, 90, 36–53. DOI:10.1016/j.compedu.2015.09.005

Hogan, A., Blomqvist, E., Cochez, M., d'Amato, C., Melo, G. D., Gutierrez, C., Kirrane, S., Gayo, J. E. L., Navigli, R., Neumaier, S., Ngomo, A.-C. N., Polleres, A., Rashid, S. M., Rula, A., Schmelzeisen, L., Sequeda, J., Staab, S., & Zimmermann, A. (2021). AIs. *ACM Computing Surveys*, 54(4), 1–37. DOI:10.1145/3447772

Holland, N. (2023). *New Holland previews next-generation flagship combine in bold statement of intent at Agritechnica | New Holland UK.* https://agriculture.newholland .com/en-gb/europe/new-holland-world/news/2023/new-holland-previews-next -generation-flagship-combines-at-agritechnica

Holzinger, A., Saranti, A., Hauschild, A. C., Beinecke, J., Heider, D., Roettger, R., . . . Pfeifer, B. (2023, August). Human-in-the-loop integration with domain-AIs for explainable federated deep learning. In *International Cross-Domain Conference for Machine Learning and Knowledge Extraction* (pp. 45-64). Cham: Springer Nature Switzerland. DOI:10.1007/978-3-031-40837-3_4

Hongyan, G. A. O. (2009, August). A simple multi-sensor data fusion algorithm based on principal component analysis. In *2009 ISECS International Colloquium on Computing, Communication, Control, and Management* (Vol. 2, pp. 423-426). IEEE. DOI:10.1109/CCCM.2009.5267459

Hoyo-Montaño, J. A., Valencia-Palomo, G., Galaz-Bustamante, R. A., García-Barrientos, A., & Espejel-Blanco, D. F. (2019). Environmental impacts of energy saving actions in an academic building. *Sustainability (Basel)*, 11(4), 989. DOI:10.3390/su11040989

Huang, H., Sun, L., Du, B., Liu, C., Lv, W., & Xiong, H. (2021, August). Representation learning on AIs for node importance estimation. In *Proceedings of the 27th ACM SIGKDD Conference on Knowledge Discovery & Data Mining* (pp. 646-655).

Hussain, M. I. (2017). Internet of Things: challenges and research opportunities. *CSI transactions on ICT, 5*, 87-95.

Hussain, Z., Babe, M., Saravanan, S., Srimathy, G., Roopa, H., & Boopathi, S. (2023). Optimizing Biomass-to-Biofuel Conversion: IoT and AI Integration for Enhanced Efficiency and Sustainability. In *Circular Economy Implementation for Sustainability in the Built Environment* (pp. 191–214). IGI Global.

Hussain, A. J., Al-Fayadh, A., & Radi, N. (2018). Image compression techniques: A survey in lossless and lossy algorithms. *Neurocomputing*, 300, 44–69. DOI:10.1016/j.neucom.2018.02.094

Hussain, A., Ansari, H. W. A., Nasir, H., & Maqbool, M. Q. (2023). Developing a Model for the Adoption of Industrial Revolution 5.0 Among Malaysian Manufacturing SMEs for Sustainable Growth. In *Opportunities and Challenges of Business 5.0 in Emerging Markets* (pp. 40–57). IGI Global. DOI:10.4018/978-1-6684-6403-8.ch003

Hussain, M., Zhu, W., Zhang, W., & Abidi, S. M. R. (2018). Student Engagement Predictions in an e-Learning System and Their Impact on Student Course Assessment Scores. *Computational Intelligence and Neuroscience*, 2018(1), 634–645. DOI:10.1155/2018/6347186 PMID:30369946

Husson, O. (2013). Redox potential (Eh) and pH as drivers of soil/plant/microorganism systems: A transdisciplinary overview pointing to integrative opportunities for agronomy. *Plant and Soil*, 362(1–2), 389–417. DOI:10.1007/s11104-012-1429-7

Hu, X., Liu, Y., Tang, B., Yan, J., & Chen, L. (2023). Learning dynamic ML for overtaking strategy in autonomous driving. *IEEE Transactions on Intelligent Transportation Systems*, 24(11), 11921–11933. DOI:10.1109/TITS.2023.3287223

Hwang, K., & Chen, M. (2017). *Big-data analytics for cloud, IoT and cognitive computing.* John Wiley & Sons.

Idoje, G., Dagiuklas, T., & Iqbal, M. (2021). Survey for smart farming technologies: Challenges and issues. *Computers & Electrical Engineering*, 92, 107104. DOI:10.1016/j.compeleceng.2021.107104

Ipate, G., Voicu, G., & Dinu, I. (2015). Research on the use of drones in precision agriculture. *University Politehnica of Bucharest Bulletin Series*, 77(4), 1–12.

Iqbal, H. M., Parra-Saldivar, R., Zavala-Yoe, R., & Ramirez-Mendoza, R. A. (2020). Smart educational tools and learning management systems: Supportive framework. *International Journal on Interactive Design and Manufacturing*, 14(4), 1179–1193. DOI:10.1007/s12008-020-00695-4

Iqbal, T., Ghaffar, A. M., Ur Rehman, U., Saeed, Y., Aqib, M., Iqbal, F., & Saleem, S. R. (2022). Development of Real Time Seed Depth Control System for Seeders. *PAPC*, 7, 7. Advance online publication. DOI:10.3390/environsciproc2022023007

Irpan, M., & Shaddiq, S. (2024). Industry 4.0 and Industry 5.0—Inception, Conception, Perception, and Rethinking Loyalty Employment. *International Journal of Economics, Management, Business, and Social Science*, 4(1), 95–114.

Islam, M. S., Amin, S., Arifuzzaman, M., Rahman, M. H., & Hossain, R. (2023). *Automatic Train Wash Plant on Metro System* (Doctoral dissertation, Sonargoan University (SU)).

Ismail, M. M., Ahmed, Z., Abdel-Gawad, A. F., & Mohamed, M. (2024). Toward Supply Chain 5.0: An Integrated Multi-Criteria Decision-Making Models for Sustainable and Resilience Enterprise. *Decision making: applications in management and engineering, 7*(1), 160-186.

Ismaili, J., & Ibrahimi, E. H. O. (2017). Mobile learning as alternative to assistive technology devices for special needs students. *Education and Information Technologies*, 22(3), 883–899. DOI:10.1007/s10639-015-9462-9

Jagatheesaperumal, S. K., Pham, Q.-V., Ruby, R., Yang, Z., Xu, C., & Zhang, Z. (2022). Explainable AI over the Internet of Things (IoT): Overview, state-of-the-art and future directions. *IEEE Open Journal of the Communications Society*, 3, 2106–2136. DOI:10.1109/OJCOMS.2022.3215676

Janardhana, K., Singh, V., Singh, S. N., Babu, T. R., Bano, S., & Boopathi, S. (2023). Utilization Process for Electronic Waste in Eco-Friendly Concrete: Experimental Study. In *Sustainable Approaches and Strategies for E-Waste Management and Utilization* (pp. 204–223). IGI Global.

Jat, D. S., Limbo, A. S., & Singh, C. (2021). Internet of Things for Automation in Smart Agriculture: A Technical Review. In *Research Anthology on Recent Trends* (Vol. 1). Tools, and Implications of Computer Programming. DOI:10.4018/978-1-6684-3694-3.ch025

Javaid, M., Haleem, A., Singh, R. P., & Suman, R. (2022). Enhancing smart farming through the applications of Agriculture 4.0 technologies. *International Journal of Intelligent Networks*, 3, 150–164. DOI:10.1016/j.ijin.2022.09.004

Jeba, N., & Rathi, S. (2021). Effective data management and real-time analytics in internet of things. *International Journal of Cloud Computing*, 10(1-2), 112–128. DOI:10.1504/IJCC.2021.113994

Jiang, Q., Zhou, X., Wang, R., Ding, W., Chu, Y., Tang, S., Jia, X., & Xu, X. (2022). Intelligent monitoring for infectious diseases with fuzzy systems and edge computing: A survey. *Applied Soft Computing*, 123, 108835. DOI:10.1016/j.asoc.2022.108835

Jiao, Y., Wang, P., Feng, S., & Niyato, D. (2018). Profit maximization mechanism and data management for data analytics services. *IEEE Internet of Things Journal*, 5(3), 2001–2014. DOI:10.1109/JIOT.2018.2819706

Jillahi, K. B., & Iorliam, A. (2024). A Scoping Literature Review of Artificial Intelligence in Epidemiology: Uses, Applications, Challenges and Future Trends. *Journal of Computing Theories and Applications*, 2(2), 204–228. DOI:10.62411/jcta.10350

Ji, S., Pan, S., Cambria, E., Marttinen, P., & Philip, S. Y. (2021). A survey on AIs: Representation, acquisition, and applications. *IEEE Transactions on Neural Networks and Learning Systems*, 33(2), 494–514. DOI:10.1109/TNNLS.2021.3070843 PMID:33900922

Jokubauskis, D. (2020). *Development and applications of compact spectroscopic terahertz imaging systems using principles of optical beam engineering* (Doctoral dissertation, Vilniaus universitetas).

Jolles, J. W. (2021). Broad-scale applications of the Raspberry Pi: A review and guide for biologists. *Methods in Ecology and Evolution*, 12(9), 1562–1579. DOI:10.1111/2041-210X.13652

Jordan, A. A., Pegatoquet, A., Castagnetti, A., Raybaut, J., & Le Coz, P. (2020). Deep learning for eye blink detection implemented at the edge. *IEEE Embedded Systems Letters*, 13(3), 130–133. DOI:10.1109/LES.2020.3029313

Jung, T., Li, X.-Y., Wan, Z., & Wan, M. (2014). Control cloud data access privilege and anonymity with fully anonymous attribute-based encryption. *IEEE Transactions on Information Forensics and Security*, 10(1), 190–199. DOI:10.1109/TIFS.2014.2368352

Jung, W.-K., Kim, D.-R., Lee, H., Lee, T.-H., Yang, I., Youn, B. D., Zontar, D., Brockmann, M., Brecher, C., & Ahn, S.-H. (2021). Appropriate smart factory for SMEs: Concept, application and perspective. *International Journal of Precision Engineering and Manufacturing*, 22(1), 201–215. DOI:10.1007/s12541-020-00445-2

Kakamoukas, G., Sariciannidis, P., Livanos, G., Zervakis, M., Ramnalis, D., Polychronos, V., Karamitsou, T., Folinas, A., & Tsitsiokas, N. (2019). A Multi-collective, IoT-enabled, Adaptive Smart Farming Architecture. *2019 IEEE International Conference on Imaging Systems and Techniques (IST)*, 1–6. DOI:10.1109/IST48021.2019.9010236

Kamenskih, A. (2022). The analysis of security and privacy risks in smart education environments. *Journal of Smart Cities and Society*, 1(1), 17–29. DOI:10.3233/SCS-210114

Kamruzzaman, M., Alanazi, S., Alruwaili, M., Alshammari, N., Elaiwat, S., Abu-Zanona, M., Innab, N., Mohammad Elzaghmouri, B., & Ahmed Alanazi, B. (2023). AI-and IoT-assisted sustainable education systems during pandemics, such as COVID-19, for smart cities. *Sustainability (Basel)*, 15(10), 8354. DOI:10.3390/su15108354

Karale, A.. (2023). Smart billing cart using RFID, YOLO and deep learning for mall administration. *International Journal of Instrumentation and Innovation Sciences*, 8(2).

Karesh, W. B., Dobson, A., Lloyd-Smith, J. O., Lubroth, J., Dixon, M. A., Bennett, M., Aldrich, S., Harrington, T., Formenty, P., Loh, E. H., Machalaba, C. C., Thomas, M. J., & Heymann, D. L. (2012). Ecology of zoonoses: Natural and unnatural histories. *Lancet*, 380(9857), 1936–1945. DOI:10.1016/S0140-6736(12)61678-X PMID:23200502

Karimi, A.-H., Schölkopf, B., & Valera, I. (2021). Algorithmic recourse: from counterfactual explanations to interventions. Proceedings of the 2021 ACM conference on fairness, accountability, and transparency.

Kasat, K. (2023). Implementation and recognition of waste management system with mobility solution in smart cities using Internet of Things. In *2023 Second International Conference on Augmented Intelligence and Sustainable Systems (ICAISS)* (pp. 1661-1665). Trichy, India. DOI:10.1109/ICAISS58487.2023.10250690

Kaur, A., Bhatia, M., & Stea, G. (2022). A survey of smart classroom literature. *Education Sciences*, 12(2), 86. DOI:10.3390/educsci12020086

Kawamura, T., Egami, S., Matsushita, K., Ugai, T., Fukuda, K., & Kozaki, K. (2022, October). Contextualized scene AIs for xai benchmarking. In *Proceedings of the 11th International Joint Conference on AIs* (pp. 64-72).

Kazi, K. S. (2022). Smart grid energy-saving technique using machine learning. *Journal of Instrumentation Technology and Innovations*, 12(3), 1–10.

Kazi, K. S. (2023). Detection of malicious nodes in IoT networks based on throughput and ML. *Journal of Electrical and Power System Engineering*, 9(1), 22–29.

Kazi, K. S. (2024a). Artificial intelligence (AI)-driven IoT (AIIoT)-based agriculture automation. In Satapathy, S., & Muduli, K. (Eds.), *Advanced Computational Methods for Agri-Business Sustainability* (pp. 72–94). IGI Global., DOI:10.4018/979-8-3693-3583-3.ch005

Kazi, K. S. (2024b). IoT driven by machine learning (MLIoT) for the retail apparel sector. In Tarnanidis, T., Papachristou, E., Karypidis, M., & Ismyrlis, V. (Eds.), *Driving Green Marketing in Fashion and Retail* (pp. 63–81). IGI Global., DOI:10.4018/979-8-3693-3049-4.ch004

Kazi, K. S. L. (2022). Predict the severity of diabetes cases using K-means and decision tree approach. *Journal of Advances in Shell Programming*, 9(2), 24–31.

Kazi, K. S., Liyakat, S., & Sridevi, M. (2023). HEECCNB: An efficient IoT-cloud architecture for secure patient data transmission and accurate disease prediction in healthcare systems. In *2023 Seventh International Conference on Image Information Processing (ICIIP)* (pp. 407-410). Solan, India. DOI:10.1109/ICIIP61524.2023.10537627

Kazi, K. S., Liyakat, S., Sridevi, M., Saha, B., Reddy, S. R., & Shirisha, N. (2023). Fruit grading disease detection and an image processing strategy. *Journal of Image Processing and Artificial Intelligence*, 9(2), 17–34.

Keeling, M. J., & Eames, K. T. (2005). Networks and epidemic models. *Journal of the Royal Society, Interface*, 2(4), 295–307. DOI:10.1098/rsif.2005.0051 PMID:16849187

Kenny, U., & Regan, Á. (2021). Co-designing a smartphone app for and with farmers: Empathising with end-users' values and needs. *Journal of Rural Studies*, 82, 148–160. DOI:10.1016/j.jrurstud.2020.12.009

Khaira, A. (2024). From 3D to 4D: The Evolution of Additive Manufacturing and Its Implications for Industry 5.0. In *Emerging Technologies in Digital Manufacturing and Smart Factories* (pp. 39-53). IGI Global.

Khanh Duy, T., Küng, J., & Huu Hanh, H. (2021). Survey on iot data analytics with semantic approaches. The 23rd International Conference on Information Integration and Web Intelligence. DOI:10.1145/3487664.3487785

Khan, M. A., & Salah, K. (2018). IoT security: Review, blockchain solutions, and open challenges. *Future Generation Computer Systems*, 82, 395–411. DOI:10.1016/j.future.2017.11.022

Kigambiroha, M. (2023). *Motor cycle theft control system using RFID, GSM and GPS technology.*

Kim, J. E., Henson, C., Huang, K., Tran, T. A., & Lin, W. Y. (2021). Accelerating road sign ground truth construction with AI and machine learning. In *Intelligent Computing:Proceedings of the 2021 Computing Conference,* Volume 2 (pp. 325-340). Springer International Publishing.

Kim, Y., & Bang, H. (2018). Introduction to Kalman filter and its applications. *Introduction and Implementations of the Kalman Filter*, 1, 1–16.

King, R. C., Villeneuve, E., White, R. J., Sherratt, R. S., Holderbaum, W., & Harwin, W. S. (2017). Application of data fusion techniques and technologies for wearable health monitoring. *Medical Engineering & Physics*, 42, 1–12. DOI:10.1016/j.medengphy.2016.12.011 PMID:28237714

kinze. (n.d.). 3665 Planter. *Kinze*. Retrieved April 23, 2024, from https://www.kinze.com/planters/3665-planter/

Kizilcec, R. F., & Lee, H. (2022). Algorithmic fairness in education. In *The ethics of artificial intelligence in education* (pp. 174–202). Routledge. DOI:10.4324/9780429329067-10

Kleinberg, J., Mullainathan, S., & Raghavan, M. (2016). Inherent trade-offs in the fair determination of risk scores. *arXiv preprint arXiv:1609.05807*.

Kolanowski, K., Świetlicka, A., Kapela, R., Pochmara, J., & Rybarczyk, A. (2018). Multisensor data fusion using Elman neural networks. *Applied Mathematics and Computation*, 319, 236–244. DOI:10.1016/j.amc.2017.02.031

Kosgiker, G., Kumtole, S., Sunil Shinde, S., Sunil Shinde, S., Nagrale, M., & Kutubuddin, K. (2023). Monitoring fresh fruit and food using IoT and machine learning to improve food safety and quality. Tuijin Jishu/Journal of Propulsion Technology, 44(3), 2927-2931.

Koshariya, A. K., Kalaiyarasi, D., Jovith, A. A., Sivakami, T., Hasan, D. S., & Boopathi, S. (2023). AI-Enabled IoT and WSN-Integrated Smart Agriculture System. In *Artificial Intelligence Tools and Technologies for Smart Farming and Agriculture Practices* (pp. 200–218). IGI Global. DOI:10.4018/978-1-6684-8516-3.ch011

Kotikangas, M. (2023). Utilization of digital twin for customer tailored variable speed drive.

Kotkar, V. A., & Gharde, S. S. (2013). *Review of various image contrast enhancement techniques.*

Kraft, M., Bai, J., Mosbach, S., Taylor, C., Karan, D., Lee, K. F., ... Lapkin, A. (2023). From Platform to AI: Distributed Self-Driving Laboratories.

Kralj, D., & Aralica, K. (2022, September). Industry 5.0 from the Perspective of Safety at Work. In *Occupational Safety and Health,Proceedings of the 8th International Professional and Scientific Conference,Zadar, Croatia* (pp. 21-24).

Kralj, D., & Aralica, K. (2023). Safety at work within industry 5.0-quo vadis. *Sigurnost: časopis za sigurnost u radnoj i životnoj okolini, 65*(3), 317-324.

Kristoffersen, E., Blomsma, F., Mikalef, P., & Li, J. (2020). The smart circular economy: A digital-enabled circular strategies framework for manufacturing companies. *Journal of Business Research*, 120, 241–261. DOI:10.1016/j.jbusres.2020.07.044

KSL. (2022). IoT-based weather prototype using WeMos. *Journal of Control and Instrumentation Engineering*, 9(1), 10–22.

Kumar, M., Kumar, K., Sasikala, P., Sampath, B., Gopi, B., & Sundaram, S. (2023). Sustainable Green Energy Generation From Waste Water: IoT and ML Integration. In *Sustainable Science and Intelligent Technologies for Societal Development* (pp. 440–463). IGI Global.

Kumar, P. R., Meenakshi, S., Shalini, S., Devi, S. R., & Boopathi, S. (2023). Soil Quality Prediction in Context Learning Approaches Using Deep Learning and Blockchain for Smart Agriculture. In *Effective AI, Blockchain, and E-Governance Applications for Knowledge Discovery and Management* (pp. 1–26). IGI Global. DOI:10.4018/978-1-6684-9151-5.ch001

Kumar, P., Sampath, B., Kumar, S., Babu, B. H., & Ahalya, N. (2023). Hydroponics, Aeroponics, and Aquaponics Technologies in Modern Agricultural Cultivation. In *IGI: Trends, Paradigms, and Advances in Mechatronics Engineering* (pp. 223–241). IGI Global.

Kumar, R. (2018). Bilingual Domain-Independent Natural Language Interface to Database.

Kumar, R., Sinwar, D., Pandey, A., Tadele, T., Singh, V., & Raghuwanshi, G. (2022). IoT Enabled Technologies in Smart Farming and Challenges for Adoption. In Pattnaik, P. K., Kumar, R., & Pal, S. (Eds.), *Internet of Things and Analytics for Agriculture* (Vol. 3, pp. 141–164). Springer Singapore. DOI:10.1007/978-981-16-6210-2_7

Kumar, S., Meena, R. S., Sheoran, S., Jangir, C. K., Jhariya, M. K., Banerjee, A., & Raj, A. (2022). Remote sensing for agriculture and resource management. In *Natural Resources Conservation and Advances for Sustainability* (pp. 91–135). Elsevier. DOI:10.1016/B978-0-12-822976-7.00012-0

Kumar, S., Sharma, D., Rao, S., Lim, W. M., & Mangla, S. K. (2022). Past, present, and future of sustainable finance: Insights from big data analytics through machine learning of scholarly research. *Annals of Operations Research*, 1–44. DOI:10.1007/s10479-021-04410-8 PMID:35002001

Kusiak, A. (2024). Federated explainable artificial intelligence (fXAI): A digital manufacturing perspective. *International Journal of Production Research*, 62(1-2), 171–182. DOI:10.1080/00207543.2023.2238083

Kusner, M. J., Loftus, J., Russell, C., & Silva, R. (2017). Counterfactual fairness. *Advances in Neural Information Processing Systems*, 30.

Kutubuddin, K. S. (2022). Business mode and product life cycle to improve marketing in healthcare units. *E-Commerce for Future & Trends*, 9(3), 1–9.

Kutubuddin, K. S. (2023). Nanotechnology in precision farming: The role of research. *International Journal of Nanomaterials and Nanostructures*, 9(2). Advance online publication. DOI:10.37628/ijnn.v9i2.1051

Kwet, M., & Prinsloo, P. (2020). The 'smart' classroom: A new frontier in the age of the smart university. *Teaching in Higher Education*, 25(4), 510–526. DOI:10.1080/13562517.2020.1734922

LaDeau, S. L., Glass, G. E., Hobbs, N. T., Latimer, A., & Ostfeld, R. S. (2011). Data–model fusion to better understand emerging pathogens and improve infectious disease forecasting. *Ecological Applications*, 21(5), 1443–1460. DOI:10.1890/09-1409.1 PMID:21830694

Lal, R., Reicosky, D. C., & Hanson, J. D. (2007). Evolution of the plow over 10,000 years and the rationale for no-till farming. *Soil & Tillage Research*, 93(1), 1–12. DOI:10.1016/j.still.2006.11.004

Larose, D. T., & Larose, C. D. (2014). *Discovering knowledge in data: an introduction to data mining* (Vol. 4). John Wiley & Sons. DOI:10.1002/9781118874059

Lawson, A. B. (2018). *Bayesian disease mapping: hierarchical modeling in spatial epidemiology. Chapman and Hall/CRC.*

Le Hesran, C., Ladier, A.-L., Botta-Genoulaz, V., & Laforest, V. (2020). A methodology for the identification of waste-minimizing scheduling problems. *Journal of Cleaner Production*, 246, 119023. DOI:10.1016/j.jclepro.2019.119023

Lecue, F. (2020). On the role of AIs in explainable AI. *Semantic Web*, 11(1), 41–51. DOI:10.3233/SW-190374

Lee, L. M. (2019). Public health surveillance: Ethical considerations. *The Oxford handbook of public health ethics*, 320.

Lee, S., & Manfredi, L. R. (2021). Promoting recycling, reducing and reusing in the School of Design: A step toward improving sustainability literacy. *International Journal of Sustainability in Higher Education*, 22(5), 1038–1054. DOI:10.1108/IJSHE-11-2020-0443

Lee, W. S., Alchanatis, V., Yang, C., Hirafuji, M., Moshou, D., & Li, C. (2010). Sensing technologies for precision specialty crop production. *Computers and Electronics in Agriculture*, 74(1), 2–33. DOI:10.1016/j.compag.2010.08.005

Lee, Y. H. (2018). An overview of meta-analysis for clinicians. *The Korean Journal of Internal Medicine*, 33(2), 277–283. DOI:10.3904/kjim.2016.195 PMID:29277096

Leimu, R., & Koricheva, J. (2004). Cumulative meta–analysis: A new tool for detection of temporal trends and publication bias in ecology. *Proceedings of the Royal Society of London. Series B, Biological Sciences*, 271(1551), 1961–1966. DOI:10.1098/rspb.2004.2828 PMID:15347521

Lescano, A. G., Larasati, R. P., Sedyaningsih, E. R., Bounlu, K., Araujo-Castillo, R. V., Munayco Escate, C. V., Soto, G., Mundaca, C. C., & Blazes, D. L. (2008, December). Statistical analyses in disease surveillance systems. *BMC Proceedings*, 2(S3), 1–6. DOI:10.1186/1753-6561-2-s3-s7 PMID:19025684

Li, A., Wang, X., Wang, W., Zhang, A., & Li, B. (2019). A survey of relation extraction of AIs. In *Web and Big Data: APWeb-WAIM 2019 International Workshops, KGMA and DSEA, Chengdu, China, August 1–3, 2019, Revised Selected Papers 3* (pp. 52-66). Springer International Publishing.

Li, X., Liu, J., Li, J., Yu, W., Cao, Z., Qiu, S., . . . Jiao, X. (2023, August). ML Structure-Based Implicit Risk Reasoning for Long-Tail Scenarios of Automated Driving. In *2023 4th International Conference on Big Data, Artificial Intelligence and Internet of Things Engineering (ICBAIE)* (pp. 415-420). IEEE.

Li, C. (2020). Information processing in Internet of Things using big data analytics. *Computer Communications*, 160, 718–729. DOI:10.1016/j.comcom.2020.06.020

Li, M., Wang, H., Dai, H., Li, M., Gu, R., Chen, F., & Chen, G. (2024). A Survey of Multi-Dimensional Indexes: Past and Future Trends. *IEEE Transactions on Knowledge and Data Engineering*, 36(8), 3635–3655. DOI:10.1109/TKDE.2024.3364183

Limbo, A., Suresh, N., Ndakolute, S.-S., Hashiyana, V., Haiduwa, T., & Ujakpa, M. M. (2021). Smart irrigation system for crop farmers in Namibia. In *Transforming the Internet of Things for Next-Generation Smart Systems*. DOI:10.4018/978-1-7998-7541-3.ch008

Lin, J. S., Burkom, H. S., Murphy, S. P., Elbert, Y., Hakre, S., Babin, S. M., & Feldman, A. B. (2006). *Bayesian fusion of syndromic surveillance with sensor data for disease outbreak classification.* In Life Science Data Mining (pp. 119-141). DOI:10.1142/9789812772664_0006

Lin, L., & Chu, H. (2018). Quantifying publication bias in meta-analysis. *Biometrics*, 74(3), 785–794. DOI:10.1111/biom.12817 PMID:29141096

Lioutas, E. D., & Charatsari, C. (2020). Smart farming and short food supply chains: Are they compatible? *Land Use Policy*, 94, 104541. DOI:10.1016/j.landusepol.2020.104541

Li, S., Iqbal, M., & Saxena, N. (2022). Future industry internet of things with zero-trust security. *Information Systems Frontiers*, 1–14. DOI:10.1007/s10796-021-10199-5

Li, S., Li, J., Yu, S., Wang, P., Liu, H., & Yang, X. (2023). Anti-Drift Technology Progress of Plant Protection Applied to Orchards: A Review. *Agronomy (Basel)*, 13(11), 2679. DOI:10.3390/agronomy13112679

Liu, H., Li, Y., Hong, R., Li, Z., Li, M., Pan, W., Glowacz, A., & He, H. (2020). AI analysis and visualization of research trends on driver behavior. *Journal of Intelligent & Fuzzy Systems*, 38(1), 495–511. DOI:10.3233/JIFS-179424

Liu, J., Huang, J., Sun, R., Yu, H., & Xiao, R. (2020). Data fusion for multi-source sensors using GA-PSO-BP neural network. *IEEE Transactions on Intelligent Transportation Systems*, 22(10), 6583–6598. DOI:10.1109/TITS.2020.3010296

Liu, J., Zhang, X., Li, Y., Wang, J., & Kim, H. J. (2019). Deep learning-based reasoning with multi-ontology for IoT applications. *IEEE Access : Practical Innovations, Open Solutions*, 7, 124688–124701. DOI:10.1109/ACCESS.2019.2937353

Liu, L.-W., Ma, X., Wang, Y.-M., Lu, C.-T., & Lin, W.-S. (2021). Using artificial intelligence algorithms to predict rice (Oryza sativa L.) growth rate for precision agriculture. *Computers and Electronics in Agriculture*, 187, 106286. DOI:10.1016/j.compag.2021.106286

Liu, Q., Li, X., Tang, Y., Gao, X., Yang, F., & Li, Z. (2023). ML Reinforcement Learning-Based Decision-Making Technology for Connected and Autonomous Vehicles: Framework, Review, and Future Trends. *Sensors (Basel)*, 23(19), 8229. DOI:10.3390/s23198229 PMID:37837063

Liu, S., Baret, F., Allard, D., Jin, X., Andrieu, B., Burger, P., Hemmerlé, M., & Comar, A. (2017). A method to estimate plant density and plant spacing heterogeneity: Application to wheat crops. *Plant Methods*, 13(1), 38. DOI:10.1186/s13007-017-0187-1 PMID:28529535

Liu, X., Dastjerdi, A., & Buyya, R. (2016). Stream processing in IoT: Foundations, state-of-the-art, and future directions. In *Internet of Things* (pp. 145–161). Elsevier. DOI:10.1016/B978-0-12-805395-9.00008-3

Liyakat, K. K. S. (2023). IoT-based Arduino-powered weather monitoring system. *Journal of Telecommunication Study*, 8(3), 25–31. DOI:10.46610/JTC.2023. v08i03.005

Liyakat, K. K. S. (2023). Machine learning approach using artificial neural networks to detect malicious nodes in IoT networks. In Shukla, P. K., Mittal, H., & Engelbrecht, A. (Eds.), *Computer Vision and Robotics. CVR 2023. Algorithms for Intelligent Systems*. Springer., DOI:10.1007/978-981-99-4577-1_3

Liyakat, K. K. S. (2024). Explainable AI in healthcare. In Anitha, A., & Debi Prasanna Acharjya, K. (Eds.), *Explainable Artificial Intelligence in Healthcare Systems* (pp. 271–284).

Liyakat, K. K. S. (2024). Machine learning approach using artificial neural networks to detect malicious nodes in IoT networks. In Udgata, S. K., Sethi, S., & Gao, X. Z. (Eds.), *Intelligent Systems. ICMIB 2023. Lecture Notes in Networks and Systems* (Vol. 728, pp. 1–20). Springer. DOI:10.1007/978-981-99-3932-9_12

Lodi, G., Aniello, L., Di Luna, G. A., & Baldoni, R. (2014). An event-based platform for collaborative threats detection and monitoring. *Information Systems*, 39, 175–195. DOI:10.1016/j.is.2013.07.005

Lo, H. W., Chan, H. W., Lin, J. W., & Lin, S. W. (2024). Evaluating the interrelationships of industrial 5.0 development factors using an integration approach of Fermatean fuzzy logic. *Journal of Operations Intelligence*, 2(1), 95–113. DOI:10.31181/ jopi21202416

Lourenço, C., Tatem, A. J., Atkinson, P. M., Cohen, J. M., Pindolia, D., Bhavnani, D., & Le Menach, A. (2019). Strengthening surveillance systems for malaria elimination: A global landscaping of system performance, 2015–2017. *Malaria Journal*, 18(1), 1–11. DOI:10.1186/s12936-019-2960-2 PMID:31533740

Lucivero, F. (2020). Big data, big waste? A reflection on the environmental sustainability of big data initiatives. *Science and Engineering Ethics*, 26(2), 1009–1030. DOI:10.1007/s11948-019-00171-7 PMID:31893331

Lukovnikov, D. (2022). Deep learning methods for semantic parsing and question answering over AIs (Doctoral dissertation, Universitäts-und Landesbibliothek Bonn).

Lu, Y., Yang, L., Shi, B., Li, J., & Abedin, M. Z. (2022). A novel framework of credit risk feature selection for SMEs during industry 4.0. *Annals of Operations Research*, 1–28. DOI:10.1007/s10479-022-04849-3 PMID:35910041

Luyckx, M., & Reins, L. (2022). The Future of Farming: The (Non)-Sense of Big Data Predictive Tools for Sustainable EU Agriculture. *Sustainability (Basel)*, 14(20), 12968. DOI:10.3390/su142012968

Lv, Z. (2023). Digital Twins in Industry 5.0. *Research, 6*, 71.

Mafata, M., Brand, J., Kidd, M., Medvedovici, A., & Buica, A. (2022). Exploration of data fusion strategies using principal component analysis and multiple factor analysis. *Beverages*, 8(4), 66. DOI:10.3390/beverages8040066

Magadum, P. K. (2024). Machine learning for predicting wind turbine output power in wind energy conversion systems. Grenze International Journal of Engineering and Technology, 10(1), 2074-2080. https://thegrenze.com/index.php?display=page&view=journalabstract&absid=2514&id=8

Magnani, M., & Montesi, D. (2010). A survey on uncertainty management in data integration. *ACM Journal of Data and Information Quality*, 2(1), 1–33. DOI:10.1145/1805286.1805291

Maguluri, L. P., Ananth, J., Hariram, S., Geetha, C., Bhaskar, A., & Boopathi, S. (2023). Smart Vehicle-Emissions Monitoring System Using Internet of Things (IoT). In *Handbook of Research on Safe Disposal Methods of Municipal Solid Wastes for a Sustainable Environment* (pp. 191–211). IGI Global.

Maguluri, L. P., Arularasan, A., & Boopathi, S. (2023a). Assessing Security Concerns for AI-Based Drones in Smart Cities. In *Effective AI, Blockchain, and E-Governance Applications for Knowledge Discovery and Management* (pp. 27–47). IGI Global. DOI:10.4018/978-1-6684-9151-5.ch002

Mahler, R. P. (1996, June). Unified data fusion: fuzzy logic, evidence, and rules. In *Signal Processing, Sensor Fusion, and Target Recognition V* (Vol. 2755, pp. 226–237). SPIE. DOI:10.1117/12.243164

Mahon, L., Giunchiglia, E., Li, B., & Lukasiewicz, T. (2020, December). AI extraction from videos. In *2020 19th IEEE International Conference on Machine Learning and Applications (ICMLA)* (pp. 25-32). IEEE.

Malathi, J., Kusha, K., Isaac, S., Ramesh, A., Rajendiran, M., & Boopathi, S. (2024). IoT-Enabled Remote Patient Monitoring for Chronic Disease Management and Cost Savings: Transforming Healthcare. In *Advances in Explainable AI Applications for Smart Cities* (pp. 371–388). IGI Global.

Malawade, A. V., Yu, S. Y., Hsu, B., Muthirayan, D., Khargonekar, P. P., & Al Faruque, M. A. (2022). Spatiotemporal scene-ML embedding for autonomous vehicle collision prediction. *IEEE Internet of Things Journal*, 9(12), 9379–9388. DOI:10.1109/JIOT.2022.3141044

Ma, M., Wang, P., & Chu, C.-H. (2013). Data management for internet of things: Challenges, approaches and opportunities. 2013 IEEE International conference on green computing and communications and IEEE Internet of Things and IEEE cyber, physical and social computing.

Manjunatha, P., Verma, A. K., & Srividya, A. (2008, December). Multi-sensor data fusion in cluster based wireless sensor networks using fuzzy logic method. In *2008 IEEE region 10 and the third international conference on industrial and information systems* (pp. 1-6). IEEE. DOI:10.1109/ICIINFS.2008.4798453

Maraveas, C., Konar, D., Michopoulos, D. K., Arvanitis, K. G., & Peppas, K. P. (2024). Harnessing quantum computing for smart agriculture: Empowering sustainable crop management and yield optimization. *Computers and Electronics in Agriculture*, 218, 108680. DOI:10.1016/j.compag.2024.108680

Marinakis, V. (2020). Big data for energy management and energy-efficient buildings. *Energies*, 13(7), 1555. DOI:10.3390/en13071555

Marjani, M., Nasaruddin, F., Gani, A., Karim, A., Hashem, I. A. T., Siddiqa, A., & Yaqoob, I. (2017). Big IoT data analytics: Architecture, opportunities, and open research challenges. *IEEE Access : Practical Innovations, Open Solutions*, 5, 5247–5261. DOI:10.1109/ACCESS.2017.2689040

Markus, K. A. (2021). Causal effects and counterfactual conditionals: Contrasting Rubin, Lewis and Pearl. *Economics and Philosophy*, 37(3), 441–461. DOI:10.1017/S0266267120000437

Maroof, M. A., & Kapate, S. (2023). *Exploring Dynamics of Industry 5.0*. World Journal of Management and Economics.

Martinelli, F., Scalenghe, R., Davino, S., Panno, S., Scuderi, G., Ruisi, P., Villa, P., Stroppiana, D., Boschetti, M., Goulart, L. R., Davis, C. E., & Dandekar, A. M. (2015). Advanced methods of plant disease detection. A review. *Agronomy for Sustainable Development*, 35(1), 1–25. DOI:10.1007/s13593-014-0246-1

Martín-Gutiérrez, J., Fabiani, P., Benesova, W., Meneses, M. D., & Mora, C. E. (2015). Augmented reality to promote collaborative and autonomous learning in higher education. *Computers in Human Behavior*, 51, 752–761. DOI:10.1016/j.chb.2014.11.093

Masenya, T. M., & Chisita, C. T. (2022). Futurizing library services in a technology-driven dispensation: Reflections on selected academic libraries in Zimbabwe and South Africa. In *Innovative technologies for enhancing knowledge access in academic libraries* (pp. 1–21). IGI Global. DOI:10.4018/978-1-6684-3364-5.ch001

Matthew, U. O., Kazaure, J. S., & Okafor, N. U. (2021). Contemporary development in E-Learning education, cloud computing technology & internet of things. *EAI Endorsed Transactions on Cloud Systems*, 7(20), e3–e3.

Mawgoud, A. A., Taha, M. H. N., & Khalifa, N. E. M. (2020). Security threats of social internet of things in the higher education environment. *Toward Social Internet of Things (SIoT): Enabling Technologies, Architectures and Applications: Emerging Technologies for Connected and Smart Social Objects*, 151-171.

Maybeck, P. S. (1990). The Kalman filter: An introduction to concepts. In *Autonomous robot vehicles* (pp. 194–204). Springer New York. DOI:10.1007/978-1-4613-8997-2_15

McMichael, A. J. (2004). Environmental and social influences on emerging infectious diseases: Past, present and future. *Philosophical Transactions of the Royal Society of London. Series B, Biological Sciences*, 359(1447), 1049–1058. DOI:10.1098/rstb.2004.1480 PMID:15306389

Mekonnen, Y., Namuduri, S., Burton, L., Sarwat, A., & Bhansali, S. (2020). Review—Machine Learning Techniques in Wireless Sensor Network Based Precision Agriculture. *Journal of the Electrochemical Society*, 167(3), 037522. DOI:10.1149/2.0222003JES

Mershad, K., Damaj, A., Wakim, P., & Hamieh, A. (2020). LearnSmart: A framework for integrating internet of things functionalities in learning management systems. *Education and Information Technologies*, 25(4), 2699–2732. DOI:10.1007/s10639-019-10090-6

Metje-Sprink, J., Menz, J., Modrzejewski, D., & Sprink, T. (2019). DNA-Free Genome Editing: Past, Present and Future. *Frontiers in Plant Science*, 9, 1957. DOI:10.3389/fpls.2018.01957 PMID:30693009

Meyes, R., Lu, M., de Puiseau, C. W., & Meisen, T. (2019). Ablation studies in artificial neural networks. *arXiv preprint arXiv:1901.08644*.

Millard, J. (2023). Exploring the impact of digital transformation on public governance.

Millard, J. (2023). Impact of digital transformation on public governance. *Joint Research Centre (Seville site)*.

Miller, J. C. (2013). *Laser ablation: principles and applications* (Vol. 28). Springer Science & Business Media.

Mini, G. V., & Viji, K. A. (2017). A comprehensive cloud security model with enhanced key management, access control and data anonymization features. *International Journal of Communication Networks and Information Security*, 9(2), 263.

Miorandi, D., Sicari, S., De Pellegrini, F., & Chlamtac, I. (2012). Internet of things: Vision, applications and research challenges. *Ad Hoc Networks*, 10(7), 1497–1516. DOI:10.1016/j.adhoc.2012.02.016

Mishra, N., Lin, C.-C., & Chang, H.-T. (2014). A cognitive oriented framework for IoT big-data management prospective. 2014 IEEE International Conference on Communiction Problem-solving.

Mishra, P., & Singh, G. (2023). Energy management systems in sustainable smart cities based on the internet of energy: A technical review. *Energies*, 16(19), 6903. DOI:10.3390/en16196903

Mishra, S., Mishra, B. K., Tripathy, H. K., & Dutta, A. (2020). Analysis of the role and scope of big data analytics with IoT in health care domain. In *Handbook of data science approaches for biomedical engineering* (pp. 1–23). Elsevier. DOI:10.1016/B978-0-12-818318-2.00001-5

Misra, N., Dixit, Y., Al-Mallahi, A., Bhullar, M. S., Upadhyay, R., & Martynenko, A. (2020). IoT, big data, and artificial intelligence in agriculture and food industry. *IEEE Internet of Things Journal*, 9(9), 6305–6324. DOI:10.1109/JIOT.2020.2998584

Mistry, I., Tanwar, S., Tyagi, S., & Kumar, N. (2020). Blockchain for 5G-enabled IoT for industrial automation: A systematic review, solutions, and challenges. *Mechanical Systems and Signal Processing*, 135, 106382. DOI:10.1016/j.ymssp.2019.106382

Mitropoulou, K., Kokkinos, P., Soumplis, P., & Varvarigos, E. (2024). Anomaly Detection in Cloud Computing using AI Embedding and Machine Learning Mechanisms. *Journal of Grid Computing*, 22(1), 6. DOI:10.1007/s10723-023-09727-1

Mladineo, M., Celent, L., Milković, V., & Veža, I. (2024). Current State Analysis of Croatian Manufacturing Industry with Regard to Industry 4.0/5.0. *Machines (Basel)*, 12(2), 87. DOI:10.3390/machines12020087

Mogas, J., Palau, R., Fuentes, M., & Cebrián, G. (2022). Smart schools on the way: How school principals from Catalonia approach the future of education within the fourth industrial revolution. *Learning Environments Research*, 25(3), 875–893. DOI:10.1007/s10984-021-09398-3

Mohamed, E. S., Belal, A., Abd-Elmabod, S. K., El-Shirbeny, M. A., Gad, A., & Zahran, M. B. (2021). Smart farming for improving agricultural management. *The Egyptian Journal of Remote Sensing and Space Sciences*, 24(3), 971–981. DOI:10.1016/j.ejrs.2021.08.007

Mohamed, M. (2023). Agricultural Sustainability in the Age of Deep Learning: Current Trends, Challenges, and Future Trajectories. *Sustainable Machine Intelligence Journal*, 4. Advance online publication. DOI:10.61185/SMIJ.2023.44102

Mohammadian, H. D., & Rezaie, F. (2020). The role of IoE-Education in the 5 th wave theory readiness & its effect on SME 4.0 HR competencies. *2020 IEEE Global Engineering Education Conference (EDUCON)*, 1604–1613. DOI:10.1109/EDUCON45650.2020.9125249

Mohd Hanafiah, N., Mispan, M. S., Lim, P. E., Baisakh, N., & Cheng, A. (2020). The 21st Century Agriculture: When Rice Research Draws Attention to Climate Variability and How Weedy Rice and Underutilized Grains Come in Handy. *Plants*, 9(3), 365. DOI:10.3390/plants9030365 PMID:32188108

Mohd Yamin, M. N., Ab. Aziz, K., Gek Siang, T., & Ab. Aziz, N. A. (2023). Determinants of Emotion Recognition System Adoption: Empirical Evidence from Malaysia. *Applied Sciences (Basel, Switzerland)*, 13(21), 11854. DOI:10.3390/app132111854

Mohr, S., & Kühl, R. (2021). Acceptance of artificial intelligence in German agriculture: An application of the technology acceptance model and the theory of planned behavior. *Precision Agriculture*, 22(6), 1816–1844. DOI:10.1007/s11119-021-09814-x

Moin, A. (2021). Data analytics and machine learning methods, techniques and tool for model-driven engineering of smart iot services. 2021 IEEE/ACM 43rd International Conference on Software Engineering: Companion Proceedings (ICSE-Companion).

Monninger, T., Schmidt, J., Rupprecht, J., Raba, D., Jordan, J., Frank, D., Staab, S., & Dietmayer, K. (2023). Scene: Reasoning about traffic scenes using heterogeneous ML neural networks. *IEEE Robotics and Automation Letters*, 8(3), 1531–1538. DOI:10.1109/LRA.2023.3234771

Morain, S. A., & Budge, A. M. (Eds.). (2012). *Environmental tracking for public health surveillance*. CRC Press. DOI:10.1201/b12680

Morais, R., Fernandes, M. A., Matos, S. G., Serôdio, C., Ferreira, P. J. S. G., & Reis, M. J. C. S. (2008). A ZigBee multi-powered wireless acquisition device for remote sensing applications in precision viticulture. *Computers and Electronics in Agriculture*, 62(2), 94–106. DOI:10.1016/j.compag.2007.12.004

Mun, S. H., & Abdullah, A. H. (2016). A review of the use of smart boards in education. 2016 IEEE 8th international conference on engineering education (ICEED). PMID:27822404

Mupepi, M. (2017). *Effective talent management strategies for organizational success*. IGI Global. DOI:10.4018/978-1-5225-1961-4

Murray, E. A. (1996). What have ablation studies told us about the neural substrates of stimulus memory? Seminars in Neuroscience.

Muzammal, M., Talat, R., Sodhro, A. H., & Pirbhulal, S. (2020). A multi-sensor data fusion enabled ensemble approach for medical data from body sensor networks. *Information Fusion*, 53, 155–164. DOI:10.1016/j.inffus.2019.06.021

Muzayanah, R., Lestari, A. D., & Muslim, M. A. (2024). IoT-Integrated Smart Attendance and Attention Monitoring System For Primary and Secondary School Classroom Management. *Journal of Electronics Technology Exploration*, 2(1), 21–25. DOI:10.52465/joetex.v2i1.381

Mwabukusi, M., Karimuribo, E. D., Rweyemamu, M. M., & Beda, E. (2014). Mobile technologies for disease surveillance in humans and animals: Proceedings. *The Onderstepoort Journal of Veterinary Research*, 81(2), 1–5. DOI:10.4102/ojvr. v81i2.737 PMID:25005126

Nagrale, M. (2024). Internet of robotic things in cardiac surgery: An innovative approach. *African Journal of Biological Sciences*, 6(6), 709–725. DOI:10.33472/ AFJBS.6.6.2024.709-725

Nair, A., Pillai, S. V., & Senthil Kumar, S. A. (2024). Towards emerging Industry 5.0–a review-based framework. *Journal of Strategy and Management*.

Narang, N. K. (2022). Mentor's Musings on Disruptive Technologies and Standards Interplay in Industrial Transformation. *IEEE Internet of Things Magazine*, 5(1), 4–12. DOI:10.1109/MIOT.2022.9773142

Narkhede, G. B., Pasi, B. N., Rajhans, N., & Kulkarni, A. (2024). Industry 5.0 and sustainable manufacturing: A systematic literature review. *Benchmarking*. Advance online publication. DOI:10.1108/BIJ-03-2023-0196

Natalia, T., Pathani, A., Dhaliwal, N., Rajasekhar, N., & Khatkar, M. (2024). Block-chain Integration in Industry 5.0: A Security Experiment for Resilience Assessment. In *BIO Web of Conferences* (Vol. 86, p. 01070). EDP Sciences.

Natalia, V., Bisht, Y. S., Prabhakar, P. K., Arora, R., Mishra, S. K., & Rajasekhar, N. (2024). AI and Autonomous Systems: An Experiment in Industry 5.0 Transformation. In *BIO Web of Conferences* (Vol. 86, p. 01094). EDP Sciences.

Nazari, M. (2017). *Infrared Matrix-Assisted Laser Desorption Electrospray Ionization (IR-MALDESI): Development and Applications in Metabolomics, Mass Spectrometry Imaging, and Direct Analysis.* North Carolina State University.

Neeraja, P. R. (2024). DL-based somnolence detection for improved driver safety and alertness monitoring. In 2024 IEEE International Conference on Computing, Power and Communication Technologies (IC2PCT) (pp. 589-594). Greater Noida, India. DOI:10.1109/IC2PCT60090.2024.10486714

Nel-Sanders, D. (2023). Revolutionising Public Private Partnerships: A Transition to the Fifth Industrial Revolution. *International Journal of Innovation in Management. Economics and Social Sciences*, 3(1), 12–29.

Nerkar, P. M. (2023). Predictive data analytics framework based on heart healthcare system (HHS) using machine learning. Journal of Advanced Zoology, 44(Special Issue 2), 3673-3686.

Netherton, T., & Netherton, T. J. (2021). A fully-automated, deep learning-based framework for ct-based localization, segmentation, verification and planning of metastatic vertebrae.

Nguyen, B. T. (2011). *Face-to-face, blended, and online instruction: Comparison of student performance and retention in higher education.* University of California.

Nguyen, D. C., Ding, M., Pathirana, P. N., Seneviratne, A., Li, J., & Poor, H. V. (2021). Federated learning for internet of things: A comprehensive survey. *IEEE Communications Surveys and Tutorials*, 23(3), 1622–1658. DOI:10.1109/COMST.2021.3075439

Nickel, M., Murphy, K., Tresp, V., & Gabrilovich, E. (2015). A review of relational machine learning for AIs. *Proceedings of the IEEE*, 104(1), 11–33. DOI:10.1109/JPROC.2015.2483592

Nishanth, J., Deshmukh, M. A., Kushwah, R., Kushwaha, K. K., Balaji, S., & Sampath, B. (2023). Particle Swarm Optimization of Hybrid Renewable Energy Systems. In *Intelligent Engineering Applications and Applied Sciences for Sustainability* (pp. 291–308). IGI Global. DOI:10.4018/979-8-3693-0044-2.ch016

Nnebue, C., Onwasigwe, C., Adogu, P., & Adinma, E. (2014). Challenges of data collection and disease notification in Anambra State, Nigeria. *Tropical Journal of Medical Research*, 17(1), 1–6. DOI:10.4103/1119-0388.130173

Noura, M., Atiquzzaman, M., & Gaedke, M. (2019). Interoperability in internet of things: Taxonomies and open challenges. *Mobile Networks and Applications*, 24(3), 796–809. DOI:10.1007/s11036-018-1089-9

Nyemba, W. R., Chikuku, T., Chiroodza, J. R., Dube, B., Carter, K. F., Mbohwa, C., & Magombo, L. (2020). Industrial design thinking and innovations propelled by the Royal Academy of Engineering in Sub-Saharan Africa for capacity building. *Procedia CIRP*, 91, 770–775. DOI:10.1016/j.procir.2020.02.233

Oktian, Y. E., Lee, S.-G., & Lee, B.-G. (2020). Blockchain-based continued integrity service for IoT big data management: A comprehensive design. *Electronics (Basel)*, 9(9), 1434. DOI:10.3390/electronics9091434

Olsson, J. (2014). 6LoWPAN demystified. *Texas Instruments*, 13, 1–13.

Omotayo, T., Moghayedi, A., Awuzie, B., & Ajayi, S. (2021). Infrastructure elements for smart campuses: A bibliometric analysis. *Sustainability (Basel)*, 13(14), 7960. DOI:10.3390/su13147960

Onyekwelu, R. U., & Obikeze, A. J. (2023). *E-Administration And Service Delivery: A Study Of Joint Admissions And Matriculation Board*. JAMB.

Owusu, P. K., Nortey, D. N. N., Koffie-Ocloo, D., & Afriyie, G. O. (2023, December). Evaluating customer satisfaction with AI chatbot interactions in the Ghanaian insurance industry: Focusing on Star Assurance Ltd. In *Conference proceedings edited by* (p. 43).

Pace, P., Aloi, G., Gravina, R., Caliciuri, G., Fortino, G., & Liotta, A. (2018). An edge-based architecture to support efficient applications for healthcare industry 4.0. *IEEE Transactions on Industrial Informatics*, 15(1), 481–489. DOI:10.1109/TII.2018.2843169

Padhiary, M., Kyndiah, A. K., Kumara, R., & Saha, D. (2024). Exploration of electrode materials for in-situ soil fertilizer concentration measurement by electrochemical method. *International Journal of Advanced Biochemistry Research*, 8(4), 539–544. DOI:10.33545/26174693.2024.v8.i4g.1011

Padhiary, M., Rani, N., Saha, D., Barbhuiya, J. A., & Sethi, L. N. (2023). Efficient Precision Agriculture with Python-based Raspberry Pi Image Processing for Real-Time Plant Target Identification. *International Journal of Research and Analytical Review*, 10(3), 539–545. http://doi.one/10.1729/Journal.35531

Padhiary, M., & Roy, P. (2024). Advancements in Precision Agriculture: Exploring the Role of 3D Printing in Designing All-Terrain Vehicles for Farming Applications. *International Journal of Scientific Research*, 13(5), 861–868.

Padhiary, M., Saha, D., Kumar, R., Sethi, L. N., & Kumar, A. (2024). Enhancing precision agriculture: A comprehensive review of machine learning and AI vision applications in all-terrain vehicle for farm automation. *Smart Agricultural Technology*, 8, 100483. DOI:10.1016/j.atech.2024.100483

Padhiary, M., Sethi, L. N., & Kumar, A. (2024). Enhancing Hill Farming Efficiency Using Unmanned Agricultural Vehicles: A Comprehensive Review. *Transactions of the Indian National Academy of Engineering : an International Journal of Engineering and Technology*, 9(2), 253–268. DOI:10.1007/s41403-024-00458-7

Padmavathi, G., Subashini, P., & Lavanya, P. K. (n.d.). *Performance evaluation of the various edge detectors and filters for the noisy IR images.*

Padmavathi, K., Deepa, C., & Prabhakaran, P. (2020). Internet of Things (IoT) and Big Data: Data Management, Analytics, Visualization and Decision Making. In *The Internet of Things and Big Data Analytics* (pp. 217–246). Auerbach Publications. DOI:10.1201/9781003036739-10

Palleja, T., Tresanchez, M., Llorens, J., & Saiz-Vela, A. (2023). Design and characterization of a real-time capacitive system to estimate pesticides spray deposition and drift. *Computers and Electronics in Agriculture*, 207, 107720. DOI:10.1016/j.compag.2023.107720

Pandita, A., & Kiran, R. (2023). The technology interface and student engagement are significant stimuli in sustainable student satisfaction. *Sustainability (Basel)*, 15(10), 7923. DOI:10.3390/su15107923

Pang, T. Y., Lee, T. K., & Murshed, M. (2023). Towards a New Paradigm for Digital Health Training and Education in Australia: Exploring the Implication of the Fifth Industrial Revolution. *Applied Sciences (Basel, Switzerland)*, 13(11), 6854. DOI:10.3390/app13116854

Pan, J. Z., Vetere, G., Gomez-Perez, J. M., & Wu, H. (Eds.). (2017). *Exploiting linked data and AIs in large organisations* (p. 281). Springer. DOI:10.1007/978-3-319-45654-6

Papadopulos, J., & Christiansen, J. (2023). Conversational AI Workforce Revolution: Exploring the Effects of Conversational AI on Work Roles and Organisations.

Papenmeier, A., Englebienne, G., & Seifert, C. (2019). How model accuracy and explanation fidelity influence user trust. *arXiv preprint arXiv:1907.12652.*

Paquet, C., Coulombier, D., Kaiser, R., & Ciotti, M. (2006). Epidemic intelligence: A new framework for strengthening disease surveillance in Europe. *Eurosurveillance*, 11(12), 5–6. DOI:10.2807/esm.11.12.00665-en PMID:17370970

Paradiso, R., & Proietti, S. (2022). Light-Quality Manipulation to Control Plant Growth and Photomorphogenesis in Greenhouse Horticulture: The State of the Art and the Opportunities of Modern LED Systems. *Journal of Plant Growth Regulation*, 41(2), 742–780. DOI:10.1007/s00344-021-10337-y

Paramasivam, B. (2020). Investigation on the effects of damping over the temperature distribution on internal turning bar using Infrared fusion thermal imager analysis via SmartView software. *Measurement*, 162, 107938. DOI:10.1016/j.measurement.2020.107938

Parikh, D., & Polikar, R. (2007). An ensemble-based incremental learning approach to data fusion. *IEEE Transactions on Systems, Man, and Cybernetics. Part B, Cybernetics*, 37(2), 437–450. DOI:10.1109/TSMCB.2006.883873 PMID:17416170

Partel, V., Costa, L., & Ampatzidis, Y. (2021). Smart tree crop sprayer utilizing sensor fusion and artificial intelligence. *Computers and Electronics in Agriculture*, 191, 106556. DOI:10.1016/j.compag.2021.106556

Pearl, J. (2000). Models, reasoning and inference. *Cambridge, UK: Cambridge University Press*.

Pearl, J. (2009). Causal inference in statistics: An overview. *Statistics Surveys*, 3(none), 96–146. DOI:10.1214/09-SS057

Pearl, J. (2009). *Causality*. Cambridge university press. DOI:10.1017/CBO9780511803161

Pearl, J. (2019). The seven tools of causal inference, with reflections on machine learning. *Communications of the ACM*, 62(3), 54–60. DOI:10.1145/3241036

Pearl, J., & Mackenzie, D. (2018). *The book of why: the new science of cause and effect*. Basic books.

Pedro, A., Pham-Hang, A. T., Nguyen, P. T., & Pham, H. C. (2022). Data-driven construction safety information sharing system based on linked data, ontologies, and AI technologies. *International Journal of Environmental Research and Public Health*, 19(2), 794. DOI:10.3390/ijerph19020794 PMID:35055616

Peng, H., Ma, S., & Spector, J. M. (2019). Personalized adaptive learning: An emerging pedagogical approach enabled by a smart learning environment. *Smart Learning Environments*, 6(1), 1–14. DOI:10.1186/s40561-019-0089-y

Pereira Perdigao, G. (2018). Internship and master thesis: Concept of Operation: Unmanned Maintenance Dredging.

Perera, C., Zaslavsky, A., Christen, P., & Georgakopoulos, D. (2013). Context aware computing for the internet of things: A survey. *IEEE Communications Surveys and Tutorials*, 16(1), 414–454. DOI:10.1109/SURV.2013.042313.00197

Periasamy, J. K., Subhashini, S., Mutharasu, M., Revathi, M., Ajitha, P., & Boopathi, S. (2024). Synergizing Federated Learning and In-Memory Computing: An Experimental Approach for Drone Integration. In *Developments Towards Next Generation Intelligent Systems for Sustainable Development* (pp. 89–123). IGI Global. DOI:10.4018/979-8-3693-5643-2.ch004

Pervaiz, F., Pervaiz, M., Rehman, N. A., & Saif, U. (2012). FluBreaks: Early epidemic detection from Google flu trends. *Journal of Medical Internet Research*, 14(5), e2102. DOI:10.2196/jmir.2102 PMID:23037553

Phalkey, R. K., Yamamoto, S., Awate, P., & Marx, M. (2015). Challenges with the implementation of an Integrated Disease Surveillance and Response (IDSR) system: Systematic review of the lessons learned. *Health Policy and Planning*, 30(1), 131–143. DOI:10.1093/heapol/czt097 PMID:24362642

Plageras, A. P., Psannis, K. E., Ishibashi, Y., & Kim, B. G. (2016, October). IoT-based surveillance system for ubiquitous healthcare. In *IECON 2016-42nd Annual Conference of the IEEE Industrial Electronics Society* (pp. 6226-6230). IEEE. DOI:10.1109/IECON.2016.7793281

Plageras, A. P., Psannis, K. E., Stergiou, C., Wang, H., & Gupta, B. B. (2018). Efficient IoT-based sensor BIG Data collection–processing and analysis in smart buildings. *Future Generation Computer Systems*, 82, 349–357. DOI:10.1016/j.future.2017.09.082

Ploennigs, J., Semertzidis, K., Lorenzi, F., & Mihindukulasooriya, N. (2022, October). Scaling AIs for automating AI of digital twins. In *International Semantic Web Conference* (pp. 810-826). Cham: Springer International Publishing.

Polikar, R., Topalis, A., Parikh, D., Green, D., Frymiare, J., Kounios, J., & Clark, C. M. (2008). An ensemble based data fusion approach for early diagnosis of Alzheimer's disease. *Information Fusion*, 9(1), 83–95. DOI:10.1016/j.inffus.2006.09.003

Polonsky, J. A., Baidjoe, A., Kamvar, Z. N., Cori, A., Durski, K., Edmunds, W. J., ... & Jombart, T. (2019). *Outbreak analytics: a developing data science for informing the response to emerging pathogens*. Philosophical Transactions of the Royal Society B, 374(1776), 20180276.

Poornima, G., Janardhanachari, V., & Sakkari, D. S. (2023). Data Management for IoT and Digital Twin. In *New Approaches to Data Analytics and Internet of Things Through Digital Twin* (pp. 28–45). IGI Global.

Pradeepa, M. (2022). Student health detection using a machine learning approach and IoT. In 2022 IEEE 2nd Mysore Subsection International Conference (MysuruCon). DOI:10.1109/MysuruCon55714.2022.9972445

Prasad, K. R., Karanam, S. R., Ganesh, D., Liyakat, K. K. S., Talasila, V., & Purushotham, P. (2024). AI in public-private partnership for IT infrastructure development. *The Journal of High Technology Management Research*, 35(1), 100496. DOI:10.1016/j.hitech.2024.100496

Prior, T., Giurco, D., Mudd, G., Mason, L., & Behrisch, J. (2012). Resource depletion, peak minerals and the implications for sustainable resource management. *Global Environmental Change*, 22(3), 577–587. DOI:10.1016/j.gloenvcha.2011.08.009

Proppe, D. S., Pandit, M. M., Bridge, E. S., Jasperse, P., & Holwerda, C. (2020). Semi-portable solar power to facilitate continuous operation of technology in the field. *Methods in Ecology and Evolution*, 11(11), 1388–1394. DOI:10.1111/2041-210X.13456

Puranik, T. A., Shaik, N., Vankudoth, R., Kolhe, M. R., Yadav, N., & Boopathi, S. (2024). Study on Harmonizing Human-Robot (Drone) Collaboration: Navigating Seamless Interactions in Collaborative Environments. In *Cybersecurity Issues and Challenges in the Drone Industry* (pp. 1–26). IGI Global.

Qiang, Y., Wang, X., Liu, X., Wang, Y., & Zhang, W. (2024). Edge-enhanced ML Attention Network for driving decision-making of autonomous vehicles via Deep Reinforcement Learning. *Proceedings of the Institution of Mechanical Engineers, Part D: Journal of Automobile Engineering*.

Radin, J. M., Wineinger, N. E., Topol, E. J., & Steinhubl, S. R. (2020). Harnessing wearable device data to improve state-level real-time surveillance of influenza-like illness in the USA: A population-based study. *The Lancet. Digital Health*, 2(2), e85–e93. DOI:10.1016/S2589-7500(19)30222-5 PMID:33334565

Raheman, F. (2022). Sharonomics: A Radical Economic Theory for the Next Industrial Revolution and Beyond. *Theoretical Economics Letters*, 12(6), 1710–1748. DOI:10.4236/tel.2022.126094

Rahier, T. (2018). *Bayesian networks for static and temporal data fusion* (Doctoral dissertation, Université Grenoble Alpes).

Rahmani, A. M., Gia, T. N., Negash, B., Anzanpour, A., Azimi, I., Jiang, M., & Liljeberg, P. (2018). Exploiting smart e-Health gateways at the edge of healthcare Internet-of-Things: A fog computing approach. *Future Generation Computer Systems*, 78, 641–658. DOI:10.1016/j.future.2017.02.014

Rahman, N. A. A., Abdullah, M. A., Hassan, A., & Mahroof, K. (2023). *17 Hard Hit by Halal Meat Cartel Controversy*. Technologies and Trends in the Halal Industry.

Raja Gopal, S., & Prabhakar, V. S. V. (2022). Intelligent edge based smart farming with LoRa and IoT. *International Journal of System Assurance Engineering and Management*. Advance online publication. DOI:10.1007/s13198-021-01576-z

Rajesh, P. V., Ashvin, J., Harish, M., Kishore, G., & Nidheesh, S. (2024). Fabrication of Equipment and IoT-Assisted Monitoring for Enhanced Zero-Till Farming. In *Emerging Technologies and Marketing Strategies for Sustainable Agriculture* (pp. 209–233). IGI Global. DOI:10.4018/979-8-3693-4864-2.ch011

Raji, E., Ijomah, T. I., & Eyieyien, O. G. (2024). Data-Driven decision making in agriculture and business: The role of advanced analytics. *Computer Science & IT Research Journal*, 5(7), 1565–1575. DOI:10.51594/csitrj.v5i7.1275

Raj, M., Gupta, S., Chamola, V., Elhence, A., Garg, T., Atiquzzaman, M., & Niyato, D. (2021). A survey on the role of Internet of Things for adopting and promoting Agriculture 4.0. *Journal of Network and Computer Applications*, 187, 103107. DOI:10.1016/j.jnca.2021.103107

Rajput, S., & Singh, S. P. (2020). Industry 4.0 Model for circular economy and cleaner production. *Journal of Cleaner Production*, 277, 123853. DOI:10.1016/j.jclepro.2020.123853

Randhawa, S., & Jain, S. (2017). Data aggregation in wireless sensor networks: Previous research, current status and future directions. *Wireless Personal Communications*, 97(3), 3355–3425. DOI:10.1007/s11277-017-4674-5

Rani, S., & Srivastava, G. (2024). Secure hierarchical fog computing-based architecture for industry 5.0 using an attribute-based encryption scheme. *Expert Systems with Applications*, 235, 121180. DOI:10.1016/j.eswa.2023.121180

Rasheed, M. W., Tang, J., Sarwar, A., Shah, S., Saddique, N., Khan, M. U., Imran Khan, M., Nawaz, S., Shamshiri, R. R., Aziz, M., & Sultan, M. (2022). Soil Moisture Measuring Techniques and Factors Affecting the Moisture Dynamics: A Comprehensive Review. *Sustainability (Basel)*, 14(18), 11538. DOI:10.3390/su141811538

Raspberry Pi Foundation. (n.d.). *Raspberry Pi 4 Tech Specs*. Retrieved 20 June 2024, from https://www.raspberrypi.com/products/raspberry-pi-4-model-b/specifications/

Rathore, M. M., Ahmad, A., Paul, A., & Rho, S. (2016). Urban planning and building smart cities based on the internet of things using big data analytics. *Computer Networks*, 101, 63–80. DOI:10.1016/j.comnet.2015.12.023

Rathore, M. M., Paul, A., Hong, W.-H., Seo, H., Awan, I., & Saeed, S. (2018). Exploiting IoT and big data analytics: Defining smart digital city using real-time urban data. *Sustainable Cities and Society*, 40, 600–610. DOI:10.1016/j.scs.2017.12.022

Ravisankar, A., Sampath, B., & Asif, M. M. (2023). Economic Studies on Automobile Management: Working Capital and Investment Analysis. In *Multidisciplinary Approaches to Organizational Governance During Health Crises* (pp. 169–198). IGI Global.

Ray, D. (2016). Cloud adoption decisions: Benefitting from an integrated perspective. *Electronic Journal of Information Systems Evaluation, 19*(1), 3-21.

Razzaq, M. A., Gill, S. H., Qureshi, M. A., & Ullah, S. (2017). Security issues in the Internet of Things (IoT): A comprehensive study. *International Journal of Advanced Computer Science and Applications*, 8(6), 383.

Reddy, C. K. K., Anisha, P. R., Khan, S., Hanafiah, M. M., Pamulaparty, L., & Mohana, R. M. (Eds.). (2024). *Sustainability in Industry 5.0: Theory and Applications*. CRC Press.

Ren, W., Tong, X., Du, J., Wang, N., Li, S., Min, G., & Zhao, Z. (2021). Privacy enhancing techniques in the internet of things using data anonymisation. *Information Systems Frontiers*, 1–12. DOI:10.1007/s10796-021-10116-w

Ribeiro, M. T., Singh, S., & Guestrin, C. (2016). Why should i trust you?" Explaining the predictions of any classifier. Proceedings of the 22nd ACM SIGKDD international conference on knowledge discovery and data mining.

Rinat, K., Thakur, G., Gupta, M., Madhuri, T. N. P., & Bansal, S. (2024). Comparative Analysis of Big Data Computing in Industry 4.0 and Industry 5.0: An Experimental Study. In *BIO Web of Conferences* (Vol. 86, p. 01068). EDP Sciences.

Rincón, V. J., Grella, M., Marucco, P., Alcatrão, L. E., Sanchez-Hermosilla, J., & Balsari, P. (2020). Spray performance assessment of a remote-controlled vehicle prototype for pesticide application in greenhouse tomato crops. *The Science of the Total Environment*, 726, 138509. DOI:10.1016/j.scitotenv.2020.138509 PMID:32305758

Ritchie, J. T., & Nesmith, D. S. (2015). Temperature and Crop Development. In Hanks, J., & Ritchie, J. T. (Eds.), *Agronomy Monographs* (pp. 5–29). American Society of Agronomy, Crop Science Society of America, Soil Science Society of America. DOI:10.2134/agronmonogr31.c2

Robertson, C., Nelson, T. A., MacNab, Y. C., & Lawson, A. B. (2010). Review of methods for space–time disease surveillance. *Spatial and Spatio-temporal Epidemiology*, 1(2-3), 105–116. DOI:10.1016/j.sste.2009.12.001 PMID:22749467

Rodney, B. D. (2020). Understanding the paradigm shift in education in the twenty-first century: The role of technology and the Internet of Things. *Worldwide Hospitality and Tourism Themes*, 12(1), 35–47. DOI:10.1108/WHATT-10-2019-0068

Rodríguez, A. I., Riaza, B. G., & Gómez, M. C. S. (2017). Collaborative learning and mobile devices: An educational experience in Primary Education. *Computers in Human Behavior*, 72, 664–677. DOI:10.1016/j.chb.2016.07.019

Rosenzweig, C., & Tubiello, F. N. (2007). Adaptation and mitigation strategies in agriculture: An analysis of potential synergies. *Mitigation and Adaptation Strategies for Global Change*, 12(5), 855–873. DOI:10.1007/s11027-007-9103-8

Rossi, S., & Caffi, S. (2019). Critical Success Factors for the Adoption of Decision Tools in IPM. *Agronomy (Basel)*, 9(11), 710. DOI:10.3390/agronomy9110710

Saberi, S., Kouhizadeh, M., Sarkis, J., & Shen, L. (2019). Blockchain technology and its relationships to sustainable supply chain management. *International Journal of Production Research*, 57(7), 2117–2135. DOI:10.1080/00207543.2018.1533261

Saha, D., Padhiary, M., Barbhuiya, J. A., Chakrabarty, T., & Sethi, L. N. (2023). Development of an IOT based Solenoid Controlled Pressure Regulation System for Precision Sprayer. *International Journal for Research in Applied Science and Engineering Technology*, 11(7), 2210–2216. DOI:10.22214/ijraset.2023.55103

Sahu, P., Singh, S., & Kumar, P. (2019). Challenges and Issues in Securing Data Privacy in IoT and Connected Devices. 2019 6th International Conference on Computing for Sustainable Global Development (INDIACom).

Saini, M. K., & Goel, N. (2019). How smart are smart classrooms? A review of smart classroom technologies. *ACM Computing Surveys*, 52(6), 1–28. DOI:10.1145/3365757

Salam, A. (2024). Internet of Things for Water Sustainability. In A. Salam, *Internet of Things for Sustainable Community Development* (pp. 113–145). Springer International Publishing. DOI:10.1007/978-3-031-62162-8_4

Saleem, A. N., Noori, N. M., & Ozdamli, F. (2022). Gamification applications in E-learning: A literature review. *Technology. Knowledge and Learning*, 27(1), 139–159. DOI:10.1007/s10758-020-09487-x

Sampath, B., Sureshkumar, T., Yuvaraj, M., & Velmurugan, D. (2021). Experimental Investigations on Eco-Friendly Helium-Mist Near-Dry Wire-Cut EDM of M2-HSS Material. *Materials Research Proceedings*, 19, 175–180.

Sankar, K. M., Booba, B., & Boopathi, S. (2023). Smart Agriculture Irrigation Monitoring System Using Internet of Things. In *Contemporary Developments in Agricultural Cyber-Physical Systems* (pp. 105–121). IGI Global. DOI:10.4018/978-1-6684-7879-0.ch006

Saputro, E. P. (2024). Kolaborasi Manusia Dan Sumber Daya Robotik Menuju Masa Depan Manufaktur Berkelanjutan Industri 5.0. *Innovative: Journal Of Social Science Research*, 4(1), 2504–2516.

Sarker, I. H. (2021). Machine Learning: Algorithms, Real-World Applications and Research Directions. *SN Computer Science*, 2(3), 160. DOI:10.1007/s42979-021-00592-x PMID:33778771

Sasaki, Y. (2021). A survey on IoT big data analytic systems: Current and future. *IEEE Internet of Things Journal*, 9(2), 1024–1036. DOI:10.1109/JIOT.2021.3131724

Satav, S. D., Lamani, D., Harsha, K., Kumar, N., Manikandan, S., & Sampath, B. (2023). Energy and Battery Management in the Era of Cloud Computing: Sustainable Wireless Systems and Networks. In *Sustainable Science and Intelligent Technologies for Societal Development* (pp. 141–166). IGI Global.

Saura, J. R., Palacios-Marqués, D., & Ribeiro-Soriano, D. (2023). Digital marketing in SMEs via data-driven strategies: Reviewing the current state of research. *Journal of Small Business Management*, 61(3), 1278–1313. DOI:10.1080/00472778.2021.1955127

Sayyad, L. (2023). Home automation system based on GSM. *Journal of VLSI Design Tools & Technology*, 13(3), 7–12. DOI:10.37591/jovdtt.v13i3.7877

Sazu, M. H., & Jahan, S. A. (2022). High efficiency public transportation system: role of big data in making recommendations. *Journal of process management and new technologies, 10*(3-4), 9-21.

Schier, M., Reinders, C., & Rosenhahn, B. (2023). Deep reinforcement learning for autonomous driving using high-level heterogeneous ML representations. *International Conference on Robotics and Automation (ICRA)*.

Schoeffer, J., & Kuehl, N. (2021). Appropriate fairness perceptions? On the effectiveness of explanations in enabling people to assess the fairness of automated decision systems. Companion Publication of the 2021 Conference on Computer Supported Cooperative Work and Social Computing. DOI:10.1145/3462204.3481742

Schröder, A. J., Cuypers, M., & Götting, A. (2024). From Industry 4.0 to Industry 5.0: The Triple Transition Digital, Green and Social. In *Industry 4.0 and the Road to Sustainable Steelmaking in Europe: Recasting the Future* (pp. 35–51). Springer International Publishing. DOI:10.1007/978-3-031-35479-3_3

Selvakumar, S., Shankar, R., Ranjit, P., Bhattacharya, S., Gupta, A. S. G., & Boopathi, S. (2023). E-Waste Recovery and Utilization Processes for Mobile Phone Waste. In *Handbook of Research on Safe Disposal Methods of Municipal Solid Wastes for a Sustainable Environment* (pp. 222–240). IGI Global. DOI:10.4018/978-1-6684-8117-2.ch016

Selvarajan, S., Manoharan, H., & Shankar, A. (2024). SL-RI: Integration of supervised learning in robots for industry 5.0 automated application monitoring. *Measurement. Sensors*, 31, 100972. DOI:10.1016/j.measen.2023.100972

erban, R.-A. (2017). The impact of big data, sustainability, and digitalization on company performance. *Studies in Business and Economics*, 12(3), 181–189. DOI:10.1515/sbe-2017-0045

Shafer, G. (1992). Dempster-shafer theory. Encyclopedia of artificial intelligence, 1, 330-331.

Shah, A. S., Nasir, H., Fayaz, M., Lajis, A., & Shah, A. (2019). A review on energy consumption optimization techniques in IoT based smart building environments. *Information (Basel)*, 10(3), 108. DOI:10.3390/info10030108

Shaheb, R., Venkatesh, R., & Shearer, S. A. (2021). A Review on the Effect of Soil Compaction and its Management for Sustainable Crop Production. *Journal of Biosystems Engineering*, 46(4), 417–439. DOI:10.1007/s42853-021-00117-7

Shanwad, U., Patil, V., Dasog, G., Mansur, C., & Shashidhar, K. (2002). Global positioning system (GPS) in precision agriculture. *Proceedings of Asian GPS Conference*, 1.

Sharma, A., & Singh, B. (2022). Measuring Impact of E-commerce on Small Scale Business: A Systematic Review. *Journal of Corporate Governance and International Business Law*, 5(1).

Sharma, N., Acharya, S., Kumar, K., Singh, N., & Chaurasia, O. P. (2018). Hydroponics as an advanced technique for vegetable production: An overview. *Journal of Soil and Water Conservation*, 17(4), 364–371. DOI:10.5958/2455-7145.2018.00056.5

Sharma, S., Henderson, J., & Ghosh, J. (2020). CERTIFAI: A common framework to provide explanations and analyse the fairness and robustness of black-box models. *Proceedings of the AAAI/ACM Conference on AI, Ethics, and Society.* DOI:10.3233/JIFS-202503

Sheikholeslami, S. (2019). Ablation programming for machine learning.

Sheikholeslami, S., Meister, M., Wang, T., Payberah, A. H., Vlassov, V., & Dowling, J. (2021). Autoablation: Automated parallel ablation studies for deep learning. *Proceedings of the 1st Workshop on Machine Learning and Systems.* PMID:33923270

Shekarpour, S., Nadgeri, A., & Singh, K. (2020). QA2Explanation: Generating and Evaluating Explanations for Question Answering Systems over AI. *arXiv preprint arXiv:2010.08323.*

Shemshack, A., & Spector, J. M. (2020). A systematic literature review of personalized learning terms. *Smart Learning Environments*, 7(1), 33. DOI:10.1186/s40561-020-00140-9

Shi, H., Zhang, Y., Xu, Z., Xu, X., & Qi, L. (2022). Multi-source temporal AI embedding for edge computing enabled internet of vehicles. *Neurocomputing*, 491, 597–606. DOI:10.1016/j.neucom.2021.12.036

Shinde, P. P., & Shah, S. (2018). A Review of Machine Learning and Deep Learning Applications. *2018 Fourth International Conference on Computing Communication Control and Automation (ICCUBEA)*, 1–6. DOI:10.1109/ICCUBEA.2018.8697857

Shweta, K. (2022). Automatic wall painting robot. *Journal of Image Processing and Intelligent Remote Sensing*, 2(6).

Siebald, H., Hensel, O., Beneke, F., Merbach, L., Walther, C., Kirchner, S. M., & Huster, J. (2017). Real-Time Acoustic Monitoring of Cutting Blade Sharpness in Agricultural Machinery. *IEEE/ASME Transactions on Mechatronics*, 22(6), 2411–2419. DOI:10.1109/TMECH.2017.2735542

Siemens, M. C., & Hulick, D. E. (2008). A New Grain Harvesting System for Single-Pass Grain Harvest, Biomass Collection, Crop Residue Sizing, and Grain Segregation. *Transactions of the ASABE*, 51(5), 1519–1527. DOI:10.13031/2013.25300

Silva, B. N., Khan, M., & Han, K. (2020). Integration of Big Data analytics embedded smart city architecture with RESTful web of things for efficient service provision and energy management. *Future Generation Computer Systems*, 107, 975–987. DOI:10.1016/j.future.2017.06.024

Silva, B. N., Khan, M., Jung, C., Seo, J., Muhammad, D., Han, J., Yoon, Y., & Han, K. (2018). Urban planning and smart city decision management empowered by real-time data processing using big data analytics. *Sensors (Basel)*, 18(9), 2994. DOI:10.3390/s18092994 PMID:30205499

Silvanus, S. K. (2017). *Fabrication and characterization of magnetoresponsive carbon nanotube-infused polysulfone (CNT-IPSF) nanocomposites for water purification* (Doctoral dissertation, Kenyatta University).

Singh, B. (2023). Blockchain Technology in Renovating Healthcare: Legal and Future Perspectives. In *Revolutionizing Healthcare Through Artificial Intelligence and Internet of Things Applications* (pp. 177-186). IGI Global.

Singh, B. (2019). Profiling Public Healthcare: A Comparative Analysis Based on the Multidimensional Healthcare Management and Legal Approach. *Indian Journal of Health and Medical Law*, 2(2), 1–5.

Singh, B. (2020). Global science and jurisprudential approach concerning healthcare and illness. *Indian Journal of Health and Medical Law*, 3(1), 7–13.

Singh, B. (2022). COVID-19 Pandemic and Public Healthcare: Endless Downward Spiral or Solution via Rapid Legal and Health Services Implementation with Patient Monitoring Program. *Justice and Law Bulletin*, 1(1), 1–7.

Singh, B. (2022). Relevance of Agriculture-Nutrition Linkage for Human Healthcare: A Conceptual Legal Framework of Implication and Pathways. *Justice and Law Bulletin*, 1(1), 44–49.

Singh, B. (2022). Understanding Legal Frameworks Concerning Transgender Healthcare in the Age of Dynamism. *Electronic Journal of Social and Strategic Studies*, 3(1), 56–65. DOI:10.47362/EJSSS.2022.3104

Singh, B. (2023). Federated Learning for Envision Future Trajectory Smart Transport System for Climate Preservation and Smart Green Planet: Insights into Global Governance and SDG-9 (Industry, Innovation and Infrastructure). *National Journal of Environmental Law*, 6(2), 6–17.

Singh, B. (2023). Tele-Health Monitoring Lensing Deep Neural Learning Structure: Ambient Patient Wellness via Wearable Devices for Real-Time Alerts and Interventions. *Indian Journal of Health and Medical Law*, 6(2), 12–16.

Singh, B. (2023). Unleashing Alternative Dispute Resolution (ADR) in Resolving Complex Legal-Technical Issues Arising in Cyberspace Lensing E-Commerce and Intellectual Property: Proliferation of E-Commerce Digital Economy. *Revista Brasileira de Alternative Dispute Resolution-Brazilian Journal of Alternative Dispute Resolution-RBADR*, 5(10), 81–105. DOI:10.52028/rbadr.v5i10.ART04.Ind

Singh, B. (2024). Legal Dynamics Lensing Metaverse Crafted for Videogame Industry and E-Sports: Phenomenological Exploration Catalyst Complexity and Future. *Journal of Intellectual Property Rights Law*, 7(1), 8–14.

Singh, B., & Kaunert, C. (2024). Integration of Cutting-Edge Technologies such as Internet of Things (IoT) and 5G in Health Monitoring Systems: A Comprehensive Legal Analysis and Futuristic Outcomes. *GLS Law Journal*, 6(1), 13–20. DOI:10.69974/glslawjournal.v6i1.123

Siow, E., Tiropanis, T., & Hall, W. (2018). Analytics for the internet of things: A survey. *ACM Computing Surveys*, 51(4), 1–36. DOI:10.1145/3204947

Slack, D., Hilgard, S., Jia, E., Singh, S., & Lakkaraju, H. (2020, February). Fooling lime and shap: Adversarial attacks on post hoc explanation methods. In *Proceedings of the AAAI/ACM Conference on AI, Ethics, and Society* (pp. 180-186). DOI:10.1145/3375627.3375830

Śledziewska, K., & Włoch, R. (2021). The Economics of Digital Transformation. *The disruption of.*

Śledziewska, K., & Włoch, R. (2021). The foundations of the digital economy. In *The Economics of Digital Transformation*. Taylor & Francis. DOI:10.4324/9781003144359-1

Song, M., Cen, L., Zheng, Z., Fisher, R., Liang, X., Wang, Y., & Huisingh, D. (2017). How would big data support societal development and environmental sustainability? Insights and practices. *Journal of Cleaner Production*, 142, 489–500. DOI:10.1016/j.jclepro.2016.10.091

Sonia, R., Gupta, N., Manikandan, K., Hemalatha, R., Kumar, M. J., & Boopathi, S. (2024). Strengthening Security, Privacy, and Trust in Artificial Intelligence Drones for Smart Cities. In *Analyzing and Mitigating Security Risks in Cloud Computing* (pp. 214–242). IGI Global. DOI:10.4018/979-8-3693-3249-8.ch011

Sonnenberg, M. (2012). Are you SMARTer than a SMART Board™? How to Effectively Use This Technology Tool to Communicate in a Classroom With a Diverse Group of Learners. In *Communication technology for students in special education and gifted programs* (pp. 243–248). IGI Global. DOI:10.4018/978-1-60960-878-1.ch019

Speringer, M., & Schnelzer, J. (2019). Differentiation of industry 4.0 models. *Vienna, Austria.*

Sreenivasulu, . (2022). Implementation of latest machine learning approaches for students grade prediction. *International Journal of Early Childhood Special Education*, 14(3), 9887–9894.

Srinivasan, S., Hema, D. D., Singaram, B., Praveena, D., Mohan, K. K., & Preetha, M. (2024). Decision Support System based on Industry 5.0 in Artificial Intelligence. *International Journal of Intelligent Systems and Applications in Engineering*, 12(15s), 172–178.

Stefanowski, J., Krawiec, K., & Wrembel, R. (2017). Exploring complex and big data. *International Journal of Applied Mathematics and Computer Science*, 27(4), 669–679. DOI:10.1515/amcs-2017-0046

Stehr, N. J. (2015). Drones: The newest technology for precision agriculture. *Natural Sciences Education*, 44(1), 89–91. DOI:10.4195/nse2015.04.0772

Suganya, G., Selvakumar, J. J., Varadharajan, P., & Pachiyappan, S. (2024). Skill Sets Required to Meet a Human-Centered Industry 5.0: A Systematic Literature Review and Bibliometric Analysis. *Advances in Web Technologies and Engineering*, 5(0), 231–252. DOI:10.4018/979-8-3693-0782-3.ch014

Sultanabanu, S. L. (2024). ChatGPT: An automated teacher's guide to learning. In Bansal, R., Chakir, A., Ngah, A. H., Rabby, F., & Jain, A. (Eds.), *AI Algorithms and ChatGPT for Student Engagement in Online Learning* (pp. 1–20). IGI Global. DOI:10.4018/979-8-3693-4268-8.ch001

Sun, J. C.-Y., & Hsieh, P.-H. (2018). Application of a gamified interactive response system to enhance the intrinsic and extrinsic motivation, student engagement, and attention of English learners. *Journal of Educational Technology & Society*, 21(3), 104–116.

Sun, P. (2020). Security and privacy protection in cloud computing: Discussions and challenges. *Journal of Network and Computer Applications*, 160, 102642. DOI:10.1016/j.jnca.2020.102642

Sunyaev, A., & Sunyaev, A. (2020). The internet of things. *Internet Computing: Principles of Distributed Systems and Emerging Internet-Based Technologies*, 301-337.

Svetashova, Y., Heling, L., Schmid, S., & Acosta, M. (2021). Pay-as-you-go Population of an Automotive Signal AI. *The Semantic Web: 18th International Conference, ESWC 2021, Virtual Event, June 6–10, 2021Proceedings*, 18, 717–735.

Tabrizchi, H., & Kuchaki Rafsanjani, M. (2020). A survey on security challenges in cloud computing: Issues, threats, and solutions. *The Journal of Supercomputing*, 76(12), 9493–9532. DOI:10.1007/s11227-020-03213-1

Tang, X., Sun, T., Zhu, R., & Wang, S. (2021, January). CKG: dynamic representation based on context and AI. In *2020 25th International Conference on Pattern Recognition (ICPR)* (pp. 2889-2895). IEEE.

Tang, S., Razeghi, O., Kapoor, R., Alhusseini, M. I., Fazal, M., Rogers, A. J., Rodrigo Bort, M., Clopton, P., Wang, P. J., Rubin, D. L., Narayan, S. M., & Baykaner, T. (2022). Machine learning–enabled multimodal fusion of intra-atrial and body surface signals in prediction of atrial fibrillation ablation outcomes. *Circulation: Arrhythmia and Electrophysiology*, 15(8), e010850. DOI:10.1161/CIRCEP.122.010850 PMID:35867397

Tangwannawit, P., & Saengkrajang, K. (2021). Technology Acceptance Model to Evaluate The Adoption of The Internet of Things For Planting Maize. *Life Sciences and Environment Journal, 22*, 262273. DOI:10.14456/LSEJ.2021.13

Tan, Z., Zhao, X., Fang, Y., Ge, B., & Xiao, W. (2018). AI representation via similarity-based embedding. *Scientific Programming*.

Tawalbeh, L., Muheidat, F., Tawalbeh, M., & Quwaider, M. (2020). IoT Privacy and security: Challenges and solutions. *Applied Sciences (Basel, Switzerland)*, 10(12), 4102. DOI:10.3390/app10124102

Terzieva, V., Ilchev, S., & Todorova, K. (2022). The Role of Internet of Things in Smart Education. *IFAC-PapersOnLine*, 55(11), 108–113. DOI:10.1016/j.ifacol.2022.08.057

Texier, G., Allodji, R. S., Diop, L., Meynard, J. B., Pellegrin, L., & Chaudet, H. (2019). Using decision fusion methods to improve outbreak detection in disease surveillance. *BMC Medical Informatics and Decision Making*, 19, 1–11.

Thacker, S. B., & Berkelman, R. L. (1988). Public health surveillance in the United States. *Epidemiologic Reviews*, 10(1), 164–190. DOI:10.1093/oxfordjournals.epirev. a036021 PMID:3066626

Thomas, S., Kuska, M. T., Bohnenkamp, D., Brugger, A., Alisaac, E., Wahabzada, M., Behmann, J., & Mahlein, A.-K. (2018). Benefits of hyperspectral imaging for plant disease detection and plant protection: A technical perspective. *Journal of Plant Diseases and Protection*, 125(1), 5–20. DOI:10.1007/s41348-017-0124-6

Thomasson, J. A., Baillie, C. P., Antille, D. L., McCarthy, C. L., & Lobsey, C. R. (2018). A review of the state of the art in agricultural automation. Part II: On-farm agricultural communications and connectivity. DOI:10.13031/aim.201801590

Timko, A. M. (2022). *Cybersecurity of Internet of Things Devices: A Secure Shell Implementation* [Metropolia University of Applied Sciences]. https://www.theseus.fi/handle/10024/748434

Tissenbaum, M., & Slotta, J. D. (2019). Developing a smart classroom infrastructure to support real-time student collaboration and inquiry: A 4-year design study. *Instructional Science*, 47(4), 423–462. DOI:10.1007/s11251-019-09486-1

Tönjes, R., Barnaghi, P., Ali, M., Mileo, A., Hauswirth, M., Ganz, F., Ganea, S., Kjærgaard, B., Kuemper, D., & Nechifor, S. (2014). Real time iot stream processing and large-scale data analytics for smart city applications. poster session, European Conference on Networks and Communications.

Topakci, M., Unal, I., Canakci, M., Yigit, M., & Karayel, D. (2010). Improvement of field efficiency measurement system based on GPS for precision agriculture applications. *Journal of Food Agriculture and Environment*, 8(3 & 4), 288–292.

Trappey, A. J., Liang, C. P., & Lin, H. J. (2022). Using machine learning language models to generate innovation AIs for patent mining. *Applied Sciences (Basel, Switzerland)*, 12(19), 9818. DOI:10.3390/app12199818

Trappey, A. J., Trappey, C. V., Govindarajan, U. H., Chuang, A. C., & Sun, J. J. (2017). A review of essential standards and patent landscapes for the Internet of Things: A key enabler for Industry 4.0. *Advanced Engineering Informatics*, 33, 208–229. DOI:10.1016/j.aei.2016.11.007

Triantafyllou, A., Sarigiannidis, P., & Bibi, S. (2019). Precision Agriculture: A Remote Sensing Monitoring System Architecture. *Information (Basel)*, 10(11), 348. DOI:10.3390/info10110348

Turnip, A., Pebriansyah, F. R., Simarmata, T., Sihombing, P., & Joelianto, E. (2023). Design of smart farming communication and web interface using MQTT and Node.js. *Open Agriculture*, 8(1), 20220159. DOI:10.1515/opag-2022-0159

Vacchi, M., Siligardi, C., & Settembre-Blundo, D. (2024). Driving Manufacturing Companies toward Industry 5.0: A Strategic Framework for Process Technological Sustainability Assessment (P-TSA). *Sustainability (Basel)*, 16(2), 695. DOI:10.3390/su16020695

Valeriya, G., Kirola, M., Gupta, M., Bharathi, P., & Acharya, P. (2024). Evaluating the Impact of AI-Based Sustainability Measures in Industry 5.0: A Longitudinal Study. In *BIO Web of Conferences* (Vol. 86, p. 01058). EDP Sciences.

Van der Poll, J. A. (2022). Problematizing the Adoption of Formal Methods in the 4IR–5IR Transition. *Applied System Innovation*, 5(6), 127. DOI:10.3390/asi5060127

Van Houwelingen, H. C., Arends, L. R., & Stijnen, T. (2002). Advanced methods in meta-analysis: Multivariate approach and meta-regression. *Statistics in Medicine*, 21(4), 589–624. DOI:10.1002/sim.1040 PMID:11836738

Vatin, N. I., Negi, G. S., Yellanki, V. S., Mohan, C., & Singla, N. (2024). Sustainability Measures: An Experimental Analysis of AI and Big Data Insights in Industry 5.0. In *BIO Web of Conferences* (Vol. 86, p. 01072). EDP Sciences.

Vatti, R., Vatti, N., Mahender, K., Lakshmi Vatti, P., & Krishnaveni, B. (2020). Solar energy harvesting for smart farming using nanomaterial and machine learning. *IOP Conference Series. Materials Science and Engineering*, 981(3), 032009. DOI:10.1088/1757-899X/981/3/032009

Velmurugan, M., Ouyang, C., Moreira, C., & Sindhgatta, R. (2021). Developing a fidelity evaluation approach for interpretable machine learning. *arXiv preprint arXiv:2106.08492*.

Velmurugan, K., Venkumar, P., & Sudhakara, P. R. (2021). SME 4.0: Machine learning framework for real-time machine health monitoring system. *Journal of Physics: Conference Series*, 1911(1), 012026. DOI:10.1088/1742-6596/1911/1/012026

Venkatesh, C., Jayakrishna, D., & Sivayamini, L. (2022). Design of Smart Classroom in Educational Institutes for Smart and a Sustainable Campus Based on Internet of Things. In *Modern Approaches in Machine Learning & Cognitive Science: A Walkthrough* (pp. 547–558). Springer. DOI:10.1007/978-3-030-96634-8_50

Venkateswaran, N., Kiran Kumar, K., Maheswari, K., Kumar Reddy, R. V., & Boopathi, S. (2024). Optimizing IoT Data Aggregation: Hybrid Firefly-Artificial Bee Colony Algorithm for Enhanced Efficiency in Agriculture. *AGRIS On-Line Papers in Economics and Informatics*, 16(1), 117–130. DOI:10.7160/aol.2024.160110

Verdouw, C., Tekinerdogan, B., Beulens, A., & Wolfert, S. (2021). Digital twins in smart farming. *Agricultural Systems*, 189, 103046. DOI:10.1016/j.agsy.2020.103046

Verma, S., Kawamoto, Y., Fadlullah, Z. M., Nishiyama, H., & Kato, N. (2017). A survey on network methodologies for real-time analytics of massive IoT data and open research issues. *IEEE Communications Surveys and Tutorials*, 19(3), 1457–1477. DOI:10.1109/COMST.2017.2694469

Villar, A., Paladini, S., & Buckley, O. (2023, July). Towards Supply Chain 5.0: Redesigning Supply Chains as Resilient, Sustainable, and Human-Centric Systems in a Post-pandemic World. In *Operations* []. Cham: Springer International Publishing.]. *Research Forum*, 4(3), 60. DOI:10.1007/s43069-023-00234-3

Vipin, P.-N. T. M. S. (2006). *Introduction to data mining.*

Virk, S. S., Fulton, J. P., Porter, W. M., & Pate, G. L. (2020). Row-crop planter performance to support variable-rate seeding of maize. *Precision Agriculture*, 21(3), 603–619. DOI:10.1007/s11119-019-09685-3

Von Rueden, L., Mayer, S., Beckh, K., Georgiev, B., Giesselbach, S., Heese, R., Kirsch, B., Walczak, M., Pfrommer, J., Pick, A., Ramamurthy, R., Garcke, J., Bauckhage, C., & Schuecker, J. (2021). Informed machine learning–a taxonomy and survey of integrating prior knowledge into learning systems. *IEEE Transactions on Knowledge and Data Engineering*, 35(1), 614–633. DOI:10.1109/TKDE.2021.3079836

Vorakulpipat, C., Sirapaisan, S., Rattanalerdnusorn, E., & Savangsuk, V. (2017). A Policy-Based Framework for Preserving Confidentiality in BYOD Environments: A Review of Information Security Perspectives. *Security and Communication Networks*, 2017(1), 2057260. DOI:10.1155/2017/2057260

Voss, W. G. (2016). European union data privacy law reform: General data protection regulation, privacy shield, and the right to delisting. *Business Lawyer*, 72(1), 221–234.

Wachter, S., Mittelstadt, B., & Russell, C. (2017). Counterfactual explanations without opening the black box: Automated decisions and the GDPR. *SSRN*, 31, 841. DOI:10.2139/ssrn.3063289

Wang, S., Zhang, J., Wang, P., Law, J., Calinescu, R., & Mihaylova, L. (2024). A deep learning-enhanced Digital Twin framework for improving safety and reliability in human–robot collaborative manufacturing. *Robotics and computer-integrated manufacturing, 85*, 102608.

Wang, B., Zhou, H., Li, X., Yang, G., Zheng, P., Song, C., Yuan, Y., Wuest, T., Yang, H., & Wang, L. (2024). Human Digital Twin in the context of Industry 5.0. *Robotics and Computer-integrated Manufacturing*, 85, 102626. DOI:10.1016/j.rcim.2023.102626

Wang, F., & Rudin, C. (2015). Falling rule lists. Artificial intelligence and statistics.

Wang, J., Tigelaar, D. E., Luo, J., & Admiraal, W. (2022). Teacher beliefs, classroom process quality, and student engagement in the smart classroom learning environment: A multilevel analysis. *Computers & Education*, 183, 104501. DOI:10.1016/j.compedu.2022.104501

Wang, L., Adiga, A., Chen, J., Lewis, B., Sadilek, A., Venkatramanan, S., & Marathe, M. (2022). Combining Theory and Data-Driven Approaches for Epidemic Forecasts. In *Knowledge Guided Machine Learning* (pp. 55–82). Chapman and Hall/CRC. DOI:10.1201/9781003143376-3

Wang, Z. (2008). Smart spaces: Creating new instructional space with smart classroom technology. *New Library World*, 109(3/4), 150–165. DOI:10.1108/03074800810857603

Waske, B., & Benediktsson, J. A. (2007). Fusion of support vector machines for classification of multisensor data. *IEEE Transactions on Geoscience and Remote Sensing*, 45(12), 3858–3866. DOI:10.1109/TGRS.2007.898446

Wazid, M., Das, A. K., Hussain, R., Succi, G., & Rodrigues, J. J. (2019). Authentication in cloud-driven IoT-based big data environment: Survey and outlook. *Journal of Systems Architecture*, 97, 185–196. DOI:10.1016/j.sysarc.2018.12.005

Welch, G., & Bishop, G. (1995). *An introduction to the Kalman filter*. Springer New York.

Wen, L. (2024). Design automation system synchronization for cyber physical system with dynamic voltage and frequency scaling in industry 5.0. *Measurement. Sensors*, 31, 100981. DOI:10.1016/j.measen.2023.100981

Werner, S., Rettinger, A., Halilaj, L., & Lüttin, J. (2021). RETRA: Recurrent transformers for learning temporally contextualized AI embeddings. *The Semantic Web: 18th International Conference, ESWC 2021, Virtual Event, June 6–10, 2021 Proceedings*, 18, 425–440.

Williamson, B. (2017). Big data in education: The digital future of learning, policy and practice.

Wilson, N. (2000). Algorithms for dempster-shafer theory. In *Handbook of Defeasible Reasoning and Uncertainty Management Systems: Algorithms for Uncertainty and Defeasible Reasoning* (pp. 421–475). Springer Netherlands. DOI:10.1007/978-94-017-1737-3_10

Wiseman, L., Sanderson, J., Zhang, A., & Jakku, E. (2019). Farmers and their data: An examination of farmers' reluctance to share their data through the lens of the laws impacting smart farming. *NJAS Wageningen Journal of Life Sciences*, 90–91(1), 1–10. DOI:10.1016/j.njas.2019.04.007

Wu, J. K., & Wong, Y. (2006, July). Bayesian approach for data fusion in sensor networks. *In 2006 9th International Conference on Information Fusion* (pp. 1-5). IEEE.

Xia, H., Wang, Y., Gauthier, J., & Zhang, J. Z. (2022). AI of mobile payment platforms based on deep learning: Risk analysis and policy implications. *Expert Systems with Applications*, 208, 118143. DOI:10.1016/j.eswa.2022.118143

Xiao, D., Dianati, M., Geiger, W. G., & Woodman, R. (2023). Review of ML-based hazardous event detection methods for autonomous driving systems. *IEEE Transactions on Intelligent Transportation Systems*, 24(5), 4697–4715. DOI:10.1109/TITS.2023.3240104

Xu, P., Lee, J., Barth, J. R., & Richey, R. G. (2021). Blockchain as supply chain technology: Considering transparency and security. *International Journal of Physical Distribution & Logistics Management*, 51(3), 305–324. DOI:10.1108/IJPDLM-08-2019-0234

Xu, W., Feng, L., & Ma, J. (2022). Understanding the domain of driving distraction with AIs. *PLoS One*, 17(12), e0278822. DOI:10.1371/journal.pone.0278822 PMID:36490240

Yang, C., Yu, M., Hu, F., Jiang, Y., & Li, Y. (2017). Utilizing cloud computing to address big geospatial data challenges. *Computers, Environment and Urban Systems*, 61, 120–128. DOI:10.1016/j.compenvurbsys.2016.10.010

Yang, K.-T., Wang, T.-H., & Kao, Y.-C. (2012). How an interactive whiteboard impacts a traditional classroom. *Education as Change*, 16(2), 313–332. DOI:10.1080/16823206.2012.745759

Yeh, C.-K., Hsieh, C.-Y., Suggala, A., Inouye, D. I., & Ravikumar, P. K. (2019). On the (in) fidelity and sensitivity of explanations. *Advances in Neural Information Processing Systems*, 32.

Ye, N. (2003). *The handbook of data mining*. CRC Press. DOI:10.1201/b12469

Ye, Y., He, Y., & Wang, YeKui, H. (2016). SHVC, the Scalable Extensions of HEVC, and Its Applications. *ZTE Communications*, 14(1), 24.

Yildiz, R. O., & Esmer, S. (2023). Talent management strategies and functions: A systematic review. *Industrial and Commercial Training*, 55(1), 93–111. DOI:10.1108/ICT-01-2022-0007

Yilmazoglu, M. Z. (2017). Decreasing energy consumption and carbon footprint in a school building: A comparative study on energy audits. *International Journal of Global Warming*, 13(2), 237–257. DOI:10.1504/IJGW.2017.086291

Yim, J., Udpa, S. S., Udpa, L., Mina, M., & Lord, W. (1995). Neural network approaches to data fusion. *Review of Progress in Quantitative Nondestructive Evaluation*, 14, 819–826. DOI:10.1007/978-1-4615-1987-4_102

Yousefi, M. R., & Razdari, A. M. (2015). Application of GIS and GPS in precision agriculture (a review). *International Journal of Advanced Biological and Biomedical Research*, 3(1), 7–9.

Yu, C., Wang, X., Xu, X., Zhang, M., Ge, H., Ren, J., Sun, L., Chen, B., & Tan, G. (2019). Distributed multiagent coordinated learning for autonomous driving in highways based on dynamic coordination MLs. *IEEE Transactions on Intelligent Transportation Systems*, 21(2), 735–748. DOI:10.1109/TITS.2019.2893683

Yu, S. Y., Malawade, A. V., & Faruque, M. A. A. (2023). Scene-ML Embedding for Robust Autonomous Vehicle Perception. In *Machine Learning and Optimization Techniques for Automotive Cyber-Physical Systems* (pp. 525–544). Springer International Publishing. DOI:10.1007/978-3-031-28016-0_18

Zamora-Izquierdo, M. A., Santa, J., Martínez, J. A., Martínez, V., & Skarmeta, A. F. (2019). Smart farming IoT platform based on edge and cloud computing. *Biosystems Engineering*, 177, 4–17. DOI:10.1016/j.biosystemseng.2018.10.014

Zeeshan, K., Hämäläinen, T., & Neittaanmäki, P. (2022). Internet of Things for sustainable smart education: An overview. *Sustainability (Basel)*, 14(7), 4293. DOI:10.3390/su14074293

Zezza, A., & Tasciotti, L. (2010). Urban agriculture, poverty, and food security: Empirical evidence from a sample of developing countries. *Food Policy*, 35(4), 265–273. DOI:10.1016/j.foodpol.2010.04.007

Zhai, X., Chu, X., Chai, C. S., Jong, M. S. Y., Istenic, A., Spector, M., Liu, J.-B., Yuan, J., & Li, Y. (2021). A Review of Artificial Intelligence (AI) in Education from 2010 to 2020. *Complexity*, 2021(1), 881–890. DOI:10.1155/2021/8812542

Zhang, A., Venkatesh, V., Wang, J. X., Mani, V., Wan, M., & Qu, T. (2023). Drivers of industry 4.0-enabled smart waste management in supply chain operations: A circular economy perspective in china. *Production Planning and Control*, 34(10), 870–886. DOI:10.1080/09537287.2021.1980909

Zhang, J., & Tao, D. (2021). Empowering Things With Intelligence: A Survey of the Progress, Challenges, and Opportunities in Artificial Intelligence of Things. *IEEE Internet of Things Journal*, 8(10), 7789–7817. DOI:10.1109/JIOT.2020.3039359

Zhang, Y., Yip, C., Lu, E., & Dong, Z. Y. (2022). A systematic review on technologies and applications in smart campus: A human-centered case study. *IEEE Access : Practical Innovations, Open Solutions*, 10, 16134–16149. DOI:10.1109/ACCESS.2022.3148735

Zhao, Y., Wang, Y., & Derr, T. (2023). Fairness and explainability: Bridging the gap towards fair model explanations. Proceedings of the AAAI Conference on Artificial Intelligence.

Zheng, Z., Zhou, B., Zhou, D., Soylu, A., & Kharlamov, E. (2022, October). Executable AI for transparent machine learning in welding monitoring at Bosch. In *Proceedings of the 31st ACM International Conference on Information & Knowledge Management* (pp. 5102-5103).

Zhou, B., Sun, Y., Bau, D., & Torralba, A. (2018). Revisiting the importance of individual units in cnns via ablation. *arXiv preprint arXiv:1806.02891*.

Zhou, H., Liu, Q., Yan, K., & Du, Y. (2021). Deep Learning Enhanced Solar Energy Forecasting with AI-Driven IoT. *Wireless Communications and Mobile Computing*, 2021(1), 1–11. DOI:10.1155/2021/9249387

Zhou, K., Fu, C., & Yang, S. (2016). Big data driven smart energy management: From big data to big insights. *Renewable & Sustainable Energy Reviews*, 56, 215–225. DOI:10.1016/j.rser.2015.11.050

Zhou, X. C., & Shen, H. B. (2010). Notifiable infectious disease surveillance with data collected by search engine. *Journal of Zhejiang University. Science, C*, 11, 241–248.

Zhu, Z.-T., Yu, M.-H., & Riezebos, P. (2016). A research framework of smart education. *Smart learning environments, 3*, 1-17.

Zhuang, R., Fang, H., Zhang, Y., Lu, A., & Huang, R. (2017). Smart learning environments for a smart city: From the perspective of lifelong and lifewide learning. *Smart Learning Environments*, 4(1), 1–21. DOI:10.1186/s40561-017-0044-8

Ziatdinov, R., Atteraya, M. S., & Nabiyev, R. (2024). The Fifth Industrial Revolution as a Transformative Step towards Society 5.0. *Societies (Basel, Switzerland)*, 14(2), 19. DOI:10.3390/soc14020019

Žigienė, G., Rybakovas, E., & Alzbutas, R. (2019). Artificial intelligence based commercial risk management framework for SMEs. *Sustainability (Basel)*, 11(16), 4501. DOI:10.3390/su11164501

Zikopoulos, P., & Eaton, C. (2011). *Understanding big data: Analytics for Enterprise Class Hadoop and Streaming Data*. McGraw-Hill Osborne Media.

Zitová, B., & Flusser, J. (2003). Image registration methods: A survey. *Image and Vision Computing*, 21(11), 977–1000. DOI:10.1016/S0262-8856(03)00137-9

About the Contributors

Salu George Thandekkattu is an accomplished academician with over 24 years of teaching experience in Computer Science and Computer Engineering across diverse cultural environments, including the UAE and Africa. Currently serving as an Assistant Professor at the American University of Nigeria, he has significantly contributed to the academic community through his leadership roles, including Chair of the Department of Computer Science and various committee memberships. Dr. George holds a Ph.D. in Computer Science and specializes in Internet of Things (IoT), Big Data Analytics, Data Science, and Network Security. His extensive research has been published in several international journals and conferences. He is an active member of the Association for Computing Machinery (ACM) and the Institute of Electrical and Electronics Engineers (IEEE).

Narasimha Rao Vajjhala is working as the Dean of the Faculty of Engineering and Architecture at the University of New York Tirana, Albania. He had previously worked as the Chair of Computer Science and Software Engineering programs at the American University of Nigeria. He is a senior member of ACM and IEEE. He is the Editor-in-Chief (EiC) of the International Journal of Risk and Contingency Management (IJRCM). He is also a member of the Risk Management Society (RIMS), and the Project Management Institute (PMI). He has over 23 years of experience teaching programming and database-related courses at both graduate and undergraduate levels in Europe and Africa. He has also worked as a consultant in technology firms in Europe and has experience participating in EU-funded projects. He has completed a Doctorate in Information Systems and Technology (United States); holds a Master of Science in Computer Science and Applications (India), and a Master of Business Administration with a specialization in Information Systems (Switzerland).

* * *

M. Clement Joe Anand is an Assistant Professor in the Department of Mathematics at Mount Carmel College (Autonomous), Bengaluru, Karnataka. With 12 years of teaching and research experience, he has been recognized with an honorary award from the University of Mexico, USA, by the Board of Neutrosophic Science International Association. Dr. Anand has published 50 research articles indexed in Scopus and SCI databases and holds two Indian patents. He completed a short-term course at the Indian Institute of Technology, Madras, and earned his doctoral degree from the University of Madras, Chennai. As a reviewer for several Scopus and SCI-indexed journals, Dr. Anand contributes significantly to the academic community. He has also received a research grant from the Science and Engineering Research Board (SERB), under the Department of Science and Technology (DST), Government of India.

J. Ananth is a distinguished faculty member in the Department of Marine Engineering at AMET, Deemed to be University, Chennai. His research and teaching expertise encompass marine propulsion systems, ship design, and maritime safety. Dr. Ananth is committed to advancing the field of marine engineering through his academic contributions and research initiatives.

Manmeet Kaur Arora is a Research Scholar at the School of Law, Sharda University, Greater Noida. She is a graduate of Law and has completed her Master's in Law from Amity University, Noida. Manmeet Kaur is a qualified Company Secretary Executive Programme. She has over 8+ years of Industry Experience and 1 year of experience as an Associate at a reputed IPR Law Firm. Manmeet Kaur has attended 20+ National & International Conferences, Webinars, Seminars, Symposiums, and Paper Presentations and participated in 5+ Faculty Development programs. She has over 50+ publications in various esteemed Journals and Books. She is active at the Family Dispute Resolution Clinic, Meditation Centre, Greater Noida. Manmeet Kaur has a keen interest in the areas of Corporate Law, Intellectual Property Rights, Insolvency, Artificial Intelligence, Machine Learning, and Blockchain Technology.

Gabriel Terna Ayem is an Assistant professor at the American University of Nigeria (AUN) Yola Adamawa State in the Department of Computer Science, the same University where he bagged his PhD in Computer Science in the year 2024. His research interest is in Big Data Analytics and Explainable AI. He holds an MSc degree in Computer Science from the University of Wolverhampton in the United Kingdom (UK) in 2012, and a combined bachelor's degree honors (BSc (Ed)) in Mathematics/Statistics/Computer Science at the Federal University of Agriculture Makurdi, Benue State, Nigeria in 2002. He has over 20 years of experience in academia and administration, Dr. Gabriel Ayem has held various positions including a Chief Lecturer in the Department of Computer Science at Benue State Polytechnic, Ugbokolo, Benue State, and Head of the Department of Computer Science at the same Polytechnic from 2016-2018. He has numerous articles in peer-reviewed journals, book chapters, and conferences on topics ranging from Causal Impact analysis, Structural model design validation, explainability, cloud computing architecture, implementation of Blockchain in EHR, etc. Dr. Gabriel is a member of several professional bodies, including the Nigeria Computer Society (NCS). He is also actively involved in community service, having held leadership positions in Kingdom People Assembly, a nonprofit organization aimed at empowering young talented Christians in Benue State, Nigeria. His current research interests include the application of Big Data Analytics, and explainability in the Management, and sustenance of Internet of Things (IoT) applications.

Harish BabuBachina serves as a faculty member in the Department of Automobile Engineering at VNR Vignana Jyothi Institute of Engineering and Technology in Hyderabad. With expertise in automotive technologies, vehicle dynamics, and sustainable transportation, Dr. Babu is dedicated to advancing research and education in automobile engineering, making significant contributions to both academia and industry.

Richa Bhalla is a faculty member in the Department of General Management at ISBR Business School, Bangalore. Her expertise encompasses management studies, with a particular focus on organizational behavior and strategic management. Dr. Bhalla is committed to fostering academic excellence and advancing management practices through her research and teaching activities.

Sampath Boopathi is an accomplished individual with a strong academic background and extensive research experience. He completed his undergraduate studies in Mechanical Engineering and pursued his postgraduate studies in the field of Computer-Aided Design. Dr. Boopathi obtained his Ph.D. from Anna University, focusing his research on Manufacturing and optimization. Throughout his career, Dr. Boopathi has made significant contributions to the field of engineering. He has authored and published over 225 research articles in internationally peer-reviewed journals, highlighting his expertise and dedication to advancing knowledge in his area of specialization. His research output demonstrates his commitment to conducting rigorous and impactful research. In addition to his research publications, Dr. Boopathi has also been granted one patent and has three published patents to his name. This indicates his innovative thinking and ability to develop practical solutions to real-world engineering challenges. With 17 years of academic and research experience, Dr. Boopathi has enriched the engineering community through his teaching and mentorship roles.

Eriona Çela is a distinguished academic currently serving as a Full-Time Assistant Professor at the University of New York Tirana, where she is a member of the Faculty of Law and Social Sciences in the Department of Psychology. She earned her Ph.D. in Teaching Methodology of English for Specific Purposes (ESP) from the University of Bari "Aldo Moro" in Italy, enhancing her extensive background in language education, which includes earlier degrees in English Language and Law from the University of Tirana and Business Academy College in Albania. Dr. Çela's research interests are broad and interdisciplinary, focusing on Law, Business English, Artificial Intelligence, Machine Learning, Deep Learning, Natural Language Processing, Teaching Methodology, ESP, Academic Writing, Higher Education, Plagiarism, and European Integration. She is well-versed in teaching various subjects, including Academic Writing, ESL, Business English, Law, and Legal English. She also has significant expertise in translating legal, business, and educational documents. Her academic experience spans several respected institutions, including previous roles as an Assistant Professor at the University of Luarasi, the University of Elbasan "Aleksandër Xhuvani," the University of Tirana, and the University of Durrës "Aleksandër Moisiu." In addition to her academic roles, Dr. Çela has held significant administrative positions within the Albanian Ministry of Education and Sport, contributing to integration, coordination, and project feasibility. Dr. Çela is active in the academic community as a member and managing editor of various editorial boards, including those for the European Journal of Arts, Humanities and Social Sciences, and the International Journal of Risk and Contingency Management. Her contributions to conferences and scholarly journals are numerous, underscoring her commitment to advancing research and practice in her fields of expertise. She also brings practical insights into her teaching and research from her experiences as a trainer and higher education expert involved in quality assurance and educational reforms in Albania. This rich background informs her ongoing contributions to academic discussions and policy-making in education, both in Albania and internationally.

Somu Chinnusamy is actively engaged in Research and Development at RSP Science Hub, Coimbatore. His work focuses on advancing scientific research and technological innovation. Prof. Chinnusamy is committed to making significant contributions to the scientific community through his expertise and research initiatives.

Philip Eappen is an Assistant Professor of Healthcare Management at Cape Breton University and also serves as the Director of Clinical Services and Transition to Community at the Breton Ability Center (LOA). With over a decade of experience in hospital and healthcare management operations, Dr. Eappen has a solid academic background. Prior to joining Cape Breton University, he taught healthcare management at the University of Toronto, the Southern Alberta Institute of Technology, and Fanshawe College. Dr. Eappen also worked as a Director of Health Services and Chief Administrator of Healthcare Operations at the American University of Nigeria. Additionally, he has served as a faculty member at the American University and other universities and colleges. Dr. Eappen holds a doctorate in healthcare administration from Central Michigan University in the United States, a Master of Business Administration in Healthcare Management, a Bachelor of Nursing, and a Post-Graduate Certificate in International Health. Dr. Eappen is a board director on various boards, including the American College of Healthcare Executives, Myeloma Canada, and Aplastic Anemia and Myelodysplasia Canada. Dr. Eappen is also a long-serving member of the American College of Healthcare Executives and the Canadian College of Health Leaders. His research interests are focused on healthcare innovations, particularly healthcare informatics, and he has published various articles, book chapters, and books on the subject in recent years.

Mathias M. Fonkam is an accomplished Associate Teaching Professor at Penn State University with over 20 years of experience in computer science education and as a practicing software engineer. He holds a Ph.D. in Computer Science, an M.Sc. in Systems Engineering and a BSc in Computer Engineering from Cardiff University, UK. His professional journey includes serving as the Dean at the American University of Nigeria (AUN), where he spearheaded numerous initiatives, such as developing the university's Open Source ERP System and establishing various postgraduate programs. Dr. Fonkam's research interests span AI, data science, blockchain, open-source software and systems dynamics, with over 30 publications in reputable conferences and journals. He has also contributed significantly to curriculum development and accreditation processes in Nigerian universities. Fluent in English, Portuguese, and French, Dr. Fonkam is dedicated to advancing computing education and professional development, leveraging his extensive expertise in teaching, mentoring, and research.

Shwetha G. K. is a faculty member in the Department of Computer Science and Engineering at NMAMIT, Karkala, affiliated with NITTE Deemed to be University. Her research interests encompass computer systems, software engineering, and data analytics. Prof. Shwetha G.K. is dedicated to advancing academic excellence and technological innovation through her teaching, research, and active participation in various academic projects.

Bern Igoche is a PhD Computing research student at the University of Portsmouth, with a focus on Ontologies and Semantic Web, and Data Mining & Knowledge Discovery. He holds an MSc in Information Technology Management from the University of Wolverhampton and a Bachelor's degree in Computer Science and Information Technology Education, as well as a Higher National Diploma in Business Administration/Management. With over 20 years of experience in academia and information technology, Bern has held various positions including Senior Lecturer and Director of ICT at Benue State Polytechnic, Nigeria. He has authored several books and published numerous articles in peer-reviewed journals on topics ranging from e-learning to ontology-driven knowledge discovery. Bern is a member of several professional bodies, including the Computer Professionals Registration Council of Nigeria, Nigeria Computer Society, and the British Computer Society. He is also actively involved in community service, having held leadership positions in Rotary International and other organizations. His current research interests include the application of ontologies for knowledge discovery in academic databases and the development of innovative technologies for enhancing learning and information management.

Kittisak Jermsittiparsert is a Research Fellow at Shinawatra University, Thailand, an Adjunct Professor at Sekolah Tinggi Ilmu Administrasi Abdul Haris, and an Adjunct Research Professor at Universitas Muhammadiyah Sinjai, Universitas Muhammadiyah Makassar & Universitas Muhammadiyah Sidenreng Rappang, Indonesia. Previously, he was a Full-Professor of Public Administration at Huanghe Business School, Henan University of Economics and Law, China, a Professor at Faculty of Education, University of City Island, Cyprus, a Lecturer at Faculty of Political Science, Rangsit University & College of Innovative Business and Accountancy, Dhurakij Pundit University, a Researcher at Chulalongkorn University Social Research Institute, Thailand, and an Adjunct Researcher at Ton Duc Thang University & Duy Tan University, Vietnam. He holds a Ph.D. (Social Sciences) from Kasetsart University, Thailand. His areas of expertise are Political Science, Public and Private Management, International Political Economy, and Social Research. He is named in the world's top 2% of scientists list by Stanford University, USA since 2020. Up to now, he has published more than 450 Scopus/WoS indexed documents.

Kamal Bakari Jillahi is a dedicated academic and researcher currently serving as a Lecturer in the Department of Mathematical Sciences at Taraba State University, Nigeria. He is pursuing his Ph.D. in Computer Science and holds a Master's degree in Computer Engineering from Eastern Mediterranean University. With over a decade of experience in academia and industry, Kamal specializes in Artificial Intelligence, Machine Learning, and Big Data. He has published several research papers in international conferences and journals, focusing on the application of AI in various domains. Kamal is a Chartered Member of the Nigerian Computer Society and is proficient in multiple languages, including English, Arabic, and French.

Monish Kumar K. is a dedicated faculty member in the Department of Civil Engineering at Sri Jayachamarajendra College of Engineering, JSSSTU, Mysuru. His research and teaching expertise span various civil engineering disciplines, with a particular focus on sustainable infrastructure and construction technology. Prof. Kumar K is committed to advancing knowledge and practice in his field through rigorous research and a commitment to academic excellence.

Christian Kaunert is Professor of International Security at Dublin City University, Ireland. He is also Professor of Policing and Security, as well as Director of the International Centre for Policing and Security at the University of South Wales. In addition, he is Jean Monnet Chair, Director of the Jean Monnet Centre of Excellence and Director of the Jean Monnet Network on EU Counter-Terrorism (www.eucter.net).

Kutubuddin Kazi holds a B.E., M.E., and Ph.D. in Electronics and Telecommunication Engineering. He is currently serving as a Professor and Head of the Department of Electronics and Telecommunication Engineering and has previously held the position of Dean of Research and Development. As a Post-Doctoral Fellow, Dr. Liyakat focuses on IoT applications in healthcare. He has an extensive publication record, with over 110 research papers in various journals and 11 books in the field of engineering. Dr. Liyakat has been awarded 15 Indian patents, 2 South African granted patents, 2 Indian copyright patents, and 8 UK granted patents, all related to IoT in healthcare. Additionally, he serves as a reviewer for Scopus-indexed conferences and journals and is a member of the editorial board for several academic journals.

Sahil Lal is a Research Scholar at School of Law, Sharda University. He pursued his graduation from National Law University, Lucknow and completed his Master's in Law from Gujarat National Law University, Gandhinagar. Sahil has completed a certificate course on 'AI & Law' from Lund University, Sweden and on 'Cyber Law' from Indian Law Institute, New Delhi. Sahil Lal is a qualified UGC-NET & JRF candidate. He has a 10+ year Industry Experience and is an active member of Family Dispute Resolution Clinic, Mediation Center, Greater Noida. Sahil has attended 20+ International & National Conferences along with Paper Presentation and has also participated in more than 5+ Faculty Development Programme. Mr. Sahil has more than 50+ publications in various esteemed Journals & Books. Mr. Sahil has a keen interest in area of Artificial Intelligence, Machine Learning, Robotics, Block-Chain Technology and Intellectual Property Rights.

Anton Limbo is a Lecturer and Researcher at the University of Namibia's Department of Computing, Mathematics, and Statistics. His research is centred on the innovative applications of the Internet of Things (IoT) within the field of ICT for Development (ICT4D), with a particular emphasis on Smart Agriculture, Smart Healthcare, Smart Home-Care Giving, and Home Automation. Through his work, Anton has significantly contributed to the academic community by publishing numerous papers that underscore the critical need for ongoing research in applying IoT technologies to improve the quality of life in the developing world. In addition to his research, Anton plays other roles such as coordinating and administering the University of Namibia's High-Performance Computing (HPC) system, which is instrumental in advancing computational research, including data modelling, simulations, and training artificial intelligence models. His efforts are paving the way for enhanced research capabilities and technological advancements in Namibia. Anton also serves as a member of the Cybersecurity Curriculum Advisory Board and Namibia 4th Industrial Revolution Taskforce.

Sherif M. Ismail is a distinguished faculty member at the American University in Cairo. His academic focus includes [specific field or research interests, if known]. Prof. Ismail is committed to advancing knowledge and contributing to academic excellence through his research, teaching, and professional activities.

H. Mickle Aancy is a distinguished faculty member in the Department of MBA at Panimalar Engineering College, Chennai. Her expertise spans business administration, management strategies, and organizational leadership. Prof. Aancy is dedicated to fostering academic excellence and advancing the professional development of her students through her teaching and research endeavors.

Ananias Ndemuweda Nakale is a Scholar and IT professional with a deep interest in the intersection of technology, AI, and agriculture. Holding a Bachelor's degree with Honours from the University of Namibia and a Google IT Support Professional Certificate, Ananias has built a strong foundation in the IT field. His innovative undergraduate thesis, entitled "Design and Development of an AI-Based Mobile Application for Identifying Namibia Insect Pests," demonstrates his commitment to leveraging technology for practical agricultural solutions. Currently, he works as a Business Support Analyst at Letshego Bank, where he focuses on optimising business processes and addressing user needs. His dedication to furthering his expertise is evident as he pursues a Master's degree in Computer Science, deepening his knowledge and capabilities in the field. Outside of his professional endeavours, Ananias is passionate about finding creative solutions to challenges in technology and agriculture, continually exploring advancements in AI to improve the intersection of these fields.

P. Nisha is a respected faculty member in the Department of Electrical and Electronics Engineering at St. Joseph's Institute of Technology, Chennai. Her expertise encompasses electrical systems and electronics, with a focus on innovative solutions and technological advancements. Prof. Nisha is dedicated to promoting academic and research excellence within her field.

Maria Ndapewa Ntinda is a senior lecturer in the Department of Computing, Mathematical, and Statistical Sciences at the University of Namibia. With a deep commitment to leveraging technology for social good, Maria has been involved in numerous projects to apply Information and Communication Technology (ICT) to address real-world challenges, particularly in developing nations. Her research interests have recently expanded to include the application of Artificial Intelligence (AI) and the Internet of Things (IoT) in agriculture. She explores how these technologies can enhance agricultural productivity, sustainability, and food security in developing regions. Maria is also researching the potential of digital tourism and how digital platforms and AI-driven solutions can revolutionise the tourism industry, especially in promoting cultural heritage and supporting eco-tourism across Africa. In addition to her work in these areas, Maria is passionate about bridging the gap between the Software Engineering (SE) industry and academia. Her research in computing education is deeply rooted in understanding how ICT for Development (ICT4D) can be used to address socio-economic challenges in the Global South. Through her work, Maria aims to ensure that technological innovations, particularly in AI and IoT, are not just theoretical advancements but practical tools that contribute meaningfully to communities' socio-economic development.

Mrutyunjay Padhiary is an honoured Assistant Professor in the Department of Agricultural Engineering at Assam University, Silchar, India, possessing a solid academic background that includes a B.Tech from Orissa University of Agriculture & Technology, Bhubaneswar, India; an M.Tech from the prestigious Indian Institute of Technology Kharagpur; and a PhD in precision agriculture from Assam University. He has been a dedicated academic at Assam University since 2008 and has over 18 years of expertise. Among his prior appointments were notable roles in teaching and research at the Faculty of Technology, UBKV in West Bengal, and Tribhuban University in Nepal and also has experience from IIT Kharagpur as a researcher. He has received numerous honours, including an International NUS Research Fellowship and a perfect score on the 2001 GATE Exam, attesting to his competence in precision agriculture. He has authored multiple publications in prestigious journals and is a life member of the Indian Society of Agricultural Engineers. He has made significant contributions to the fields of biofuel production, AI vision, aquaculture, precision farming, farm automation, and artificial intelligence. Furthermore, he has undertaken academic travel overseas, where he worked for a long time at the National University of Singapore, performing biofuel research. Additionally, he is currently working in several research projects, which range from autonomous surface vessels to Precision Agriculture All-Terrain Vehicles.

Rajasekhara Mouly Potluri is an experienced academician and researcher with an illustrious career spanning thirty-three years in industry and academia across ten countries. Currently serving as a Professor of Management and Marketing at the Business School of Kazakh-British Technical University in Almaty, Kazakhstan, and holds a Ph.D. and M. Phil. in Management/Marketing from Shivaji University. He also earned an MBA in Marketing and a Master of Commerce in Banking from Andhra University, India. Prof. Raj has made significant contributions to scholarly literature with over a hundred and twenty-five publications, including research articles, books, book chapters, and case studies. His work appears in prestigious peer-reviewed journals indexed in Scopus, ABDC, SSCI, IEEE, KCI, and international conferences. He has been honored with over twenty Best Research Paper Awards and Academic Service Excellence Awards, underscoring his impactful research contributions. His research interests encompass Marketing, Islamic Marketing, Corporate Social Responsibility (CSR) and Sustainability, Human Resource Management (HRM) & Organizational Behavior (OB), and Entrepreneurship. Prof. Raj continues to enrich the academic community with his extensive knowledge and research contributions, aiming to advance understanding and practices in his areas of expertise globally.

Kokila Radhakrishnan is a prominent faculty member at the School of Computer Applications, Dayananda Sagar University, Bengaluru. Her research is centered on computer science and applications, with a particular focus on software engineering and data analysis. Dr. Kokila is committed to advancing the field through innovative research and comprehensive teaching.

Sandip Rakshit is Associate Professor at Rabat Business School, International University of Rabat. He has experience and expertise of teaching & research in American, Australian & French universities in India, Vietnam, Morocco, UAE, Singapore and Africa. Ph.D. in Computer Science (Information Systems) from Jadavpur University, India, and Ph.D. in Management (Business & Technology) from Indian Institute of Technology, Dhanbad; in along with 22+ years of teaching experience. He has published several research papers in leading international journals, including Industrial Marketing Management, Technological Forecasting and Social Change, Journal of Business Research, and Technovation.

G. Nageswara Rao is a faculty member in the Department of Electrical and Electronics Engineering at Lakireddy Bali Reddy College of Engineering, Mylavaram. His research interests include electrical systems, power electronics, and renewable energy technologies. Dr. Rao is dedicated to enhancing academic and research initiatives in his field through his expertise and contributions.

Padmavathy S. is a faculty member in the Department of Management Studies at Kongu Engineering College, Erode. Her expertise includes a broad range of management disciplines, with a particular focus on organizational behavior and strategic management. Prof. Padmavathy S makes significant contributions to the academic community through her research, teaching, and active involvement in management education.

Bhupinder Singh is working as Professor at Sharda University, India. Also, Honorary Professor in University of South Wales UK and Santo Tomas University Tunja, Colombia. His areas of publications as Smart Healthcare, Medicines, fuzzy logics, artificial intelligence, robotics, machine learning, deep learning, federated learning, IoT, PV Glasses, metaverse and many more. He has 3 books, 139 paper publications, 163 paper presentations in international/national conferences and seminars, participated in more than 40 workshops/FDP's/QIP's, 25 courses from international universities of repute, organized more than 59 events with international and national academicians and industry people's, editor-in-chief and co-editor in journals, developed new courses. He has given talks at international universities, resource person in international conferences such as in Nanyang Technological University Singapore, Tashkent State University of Law Uzbekistan; KIMEP University Kazakhstan, All'ah meh Tabatabi University Iran, the Iranian Association of International Criminal law, Iran and Hague Center for International Law and Investment, The Netherlands, Northumbria University Newcastle UK,

P. Sukania is a faculty member in the Department of Mathematics at R.M.K. Engineering College, Kavarapettai. Her academic focus encompasses applied mathematics, mathematical modeling, and computational techniques. Prof. Sukania is committed to advancing mathematical education and research, making significant contributions to both the academic community and the broader field of mathematics.

A. Vellingiri is a distinguished faculty member in the Department of Electronics and Communication Engineering at Bannari Amman Institute of Technology, Erode. His research interests focus on advanced electronics, communication systems, and signal processing. With a strong academic background and extensive experience, Prof. Vellingiri makes significant contributions to his field through both teaching and research.

Index

Symbols

5G connectivity 69, 219, 227

A

Administrative Efficiency 27
Agricultural Productivity 78, 106, 110,
    112, 114, 117, 128, 330
Agriculture 4.0 137, 144, 163, 164, 168
Agriculture Industry 329, 330
Area Under Curve (AUC) 260, 277
Artificial Intelligence (AI) 3, 15, 19, 20,
    24, 46, 48, 49, 69, 71, 73, 75, 80, 81,
    88, 91, 94, 99, 100, 102, 104, 105,
    111, 115, 137, 139, 140, 143, 144,
    149, 154, 163, 165, 167, 168, 172,
    173, 201, 202, 204, 205, 227, 230,
    267, 271, 275, 280, 281, 282, 284,
    285, 287, 289, 292, 293, 294, 296,
    303, 309, 313, 316, 317, 318, 327,
    345, 346, 353, 374, 377, 378, 379, 380
Artificial Intelligence of Things 143, 144,
    163, 167, 168
Autonomous Vehicles (AV) 83, 100, 215,
    227, 279, 280, 281, 282, 283, 284,
    285, 287, 288, 289, 290, 291, 295,
    296, 298, 299

B

Big Data Analytics 126, 169, 170, 171,
    172, 173, 174, 175, 181, 197, 199,
    201, 203, 221, 223, 224, 225, 226,
    227, 303, 319, 340

C

Circular Economy 51, 52, 53, 54, 68, 69,
    72, 73, 74, 75, 76, 101, 102
Clean Technologies 51, 52, 58, 59, 62, 64,
    65, 66, 67, 71, 76
Cloud 8, 17, 22, 46, 47, 69, 73, 75, 95, 98,
    105, 128, 144, 167, 199, 201, 202,
    205, 218, 222, 223, 225, 226, 229,
    242, 245, 267, 270, 276, 277, 284,
    287, 288, 295, 302, 303, 307, 308,
    319, 335, 336, 346, 348, 358, 367,
    370, 371, 377, 379
Crop Monitoring 80, 140, 145
Customer Experience 380
Cybersecurity 103, 105, 128, 152, 166,
    173, 174, 288, 299, 303, 307, 332,
    333, 343, 348, 368, 375

D

Data-Driven 27, 28, 29, 30, 32, 35, 36,
    37, 44, 48, 49, 65, 82, 85, 93, 95, 96,
    101, 113, 119, 120, 121, 140, 166,
    171, 209, 219, 221, 222, 275, 286,
    295, 307, 329, 330, 331, 332, 334,
    339, 340, 348, 375, 379
Data-Driven Decision-Making 27, 28,
    29, 30, 32, 36, 44, 49, 65, 82, 85, 93,
    330, 339, 340
Data Management 88, 97, 98, 158, 199,
    202, 209, 210, 211, 212, 213, 214, 216,
    217, 218, 219, 220, 221, 222, 223,
    224, 226, 227, 231, 244, 245, 269, 307
Decision-Making 27, 28, 29, 30, 32, 36,
    43, 44, 49, 65, 80, 82, 85, 91, 93, 95,
    100, 101, 106, 110, 116, 123, 124,
    126, 143, 145, 146, 147, 153, 155,
    156, 161, 162, 169, 171, 172, 174,
    175, 193, 210, 212, 214, 215, 216,
    219, 232, 236, 242, 243, 246, 249,
    288, 289, 295, 296, 299, 309, 310, 312,
    319, 326, 330, 333, 339, 340, 356, 380
Deep Learning 73, 75, 103, 104, 109, 119,
    136, 138, 139, 140, 167, 179, 204, 207,
    214, 215, 227, 247, 292, 293, 294, 295,
    297, 305, 312, 314, 318, 345
Drones 77, 78, 79, 80, 81, 82, 83, 85, 86,
    87, 88, 89, 90, 91, 92, 93, 94, 95, 97,
    98, 102, 104, 105, 106, 107, 111,
    113, 120, 124, 125, 126, 140, 168,
    171, 326, 329